Instructor's Manual

to accompany

Case Studies in Finance
Managing for Corporate
Value Creation

Robert Bruner
University of Virginia

IRWIN

Homewood, IL 60430
Boston, MA 02116

Printed in the United States of America.

ISBN 0–256–07527–1

1 2 3 4 5 6 7 8 9 0 MG 6 5 4 3 2 1 0 9

A NOTE FROM THE EDITOR:

Thank you for adopting <u>Case Studies in Finance: Managing for Corporate Value Creation.</u> We are confident you will be pleased with your selection. Immediately following this note are two copies of a survey. Upon completion of your course for which you use Bruner please take 5-10 minutes to provide us with your comments. We are dedicated to continuous improvement and your suggestions will be helpful. Save the second survey for comments you may have after teaching from the book a second time.

Survey of Instructors

Your evaluation of the cases in <u>Case Studies in Finance: Managing for Corporate Value Creation</u> would be most helpful. AT THE END OF THE COURSE in which you USED this book, please complete the brief survey below, fold it as indicated on the back, and return it postpaid to Michael Junior, Editor, Richard D. Irwin Inc.

Instructor's Name_____

School_____ Telephone Number_____

The course was (circle one of each pair): required/elective, undergraduate/graduate, first course/second course.

Number of students enrolled annually in this course:_____

Evaluation of Individual Cases

1. Please draw a line through the names of the cases you did <u>not</u> use.
2. Write a plus sign, "+", next to the names of the top quartile of cases, i.e. which were most successful (defined any way you like).
3. Write a minus sign, "-", next to the names of the bottom quartile of cases, i.e. which were least successful.

Cases in the Case Book

1.	Walt Disney Productions	25.	Southboro Corp.
2.	Peter Lynch	26.	Morgan Stanley Group
3.	The Financial Detective	27.	Spiegel, Inc.
4.	Johnson's Nursery	28.	Intro to Debt Policy
5.	Alfin Fragrances Inc.	29.	Tonka Corp.
6.	Padgett Blank Book Company	30.	Coleco
7.	Atlantic Southeast Airlines	31.	Design Technologies
8.	L.S. Starrett Company	32.	Delta and Eastern
9.	DeLaurentiis	33.	Johnstown Corp.
10.	Columbia Mills, Inc.	34.	Merit Marine
11.	Blue Cross and Blue Shield	35.	Chrysler's Warrants
12.	Teletech Corporation	36.	Flowers Inds.
13.	General Motors Corporation, 1988	37.	British Petroleum
14.	The Investment Detective	38.	Brunswick Fed. S&L
15.	Westfield Inc.	39.	Emerson Electric
16.	Boggs Mineral Company	40.	Merchants Cotton
17.	Sandbridge Company (A)	41.	Gifford Bunsen
18.	Palmetto Shipping & Stevedoring	42.	Boston Celtics
19.	Sprigg Lane Group (A)	43.	Societe Generale (A)
20.	Enercon Corporation	44.	Bumble Bee Seafoods
21.	Iskall Arno, Inc. (Abridged)	45.	Aqua Company (A)
22.	Brown-Forman Distillers	46.	Sybron Corporation
23.	E.I. DuPont: 1909	47.	Hybritech Inc. (A)
24.	Cleveland-Cliffs Iron Company		

Cases in Instructor's Manual

Peachtree National Bank	Hybritech Inc. (B)
Societe Generale (B)	Colt Industries
Aqua Company (B)	Enigma Engineering
Eli Lilly & Company	

Please take a moment to jot some comments on the most and least successful cases.

Evaluation of Students' Diskettes

I did/did not (circle one) make the Lotus spreadsheets available to the students.

If not, why?

If you did use the student diskettes, what was your experience?

Evaluation of the Entire Case Book and Instructor's Manual

	Poor				Excellent
1. In **absolute terms**, I think the casebook is: (circle one)	1	2	3	4	5
2. In **absolute terms**, I think the instructor's manual is: (circle one)	1	2	3	4	5

3. Please rate this selection of cases along the following dimensions:

	Low				High
Content/Substance of Case Problems	1	2	3	4	5
Contemporary Relevance	1	2	3	4	5
Difficulty	1	2	3	4	5

4. Please tell us how helpful were various features of the instructor's manual:

	Not Useful				Very Useful
Suggested Assignment Questions	1	2	3	4	5
Hypothetical Teaching Plans	1	2	3	4	5
Case Analyses	1	2	3	4	5
Instructor's Models on Diskette	1	2	3	4	5
Notes: Teaching and Course Design	1	2	3	4	5

5. What other casebooks have you used? How does this casebook compare to those?

6. In what subject areas is the casebook strongest? Weakest?

7. What changes would you recommend for the second edition?

- -

(fold over and tape closed)

Your evaluation of the cases in <u>Case Studies in Finance: Managing for Corporate Value Creation</u> would be most helpful. AT THE END OF THE COURSE in which you USED this book, please complete the brief survey below, fold it as indicated on the back, and return it postpaid to Michael Junior, Editor, Richard D. Irwin Inc.

Instructor's Name_____

School_____ Telephone Number_____

The course was (circle one of each pair): required/elective, undergraduate/graduate, first course/second course.

Number of students enrolled annually in this course:_____

Evaluation of Individual Cases

1. Please draw a line through the names of the cases you did <u>not</u> use.
2. Write a plus sign, "+", next to the names of the top quartile of cases, i.e. which were most successful (defined any way you like).
3. Write a minus sign, "-", next to the names of the bottom quartile of cases, i.e. which were least successful.

Cases in the Case Book

1.	Walt Disney Productions	25.	Southboro Corp.
2.	Peter Lynch	26.	Morgan Stanley Group
3.	The Financial Detective	27.	Spiegel, Inc.
4.	Johnson's Nursery	28.	Intro to Debt Policy
5.	Alfin Fragrances Inc.	29.	Tonka Corp.
6.	Padgett Blank Book Company	30.	Coleco
7.	Atlantic Southeast Airlines	31.	Design Technologies
8.	L.S. Starrett Company	32.	Delta and Eastern
9.	DeLaurentiis	33.	Johnstown Corp.
10.	Columbia Mills, Inc.	34.	Merit Marine
11.	Blue Cross and Blue Shield	35.	Chrysler's Warrants
12.	Teletech Corporation	36.	Flowers Inds.
13.	General Motors Corporation, 1988	37.	British Petroleum
14.	The Investment Detective	38.	Brunswick Fed. S&L
15.	Westfield Inc.	39.	Emerson Electric
16.	Boggs Mineral Company	40.	Merchants Cotton
17.	Sandbridge Company (A)	41.	Gifford Bunsen
18.	Palmetto Shipping & Stevedoring	42.	Boston Celtics
19.	Sprigg Lane Group (A)	43.	Societe Generale (A)
20.	Enercon Corporation	44.	Bumble Bee Seafoods
21.	Iskall Arno, Inc. (Abridged)	45.	Aqua Company (A)
22.	Brown-Forman Distillers	46.	Sybron Corporation
23.	E.I. DuPont: 1909	47.	Hybritech Inc. (A)
24.	Cleveland-Cliffs Iron Company		

Cases in Instructor's Manual

Peachtree National Bank	Hybritech Inc. (B)
Societe Generale (B)	Colt Industries
Aqua Company (B)	Enigma Engineering
Eli Lilly & Company	

<u>Please take a moment to jot some comments on the most and least successful cases.</u>

Evaluation of Students' Diskettes

I did/did not (circle one) make the Lotus spreadsheets available to the students.

If not, why?

If you did use the student diskettes, what was your experience?

Evaluation of the Entire Case Book and Instructor's Manual

	Poor				Excellent
1. In **absolute terms**, I think the casebook is: (circle one)	1	2	3	4	5
2. In **absolute terms**, I think the instructor's manual is: (circle one)	1	2	3	4	5

3. Please rate this selection of cases along the following dimensions:

	Low				High
Content/Substance of Case Problems	1	2	3	4	5
Contemporary Relevance	1	2	3	4	5
Difficulty	1	2	3	4	5

4. Please tell us how helpful were various features of the instructor's manual:

	Not Useful				Very Useful
Suggested Assignment Questions	1	2	3	4	5
Hypothetical Teaching Plans	1	2	3	4	5
Case Analyses	1	2	3	4	5
Instructor's Models on Diskette	1	2	3	4	5
Notes: Teaching and Course Design	1	2	3	4	5

5. What other casebooks have you used? How does this casebook compare to those?

6. In what subject areas is the casebook strongest? Weakest?

7. What changes would you recommend for the second edition?

- -

(fold over and tape closed)

Preface

I learned to design case courses and teach cases through a process of trial-and-error and apprenticeship. My goal in writing this manual was to accelerate the learning process for others.

• The *teaching notes* aim to show a plan and some calculations that work in the classroom. Many case teachers prefer no formal teaching plan. Each to his or her own taste. The plans are offered simply to help the instructor envision how the case might play in the classroom. Ultimately, the mark of a good instructor's manual is the dust it gathers, for most case teachers develop their own approaches, plans, and notes.

• The "Note on Developing a Case-Method Teaching Plan" is offered to help the first-time instructor make the transition from the notes in this manual to a set of customized notes.

• The "Note on Designing a Case-Method Course" covers a number of considerations useful in fashioning a series of cases into a coherent course of study. This note contains tables that allow the instructor to cross-reference the cases quickly by subject, general task, and textbook readings.

• "Case Study with the Aid of a Personal Computer: Note on Using the Disk Files" describes the use, contents, and method of accessing Lotus spreadsheets that support the cases and teaching notes and are available on diskettes from Irwin.

• The note, "Equity Costs: Some Conventions on Using the CAPM," describes the two approaches used most frequently in the teaching notes. The aim is to alert the instructor to the multiple approaches possible.

USING THE SUPPLEMENTAL CASES PROVIDED IN THE INSTRUCTOR'S MANUAL

This manual contains five companion cases ["Peachtree National Bank", "Societe Generale de Belgique" (B), "Aqua Company" (B), "Eli Lilly and Company," and "Hybritech Incorporated" (B)] and one technical note ("Leveraged Employee Stock Ownership Plans") for optional use with cases appearing in the case book. These cases are published here, rather than in the case book, because they present information that would affect student preparation and discussion of the primary cases. The instructor is cautioned not to distribute the companion cases in general fashion (i.e., at the start of the semester) without first consulting the respective teaching notes about the use of the companion cases.

The manual also contains two cases and their teaching notes ("Colt Industries" and "Enigma Engineering") offered for possible use in examinations or in the regular classroom setting.

The student disk files supporting the companion and exam cases are to be found on the instructor's disk.

PERMISSION TO DUPLICATE CASES IN THE INSTRUCTOR'S MANUAL

The Darden Graduate Business School Sponsors of the University of Virginia and Richard D. Irwin, Inc., grant permission to duplicate the cases in this instructor's manual, *provided* that *Case Studies in Finance: Managing for Corporate Value Creation* has been adopted as a required text in the course for which the copies are made, and the number of copies made does not exceed the enrollment of the course. In circumstances other than these, the instructor may obtain loose-leaf copies and/or site licenses for duplicating cases by contacting Ann Morris, Darden Educational Materials Services, The Darden School, Box 6550, Charlottesville, Virginia 22906. [Telephone: (804) 924-3638].

ACKNOWLEDGEMENTS

Each teaching note bears an acknowledgement of my debt to particular colleagues, research assistants, and students. My research assistant for this manual, Michael J. Nagle, influenced virtually every item in some way and prepared the accompanying diskettes. I am especially grateful for his attention to detail. Bette Collins edited the entire book, ensuring consistency of style and typographic presentation, supported by Kathleen Collier, Kim Langford, Zee Watson, and Dot Govoruhk. Their patience and good humor were highly valued.

Although my helpers and I have strived to eliminate errors in both the cases and notes, some errors and omissions seem to evade the most careful screening. If you find some, or if you have any comments or suggestions on the cases or notes, please let me know. I hope you enjoy using the cases.

Robert F. Bruner
The Darden School
University of Virginia
Box 6550
Charlottesville, VA 22906

Contents

Note on Developing a Case-Method Teaching Plan

The case method at its best is student driven rather than instructor driven. Some of the best case teachers recognize this truth and, practically speaking, are minimalists when it comes to planning individual classes. Why, then, should one plan?

First and foremost, a plan imposes a discipline on one's own preparation of a case. Anticipating specific topics of discussion helps target your analysis effectively. Second, a plan can help anticipate areas of difficulty for the students. And third, the plan can serve as a compass for more active discussion leadership if the discussion loses its steam.

From this perspective, *the teaching plan is not a script*. I have used the suggested teaching plans in this manual and have also departed from them freely, as the needs of the students and my own teaching goals required. Moreover, any time I teach a case, I am bound to tailor the teaching plan in ways suggested by the following questions:

- Whom am I teaching? What are their goals? Needs? Skills? An assessment of the course client is the origin of any plan. For instance, MBA students generally have an appetite for learning hard skills and conceptual frameworks. Business executives, on the other hand, eschew frameworks and seek to obtain practical solutions to problems they encounter.

- Why is this case in the course? What are my teaching objectives in this case? Many of the cases in this book are rich enough on a stand-alone basis to carry many teaching points. The relevant task of teaching the case is not maximization, however, but optimization; shoe-horning in all possible teaching points is less desirable than making a lasting impression of a few key points. The selection of specific teaching objectives should be dictated by the needs of the students and the conceptual flow of the course. The success of subsequent cases may depend on consolidation of earlier teaching points and/or the introduction of new ideas.

- What question or statement is the most effective way to open the discussion? I believe this question is the most difficult to answer in developing a teaching plan. A good opener sets the stage, raises the curtain effectively, and builds drama. Bad openers mire the discussion in trivial issues or issues that are substantive but far afield from the objectives of the discussion. The opener should be tailored to the nature of the case: Where the case problem is clearly defined and specific figure analysis is to be done, I favor openers that help establish the relevance of the analysis and launch the discussion into the figures. For cases where the challenge is to define the problem, I favor openers that bring out the richness and complexity of the situation.

- What questions are appropriate in the middle of the discussion? A former Dean of the Darden School used to say, "Never ask a question for which you don't know the answer." Random questioning can send a discussion far off course. Like the opener, questions for the body of the case discussion should be motivated by the teaching objectives of the case and the needs of the students. Regarding student needs, for instance, it pays to pause in the discussion and ask students to define new technical terms that may have come up.

1

- How should I close the discussion? Some instructors believe that closure (in the form of class consensus or summary of teaching points) is unnecessary. What matters to them is the process of debate that occurred in the body of the case discussion. I prefer a formal closure as a way of concluding any drama that may have been created during the discussion. As the teaching plans in this manual show, one can use devices such as a vote of the class on a decision, the presentation of the epilogue to the case, and/or discussion of summary points--either by the students or the instructor. Used in this way, the closing is a learning opportunity for the students; indeed, the sharp reversals from expectations in some of the epilogues often leave the most lasting impressions of a case discussion.

The teaching plans here are guides; they will not suit every instructor and every situation. I hope you find them helpful, however, as a beginning in shaping your own teaching plans.

Note on Designing a Case-Method Course

> Professor Summerlee gave a snort of impatience. "We have
> spent two long days in explorations," said he, "and we are
> no wiser as to the actual geography of the place than when
> we started... The farther we go the less likely it is that
> we will get any general view..."
>
> "I am surprised, sir," boomed Challenger, stroking his
> majestic beard, "that any man of science should commit
> himself to so ignoble a sentiment... I absolutely refuse to
> leave until we are able to take back with us something in
> the nature of a chart."
>
> Sir Arthur Conan Doyle, *The Lost World*

Studying by the case method is like map making by sailing up a coast. The student sees the immediate landscape (the case), but he or she may not gain a sense of the continent until the end of the course. I believe it helps for the guide/instructor to have the satellite photo in mind with which to aid the process of discovery. The purpose of this note, therefore, is to highlight some considerations worth bearing in mind as you design the map of case discussions.

The most successful case-method courses have in common many of the following attributes:

A CONCEPTUAL OR TOPICAL FLOW

There is a physics of case-method course design in which the entropy of eclecticism pulls hard at virtually any structure imposed on the course. Eclecticism is driven by sentiments and situations common to most case teachers: a list of favorite cases; the absence of good cases on particular topics; the natural reluctance to dally with new and uncertain teaching materials; the belief that, in the case method, it is the students' responsibility to figure things out for themselves; and the awkwardness with which corporate finance fits into a linear course plan.[1]

Nevertheless, a good course has a beginning, middle, and end; it *flows*. An important benefit of design is that it fosters the students' trust and respect for the instructor, which can yield huge dividends when it comes time to convey difficult concepts or techniques. More importantly, if topics are structured on top of each other, each new module of cases reinforces the work in earlier modules; the learning gain is multiplicative rather than merely additive.

Two tables can help you begin the process of structuring your course. The list of cases in Exhibit A presents the cases in the eight modules grouped by the primary subject of each case. It thus provides a quick reference. Because

---

[1]There are at least two classic course-planning dilemmas in corporate finance: (1) whether to teach cost of capital before capital structure and (2) whether to teach dividend policy before capital structure. In any discussion among finance colleagues, the choice comes down to a matter of "tastes great" versus "less filling," personal preferences.

most of the cases in fact raise several issues, however, both explicitly and implicitly, Exhibit B cross-references the cases by various subject areas and indicates how significant the subject is in each case.

CAREFULLY DESIGNED BEGINNINGS AND ENDINGS

The opening and closing of a course (and of modules within it) present excellent opportunities to frame the subject matter of the course. At the opening, one creates expectations about the contents of the course and the effort necessary to absorb the contents. Above all, the course opener should convey some of the intellectual excitement inherent in corporate finance. At the closing, one has the opportunity to summarize and build student self-confidence in mastery of the material.

One strategy for exploiting these opportunities is to use comprehensive cases to open the course. For instance, "Walt Disney Productions, June 1984," "Societe Generale de Belgique" (A), and "Spiegel Inc." raise a host of issues surrounding value creation for shareholders and the estimation of that value; these cases involve the assessment of complex situations rather than heavy number crunching. Thus, I believe them to be compelling and challenging[2] course-openers.

Many instructors prefer the opposite opening strategy. They use a relatively simple case, seeking to minimize possible confusion at the start of the course and giving even mere novices a sense of accomplishment on the opening day.

At the close of a course, comprehensive cases help review the terrain covered by the course and build student confidence. Merger or divestiture cases (e.g., "Brown-Forman," "Hybritech" (A), "Sybron") provide a good synthesis of valuation and strategy. Merchant-banking cases such as "Aqua" (A) and (B), "Bumble Bee Seafoods," "Design Technologies," or "Enigma Engineering" invite a synthesis of valuation, capital structure, and financing tactics.

VARIETY IN DELIVERY

Variety enlivens student participation and learning. Within a course, an instructor can design in considerable variety along the following dimensions:

Format

A steady stream of standard case discussions could be leavened with classes based on team presentations (e.g., "Delta/Eastern"), extended role-plays (e.g., "Morgan Stanley," "Iskall Arno"), or negotiation exercises (e.g., "Hybritech" and "Lilly").

---

[2]In the spirit of showing a climber the height of the mountain, I prefer to use challenging course openers. My expectation is that the class will not gain full closure on the case, but will raise a number of themes and issues to be dealt with throughout the course. The opener, in effect, becomes a foil for the course (e.g., "We've seen this before, in Disney...").

Exhibit C lists the cases according to three categories of challenge: figure analysis, interpretation, and problem identification.

Task

Students appreciate a mixture of number-crunching problem situations with cases in which interpretation and the exercise of managerial judgment are important. For instance, the module on financial analysis and forecasting offers cases requiring both modeling (e.g., "Alfin," "Columbia Mills") and interpretation ("DeLaurentiis" or "Padgett"). My own approach is to load the front end of a module with number-crunching cases and then follow with interpretive cases.

Pacing/Intensity

By and large, the cases in this collection are challenging. Thus students welcome periodic "breathers" and opportunities to dwell more carefully than usual on a complex situation. Some of the shorter cases in the collection (e.g., "DuPont," "Financial Detective," "Investment Detective") may be considered breathers. Other cases (e.g., "Southboro," "Design Technologies") are rich enough to be taught over two class periods if time permits detailed exploration. Another two-day arrangement can be used for sequel cases, which might require somewhat less preparation time for the student on the second day (e.g., "Hybritech" (A) and (B), "Aqua" (A) and (B), "Societe Generale" (A) and (B), and "Columbia" and "Peachtree").

Direction/Ambiguity

Another dimension of variation is the degree to which the instructor "sets up" the case discussion--that is, through choice of problem or use of advance assignment questions. This collection contains a number of relatively ambiguous, less directive cases, such as "Disney," "Societe Generale," "Spiegel," and "Southboro," which are useful vehicles for problem identification, for which skill the case method is ideal.

Variation of Unknowns

An instructor tries to reinforce what has come before in a course without being repetitious. It may help to have one day's case solve for B given A, and the next day's solve for A given B. Cases that pair up like this are "Merchants Cotton" and "Emerson Electric," "Westfield" and "Boggs," "Padgett" and "Columbia," "Teletech" and "General Motors," and "Tonka" and "Coleco."

HELPING THE STUDENTS HELP THEMSELVES

In the case method, one often observes that the hardest won insights are the best learned. Unfortunately, this kind of "best learning" is difficult to stimulate; the instructor must walk a thin line between giving away too much and giving away too little. Ultimately, I believe the best one can do is help prepare students for the process of self-discovery in the following ways:

Collateral Readings

Where especially useful, some of the teaching notes cite articles that can help set the conceptual underpinning for the case. An alternative is to assign or suggest textbook chapters, although this method has the disadvantage that the student might assume the case is an extended problem meant to exercise a specific technique in the chapter, which no true case study will do effectively.

For your reference, Exhibit D cross-tabulates the cases in this collection with chapters in leading corporate finance texts.

Course Tracking

Preparing a syllabus and sending periodic memos to students can help them track the flow of the course and follow the progressive structure of concepts and techniques. Memos should not present case solutions, but should remind students about ideas/techniques/terms recently presented and worth thinking about further.

Study Groups

Small group discussions before class can be an extremely effective device for building self-confidence and student mastery of the material. The instructor can encourage the voluntary formation of these groups simply by suggesting the idea and letting motivated individuals do the rest. In my experience, a significant percentage of students will participate in study groups. (Incidentally, when study groups are used, the instructor will need to establish the norm that every student is individually accountable for class preparation; one needs to discourage free riding.)

Feedback

Quizzes, exams, and written and oral comments on class participation can give students a sense of their grasp of the material and can motivate students' efforts to consolidate course material periodically.

The best case-method course maps grow out of relentless tinkering. Thus I encourage you to experiment--using these cases in whatever combinations make sense to you. As Doyle's Challenger would say, however, refuse to leave without a chart.

EXHIBIT A   Primary Subject of Each Case

I. SETTING SOME THEMES

1.	Walt Disney Productions, June 1984	Value creation
2.	Peter Lynch and the Fidelity Magellan Fund	Market efficiency

II. FINANCIAL ANALYSIS AND FORECASTING FUNDS NEEDS

3.	The Financial Detective	Financial ratios
4.	Johnson's Nursery	Cash-flow forecasting
5.	Alfin Fragrances, Inc.	Cash flow and valuation
6.	Padgett Blank Book Company	Funds needs and growth
7.	Atlantic Southeast Airlines	Sensitivity tests of funds needs
8.	L. S. Starrett Company	Employee stock ownership loan
9.	De Laurentiis Entertainment Group, Inc.	Funds needs and strategy
10.	Columbia Mills, Inc.	Funds needs and cyclical risk

III. COST OF CAPITAL

11.	Blue Cross and Blue Shield of Virginia	Opportunity cost
12.	Teletech Corporation	Divisional hurdle rates
13.	General Motors Corporation, 1988	Cost of equity

IV. CAPITAL BUDGETING AND RESOURCE ALLOCATION

14.	The Investment Detective	Techniques of analysis
15.	Westfield Inc.	Product substitution
16.	Boggs Mineral Company	Cash flows and standard costs
17.	Sandbridge Company (A)	Evaluation of new technology
18.	Palmetto Shipping & Stevedoring Co., Inc.	Rent-versus-buy evaluation
19.	Sprigg Lane (A)	Risk analysis and project evaluation
20.	Enercon Corporation	Synergies and project interdependencies
21.	Iskall Arno, Inc. (Abridged)	Comprehensive resource allocation
22.	Brown-Forman Distillers Corporation	Valuing acquisition target

V. MANAGEMENT OF SHAREHOLDERS' EQUITY

23.	E. I. du Pont de Nemours Powder Company: 1909	Dividend irrelevance
24.	Cleveland-Cliffs Iron Company	Value conservation
25.	Southboro Corporation	Signaling, clienteles, and financing
26.	Morgan Stanley Group, Inc.	Initial public offering
27.	Spiegel, Inc. (Abridged)	Strategy and timing in equity issues

VI. CORPORATE DEBT POLICY

28.	Introduction to Debt Policy and Value	Debt tax shields
29.	Tonka Corporation	Debt tax shields and strategy
30.	Coleco Industries, Inc.	Costs of financial distress
31.	Design Technologies, Inc.	Allocating value
32.	Delta and Eastern Airlines	Comprehensive financial strategy
33.	Johnstown Corporation	Debt versus equity financing

VII. FINANCING TACTICS AND INSTRUMENTS

VIII. MERGERS, ACQUISITIONS, AND RESTRUCTURINGS

CASES IN THE INSTRUCTOR'S MANUAL

This index lists cases by topic, indicating where the subject is a prominent issue (in boldface type) or implicit (plain type). The case numbers are found in Exhibit A of this note.

<u>Topic</u>	<u>Case Numbers</u>
Basic Financial Analysis (Historical Performance)	
Realized versus required returns	**1, 2, 5, 7, 8, 12, 14, 32, 43, 49,** 22
Ratio analysis	**3, 6,** 8, 25, 27
Sources and uses of funds	**4, 6,** 10, 32
Breakeven analysis	**4,** 15, 17
Investment Issues	
Project evaluation	**14–21,** 25, 40
Securities valuation	**2, 24, 26, 27, 29, 31, 33, 35–39, 41, 42, 44, 45, 47, 50–54,** 5, 9, 13, 22, 23, 24, 28, 43, 49
Cost of capital	**11–13, 22, 44, 45,** 1, 15, 19, 20, 21, 26, 31, 33, 41, 47, 50–54
Risk and sensitivity analysis	**6, 7, 9, 10, 19, 30–33, 41, 44, 45, 48, 50–54,** 4, 8, 34, 39, 40
Firm valuation	**1, 2, 5, 9, 22, 23, 24, 26–31, 33, 42–47, 49–54,** 12, 13, 21, 25, 32

Financing Decisions

    Debt policy/capital structure   **28–33, 44, 45, 53, 54**, 3, 4, 6–10

    Dividend policy   **23, 25, 32**, 4, 6, 8, 10

    Issuing equity/going public   **26, 27, 33, 37, 42**

    Repurchasing equity   **8, 24, 53**

    Bank lending decisions   **5–10, 31, 34, 44, 48**, 30

    Issuing long-term debt   **34, 36, 38, 39, 40, 41, 44, 45, 51, 52, 53, 54**

    Agency problems   **6, 26, 30**, 1, 10, 48, 31, 42

    Capital-market signaling   **1, 2, 25**, 24, 26, 27

Corporate Restructuring

    Mergers and acquisitions   **1, 22, 24, 31, 42–47, 49–52, 54**

    Leveraged acquisitions/buyouts   **31, 44, 45, 46**

    Divestitures   **44, 46**, 31

    Conversion to limited partnership   **42**, 54

    Employee stock ownership   **8**, 26

Capital Markets

    Efficiency   **2, 5, 39–41, 46**

    Institutions and structure   **2, 26, 38–41**, 13, 27

International Finance   **37, 39, 40, 43, 49**, 7, 27

Option Valuation	**33, 35, 36, 37, 38, 52,** 30
Working-Capital Management	**3-10, 34, 48**
Public Policy, Ethical Concerns	**5, 9, 11, 21, 32, 35, 37, 43, 49,** 24, 33, 38

EXHIBIT C Cases Indexed by Type of Challenge

The following table catalogues the cases by type of analytical challenge each case pose:*

• The Type I case presents a clearly defined problem; the figure analysis to be done is specified.

• In the Type II case, the problem is clearly defined, and some finished figure work is presented; the student must interpret the results and/or perform a sensitivity analysis.

• In the Type III case, the student must define the problem and choose an analytical approach; sometimes implementation of a recommendation is an important element of the problem.

Type I	Type II	Type III
Alfin Fragrances	Disney	Cleveland-Cliffs
Columbia Mills	Financial Detective	Southboro
Peachtree National	Johnson's Nursery	Spiegel
General Motors	Padgett Blank Book	Delta and Eastern
Investment Detective	Atlantic Southeast	Boston Celtics
Westfield	Starrett	Societe Generale (A) & (B)
Boggs Mineral	De Laurentiis	Sybron
Sandbridge	Blue Cross	Hybritech (A)
Palmetto	Teletech	Eli Lilly
Brown-Forman	Sprigg Lane (A)	Johnstown
E. I. du Pont	Enercon	
Morgan Stanley	Iskall Arno	
Debt Policy & Value	Tonka	
Gifford Bunsen	Coleco	
Hybritech (B)	Merit Marine	
Chrysler's Warrants	Flowers Inds.	
British Petroleum	Brunswick	
Emerson Electric	Aqua (A) and (B)	
Merchants Cotton	Colt Inds.	
	Enigma Engineering	
	Bumble Bee	

*My colleague, William Rotch, developed this scheme.

12

The three graduate textbooks referred to here are:

Brealey, R. A., and Myers, S. C. *Principles of Corporate Finance*. 3rd Edition.
New York: McGraw-Hill, 1988.

Weston, J. F., and Copeland, T. E. *Managerial Finance*. 8th Edition.
Chicago: Dryden Press, 1986.

Ross, S. A., and Westerfield, R. W. *Corporate Finance*. 1st Edition. St.
Louis: Times Mirror/Mosby, 1988.

		Chapters in:		
		Brealey & Meyers	Ross & Westerfield	Weston & Copeland
I.	Setting Themes	1, 11, 33, 36	1	1
II.	Financial Analysis	27–32	2, 22–25	2, 8–15
III.	Cost of Capital	7, 8	6–8	16–21
IV.	Capital Budgeting	2–6, 10–12	3–5, 9–11	5–7, 23
V.	Equity Management	16	15, 16	22
VI.	Debt Policy	17, 18, 19	14	20–21
VII.	Financing Tactics	13–15, 20–26, 34	12–13, 17–21, 28	24–29, 32
VIII.	Mergers	33	26	23, 30–31

Case Study with the Aid of a Personal Computer: Note on Using the Disk Files

The advent of the personal computer has revolutionized corporate financial analysis. Used properly[1] in a training setting, the computer can help the student attain insights faster and more surely than through calculations by hand. With the diffusion of the personal computer throughout the corporate work place, computer-based case analysis is increasingly relevant. A chief barrier to the use of computers in case study, however, is data entry. The diskettes accompanying this instructor's manual help surmount that barrier.

WHAT THE DISKS CONTAIN

You will find two types of disks:

1. disks for ordinary *student* access. Student disks offer Lotus spreadsheet files containing the primary exhibits of every case. Some of these student files contain exercisable models, which allow the student to test ideas with minimum setup time. However, *none of the student files contains suggestions for analysis that are not already in the case.* The student files are not answer cribs;

2. a disk for the *instructor*. This disk contains the completed Lotus models that generated the analysis in many of the teaching notes. These models can help the instructor in many ways, including saving setup time, affording examination of the computations underlying the teaching notes, and enabling "what-if" analysis and customization. At the instructor's discretion, some of these models could be provided to students to help channel their analysis in specific ways. Finally, the instructor's disk contains exhibit files for those cases published in the instructor's manual (i.e., the suggested exam cases and the sequel cases).

Exhibit A of this note lists the files contained on the disks and their corresponding cases.

EQUIPMENT AND SOFTWARE

You will need an IBM personal computer or one that is IBM compatible. Also required is a copy of Lotus 1-2-3 Software (edition 2.0 or higher).

---

[1]"Proper use" requires thoughtful guidance of the student by the instructor. Computer-based case analysis offers many traps for the student. The classic traps are (1) focusing on programming instead of financial analysis and (2) "data dredging" or "analysis paralysis" (i.e., focusing on financial analysis, but without direction). The instructor can help students skirt these problems by suggesting that the students use the disks only if they have an understanding of Lotus and by setting a standard for case discussion that students may only discuss *financial insights* and not the modeling techniques by which they derived them.

ACCESSING THE FILES

The first time you access the files you will need to unarchive the disks. This time only, you will need a computer with two disk drives (e.g., one hard drive and one floppy, or two floppy disk drives). You will need to unarchive the files only once.

To begin the process of unarchiving, place any disk in a floppy drive, make that drive the default drive, and type README and press the <ENTER> key.

FINDING YOUR WAY WITHIN EACH FILE

Each file has a contents screen at the "home" position (i.e., cell A1) which shows:

- the name of the file,
- the title of the case, and
- the contents of the Lotus worksheet file indicating the location of the various exhibits in the spreadsheet.

Once you are in the file, you can find your way quickly to each exhibit by using the range names indicated in the contents section along with the GOTO (F5) key. For instance, suppose you wish to go to Exhibit 4 in a worksheet, and that its range name is "EXH4"; from any position in the spreadsheet, you can access that exhibit by typing:

F5
EXH4 <enter>

SUGGESTIONS ON ADMINISTERING STUDENT USE OF THE DISKS

Students should be expected to work on their own disks and, therefore, will need access to these disks only long enough to make a copy. Perhaps the best method of distributing the files is through a personal computer network, if one is available at your school. Alternatively, copies of the disks can be placed on reserve at the circulation desk of your library, or with a secretary or teaching assistant.

Make one or more back-up copies of the files, and store the original disks in a safe and secure place.

Case Number	Item	Student Worksheet (____.WK1)	Instructor Worksheet* (____.WK1)

Items in the Casebook

Case Number	Item	Student Worksheet	Instructor Worksheet*
1.	Walt Disney Productions, June 1984	DISNEY	none
2.	Peter Lynch and the Fidelity Magellan Fund	LYNCH	none
3.	The Financial Detective	DETECT	none
4.	Johnson's Nursery	JOHNNUR	JOHNURTN
5.	Alfin Fragrances, Inc.	ALFIN	ALFINTN
6.	Padgett Blank Book Company	PADGETT	none
7.	Atlantic Southeast Airlines	ASA	none
8.	The L. S. Starrett Company	STARRETT	STARRETTN
9.	De Laurentiis Entertainment Group, Inc.	DEG	none
10.	Columbia Mills, Inc.	COLMILLS	none
11.	Blue Cross and Blue Shield of Virginia	BLUCROSS	none
12.	Teletech Corporation	TELETECH	none
13.	General Motors Corporation, 1988	GENMOT	none
14.	The Investment Detective	INDETECT	INVDETTN
15.	Westfield Inc.	WESTFLD	none
16.	Boggs Mineral Company	BOGGS	none
17.	Sandbridge Company (A)	SANDBRDG	SANDBGTN
18.	Palmetto Shipping & Stevedoring Co., Inc.	PALMETTO	PALMETTN
19.	Sprigg Lane (A)	SPRIGG	none
20.	Enercon Corporation	ENERCON	none
21.	Iskall Arno, Inc. (Abridged)	ISKALL	none
22.	Brown-Forman Distillers Corporation	BROWNFOR	BROFORTN
23.	E. I. du Pont de Nemours Powder Company: 1909	DUPONT	none
24.	Cleveland-Cliffs Iron Company	CLEVE	none
25.	Southboro Corporation	SOUTH	SBOROTN
26.	Morgan Stanley Group, Inc.	MORGAN	none
27.	Spiegel, Inc. (Abridged)	SPIEGEL	SPIEGELTN
28.	Introduction to Debt Policy and Value	DEBTPOL	DEBTPOTN
29.	Tonka Corporation	TONKA	none
30.	Coleco Industries, Inc.	COLECO	none
31.	Design Technologies, Inc.	DESIGN	DESTECTN
32.	Delta and Eastern Airlines	DELEAST	none
33.	Johnstown Corporation	JOHNS	JOHNSTN
34.	Merit Marine Corporation	MERIT	none
35.	Chrysler's Warrants: September 1983	CHRYSLER	none
36.	Flowers Industries, Inc. (Abridged)	FLOWERS	FLOWRSTN
37.	British Petroleum Company, Ltd.	BRITPET	BRITPETN
38.	Brunswick Federal Savings and Loan Ass'n	BRUNSWCK	BRUNSWTN
39.	Emerson Electric Company	EMERSON	none
40.	Merchants Cotton Company	MERCHANT	none
41.	Gifford Bunsen and Company	BUNSEN	BUNSENTN

Case Number	Item	Student Worksheet	Instructor Worksheet
42.	Boston Celtics Limited Partnership	CELTICS	none
43.	Societe Generale de Belgique (A)	SGB	none
44.	Bumble Bee Seafoods, Inc.	BUMBLE	BUMBLETN
45.	Aqua Company (A)	AQUA	AQMODLTN AQUATN
46.	Sybron Corporation	SYBRON	SYBRONTN
47.	Hybritech, Inc. (A)	HYBTECH	HYBRIATN

Items in the Instructor's Manual**

48.	Peachtree National Bank	PEACH	none
49.	Societe General de Belgique (B)	none	none
50.	Aqua Company (B)	none	AQMODLTN AQUATN
51.	Eli Lilly and Company	LILLY	LILLYTN
52.	Hybritech, Inc. (B)	HYBRIB	HYBRIBTN
53.	Colt Industries	COLT	none
54.	Enigma Engineering	ENIGMA	ENIGMATN

*Instructor's worksheets are to be found on the instructor's disk.

**Student worksheets for these items are *not* found on the student diskettes; they are on the instructor's diskette.

Equity Costs: Some Conventions on Using the CAPM

One of the daunting aspects of preparing teaching notes for case studies in corporate finance is estimating equity costs satisfactorily with the capital-asset-pricing model (CAPM). Although the model itself is well understood, the theory says nothing about *which* risk-free rates, market premia, and betas to use in the model. There is an abundance of possibilities, and any sampling of academicians and practitioners will summon forth many combinations and permutations of methods. Rather than use all approaches pell-mell, these notes adhere to a few conventions. Armed with an understanding of the conventions underlying these notes, the instructor can follow the analysis more directly and, if desired, customize more easily.

COMBINATIONS OF RISK-FREE RATE AND MARKET PREMIUM

Many of the cases present a range of risk-free (i.e., U.S. government) rate alternatives, and the arithmetic and geometric mean market premia as of the date of the case. The teaching notes draw on the following two combinations:[1]

Short-Term Risk-Free Rate and Arithmetic Market Premium

The argument for this approach is that short-term rates are the best proxy for riskless rates: as obligations of the U.S. government, short-term rates are the closest to being default free; as short-term rates, they sustain little risk of illiquidity or capital loss because of sudden rises in market yields. For the purposes of these notes, "short term" is defined as 90 to 360 days.
The corresponding market premium used is the arithmetic average premium estimated over the long term (e.g., 1926 to the date of the case); for the period through 1988, this average has been estimated to be 8.4 percent.[2] If there is a bias in academia and in practice, it is toward the arithmetic premium, because when compounded over many periods, an arithmetic mean return is the one that gives the *mean* of the probability distribution of ending values; it equates the present value of an investment with its expected future value.

Long-Term Risk-Free Rate and Geometric Mean Market Premium

Partisans of the long-term risk-free rate argue that most corporate investments are for the long term, and that the long rate better matches the term of the asset being valued. According to this view, investors want to earn a market risk premium equal to the compound rate of return (over time) that the stock market has earned over and above returns on long-term bonds. For the purposes of these notes, "long term" is defined as 20 or 30 years.

---

[1]The analysis for "Aqua" (A) and (B) relies on a third approach, described in "Diversification, the Capital Asset Pricing Model, and the Cost of Equity Capital," a note published by Harvard Business School (9-276-183).

[2]The source for the estimated market premia is *Stocks, Bonds, Bills and Inflation,* which was originally prepared by Ibbotson and Sinquefield and published by the Institute of Chartered Financial Analysts in Charlottesville, Virginia. Starting in 1984, the data have been updated and published annually in a yearbook of the same name by Ibbotson Associates, Chicago, Illinois.

If one uses the yield on long-term U.S. government bonds as the estimate for the risk-free rate, then one should estimate the market premium (annualized compound rate) over a "typical" period of the same length. For instance, if you use the 30-year "long bond" as the basis for the risk-free rate, then you might average the compound rates for the periods 1925 to 1956 and 1956 to 1986. As a convenient approximation, you could simply use the geometric average over the entire period. For the years 1926 to 1988, the geometric mean market premium was 5.4 percent.

SELECTION OF BETA

At any time, you can uncover a range of estimated betas for many large companies published by statistical services, financial institutions, and consulting firms. Most betas quoted in these cases come from *Value Line Investment Survey*, a selection made on the basis of ready accessibility to students in the hope that it might stimulate their further research.

In a few instances, betas are drawn from *MediaGeneral Industriscope*, which publishes two betas for every company, "Up-market" and "Down-market." This form of presentation helps impress on students the basic variability in beta estimates. When confronted with these variations, there are two solutions: (1) if one is valuing a long-term asset, then it makes sense to average the estimates on the assumption that the market will fluctuate over time, causing beta to oscillate around its mean; (2) if the analytical task involves the shorter term, one can simply choose the beta consistent with current market conditions.

CAVEAT

None of these conventions is "correct." Research shows that market premia vary through time. Moreover, the CAPM only approximates market reality. Lacking a perfect forecast of equity returns, the analyst is left to wrestle estimated required returns from arguable conventions such as those described here.

Walt Disney Productions, June 1984

SYNOPSIS AND OBJECTIVES

This case is set in the midst of the attempted takeover of Walt Disney Productions by the raider Saul Steinberg in June 1984. Disney's chief executive officer ponders whether to fight the takeover or pay "greenmail." One significant influence on the decision is the "true" value of the firm. The case offers, either directly or through analysis, several estimates of value. The valuation question invites a review of Disney's past performance and current competitive position. Other significant influences on the decision are the ethics and economics of paying greenmail. The rich range of issues raised in the case (strategy, valuation, performance measurement, and ethics) help make it an effective first case, review case, or final exam in a corporate finance course.

The case was written and has been taught successfully to

* motivate a discussion of "excellence" from a corporate financial point of view and of the ways in which excellence might be measured;

* review and compare various valuation methodologies and suggest some explanations for the disparities among the results;

* show that corporate value depends heavily on industry conditions and the strategic choices managers make;

* estimate the economic costs of greenmail and discuss their influence on the morality of greenmail payment.

STUDY QUESTIONS

1. What are Disney's major business segments, and what is Disney's relative competitive position in each? How well has Disney performed in the segments and in the aggregate? What criteria should you use to judge performance?

2. What is Disney's apparent business strategy?

3. Is Disney a "growth company"? What should define a growth company?

4. Why was this "excellent company" the target of a takeover attempt?

5. Should Disney repurchase Saul Steinberg's shares?

   a. If so, what should be the repurchase price? How will the price of Disney's shares respond to the purchase announcement? Does the repurchase represent a transfer of wealth?

Teaching note written by Robert F. Bruner. Copyright (c) 1987 by the Darden Graduate Business School Sponsors, Charlottesville, VA.

b.   If not, and if Steinberg completes his takeover, what are the wealth
      consequences for Steinberg? For the former public shareholders?

TEACHING PLAN

An 80-minute discussion of this case could have many possible structures.
The following is one outline, which the author has used with some success. As a
means of accelerating the discussion and focusing it on the underlying valuation
problem, I begin the class with the various Disney share values given in the
case already listed on a chalkboard (see Exhibit A). I then ask the following
questions:

(15 minutes) As Disney's CEO, would you buy back the Disney shares from Saul
      Steinberg? Why? Why not? Take a vote.

(10 minutes) What is the meaning of these different valuations? Why not just
      ask an accountant to tell us what Disney is worth? How, in an efficient
      stock market, can there be a valuation discrepancy this big?

(10 minutes) Ron Miller, the CEO, said, "We have created unique value along
      with competitive and strategic advantage...." What are the unique value and
      advantage to which he refers? Please be as specific as you can in each
      business segment.

(10 minutes) Over the years, what role has Disney's management played in the
      development of this value and advantage?

(15 minutes) Is Disney excellent in financial terms? How do you define
      excellence?

(5 minutes) Why isn't operational success automatically accompanied by
      financial success?

(15 minutes) Should Ron Miller pay greenmail? Take a vote again.

        Pick a "Yes" voter: At what price? What will happen to
        the share price of the remaining shares? Why? How does
        management's interest differ from the shareholders' on this
        question?

        Pick a "No" voter: Why not? What are the eventual payoffs
        to the public shareholders? To Steinberg? To the
        employees?

The closing vote is unlikely to reveal a consensus, although the vote is
useful as a springboard to a brief survey by the instructor of Disney's history
subsequent to June 11, 1984. The epilogue (to follow) serves as an effective
summation of many of the issues raised in the case and is, I believe, a more
effective closing than a conceptual statement by the instructor.

21

ANALYSIS

Valuation Problem

As students work to establish the true value of Walt Disney Productions, the range of values given in Exhibit A frame the main dilemma in the case. They should quickly delete from the list book value per share and the April 1983 stock price, on the grounds that they reflect past performance or outdated investor expectations. Steinberg's bid prices may be driven more by bargaining strategy than by intrinsic values although plainly the acquisition of Gibson Greetings is to Steinberg a value-destroying investment. On the other hand, Steinberg's cost basis ($63.25/share) is an extremely useful reference point, because it reveals the foundation on which he believed he could still make a profit. The estimates of securities analysts at C. J. Lawrence ($64-$99/share) and Goldman, Sachs ($75/share) support the views that Steinberg did not overpay for his shares and that the shares might be worth considerably more than he paid.

Students may choose to augment this range of values with their own estimates. For instance, multiplying the forecasted EPS of $3.10 (David Londoner, case Exhibit 13) to $3.25 (Richard Simon, case text) times P/E multiples of 15 to 20 times gives share values ranging from $46.50 to $65.00. Sometimes students choose to capitalize profits or dividends at the difference between the cost of equity capital and the expected growth rate. The resulting share values are ordinarily quite low.

The disparity among the valuations is simply because Disney is worth one thing on a business-as-usual basis and something much higher if restructured, which is the thrust of the article in case Exhibit 13.

Assessment of Performance and Defining "Excellence"

Another way to rationalize the disparity in valuations is to adjust Disney's book value of equity for the wide differences between historical cost and current estimated value of certain assets, such as Disneyland, the film library, and the firm's enormous holdings of raw land. The calculation in Exhibit B suggests that, based on certain assumptions, the current book value of the company is $66.52 per share, not $40.58 per share as the balance sheet would suggest. This adjusted book value is still at the lower end of the range of asset-based valuations ($64.00-$99.00) suggested by C. J. Lawrence & Company. Furthermore, the calculation in Exhibit B ignores any benefits that could be gained from exploiting Disney's existing unused debt capacity. Even recognizing that the adjusted book-value estimate may be conservative, Disney's stock price before the takeover play began ($52.625) compares unfavorably with the adjusted book value. The resulting market-to-book value ratio is .79.

The ratio of stock price to adjusted book value is an appealing measure of performance. Intuitively, market-to-book ratios greater than 1 suggest that each dollar of profit retained in the firm is converted into more than a dollar of market value—which is *value creation*. Conversely, a market-to-book ratio less than 1 suggests that each dollar retained amounts to less than a dollar in market value—*value destruction*. The sources of value creation and destruction have been discussed at length elsewhere (see William Fruhan, *Financial Strategy*, Irwin, 1979); simply stated, however, the essential ingredient in value creation is the ability to earn rates of return in excess of those required by investors. As Exhibit C shows, over a sample of firms, higher market-to-book ratios are associated with higher "spreads" (i.e., positive differences between realized returns and required returns).

Exhibit D compares Disney's realized returns on equity with the returns required by Disney's equity-holders (i.e., the cost of equity). Equity costs may be calculated by using the data in case Exhibit 6 in the capital-asset-pricing model; returns on equity are also available in case Exhibit 6. Exhibit D shows that, for a considerable time, Disney has failed to perform up to the standard set by its shareholders. Worse yet, over the years 1981 to 1983, Disney even failed to earn the rate of return available on one-year U.S. Treasury bills.

There are several possible explanations for this performance. One is that the company may have foundered in the absence of a strong and creative leader. Walt Disney died in 1966, the last year of true supernormal performance. The commentaries quoted from *Newsweek* and *Business Week* in the case lend some support to this view. In terms of the value-creation framework, one could argue that Walt Disney's personal creative genius was the source of the firm's high realized returns. Other examples of this phenomenon in business history—such as Thomas Edison and Edwin Land—indicate that this "Great Leader Theory" is serious and meaningful, although the case gives no specific guidance about the areas of leadership failure after 1966.

An alternative interpretation of this performance is that it reflects managerial inefficiency, i.e., the failure to employ assets in their highest valued uses. Substantial evidence in Disney's history supports this interpretation. Case Exhibit 6 shows that, from 1965 to 1971, Disney's asset-utilization ratio fell to a third of what it had been. This decline coincided with the firm's investment in Florida and development of Disney World. Another shock occurred in the early 1980s when the firm's pretax profit margin fell from 27.12 percent (1980) to 12.5 percent (1983). This decline coincided with the opening of EPCOT Center and various setbacks in the firm's filmed entertainment division. The case indicates that the film segment once showed a 56 percent pretax return on investment; now its returns are negative. Similarly, theme parks returned 15.7 percent on assets (pretax) in 1978; compared with a 10 percent pretax return at the time of the case. The case suggests that, at the margin, the investment in parks is, in fact, even lower: EPCOT was returning $80 million (pretax) on assets of $1.9 billion. The fact that Walt Disney personally approved the firm's massive entry into Florida dampens some of the force of the Great Leader Theory. Plainly, the firm was taking major gambles that were not paying off.

Assessment of Strategy and Competitive Position

Did Disney "create unique value along with competitive and strategic advantage?" As Disney's large fund of creative capital suggests, it had in the past. The real question is how well management would use that capital for the survival of the firm and prosperity of its stakeholders. Exhibit E presents a model chalkboard layout for the history and current position of Disney's businesses. Plainly, the company has to respond to changing consumer demographics in filmed entertainment and to the combination of growing capacity and maturing demand in theme parks. Real estate development, however, requires different skills from those of the past and a different commitment of financial capital. It is a related business only in the sense that it may integrate the theme parks more effectively and profitably into their surrounding areas. Walt Disney Productions may have been taking a large leap into this new area, however, possibly at the expense of new creative projects and effective use of its existing creative capital (e.g., the artistic staff and film library). The current strategy might be characterized as an evolution away from operations based on creative capital and toward operations based on real property.

One might argue that Disney Productions has been paying its dues over the past 15 years for this strategic refocus and is now poised for lift-off into profitability based on real estate. The Florida theme parks are in place, and the nearby raw land remains to be developed. According to this argument, Saul Steinberg waited to raid Disney until the heavy investment phase was completed; if only the development revenues were arriving more quickly, the stock market would see the firm for its tremendous potential.

Securities analyst Richard Simon implies in the case that there is a more profitable alternative to the real estate-based strategy: refocus on creative capital with particular emphasis on filmed entertainment and communications (e.g., pay TV). Obviously, this route carries large risks as well as potentialities. Cable programming services are proliferating (see case Exhibit 4). Theme-park attendance appears to have leveled off for Disney (case Exhibit 7), and for the industry, growth is low and mature (see case Exhibit 11). As a film distributor, Disney's market share is low and declining (case Exhibit 9). The profitability of film production is highly volatile (see case Exhibit 8), and film inventory is large in relation to film revenues. This situation would not seem to be one in which to make much money. The main counter to all these arguments is that film entertainment was a profitable strategic focus at one time in Disney's past and perhaps it could be so again.

The Issue of Excellence

As the opening quotation of the case suggests, Peters and Waterman [*In Search of Excellence* (Harper & Row, 1982)] included Disney in their pantheon of "America's Best-Run Companies." Most consumers of the firm's services would be prone to agree with this assessment; in discussions of this case, several students will usually comment glowingly on the firm's animated films and theme parks. In this context, one of the larger questions the case poses is why this excellent company is the target of a takeover attempt.

The answer depends heavily on what we mean by excellence in business. Peters and Waterman focus in their highly popular book on aspects of the process of managing rather than on goal achievement. Business excellence, they say, is characterized by simple organization, lean staff, a bias for action rather than analysis, and emphasis on product quality based on respect for individual workers, fawning attention to customers, etc. Disney ranked high on several of these criteria. This approach is a means-oriented view of excellence, however, that says little about the achievement of ultimate objectives.

From an administrative point of view, the goals of the firm should be to create investment value for shareholders, to create value (or meaning) for employees, and to deliver value to customers. These competing goals must be balanced. A strategy of profiting any two stakeholder groups at the expense of the third is unsustainable in the long run; eventually, the slighted party will react.

Excellence defined in terms of value creation and delivery is a subject about which corporate finance has much to say. The value-creation framework suggests that premium (i.e., above-book-value) stock prices result from achieving large positive spreads between realized returns on equity and the returns required by equity-holders. Stocks selling below book value are associated with negative spreads. Thus, the value-creation framework focuses attention on the fundamental opportunities and constraints of the firm, along with the choices managers make.

Defining excellence in corporate financial terms suggests that Disney was not excellent, at least not in delivering value to investors (see Exhibit D). Disney seems to have succeeded in satisfying employees and customers, but not shareholders. Indeed, the opportunity to unlock the latent, undelivered value for shareholders finally became apparent enough to entice a raider into play. In other words, Disney was attacked because it was *not* excellent.

Paying Greenmail

Greenmail is the payment of a premium share price by a takeover target to a hostile buyer for the buyer's accumulated shares in the target. Paying greenmail is considered unethical for four main reasons. First, it is a discriminatory payment; not all public shareholders enjoy the right to sell their shares to the company at the price paid to the greenmailer. This fact is especially painful to professional arbitrageurs. Second, it is viewed as the triumph of agents' self-interest: senior managers rarely welcome the consequences of a hostile takeover and, so it is argued, sacrifice shareholders' wealth to preserve their jobs. Third, it is believed to effect significant transfers of wealth from the remaining public shareholders to a more powerful raider. Fourth, greenmail payments (like blackmail) are actions not freely conceived and may set the pattern for further intimidation; expediency is a bad precedent. Against such a list, there appear to be no conditions under which management would be justified in paying greenmail. The objective of any class discussion of the ethics of paying greenmail should be to show that such a conclusion is not strictly true.

There may be circumstances in which public shareholders would be better off after the greenmail payment *even if* they were discriminated against, their agents acted in self-interest, and the action was not freely taken. A decision involves weighing the evident costs of greenmail versus the potential benefits. Some students may argue that it is impossible to place a price on discrimination or the loss of free choice and that managerial self-interest is always bad. Yet, in many ways each day, individuals submit to discrimination or loss of choice to enhance their own welfare. Furthermore, managerial self-interest is not *per se* harmful to shareholders; there is bound to be a wide range of decisions in which managerial and shareholder self-interest coincide.

The key question is whether shareholders receive any benefits to offset the costs of greenmail. Specifically, will the remaining shareholders be better or worse off after the payment than before? The Disney case facts imply that management may have had an estimate of the intrinsic value of the firm that was materially higher than the *ex ante* share price or a potential greenmail price per share (see Exhibit A). Under this circumstance, any repurchase of shares at a price less than intrinsic value will transfer wealth from the selling shareholders (i.e., the greenmailer) *to* the remaining public shareholders. The amount of the wealth transfer per share remaining will be:

$$\frac{[(\text{Intrinsic value/Share} - \text{Cash paid/Share}) \times \text{Shares bought}]}{\text{Shares remaining outstanding}}$$

The numerator of this equation suggests that the total wealth transferred depends on the difference between what the greenmailer (e.g., Steinberg) would have received had he "bought and held" versus what he actually received. If the wealth transfer is positive and material, it could be "right" for managers to pay greenmail.

The instructor will want to hedge any strong statement in favor of greenmail because managers actually do have alternatives to paying it. The first is to announce and execute a restructuring of the firm along the lines the raider would have to effect to unlock latent value. This move allows both the raider and the public to participate in the benefits. The second alternative is to

25

offer to repurchase shares from the public instead of the greenmailer, as happened in the case of T. Boone Pickens' attempted raid on Unocal. This move siphons cash to the public at the expense of the raider and, in fact, enhances the freedom of choice of the public shareholder: he or she can elect to receive the greenmailer's price per share or hold onto the shares in hopes of eventually receiving the intrinsic value per share. Because these alternatives exist in theory, it may be useful for the instructor to dwell briefly on the effects they might have on the firm, its shareholders, and the raider. The decision to pay greenmail versus its alternatives ultimately depends on the wealth-creation/ wealth-transfer effects each choice may have. Because the case presents no details on the wealth effects of the alternatives to greenmail, the class is left to speculate. The virtue of doing so is to temper any seemingly doctrinaire support in favor of paying greenmail.

The chief objection to this wealth-transfer-based line of analysis is that stock prices usually *fall* after greenmail is paid. This could happen for two reasons. First, greenmail payment takes a target company "out of play" (i.e., it removes the immediate threat of takeover. Terminating the action process induces frantic selling of arbitrageurs. The market in the firm's stock is equilibrating away from one highly opportunistic clientele back toward longer term investors. A second explanation for the price decline is an inevitable information asymmetry: investors cannot know as much about a firm's prospects as managers. The problem is essentially one of signaling or investor relations, which, by and large, firms do poorly. Even if management *never* talks to shareholders, however, and instead waits for intrinsic value eventually to become manifest in operating performance, it still makes economic sense to pay greenmail if the wealth transfer to the remaining shareholders is positive.

Should Ron Miller pay greenmail to Saul Steinberg? The answer is "yes," assuming (1) that the price paid per Steinberg share is less than the intrinsic value, (2) that Miller makes it a top priority to realize the intrinsic value for remaining shareholders (via operational changes and better investor relations), and (3) that the effect on share price is superior to restructuring or other defenses. What should the price be? It should be as low as possible consistent with an incentive for Steinberg to sell--certainly no higher than the estimated intrinsic value. Raiders and arbitrageurs look for annualized rates of return above 50 percent. Assuming Steinberg bought his shares on March 1, 1984, his holding period to the date of the case was 103 days. Thus, he would seek an interim gain of 14 percent in order to achieve an annualized gain of 50 percent. Steinberg's apparent cost basis was $63.25, suggesting a greenmail price of $72.11 (114 percent of cost). At a greenmail price of $77.45, Steinberg would receive an annualized rate of return of 77.96 percent.

The decision to pay greenmail is difficult because of ambiguity and the conflicting tugs of various arguments; but wrestling with these unenviable problems is what chief executives are paid for. Although the economic analysis outlined here sheds light on the consequences of paying greenmail, nothing noted here should be construed as suggesting that the decision can be reduced to a simple rule of thumb.

EPILOGUE

On June 12, 1984, Disney's CEO announced an agreement to buy Steinberg's 4.2 million shares for $325.3 million or $77.45 per share. On that day, Disney shares closed at $49, down $5.25 or 9.7 percent from the previous close. Two days later, the first of many shareholder lawsuits protesting the payment was filed. The lawsuits had virtually no effect on the greenmail payment.

On July 17, Irwin Jacobs, charging that Disney was overpaying for Gibson Greetings, announced a hostile tender offer. A month later, Disney canceled its planned acquisition of Gibson--but Jacobs continued with his tender offer. Eventually, Jacobs' shares were bought at cost by the Bass brothers, who, as previous owners of Arvida, had become large shareholders in Disney.

Apparently sensing that the two raids indicated fundamental problems in management, the board of directors fired Ronald Miller as CEO on September 7, 1984. Two directors who helped in the takeover defense quit in January 1985. The chief financial officer, the head of the pay TV division, and other managers left within a year of Miller's departure. A major management house cleaning had thus taken place following the raids.

More importantly, the focus of the firm's strategy shifted from real property back to creative capital. The new CEO, Michael Eisner, was hired from Paramount; the president came from Fox Films. Losing no time, in November 1984, they announced aggressive film-production plans: a target of 15 releases per year (up from 4 films per year), which would put Disney back in the class of major producers. The films were to be financed through limited partnerships.

The renewed emphasis on films was prescient. In early 1985, two major takeovers rocked the film industry: Turner Broadcasting bought MGM/United Artists and Rupert Murdoch bought half of Twentieth Century Fox. Generally, securities analysts believed that film companies were attractive investments because of a rising consumer appetite for movies and home video entertainment.

The development of theme parks and surroundings would continue as planned, including a new Disneyland near Paris, but management announced in May 1985 that it was studying sales/leasebacks of its theme parks, which would raise more than $2 billion. Finally, in December 1986, Disney announced that it was considering selling or splitting off its Arvida real estate unit. These and other proposals indicated a tightening of asset management--a challenge the firm had ignored during the preceding 20 years.

Within 11 months of the greenmail decision, Disney's stock was trading around $85 per share. Adjusting for a four-for-one stock split in early 1986, Disney shares have traded above $85 since this episode, and on September 2, 1987, closed at $307.50.

EXHIBIT A   Selected Values and Bids for Disney Stock

$84.38	Stock price in April 1983
$64–$99.00	C. J. Lawrence estimate
$75.00	Goldman Sachs estimate
$72.50	Steinberg's bid if Gibson not acquired
$67.50	Steinberg's bid if Gibson acquired
$63.25	Steinberg's apparent cost basis
$54.25	Stock price June 11, 1984
$47.50	Stock price November 10, 1983
$40.58	Book value/share December 31, 1983

EXHIBIT B Calculation of Disney's Adjusted Book Value per Share

Book value of equity as reported September 30, 1983*	$1,400,528,000
Disneyland**	120,000,000
Film library†	275,000,000
Raw land††	500,000,000
Adjusted book value	$2,295,528,000
Number of common shares	34,509,171
Adjusted book value per share	$66.52

---

*Case Exhibit 2.

**Case text. Disneyland was carried on the books at $20 million, although it was estimated to be worth $140 million.

†Film library was apparently carried at zero historical cost, consistent with industry practice of rapid amortization of film production costs (balance sheet, case Exhibit 2, shows no value broken out for film library). However, case Exhibit 10 suggests that the film library was worth $275 million. The annuity value of old but successful films is immediately apparent from case Exhibit 3, which presents the annual revenues from releases of "Snow White."

††Most of Disney's raw land was acquired in the mid- and late 1960s as part of its Florida projects. The general level of prices (e.g., Consumer Price Index) rose approximately three times between the late-1960s and the mid-1980s. The assumption here is that the raw land was acquired at one-third of its value estimated today. The case mentions that the raw land is believed to be worth $300–$700 million. Assuming the $700 million value and a $200 million cost (about one-third), the valuation adjustment would be $500 million.

EXHIBIT C Profitability and Value of DJIA Companies, Winter 1984

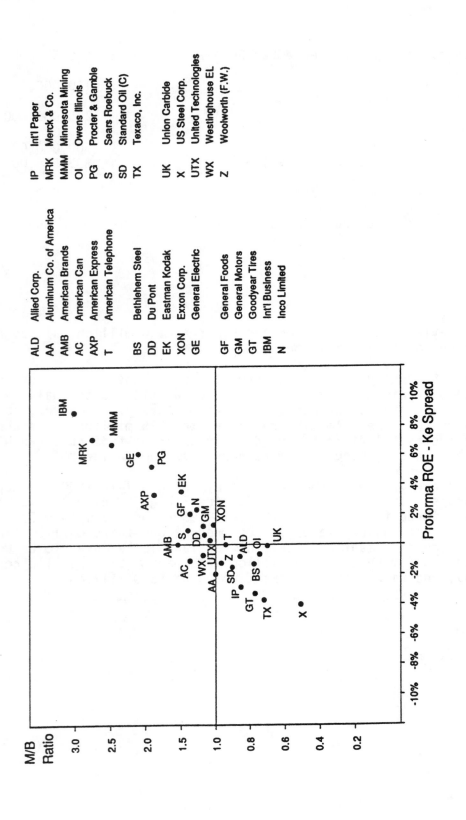

Source: Marakon Associates

EXHIBIT D Walt Disney Productions Annual Return on Equity Compared to Cost of Equity

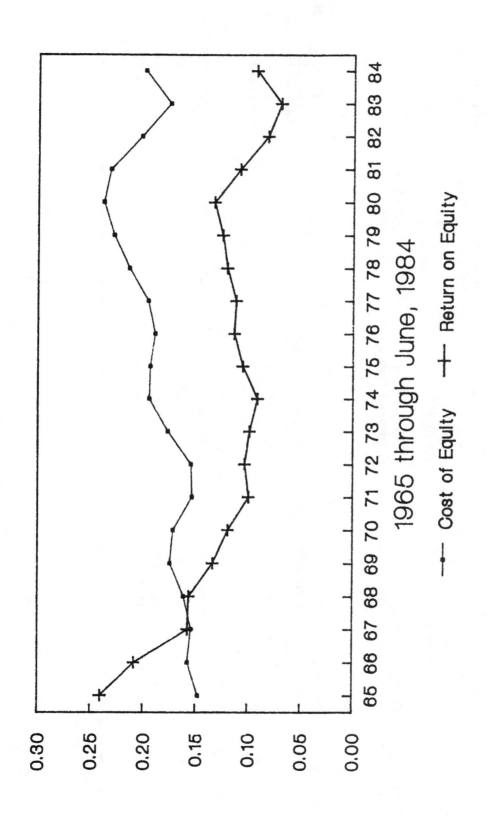

1965 through June, 1984

— Cost of Equity + Return on Equity

EXHIBIT E Business Segments and Strategy

Segment	Filmed Entertainment	Theme Parks	Consumer Products	Real Estate
Entry	Animation 1928 Wonderful World (TV) 1961–81 Disney Channel 1979 Touchstone Films 1979	Disneyland 1954 Disneyland 1972 EPCOT 1982 Tokyo 1983	Gibson Greetings 1984	28,000 Acres in Orlando, 1968 Arvida 1984
Industry Situation	Changing demographics Consolidation in films Heavy competition in cable Large risks	25 Parks Saturated Demand Low Growth	Highly Competitive Easy Entry	
Disney Position	Dominant family brand Trademarked animated characters Valuable film library	Leading franchise Well-positioned in Florida and Southern Calif.	Ancillary	Huge position in Florida Determines land values around Orlando
Strategy	Shift to target more mature audiences Exploit film library	Spend aggressively to maintain/improve existing parks	Protect trademarks Exploit characters	Develop slowly and selectively
Red Flags	Erosion of creative talent Recent big film losses	Flat growth, even with EPCOT		Huge capital requirements Long time to pay off

Peter Lynch and the Fidelity Magellan Fund

SYNOPSIS AND OBJECTIVES

The manager of the Fidelity Magellan Fund, Peter Lynch, announced in February 1988 that his long-term goal was to beat the return on the market by 5-6 percentage points annually. The student must decide whether, in the spring of 1988, the Magellan Fund deserves continued heavy investment by individual investors. To motivate a discussion of the reasonableness of "beating the market," the case presents background information on the U.S. equity markets, the mutual fund industry and its performance, and the stock market crash of October 1987.

The case is intended to provide a nontechnical introduction to the U.S. equity markets and to lay the foundation for some basic concepts in finance. Ideally, the case would appear early in an introductory course in finance. Specifically, this case has been used to

- motivate a discussion of the concept of capital-market efficiency;

- impart some recent capital market history—in particular, regarding the bull market of 1982-87 and the crash of October 1987;

- define the influence of institutions in the U.S. equity markets and the relative importance of pension funds, mutual funds, and individual investors in setting prices of equities. (An important part of this point is to establish the concept of "lead steers.");

- introduce a basic concept of valuation: that the value of a firm will be equal to the sum of the values of its assets, as illustrated by the net asset valuation of mutual funds;

- exercise one measure of investment performance: total percentage rate of return of a fund less the total return of a broad market index (e.g., the Standard & Poor's 500) or less the return on a group of funds with similar investment objectives.

STUDY QUESTIONS

1. How easy to achieve will Peter Lynch's long-term goal be? Is it reasonable?

2. How well has the Magellan Fund performed over the last 10 years? Please be specific in your assessment: what does "good performance" mean to you, and how do you measure it?

Teaching note written by Robert F. Bruner. Copyright (c) 1988 by the Darden Graduate Business School Sponsors, Charlottesville, VA.

3. Suppose you advise wealthy individuals in the area of equity investments. Would you recommend investment in the Magellan Fund? In any "growth" fund? What beliefs about the equity markets does your answer reflect?

Students who are new to the subject of finance may find useful a reference to one or more dictionaries of financial terms, such as *Barrons Dictionary of Finance and Investment Terms* (John Downes and Jordan Elliot Goodman, Woodbury, CT: Barron's Educational Series, 1985) or *Dictionary of Banking and Finance* (edited by Lewis E. Davids, Totowa, NJ: Littlefield, Adams & Co., 1978).

TEACHING PLAN

Assuming the case is taught early in an introductory finance course, the author's strategy is to exploit the descriptive elements of the case first, then move into the analytical aspects, and finally end with the decision and recommendation. The reason is that novices to finance may need reinforcement of some core knowledge about the equity markets and mutual funds before tackling the problems of measuring performance. Throughout the discussion, the instructor should solicit definitions of financial terms from the students. The following outline of questions and discussion follows that strategy:

(5 minutes) What is Fidelity Management Research? Magellan?

(10 minutes) Are they material players in the U.S. equity markets? Who are the major players in equities? What is the structure of the equity investment market?

(15 minutes) What do you need to do well to succeed or merely survive as an investment manager in this market? How would you define "excellent performance"?

(5 minutes) What is Peter Lynch's strategy?

(15 minutes) How well has Magellan done?

(15 minutes) How realistic is Lynch's goal?

(10 minutes) If markets are efficient, what is the role for the manager?

(5 minutes) Would you invest in Magellan? Close with a vote, yes or no.

Discussing the performance of the Fidelity Magellan Fund since the date of the case (see the epilogue) is a useful vehicle for closing comments supporting and opposing the notion of capital-market efficiency.

ANALYSIS

Descriptive Points

An important objective of the case is to introduce the novice to the structure of the U.S. capital markets. This foundation is useful for the student later in a course when he or she encounters concepts founded on capital-market efficiency, investor rationality, and perfect competition. The case conveys the role of arbitrage driven by huge volumes of money (managed by institutional investors) setting prices in the markets.

Simple demographics are an important descriptive element. The capital market can be segmented into the stock, bond, and money markets. Within the stock market, there are major segments by type of player: pension funds, mutual funds, and individuals. The mutual fund segment, in turn, can be broken down by investment objective: growth, income, etc. The magnitude of the market (in terms of dollars and people) and the heterogeneity of investors underscore the difficulty of achieving consistently superior performance.

Another important descriptive element is recent capital-market history, including the bull market from 1982 to 1987 and the crash in October 1987. Here the novice confronts the dynamic nature of the market and the essential challenge to investors posed by changing conditions. These conditions can motivate a discussion of market timing and technical analysis as investment strategies and the relative significance of the basic buy-and-hold strategy.

A third descriptive element concerns the structure of the mutual-fund-management industry itself. One could characterize money management as a cottage industry—thousands of small firms and relatively easy entry—but such a view is misleading. It ignores the huge barriers that block entry into the group of large mutual fund managers, including reputation (past success); investment know-how; economies of scale in administration, trading, and research; and some skill in market segmentation of investors. Despite these barriers, sustaining a comparative advantage in the competition for the management of investors' funds remains difficult. Fidelity may be the largest mutual fund manager, but its primacy is not assured.

Lynch's Strategy and Performance: The Measurement Issue

Much of Peter Lynch's past performance is founded on the following management approach: (1) stay fully invested (minimize cash); (2) pick stocks based on their "fundamentals"; (3) emphasize growth companies; and (4) trade frequently (do not avoid high turnover). With this strategy, Lynch seeks to beat the market by 5-6 percentage points per year over the long term.

Up to the date of the case, Lynch's strategy seems to have served him well. The statistics are indisputable: over the past 10 years, the Magellan Fund ranks number one among all equity funds in total return. More careful examination reveals, however, that most of the success is attributable to returns in the first five years of that period. Exhibit A, Magellan's total and excess returns by year, shows a slow downward trend in both measures over time. It turns out that this trend correlates significantly with the growth in Magellan's size. Exhibit B associates the returns with asset size of the fund and shows an even more pronounced downward trend in returns. Finally, Exhibit C computes the average excess returns for the five-year period (ending each year, 1981 to 1987) and also weights those returns by the size of the fund; here the downward trend is most clearly pronounced. In essence, the figures show that Magellan's performance regresses toward the "average" return for the market as the fund's size increases. This trend should be no surprise: at a fund size of $11 billion, Magellan must be approximating an index fund, representative of the market at large. There may not be enough small, aggressive growth companies for Magellan to invest in; thus Lynch's promise of 5-6 percent excess returns depends on his market-timing ability.

Market Efficiency

Lynch's apparent strategy and the evident source of his excess returns in the future vary sharply from conventional views about the efficiency of the stock market. This insight is intended to motivate a debate about the practicality of stock market efficiency. The instructor may find novices quite ready to embrace the concept of efficiency (depending on their exposure to the concept in textbooks or other readings), thus making it necessary to play the devil's advocate on Lynch's behalf in order to stimulate debate. A key insight to emerge from such a debate must be that efficiency is assured only if there are enough Peter Lynchs in the market who invest in the expectation of earning excess returns. In other words, the existence of Peter Lynch is no mark of market inefficiency.

The real issue is the consistency with which Lynch earns his returns. The case presents academic findings (footnote 9) which suggest that mutual funds do not earn excess returns on a risk-adjusted basis. And a simple inspection of case Exhibit 6 (see now "+/- S&P 500 %") reveals that, over the past five years, Magellan has no consistent pattern of superior performance.

EPILOGUE

From March 1988 to June 1989, Magellan Fund posted superior returns compared with the market as a whole, summarized in the following table:

	Magellan	S&P 500
Mar. 1988 – Mar. 1989:	+13.75%	+6.75%
June 1988 – June 1989:	+22.19%	+18.07%

Exhibit D presents the performance of Magellan on a monthly basis over this period.

In April 1989, *Forbes* magazine published an article[1] consistent with the analysis here (i.e., that given Magellan's size, Lynch's performance would probably increasingly mirror the performance of the market as a whole). Evidently, Peter Lynch bristled at this observation. He replied in the same article,

> In a golf analogy, I shot a bunch of 68s and everybody in the field was shooting 80s. And now I'm shooting 75s and everybody else is still shooting in the mid-80s. And you're saying, "What's wrong with your golf game?" I still think Magellan can beat the market.

---

[1]Jonathan Clements, "Can Lynch Live Up to His Reputation?" April 3, 1989, pp. 174-76.

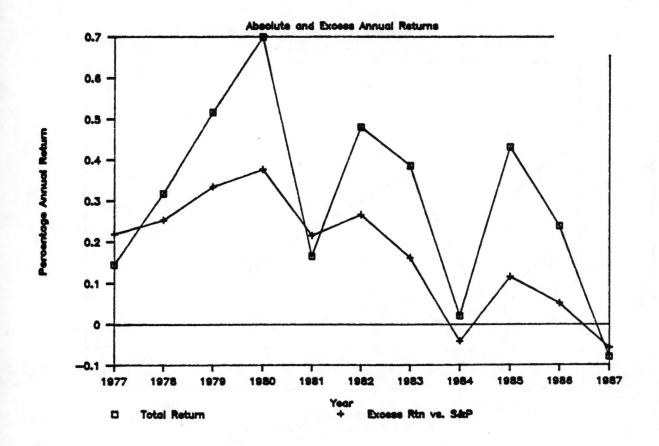

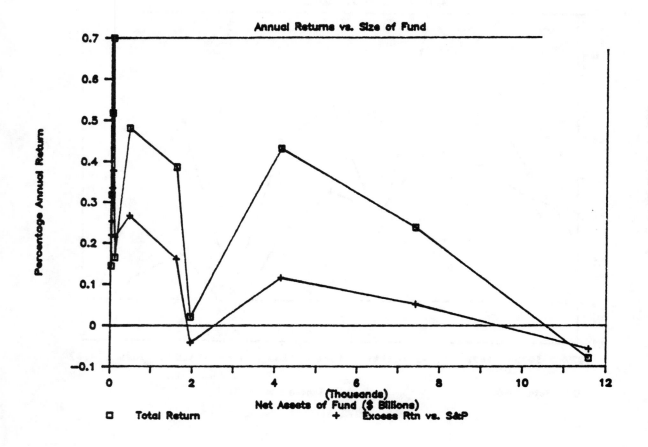

Annual Returns vs. Size of Fund

EXHIBIT C   Excess Returns, Five-Year Windows

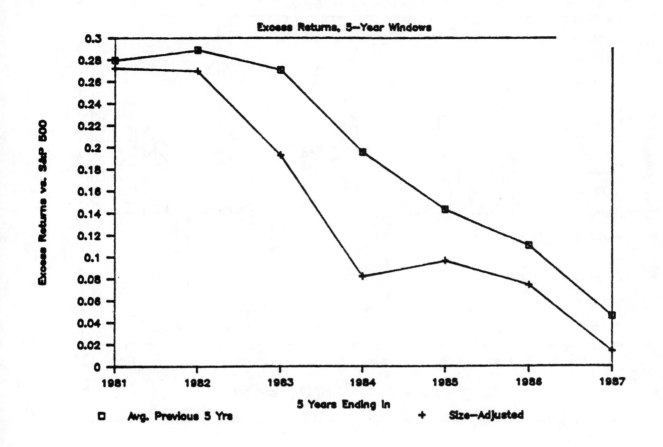

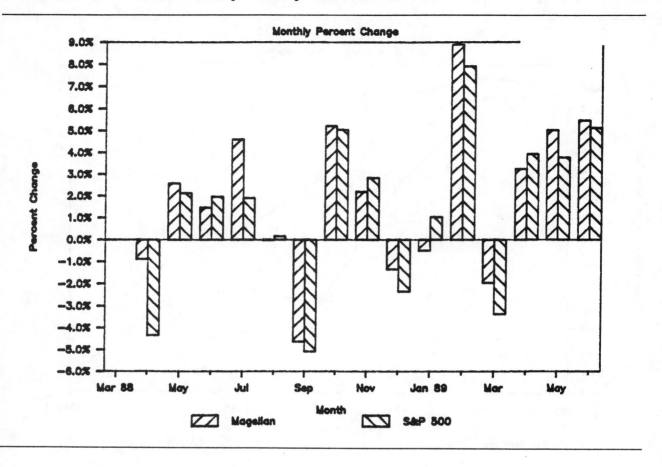

The Financial Detective

SYNOPSIS AND OBJECTIVES

The student is presented financial ratios for eight pairs of unidentified companies and asked to mate the description of the company with the financial profile apparent in the ratios. The primary objective of this case is to introduce students to financial-ratio analysis--in particular, the range of ratios and the insights each affords. Important substantive insights may also be drawn from the case. First, the economics of individual industries accounts for significant variation in financial ratios because of, for instance, differences in technologies, product characteristics, and competitive structures. Second, financial performance results from managerial choices; within industries, the wide variation in financial ratios is often a result of differences in corporate strategy.

STUDY QUESTIONS

The problem in this case is self-explanatory; no formal assignment questions are required. However, depending on the level of the students, the instructor may choose to assign different subgroups of the class to deal with specific industries.

TEACHING PLAN

Discussion of this case is straightforward: one simply proceeds through the eight industries. There are, however, several approaches in leading the discussion that can enhance the learning experience.

First, one should call on a different student to resolve the question in each industry. This case is an excellent vehicle for bringing out the quiet or less confident student through a "cold call"; the task is objective, so the personal exposure is limited. If one asks the students to choose the industry they wish to address, the easier industry pairs (appliances, computers, retailing, hotels) tend to be dispatched first, while the harder pairs (drugs, electronics, newspapers, transportation) will be dealt with later in the discussion. The result is good pacing: the easy comparisons build student confidence to tackle the harder comparisons, and the harder comparisons lay the groundwork for closing comments by the instructor.

Second, it makes sense to format the chalkboards in advance of class, writing the industry names as column headings, with the company letters below them. Under each of the company letters, the instructor records the salient characteristics mentioned by the student. When the student exhausts the important observations, the instructor can ask the student to identify the company in each pair.

With regard to any given industry, the best approach is to invite a student to list the salient qualitative features of each company. This approach tends

---

Teaching note written by Robert F. Bruner. Copyright (c) 1989 by the Darden Graduate Business School Sponsors, Charlottesville, VA.

to focus the discussion on the key issues and discourages a mind-numbing recitation of the numbers.

Third, suspense is a useful tool in this case. Students often ask for the correct answers as each industry is discussed. By deferring the correct answers until the end, however, the instructor can use them as a platform on which to make some general summary comments on the nature of ratio analysis.

Fourth, time management is a challenge in this case. The early (easy) industries can absorb more time than they objectively require. The harder industry comparisons deserve more time, simply because, with them, the students learn more about the limitations of ratio analysis. Moreover, since the case raises many mechanical and substantive issues, it is worth leaving 15 minutes at the end of class to survey the issues and get closure on them.

ANALYSIS

Comparisons Among Industries

This case is primarily about the effect of managerial strategy on financial ratios, but it also affords several insights about the effect of industry differences on financial ratios. For instance, differences in *asset intensity* can produce dramatically different asset structures [compare the percentages of inventory and net property, plant, and equipment (PP&E) for hotels or transportation with appliances or health products]. The rate of *technological change* can manifest itself in several ways, perhaps most prominently in spending for research and development (R&D) companies (compare computer or the firms in health products) and in the reinvestment rate required to stay competitive (compare dividend-payout ratios for computers and appliances). *Industry structure* is believed to affect profitability through the pricing power of the firm. The newspaper industry can be characterized as locally oligopolistic (in some areas, monopolistic); the appliance industry is much more competitive in structure. The gross profit margins of the two industries differ substantially.

The general insight for students must be that, in conducting the financial analysis of a firm, one must understand the nature of the industry.

Comparisons of Pairs of Firms Within Industries

Turning to the pairwise comparison, we seek to impress upon students the impact different business strategies have on the financial ratios of the firm.

Health products: Firms A and B. Company A is Johnson & Johnson, the manufacturer of nonprescription drugs, health and beauty aids, and other consumer products. Company B is Baxter Travenol, which manufactures patented prescription drugs and has recently acquired American Hospital Supply. Perhaps the most significant difference between these firms is in their customer focus: J&J sells to consumers, while Baxter sells to institutions and doctors.

Company A bears the profile of a consumer-oriented firm. *Gross profit/sales* for company A is significantly higher than for B. A's products are branded (e.g., Tylenol) and command a price premium. B's products are patented and should also command a price premium, although the margins in this sector are probably offset by the lower margins of the hospital-supply company.

The higher selling, general, and administrative expense *(SG&A)/sales* for company A reflects differences in marketing strategies. Company A brands its products and markets with the benefit of advertising through standard consumer-products channels. Company B markets largely through a direct sales force. One may assume that selling direct is cheaper (in absolute terms) than to brand-

42

advertise and sell. A second reason SG&A might be higher for company A is that J&J is organized into 165 discrete companies (each with its own administration); company B is organized centrally. Company A's decentralization may result in higher administration expenses.

Sales/Assets is greater for company A, perhaps reflecting its mass-market, high-volume orientation.

While *receivables/sales* for the two companies are similar, company A turns them almost twice as fast (8.41x versus 4.87x). Also, the *days sales outstanding* (DSO) for company A is considerably shorter than for company B (43 days versus 75 days). This difference probably reflects the clientele: A sells to retailers, who are high-turnover oriented, while B sells to institutions, who may take longer to pay, and to druggists, who simply may require longer payment terms to finance their inventory of ethical drugs.

One anomaly that may throw students is that *R&D expense/sales* is lower for company B, the pharmaceutical company (3.2 percent versus 7.7 percent). One possible explanation is that Baxter may spend a high amount on R&D in its pharmaceutical segment, but this expense is masked by the high volume of sales in its hospital-supply segment. This anomaly highlights a worthy caveat to students: One needs to understand the underlying business portfolio of the company whose ratios one is analyzing.

Finally, the case states that, as a result of the recent acquisition, the pharmaceuticals company has significant goodwill on its books. This appears as a large difference in the *other assets* line (40.6 percent versus 15.6 percent).

Appliances: Firms C and D. Company C is Maytag, the firm that sets itself apart as a high-quality product manufacturer. Company D is Whirlpool, which markets under the Roper and Kitchen-Aid brands as well as its own name and manufactures Kenmore appliances for Sears Roebuck. Many of the differences between these two firms may be attributed to strategic choices about quality production and channels of marketing. To sharpen this distinction, one can ask the students what a Sears might stipulate in a private-label supply contract. (Sears might offer predictable demand and faster payment in return for lower price.)

Receivables/Assets is lower for D than C, which reflects the different customer bases of the two firms: D gets paid faster under its private-label contract. This difference is also apparent in the lower *DSO* for D, as well as the higher *receivables turnover*.

Cost of goods sold (COGS)/sales is lower for C because it charges higher prices for its higher quality.[1] This explanation could also apply to company C's higher *sales/assets*.

The combination of higher net margin and higher asset turnover in company C leads to a 10-percentage-point difference in *return on assets* and a 22-point difference (the largest in the exhibit) in *return on equity* from company D's. These huge differences in return probably explain the large difference in *market/book* ratios for the two firms (5.16x for company C and 1.91x for D).

Computers: Firms E and F. Company E is Control Data Corporation (CDC), a manufacturer of large, general-use computers and related software, and a provider

---

[1]Assuming that both firms have the same costs. The alternative explanation is that company C has lower costs and the same prices. While this ambiguity cannot be resolved by case facts, the interpretation in the text is more consistent with the quality rationale.

of financial services. Company F is Cray Research, a manufacturer of supercomputers. The essential difference that motivates our conclusions here is *product focus*: Cray has a narrowly defined product line, while CDC produces a broad line of computers, only one segment of which is supercomputers. Cray is the acknowledged volume and quality leader for its segment.

The most striking difference between the two companies is *gross profits/sales*--a spread of 34 percentage points. Company F, which enjoys the higher ratio, exploits premium pricing power for its product.

On the other hand, because F defines its customer market narrowly, it sells fewer units and enjoys a lower aggregate sales volume. Company F's products are, comparatively speaking, big-ticket items. These characteristics are apparent in its lower *sales/assets* ratio (76 percent versus 128 percent).

The two firms market their products differently. CDC, the broad-line manufacturer identified as company E, relies on much more proactive direct sales activity than does Cray. The specialty manufacturer lets the product sell itself. This difference is reflected in the comparatively lower *SG&A/sales* ratio for company F, the specialized manufacturer.

Retailing: Firms G and H. Company G, Wal-Mart, owns a chain of discount department and drug stores. Company H is a fuller price department-store chain. The essential strategic differences are in product pricing (discount versus full price), service level (bare bones versus full), on-site versus catalogue sales, leasing versus outright ownership of PP&E, and perhaps in market positioning (suburban/rural versus urban).

The discounter offers low prices in return for receiving high sales volume. The full-service department store offers fuller pricing but also fuller service, such as credit. This basic difference is apparent in the *sales/assets* ratio (the discounter has much higher asset turns) and in *receivables turnover* and *DSO* (the discounter gives little credit, so DSO is only two, and turnover is extremely high).

One might interpret the catalogue sales to contribute to more rapid *inventory turnover* for the full-line firm. The higher *inventory/assets* for the discounter may be attributable to its need to maintain stocks in many small outlets.

The issue of leasing that the case raises is complicated by no clear indication of whether these are operating or capitalized leases. One could assume, given the long-term nature of the commitment, that the store leases would need to be capitalized, in which case the obligation would be listed in *other liabilities* and the asset would be listed in *other assets*. Company H fits this profile: it has little net PP&E and much more "other" assets and liabilities.

Electronics: Firms I and J. Company I is Motorola, which has two principal segments--semiconductors, and radio and television equipment. Company J is Texas Instruments, which produces semiconductors as well as consumer products that use its semiconductors (e.g., hand-held calculators). As the product mix of the two companies implies, the main issue in this comparison is the relative degree of diversification away from the semiconductor business--a high-volume, commodity product. Company I is relatively more diversified than company J.

The lower *gross profit margin* of company J is consistent with a strong commitment to the commodity semiconductors segment. Company I's higher gross margin is offset by higher *SG&A expense/sales* which is consistent with the marketing expenses necessary to sell branded products.

A second area of difference is in the liquidity and leverage of the two firms. The case suggests that the firm producing calculators is "financially conservative." This conservatism is reflected in firm J's *quick ratio* and *current ratio* and its greater reliance on long-term debt as opposed to short-term instruments for financing (see ratio of *long-term debt/assets*).

In other respects, the two firms have remarkably similar financial characteristics, which makes this comparison one of the more difficult to settle.

Hotels: Firms K and L. Company K, Hilton, operates a chain of high-quality hotels worldwide and a smaller line of casinos. Company L is Marriott, which is about equally committed to hotels and food-service operations. The strategic and economic differences between these two firms lie in the extent of each's commitment to hotels (a highly asset-intensive business) as opposed to service operations.

Firm K fits the profile of the hotel/casino business: high *gross and net margins*, high *quick and current ratios* (perhaps reflecting its casino business), and a relatively low *sales/assets* ratio, reflecting high asset intensity.

Firm L looks more like a service business. Its profit margins are smaller than firm K, but its *sales/assets* ratio is much larger, which reflects a smaller asset base than the other firm. Firm L finances itself more aggressively— showing *equity/assets* of only 15 percent, long-term debt/equity of 308 percent, and much lower *current* and *quick ratios* than firm K.

Newspapers: Firms M and N. Company M is Lee Enterprises, owner of a number of small newspapers in the Midwest. Company N is the New York Times Company. The strategic difference between these two entities is along the centralization/decentralization dimension. As stated in the text, the company with the flagship newspaper has a centralized, well-managed inventory system.

Company N corresponds to the profile of the centralized publisher: its *inventory turnover* is 47 times per year—nearly weekly. And as a percentage of assets, inventory of company N is less than half of company M.

In comparison, company M bears some of the features of a decentralized operation, perhaps built by acquisition. *Other assets* compose almost 62 percent of total assets, which suggests the existence of substantial goodwill created by acquisitions, or equity interests in unconsolidated subsidiaries. Consistent with the capital intensity of multiplant newspaper publishing, *sales/assets* of company M is lower than company N. Company N may be able to achieve some economies of scale by publishing from one central location. Offsetting company M's lower asset turnover is its higher profitability: *gross margin* and *net margin* are higher for the decentralized publisher; competition may be less intense outside the major metropolitan newspaper markets.

Transportation: Firms O and P. Company O is the Santa Fe Southern Pacific Corporation; Company P is Yellow Freight Trucking Company. The strategic difference suggested by the case is in their asset bases. Because of technological differences, railroads are considerably more capital intensive than trucking companies. In addition, the case suggests that a material portion of the railroad's business is based in real estate and natural resources.

Company P fits the profile of a trucking company. Its *receivables/assets* ratio is higher and *net profit margin* is lower than company O, which is consistent with the sharper competition in the deregulated trucking environment of the late 1980s. Company O has the earmarks of an asset-intensive company: *net PP&E/assets* is almost 10 percentage points higher than for company P, and *sales/assets* is about a quarter of company P's.

Some Closing Points

After the industries have been surveyed and the identities of the firms revealed, a useful closing for the instructor is to summarize the kinds of determinants of the big differences between firms in the same industries:

Market Positioning/Customer Focus

Consumer versus institutional (health)
Captive versus noncaptive supplier (appliances)
Discount versus full-price (retailing)
Single high profile versus diversified low profile (newspapers)

Product Mix

Specialty versus full line (computers)
Bare-bones service versus full service (retailing)
Vertical integration versus diversified product mix (electronics)

Asset Mix

Asset intensity versus service intensity (hotels, transportation)

Financial Policy

Conservatism versus aggressiveness (electronics)
Liquidity (computers, retailing, electronics, hotels)
Debt versus equity (retailing, electronics, hotels)
Off-balance-sheet financing (retailing, hotels)

It is important for students to observe that all these elements are largely based on decisions managers make, as opposed to luck or the dictates of the environment. To grasp the relationship between managerial choice and financial performance is to lay the groundwork for understanding the rich range of alternatives at management's disposal for achieving financial goals.

At the closing, the instructor can also make a number of observations about the art of ratio analysis. For instance:

- Ratio analysis is only as good as the financial statements underlying it. In particular, one needs to understand the accounting policies that generated the statements. The various treatments of goodwill, lease obligations, equity interests in subsidiaries, patent values, and operating licenses appear in the company discussions. In addition, the absence of data (the "NAv." in case Exhibit 1) can frustrate ratio analysis.

- Frameworks such as the DuPont System of ratios and the four categories of ratios (activity, profitability, liquidity, and leverage) are useful organizing schemes for an analysis.

- Naive ratio analysis can absorb considerable time, as one seeks to find a pattern (any pattern!) in a blizzard of numbers. Effort is economized by thinking first about the underlying business that generated the ratios.

Johnson's Nursery

SYNOPSIS AND OBJECTIVES

The proprietor of a small wholesale plant nursery is considering his projected financial performance in 1984. In the wake of three years of losses and mounting debt, he must (1) review the profit contribution of individual products, (2) estimate the breakeven sales volume, and (3) forecast his firm's balance sheet in order to determine his ability to repay debt. Ultimately, the student must recommend a course of action for the proprietor to respond to the impending financial crisis. The case is intended to serve as an introduction to financial analysis and forecasting.

STUDY QUESTIONS

1. Why has this firm found borrowing necessary? Will it need to borrow in 1984? How much? Why? Will the firm's financing needs vary during 1984?

2. What sales volume must Dave Johnson achieve in order to net a profit?

3. Which of the firm's products are most profitable?

4. Prepare an action plan for Johnson covering product mix, expense management, asset growth, and debt repayment.

TEACHING PLAN

(10 minutes)   What is the condition of Johnson's Nursery? Why is it losing money?

(15 minutes)   What is the nursery's breakeven volume?

(10 minutes)   Which products are most profitable? Would you recommend a shift in the product mix?

(35 minutes)   Can the nursery repay any of its debt in 1984? What assumptions are crucial here?

(10 minutes)   What action would you recommend Johnson take in response to the situation?

Teaching note written by Robert F. Bruner. Copyright (c) 1988 by the Darden Graduate Business School Sponsors, Charlottesville, VA.

ANALYSIS

Breakeven Analysis

Exhibit A shows that the breakeven sales volume for Johnson's Nursery is $91,909, assuming that the mix of sizes sold is the same as in case Exhibit 6 and assuming that fixed costs of $54,824 (measured over 11 months) represent the experience of an entire year. If one annualizes the fixed costs, the breakeven plant sales volume is $100,264.88. Because the contribution margins for all sizes are very close (as shown in case Exhibit 5), the breakeven will not vary greatly with mix. The contribution margins do decrease slightly, however, for the larger container sizes because of the time involved in growing the plants to reach the necessary size.

The cost accounting in case Exhibit 5 is also useful for examining the costs of holding inventory. Margins deteriorate sharply if the quarts and gallons are held longer than a year and if the 2- and 3-gallon sizes are held longer than two years. Exhibit B shows the "next-year" costs and margins for all sizes, assuming that the same amounts of fertilizer and chemicals, variable labor, and nursery supplies are used. (Plant losses for an additional year were omitted to be conservative.) If inventory is held an additional year, margins decline to around 30 to 40 percent from an average of 60 percent.

The probability of breaking even will vary with market conditions. Because demand is cyclical with housing starts, Johnson's Nursery should break even when the economy is doing well. The breakeven sales volume of $91,909–$100,264.88 compares favorably with forecasted 1984 plant sales of $143,367 and gross sales of $166,236. If housing starts decline, however, Johnson's Nursery may not reach breakeven sales. And attempting to reach breakeven by cutting prices could prove futile: competition is keen even in bouyant economic conditions. The breakeven sales level is also sensitive to changes in fixed costs. As the nursery expands, fixed costs will rise.

Debt Repayment

An important insight is that the "income statement" forecast in case Exhibit 4 is essentially a partial cash-flow forecast, because of the cash basis of accounting used for inventory and expenses. Missing from Exhibit 4 to make it a true cash-flow forecast are certain balance-sheet changes, such as payroll withholding, additions to accounts receivable, and additions to net fixed assets.

Exhibit C presents the forecasted income statement and cash budget for the firm on a monthly and annual basis. Additions to net fixed assets of $7,000 are assumed to be spread evenly over February and March, assuming that Johnson will want his asset additions in place before his business season begins in earnest. Accounts receivable are also calculated on a T-account basis, and assuming that the average days' sales outstanding of 16 days will hold through the year. At the end of every month, 16 days out of 30 days' sales are assumed to be carried into the next month.

Exhibit C shows that the nursery's cash balance troughs in March at -$24,207,[1] although by December it recovers to a modest positive sum of $6,411.

---

[1] The instructor should note that the cash budget in Exhibit C ignores minimum cash balances necessary to run the firm. For instance, if Johnson needs at least $1,000 in the cash account, the firm's financing need at the end of March will be $25,207, instead of the $24,207 shown in the exhibit.

The cause of the big seasonal variation in cash is seasonal variation in operating cash flow and accounts receivable, and it is exacerbated by the timing of the capital expenditures.

The policy implications of Exhibit C are that Johnson probably cannot repay much, if any, of the nursery's debt outstanding over the next year.[2] Moreover, Johnson will apparently need every penny of his current capital (plus a little help from his bank's line of credit) to weather the seasonal cash needs. In essence, all the nursery's internally generated cash is going back into the firm. At this rate, it is not clear when Johnson can give himself a raise (unless the nursery is prepared to borrow to do so).

Investment Analysis

What kind of an investment is the nursery for Johnson's father? Any analysis must focus on the true economic base of the firm and, therefore, must include the value of the land, roughly $360,000, and contributed capital of $221,747.87. On this investment base of $581,747.87, Mr. Johnson will receive interest of $26,100, lease income of $100, less the taxes he must pay on the forecasted income of $18,118, roughly $8,300. In all, Mr. Johnson will earn about 3 percent on his investment in 1984.

How much longer will Mr. Johnson tolerate the low rate of return? Are there not higher valued uses for the 600 acres of land he owns? Can Mr. Johnson's son begin to use the land and capital more productively than in the past? The case gives little information by which to resolve these questions, although the pressure implicit in these questions adds some urgency to the analysis.

Industry Analysis and Competitive Position

The wholesale nursery industry is highly competitive because the wholesalers have little power over their customers or suppliers. The case states that each retail nursery may buy from as many as 10 wholesalers. The wholesalers essentially function as order takers; they can do little to influence the demand for their products. In addition, wholesale nurseries are usually too small to win discounts from suppliers of fertilizer, chemicals, potting media, and containers. It is also fairly easy for new people to enter the wholesale nursery business. Setting up a nursery does not involve a huge capital investment initially. The main barrier to entry is the availability of suitable land.

The key success factors in the wholesale nursery business are a large and varied inventory, competitive prices, and high quality. A reputation for quality and a large inventory are factors that can only be established over several years, so a relatively new nursery like Johnson's will have trouble competing with the larger nurseries in the near term.

Major Alternatives

Johnson is dealing with the basic tension between growth ambitions and profitability of the business. In response, an outside adviser (such as a business student) might counsel some of the following:

---

[2]Again, assuming Johnson needs a minimum cash balance of $1,000, he could repay only about $5,400, at which annual rate it would take him about 41 years to extinguish the debt.

Diversify. Novices to finance are often prone to solve a problem by running away from it. The rationales for diversification are (1) smooth out the cyclicality of the business and (2) find a "cash cow" that would help finance the growth of the nursery. This approach ignores the fact, however, that Mr. Johnson can diversify simply by investing in a portfolio of publicly traded common stocks. For Dave Johnson's father to diversify through the nursery, there should be some unusual opportunities to create value, such as through the exploitation of special skills, but it is not clear what such skills might be. The bigger problem with a strategy of diversification is that it drains needed capital away from the growth of the nursery and thus is likely to worsen, rather than alleviate, the problem.

Integrate forward into retail. One variation on the previous idea is that the nursery should buy a retail nursery. The rationale is that retailers appear to have the market power in this industry and that integration would appropriate some of that power to Johnson. Another rationale is that it captures the profit margins of both the wholesale and retail businesses. The offsetting features are that forward integration is bound to lengthen the nursery's cash cycle and generally worsen the cash constraint. Moreover, retailing might require a set of skills (e.g., merchandising, advertising) that are relatively new to Johnson.

Slow the rate of growth and harvest. If growth creates the cash drain, perhaps a no-growth strategy will allow the nursery to release cash. For instance, case Exhibit 3 suggests that in 1984 the investment in inventory would grow, requiring an incremental investment of about $11,000 (based on variable costs only). This cash could be diverted to the repayment of the firm's liabilities, although it would take 20 years to do so at this rate. In the meantime, Johnson would have to stifle his hopes for a raise and his goal of achieving $1 million in sales.

Liquidate. Some students may suggest that Johnson exit the business altogether. These students will cite the low rate of return to Dave's father and the belief that Dave Johnson should have more progress to show for three years' work. In this view, Johnson's Nursery is a marginal business and is liable to be so for the foreseeable future. The financial consequences of this approach for Johnson's father may be roughed out as indicated in Exhibit D. Even assuming some fairly liberal liquidation recovery percentages, the nursery would probably fetch only about $185,000, which, compared with liabilities of $223,932.87 (mostly held by Mr. Johnson), suggests liquidation would yield a tax writeoff of about $40,000. Beyond the financial consequences, liquidation fails to serve the personal goals of Dave Johnson himself.

Continue to grow, practice patience. The nursery is at a difficult stage of its life. Growth never comes easily. As order sizes grow, the nursery's need to extend credit will probably grow as well, increasing the financing requirements of the nursery. If Dave Johnson and his father are willing to sacrifice now (in the form of low returns and low salary), then perhaps the firm will grow to a level at which higher rewards may be reaped. It is clear from what little is revealed about the industry, that larger scale brings with it some cost economies and some competitive power. This line of argument would assert that the nursery is a marginal operation only temporarily. Focused growth is probably the only route by which Johnson's goals may be obtained within the constraints he is under. Clearly, however, if this course is adopted, Dave must work hard to enhance the profitability of the business.

Operating Recommendations

Within the current business of Johnson's Nursery, at least two small changes in business management could improve operations:

- forecast sales based on housing starts. While forecasting the economy a year in advance is difficult, Johnson should attempt to adjust his business's growth according to the economy to avoid unsold inventory at the end of each season;

- reduce prices at the end of a season to reduce inventory. Because margins deteriorate when inventory is held, Johnson should calculate the breakeven price at which he would be better off selling a plant this year than waiting until next year.

EPILOGUE

In fiscal 1988, Johnson's Nursery's gross sales had grown to $500,000, reflecting a 45 percent compound rate of growth since 1983. Profit margins remained robust and afforded an important source of financing for the firm's growth. Other sources were secured loans from a bank. Loans from Dave Johnson's father to the nursery had not been amortized materially. By 1988, Dave Johnson had purchased his father's equity interest and had reorganized the nursery as an ordinary corporation.

EXHIBIT A   Breakeven Sales Volume Using 1984 Data

1984 Average Contribution Ratio:

	Contribution (dollars/unit) [case Exhibit 5]	Sales Volume (units) [case Exhibit 6]	Contribution (dollars)
Quart	$.484	33,810	$16,364
Gallon	$.946	26,358	24,935
2-Gallon	$1.932*	15,036	29,050
3-Gallon	$2.423*	6,235	15,107
		Total	$85,456

1984 plant sales (case Exhibit 4): $143,267

Contribution/sales ratio: $85,456/143,267 = 59.65%

11-Month Breakeven

Fixed costs (11-month data, case Exhibit 5): $ 54,824

Breakeven (using 11-month fixed costs): $54,824/.596 = $91,909.50

12-Month Breakeven

Fixed costs for 12 months
[$54,824/(11/12)]: 59,808.00

Breakeven (using 12-month fixed costs): $59,808.00/.596 = $100,264.88

---

*The unit contribution for the 2- and 3-gallon sizes was derived as an average of the dollar contributions based on propagation from quarts and gallons.

EXHIBIT B   Second-Year Contribution*

	Quart	Gallon	2-Gallon		3-Gallon	
			Quart	Gallon	Quart	Gallon
First-year variable costs	$0.316	$0.604	$1.214	$1.423	$1.738	$1.916
Second-year variable costs:						
Fertilizer and chemicals	.017	.044	.085	.085	.128	.128
Labor	.103	.257	.515	.515	.773	.773
Nursery supplies	.02	.049	.1	.1	.15	.15
Total variable costs of plant	.456	.954	1.914	2.123	2.789	2.967
Price	.8	1.55	3.25	3.25	4.25	4.25
Contribution ($)	$0.344	$0.596	$1.336	$1.127	$1.461	$1.283
(%)	43	38.5	41.1	34.7	34.4	30.2

*Actual 12-month margins would be somewhat lower. Cost information is for 11 months.

EXHIBIT C   Pro Forma Income Statement and Cash Budget for Fiscal Year 1984*

	Jan.	Feb.	Mar.	Apr.	May	Jun.	Jul.	Aug.	Sep.	Oct.	Nov.	Dec.
Gross sales:												
Plants	$3,000	$6,000	$18,170	$12,757	$12,757	$12,757	$10,540	$10,540	$10,540	$15,402	$15,402	$15,402
Freight	120	240	727	510	510	510	422	422	422	616	616	616
Soil		870	990	315	649	1,567	336	1,154	757	0	0	0
Retail			200	500	500	200	0	0	300	400	100	0
Landscaping	500	500	500	500	500	500	500	500	500	500	500	500
Rewholesale	200	200	200	200	200	200	200	200	200	200	200	200
Total	3,820	7,810	20,787	14,782	15,116	15,734	11,998	12,816	12,719	17,118	16,818	16,718
Operating expenses:												
Salaries and FICA	3,414	3,414	4,802	3,841	4,268	5,335	5,335	5,335	4,268	3,841	3,841	3,841
Nursery supplies	5,820	2,539	7,563	856	1,107	4,995	872	1,486	6,638	620	2,920	620
Interest, G. Johnson												
Note 1	1,075	1,075	1,075	1,075	1,075	1,075	1,075	1,075	1,075	1,075	1,075	1,075
Note 2	400	400	400	400	400	400	400	400	400	400	400	400
Note 3	700	700	700	700	700	700	700	700	700	700	700	700
Attorney and accountant	400											
Truck rental	300	300	300	300	300	300	300	300	300	300	300	300
Insurance	200	400	150	150	150	150	150	150	150	150	150	150
Utilities	425	425	425	425	425	425	425	425	425	425	425	425
Supplies	65	65	65	65	65	65	65	65	65	65	65	65
Freight	225	450	1,363	957	957	957	791	791	791	1,155	1,155	1,155
Tools and maintenance	225	225	225	225	225	225	225	225	225	225	225	225
License and taxes	5	5	5	5	5	5	5	5	5	5	5	5
Membership dues	0	0	0	0	0	0	0	50	0	0	0	50
N.C. sales tax	15	15	15	15	15	15	15	15	15	15	15	15
Travel and computer	225	225	25	25	25	25	25	225	25	25	25	25
Advertising	100	100	100	100	100	100	100	100	100	100	100	100
Bank fees	5	5	5	5	5	5	5	5	5	5	5	5
Retail	0	0	20	50	50	20	0	0	30	40	10	5
Landscaping	375	375	375	375	375	375	375	375	375	375	375	375
Rewholesale	150	150	150	150	150	150	150	150	150	150	150	150
Total	14,124	10,868	17,763	9,719	10,397	15,322	11,013	11,877	15,742	9,671	11,941	9,681
Net income	(10,304)	(3,058)	3,024	5,063	4,719	412	985	939	(3,023)	7,447	4,877	7,037

EXHIBIT C (continued)

	Jan.	Feb.	Mar.	Apr.	May	Jun.	Jul.	Aug.	Sep.	Oct.	Nov.	Dec.
Memo: Accounts receivable**												
Beginning balance	$3,552.0	$2,037.3	$4,165.3	$11,086.4	$7,883.7	$8,061.9	$8,391.5	$6,398.9	$6,835.2	$6,783.5	$9,129.6	$8,969.6
Plus sales	3,820.0	7,810.0	20,787.0	14,782.0	15,116.0	15,734.0	11,998.0	12,816.0	12,719.0	17,118.0	16,818.0	16,718.0
Less collections 14/30 current-mo. sales	(1,782.7)	(3,644.7)	(9,700.6)	(6,898.3)	(7,054.1)	(7,342.5)	(5,599.1)	(5,980.8)	(5,935.5)	(7,988.4)	(7,848.4)	(7,801.7)
Last-month balance	(3,552.0)	(2,037.3)	(4,165.3)	(11,086.4)	(7,883.7)	(8,061.9)	(8,391.5)	(6,398.9)	(6,835.2)	(6,783.5)	(9,129.6)	(8,969.6)
Ending balance	2,037.3	4,165.3	11,086.4	7,883.7	8,061.9	8,391.5	6,398.9	6,835.2	6,783.5	9,129.6	8,969.6	8,916.3
Change in accts. receivable	(1,514.7)	2,128.0	6,921.1	(3,202.7)	178.1	329.6	(1,992.5)	436.3	(51.7)	2,346.1	(160.0)	(53.3)
Memo: Cash flow (CF) and financing need												
CF from operations	(10,304.0)	(3,058.0)	3,024.0	5,063.0	4,719.0	412.0	985.0	939.0	(3,023.0)	7,447.0	4,877.0	7,037.0
Plus payroll withholding+	271.1	271.1	271.1	313.4	313.4	313.4	348.2	348.2	348.2	268.6	268.6	268.6
Less payroll withholding pay't	(839.0)	0.0	0.0	(813.3)	0.0	0.0	(940.1)	0.0	0.0	(1,044.6)	0.0	0.0
Less addns. to accts. receivable	1,514.7	(2,128.0)	(6,921.1)	3,202.7	(178.1)	(329.6)	1,992.5	(436.3)	51.7	(2,346.1)	160.0	53.3
Less addns. to fixed assets	0.0	(3,500.0)	(3,500.0)	0.0	0.0	0.0	0.0	0.0	0.0	0.0	0.0	0.0
Cash flow	(9,357.2)	(8,414.9)	(7,126.0)	7,765.8	4,854.2	395.8	2,385.6	850.9	(2,623.1)	4,324.9	5,305.6	7,358.9
Beginning cash	691.1	(8,666.1)	(17,081.0)	(24,207.0)	(16,441.2)	(11,587.0)	(11,191.2)	(8,805.6)	(7,954.7)	(10,577.7)	(6,252.9)	(947.3)
Plus cash flow	(9,357.2)	(8,414.9)	(7,126.0)	7,765.8	4,854.2	395.8	2,385.6	850.9	(2,623.1)	4,324.9	5,305.6	7,358.9
Ending cash	(8,666.1)	(17,081.0)	(24,207.0)	(16,441.2)	(11,587.0)	(8,805.6)	(7,954.7)	(10,577.7)	(10,577.7)	(6,252.9)	(947.3)	6,411.7

55

EXHIBIT C (continued)

*Depreciation is not reflected in this cash budget because it affects only Johnson's tax exposure, not the Nursery's. The nursery was organized as a Subchapter S Corporation. In effect, the nursery was treated as a partnerhsip for tax purposes.

**The accounts receivable experience assumes a continuation of 1983's 16 days' sales outstanding. Thus, for each month's sales, 14 days' sales of that month's sales will have been collected at month's end, and 16 days' sales will remain outstanding.

+The analysis assumes that 7 percent of each month's salaries will be withheld for taxes (this was the experience in 1983). Payroll taxes are assumed to be paid on the first day of each new quarter, in arrears.

EXHIBIT D   Liquidation Analysis

Item	Cash Proceeds
Inventory (80% of $171,736, 1984 ending balance based on case Exhibit 3)	$137,389.00
Cash (100% of 1984 ending balance from Exhibit C)	6,411.70
Accounts receivable (80% of $8,916, 1984 ending balance from Exhibit C)	7,132.80
Equipment (80% of $25,173.45, 1983 ending balance plus new capital invested in 1984)	20,138.76
Other fixed assets (30% of $40,029.28, 1983 ending balance)	12,138.76
Other assets (25% of $3,215, 1983 ending balance)	803.75
Total liquidation value	$183,884.79

Alfin Fragrances, Inc.

SYNOPSIS AND OBJECTIVES

In February 1986, Alfin, an importer and marketer of perfumes, introduces a skin cream with certain purported medicinal qualities that reduce wrinkles. The product is considered a major breakthrough as an over-the-counter therapy and offers huge potential sales. The student must estimate Alfin's funding needs and the value of its common stock.

The case is nominally an exercise of quantitative techniques: financial forecasting and simple equity valuation. Yet it also contains several hidden insights and opportunities, including: (1) the similarity of results obtained by forecasts of cash budgets and balance sheets; (2) the crucial role of sensible judgment in forecasting--especially in the decisions involving sales growth and the scrutiny of balance-sheet assumptions; (3) an illustration of a high-growth company with *no* external financing needs [which serves as a useful contrast to "Johnson's Nursery" (Case 4) and "De Laurentiis Entertainment Group, Inc." (Case 9)]; (4) an illustration of capital-market irrationality; and (5) an opportunity to wrestle with ethical concerns in product design, marketing, and the possible sale of overvalued securities.

STUDY QUESTIONS

1. How well has Alfin performed in the past?

2. What strategy should Alfin pursue to introduce Glycel? In particular, how aggressive should Alfin's new-product introduction be? Why? What are the arguments in favor of a fast or slow rate of growth?

3. What will Alfin's requirements for external capital be for the next three years?

4. Should Alfin sell equity in 1986? Assuming that the growth rates in the case are representative of market expectations for Alfin, what is the cost of Alfin's equity capital?

TEACHING PLAN

(20 minutes) What explains Alfin's success to date? What has been Alfin's strategy? Why haven't Alfin's competitors appropriated Alfin's returns?

(10 minutes) What is Glycel? How is it different from perfumes? How should Alfin introduce Glycel?

(35 minutes) Assuming Alfin pursues a strategy for Glycel consistent with the analyst's comments in the Sales Prospects section of the case, what will Alfin's financing need be?

Teaching note written by Robert F. Bruner. Copyright (c) 1988 by the Darden Graduate Business School Sponsors, Charlottesville, VA.

(15 minutes) At $67.50 per share, is the equity fairly priced? Would you buy shares at the current level?

The instructor can gain closure on the discussion by taking a vote of the students, and then present the epilogue of the case.

ANALYSIS

Alfin's Successful Performance

An interesting and useful foundation for the case discussion is a review of the sources of Alfin's past success. Such a recap helps moderate the skepticism of the doubters in the class and draws in the timid, undecided, and optimistic students. Later, the turnabout resulting from the forecast and valuation leaves a large impression.

Alfin's past success can be measured many ways. The compound rates of growth in net income and earnings per share (EPS) were 60.8 and 39.8 percent, respectively. This success compares with an average annual rate of growth in the cosmetics industry of about 4 percent over the years 1982–86 (see case Exhibit 5). In addition, the company sports a 13.1x market-to-book value ratio and a 53x price-to-earnings (P/E) ratio, both of which are arresting in light of the much smaller figures given for other firms in the cosmetics and pharmaceuticals industries (see case Exhibit 2). This performance has been achieved not by financial gimickry (see the comparatively low dividend and debt/equity figures in case Exhibit 2), but rather by careful operating management, as shown by the firm's comparatively high growth rate and operating margin.

The strategy underlying Alfin's historical performance can be abstracted from the text and exhibits of the case. Elements of the strategy would include the following:

Niche play. Alfin focuses on market and product segments not occupied by other major players. The key to this strategy is in acquiring exclusive licenses.

High price/high margin focus. Almost all of Alfin's products are sold through fancy department stores and specialty counters. Given the exclusive nature of the product, the company is able to command huge margins, as evidenced by the 75 percent gross margin in the firm's income statement.

Focus on distribution, not manufacturing. Alfin's products are apparently relatively easy to make; the value added appears to be in branding and distribution.

Careful asset and expense management. Given its aversion to manufacturing, the firm has relatively few tangible assets. In addition, Alfin's managers seem to control the firm's inventories and receivables well, which in a distribution-oriented company is a key to success.

The instructor might consider asking the students to vote a letter grade for Alfin's management. On the basis of past performance, the grade is usually quite high.

Glycel

The new product, on which Alfin's inflated stock price seems based, is unlike any product the firm has sold previously. A comparison of Glycel and perfumes raises these contrasting points:

Glycel	Perfumes
Therapeutic properties	Cosmetic only
• Restorative	
• May require FDA approval	
Patentable	Not patentable
Performance advertising	Image advertising
• Doctor endorses	• Actress endorses

Plainly, Alfin is entering a new arena, which may require new managerial skills. Given the fact that Glycel can be marketed through the same channels, however, it seems to offer an excellent fit with the firm's existing strategy. Moreover, the huge sales potential promises to transform the company from a relatively small player in cosmetics to a large and rapidly growing firm.

Financial Forecast

Case Exhibit 11 presents the student with a completed estimate of the residual capital required in 1986. Thus the exhibit is a relatively straightforward illustration of the percentage-of-sales forecasting technique (at least, for the income-statement portion of the exhibit). By adding back noncash charges and subtracting capital expenditures and debt payments, case Exhibit 11 arrives at an estimate of residual cash flow (i.e., the funds required to support the firm over the next year). This exhibit also lays the foundation for the subsequent question regarding the value of Alfin's equity, because residual cash flow is the stream to be discounted in valuing Alfin's common stock. The instructor may choose to concentrate on the mechanics of case Exhibit 11 if this is the students' first encounter with financial forecasting.

Exhibit A of this note expands on the forecast. Many of the ratios used in preparing this forecast are given in lines 27–35 of the exhibit. The forecast reveals that the external financing needs over the forecast period are nil. Line 13 shows the cash balance increasing dramatically, while the debt (line 22) falls to zero. The residual cash flow (line 44) is basically zero—a significant difference from case Exhibit 11, which forecasted an external need of $2.9 million. The key difference between that exhibit and this analysis is in the assumption of additions to working capital. In case Exhibit 11, the analyst assumed that working capital would remain at 61 percent of sales—that is, management would want to maintain its huge balance of short-term investments in constant proportion to sales. This analysis assumes that *noncash working capital* remains at 19 percent of sales (see lines 31–33 and 35). The cash balance in this forecast is thus a plug (see line 13). Naive students will automatically take the assumption (61 percent) given in the case, but this makes no sense, since it would require the firm to borrow simply to increase its cash balance.

In this case, therefore, students can learn the value of questioning assumptions embedded in financial forecasts. By relaxing the assumption about short-term investments, Exhibit A reveals that Alfin will be a net cash generator, a net lender. Overall, Alfin is a "self-basting turkey," so profitable that it throws off more cash than it needs to grow.

A serious implication of Exhibit A is that Alfin may not have the opportunities for reinvestment at the high rate of return embedded in Glycel. This doubt leads naturally to the question of the value of Alfin's stock.

Valuation

The bottom panel of Exhibit A (lines 50-56) contains the cash flows to equity-holders to be discounted. While the annual flows follow directly from the forecasts of residual cash flow, the terminal-value estimate requires more judgment. At the terminus, Exhibit A assumes that investors receive dividends of $20.2 million in excess cash from the company and also receive the proceeds of the sale of all their stock. The stock, at the end of 1988, is estimated to be worth about $113 million or $25.80 per share in present value terms, consistent with a P/E ratio of about 14.8x 1986 estimated EPS. This terminal value was estimated by capitalizing net income for 1989 at the difference between cost of equity of 16 percent[1] and a long-term growth rate of 7.0 percent.

Obviously, the terminal value is the "tail that wags the dog," and its assumptions will warrant extensive debate. Such debate is rendered moot, however, by the fact that rather aggressive assumptions are required to realize a discounted cash flow (DCF) value per share of $67.25. For instance, a constant future growth rate of 12.7 percent is needed. In simple terms, Alfin's stock price has apparently become detached from the economic reality of Glycel.

Perhaps the coldly rational action would be to exploit the arbitrage opportunity by selling common stock to finance Glycel, thus effecting a wealth transfer from new to old shareholders. One wonders, however, how long it would take Alfin to lose the confidence of the investment community once its self-interested opportunism was recognized for what it was.

EPILOGUE

Alfin proceeded to introduce Glycel. The company's advertising began to draw criticism from industry experts and other skin-care companies by May 1986. In April 1987, the FDA sent a letter to Alfin requiring that the company apply for "new drug" status for Glycel--a procedure that was likely to take several years to complete. Alfin's advertising became the subject of a New York State investigation in May 1987 to determine whether Glycel retarded or corrected aging, as the company appeared to advertise. In July 1987, with sales waning, Alfin's board agreed to discontinue all its skin-care operations. Exhibit B

---

[1]The cost of equity was estimated using the capital-asset pricing model, where the parameters were: $B = .85$, $R_f = 8.7$ percent, and $R_m-R_f = 8.6$ percent. This gives a K_e of 16.0 percent.

extends case Exhibit 1 through the subsequent period. Quarterly results for the company were as follows:

	Net Income	Stock Price	S&P 500
4/30/86	$1.993 million	$29.500	$247.35
7/31/86	1.070	19.375	236.12
10/31/86	0.148	15.875	243.98
1/31/87	-1.417	8.750	274.08
4/30/87	-3.409	5.625	288.36
7/31/87	-8.890	4.250	318.66
10/31/87	1.066	4.500	251.79
1/31/88	0.236	3.000	257.07
4/29/88	0.136	3.750	261.33
7/31/88	$0.020 million	$ 3.500	$266.02

Analysis of Projected Cash Flows: Credit and Valuation (assuming no sale of new common shares; dollars in thousands except per share data)

Key Assumptions

Annual sales growth 1987, 1988	29.5%
Gross profit/sales	75.0%
Cash-flow growth after 1988	7.0%
Cost of equity	16.0%

Other assumptions: See Notes and "Financial Ratios" section.

Line No. and Item	1983	1984	1985	1986e	1987e	1988e
Income Statements						
1 Sales	$11,922	$18,107	$21,297	$34,000	$44,030	$57,019
2 Cost of goods sold	3,465	4,911	5,330			
3 Gross profit	8,456	13,196	15,967	25,500	33,023	42,764
4 SG&A	5,513	7,539	8,722	15,300	19,814	25,658
5 Operating profit	2,943	5,657	7,245	10,200	13,209	17,106
6 Net interest income	191	734	785	645	634	951*
7 Other income	173	200	212	220	220	220
8 Minority interest	0	0	29	29	0	0
9 Profit before taxes (PBT)	3,306	6,591	8,272	11,094	14,063	18,277
10 Taxes (@48%)	1,652	3,207	3,994	5,325	6,750	8,773
11 Net income	$1,654	$3,384	$4,278	$5,769	$7,313	$9,504
Number of shares		3,252.1	3,309.7	3,310	3,310	3,310
12 Memo: EPS	$0.65	$1.08	$1.27	$1.74	$2.21	$2.87
Balance Sheets						
13 Cash and investments	$9,198	$9,634	$10,575	$15,855	$22,736	
14 Accts. receivable (A/R)	1,905	3,480	5,440	7,045	9,123	
15 Inventories	2,900	5,023	7,820	10,127	13,114	
16 Other current assets (CA)	342	154	340	440	570	
17 Gross fixed assets	1,912	2,042	2,542	3,302	4,276	
18 Net fixed assets (FA)	1,649	1,574	1,587	1,715	1,869**	
19 Other long-term (LT) assets	143	4,625	4,625	4,625	4,625	
20 Total assets	$16,038	24,498	$30,387	$39,806	$52,038	
21 Payables and accruals	$ 2,965	$ 4,389	$ 7,140	$ 9,246	$11,974	
22 Current and LT debt	1,278	2,631	0	0	0	
23 Other LT Liabs.	20	485	485	485	485	
24 Equity	11,775	16,993	22,762	30,075	39,579	
26 Total liabs. and equity	$16,038	$24,498	$30,387	$39,806	$52,038	

63

	1984	1985	1986e	1987e	1988e
Financial Ratios					
27 Gross profit/sales	72.9%	75.0%	75.0%	75.0%	75.0%
28 SG&A/sales	41.6	41.0	45.0	45.0	45.0
29 Int. income/cash	8.0	8.1	6.1	4.0	4.2
30 Taxes/PBT	48.7	48.3	48.0	48.0	48.0
31 Accts. rec/sales	10.5	16.3	16.0	16.0	16.0
32 Invent./sales	16.0	23.6	23.0	23.0	23.0
33 Other CA/sales	1.9	0.7	1.0	1.0	1.0
34 Gross FA/sales	10.6	9.6	7.5	7.5	7.5
35 Pay. and accrus./sales	16.4	20.6	21.0	21.0	21.0
External Financing Requirements					
36 Net income			$5,769	$7,313	$9,504
37 Plus: Depreciation and amortization			$487	$633	$819**
38 Less: Addns. to A/R, inv. and other CA			($4,943)	($4,012)	($5,196)
39 Plus: Addns. to accts pay. and accruals			$2,751	$2,106	$2,728
40 Less: Cap. expend.			($500)	($760)	($974)
41 Less: Addn. to other assets			$0	$0	$0
42 Less: Debt amortization			($2,631)	$0	$0
43 Less: Incr. in cash and investments			($941)	($5,280)	($6,881)
44 Residual cash flow			($ 8)	($ 0)	$ 0
Memo: Cash account					
45 Beginning cash balance			$ 9,644	$10,577	$15,857
Plus: Residual CF			(8)	(0)	0
Plus: Extra increase in cash			941	5,280	6,881
46 Ending cash			$10,577	$15,857	$22,738
47 Debt	$1,281	$2,631	$0	$0	$0
48 Equity	$11,775	$16,993	$22,762	$30,075	$39,579
49 Debt/equity ratio	10.9%	15.5%	0.0%	0.0%	0.0%
Estimate of Share Value					
50 Cash flow to equity			($8)	($0)	$0
51 Extra dividend of terminal excess cash					$20,286†
52 Terminal value					$112,992††
53 Total cash flow			($8)	($0)	$133,278
54 DCF		$85,379	DCF of cash flows for 1986–88.		
55 Number of shares		3,309.7			
56 Value per share		$25.80			

EXHIBIT A (continued)

Notes

* Net interest income is calculated as the difference between interest income and interest expense. Interest income is equal to 6% times the balance of cash and investments outstanding at the end of the prior year. Interest expense is equal to 9.9% times debt outstanding at the end of the prior year.

** Depreciation expense for 1986 is taken from case Exhibit 11. For 1987 and 1988, the ratio of depreciation to gross fixed assets is assumed to hold constant at the 1986 level, 19.7%. Net fixed assets was calculated by summing the NFA balance at the end of the prior period plus the change in gross fixed assets, less depreciation for the period.

† The dividend of excess cash assumes that cash required is equal to 10% of total assets.

†† Terminal value was estimated by capitalizing (1+g) x Net income(1988) at the difference between the cost of equity and the long-term growth rate (see Key Assumptions at top of the exhibit).

EXHIBIT B Alfin Stock Prices, 1986-87, Adjusted for 2-for-1 Stock Split,
February 21, 1986

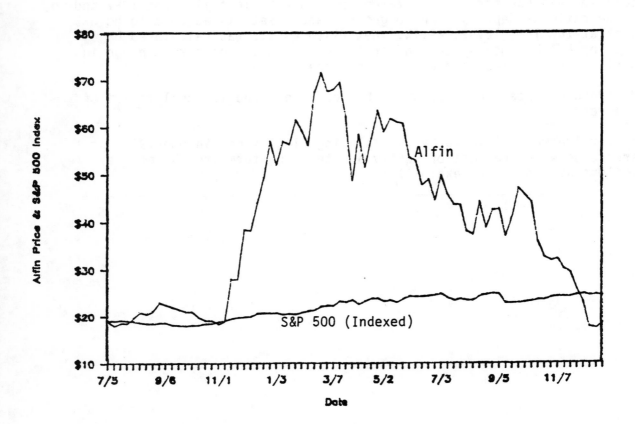

Source: *ISL Daily Stock Price Index*.

Padgett Blank Book Company

SYNOPSIS AND OBJECTIVES

A small manufacturer of notebooks and other stationery products has been financing its growth-by-acquisition strategy by means of 90-day notes to a commercial bank. The banker seeks to restructure the credit, placing it on a long-term basis. The tasks of the student are to (1) evaluate the strategy and financial performance of the company to date, (2) study the detailed financial forecasts and sensitivity analyses (given in the case), and (3) recommend a structure for the loan and plan of action for the banker.

The case has been used to exercise students' financial-forecasting and -analysis skills and to introduce some basic principles of debt structuring. In addition, the case raises several issues concerning the relationship between the banker and debtor. Finally, inflation appears as an implicit issue in the forecast assumptions; the case thus affords an opportunity to discuss the financial effects of inflation.

STUDY QUESTIONS

Because much of the computation is complete in this case, an appropriate approach is to direct students toward the judgmental issues of problem definition and resolution, with the aid of less directive study questions than are often used:

1. Why should Francis Libris, the banker, seek to structure Padgett's loan on a "more orderly basis"?

2. Why does Padgett need a loan? How fast can it repay?

3. What should Libris propose as terms for the new loan structure?

TEACHING PLAN

This case is rich enough to support a discussion stretched over two class periods. However, what follows is an outline for a one-class discussion. The outline may be extended by inviting students to prepare their own financial forecasts based on alternative assumptions.

(10 minutes) Why should Libris seek to put the loan to Padgett on a "more orderly basis"? The basic notion of loan structuring needs to surface here.

(20 minutes) How well has Padgett done? Is it a customer relationship worth keeping? This part of the discussion should review salient aspects of Padgett's industry, strategy, strengths and weaknesses, historical performance, and bank relationship.

Teaching note written by Robert F. Bruner. Copyright (c) 1989, by the Darden Graduate Business School Sponsors, Charlottesville, VA.

(35 minutes) What are Padgett's prospects for servicing the $7.2 million in debt? How much cash will Padgett throw off? What could go wrong? This segment should involve a review of Padgett's preliminary projection (case Exhibit 4) and Libris's re-forecast (case Exhibit 6). Students may benefit from a discussion of the structure of the forecasts as well as scrutiny of forecast assumptions.

(15 minutes) What might Libris recommend to Padgett as remedies to this situation? In essence, Libris must propose some combination of working-capital loan and term loan, possibly combined with some form of asset redeployment to release cash.

The instructor can close the discussion by comparing the more tailored recommended loan structure to the current 90-day note structure. This comparison then becomes a platform for summarizing the disciplining role of the banker and the advantages of artful tailoring of loan terms.

ANALYSIS

Historical Analysis of Company

Padgett is a closely held company whose shares nonetheless trade over the counter. The dominant family has a desire for dividends and probably is averse to issuing stock to finance the firm's growth. Given this constraint on the growth of equity, Windsor Trust must provide the necessary capital.

Padgett, however, may need a banker who is more than just a provider of capital. Padgett's management is professional but not financially oriented. Evidence of this appears in two areas. First, the firm's policy of level production (in order to reduce unit costs) induces a seasonal cycle in borrowing, peaking in late summer or early fall. While many firms wittingly adopt a level production policy, in Padgett's case there is no clear evidence that management understands the financial requirements this policy creates. Second, few of the firm's customers take the discount for early payment; instead, they stretch the payment for an additional 30 days—reflecting the nature of the firm's customer base, severe competition, or management laxity.

Padgett is a player in a highly competitive but consolidating industry. The company's strategy is to buy small companies fitting Padgett's product or marketing needs. However, the execution of this strategy appears to be impulsive (Padgett bought Tri-State Tablet Company on short notice), although the suddenness of purchases is probably also a result of the surprise appearance of acquisition opportunities and the desire to pre-empt competitors. The possibility of continued growth by acquisition is an important wild card in the analysis of Padgett's prospects and ability to service debt.

Padgett's historical financial performance (see case Exhibit 3) is not completely encouraging. Its sales growth is erratic, perhaps reflecting variable inflation rates and the acquisition. Liquidity is worsening: the quick ratio has fallen from 2.7x to .8x. Operating expenses as a percent of sales have been rising over the past three years from 22.1 to 26.5 percent. And financial leverage is up dramatically, from debt/total capital of 22 percent to 67 percent. However, the trend in return on equity is rising. As the Du Pont ratio analysis in Exhibit A shows, this trend results from increased leverage.

Bank Relationship

Windsor Trust is Padgett's only lending bank, although other banks appear to be trying to gain Padgett's business. Padgett has deposited substantial state and federal tax payments with Windsor and maintains average collected balances of $755,000 (including subsidiaries). Loan balances have grown from $3.3 million to $7.2 million; the last loan clean-up occurred three years ago.

Libris's goals consist of (1) not losing the account to Phoenix Bank of Manhattan or to an insurance company and (2) working "quickly toward a satisfactory resolution of the loan structure."

Assessment of Financial Forecast

Exhibit B summarizes the results of case Exhibit 6, which gives Padgett's forecasted funds needed or generated by rate of growth of the business. At a 5 percent growth rate over the 1989-92 period, Padgett can apparently repay $4.3 million in debt. In contrast, if Padgett grows at 10 percent, it will release only $1.31 million in debt. And at a 15 percent growth rate, Padgett will actually require $2.13 million more in debt. The higher the growth rate, the higher the need for bank debt. (This discussion provides an important learning opportunity for students who may not have recognized this relationship.)

In short, at the lower, more optimistic growth rate, Padgett will have $2.9 million unpaid by the end of 1992; as the growth rate increases, the unpaid balance and time to clean up grow. Moreover, the forecast ignores the incremental seasonal financing peak of $2 million, which would surely lift Padgett's total financing needs at the seasonal peak above the $8 million lending limit set by the bank. This situation is intolerable for a bank that defines its role as a short-term lender.

Restructuring Alternatives and Recommendations

Possible sources of funds include (1) the sale of the plant for $.7 million, (2) borrowing by the Canadian subsidiary and up-streaming $1 million to the parent, (3) obtaining a $2 million mortgage on the real estate, (4) $.5 million from the switch to LIFO, and (5) better control of accounts receivable to improve cash flow and reduce seasonal cash needs. These actions yield $4.2 million in funds that could be applied to the $7.45 million currently outstanding.

Exhibit C presents each of the year-end debt balances reduced by $4.2 million. At a 5 percent growth rate, the loan is cleaned up by the end of the third year. At 10 percent growth, the balance falls to $1.95 million, although the rate of amortization is slow: it will take 6-7 years to amortize the debt. At a 15 percent growth rate, the debt balance grows from $3.25 million initially to $5.38 million, better than the balances under no restructuring but not acceptable as a short-term credit.

Given that 5 percent growth is consistent with a minimal, embedded rate of inflation in the United States, we must conclude that Padgett is a candidate for long-term capital. If Padgett continues to resist this suggestion, Libris could propose a curtailment of dividends (or at least dividend increases), stretching accounts payable, or reducing capital expenditures to a level below depreciation.

The menu of possible actions casts Libris into the role of financial advisor rather than friendly commercial banker. To help develop a reasonable plan, Libris must prepare to speak up about corporate policies well beyond the use of bank debt. This makes Libris somewhat of a disciplinarian.

EXHIBIT A Du Pont Ratio Analysis

Year	Return on Equity	Profit/ Sales	Sales/ Assets	Assets/ Equity
1971	.133	.076	1.40	1.22
1972	.114	.066	1.407	1.206
1973	.13	.058	1.484	1.46
1974	.146	.063	1.33	1.67

	1989	1990	1991	1992	Cumulative Change
5 Percent Growth					
Budgeted short-term notes	7.45	6.29	5.50	4.35	
Excess cash	0	.01	.73	1.24	
Net need	7.45	6.28	4.77	3.11	
Change in balance		(1.13)	(1.51)	(1.66)	(4.30)
10 Percent Growth					
Budgeted short-term notes	7.45	6.29	5.50	4.35	
Cash deficit	0	1.02	1.29	1.80	
Net need	7.45	8.30	8.94	9.58	
Change in balance		(.15)	(.55)	(.61)	(1.31)
15 Percent Growth					
Budgeted short-term notes	7.45	6.29	5.50	4.35	
Cash deficit	0	2.01	3.44	5.23	
Net need	7.45	8.30	8.94	9.58	
Change in balance		+.85	+.64	+.64	+2.13

Note: This analysis ignores:

- seasonal peak borrowing needs, $2 million;

- possibility of reducing capital expenditures to a level below annual depreciation charges;

- possible stretching of accounts payable;

- possible reduction in dividends.

EXHIBIT C   Summary of Funds Needed/Generated Revised to Reflect Application of
            Restructuring Proceeds

Estimate of
Restructuring Proceeds

Switch to LIFO	$.5 million
Sale of plant	.7
Canadian subsidiary	
Borrows and	
up-streams	1.0
Real estate	
mortgage	2.0
Total	$4.2 million

Revised Estimate of Ending Debt Balance

	1989	1990	1991	1992
5 percent growth	$3.25	$2.08	$0.57	0
10 percent growth	3.25	3.10	2.55	$1.95
15 percent growth	$3.25	$4.10	$4.74	$5.38

Note: This analysis ignores:

- seasonal peak borrowing needs, $2 million;

- possibility of reducing capital expenditures to a level
  below annual depreciation charges;

- possible stretching of accounts payable;

- possible reduction in dividends.

Atlantic Southeast Airlines

SYNOPSIS AND OBJECTIVES

A loan officer of Wachovia Bank must decide in 1985 whether to participate in a $19.2 million loan to this commuter airline (ASA) based in Atlanta. The purpose of the loan is to finance the purchase of six new airplanes to be produced by a manufacturer in Brazil.

The objective of the case is to exercise students' credit-analysis skills, particularly the sensitivity analysis of financial forecasts based on scenario assumptions. The case provides students a "base-case" financial forecast on which to conduct a sensitivity analysis.

STUDY QUESTIONS

1.   What is ASA's strategy? How well has it performed? How closely does ASA conform to the profile of successful commuter airline?

2.   What is the likelihood that ASA can repay the loan? What risks do you perceive in this situation? How vulnerable to those risks is ASA's ability to repay the loan?

3.   Should Wachovia participate in the credit?

TEACHING PLAN

The following questions can be used to motivate an 80-minute discussion of the case:

(20 minutes) Why does ASA need to borrow? Is the purchase of the airplanes consistent with its strategy; with the changing industry conditions? What are the risks associated with the investment?

(20 minutes) How well has ASA done? What are the key determinants of ASA's performance?

(40 minutes) Can ASA repay the loan? How robust are your conclusions about the risks outlined earlier? What is your recommendation?

Because much of the learning gain from this case comes from sensitivity and scenario analysis, the instructor may wish to assign beforehand the revised forecasts in Exhibits A-R of this note--a more directive approach to the analysis than usually, which allows one to give more attention in class to the qualitative and decisional aspects of the problem. If, however, the emphasis is on forecasting mechanics, the instructor will want to focus on student-produced forecasts and their generation with a personal computer.

Teaching note written by David Jarrett and Robert F. Bruner. Copyright (c) 1988 by the Darden Graduate Business School Sponsors, Charlottesville, VA.

ANALYSIS

Atlantic Southeast Airlines has demonstrated rapid growth and strong profitability throughout its brief history. The question facing Rick Spangler is whether the airline can continue building a pattern of successful performance during the ten years the loan is outstanding. This issue can be evaluated by five kinds of analysis:

• assessment of company and industry,

• evaluation of current financial condition,

• forecasts of future financial condition,

• consideration of risks associated with the loan, and

• understanding of the loan in the context of Wachovia's relationship with ASA.

The results of these five analyses will provide the basis for a decision on participation in the loan.

Company and Industry

The case lists six attributes that will identify a successful company in the modern commuter airline industry. The following paragraphs evaluate ASA by each of these attributes:

Sustainable size. ASA is 18th in size among almost 200 carriers competing in the industry. Even though consolidation is expected to reduce the number of carriers to 100 by 1993, ASA's current position in the top 10 percent would indicate it is large enough to remain competitive in future years. The company has an additional advantage in having as its market the Southeast, a region that is growing more rapidly than the nation as a whole.

Quality management. Based on the reports of the financial analysts, management skill is a major strength for ASA. The top executives have experience in running an established airline and have better business sense than most of their counterparts. While the management has seized available opportunities to expand routes, the company has not grown faster than prudent use of its financial resources would allow. The company's quick response to the tax-credit mistake and engine failures indicates integrity and responsiveness to constituents—whether financial analysts or worried passengers—that reflect an underlying sensitivity to the marketplace in which it competes.

Modern aircraft. The airline is attempting to modernize its fleet through this loan. All three of the airplane models it uses now are widely used by commuter airlines, and ASA is trying to gain an advantage over its competition by purchasing the Brasilias, which appear to be the finest planes available for the airline's route system. Because of expansion, the company will continue using its older planes, but most of these are leased rather than owned, which minimizes the risk on the part of ASA. The one-year leases on the Shorts 360s are an especially good deal. If the airline does continue to expand, it may also be able to purchase good planes at bargain prices from other airlines who are not as successful as ASA.

Strong capital base. In an industry that is, in general, highly leveraged and financially unsteady, ASA has placed itself in a sound capital position. For example, the ratio of long-term debt to owners' equity has fallen from 3.27 in 1981 to 0.40 in 1984, a remarkable achievement in any industry. If ASA were to maintain its present debt level another year, the strength of the anticipated 1985 earnings alone would further reduce the ratio to 0.27. Unless earnings disappear, ASA has more than enough capital for continued operations and adequate resources for additional expansions.

Well-defined market niche. ASA has created market niches both in geography and the kind of traveler that takes its flights. The airline's route system covers a radius of 250 miles around Atlanta, with service from the Memphis hub expanding the base from the Deep South to the middle South. The Southeast's business growth and large proportion of small cities will help a commuter airline like ASA develop. In addition to its regional base, 80 percent of ASA passengers are in the relatively stable business and military segments of the market.

Link with major carrier. The working agreement ASA has with Delta provides both airlines an excellent partnership. Delta is a dominant carrier in the South, and ASA will be the airline of choice for people selecting commuter flights to and from Atlanta to the small cities of the deep South. Delta will benefit because cost-efficient ASA can keep Delta's competitors out of markets it cannot service profitably but is unwilling to concede to another major competitor.

The condition of the commuter-airline industry during the next ten years will play an important part in whether the airline can expect continued success. The Airline Deregulation Act of 1978 gave the industry its present shape, and the embryonic stage of the industry can be said to have begun then. The industry is now in a growth stage, most clearly seen in the rise in passenger revenue-miles and the elimination of weaker carriers. A critical question is: when will the industry reach maturity? That is, when will demand flatten and margins begin to contract as companies fight for survival? Because the largest source of demand has been the divestment of marginal routes by major carriers, maturity appears likely to occur soon. Most major carriers probably have already ended service on most of the routes they plan to eliminate.

During much of the repayment period of this loan, then, the industry is likely to be in a mature stage. In maturity, market expansion would probably be limited to three possible sources:

- passengers choosing more frequently to fly to a major airport than drive,

- extension of service to communities where air service doesn't exist, and

- taking shorter routes from major airlines by competing on the basis of price.

The first of these three potential sources of expansion is linked to the strength of the economy. The prosperity during the two years preceding March 7, 1985, suggests, however, that little more growth can be expected purely from economic conditions; in fact, a downturn could produce a decline in passenger revenue-miles, particularly in the nonbusiness-traveler segment of the market. During the 1981-82 recession and concurrent air traffic controllers' strike, revenue passenger-miles fell roughly 5 percent for airlines like Delta. Commuter airlines might expect at least that much loss (or reduction in growth) from the next recession. They were less affected than the majors during the last recession only because the commuter-airline industry was still growing rapidly at the time.

More likely sources of passenger development are extensions of service, but the costs of serving smaller markets may be too much for the commuter airlines to handle, just as service to commuter airlines' current markets became prohibitively expensive for the major carriers. The third possibility has the highest risks and rewards. With new planes like the Brasilia, commuter airlines might be able to fly major airlines' shorter runs in a little more time but at a far lower price. A commuter airline using this strategy risks severe retaliation, however, especially if the major airline that is undercut is the partner of the commuter carrier.

None of these sources of expansion seems extremely promising; so growth in the industry will almost certainly slow. Individual airlines, however, may continue to build volume as some of the more poorly managed airlines drop out of the market. If ASA were to continue expanding, perhaps by opening a third hub, it has the management strength and financial depth to continue growing faster than the market as a whole. But growth, both for ASA and for its competitors, may come at the cost of reduced margins.

The pace of ASA's growth is important, because it will dictate the company's need for additional aircraft. Given the maximum flying hours of 9 per day and ASA's current fleet of 26 planes, and assuming that service is reduced by half on weekends (making for effectively six full flying days each week), the airline's capacity is:

$$9 \text{ hours/plane/day} \times 26 \text{ planes} \times 313 \text{ days/year} = 73,242 \text{ hours}$$

each year. Based on the 1985 pro forma operating statistics, ASA can provide about 4,900 available passenger miles (APMs) per hour of flying time. Multiplying APMs per hour by the hours per year gives 359 million available passenger miles during 1985. That capacity would be adequate to handle the 175 million revenue passenger-miles (RPMs) anticipated in 1985, but not the 238 million anticipated in 1986. The 238 million RPMs would work out to a load factor of 66.3 percent; a load factor that high would invite a larger carrier to take ASA's better routes. The purchase of the 10 Brasilias is therefore a timely one.

Once in service, the new Brasilias will expand ASA's capacity to

$$9 \text{ hours/plane/day} \times 36 \text{ planes} \times 313 \text{ days/year} = 101,412 \text{ hours}$$

each year, or 497 million APMs. Assuming that 50 percent is as high a load factor as a commuter airline could accept without risking competition from larger airlines, ASA could handle 249 million RPMs per year. The airline expects that level of demand by 1987. An important issue for financial analysis is whether ASA will have the cash flow to finance the acquisition of the additional planes.

Financial Analysis

The company's present financial condition may be evaluated by ratios measuring liquidity, leverage, operating efficiency, and use of capital as follows:

	1981	1982	1983	1984
Current ratio	1.07	2.30	1.46	1.86
Debt/net worth	7.85	2.54	1.14	1.08
Return on sales	15.6%	11.2%	7.6%	12.1%
Return on equity	94.8%	20.6%	14.0%	29.1%

In an industry where most companies are highly leveraged and financially vulnerable, ASA has *solid liquidity and leverage* ratios. The company has restored a balance between debt and equity in its capital structure in three years while maintaining its cash position. This fact is especially impressive in light of the industry's debt-to-net worth ratio of 2.0. ASA's return on sales and return on equity have been more variable, partly because of the timing of investment tax credits associated with the purchase of new airplanes. Return on sales, however, compares favorably with the 1983 regional industry average of 2.9 percent.

Return on equity is above ASA's recent cost of equity, as calculated using the capital-asset-pricing model:

$$K_e = \text{Riskless return} + \text{Beta (Arithmetic average market premium)}$$

$$= 7.7 + 1.5\ (8.6)$$

$$= 20.6 \text{ percent}$$

using the six-month Treasury bill rate of December 1984 as the riskless return, the long-term arithmetic market premium of 8.6 percent, and 1.5 as a beta to reflect the volatility of the commuter-airline industry. (Case Exhibit 6 reports Delta's beta as 1.2, which seems about average for the major carriers.) A 29 percent return on equity is impressive by comparison.

Comparing 1984 fiscal-year data for ASA and Metro Airlines reveals additional strength in ASA's position:

	Metro Airlines	ASA
Current ratio	0.64	1.86
Debt/net worth	1.89	1.08
Return on sales	0.02%	12.1%
Return on equity	0.07%	29.1%

Based on the first six months' data for Metro Airlines' 1985 fiscal year, however, Metro is showing rapid improvement:

	Metro Airlines	
	April 1984	October 1984
Current ratio	0.64	0.92
Debt/net worth	1.89	1.59
Return on sales	0.02%	10.3%
Return on equity	0.07%	23.0%

These financial data suggest that Metro's working arrangement with Eastern is rapidly making Metro a viable competitor with ASA, even though ASA has a significant head start and solid financial strength.

Analysis of Pro Formas

While the pro forma financial statements and operating statistics provided by the company provide a good starting point in analyzing the risk associated with lending to ASA, there are a number of problems in using them as presented. From an operating standpoint, to assume that the spread between load factor and breakeven load factor will increase from 6.4 percentage points to 10 percentage points is not conservative. While ASA will reap the benefits of having a more efficient fleet of airplanes, the environmental indicators suggest that translating that advantage to a larger spread will be very difficult.

To imagine ASA operating at a load factor of 50 percent, as desirable as that goal is, is also difficult. For a commuter airline to achieve load factors that high, it must drop some marginally profitable routes or flights. While this step will increase ASA earnings in the short term, the airline may need to fly some of those runs to keep a competitor from increasing its presence in that market. As noted earlier, once a commuter airline's average load factor starts climbing near the 50 percent range, larger airlines can think about making money on that carrier's above-average routes, where the load factor may be as high as 60 percent. Because a commuter airline can compete with a large regional or major carrier for any given route only on price, ASA would have to slash margins to hold share. In addition, Delta may pressure ASA to keep prices down on all but monopoly routes, which would further depress margins. Under these conditions, the company is unlikely to increase its operating margins from 17 percent in 1985 to 23 percent in 1989.

The balance sheet reveals another problem. The expenditure of zero cash for property and equipment from 1986 to 1989 will not happen; to remain competitive, ASA will have to spend at least some money on property and equipment. The airline may choose to replace the older planes in its fleet or, in the event of further growth, either purchase or lease additional planes. Any of these moves would result in another fixed-asset addition or income-statement charge. Furthermore, the company will not have $67 million in its cash account in 1989. That cash will either not be generated, or it will be spent on increasing the airline's business activity, which will change the lending risk in unforeseeable ways.

On the other hand, ASA's projections for declining growth in RPMs are reasonable, given the flattening demand that will occur across the industry when maturity occurs. This airline does have a reputation for growing faster than the market, however, so an important test in sensitivity analysis will be assessing to what extent further growth would erode ASA's cash position.

Revised Pro Formas

Changing the operating margin and property-and-equipment numbers on the pro formas will rectify the starting point for evaluating ASA's future financial condition. Exhibits A and B present the adjusted "base case" forecasts. The revised income statements (Exhibit A) begin by using the annual RPM figures as given and assuming a yield of 39.5 cents per mile, based on an average fare of $70 dollars and average haul of 180 miles. Inflation is assumed to be negligible. Passenger revenues are derived by multiplying RPMs by yield, while other revenues are assumed to be 3 percent of passenger revenues. The cost of flying operations is 25 percent of sales, maintenance cost is 11 percent of sales, and indirect expenses, which include such items as gate fees and terminal expenses, run 31 percent of sales.

As noted earlier, the effect of growing demand on ASA's needs for additional aircraft will influence the company's future cash needs. This factor has been taken into account in the revised pro formas by making the aircraft lease and depreciation figures on the income statements dependent on the number of RPMs flown in a given year. The purchase of the 10 Brasilias is assumed to be adequate to provide capacity for 1985 and 1986. Beyond that time, the decision to buy or lease additional aircraft will depend on the growth in RPMs. ASA will need an additional 30 seats in capacity for every 9 million additional RPMs. This guideline was determined by looking at case Exhibit 11, which indicates that the 10 new Brasilias are projected to fly 6.75 million miles per year. Assuming that this mileage is their maximum per year, one plane has the capability to fly 675,000 miles annually, which converts to RPMs as

675,000 miles/plane/year x 30 seats/plane x .43 load factor

or about 9 million RPMs. A further assumption is that ASA will buy/lease planes to meet future capacity demands in a 50/50 ratio. The cost of purchasing 30 seats is assumed to be $5.25 million, while lease costs are set at $600,000 per year.

Other items on the revised income statements are unchanged from the company's pro formas. A tax rate of 50 percent is assumed, although all available investment tax credits are used in computing net income in 1985 and 1986.

On the balance sheets (Exhibit B), cash is a plug figure. Accounts receivable are assumed to be 10 percent of revenue, or 36.5 days of sales. Expendable parts and other current assets are taken from the company's projections. The property-and-equipment and depreciation figures are taken as given in years 1985 and 1986 and increased in later years by the value of the planes to be purchased based on the decision rule stated here.

All liabilities are taken as given in the company projections except accounts payable, which is set at 7 percent of the total operating expenses, or 25.5 days. In the owners' equity section, retained earnings is adjusted by the income as recomputed on the revised income statements.

The altered assumptions in this revised base case reduce income growth to a crawl over the period as the investment tax credits from the purchase of the Brasilias are exhausted. (This projection is conservative in that it doesn't account for a tax credit on future purchases of planes.) The cash balance, however, falls only from $67.4 million to $43.7 million. ASA should have no problems repaying the loan under this scenario, as illustrated by the following ratios:

	1984	1985	1987	1989
Current ratio	1.86	1.93	2.20	3.00
Debt/net worth	1.08	1.78	1.60	1.11
Return on sales	15.6%	12.1%	5.6%	6.2%
Return on equity	29.1%	31.8%	14.7%	13.2%
Debt coverage	4.9	2.7	2.3	2.5

Liquidity improves markedly over a period in which the company once again successfully levers and unlevers itself in a span of three years. Return on sales falls as the investment tax credits run out, while the decline in return on equity is almost inevitable given ASA's policy of retaining all its earnings as equity. The company's earnings growth doesn't look especially impressive under this conservative scenario, but solid debt-coverage ratios indicate that ASA is still a reasonable credit risk.

Sensitivity Analysis

Four conditions might change the financial outlook for ASA: higher than expected growth, wage and price inflation, increased competition, and economic recession. Each will be examined in turn.

Growth. Large carriers are probably finished with their divestiture of marginal routes; the company-furnished pro formas are generally correct in their assessment that ASA cannot continue growing at its historical rate. The uncertainty concerns when the slowdown will come and how sharp it will be.

Exhibits C through H present three growth scenarios, two with faster growth than the base case and one with slower growth. The key figure is the cash remaining on the balance sheet in the final year, 1989. In all cases, the cash balance remains large, although the most severe strain on ASA's liquidity comes with the highest growth. The size of the cash balance in Exhibit D, however, suggests that, unless the industry expands more than expected or ASA further widens the difference between its growth and the market's growth, the company can remain liquid.

Inflation. Inflation generally improves a company's cash position, and ASA is no exception. Exhibits I and J are based on the assumptions used in the high-growth case described earlier (Exhibits C and D) plus inflation. Increasing the assumed inflation rate from zero to 10 percent in effect improves the company's cash position by $23.2 million. However, these inflation scenarios ignore the possibility that load factor will decrease if consumers drive to major airports instead of fly.

Competition. Increased competition can be expected to result in smaller operating margins. This circumstance is likely because of the rapid expansion of Metro Airlines and its connection with Eastern in serving the Atlanta market. Two relevant scenarios are portrayed in Exhibits K through N—one where the operating efficiency ratios are worsened by 10 percent (the "competition" case), the other where these ratios are reduced by 20 percent (the "high-competition" case).

The competition case uses the high-growth assumptions presented in Exhibits C and D on the premise that no situation would be more constraining in terms of cash generation than this one. The final-year cash balance is reduced from $23.0 million to $4.4 million with 10 percent ratio deterioration, which would effectively reduce gross margin by 20 percent. With ASA's growth, however, the company would still have additional debt and equity capacity, and the lending risk remains relatively small.

The high-competition case is more sobering. Conditions of extreme price competition are unlikely to occur as long as extraordinary growth occurs; so the moderate growth scenario is used as the foundation for this forecast. With 20 percent ratio deterioration--40 percent margin compression--the cash balance is reduced to only $1.4 million. Were these conditions to persist over a long period, ASA might have a difficult time meeting all its obligations, especially because ASA's lackluster income performance would make taking on additional debt or equity an expensive proposition. If these conditions existed, however, many of ASA's financially weaker competitors would be forced to halt operations. ASA would then face less competition and be able to increase margins to historical levels. The lending concern here is whether ASA can sustain margin compression for two or three years; based on these scenarios, it stands a good chance.

Recession. The recession scenarios involve changing two of the variables with the biggest influence on ASA's cash position: operating margins and growth rates. Recession would reduce demand for commuter air service, as stated in the case, because many passengers would simply drive to a major airport. Reduced demand would then place downward pressure on operating margins as carriers fought to maintain high enough load factors to survive the downturn. Offsetting this scenario perhaps is the fact that 80 percent of ASA's passengers are business travellers and military personnel, who may be more recession-resistant than pleasure travellers.

The "mild-recession" case (Exhibits O and P) assumes a moderate disruption of the growth pattern assumed in the moderate-growth case. RPMs actually decline 5 percent in 1988 and fail to rebound the following year. In addition, there is a 10 percent operating-ratio deterioration. The "deep-recession" case (Exhibits Q and R) assumes even slower growth and 20 percent ratio deterioration. In both cases, cash balances remain positive, even though profitability takes a beating.

The implications of these various scenarios are summarized in Exhibit S, which calculates the ratios that compose the five numerical convenants placed on ASA by the loan agreement. In all cases but the high-competition and deep-recession cases, ASA remains within the covenants. Even though both the high-competition and deep-recession scenarios are truly worst cases, the only serious default conditions take place in the deep-recession case. This sensitivity analysis suggests that quite a rare set of circumstances would be required to put ASA under. In all but the worst cases, the company can withstand high growth, inflation, fiercer competition, and recession and still have the cash to pay the interest and principal of the loan on schedule.

Risk Analysis

Another way of examining the airline's creditworthiness is to examine other risks that might give ASA difficulty in repaying its loan to Wachovia. The risks facing ASA (and, by extension, Wachovia) may be classified as company-specific, industry, and lending risks.

Making this loan carries with it five potential risks. The first one is a potential end to ASA's working agreement with Delta Air Lines. ASA could find itself with little demand for its services should Delta walk away—particularly if Delta chose to align itself with another commuter carrier. Given ASA's performance and Delta's record of never canceling an agreement with a commuter partner, however, this risk is minimal. Delta would have to pay dearly to try to defend its competitive position by flying those commuter routes itself or buying or creating a commuter subsidiary to fly them for it.

The second risk is that ASA management will overextend its financial resources. The airline has grown rapidly, and one apparent key to its success has been its ability to sustain that growth. This loan would fund a purchase that would expand the airline's capacity by 39 percent, but given the airline's historical growth in RPMs of 110 percent per year, an addition of this magnitude seems conservative. In addition, ASA leases many of the airplanes it presently flies; holding 8 of them, or 36.5 percent of its available seats, on one-year leases gives it unusual flexibility if demand slackens. While ASA would have less income in a downturn to cover the fixed principal and interest payments caused by its purchase of the Brasilias, it would also have a more cost-efficient fleet and higher margins to help pay for the new planes. The recession scenarios suggest that ASA can generate cash despite slow demand even with the higher number of planes caused by the purchase this loan is funding.

The third company-specific risk concerns the quality of the plane ASA has chosen to buy. While the Brasilia seems ideal for ASA's route system, it has never been commercially flown. The best estimate of its success is the encouraging track record of the Bandeirante, particularly the indication that no structural flaw will be cited in the Bandeirante crash in December 1984. The fact that more than 100 orders have been placed to Embraer for the new airplanes also creates confidence in ASA's judgment. Nevertheless, management's decision to gain the advantage of being among the first with a superior plane still carries with it a risk that the plane will not perform to expectations.

An extension of this risk is that the regulatory or antitrust philosophy of the government will change in a way that would prohibit working agreements such as the one between Delta and ASA.

The final company-specific risk is that ASA's three founding executives will not be around for the duration of the loan agreement. One or more of the present managers might leave the company for a number of reasons: an internal dispute, death, the desire to move on to a new challenge. While these possibilities exist in any company, management continuity is crucial in this industry, where good business sense, a commodity that separates successful companies from unsuccessful ones, is scarce. The risk may be reduced, in that three executives, not merely one, have shaped the airline into its current form and that they have had six years to train subordinates who could by now be ready to step into positions requiring a strategic focus.

Beyond these company-specific risks lie industry risks that will face all carriers as the commuter-airline industry matures. The first, which may have direct implications for ASA management, is the expected consolidation of the industry. The way in which the industry contracts will influence the viability of ASA and, by extension, the likelihood that Wachovia will have its loan repaid. Consolidation may occur either through groups of small carriers merging and becoming bigger carriers or through the major carriers making subsidiaries of their partner commuter airlines. Because ASA's greatest strength is its management, the greatest threat to it would be a business combination that removed management control from the founders. The potentially large balance the company could have in its cash account could encourage an unfriendly acquisition, although the inherent riskiness of a commuter airline might discourage a takeover by a company outside the industry. If ASA were acquired from within the industry, one would expect the new management to have some ability to run it.

The future structure of the industry will affect ASA in other ways. For example, ASA employees may tire of the two-tiered wage system developing in the industry and insist on future union representation, which would greatly diminish the airline's current cost advantage. Another possible source of failure on ASA's part would be mergers that would expand commuter carriers from one- and two-hub operations to multi-hubbed networks operating in different regions of the country. Because part of ASA's success has come from its management's knowledge of the Southeast, expansion beyond that region carries an additional risk for the airline.

Another risk involves possible competition within the Atlanta market. If the Southeast continues to grow faster than other regions of the country, a struggling carrier with many routes in the Northeast or Midwest might attempt to enter the Atlanta market with force in an effort to take part of the market from Delta and Eastern. Although ASA would lose revenue if competition increased in Atlanta, it has an advantage over Metro Express in that Delta is financially stronger than Eastern and would presumably be better able to defend its position than its weaker competitor.

Another risk faced by every management team in the airline industry is the possibility that a major air disaster will bring unfavorable publicity and a resultant decline in traffic and revenue for the carrier involved. This risk is perhaps greater for a commuter carrier than for a major airline, because many fliers feel less than secure in small, propeller-driven planes; in addition, commuter carriers lack the years of name recognition and trust that allow major airlines to continue operating successfully after these disasters. While no evidence exists on how ASA management would handle a plane crash, its reaction—rapid and confidence-restoring—to the two adverse situations it has faced in recent years is encouraging and provides some assurance that the airline could handle a more difficult problem with similar effectiveness.

The final industry characteristic affecting ASA would be changes in the regulatory environment. Because the industry has taken its modern form only recently, it is difficult to assess how the government will respond to price levels on monopoly routes or to possible future charges of safety problems. While federal authorities are unlikely to take pricing decisions from the hands of the commuter carriers, they may act to promote increased competition within the industry, which would reduce margins and increase individual carriers' vulnerability in a recession.

Wachovia also faces a number of lending risks. First of all, ten years is a long commitment for a bank, the kind of commitment typically made to a company in which the bank places great confidence. In this case, ASA is only six years old, and while it has done very well so far, there is not the track record one would hope for in making a loan of this duration.

Another concern for Wachovia is the South American exposure of interest payments. This bank, like most others its size with its risk profile, is attempting to limit South American exposure. The exposure created in this loan is acceptable, however, for two reasons. First, the Brazilian government has never failed to pay interest or principal on time under the FINEX program, even during the debt crisis in 1982. This record suggests that only an enormous financial shock within Brazil could cause nonrepayment. Second, FINEX is responsible for only a portion of the interest payments. If LIBOR is assumed to be 10 percent during the period of the loan, Wachovia's exposure is only 4.25 percent of the outstanding principal, a sum of $124,312 during the first year and less than that amount afterward; there is no foreign exposure of principal.

The other lending risk facing Wachovia is a common one, that of being a participant rather than a lead bank in a loan. Because Winston-Salem is geographically removed from Atlanta, Wachovia's ability to keep in touch with the company and assess its current position is limited. To a significant extent, it must rely on the covenants that Lloyd's has negotiated to protect it from the risks associated with making this loan.

Relationship Analysis

Wachovia is at a critical time in its relationship with ASA. If the bank rejects the loan, it will lose its best chance of a long-term relationship with the company. The two parties have been getting to know each other for the past two years, and if Wachovia cannot be counted on to come through with financing now, ASA will probably seek other banks to do business with. This likelihood is increased by the fact that Trust Company Bank has been offered a part of the loan and, as agent bank, will feel an obligation to accept, even if it believes the loan decision is a difficult call. Should Wachovia back away, it will reinforce the position of Trust Company as the bank ASA can count on when it has financing needs.

Should Wachovia accept the loan, its relationship with ASA could expand significantly. It is the only other regional bank among those invited to be participants and, as such, makes a likely alternative if Trust Company loses interest in the relationship or if Wachovia can offer a more attractive long-term relationship. ASA is apparently impressed with Wachovia, so even if the bank doesn't gain a position as agent bank, it is likely to receive future invitations to participate in multi-institution loans. As ASA continues growing and stabilizes in a maturing market, future loans—loans more closely fitting Wachovia's risk profile—are likely to carry less risk than the present one.

The Decision

Atlantic Southeast Airlines is a strong company in a difficult industry. It meets the six qualifications for success set forth in the case, although the changing shape of the industry will have an uncertain influence on the airline's ability to continue doing so. One likely outcome of the changed environment will be a slowing of the growth the industry has experienced in the seven years since deregulation. Because slower growth usually means smaller cash requirements, this condition will improve ASA's ability to repay the loan. The company also has considerable financial strength: it is liquid and well capitalized and has strong performance ratios. This strength is particularly evident when ASA is compared with its principal competitor, Metro Airlines.

Because of the high level of uncertainty in the company and industry's future, the most crucial basis for making a lending decision is the quality of the management. The three founders of ASA will determine how well the airline reacts to its changing environment and whether it will continue to operate profitably. The earnings performance of the company and the reputation of its executives are excellent, which indicates that ASA would be well positioned to ride out any storm that might come its way. Based on the company's past performance, its current financial strength, and the ability of its executives, students usually decide to make the loan.

EXHIBIT A   Revised ASA Pro Forma Income Statements: Base Case (thousands of dollars)

Flying operations cost/sales	25%	Average fare	$70		
Maintenance cost/sales	11%	Length of haul	180 miles		
Indirect expenses/sales	31%	Inflation	0%		

	1985	1986	1987	1988	1989
Real growth from prev. year	--	36%	11%	5%	4%
Revenue passenger-miles	175	238	264	277	288
Operating revenues:					
Passenger	$68,056	$92,556	$102,737	$107,874	$112,188
Other	2,042	2,777	3,082	3,236	3,366
Total operating revenues	70,097	95,332	105,819	111,110	115,554
Operating expenses:					
Aircraft leases	9,080	9,650	12,127	12,494	12,802
Flying operations	17,524	23,833	26,455	27,777	28,889
Maintenance	7,711	10,487	11,640	12,222	12,711
Indirect expenses	21,730	29,553	32,804	34,444	35,822
Depreciation	2,443	7,357	7,334	7,591	7,807
Total operating expenses	58,488	80,880	90,360	94,529	98,030
Operating income	11,609	14,453	15,549	16,581	17,524
Nonoperating expense	1,530	3,320	3,600	3,450	3,300
Profit before tax	10,727	11,133	11,859	13,131	14,224
Income tax provision	2,243	3,486	5,929	6,566	7,112
Net income	$8,485	$7,646	$5,929	$6,566	$7,112

EXHIBIT B   Revised ASA Pro Forma Balance Sheets: Base Case (thousands of dollars)

	1985	1986	1987	1988	1989
ASSETS					
Current assets:					
Cash	$15,067	$24,038	$27,131	$34,746	$43,736
Accounts receivable	7,010	9,533	10,582	11,111	11,555
Expendable parts	1,500	1,650	1,900	1,950	2,000
Other current assets	700	750	800	800	800
Total current assets	24,277	35,971	40,413	48,607	58,091
Property and equipment	50,996	71,796	79,432	83,284	86,521
Less depreciation	7,256	12,163	19,497	27,088	34,895
Net prop. and equipment	43,740	59,633	59,935	56,197	51,626
Deposits	1,140	--	--	--	--
Deferred charges	4,800	4,600	4,400	4,200	4,000
Total assets	$74,295	$100,204	$104,748	$109,003	$113,717
LIABILITIES AND OWNERS' EQUITY					
Current liabilities:					
Current long-term debt	$4,020	$5,824	$5,867	$5,914	$5,964
Accounts payable	4,387	6,066	6,777	7,090	7,352
Air-traffic liability	2,000	2,600	3,000	3,200	3,250
Accrued expenses	1,500	1,800	1,960	2,000	2,050
Other	650	700	750	750	750
Total current liabs.	12,557	16,990	18,354	18,954	19,366
Long-term debt	29,800	39,050	33,200	27,300	21,400
Deferred income taxes	5,240	9,820	12,920	15,910	19,000
Total liabilities	47,597	65,860	64,474	62,164	59,766
Owners' equity:					
Common stock	400	400	400	400	400
Capital in excess of par	8,177	8,177	8,177	8,177	8,177
Retained earnings	18,121	25,767	31,697	38,262	45,374
Total owners' equity	26,698	34,344	40,274	46,839	53,951
Total liabs. and owners' equity	$74,295	$100,204	$104,748	$109,003	$113,717

EXHIBIT C   Revised ASA Pro Forma Income Statements: High-Growth Case (thousands of dollars)

Flying operations cost/sales	25%	Average fare	$70		
Maintenance cost/sales	11%	Length of haul	180 miles		
Indirect expenses/sales	31%	Inflation	0%		

	1985	1986	1987	1988	1989
Real growth from prev. year	--	36%	22%	18%	15%
Revenue passenger-miles	175	238	290	343	394
Operating revenues:					
Passenger	$68,056	$92,556	$112,918	$133,243	$153,229
Other	2,042	2,777	3,388	3,997	4,597
Total operating revenues	70,097	95,332	116,305	137,240	157,826
Operating expenses:					
Aircraft leases	9,080	9,650	12,854	14,306	15,734
Flying operations	17,524	23,833	29,076	34,310	39,457
Maintenance	7,711	10,487	12,794	15,096	17,361
Indirect expenses	21,730	29,553	36,055	42,544	48,926
Depreciation	2,443	7,357	7,843	8,859	9,859
Total operating expenses	58,488	80,880	98,622	115,117	131,336
Operating income	11,609	14,453	17,683	22,124	26,490
Nonoperating expense	1,530	3,320	3,600	3,450	3,300
Profit before tax	10,727	11,133	14,083	18,674	23,190
Income tax provision	2,243	3,486	7,042	9,337	11,595
Net income	$8,485	$7,646	$7,042	$9,337	$11,595

EXHIBIT D Revised ASA Pro Forma Balance Sheets: High-Growth Case (thousands of dollars)

	1985	1986	1987	1988	1989
ASSETS					
Current assets:					
Cash	$15,067	$24,038	$20,687	$20,310	$23,422
Accounts receivable	7,010	9,533	11,631	13,724	15,783
Expendable parts	1,500	1,650	1,900	1,950	2,000
Other current assets	700	750	800	800	800
Total current assets	24,277	35,971	35,018	36,784	42,005
Property and equipment	50,996	71,796	87,068	102,312	117,301
Less depreciation	7,256	12,163	20,006	28,865	38,724
Net prop. and equipment	43,740	59,633	67,062	73,446	78,577
Deposits	1,140	--	--	--	--
Deferred charges	4,800	4,600	4,400	4,200	4,000
Total assets	$74,295	$100,204	$106,480	$114,430	$124,582
LIABILITIES AND OWNERS' EQUITY					
Current liabilities:					
Current long-term debt	$4,020	$5,824	$5,867	$5,914	$5,964
Accounts payable	4,387	6,066	7,397	8,634	9,850
Air-traffic liability	2,000	2,600	3,000	3,200	3,250
Accrued expenses	1,500	1,800	1,960	2,000	2,050
Other	650	700	750	750	750
Total current liabs.	12,557	16,990	18,974	20,498	21,864
Long-term debt	29,800	39,050	33,200	27,300	21,400
Deferred income taxes	5,240	9,820	12,920	15,910	19,000
Total liabilities	47,597	65,860	65,094	63,708	62,264
Owners' equity:					
Common stock	400	400	400	400	400
Capital in excess of par	8,177	8,177	8,177	8,177	8,177
Retained earnings	18,121	25,767	32,809	42,146	53,741
Total owners' equity	26,698	34,344	41,386	50,723	62,318
Total liabs. and owners' equity	$74,295	$100,204	$106,480	$114,431	$124,582

EXHIBIT E Revised ASA Pro Forma Income Statements: Moderate-Growth Case
(thousands of dollars)

Flying operations cost/sales	25%	Average fare	$70		
Maintenance cost/sales	11%	Length of haul	180 miles		
Indirect expenses/sales	31%	Inflation	0%		

	1985	1986	1987	1988	1989
Real growth from prev. year	--	36%	16%	11%	9%
Revenue passenger-miles	175	238	276	306	334
Operating revenues:					
Passenger	$68,056	$92,556	$107,364	$119,175	$129,900
Other	2,042	2,777	3,221	3,575	3,897
Total operating revenues	70,097	95,332	110,585	122,750	133,797
Operating expenses:					
Aircraft leases	9,080	9,650	12,458	13,301	14,067
Flying operations	17,524	23,833	27,646	30,687	33,449
Maintenance	7,711	10,487	12,164	13,502	14,718
Indirect expenses	21,730	29,553	34,281	38,052	41,477
Depreciation	2,443	7,357	7,565	8,156	8,692
Total operating expenses	58,488	80,880	94,115	103,700	112,404
Operating income	11,609	14,453	16,470	19,050	21,393
Nonoperating expense	1,530	3,320	3,600	3,450	3,300
Profit before tax	10,727	11,133	12,870	15,600	18,093
Income tax provision	2,243	3,486	6,435	7,800	9,047
Net income	$8,485	$7,646	$6,435	$7,800	$9,047

EXHIBIT F   Revised ASA Pro Forma Balance Sheets: Moderate-Growth Case (thousands of dollars)

	1985	1986	1987	1988	1989
ASSETS					
Current assets:					
Cash	$15,067	$24,038	$24,202	$28,330	$35,063
Accounts receivable	7,010	9,533	11,059	12,275	13,380
Expendable parts	1,500	1,650	1,900	1,950	2,000
Other current assets	700	750	800	800	800
Total current assets	24,277	35,971	37,961	43,355	51,243
Property and equipment	50,996	71,796	82,903	91,760	99,805
Less depreciation	7,256	12,163	19,728	27,884	36,577
Net prop. and equipment	43,740	59,633	63,174	63,876	63,228
Deposits	1,140	--	--	--	--
Deferred charges	4,800	4,600	4,400	4,200	4,000
Total assets	$74,295	$100,204	$105,535	$111,431	$118,471
LIABILITIES AND OWNERS' EQUITY					
Current liabilities:					
Current long-term debt	$4,020	$5,824	$5,867	$5,914	$5,964
Accounts payable	4,387	6,066	7,059	7,777	8,430
Air-traffic liability	2,000	2,600	3,000	3,200	3,250
Accrued expenses	1,500	1,800	1,960	2,000	2,050
Other	650	700	750	750	750
Total current liabs.	12,557	16,990	18,636	19,641	20,444
Long-term debt	29,800	39,050	33,200	27,300	21,400
Deferred income taxes	5,240	9,820	12,920	15,910	19,000
Total liabilities	47,597	65,860	64,756	62,851	60,844
Owners' equity:					
Common stock	400	400	400	400	400
Capital in excess of par	8,177	8,177	8,177	8,177	8,177
Retained earnings	18,121	25,767	32,202	40,002	49,049
Total owners' equity	26,698	34,344	40,779	48,579	57,626
Total liabs. and owners' equity	$74,295	$100,204	$105,535	$111,430	$118,470

EXHIBIT G   Revised ASA Pro Forma Income Statements: Low-Growth Case (thousands
of dollars)

Flying operations cost/sales	25%	Average fare	$70	
Maintenance cost/sales	11%	Length of haul	180 miles	
Indirect expenses/sales	31%	Inflation	0%	

	1985	1986	1987	1988	1989
Real growth from prev. year	--	30%	10%	3%	0%
Revenue passenger-miles	175	228	250	258	258
Operating revenues:					
Passenger	$68,056	$88,472	$97,319	$100,239	$100,239
Other	2,042	2,654	2,920	3,007	3,007
Total operating revenues	70,097	91,126	100,239	103,246	103,246
Operating expenses:					
Aircraft leases	9,080	9,650	11,740	11,949	11,949
Flying operations	17,524	22,782	25,060	25,812	25,812
Maintenance	7,711	10,024	11,026	11,357	11,357
Indirect expenses	21,730	28,249	31,074	32,006	32,006
Depreciation	2,443	6,949	7,063	7,209	7,209
Total operating expenses	58,488	77,653	85,964	88,333	88,333
Operating income	11,609	13,473	14,275	14,913	14,913
Nonoperating expense	1,530	3,320	3,600	3,450	3,300
Profit before tax	10,727	10,153	10,675	11,463	11,613
Income tax provision	2,243	2,997	5,338	5,732	5,807
Net income	$8,485	$7,157	$5,338	$5,732	$5,807

EXHIBIT H   Revised ASA Pro Forma Balance Sheets: Low-Growth Case (thousands of dollars)

	1985	1986	1987	1988	1989
ASSETS					
Current assets:					
Cash	$15,067	$23,727	$27,007	$35,162	$45,668
Accounts receivable	7,010	9,113	10,024	10,325	10,325
Expendable parts	1,500	1,650	1,900	1,950	2,000
Other current assets	700	750	800	800	800
Total current assets	24,277	35,240	39,731	48,237	58,793
Property and equipment	50,996	71,796	78,431	80,621	80,621
Less depreciation	7,256	12,163	19,226	26,435	33,645
Net prop. and equipment	43,740	59,633	59,205	54,186	46,977
Deposits	1,140	--	--	--	--
Deferred charges	4,800	4,600	4,400	4,200	4,000
Total assets	$74,295	$99,473	$103,336	$106,623	$109,770
LIABILITIES AND OWNERS' EQUITY					
Current liabilities:					
Current long-term debt	$4,020	$5,824	$5,867	$5,914	$5,964
Accounts payable	4,387	8,824	6,447	6,625	6,625
Air-traffic liability	2,000	2,600	3,000	3,200	3,250
Accrued expenses	1,500	1,800	1,960	2,000	2,050
Other	650	700	750	750	750
Total current liabs.	12,557	16,748	18,024	18,489	18,639
Long-term debt	29,800	39,050	33,200	27,300	21,400
Deferred income taxes	5,240	9,820	12,920	15,910	19,000
Total liabilities	47,597	65,618	64,144	61,699	59,039
Owners' equity:					
Common stock	400	400	400	400	400
Capital in excess of par	8,177	8,177	8,177	8,177	8,177
Retained earnings	18,121	25,278	30,615	36,347	42,153
Total owners' equity	26,698	33,855	39,192	44,924	50,730
Total liabs. and owners' equity	$74,295	$99,473	$103,336	$106,623	$109,769

EXHIBIT I Revised ASA Pro Forma Income Statements: Inflation Case (thousands of dollars)

Flying operations cost/sales	25%	Average fare	$70
Maintenance cost/sales	11%	Length of haul	180 miles
Indirect expenses/sales	31%	Inflation	0%

	1985	1986	1987	1988	1989
Real growth from prev. year	--	36%	22%	18%	15%
Revenue passenger-miles	175	238	290	343	394
Operating revenues:					
Passenger	$68,056	$101,811	$136,631	$177,346	$224,343
Other	2,042	3,054	4,099	5,320	6,730
Total operating revenues	70,097	104,865	140,729	182,667	231,073
Operating expenses:					
Aircraft leases	9,080	9,650	12,854	14,306	15,734
Flying operations	17,524	26,216	35,182	45,667	57,768
Maintenance	7,711	11,535	15,480	20,093	25,418
Indirect expenses	21,730	32,508	43,626	56,627	71,633
Depreciation	2,443	7,357	7,843	8,859	9,859
Total operating expenses	58,488	87,267	114,986	145,552	180,412
Operating income	11,609	17,599	25,743	37,114	50,662
Nonoperating expense	1,530	3,320	3,600	3,450	3,300
Profit before tax	10,727	14,279	22,143	33,664	47,362
Income tax provision	2,243	5,059	11,072	16,832	23,681
Net income	$8,485	$9,219	$11,072	$16,832	$23,681

EXHIBIT J   Revised ASA Pro Forma Balance Sheets: Inflation Case (thousands of dollars)

	1985	1986	1987	1988	1989
ASSETS					
Current assets:					
Cash	$15,067	$23,727	$27,007	$35,162	$45,668
Accounts receivable	7,010	10,487	14,073	18,267	23,107
Expendable parts	1,500	1,650	1,900	1,950	2,000
Other current assets	700	750	800	800	800
Total current assets	24,277	38,024	49,848	52,166	70,869
Property and equipment	50,996	71,796	87,068	102,312	117,301
Less depreciation	7,256	12,163	20,006	28,865	38,724
Net prop. and equipment	43,740	59,633	67,062	73,446	78,577
Deposits	1,140	--	--	--	--
Deferred charges	4,800	4,600	4,400	4,200	4,000
Total assets	$74,295	$102,257	$113,310	$129,812	$153,446
LIABILITIES AND OWNERS' EQUITY					
Current liabilities:					
Current long-term debt	$4,020	$5,824	$5,867	$5,914	$5,964
Accounts payable	4,387	6,545	8,624	10,916	13,531
Air-traffic liability	2,000	2,600	3,000	3,200	3,250
Accrued expenses	1,500	1,800	1,960	2,000	2,050
Other	650	700	750	750	750
Total current liabs.	12,557	17,469	20,201	22,780	25,545
Long-term debt	29,800	39,050	33,200	27,300	21,400
Deferred income taxes	5,240	9,820	12,920	15,910	19,000
Total liabilities	47,597	66,339	66,321	65,990	65,945
Owners' equity:					
Common stock	400	400	400	400	400
Capital in excess of par	8,177	8,177	8,177	8,177	8,177
Retained earnings	18,121	27,340	38,412	55,244	78,925
Total owners' equity	26,698	35,917	46,989	63,821	87,502
Total liabs. and owners' equity	$74,295	$102,256	$113,310	$129,811	$153,447

EXHIBIT K   Revised ASA Pro Forma Income Statements: Competition Case (thousands of dollars)

Flying operations cost/sales	27.5%	Average fare	$70		
Maintenance cost/sales	12.1%	Length of haul	180 miles		
Indirect expenses/sales	34.1%	Inflation	0%		

	1985	1986	1987	1988	1989
Real growth from prev. year	--	36%	22%	18%	15%
Revenue passenger-miles	175	238	290	343	394
Operating revenues:					
Passenger	$68,056	$92,556	$112,918	$133,243	$153,229
Other	2,042	2,777	3,388	3,997	4,597
Total operating revenues	70,097	95,332	116,305	137,240	157,826
Operating expenses:					
Aircraft leases	9,080	9,650	12,854	14,306	15,734
Flying operations	19,277	26,216	31,984	37,741	43,402
Maintenance	8,482	11,535	14,073	16,606	19,097
Indirect expenses	23,903	32,508	39,660	46,799	53,819
Depreciation	2,443	7,357	7,843	8,859	9,859
Total operating expenses	63,185	87,267	106,415	124,312	141,911
Operating income	6,913	8,065	9,891	12,929	15,916
Nonoperating expense	1,530	3,320	3,600	3,450	3,300
Profit before tax	5,383	4,745	6,291	9,479	12,616
Income tax provision	0	0	3,008	4,739	6,308
Net income	$5,383	$4,745	$3,282	$4,739	$6,308

EXHIBIT L   Revised ASA Pro Forma Balance Sheets: Competition Case (thousands of
          dollars)

	1985	1986	1987	1988	1989
ASSETS					
Current assets:					
Cash	$15,067	$21,616	$14,612	$9,742	$7,670
Accounts receivable	7,010	9,533	11,631	13,724	15,783
Expendable parts	1,500	1,650	1,900	1,950	2,000
Other current assets	700	750	800	800	800
Total current assets	24,277	33,549	28,943	26,216	26,253
Property and equipment	50,996	71,796	87,068	102,312	117,301
Less depreciation	7,256	12,163	20,006	28,865	38,724
Net prop. and equipment	43,740	59,633	67,062	73,446	78,577
Deposits	1,140	--	--	--	--
Deferred charges	4,800	4,600	4,400	4,200	4,000
Total assets	$74,647	$97,782	$100,405	$103,862	$108,830
LIABILITIES AND OWNERS' EQUITY					
Current liabilities:					
Current long-term debt	$4,020	$5,824	$5,867	$5,914	$5,964
Accounts payable	4,739	6,545	7,981	9,323	10,643
Air-traffic liability	2,000	2,600	3,000	3,200	3,250
Accrued expenses	1,500	1,800	1,960	2,000	2,050
Other	650	700	750	750	750
Total current liabs.	12,909	17,469	19,558	21,187	22,657
Long-term debt	29,800	39,050	33,200	27,300	21,400
Deferred income taxes	5,240	9,820	12,920	15,910	19,000
Total liabilities	47,949	66,339	65,678	64,397	63,057
Owners' equity:					
Common stock	400	400	400	400	400
Capital in excess of par	8,177	8,177	8,177	8,177	8,177
Retained earnings	18,121	22,866	26,149	30,888	37,196
Total owners' equity	26,698	31,443	34,726	39,465	45,773
Total liabs. and owners' equity	$74,647	$97,782	$100,404	$103,862	$108,830

EXHIBIT M   Revised ASA Pro Forma Income Statements: High-Competition Case
            (thousands of dollars)

Flying operations cost/sales	30.0%	Average fare	$70		
Maintenance cost/sales	13.2%	Length of haul	180 miles		
Indirect expenses/sales	37.2%	Inflation	0%		

	1985	1986	1987	1988	1989
Real growth from prev. year	--	36%	16%	11%	9%
Revenue passenger-miles	175	238	276	306	334
Operating revenues:					
Passenger	$68,056	$92,556	$107,364	$119,175	$129,900
Other	2,042	2,777	3,221	3,575	3,897
Total operating revenues	70,097	95,332	110,585	122,750	133,797
Operating expenses:					
Aircraft leases	9,080	9,650	12,458	13,301	14,067
Flying operations	21,029	28,600	33,176	36,825	40,139
Maintenance	9,253	12,584	14,597	16,203	17,661
Indirect expenses	26,076	35,464	41,138	45,663	49,773
Depreciation	2,443	7,357	7,565	8,156	8,692
Total operating expenses	67,881	93,654	108,934	120,148	130,333
Operating income	2,216	1,678	1,652	2,602	3,465
Nonoperating expense	1,530	3,320	3,600	3,450	3,300
Profit before tax	686	(1,642)	(1,948)	(848)	165
Income tax provision	0	(821)	(974)	(424)	0
Net income	$686	($821)	($974)	($424)	$165

EXHIBIT N   Revised ASA Pro Forma Balance Sheets: High-Competition Case
            (thousands of dollars)

	1985	1986	1987	1988	1989
ASSETS					
Current assets:					
Cash	$15,067	$16,529	$9,437	$5,463	$3,425
Accounts receivable	7,010	9,533	11,059	12,275	13,380
Expendable parts	1,500	1,650	1,900	1,950	2,000
Other current assets	700	750	800	800	800
Total current assets	24,277	38,462	23,196	20,488	19,605
Property and equipment	50,996	71,796	82,903	91,760	99,805
Less depreciation	7,256	12,163	19,728	27,884	36,577
Net prop. and equipment	43,740	59,633	63,174	63,876	63,228
Deposits	1,140	--	--	--	--
Deferred charges	4,800	4,600	4,400	4,200	4,000
Total assets	$74,999	$92,695	$90,770	$88,564	$86,833
LIABILITIES AND OWNERS' EQUITY					
Current liabilities:					
Current long-term debt	$4,020	$5,824	$5,867	$5,914	$5,964
Accounts payable	5,091	7,024	8,170	9,011	9,775
Air-traffic liability	2,000	2,600	3,000	3,200	3,250
Accrued expenses	1,500	1,800	1,960	2,000	2,050
Other	650	700	750	750	750
Total current liabs.	13,261	17,948	19,747	20,875	21,789
Long-term debt	29,800	39,050	33,200	27,300	21,400
Deferred income taxes	5,240	9,820	12,920	15,910	19,000
Total liabilities	48,301	66,818	65,867	64,085	62,189
Owners' equity:					
Common stock	400	400	400	400	400
Capital in excess of par	8,177	8,177	8,177	8,177	8,177
Retained earnings	18,121	17,300	16,326	15,902	16,066
Total owners' equity	26,698	25,877	24,903	24,479	24,643
Total liabs. and owners' equity	$74,999	$92,695	$90,770	$88,564	$86,832

EXHIBIT O   Revised ASA Pro Forma Income Statements: Mild-Recession Case
            (thousands of dollars)

Flying operations cost/sales	27.5%	Average fare	$70		
Maintenance cost/sales	12.1%	Length of haul	180 miles		
Indirect expenses/sales	34.1%	Inflation	0%		

	1985	1986	1987	1988	1989
Real growth from prev. year	--	36%	16%	-5%	0%
Revenue passenger-miles	175	238	276	262	262
Operating revenues:					
Passenger	$68,056	$92,556	$107,364	$101,996	$101,996
Other	2,042	2,777	3,221	3,060	3,060
Total operating revenues	70,097	95,332	110,585	105,056	105,056
Operating expenses:					
Aircraft leases	9,080	9,650	12,458	12,458	12,458
Flying operations	19,277	26,216	30,411	28,890	28,890
Maintenance	8,482	11,535	13,381	12,712	12,712
Indirect expenses	23,903	32,508	37,710	35,824	35,824
Depreciation	2,443	7,357	7,565	7,297	7,297
Total operating expenses	63,185	87,267	101,525	97,181	97,181
Operating income	6,913	8,065	9,061	7,875	7,875
Nonoperating expense	1,530	3,320	3,600	3,450	3,300
Profit before tax	10,727	4,745	5,461	4,425	4,575
Income tax provision	2,243	293	2,730	2,212	2,287
Net income	$8,485	$4,453	$2,730	$2,212	$2,287

EXHIBIT P   Revised ASA Pro Forma Balance Sheets: Mild-Recession Case (thousands of dollars)

	1985	1986	1987	1988	1989
ASSETS					
Current assets:					
Cash	$15,067	$21,323	$17,860	$25,123	$32,197
Accounts receivable	7,010	9,533	11,059	10,506	10,506
Expendable parts	1,500	1,650	1,900	1,950	2,000
Other current assets	700	750	800	800	800
Total current assets	24,277	33,256	31,619	38,379	45,503
Property and equipment	50,996	71,796	82,903	82,903	82,903
Less depreciation	7,256	12,163	19,728	27,025	34,323
Net prop. and equipment	43,740	59,633	63,174	55,878	48,580
Deposits	1,140	--	--	--	--
Deferred charges	4,800	4,600	4,400	4,200	4,000
Total assets	$74,295	$97,489	$99,193	$98,457	$98,083
LIABILITIES AND OWNERS' EQUITY					
Current liabilities:					
Current long-term debt	$4,020	$5,824	$5,867	$5,914	$5,964
Accounts payable	4,387	5,824	7,614	7,289	7,289
Air-traffic liability	2,000	2,600	3,000	3,200	3,250
Accrued expenses	1,500	1,800	1,960	2,000	2,050
Other	650	700	750	750	750
Total current liabs.	12,557	16,748	19,191	19,153	19,303
Long-term debt	29,800	39,050	33,200	27,300	21,400
Deferred income taxes	5,240	9,820	12,920	15,910	19,000
Total liabilities	47,597	65,618	65,311	62,363	59,703
Owners' equity:					
Common stock	400	400	400	400	400
Capital in excess of par	8,177	8,177	8,177	8,177	8,177
Retained earnings	18,121	22,574	25,304	27,516	29,804
Total owners' equity	26,698	31,151	33,881	36,093	38,381
Total liabs. and owners' equity	$74,295	$96,769	$99,192	$98,456	$98,084

EXHIBIT Q   Revised ASA Pro Forma Income Statements: Deep-Recession Case
            (thousands of dollars)

Flying operations cost/sales	30.0%	Average fare	$70		
Maintenance cost/sales	13.2%	Length of haul	180 miles		
Indirect expenses/sales	37.2%	Inflation	0%		

	1985	1986	1987	1988	1989
Real growth from prev. year	--	36%	16%	-15%	-5%
Revenue passenger-miles	175	238	276	235	223
Operating revenues:					
Passenger	$68,056	$92,556	$107,364	$91,260	$86,697
Other	2,042	2,777	3,221	2,738	2,601
Total operating revenues	70,097	95,332	110,585	93,998	89,298
Operating expenses:					
Aircraft leases	9,080	9,650	12,458	12,458	12,458
Flying operations	21,029	28,600	33,176	28,199	26,789
Maintenance	9,253	12,584	14,597	12,408	11,787
Indirect expenses	26,076	35,464	41,138	34,967	33,219
Depreciation	2,443	7,357	7,565	7,565	7,565
Total operating expenses	67,881	93,654	108,934	95,597	91,818
Operating income	2,216	1,678	1,652	(1,599)	(2,521)
Nonoperating expense	1,530	3,320	3,600	3,450	3,300
Profit before tax	10,727	(1,642)	(1,948)	(5,049)	(5,821)
Income tax provision	2,243	(2,901)	(974)	(2,525)	(2,910)
Net income	$8,485	$1,259	($974)	($2,525)	($2,910)

EXHIBIT R   Revised ASA Pro Forma Balance Sheets: Deep-Recession Case   (thousands of dollars)

	1985	1986	1987	1988	1989
ASSETS					
Current assets:					
Cash	$15,067	$18,609	$11,517	$14,743	$17,074
Accounts receivable	7,010	9,533	11,059	9,400	8,930
Expendable parts	1,500	1,650	1,900	1,950	2,000
Other current assets	700	750	800	800	800
Total current assets	24,277	30,542	25,276	26,893	28,804
Property and equipment	50,996	71,796	82,903	82,903	82,903
Less depreciation	7,256	12,163	19,728	27,293	34,858
Net prop. and equipment	43,740	59,633	63,174	55,610	48,045
Deposits	1,140	--	--	--	--
Deferred charges	4,800	4,600	4,400	4,200	4,000
Total assets	$74,999	$94,775	$92,850	$86,703	$80,849
LIABILITIES AND OWNERS' EQUITY					
Current liabilities:					
Current long-term debt	$4,020	$5,824	$5,867	$5,914	$5,964
Accounts payable	5,091	7,024	8,170	7,170	6,886
Air-traffic liability	2,000	2,600	3,000	3,200	3,250
Accrued expenses	1,500	1,800	1,960	2,000	2,050
Other	650	700	750	750	750
Total current liabs.	13,261	17,948	19,747	19,034	18,900
Long-term debt	29,800	39,050	33,200	27,300	21,400
Deferred income taxes	5,240	9,820	12,920	15,910	19,000
Total liabilities	48,301	66,818	65,867	62,244	59,300
Owners' equity:					
Common stock	400	400	400	400	400
Capital in excess of par	8,177	8,177	8,177	8,177	8,177
Retained earnings	18,121	19,380	18,406	15,881	12,971
Total owners' equity	26,698	27,957	26,983	24,458	21,548
Total liabs. and owners' equity	$74,999	$94,775	$92,850	$86,702	$80,848

EXHIBIT S   Covenant Compliance Summary for 1989 Projections

Covenant:	Long-Term Debt to Net Worth	Liabilities to Net Worth	Current Ratio	Fixed-Charge Coverage	Minimum Net Worth*
Case:					
Base	0.32	0.88	4.2	4.7	$67.6
High growth	0.33	0.96	2.0	5.7	$64.2
Moderate growth	0.36	1.01	2.6	4.6	$59.4
Low growth	0.41	1.12	3.3	3.3	$52.0
Inflation	0.23	0.72	2.9	9.9	$90.5
Competition	0.47	1.35	1.1	3.9	$45.7
High competition	0.83	2.34	0.9	1.6	$25.6
Recession	0.56	1.52	2.4	2.1	$38.4
Deep recession	1.07	2.87	1.5	0.4	$20.0

*Millions of dollars.

The L. S. Starrett Company

SYNOPSIS AND OBJECTIVES

Wachovia Bank must decide on two loan requests from L. S. Starrett. The first is a term loan to a new employee stock ownership plan (ESOP) that Starrett plans to establish. The second is a revolving loan to the parent to ensure liquidity because the parent intends to repurchase outstanding shares. The case presents students with tasks of credit analysis and valuation of common stock. It can be used to:

- illustrate the credit and valuation effects of ESOPs;

- explore the effect of leverage on stock prices;

- consider the use of ESOPs as takeover defenses and the larger issue of managerial entrenchment.

STUDY QUESTIONS

As background, students may find useful the note, "Leveraged Employee Stock Ownership Plans" which is provided as a supplement in this instructor's manual and may be reproduced for classroom purposes. The note provides a succinct introduction to the subject. A more detailed presentation is "Leveraged ESOPs and Corporate Restructuring," by Robert F. Bruner, *Continental Bank Journal of Applied Corporate Finance*, Winter 1988. This article develops a wide range of corporate financial considerations related to ESOPs.

1. How does a leveraged ESOP work? Diagram for yourself the flow of funds and securities among employer, ESOP, and bank. How is an ESOP accounted for on the balance sheet?

2. How, if at all, will the ESOP-and-share-repurchase restructuring affect Starrett's stock price? Is the tender offer at $30 a share fairly priced? What is it that creates the value, if any, in this restructuring? (Assume that the company repurchases outstanding stock amounting to 600,000 shares.)

3. Who benefits most from this transaction: old shareholders, ESOP participants, creditors, management? Why?

4. Should Wachovia make the loans? Are the credit risks material? Are the covenants and pricing appropriate?

TEACHING PLAN

(15 minutes) How does a leveraged ESOP work?

Teaching note written by Robert F. Bruner. Copyright (c) 1989 by the Darden Graduate Business School Sponsors, Charlottesville, VA.

(10 minutes) What kind of company is Starrett? Why does it want an ESOP? Should Doug Starrett worry about a threat of takeover?

(25 minutes) Will this restructuring create value?

(20 minutes) How will the value created in this restructuring be allocated among the players?

(10 minutes) Should Wachovia make either loan, or both? Why?

The class may be closed with a presentation of the outcome presented in the epilogue of this note and comments about the growing attractiveness for banks of ESOP-related loans.

ANALYSIS

The case affords many opportunities for analysis. The following discussion will focus on a range of topics: (1) the credit and loan evaluation of Starrett, (2) the use of an ESOP as an antitakeover device, and (3) the allocation of value among the various stakeholders in the company (shareholders, employees, management).

Credit Evaluation

The credit request consists of two loans: (1) a 10-year, $18 million term loan to the ESOP to finance its purchase of 600,000 shares at $30 a share, and (2) a $15 million, 2-year revolving loan/5-year term loan that would ensure the company's liquidity as it prepares to repurchase 600,000 to 800,000 shares for $18 to $24 million.

Historical analysis and current standing. A cursory examination of Starrett makes the decision on the $18 million ESOP loan elementary. The firm had no debt at fiscal-year-end 1984 [it had committed to a $7.5 million industrial revenue bond (IRB) that would show up in December 1984] and had $22.9 million in cash and short-term investments. In addition, the firm's net margin remained healthy (above 7 percent) during the 1982-83 recession (see Exhibit A), the worst decline in the industry since 1949. The firm had historically been extremely liquid, as evidenced by its current-ratio range from a low of 2.88 to a high of 5.09 during the last 10 years (see case Exhibit 1). Steady profits and moderate capital expenditures allowed the company to fund all its domestic growth internally, although before 1978 it used debt to fund its foreign operations.

There are, however, aspects of Starrett that might give a conservative lending institution pause. First, the case suggests that a management change is to be expected in the near future. Second, the "excess cash" on the firm's books could easily dwindle as the following likely-case/worst-case[1] comparison suggests:

---

[1]Under the most likely scenario, Starrett sells the 600,000 shares to the ESOP and repurchases a like number at the same price; the two possible acquisitions are concluded for $10 million, and no premium is necessary to repurchase shares. Under the worst-case scenario, Starrett repurchases 800,000 shares for $24 million, makes the acquisitions, and is forced by competing bids to increase its tender offer by $2 a share.

Pro Forma Cash Balance
(in millions of dollars)

	Likely Case	Worst Case
Cash balance (9/30/84)	$22.9	$22.9
Proceeds from ESOP	18.0	18.0
Repurchase	(18.0)	(24.0)
Possible acquisition	(10.0)	(10.0)
Tender price increased to $32/share	0.0	(1.6)
Pro forma cash balance	$12.8	$ 5.3

Even though the company would still have cash under the worst-case scenario, the amount would be significantly less than in the likely scenario.

The third insight about Starrett is that it may not be the good performer that cursory examination suggests and that there may be good grounds for fear of a takeover. Exhibit A shows that Starrett's cost of equity consistently exceeded its return on equity, sometimes by as much as 50 percent. Because Starrett used no debt in its capital structure between 1981 and 1984, its return on equity was significantly lower than if the firm had been leveraged. A second reason for the relatively low return on equity is that the firm has such a large portion of its asset base (21 percent at FYE 1984) in low-yielding, short-term government securities.

Cash-flow assessment. Exhibits B and C present forecasts of Starrett's income statements and balance sheets, respectively, assuming the ESOP and share repurchase. These two exhibits are modifications of case Exhibits 5 and 6 to reflect payments to the ESOP, introduction of ESOP debt, and adjustment of equity accounts. Note that Exhibit B is based on an assumed gross margin rather than the actual numbers from case Exhibit 5, which creates some differences from Exhibit 5, but they are minor.

Exhibits B and C reveal that Starrett can comfortably service the ESOP debt while paying dividends and investing in assets; the revolver is not drawn down and short-term investments increase by about $8 million over the 1985-89 period. The interest and fixed-charges coverage ratios given in Exhibit D suggest a wide margin of comfort, although the restructuring changes the capitalization and coverage ratios significantly in 1986 (the first full year of debt service) versus 1984. By 1989, the capitalization ratios will still not have recovered to their initial levels, i.e., the all-equity capital structure.

A rough sensitivity analysis confirms the coverage-ratio analysis. For instance, one can calculate the level of earnings before interest and taxes at which Starrett just breaks even on its ESOP payments, capital expenditures, and additions to working capital. Using the figures for 1986, the breakeven EBIT is $15.3 million.[2] This represents a 36 percent discount from forecasted operating profit--evidently healthy cushion. If sales for 1986 hold constant at $132.7

---

[2]The breakeven formula is
$$(\text{EBIT} - \text{IRB} - \text{ESOP})(1\text{-Tax rate}) - \text{Capital expenditure} + \text{Depreciation}$$
$$- \text{Additions to working capital} - \text{ IRB amortization} = 0$$

million, this EBIT implies a contraction in operating profit from 17.56 percent to 11.5 percent. As Exhibit D reveals, Starrett's operating margin fell to 12.66 percent in 1982, still above the expected breakeven for 1986.

IRB covenant analysis. The following table reveals that Starrett will probably hurdle only three of the proposed IRB covenants successfully and will default (by a whisker) on the fourth covenant in 1985:

IRB Loan Covenants
Projected at FYE 1985

Existing Covenants	No ESOP; No Repurchase	ESOP Buys 600,000 Shares; Same Number Repurchased
Current ratio > 2.5	4.64	3.91
Total liabilities < .8 of tangible net worth	23.2%	69%
Net working capital > $45 mm	$69.5 mm	$67.7 mm
Tangible net worth > $70 mm	$79.2 mm	$69.1 mm

Given that the existing IRB covenants did not anticipate the ESOP or share repurchase, they will need to be renegotiated in anticipation of the transactions.[3]

Credit decision. The credit decision should address the two loans separately. The ESOP loan request is reasonable in light of the apparent robustness of the firm to market adversity, strength of cash flow, and balance-sheet strength. Covenants will need to be tailored to the contemplated restructuring.

The second loan, the revolver/term, may stimulate greater discussion within the lending group. The purpose of this loan is to support the liquidity of the firm during and after the restructuring. As the worst-case analysis in the Credit Evaluation section suggests, however, the down-side outcome is not drastic. Nominally, the second loan is an insurance policy for the restructuring, but its likely economic purpose is to ensure the firm's liquidity for the acquisition of an as-yet-to-be-named firm. Do the banks want to finance an acquisition sight unseen? The answer depends on the probability that the revolver will be used. As Exhibit C suggests, the revolver will not be used. Therefore, the revolver may simply be a way to augment the fee income of the lenders. With proper covenants and in light of strong basic cash flow, the decision on this second loan should also probably be positive.

Given Wachovia's conservative lending policies, its uncertainty about Starrett managerial succession, its relatively new relationship with Starrett, and the long term of the proposed debt, Wachovia might feel comfortable taking

---

[3] In response to this prospect, Wachovia proposed the following bank covenants: (1) minimum working capital of $35 million, (2) minimum net worth of $50 million plus 50 percent of net income beginning in FY 1985, (3) total liabilities no more than 90 percent of tangible net worth, (4) minimum current ratio of 2.75, (5) no sale/leasebacks greater than $500,000, (6) no entry into new lines of business, and (7) minimum fixed-charge coverage of 3 times, where coverage is computed as:

$$\frac{PBT + ESOP\ contribution + Interest\ expense + Lease\ payments}{Interest + ESOP\ contribution + Lease\ payments}$$

only a small participation in the credit. (In fact, Wachovia decided to take only a $2 million participation from the Bank of Boston.)

The ESOP as an Antitakeover Tactic

Increasingly in the mid-1980s, firms were using ESOPs to restructure their equity clientele and, especially, to reduce the threat of hostile takeovers. Starrett's move in 1984 presaged a wave of ESOPs established well in advance of takeover attempts as a precaution. ESOPs have also been established in the *midst* of takeover battles. For example, in 1988, Polaroid Corporation established an ESOP during a raid by Shamrock and successfully thwarted the attack. Polaroid's success inspired numerous other large firms.

The ESOP may have several beneficial effects in a contest for control: (1) if the ESOP is issued new shares, the attacker's equity holdings (and voting strength) are diluted; (2) depending on the age of the ESOP, its shares could possibly be voted by management;[4] (3) depending on the shareholdings of the ESOP, it might prevent the attacker from merging with the target;[5] and (4) ESOPs can be structured with "poison pill" triggers that may give the ESOP enhanced voting power in the event of a hostile takeover attempt.

Value Creation and Allocation

Who gains and loses as a result of this restructuring is perhaps the most interesting question. Although an exact answer is difficult to give, standard valuation techniques and theories about the value of debt tax shields provide some insights.

Valuation. As a first step, Exhibits E and F present the elements of a simple discounted-cash flow (DCF) analysis based on free cash flows. The weighted-average cost of capital is calculated in Exhibit E. While it varies modestly by year, for simplicity, the annual discount rates are averaged; 15 percent is used in the free-cash-flow valuation in Exhibit F. The valuation shows a share value of $27.39 per share, suggesting that the restructuring will induce little, if any, change in share value from the current level of $27.125. However, this result masks two important effects taking place in the restructuring: (1) gains in value from the exploitation of tax shields and (2) allocation of this value to ESOP participants.

---

[4]Until employees "earn" their shares, the ESOP trustees vote them. Senior managers of the firm usually have the power to direct how the trustees vote. (By one estimate, managers control the votes in 85 percent of all ESOPs.)

[5]Merger has many advantages from a reporting, regulatory, and management-control standpoint. Most importantly, however, merger allows the attacker to exclude or "freeze out" the intransigent remaining shareholders (who did not sell their shares to the attacker), often at a share price lower than the attacker paid in the hostile tender offer. Under the Delaware Antitakeover Statutes (Delaware is the site of incorporation for the majority of large firms in the United States), 85 percent of shareholders must approve a merger. Not coincidentally, ESOPs of many public firms hold in excess of 15 percent of the shares of the firm.

Sources of value. The value of equity benefits from the subsidized interest rate (85 percent of prime), interest tax shields, the deductibility of principal payments on ESOP debt, and the deductibility of dividends to the ESOP.

- Tax Shields. Exhibit G calculates the present value of the IRB tax shield to be $1.5 million; the tax shield on the ESOP loan is worth about $8.1 million. Dividends to the ESOP are also deductible for tax purposes and generate a present value of savings in tax expense of about $4.1 million. *In toto*, this restructuring generates a present value of tax savings worth about $13.7 million.

- Interest Subsidies. Starrett will pay less-than-market rates on on the IRB and on the ESOP loan. As a result, the market values of these liabilities will be less than the face values. The difference between market and par values will accrue to common shareholders, which is demonstrated in Exhibit H, where the wealth transfer from interest-rate subsidies is $5.3 million.[6]

Exhibit H summarizes the impact of these effects. The value of the entire firm gains by $21.3 million, of which $13.7 million comes from tax shields. Paradoxically, however, the total value of equity and share value are barely changed. Where did the supposedly new value go?

Allocation of value. The simple comparison of pre- and post-restructuring share prices ignores possible transfers of value among all of the participants in the restructuring: creditors, shareholders, ESOP participants, and the government. Pairwise comparisons can help parse out the possible transfers.

Consider first the change in welfare of the public shareholders and the employees who participate in the ESOP. The wealth of the *public shareholders* as a group changes as a result of any receipts from the repurchase of shares and as a result of the change in the value of the shares they continue to hold. The *ESOP participants* are better off if the value of the ESOP's interest in Starrett is worth more than the present value of their $1.8 million pension contribution made over 10 years. Exhibit I estimates the changes in wealth for these two groups.

The ESOP participants gain significantly, $6.9 million, over the present value of their ordinary pension contributions. This gain is a result of the fact that, not only is the firm contributing the regular $1.8 million toward a reduction of the ESOP debt, but it is also paying the interest on that debt and dividends on the shares. Thus, Starrett is apparently substantially increasing the flow of value to employees, at least temporarily.

The public shareholders are marginally better off as a result of this restructuring. Predictably, the cash received from the share repurchase ($18 million) is offset by a reduction in their claim on the company. This restructuring basically represents for old shareholders a shift from securities to cash, but no meaningful change in value. (Public shareholders may benefit from the restructuring if the ESOP motivates the participants toward higher performance.)

If the banks' loans are competitively priced (as the pricing at prime and 85 percent of prime suggest), then the net present value of their loans is zero. They appropriate none of the value created in this restructuring.

---

[6]For the IRB, the wealth transfer is $2.3 million ($7.5 -$5.2). For the ESOP loan, the wealth transfer is $3 million ($18 - $15).

The loser in this transaction is the U.S. Treasury, which foregoes tax revenues with a present value of $13.7 million.

In essence, the new value created by tax shields in this transaction is transferred to ESOP participants to finance their purchase of shares. Nothing in the case or this analysis suggests that the ESOP participants will pay for their gain, either through reduced compensation or higher productivity. Any conclusion about the fairness of this result depends on one's view of who owns the property rights to Starrett's unused debt capacity.

The foregoing discussion focuses only on tax-shield effects and ignores other possible (and imponderable) effects such as more closely aligning interests of employees and shareholders or possible signals of Starrett's future prospects.

EPILOGUE

Wachovia and the Bank of Boston extended the loans along the terms outlined in the case. On November 8, 1984, Starrett announced that it was beginning a tender offer for 600,000 of its shares at $30 each, reserving the right to buy an additional 200,000 shares. The same day, the firm announced that net income for its fiscal first quarter ended September 30 had nearly doubled to $2.9 million from a year earlier. Starrett's stock price reacted as follows:

	Starrett	Standard & Poor's 500
October 1, 1984	$27.25	$164.62
12	27.75	164.18
19	28.00	167.96
26	27.50	165.29
November 2	27.25	167.42
7	29.375	169.17
8	29.625	168.68
9	29.75	167.60
16	29.875	164.10
23	29.875	166.92
30	30.25	163.58
December 7	$30.00	$162.26

The upward trend of Starrett's stock price over this period is consistent with the hypothesis that the restructuring released new information about the intrinsic value of the company.

On December 4, Starrett announced that the firm's tender offer had attracted only 341,514 shares. Other private purchases raised the total shares purchased for the treasury to 547,703. The total cost of the purchase of treasury stock was $16,439,000.

The firm's ESOP purchased 406,500 shares, instead of the 600,000 shares originally planned, for $11,051,000. The ESOP funded this purchase with a bank loan of $10,850,000 and with other sources such as the dividend on the shares purchased and the regular pension contribution from the company.

EXHIBIT A Ratio Analysis of Historical Performance

	Fiscal Year Ended June 30				3 Months Ended September 30	
	1981	1982	1983	1984	1983	1984
Return on sales	11.3%	10.0%	7.0%	8.1%	6.6%	10.8%
Return on equity	19.1%	14.6%	8.0%	10.9%	7.6%	14.6%
Return on assets	14.5%	11.5%	6.6%	9.8%	6.4%	12.0%
Current ratio	4.11	4.38	5.09	4.46	5.57	4.46
Sales/assets	1.29	1.15	0.94	1.08	0.99	1.11
Inventory turnover	2.0	1.9	1.3	1.9	--	--
Total liabilities/equity	0.31	0.27	0.22	0.23	0.19	0.20
Interest coverage	34.4	84.4	45.5	132.4	--	--
Dividend payout	28.4%	36.0%	62.1%	44.1%	65.8%	32.4%
EBIAT/net assets	18.6%	13.3%	8.2%	11.0%	--	--
K_e	19.7%	18.6%	16.6%	17.8%	--	--
Beta	0.75	0.70	0.75	0.65	--	--
Risk free	13.4%	12.8%	11.2%	12.4%	--	--
$R_m - R_f$	8.3%	8.3%	8.3%	8.3%	--	--

EXHIBIT B   Starrett Pro Forma Income Statements for the Year Ended June 30
            ($ millions)

| | Actual 1984 | Projected | | | | |
		1985	1986	1987	1988	1989
Sales	$105.8	$120.7	$132.7	$146.0	$160.6	$176.7
Cost of sales and operating expenses	88.5	99.1	109.0	119.9	131.9	145.1
Pension expense	1.4	0.0	0.0	0.0	0.0	0.0
Operating profit	15.9	21.6	23.8	26.1	28.8	31.6
Interest income (investments)	2.2	2.6	2.8	3.0	3.3	3.7
Interest expense (IRB)	0.0	0.3	0.6	0.6	0.6	0.6
Other interest expense	0.1	0.0	0.0	0.0	0.0	0.0
Payment to ESOP:						
Principal	0.0	0.9	1.8	1.8	1.8	1.8
Interest	0.0	1.0	2.0	1.8	1.5	1.3
Dividends to ESOP	0.0	0.3	0.6	0.7	0.8	0.8
Profit before tax	18.0	21.6	21.6	24.3	27.3	30.7
Taxes	9.4	10.8	10.8	12.1	13.7	15.3
Net income	$ 8.6	$ 10.8	$ 10.8	$ 12.1	$ 13.7	$ 15.3
Shares Outstanding (000,000's)	3.744	3.744	3.744	3.744	3.744	3.744
Earnings per share	$2.27	$2.89	$2.88	$3.24	$3.65	$4.09
Dividends per share	$1.00	$1.00	$1.05	$1.16	$1.28	$1.41
Additions to Retained Earnings:						
Net income	$8.6	$10.8	$10.8	$12.1	$13.7	$15.3
Dividends to common (non-ESOP)	($3.7)	($3.4)	($3.3)	($3.6)	($4.0)	($4.4)
Addition to retained earnings	$4.9	$7.4	$7.5	$8.5	$9.6	$10.9

EXHIBIT C Starrett Pro Forma Balance Sheets for the Year Ended June 30*

	Actual 1984	Projected 1985	1986	1987	1988	1989
Cash**	$0.0	$1.5	$1.5	$1.5	$1.5	$1.5
Short-term investments (plug)	22.1	24.9	26.6	28.8	31.8	34.8
Inventory	34.2	43.7	48.1	52.9	58.1	64.0
Other current assets	20.8	20.9	23.0	25.3	27.8	30.6
Current assets	77.1	91.0	99.1	108.4	119.2	130.8
Net fixed assets and other	20.6	25.7	26.7	27.7	28.7	29.7
Total assets	$97.7	$116.7	$125.8	136.1	$147.9	$160.5
Revolving loan	$0.0	$0.0	$0.0	$0.0	$0.0	$0.0
Current liabilities	17.3	21.5	23.6	26.0	28.6	31.4
Currently due: IRB†	0.0	$0.0	$0.0	$0.0	$0.6	$0.6
Currently due: ESOP debt†	0.0	$1.8	$1.8	$1.8	$1.8	$1.8
Total current liabilities	$17.3	$23.3	$25.4	$27.8	$31.0	$33.8
Long-term debt: IRB	$0.0	$7.5	$7.5	$7.5	$6.9	$6.3
Long-term debt: ESOP	0.0	15.3	13.5	11.7	9.9	8.1
Deferred income tax	1.2	1.5	1.5	1.5	1.5	1.5
Total liabilities	$18.5	$47.6	$47.9	$48.5	$49.3	$49.7
Common stock	$4.7	$4.7	$4.7	$4.7	$4.7	$4.7
Paid-in capital	9.1	9.1	9.1	9.1	9.1	9.1
Retained earnings	69.4	76.8	84.3	92.8	102.4	113.3
Less: Treasury stock	(1.0)	(1.0)	(1.0)	(1.0)	(1.0)	(1.0)
Deferred comp. expense††	0.0	(17.1)	(15.3)	(13.5)	(11.7)	(9.9)
Foreign currency trans.	(3.0)	(3.4)	(3.9)	(4.4)	(4.9)	(5.4)
Total equity	$79.2	$69.1	$77.9	$87.7	$98.6	$110.8
Total liabilities and equity	$97.7	$116.7	$125.8	$136.1	$147.9	$160.5
Shares outstanding (000,000s)	3.744	3.744	3.744	3.744	3.744	3.744

* See case Exhibit 6.

** Cash balance for 1984 is reflected in Short-term investments.

† Drawn from amortization schedule in Exhibit I.

†† Deferred-compensation expense is the contra-equity account created by the ESOP financing.

EXHIBIT D Ratio and Covenant Analysis of Projected Financial Performance

	IRB Covenants	Actual 1984	Projected				
			1985	1986	1987	1988	1989
Return on sales	—	8.13%	8.96%	8.12%	8.32%	8.51%	8.68%
Sales/assets	—	1.10	1.14	1.20	1.27	1.32	1.38
Return on assets	—	8.94%	10.24%	9.78%	10.53%	11.27%	12.02%
Assets/equity	—	1.23	1.69	1.62	1.55	1.50	1.45
Return on equity	—	10.98%	14.76%	13.88%	14.71%	15.52%	16.28%
Operating profit/sales	—	15.03%	17.90%	17.90%	17.90%	17.90%	17.90%
Long-term debt/ total capital	—	0.00%	24.42%	20.93%	17.72%	14.37%	11.37%
Interest coverage	—	18100.00%	7911.60%	4478.94%	4853.19%	5275.54%	5745.82%
Fixed charge coverage*	—	18100.00%	947.89%	528.68%	596.90%	674.76%	762.78%
Dividend payout	—	44.05%	34.61%	36.47%	35.75%	35.07%	34.43%
Total Liabilities/ tangible net worth	.80	0.23	0.69	0.62	0.55	0.50	0.45
Current ratio	CR > 2.5	4.46	3.91	3.90	3.90	3.85	3.87
Net working capital	NWC > $45 mm	$59.8	$67.7	$73.7	$80.7	$88.2	$97.0
Tangible net worth	TNW > $70 mm	$79.2	$69.1	$77.9	$87.7	$98.6	$110.8

*Computed as described in footnote 3 of this note.

EXHIBIT E Estimation of Weighted-Average Cost of Capital (WACC) ($ millions except as noted)

	1985	1986	1987	1988	1989
Equity:					
Beginning equity	$79.2	$69.1	$77.9	$87.7	$98.6
Ending equity	$69.1	$77.9	$87.7	$98.6	$110.8
Average equity	$74.1	$73.5	$82.8	$93.1	$104.7
Debt:					
Beginning debt	$25.5	$24.6	$22.8	$21.0	$19.2
Ending debt	$24.6	$22.8	$21.0	$19.2	$16.8
Average debt	$25.1	$23.7	$21.9	$20.1	$18.0
Weighted average cost of capital:					
Interest expense	$1.4	$2.6	$2.4	$2.2	$2.0
Cost of debt (after tax)	5.40%	5.48%	5.46%	5.44%	5.50%
Debt	25.26%	24.39%	20.93%	17.75%	14.67%
Cost of equity*	17.87%	17.83%	17.67%	17.54%	17.42%
Equity	74.74%	75.61%	79.07%	82.25%	85.33%
WACC	14.72%	14.82%	15.11%	15.39%	15.67%

Average of annual WACCs (1985-89):15.14%

Estimation of Cost of Equity

Unlevered beta	0.65				
Risk-free rate	11.56%				
Risk premium	8.30%				
Average debt/equity	33.79%	32.26%	26.46%	21.58%	17.19%
Levered beta	0.76	0.75	0.74	0.72	0.71
Cost of equity	17.87%	17.83%	17.67%	17.54%	17.42%

EXHIBIT F Valuation of Equity* ($ millions)

	1985	1986	1987	1988	1989
Free-Cash-Flow Forecast:					
EBIT x (1-t)	$10.8	$11.9	$13.1	$14.4	$15.8
Change in working capital	$5.4	$4.3	$4.7	$5.2	$5.7
Increase in net fixed assets	$5.1	$1.0	$1.0	$1.0	$1.0
Free cash flow	$0.3	$6.6	$7.3	$8.2	$9.1
Terminal value				$151.3	
Total cash flow	$0.3	$6.6	$7.3	$159.5	

Present-Value Calculation:	
WACC was 5-year average =	15.14%
Present value of free cash flows	$100.8
Plus value of short-term investments	$26.4
Less debt	$24.6
Value of equity	$102.6
Per share	$27.39

*This valuation calculates the value of the operating flows and then adds the value of the short-term investments to determine the value of the firm. Also, the terminal value is estimated using the Gordon growth model and assuming the average WACC and a long-term growth rate of 9.35%.

EXHIBIT G Loan Interest and Amortization Schedule and Estimation of Present Values of Debt Tax Shields

	1984	1985	1986	1987	1988	1989	1990	1991	1992	1993	1994	1995	1996	1997	1998	1999	2000
Industrial Revenue Bond																	
Interest rate	8.50%																
Term (years)*	15																
Beginning loan balance		$7.50	$7.50	$7.50	$7.50	$7.50	$6.90	$6.30	$5.70	$5.10	$4.50	$3.90	$3.30	$2.70	$2.10	$1.50	$0.90
Principal payment		$0.00	$0.00	$0.00	$0.00	$0.60	$0.60	$0.60	$0.60	$0.60	$0.60	$0.60	$0.60	$0.60	$0.60	$0.60	$0.50
Interest payment*		$0.32	$0.64	$0.64	$0.64	$0.64	$0.59	$0.54	$0.48	$0.43	$0.38	$0.33	$0.28	$0.23	$0.18	$0.13	$0.04
Ending loan balance		$7.50	$7.50	$7.50	$7.50	$6.90	$6.30	$5.70	$5.10	$4.50	$3.90	$3.30	$2.70	$2.10	$1.50	$0.90	$0.40
Total loan cash flow		$0.3	$0.6	$0.6	$0.6	$1.2	$1.2	$1.1	$1.1	$1.0	$1.0	$0.9	$0.9	$0.8	$0.8	$0.7	$0.5
Interest Annual tax shield		$0.32	$0.64	$0.64	$0.64	$0.64	$0.59	$0.54	$0.48	$0.43	$0.38	$0.33	$0.28	$0.23	$0.18	$0.13	$0.04
Present-value, tax shield (@13.5%)	$1.5	$0.2	$0.3	$0.3	$0.3	$0.3	$0.3	$0.3	$0.2	$0.2	$0.2	$0.2	$0.1	$0.1	$0.1	$0.1	$0.0
ESOP Term Loan																	
Interest rate	11.48%																
Term (years)**	10																
Beginning loan balance		$0.0	$17.1	$15.3	$13.5	$11.7	$9.9	$8.1	$6.3	$4.5	$2.7	$0.9					
Interest payment		$1.0	$2.0	$1.8	$1.5	$1.3	$0.6	$0.5	$0.4	$0.3	$0.2	$0.1					
Principal payment†		$0.9	$1.8	$1.8	$1.8	$1.8	$1.8	$1.8	$1.8	$1.8	$1.8	$0.9					
Ending loan balance		$17.1	$15.3	$13.5	$11.7	$9.9	$8.1	$6.3	$4.5	$2.7	$0.9	($0.0)					

116

EXHIBIT G (Continued)

	1984	1985	1986	1987	1988	1989	1990	1991	1992	1993	1994	1995	1996	1997	1998	1999	2000
Interest and principal payments	$1.9	$3.8	$3.6	$3.3	$3.1	$2.4	$2.3	$2.2	$2.1	$2.0	$1.0						
Annual tax shield (tax rate = 50%)	$1.0	$1.9	$1.8	$1.7	$1.6	$1.2	$1.1	$1.1	$1.0	$1.0	$0.5						
Present value, Tax shield (@11.48%)	$8.1																

*Loan was outstanding for 6 months in 1985.

**ESOP loan would be outstanding for approximately half of fiscal year 1985.

†Assumes principal payments are made at year end.

117

EXHIBIT H   Pro Forma Book- and Market-Value Balance Sheets   before and after the Restructuring (pro forma, September 30, 1984; $ million except per share data)

	No ESOP; No Repurchase; IRB Loan	ESOP; Repurchase; IRB Loan
Book Value Balance Sheets		
Net working capital	$58.4	$65.9 (Note 1)
Net fixed assets	$21.3	$21.3
Total assets	$79.7	$87.2
Debt	$0.0	$25.5 (Note 2)
Equity	$79.7	$61.7 (Note 3)
Total capital	$79.7	$87.2
Market-Value Balance Sheets		
Net working capital	$58.4	$65.9 (Note 1)
Real assets	$43.2	$43.2 (Note 4)
Present value of tax shields of		
IRB debt	$0.0	$1.5 (See Exhibit G)
ESOP debt	$0.0	$8.1 (See Exhibit G)
Dividends to ESOP	$0.0	$4.1 (Note 5)
Total assets	$101.6	$122.9
Debt, IRB	$0.0	$5.2 (Note 6)
Debt, ESOP	$0.0	$15.0 (Note 6)
Equity	$101.6	$102.7 (Note 7)
Total capital	$101.6	$122.9
Share price:	$27.13	$27.43

Notes:

1. Net working capital is increased by the amount of the IRB loan. The case does not indicate how the proceeds of this loan are to be deployed.

2. Debt will increase by $7.5 million from the IRB loan and $18 million from the ESOP loan.

3. Book equity will decrease by the amount of the ESOP loan, through the contra-equity account, deferred compensation expense.

4. The market value of real assets is estimated as a plug figure in the no-ESOP case. This value is assumed to be unchanged by the restructuring.

5. The ESOP dividend tax shield is estimated by multiplying the assumed marginal corporate tax rate, 50%, times the present value of dividends, which was estimated by capitalizing the expected ESOP dividend for 1986 at the difference between the assumed long-term cost of equity, 17.4%, and an assumed perpetual growth rate of 10%.

6. The market value of the IRB was estimated by discounting the total cash flow of the loan (see Exhibit G) at 13.5%, the assumed unsubsidized cost of debt of Starrett. The ESOP loan is valued in a similar manner.

7. Equity in the ESOP column is a plug figure. In the no-ESOP column, equity is equal to the number of shares times the latest share price, $27.125.

EXHIBIT I   Analysis of Wealth Changes: Public Shareholders and Participants in ESOP
            ($ millions)

	Public Holders	ESOP Participants
Percentage claim on equity (post restructuring)	83.97%	16.03%
Present value of total equity	$102.7	$102.7
Value of equity claim	$86.2	$16.5
Cash from share repurchase	$18.0	$0.0
Wealth after restructuring	$104.2	$16.5
Wealth before restructuring	$101.6*	$9.6**
Change in wealth	$2.7	$6.9

*Equal to 3.744 million shares times $27.125 per share.

**The relevant wealth of the ESOP participants is the present value of their pension contributions during the term over which the loan is being amortized. This is equivalent to $1.8 million per year for 10 years, discounted at the pre-tax cost of debt, assumed to be 13.5% (the prime rate of interest).

Technical Note

Leveraged Employee Stock Ownership Plans

This note provides background information on leveraged Employee Stock Ownership Trusts (ESOTs) and Employee Stock Ownership Plans (ESOPs). An explanation of leveraged ESOPs as a financing technique, their history, uses, and advantages and disadvantages are explored, as are accounting procedures.

DESCRIPTION

ESOPs are pension programs established by corporations that allow traditional pension contributions to be reduced or eliminated and replaced by the purchase of the parent's stock for the benefit of the employees. An ESOT is established to handle the transactions and act as a shell to hold the newly acquired assets from the parent.

In a leveraged ESOP, the trust borrows funds from a qualified lender, such as a bank or an insurance company, to purchase a block of the company's shares. The company makes pension contributions to the trust to cover the interest expense and principal payments, both of which are considered tax-deductible expenses. The interest income received by the lender is 50 percent tax deductible, which allows borrowing rates to drop to 70-90 percent of prime. Contributions to cover principal reductions are limited to 25 percent of payroll expenses, excluding interest expense.

The Employee Retirement Income Security Act (ERISA) of 1974 first established ESOPs by allowing contributions by firms to the ESOTs to be tax-deductible expenses and suitable for the replacement of existing pension programs. The Deficit Reduction Act of 1984 included the 50 percent tax-exclusion rule on interest income received by lenders from ESOTs. In addition, the act made dividends paid to ESOP shareholders tax deductible if the funds are distributed to the employees.

USES OF LEVERAGED ESOPs

* To fund a leveraged buyout (LBO). The tax incentives for lenders and companies make the debt used in an LBO cheaper than otherwise, thus allowing a group using an ESOP LBO to offer a higher price.

* To establish a buyer of an unwanted division or company. In a situation where a buyer would not normally be available the workers themselves can become the buyers through an ESOP.

* To recapitalize a private firm. Tax provisions allow proceeds gained from an individual selling shares in a privately held company to an ESOT to be taxed at a capital-gains rate, which can be deferred indefinitely if the proceeds are invested in domestic marketable securities. For the favorable tax

---

Technical note written by Peter R. Hennessy, research assistant, in collaboration with Robert F. Bruner. Copyright (c) 1985 by the Darden Graduate School Sponsors, Charlottesville, VA.

121

tax treatment to be valid, the ESOT must control at least 30 percent of the company following the transaction.

- To reduce the possibility of a hostile takeover. If the ESOT accumulates enough shares, it can thwart a hostile takeover attempt.

- To improve worker productivity.

- To finance general business needs.

PREREQUISITES

- For a company to realize the maximum benefit of an ESOP, it must be in a position to take advantage of the tax benefits.

- The company must have payroll expenses large enough to support the principal payment required to amortize the ESOT debt.

ADVANTAGES

- An ESOP can improve cash flow. Traditional pension contributions represent an actual use of cash, while contributions to ESOTs are made to cover the purchase of stock for which the company has already received the cash.

- An ESOP increases the base of sympathetic shareholders.

- An ESOP allows a company to recover excess assets from an existing pension program.

- An ESOP can lead to improved worker productivity.

- An ESOP can provide an in-house market for the stock of a privately held or thinly traded company.

DISADVANTAGES

- An ESOP dilutes existing shareholders' interest and voting control if new shares are issued.

- If bad will among workers and management reaches a high enough level, the shares held by the workers may end up being voted against management's wishes.

- Private companies are obligated to repurchase shares from vested employees upon their termination or retirement, which can have a severe impact on cash flow.

- An ESOP limits the diversity of the company's pension plan to the diversity of the company.

ACCOUNTING FOR LEVERAGED ESOPs

The funds borrowed by the ESOT for the purchase of company stock must be shown as a liability on the parent's balance sheet. To offset the liability, the parent's owners' equity is reduced by the amount of the debt. The company's pension contributions to the trust are used to make interest and principal payments on the debt. As the loan is reduced by the trust, the debt on the parent's balance sheet is also reduced and owners' equity is increased. All shares held by the ESOT are considered outstanding in calculating earnings per share. Any dividends accorded these shares should be charged to retained earnings, even though they are a deduction from income for tax purposes.

De Laurentiis Entertainment Group, Inc.

SYNOPSIS AND OBJECTIVES

Bank of America must decide whether to increase and syndicate its line of credit to De Laurentiis Entertainment Group (DEG) in the fall of 1986. This problem presents an opportunity for students to (1) exercise a cash-balance forecasting model, (2) analyze industry conditions and the strategy of the firm, (3) assess past performance, and (4) assess risks and key determinants of success. The epilogue provides a cautionary tale for eager lenders. Students should emerge from a discussion of this case with a heightened awareness of the need to tailor financing and growth strategy according to the risk of the product. In this instance, high product risk and large, lumpy unit size should have dictated a greater reliance on equity capital.

STUDY QUESTIONS

1. Will the proposed $75 million line of credit satisfy DEG's financial needs over the next two years? Evaluate the forecast of DEG's cash receipts and disbursements

2. What are the risks in DEG's business and strategy? How might those risks affect the firm's financial requirements?

3. Should Bank of America extend the line to $75 million and syndicate the loan? As the agent for the lending group, would you ask for or insist on any changes in Dino De Laurentiis's strategy?

TEACHING PLAN

One approach to leading a discussion of this case is to dwell first on DEG's strategy and the likely business risks it faces. The purpose of such an opening is to build a classroom consensus on the promising features of De Laurentiis's business concept. The later reversal of this consensus during the sensitivity analysis of the forecasts and finally in the epilogue makes a large impression on students.

(10 minutes) What does it take to succeed in the film-production industry? Are there any entry barriers? What are the typical rates of return?

(15 minutes) How will De Laurentiis deviate from the standard strategy of an independent producer?

(10 minutes) What risks must De Laurentiis run as he attempts to execute his strategy?

Teaching note written by Robert F. Bruner. Copyright (c) 1988 by the Darden Graduate Business School Sponsors, Charlottesville, VA.

(20 minutes) Assuming his strategy works as planned, what will be DEG's cash needs through 1989? How is the forecasting model constructed?

(15 minutes) To variatiions in which assumptions is the forecast of financing need most sensitive? How much adversity (i.e., negative deviation from forecast) can DEG absorb?

(10 minutes) What should Bank of America do?

The instructor can close the discussion with some brief comments on financial forecasting methodology and with a review of the epilogue.

ANALYSIS

The Industry and DEG's Strategy and Risks

With his founding of DEG, De Laurentiis was breaking from the *modus operandi* of the major Hollywood film studios. Much of the Hollywood style can be explored in class from the students' common knowledge. This description would appear in a diagram such as provided in Exhibit A showing the flow of production between studio and theater. This diagram is important for establishing two insights: (1) the activities of the Hollywood studio rely heavily on the contributions of creative people (writers, directors, actors), administrators (producers), distributors, and financial institutions; the power of the studio is to assemble resources. (2) In this scheme, the distributor is extremely powerful because it acts as the gatekeeper to the theaters.

De Laurentiis's strategy is an attempt to enhance the power of his studio by (1) forward integration into film distribution (via its purchase of Embassy) and (2) the aggressive use of supplemental marketing channels such as video, cable TV, and foreign distribution. There are notable financial dimensions to this strategy. First, DEG seeks to enhance its profitability by producing films away from Hollywood (i.e., North Carolina); second, DEG seeks to self-finance aggressively through advance sales (i.e., cable, video, and foreign sales). Finally, to the degree that it needs external capital, DEG seeks to fill that need through high-wire financial acrobatics (e.g., limited partnerships, foreign financing, barter, and initial public offerings). As a result of all of this activity, DEG has become a "major international vertically and horizontally integrated entertainment entity."[1]

Another aspect of DEG's strategy is to focus on producing medium-budget films, avoiding the high-budget and high-risk blockbusters for which Hollywood was famous. De Laurentiis's films were not so expensive and, even if they failed in U.S. box offices, often had a ready market in late-night TV and foreign theaters, whose audiences were perhaps not critically discerning. The problem with the total strategy has less to do with the scale of production than with DEG's ability to withstand losses.

Risk of box office failure. The first, and basic, risk DEG faces is potential failure of its films at the box office. De Laurentiis sought to mitigate those risks by preselling his films for foreign exhibition and for

---

[1] "Horror Story, Upstart Movie Makers are Fast Fading Out After a Year's Showing," *The Wall Street Journal*, November 3, 1987, p. 1.

videotape distribution. These ancillary market sales, he said, would cover his negative costs by 135 percent. The extent of his hedge is evident in the following calculation:

Historical average cost of film negative	$ 9.7 million
Historical average prints and advertising expenses	$ 5.46
Total cost	$14.16 million
Preselling receipts (1.35 x 9.7)	−13.10
Costs to be covered by domestic theatrical exhibition	$ 1.06 million

One million dollars is a relatively small required revenue from U.S. theaters. However, required revenue could be much larger: the case suggests targeted film costs in a *range* from $13 to $18 million. The shortfall to be covered would be even higher if one added in allocated interest expense, selling, general, and administrative expense, corporate overhead, and taxes. The case suggests that about 38 percent of De Laurentiis's films produced since 1981 showed a negative gross profit. Plainly, the use of average revenues and costs could present a misleading image of risk. The risk of the individual film project is at least as relevant as the risk of the portfolio. De Laurentiis is banking on box-office success.

Another perspective on the risks inherent in DEG's strategy is afforded by an analysis of industry average-cost ratios. The case indicates that the industry average ratio of revenues to negative costs was 1.78 times. The case also indicates that De Laurentiis planned to produce films with negative costs of $8-$10 million and print-and-advertising costs of $5-$8 million. If he realized the industry average cost ratio instead of exceeding it, DEG would realize gross profits as follows in these polar scenarios.

Negative costs	$ 8 million	$10 million
Prints and advertising costs	5	8
Total costs	$13	18
Revenues (1.78 x negative costs)	$14.24	17.8
Less total costs	(13.00)	(18.0)
Gross profit	$ 1.24	− .2

The differing results stem from the magnitude of distribution costs (i.e., prints and advertising) relative to revenues. In short, DEG's strategy for realizing value is a bet on box-office success. The extra value De Laurentiis sought to create was to come through more aggressive marketing and distribution efficiencies.

Risk from integration. The basic risk of film failure at the box office is heightened in DEG's decision to integrate forward into film distribution. The economic role of the distributor was to help absorb downside risk of losses from the studios. Only very large studios had the financial capacity to sustain the losses from distribution. Clearly De Laurentiis was willing to shoulder these potential losses in hopes of maximizing the potential gains (i.e., by appropriating for DEG the roughly 33-percent-of-gross-revenues participation that another distributor would demand). In short, by integrating forward, he is widening the variance of possible outcomes from each film.

Financing risk. The two foregoing risks could place a massive demand on a studio's financial resources. The case describes De Laurentiis in the process of tapping over $200 million in financing with which to tide his firm through the start-up period. However, funds from the two limited partnerships were not committed and would not be until later in the fiscal year, after some of DEG's new films were released. Box-office failure might impair the efforts to raise new funds.

In sum, DEG has set a strategic course that accepted high business risk and high financing risk. The resolution of these risks depends on the acceptance at U.S. box offices of films to be released early in the firm's life: early failures would severely weaken the firm; early successes would substantially strengthen it. DEG's strategy has its attractive features, but it was not a formula for printing money. DEG would have to manage costs and marketing well and, most importantly, avoid box-office fiascos.

Financial Forecasts of Cash Receipts and Disbursements

Case Exhibit 6 presents the forecasted cash receipts and disbursements through February 1989. In order to calculate tax expense, an income statement is presented in case Exhibit 7 (the tax expense is then posted to case Exhibit 6). Inspection of the end-of-period cash balance line reveals that under De Laurentiis's historical average revenues and costs, the planned bank loan and existing financial slack more than cover the firm's cash needs.

Sensitivity Analysis

The forecasting model can be exercised to reveal some important insights about DEG's strategy and the risks it faces. Exhibit B summarizes the end-of-period cash balances under four scenarios plus the base case given in case Exhibit 6:

1. Revenues equal 90 percent of forecast. This case tests the robustness of DEG's cash balance to modest box-office adversity over the next two and one-half years.

2. The releases scheduled for February 1987 fail at the box office, producing only 10 percent of forecasted revenues upon release. This case tests the sensitivity of cash to a failure at a very delicate point in time.

3. DEG expands film output to 21 rather than 18.

4. No preselling revenues are received. All presales are assumed to arrive upon release.

Plainly, the cash balance of the firm is quite sensitive to failure. If revenues run at 90 percent, the firm will run out of cash between 18 and 24 months from now. If the first batch of films fail (but the rest succeed), the firm will exhaust its cash in 12-18 months—a result of an initial deep operating deficit worsened by heavy development outlays as the firm increases its unit output.

Under more aggressive growth (i.e., 21 films per year), the cash balance remains positive. Note that a difference of 3 films per year accounts for a cash balance lower by $23.4 million in February 1989.

Finally, preselling makes a material difference in cash balance by 1989. If there is no preselling, cash is lower by $9.2 million in two and one-half years.

EPILOGUE

Bank of America formed the syndicate and extended the $75 million loan. At the next fiscal year end (February 27, 1987), DEG reported a net loss of $1 million, compared with the $1.5 million loss in fiscal 1986. This loss impaired the ability of De Laurentiis Film Partners L.P. to raise its newly targeted amount of $59 million; it could raise only $23 million by the closing date of March 2, 1987. In the next quarterly report (May 31, 1987), the firm announced a loss of $15.5 million because of box-office failures. This was followed by a quarterly loss of $5 million at August 31. Other events in August 1987 were a downgrading of the firm's bond rating to CCC by Standard and Poor's and a charge by the Securities and Exchange Commission that DEG was improperly accounting for interest and overhead costs.

In early November 1987, DEG's stock was trading at $2.625, down from a high of $18, and Dino De Laurentiis hinted that he might resign. DEG's chief financial officer, James Parsons, announced his resignation on Christmas Eve, followed by De Laurentiis on February 22, 1988.

By the summer of 1988, the stock was trading at $.50 per share, and the bonds (par value $100) were trading at $14.50. In August 1988, DEG entered bankruptcy. It had not yet released its fiscal year-end financial statements but was expected to report a loss of $69 million. For the nine months ended November 30, 1987, it reported a loss of $36.2 million on revenues of $46 million. The bank syndicate managed to extricate its principal, largely because the bank loans were secured by the valuable film library.

The fall of DEG so soon after its securities offerings raises the question of fraud, but that question misses the deeper lesson—that the decline can be traced to De Laurentiis's appetite for high returns and high risks. DEG's entire strategy compounded risk upon risk and left the firm too inflexible to sustain losses. During its delicate financing phase of early 1987, DEG was walking on the razor's edge. When the revenues of DEG's first few films failed to meet expectations its downward spiral was inevitable. This scenario could have been anticipated in a careful analysis with the aid of the forecasting model.

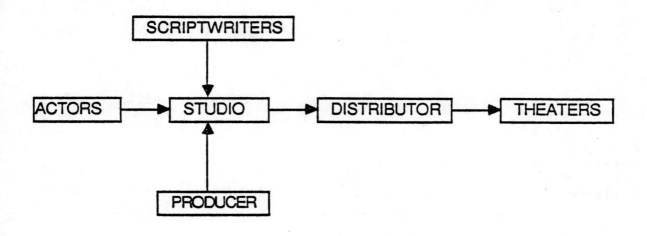

EXHIBIT B Forecasted Cash Balances Under Five Scenarios ($ millions)

	Feb. 1987	Aug. 1987	Feb. 1988	Aug. 1988	Feb. 1989
1. Base case (case Exhibit 6)	$114.8	$84.3	$49.7	$37.1	$32.1
2. Revenues 90% of forecast	106.9	67.3	22.7	−3.7	−23.3
3. Feb. 1987 releases flop (actual revenues = 10% of forecast)	52.4	15.7	−25.7	−42.1	−52.9
4. Output rises to 21 films/year	114.8	79.7	32.2	13.9	8.7
5. No preselling; revenues are received after release	$114.8	$80.1	$40.6	$27.9	$22.9

Columbia Mills, Inc.

SYNOPSIS AND OBJECTIVES

A commercial banker must review a $5 million loan request from Columbia Mills, a producer of denim cloth. The purpose of the loan is to upgrade and renovate much of the company's outdated machinery and equipment. The tasks for the student are to assess the risks and historical performance of this company and forecast Columbia's financial statements over the next few years in order to determine the firm's ability to repay the loan. The instructor should consider pairing this case with "Peachtree National Bank," case 48 in this manual, which is a sequel, but "Peachtree" should not be distributed in advance of the discussion of "Columbia Mills."

The Columbia-Peachtree case series affords an opportunity to exercise the range of students' financial-analysis and forecasting skills and invites sensitivity analysis as students address the potentially severe cyclical swings in Columbia's product and factor markets. The series' additional teaching points include replicating the origins of a troubled loan and illustrating the difficulties with which such a loan is worked out.

The objectives for "Columbia," as the first case in the series, should be to "set the stage"--i.e., analyze historical performance, risks, and financing needs. Usually a majority of students favor granting the loan.

STUDY QUESTIONS

1. Analyze the company and its request.

2. If Jay Anthony approves the request, from what should he be attempting to protect the bank? What terms could he design to accomplish this?

3. If you recommend that Anthony reject the request, what should he propose as an alternative? How should he explain these decisions to Larry Jackson and to his department head?

TEACHING PLAN

One strategy for teaching this case is first to elicit a wide range of credit insights about Columbia, as a foundation for making the credit decision. Rather than invite a student recommendation at the start of the case discussion, one could defer all conclusions until the end, when a vote is taken.

(10 minutes) What is the textile industry like? The purpose of this opening is to make a list of the industry risks.

Teaching note prepared by Robert F. Bruner, drawing extensively on notes and commentaries prepared by Bruce Boorman and William W. Sihler. Copyright (c) 1989 by the Darden Graduate Business School Sponsors, Charlottesville, VA.

(10 minutes) What is Columbia's strategy? In this segment of the discussion, another list is made suggesting that Columbia is taking actions to reduce its industry-based risks.

(10 minutes) How has the company performed under this strategy? The company performs well relative to industry averages. This assessment tends to build confidence in the reasonableness of Columbia's strategy.

(30 minutes) What is Columbia's likely financing need over the next 2-3 years? Under reasonable assumptions, the loan request of $5 million appears to be correct, and the loan can be repaid within 2-4 years.

(20 minutes) How do you come out on this? What is your recommendation? The instructor might choose to summarize the situation using the "Five Cs of Credit" (character, capital, collateral, conditions, and capacity) or some other organizing scheme. The discussion can be closed by a yes/no vote of the class on the loan.

At the end of the discussion of Columbia, the "Peachtree National Bank" case should be distributed.

ANALYSIS

The Industry

The textile industry is extremely cyclical, reflecting the effects of changing fashions and varying cotton cycles. Quality matters mainly when the fashion cycle is moving downward. The generic response to these risks is to maintain production flexibility and quality, sales diversity, and strong industry contacts. To mitigate the cotton cycle, two classic responses are to maintain financial slack and to use futures contracts. These responses do not, however, eliminate the risks. The large question posed by the industry review is whether denim is experiencing fad growth or secular growth.

The Company

Columbia has sought to mitigate these risks in a variety of ways:

- producing on contract and selling direct;

- factoring accounts receivable, which shortens the working-capital cycle;

- investing in plant to maintain its competitive position;

- purchasing cotton futures to lock in favorable prices; and

- maintaining a strong balance sheet and a reputation for quality.

Anthony is justifiably worried about the quality of management. The chairman (Jackson), who owns 21 percent of the stock, is notable mainly as the architect of the firm's unsuccessful diversification attempt. The president (Ted Baxter), on the other hand, appears to be a good manager, is young, and has an excellent understanding of the industry. Unfortunately, there is little management depth.

The borrowing need appears justified. Jackson and Baxter have demonstrated the need for Columbia to stay abreast of its competitors in terms of up-to-date equipment. With technology changing rapidly in the industry, it is imperative that Columbia have an ongoing program of equipment replacement. If it does not, its competitors will be able to take advantage of cost efficiencies derived from more modern equipment and price Columbia out of the market. This potential cost advantage is magnified when the product is a virtual commodity and the only real basis for competition is price. The need for cost parity in order to compete on a price basis is especially important to Columbia, because such a large amount of its production (over 70 percent) is concentrated in denim.

Analysis of Historical Performance

The Columbia financial statements show the marked turnaround in profitability since 1974. Dramatic sales increases of 26.7 and 52.5 percent were recorded in 1973 and 1974, respectively. These healthy sales advances were probably attributable to a combination of the stepped-up demand for denim nationally and the sizable increments to capacity provided by Columbia's plant acquisitions. Sales have begun to grow again at a 20.5 percent rate in 1976 after a slight decline in 1975.

Because of the growing demand for denim products and the cutters' apparent desire to quickly purchase enough denim to satisfy that demand, Columbia was probably producing at or near capacity in 1974 and 1975. The slight drop in the dollar amount of sales in 1975 would be explained by denim prices dropping slightly in response to the lower cotton prices of 1975. As cotton began to rise again in 1976, sales in dollars went up also.

To an extent, cost of goods sold as a percentage of sales has paralleled cotton prices, which can be seen in Exhibit A, the 1972-76 income statements restated on a percentage-of-sales basis. During 1972, Columbia was unable to take advantage of the relatively low price of cotton ($.34/lb.), probably because the new plants were not yet operating as efficiently as anticipated. Although cotton prices rose substantially in 1973 (by 63.6 percent), the gross margin grew to 9.7 percent from 6.0 percent. This improvement can probably be explained by operating efficiencies being attained in the new facilities. When cotton prices stabilized in 1974, Columbia was able to raise denim prices, and the gross margin improved to 16.8 percent. Possibly denim prices did not drop as rapidly in 1975 as the 22.1 percent decline in cotton prices, and thus the gross margin rose further to 18.5 percent. Now that cotton prices have moved upward again in 1976, the gross has dropped to 12 percent. In all, Columbia's gross margin is obviously a direct reflection of cotton prices, despite the insulation provided by the hedging activities undertaken.

In the area of operating expenses, Columbia has managed to hold the line well. Although these expenditures rose by $413,000 to 7 percent of sales in 1975, this was still below the 7.2 percent level achieved in 1972 and 1973. The 4.4 percent recorded in year-to-date 1976 is probably not accurate. Some operating expenses are being reflected on this interim statement as cost of goods sold. This expensing may also account partially for the sizable gross-margin drop in 1976. In addition, some operating expenses may not be included on the interim statement because they are, by nature, recognized at year end, such as pension or profit-sharing expenses or bonuses.

In sum, profitability has been excellent since 1973. The company earned over 9 percent before taxes in both 1974 and 1975. Tax liability was only 36 percent of pretax earnings in 1974, most likely because of tax-loss carryforwards relating to 1972 and earlier. (All these loss carryforwards have apparently now been taken.)

An examination of Exhibit B shows the financial strength Columbia has maintained throughout 1972-76. Its liquidity position has continued to improve since it bottomed out in the 1973-74 period. Both the current and quick ratios have risen, and these figures are now at levels approaching those of 1972. Factoring of receivables provides additional liquidity through the quick conversion of receivables into cash and speeds up turnover. Besides improving liquidity position, Columbia is turning its assets faster than in the past. The turnover rate dropped from 35 days to 30 days in 1976. This could be the result of Columbia getting a faster turnaround from the factor.

Until this year, inventory turnover had been at a fairly constant 44 days. In 1976, however, Columbia decreased inventory slightly despite an annualized sales growth rate of 20.5 percent. This improvement suggests that the company has adopted good inventory-management policies.

The debt/worth ratio at .51 is at a low point for the five-year period, which reflects the fact that Columbia has a fairly large amount of equity in the business even though dividend payments have been increasing over the period. At the company's low point in 1972, when dividends of $178,000 were paid after a $704,000 loss, equity was still at $7 million, and the debt/worth ratio was only at .72.

The payment of dividends in a loss year is a disturbing sign. To an extent, it shows a lack of commitment to the capital structure of the business. On the other hand, with such a large amount of equity in the company, management may have felt these dividend payments would have no adverse effect on the business. Of more concern to the bank, however, must be the fact that dividends were *increased* at a fairly healthy rate over the period. With the family orientation of the stockholder base, these dividends are probably becoming a form of income to the family members. If so, the question is whether the payments can be cut or stopped in a recession period. In effect, dividends may become fixed obligations of Columbia over the period.

By any standards, the low amount of leverage used by Columbia seems extremely conservative. Given the exceedingly cyclical nature of Columbia's industry, however, these low levels of debt serve both to minimize operating leverage and to maintain future financing flexibility. Note also that, based on the supposed "real" values of inventory and fixed assets presented in the case, Columbia's net worth is probably understated by anywhere from $3 to $5 million. If these values were added to the calculation of the debt/worth ratio, it would drop to .39.

Case Exhibit 5 traces Columbia's recent flow of funds. It shows that working capital decreased substantially during 1972 and 1973, because the $58,000 cash flow from operations plus the $406,000 net new long-term debt was insufficient to cover fixed-asset additions of $861,000 and dividends of $178,000. In 1973, fixed-asset expenditures were increased to $2,438,000 despite cash flow from operations of only $942,000 and a long-term-debt increase of only $642,000. For the second straight year, dividends paid were substantially more than net income. From Peachtree's point of view, these financial maneuverings should be somewhat disturbing. The Columbia dividend policy pays no heed to earnings. Management is also financing long-term assets through short-term sources, rather than the more conventional method.

Fortunately, the large profits generated in 1974 and 1975 were able to replenish working capital drained in the previous two years, even after yearly repayments of long-term debt of about $700,000. Although the large amount of fixed-asset additions in 1975 ($2,771,000) was, again, not funded by long-term debt, at least cash flow from operations was able to cover these additions.

Exhibit C presents a pro forma balance sheet, using the June 30, 1976, balance sheet, of Columbia as if the loan were granted. It assumes $4 million of new expenditures, $500,000 of long-term-debt repayment, and a $500,000 increase to working capital. Although some of the ratios change, they are certainly within acceptable levels to the bank.

Exhibit D provides an evaluation of Columbia's performance against Robert Morris Association (RMA) industry averages. Columbia compares favorably. Liquidity is slightly lower, but turnover ratios, especially inventory, are higher. Columbia's debt/worth ratio is in line with the other companies, indicating that the industry, in general, maintains a conservative posture toward leverage. Also, Columbia's profitability is considerably higher than the averages, perhaps reflecting that the strong demand for denim affords high profit margins.

Although reaping the rewards now from its large concentration in denim, the company is also accepting more risk. The analysis returns repeatedly to the imponderable issue of the risk in denim.

Financial Forecast

Exhibit E presents a percentage-of-sales forecast. The assumptions used were largely consistent with recent operating history. The forecast reveals a financing need by the end of 1976 of $4.75 million, which is driven substantially by the $4 million capital investment. By the end of 1977, however, the financing need has fallen to only $1.6 million, a result hinging on the important assumption that there will be no major fixed-asset additions in that year.

On the basis of this estimate, the company's request for a $5 million loan appears to be consistent with its requirements, and the company can repay the loan within the time frame.

Students may be motivated to test the robustness of this result to variations in assumptions. The key determinants of such results would be the inherent profitability of the operations and the rate of capital investment.

Peachtree National Bank Policy

The current lending posture of Peachtree is an important factor in the credit decision process. The bank is now in something of a retrenchment position: desirous of upgrading the quality of the bank's loan portfolio and not interested in making loans with more than nominal risk. On the other hand, the bank *is* interested in satisfying its established customers in their borrowing needs, given acceptable risk.

Columbia Mills is probably one of Peachtree's best customers. First and foremost, the company has dealt with the bank for 50 years. Moreover, with average collected balances of $400,000 in support of a $1.25 million credit line, this account is extremely profitable to the bank

Credit Decision

Based on the following considerations, students will tend to favor making the loan:

- Columbia's fine earnings record over the past two and a half years;

- Columbia's currently strong financial position;

- Anthony's confidence in Baxter's ability;

- the long-standing, excellent relationship Peachtree has enjoyed with Columbia;

- Columbia's commitment to the fixed-asset renovation program;

- Columbia's good current-asset management; and

- the hidden value of some of Columbia's assets.

  Offsetting these positives are several negatives:

- the uncertain direction of denim demand, in combination with Columbia's dependence on that market;

- Columbia's lack of management depth;

- the relationship between profits and cotton prices; and

- the possible role that dividends play as a form of income to many family-member stockholders.

Possibly, the loan could be structured in such a way as to mitigate many of these negatives, but as the sequel case, "Peachtree National Bank," shows, management incompetence and market cycles draw the company into financial distress.

EXHIBIT A   Income Statements, 1972–76, as a Percentage of Sales

	1972	1973	1974	1975	Jan.–June 1976
Net sales	100.00	100.00	100.00	100.00	100.00
Cost of goods sold	93.97	90.30	83.17	81.46	87.99
Gross profit	6.03	9.70	16.83	18.54	12.01
Operating expenses	7.18	7.17	6.01	6.97	4.41
Operating profit	(1.15)	2.53	10.82	11.56	7.60
Other expenses, net	1.42	2.27	1.75	1.43	–
Profit before taxes	(2.57)	.26	9.07	10.14	7.60
Taxes	--	--	3.27	4.66	3.72
Net profit	(2.57)	.27	5.80	5.48	3.88

EXHIBIT B Ratio Analysis, 1972–76

	1972	1973	1974	1975	1976*
Current ratio	2.5:1	2.0:1	1.9:1	2.0:1	2.1:1
Quick ratio	1.3:1	.7:1	1.0:1	1.0:1	1.2:1
Debt/worth ratio	0.72	0.86	0.85	0.58	0.51
Receivable turnover (days)	41.6	17.8	35.0	33.7	30.6
Inventory turnover (days)	44.5	44.9	43.4	44.9	34.1
Sales/working capital	6.6	11.1	9.9	9.5	10.0
Sales/worth	3.9	5.0	5.4	4.2	4.7
% Pretax profit/total assets	Neg.	.7	26.6	26.9	23.4
% Pretax profit/worth	Neg.	1.3	49.1	42.5	35.4

*Six-month figures.

EXHIBIT C Pro Forma Balance Sheet (thousands)*

ASSETS	6/30/76
Cash	$ 929
Accounts receivable:	
Due from factor	4,557
Other	718
Inventory	5,174
Other current	943
Total current	12,321
Fixed assets, net	11,980
Prepaid expenses	355
Def. income taxes	--
Total assets	$24,656

LIABILITIES	
Accounts payable	$ 1,301
Accrued payables	2,865
Taxes payable	--
Notes payable, banks	--
Curr. mat. LTD	706
Other current	715
Total current liabilities	5,587
Long-term debt	5,576
Def. income taxes	179
Total liabilities	11,342
Common stock	3,300
Retained earnings	10,013
Net worth	13,313
Total liabilities and worth	$24,656

*Assumptions: 1. New long-term debt of $5 million.
               2. New fixed assets of $4 million.
               3. Additional working capital of $.5 million.
               4. Long-term debt repayment of $.5 million.

EXHIBIT D Comparative Ratio Analysis

	RMA	Columbia 1976	Columbia 1975
Current ratio	2.5:1	2.1:1	2.0:1
Quick ratio	1.1:1	1.2:1	1.0:1
Debt/worth ratio	.60	.51	.58
Receivable turnover (days)	34.0	30.6	33.7
Inventory turnover (days)	64.0	34.1	44.9
Sales/working capital	4.5	10.0	9.5
Sales/worth	2.4	4.7	4.2
% Pretax profit/total assets	9.8%	36.9%	47.4%

Source: Robert Morris Associates, *Statement Studies*, 1975.

EXHIBIT E Forecasted Financing Need ($ Millions)

Year	Actual		Projected	
	1975	Jan.-June 1976	Year, 1976	1977
Sales (+10% in 1976)	$51.5	31	56.6	56.6
Gross profit (.14 x Sales)	9.5	3.7	7.9	7.9
Selling, general, and administrative (.06 x Sales)	(3.6)	(1.4)	(3.4)	(3.4)
Other expense	(.7)	0	(.7)	(.7)
Profit before tax	5.2	2.5	3.8	3.8
Tax (@48%)	2.4	1.1	1.8	1.8
Net income	2.8	1.2	2.0	2.0
Dividends	.3	.2	.35	.35
Retentions	2.5	1.0	1.65	1.65
Cash	.5	.4	.5	.5
Accounts Receivable (.093 x Sales)	4.9	5.3	5.2	5.2
Inventories (.10 x Sales)	5.2	5.2	5.6	5.6
Other current assets	.4	.9	.4	.4
Current assets	11.0	11.8	11.7	11.7
Fixed assets*	8.1	8.0	10.9	9.4
Prepaid expenses	.4	.4	.4	.4
Total assets	19.5	20.2	23.0	21.5
Accounts payable (.03 x Sales)	1.4	1.3	1.7	1.7
Accruals	1.6	2.9	1.6	1.6
Taxes payable	1.0	0	.9	.9
Other liabilities	.3	.9	.2	.2
Bank debt (curr. and LT)	2.9	1.8	NAp	NAp
Total liabilities	7.2	6.9	4.4	4.4
Common stock	3.3	3.3	3.3	3.3
Retained earnings	9.0	10.0	10.55	12.2
Total liabs. and equity	$19.5	$20.2	$18.25	$19.9
Financing need (plug)	0	0	$ 4.75	$ 1.6

*The balance for fixed assets assumes additions of $4 million in 1976 and depreciation of $1 million in 1976 and $1.5 million in 1977.

Peachtree National Bank

In early March 1978, Jay Anthony, vice president and loan officer of Peachtree National Bank, pondered what action he should take in regard to the rapidly deteriorating situation of Columbia Mills, Inc. On a routine visit to the company's headquarters the previous day, Mr. Anthony had received the unaudited financial statements for the year ended December 31, 1977, as well as further disturbing news about the company. (Columbia's summary financial statements for 1972-77 are presented in Exhibits 1 and 2.) Not only had the company's loss of $2.5 million after tax been considerably more than expected, but Columbia was experiencing severe quality-control problems, the market for its products was depressed, and management had speculated extensively in the cotton futures market with disastrous results. Management had requested an additional advance of $500,000 under its revolving-credit agreement. Columbia was currently borrowing $4.25 million of the $5.0 million limit under the agreement, which had been signed in April 1977.

Mr. Anthony knew that immediate action was required. He had not decided, however, whether it would entail just shoring up the loan agreement, or taking additional collateral, or even beginning an orderly liquidation of the bank's existing collateral. To complicate the situation further, Peachtree National was participating in this loan with another bank, Central City Bank. Hence, Mr. Anthony would have to take Central's interest into account in persuading them to go along with his decision.

BACKGROUND

Columbia Mills was primarily a producer of denim, which was sold to cutters such as Blue Bell, Inc., the H. D. Lee Company, and Genesco, Inc. It also produced fabrics for the home furnishing market and canvas for makers of tennis shoes. With over 70 percent of its production in denim, Columbia had benefited from the huge popularity of blue jeans and related products in the early to middle 1970s.

Denim was essentially an unbranded commodity; Columbia's customers were sensitive to price, quality, and delivery. Efficient, modern equipment was necessary to survive the intense competition on these dimensions from much larger companies such as Burlington Industries, Cone Mills, and J. P. Stevens. Columbia had thus found necessary an ongoing program of equipment replacement and renovation.

In late 1976, Columbia approached Peachtree, its primary bank since 1926, with a request for $5 million for equipment replacement and renovation. Mr. Anthony reviewed the request and, despite some reservations, approved the loan. He planned a tight credit agreement and a strong collateral package to mitigate

---

Case prepared by Bruce C. Boorman with the help of individuals who wish to remain anonymous. Certain aspects of the situation have been disguised to protect confidential information without changing the nature of the managerial decisions. Copyright (c) 1981 by the Darden Graduate Business School Sponsors, Charlottesville, VA.

the dangers he saw. Specifically, he identified three negative aspects of the loan:

1. An uncertainty about the future demand for denim;

2. A lack of management talent and depth at Columbia;

3. An unhealthy relationship between profitability and the price of cotton, over which Columbia had no control.

The loan package Mr. Anthony negotiated to satisfy Columbia's need for financing and to protect the bank's interests is summarized in Exhibit 3. The bank also advanced funds from time to time to cover seasonal needs. A balance of $1.5 million was outstanding at the end of 1977 on the short-term line.

Shortly after the loan agreement had been approved, Columbia asked to include Central City Bank in the financing. Central City had recently taken over Columbia's factoring business from a major New York City bank. After a period of negotiation, the banks agreed to participate on an even basis in the $5 million loan as it had originally been structured. Peachtree was named the agent bank. The loan was disbursed in mid-April 1977.

RECENT EVENTS

On a routine visit in March 1978, Mr. Anthony had been presented with the preliminary 1977 year-end financial statements. Although he had been in fairly frequent contact with Columbia's top management, Ted Baxter and Larry Jackson (president and chairman, respectively), Mr. Anthony had underestimated the magnitude of the 1977 loss, which turned out to be $2.5 million.

Probably more disturbing to Mr. Anthony, however, were the reasons behind the loss. He had assumed that the problem was in the high cotton prices of the latter part of 1976 and the first part of 1977, which textile producers were often able to pass along to their customers only on a lagged basis, if at all. Rather, the problem was that denim demand itself had slowed in 1977, as indicated by the data presented in Exhibit 4. After growing at a rate of 18.4 percent since 1969, 1977 demand growth was only 9.3 percent. In conjunction with the growing number of industry predictions calling for a decline in denim demand, the slow 1977 growth had fostered a cautious attitude on the part of the cutters, who stepped up quality-control procedures. This was the area in which Columbia suffered its most severe problems. Because of its outdated equipment, relative to competition, Columbia was unable to compete on a quality basis. When cutters began inspecting piece goods more carefully than before, Columbia products were continually found to be of poor quality. Mr. Anthony learned that a full 25 percent of the company's receivables were tied up in disputes over product quality. He also learned that Columbia's unfilled orders at year-end 1977 had dropped to 74 million square yards, as compared with 210 million square yards at the beginning of the year. This situation had deteriorated further during 1978.

In the course of his day-long visit to Columbia, Mr. Anthony was pulled aside privately by Mr. Baxter and told of another reason for Columbia's dismal 1977 performance. In the second quarter of 1977, Mr. Jackson had purchased a large amount of cotton futures, apparently believing that cotton prices would rise in the second half of 1977 and into 1978. These purchases were considerably in excess of the company's needs, clearly a speculative move on Mr. Jackson's part. The result was that Columbia was forced to take delivery of an abundance of cotton at prices considerably higher than the prevailing spot prices in the second half of 1977. In relating the story to Mr. Anthony, Mr. Baxter was obviously upset at Mr. Jackson's maneuverings. Mr. Anthony sensed a feeling of resentment by Mr. Baxter that he had not been consulted about the transaction.

The cotton-futures speculation was the most disturbing news that Mr. Anthony received during his visit. First, it raised questions about Mr. Jackson's ability and judgment. Second, and more importantly, it created doubt in Mr. Anthony's mind as to who was really running the business. For the first time, Mr. Anthony questioned how much authority Mr. Baxter had in Columbia's decision-making process. Moreover, because of the manner in which he was informed of the problem, Mr. Anthony could sense a rift growing between Mr. Jackson and Mr. Baxter over control of the company.

THE PRESENT DECISION

Because 1978 year-to-date losses of approximately $800,000 had already reduced Columbia's net worth, the loan was technically in default on the debt/worth provision of 1.0:1.0. Therefore, Mr. Anthony had the flexibility, with Central City's concurrence, of calling the loan. If Columbia could not repay the banks, they could liquidate the collateral. Mr. Anthony firmly believed that the company did not have the resources to repay its $4.25 million of bank debt. Moreover, given the dismal operating scenario, Columbia was unlikely to be able to find another lender to replace the banks.

In analyzing the bank's collateral position, Mr. Anthony did not have a recent appraisal of the Huntley and Rogers plants. He believed these plants, as going concerns, would bring around $6 million, but some industry overcapacity at present and predictions for steep drops in demand made it unlikely that a suitable purchaser would be found near that price. Mr. Anthony had no other idea of Columbia's likely liquidation value, but it would probably not repay all of the indebtedness.

A second option was presented to Mr. Anthony when Columbia requested an additional $500,000 advance on the revolving credit to replenish the company's working capital. Mr. Anthony was obviously uneasy about any new advances to the company. On the other hand, if such an advance could get Columbia through the year, the company might be able to correct its quality-control problems and minimize its losses. The advance might also provide Mr. Anthony the opportunity to revise the bank's collateral package and loan covenants and strengthen Peachtree's position. Whatever action Mr. Anthony decided to take, he knew Central City Bank had to be an integral part of the decision.

144

EXHIBIT 1   Columbia Mills, Inc., Income Statements, 1972-77 (thousands)

	1972	1973	1974	1975	1976	1977
Net sales	$27,374	$34,673	$52,885	$51,527	$60,858	$52,201
Costs of goods sold	25,724	31,311	43,982	41,974	52,831	52,440
Gross profit	1,650	3,362	8,903	9,533	8,027	(239)
Operating expenses	1,965	2,486	3,179	3,592	3,973	3,624
Operating profit	(315)	876	5,724	5,961	4,054	(3,863)
Other expenses, net	389	786	928	735	710	1,117
Profit before taxes	(704)	90	4,796	5,226	3,344	(4,980)
Taxes			1,730	2,401	1,497	(2,481)
Net profit (loss)	(704)	90	3,066	2,825	1,847	(2,499)
Dividends	178	198	259	306	340	324
Change in retained earnings	(882)	(108)	2,807	2,519	1,507	(2,823)
Depreciation	$ 762	$ 852	$ 909	$ 1,026	$ 1,084	NAv

EXHIBIT 2   Columbia Mills, Inc., Balance Sheets, as of December 31, 1972–77
            (thousands)

	1972	1973	1974	1975	1976	1977
ASSETS						
Cash	$ 420	$ 166	$ 535	$ 521	$ 441	$ 958
Accounts receivable:						
Due from factor	2,843	1,365	4,744	4,455	2,767	814
Other	322	352	393	374	838	560
Inventory, LIFO	3,180	3,903	5,303	5,231	6,555	6,383
Other current assets	182	418	301	375	774	430
Income tax refund	--	--	--	--	--	2,659
Total current assets	6,947	6,204	11,276	10,956	11,375	11,804
Fixed assets, net	4,844	6,429	6,367	8,114	8,142	9,228
Prepaid expenses	348	300	257	388	544	674
Def. income taxes	--	--	132	--	185	405
Total assets	$12,139	$12,933	$18,032	$19,458	$20,246	$22,111
LIABILITIES						
Accounts payable	$ 837	$ 1,124	$ 1,861	$ 1,408	$ 1,070	$ 1,268
Accruals	995	1,333	1,519	1,610	2,044	1,872
Taxes payable	--	--	1,694	964	266	--
Notes payable, banks	495	--	--	700	1,000	1,500
Curr. mat. LTD	428	723	724	686	4	781
Other current liabs.	56	90	123	153	187	223
Total current liabilities	2,810	3,070	5,921	5,521	4,571	5,644
Long-term debt	2,260	2,902	2,175	1,469	1,467	4,962
Def. income taxes	--	--	168	179	412	532
Total liabilities	5,070	5,972	8,264	7,169	6,450	11,138
Common stock	3,300	3,300	3,300	3,300	3,300	3,300
Retained earnings	3,769	3,661	6,468	8,989	10,496	7,673
Net worth	7,069	6,961	9,768	12,289	13,796	10,973
Total liabilities and net worth	$12,139	$12,933	$18,032	$19,458	$20,246	$22,111

AMOUNT: $5,000,000.

MATURITY: Revolving credit through December 31, 1977, converting to a
            7-year term loan at that date.

INTEREST RATE: During revolving period   Prime + 1/4
                 Term loan
                     Months   1-18   Prime + 1/4
                              19-24   Prime + 1/2
                              25-36   Prime + 3/4
                              37-84   Prime + 1

REPAYMENTS: 28 equal quarterly payments of principal and interest.

COMMITMENT FEE: 1/4 of 1% of total commitment.

SECURITY: Huntley and Rogers plants.

MAJOR COVENANTS: 1.   Minimum current ratio of 1.5:1.0.
                   2.   Minimum net worth of $10,000,000.
                   3.   Minimum cash flow/current maturities ratio of 1.0:1.0.
                   4.   Maximum debt/worth ratios of 1.0:1.0.
                   5.   Negative pledge on assets.
                   6.   No additional borrowings from any other sources.
                   7.   Quarterly statements to be provided within 30 days of
                        the end of the quarter.

EXHIBIT 4 U.S. Denim Demand, 1965-78 (millions of square yards)

1965	258
1966	296
1967	264
1968	215
1969	222
1970	283
1971	341
1972	413
1973	445
1974	505
1975	610
1976	723
1977	790

Peachtree National Bank

SYNOPSIS AND OBJECTIVES

"Peachtree" is a sequel to "Columbia Mills, Inc." (case 10), set 18 months later when the lending officer at Peachtree is considering what action he should take in regard to the rapidly deteriorating situation of Columbia Mills. The case reviews the causes of Columbia's decline and requires students to decide whether to shore up the loan agreement, seek more collateral, or begin an orderly liquidation of the existing collateral. As with the "Columbia" case, the student is required to conduct a qualitative and quantitative credit analysis.

This case is a useful introduction to the subject of financial distress and the difficulty with which a firm emerges from it. The case affords a sharp distinction between the viewpoints of borrower and lender (indeed, even between the two lenders); the case history of Columbia is riddled with agency conflicts and therefore serves as a useful foundation for a discussion later in a course on financial strategy and choice of capital structures. Ultimately, the dramatic reversal of Columbia's fortunes is itself perhaps the most salient teaching point; all too often, risk is an abstraction, assumed away under some portfolio assumption. This case makes risk immediate.

Note that the "Peachtree" case should *not* be distributed in advance of the "Columbia Mills" discussion.

STUDY QUESTIONS

1. Evaluate the terms of the loan. Did they provide protection for the dangers you saw?

2. What happened? How well did the loan design protect against these events? What could have?

3. What actions should Anthony take at this point?

4. What lessons of a general nature can you draw from this situation?

TEACHING PLAN

(15 minutes) What happened? Who discovered what? When? How much could we have foreseen? Did the banker learn early enough? Would tighter covenants have prevented this outcome? A useful opening to the discussion is to reconstruct the events, determining the extent to which the blame for the episode can be laid at the feet of the loan officer.

Teaching note written by Robert F. Bruner. Copyright (c) 1989 by the Darden Graduate Business School Sponsors, Charlottesville, VA.

(15 minutes) How serious is the default? What are the risks in continued
   operation? This line of questioning should solicit an assessment of the
   current status of the company, including the extent of the bank's current
   exposure.

(25 minutes) What are our options now? What does the inventory look like?
   What is this company worth if we liquidate? The possible actions include:
   extending more credit, raising equity, selling the company, and liquidating
   the collateral.

(20 minutes) Who has the negotiating leverage in this situation? What are
   the motivations of the various parties? The instructor should bring out the
   legal implications of default, including the power to liquidate collateral.
   However, Columbia may be able to drive a wedge between Peachtree and Central
   Bank, since they remain competitors.

(5 minutes) What should Anthony do? The instructor can solicit a few
   student recommendations and then take a vote of the class.

   The discussion can be closed with a review of the epilogue and a summary of
the agency conflicts and difficulties created by financial distress.

ANALYSIS

The Situation

   The losses in 1978 have triggered a default[1] on a loan covenant requiring a
minimum debt/worth ratio of 1.0. The loan default is the result of a number of
factors: a decline in denim demand, quality problems, operating losses,
speculation in cotton, thin management quality, and the continued payment of
dividends. Exhibit A presents sources-and-uses statements for 1976 and 1977 in
which one can see that the borrowings in 1977 essentially covered some capital
spending and the operating losses.
   In making the loan originally, many students will have made the fundamental
mistake of extrapolating linear performance (i.e., constant margins, growth,
etc.) in a cyclical industry. Moreover, many students will have assumed that
the capital investment planned by management will dramatically enhance product
quality, and will have ignored the fact that the renovation and expansion
affected a relatively small percentage of overall capacity.
   The total debt exposure appears to be closer to $7.2 million than the $4.25
million mentioned in the case.[2] The exposure includes $4.962 in long-term debt,
$1.5 million in notes payable to banks, and $.781 million in current maturities
of long-term debt.

---

[1]Some bankers call failures to meet covenant tests "technical defaults," to
distinguish them from failures to pay principal and interest on time, which are
much more tangible defaults.

[2]The case does not indicate the source of the additional $462,000 in
long-term debt. Even if it were supplied by an institution other than Peachtree
or Central City, it would still not diminish the fact that total bank debt is
considerably larger than the $5 million credit.

The value of assets in event of liquidation is probably far lower than the debt outstanding. The loan was secured by the Huntley and Rogers plants, which appear to have a net book value of $9.228 million but which seasoned lenders characterize as having a much smaller market value (closer to $1 million), because it can be difficult to sell relatively out-of-date plants in small North Carolina towns.

Other assets might carry a liquidating value of $5-$7 million, but the bank loan carries no security interest in those assets. By the date of liquidation, the cash account of the firm would probably fall to zero. The accounts receivable not due from the factor may be of questionable quality: Columbia factors its receivables with Central City who probably only accepts the good receivables. The nonfactored receivables are probably worth nothing. (In the event of liquidation, Central City might attempt to withhold its payments, $814,000,[3] to set off against loans due.) The market value of inventories may be much higher than the $6.383 million because of LIFO accounting.[4] Seasoned lenders ordinarily apply a 50 percent discount to textile inventory in liquidation. The income tax refund, whenever it arrives, is almost certainly worth book value of $2.659 million.

Strategic Alternatives

Some students will recommend immediate liquidation of collateral. Nominally, the assets may come close to repaying the $7.2 million in debt. The realities of liquidating a company suggest, however, that the banks will sustain some loan losses in the process. Liquidating the collateral would certainly trigger a formal bankruptcy proceeding, in which the banks would probably participate *pro rata* with trade creditors and employees in the proceeds from sales of the unsecured assets. Tax liabilities would take precedence in liquidation. A benevolent judge might even reserve some value for the common stockholders. The extent of the loan losses might be on the order of $1-$3 million.

Students should be reminded of the reluctance of banks to take loan write-offs; a great deal of interest income is required to make up for loan losses. Hence, there is a natural reluctance to "pull the plug" on a failing firm. Negotiated restructurings are desirable where there is some possibility of recovering the full amount of the principal (and avoiding the anger likely in small communities where the bank shuts down the largest business).

Encouraging an outright sale of the company might result in a loan loss not much different from liquidation.

Another suggestion from students would be that the company be encouraged to sell equity. In addition to bad timing, the severe dilution that an equity issue might impose on the Jackson family is bound to be vigorously opposed.

By a process of elimination, one is left with the alternative of continuing to bank Columbia, although perhaps on more careful terms than previously. One can make the case that Columbia is sick but not terminally ill. With a

---

[3]The low balance of "Due from factor" receivables at the end of 1977 was a result of low fourth-quarter sales.

[4]The per-pound cost of cotton used in valuing the inventory was 10 cents, whereas at the date of the case, cotton was selling for 39 cents. The $2 million LIFO wafer suggested in the case was actually worth more like $3-$3.5 million.

151

restoration of product quality and elimination of speculative investing in cotton futures, the cash flow would be sufficient to service a rescheduled loan. (All these moves assume, of course, that competent management is retained.) From this perspective, the relevant question is *how* to restructure the lending relationship from here on, rather than whether to terminate the relationship.

Relations Among Banks

Central City's interests and motivations differ from Peachtree's. Peachtree is a straight lender and agent for the loan. Central City is a senior lender *and* a factor of Columbia's receivables. In other words, Central City has great control over Columbia's cash. Peachtree and Central agreed that Central would share *pro rata* any set-off against the cash and factoring receivables. Nevertheless, termination of the loan would be less palatable to Central City than continuing the banking relationship.

EPILOGUE

Anthony took the view that another $500,000 in debt was not a significant change in the banks' total exposure and that extending the credit was like buying a call option on the entire principal outstanding. Anthony proceeded to renegotiate the terms of the loan, despite initial resistance from Columbia (Columbia's default basically eliminated any negotiating leverage it had).

The restructuring program included: (1) collateralizing all other assets (the income tax refund of $2.5 million was expected to arrive within 90 days of filing); (2) requiring a five-year management contract for Baxter, the competent senior manager; and (3) pressing Baxter to reduce expenses, eliminate the dividend, and continue paring down the assets.

As part of the cost-reduction program, Baxter fired the manager in charge of the dyeing operation, where many of the quality-control problems had occurred. It just so happened, however, that the fired manager was a relative of Chairman Jackson. In response, Jackson fired Baxter (actually bought out his management contract on somewhat favorable terms).

The performance of the firm gradually recovered, as the table suggests (in millions):

	1977	1978	1979	6 Months 1980
Sales	$52	$20	$30	$20
Profits	(2.4)	(4.8)	0	.5

Believing that the turnaround was successful, Columbia negotiated a new credit arrangement with a competitor of Peachtree in June 1980. Peachtree, having lost faith in Jackson as a manager, elected to abandon the credit relationship with Columbia.

In March 1981, Columbia filed for bankruptcy and was subsequently liquidated.

EXHIBIT A   Sources and Uses of Funds (thousands)

	1976	1977
SOURCES OF FUNDS		
Cash	$ 80	0
Receivables	1,224	$2,231
Inventories	0	172
Other current assets	0	344
Payables	0	198
Accruals	434	0
Bank notes	300	500
Current long-term debt	0	777
Other current liabs.	0	36
Long-term debt	0	3,495
Retained earnings	1,507	0
Def. income tax	233	120
Total Sources	$3,812	$7,873
USES OF FUNDS		
Cash	0	$ 517
Inventories	$1,324	0
Other curr. assets	399	0
Tax Refund	0	2,659
Fixed assets	28	1,086
Prepaid expenses	156	130
Def. income tax	185	220
Accounts payable	338	0
Accruals	0	172
Taxes payable	698	266
Current long-term debt	682	0
Long-term debt	2	0
Retained earnings	0	2,823
Total uses	$3,812	$7,873

Blue Cross and Blue Shield of Virginia

SYNOPSIS AND OBJECTIVES

The vice president of finance for this not-for-profit health insurance company is undertaking a review in 1983 of the appropriateness of the company's 9 percent discount rate in evaluating capital-expenditure proposals. The distinctive features of this problem are that the organization is not for profit and not taxed, and it has neither publicly traded securities nor equity, in the usual sense of the term.

The computational requirements of this BC/BS case are light; the primary task for the student is to consider the true definition of "opportunity cost of capital" and recommend a general standard. The case provides data for estimating discount rates within the general risk-premium approach and the capital-asset-pricing model (CAPM).

The case can serve several teaching objectives, including: (1) developing the concept of opportunity cost of capital, (2) illustrating the application of opportunity cost to not-for-profit settings, (3) describing managerial challenges in the health insurance industry.

STUDY QUESTIONS

1. On what was the 9 percent discount rate based?

2. Who owns Blue Cross/Blue Shield? What do the owners require?

3. What discount rate should Phyllis Wilson recommend? Why?

TEACHING PLAN

(10 minutes) What is the problem here? Why should BC/BS care what the discount rate is? The purpose of this opening is to define the question and underscore its relevance.

(20 minutes) What, if anything, is wrong with a discount rate of 9 percent? Bring out basic criticisms: (1) it is out of date; (2) it ignores higher rates of return available in alternative investments of similar risk--that is, the cost of the lost opportunity.

(10 minutes) What standard *should* BC/BS be using to determine its discount rate? What assumptions are implicit in these standards? Students will suggest at least three standards: (1) cost of funds in the market, (2) investment returns, and (3) marginal effect on subscribers.

Teaching note written by Robert F. Bruner. Copyright (c) 1989 by the Darden Graduate Business School Sponsors, Charlottesville, VA.

(10 minutes) Focusing on the market standard, what in the market is like an investment in BC/BS? How risky is BC/BS compared with these alternatives? Students will suggest similarities among a BC/BS investment, municipal bonds, and insurance companies. "Munis" and insurance companies emerge as imperfect but usable proxies for BC/BS's risk.

(10 minutes) What do you recommend? Students will combine various quantitative estimates with a certain amount of judgment. The instructor can take a vote of the class to determine the majority sentiment and to help make the transition to implementation issues.

(10 minutes) What should Wilson say in justifying this recommendation to the directors? This question serves as a check on the students' grasp of the concepts. The instructor could set this up as a role-play between Wilson and some skeptical directors.

ANALYSIS

The Setting

Although at first glance the not-for-profit setting is unorthodox, students should draw two important parallels with the standard business setting. First, the "equity" of BC/BS is the reserve fund. Aside from the relatively small mortgage, BC/BS has no other capital; practically speaking, it is an all-equity firm. Second, the "equity investors" are the subscribers, who pay more than the economic cost of the insurance in order to provide a cushion against risk. The subscribers are the residual stakeholders in the firm. The "profits" of BC/BS are additions to the reserve fund. In general, the 9 percent discount rate serves the interests of the residual stakeholders poorly.

The not-for-profit setting thus makes possible one of the important teaching points of the case: the necessity to link discount rates used to evaluate projects with the interests of the owners of the firm. In the standard business setting, students can easily repeat unthinkingly the rule that managers should work to maximize value to the owners of the firm. This case encourages students to think carefully about that rule and its implications for management action.

Critique of the 9 Percent Hurdle Rate

The new director is correct in questioning the appropriateness of the 9 percent discount rate. First, the discount rate was evidently based on historical realized returns on the investment portfolio; that is, it was a *backward-looking standard*. Even taking the most recent year, 1982, the reserve fund earned a return of 24.7 percent (case Exhibit 5); the 9 percent target appears to weight the actual returns in the distant past equally with the recent returns.

Specifically, the 9 percent discount rate nowhere reflects the changing risk profile of BC/BS. In 1982, the separate insurance entities, Blue Cross and Blue Shield, formally merged; perhaps the risk of the combined portfolio of liabilities is different from the sum of the risks of the two separate portfolios of liabilities. In 1983, The Computer Company, a Medicaid claims-processing bureau, was acquired. Finally, in 1983, BC/BS entered the consulting field through a new subsidiary, Health Risk Management. Perhaps the new activities alter the variability of cash flows in the future from what they were in the past. One hint of a resulting shift in systematic risk is the evidence in case Exhibit 9 that the average unlevered beta of insurors is .49, in contrast to .87 for computer-service companies.

Second, a rate of 9 percent compares poorly with the recent rate of *inflation* (18.9 percent) in health care costs. If BC/BS is to service its subscribers adequately in the face of this inflation, while maintaining a target capital structure, it may have to build reserves (i.e., equity) at a rate similar to inflation.

Third, the method of estimating the discount rate does not reflect *risk*; a portfolio return of 9 percent is consistent with low-risk government securities (case Exhibit 10) but less so with the risk inherent in the process that generates additions to reserves. To highlight that riskiness, one should recall that BC/BS had underwriting losses in 1980 and 1981.

Setting the Discount Rate

The balance-sheet item, "Provisions for subscriber benefits," given in case Exhibit 1 is not capital in the traditional sense and can be viewed as a direct offset against "Subscriber dues and other receivables" listed on the asset side. The firm anticipates issuing no new debt in the future in order to finance capital expenditures. Thus, BC/BS is and will remain, in essence, an all-equity firm. The implication is that the relevant cost to be estimated is the *cost of equity*.

General risk-premium approach. One rough approach to determining the cost of equity is to begin by acknowledging that equity investors in a perpetual firm should probably earn a return in excess of long-term Treasury bonds (11.66 percent) and, depending on the degree of risk, in excess of long-term industrial bonds (12.50 percent). While one cannot say exactly what the equity risk premium over these bonds should be, case Exhibit 8 suggests that, historically, a large portfolio of stocks has earned 5.7 percent (geometric means) to 7.8 percent (arithmetic means) more than long-term government debt instruments. Adding these premiums to the current rate on long-term Treasuries suggests target equity returns in the neighborhood of 17-19 percent.

CAPM approach. The case affords information sufficient to use the capital-asset-pricing model to get one fix on the cost of equity. A beta may be estimated from the information on insurance companies in case Exhibit 9. Unlevering these betas and averaging them yields an average beta for the all-equity insurance company of .49. This figure may be a slight underestimate for BC/BS, because the insurance companies in case Exhibit 9 sell a diverse line of insurance products, whereas BC/BS is a "pure play" in health insurance.

Market premiums are given in case Exhibit 8; long- and short-term Treasury rates in case Exhibit 10. We can estimate equity costs with the CAPM using either or both of these combinations: (1) geometric mean market premium and long-term Treasury rates and (2) arithmetic mean market premium and short-term Treasury rates. The following table summarizes the assumptions and results (beta = .49):

	Market Premium	Risk-Free Rate	Cost of Equity
Geometric mean	.087	.0878	.1304
Arithmetic mean	.064	.1166	.1480

These estimates are lower than those afforded by the general risk-premium approach perhaps because the CAPM approach takes into account industry-specific risk.

Differences in tax status. Some students may get confused by the fact that the sample of insurance companies consists of for-profit, taxable firms; they may insist that, because BC/BS's residual flows are before tax, the required rate of return needs to be "grossed up" to a pre-tax level. No such adjustment is required. The concept of opportunity cost tells us that residual flows of equivalent risk should be valued at equivalent discount rates. As long as we assume the sample of insurance companies is similar to BC/BS, the discount rate estimated in the preceding section is applicable to BC/BS.

CONCLUSION

A large upward revision in the discount rate for BC/BS seems justified. Although Wilson has her work cut out for her in rationalizing a large change to her fellow managers and the directors, if one reasons from the foundation concept of opportunity costs, the case for change is compelling. Without earning these apparently high rates of return, BC/BS will face increasing difficulty in forming the capital to sustain the insurance claims of its subscribers and support the growth of the company.

Teletech Corporation

SYNOPSIS AND OBJECTIVES

The vice president of finance of this large, regional telecommunications company must resolve a policy dispute in 1988 among the firm's division presidents about the appropriate cost of capital used to evaluate projects at the divisional level. Teletech consists mainly of a regulated common-carrier telecommunications division and a computer software and workstation division. The manifestly different levels of risk in the two divisions have given rise to a proposal that the firm implement a divisional capital-cost system to replace a corporatewide hurdle rate. The case also contains details about the specific calculations by which the firm estimates its corporate hurdle rate.

The case is intended to offer a general introduction to the topic of cost of capital. Almost no calculations are required of students, which allows them to wrestle with the following ideas: (1) the concept of the hurdle rate, (2) the concepts of the costs of equity and debt, (3) the weighted-average cost-of-capital formula, (4) tax adjustments, (5) the use of marginal, as opposed to average, costs and weights, and (6) the adjustment for risk in the capital-budgeting process.

STUDY QUESTIONS

Students will find collateral readings in finance textbooks to be helpful in addressing the conceptual issues in this case. Recommended are Chapter 9 in Ross and Westerfield's *Corporate Finance,* Chapter 9 in Brealey and Myers' *Principles of Corporate Finance* (3rd ed.), and Chapter 21 in Weston and Copeland's *Managerial Finance* (8th ed.).

1. In concept, what is a "hurdle rate"; how is it used; in this case, how does Teletech compute its hurdle rate? In your opinion, are the factors Teletech uses in computing its hurdle rate appropriate?

2. What would be the effect of adopting a divisional hurdle-rate system?

3. What should Barrymore recommend?

TEACHING PLAN

The following questions serve as a framework for motivating an 80-minute discussion of the case:

(5 minutes)   What is a hurdle rate?

(15 minutes)   How is the hurdle rate an issue in this case?

Teaching note written by Robert F. Bruner. Copyright (c) 1988 by the Darden Graduate Business School Sponsors, Charlottesville, VA.

(20 minutes) How does Teletech compute its hurdle rate, and what changes, if any, would you make in that computation?

(30 minutes) What are the relative merits of a divisional, as opposed to a corporatewide, hurdle-rate system? Does such a system risk mixing investment and financing decisions?

(10 minutes) What would you recommend? How would you implement it?

ANALYSIS

The case affords three important teaching points: (1) the concepts of hurdle rates and capital costs and their relevance to resource allocation, (2) the proper way to calculate the weighted-average cost of capital, and (3) risk-adjusting discount rates for use by corporations. This discussion will focus on the latter two issues.

Estimating a Hurdle Rate

Teletech uses the weighted-average cost-of-capital formula in a manner that, to a naïve student, is straightforward but that actually merits critical examination. Discussion of Teletech's calculations must focus on the choice of numbers to be used in the formula. The following opportunities for discussion arise:

- *Historical average*. The corporatewide hurdle rate is loosely derived from an average of 10 years of weighted-average capital costs. This historical average bears little relationship to current or expected capital costs.

- *Slow adjustment*. The corporatewide hurdle rate was last reviewed in 1984, yet the firm's capital costs change constantly. As case Exhibit 3 shows, the current hurdle rate of 13 percent is out of line with the latest weighted-average cost of 11.6 percent.

- *Average, not marginal, costs*. Even the calculations in case Exhibit 3 are based on the average cost of debt currently embedded in the firm's capital structure.

- *Current, not target, weights*. While the choice of weights is not a material problem at the corporate level, it emerges significantly at the divisional level. If current weights are inconsistent with targeted capital structures, then the analyst must make the difficult choice between them.

- *Inflation adjustment*. The case describes a process by which nominal future cash flows are deflated (to give real cash flows) and then discounted at nominal rates. This approach is incorrect: either real rates should be used with real flows, or nominal rates with nominal flows. As presently used, this procedure especially penalizes longer lived projects and projects whose cash flows are sensitive to inflation.

- *Taxes*. Although tax rate does not emerge as a large issue at the corporate level, the divisional discussion may wrestle with whether to use average or marginal tax rates. Finance theory favors marginal rates because of the marginal and forward-looking nature of the capital-budgeting process.

At the end of an itemized critique like this in class, the instructor may choose to summarize the elements of "good" tradecraft in using the weighted-average cost-of-capital formula.

Divisional Hurdle Rates

The debate over divisional hurdle rates essentially frames a twofold problem: (1) the concept of risk adjustment in capital budgeting and (2) the mechanics and administrative problems inherent in a divisionalized hurdle-rate system.

On the first issue, finance theory and intuition tell us that investors require higher returns as risk increases. Firms are not internally homogeneous in risk. It may be useful for the instructor to dwell on the variety of asset risks that investment projects offer--for example, engineering projects (where returns are low but relatively certain), market-expansion projects (where the returns are higher but less certain), and new-product introductions (where both returns and risks are high). The instructor can point out that, apart from new projects, each firm is really a bundle of assets--each with a different degree of risk; one can compare cash and marketable securities with accounts receivable with inventory with trademarks. To students who are new to finance, this portfolio view is often a novel and helpful way of viewing the firm.

The problem with a corporatewide hurdle rate is that it superimposes one required rate of return (and its implicitly associated risk level) on all projects. Graphically, this effect is represented by line A-B in Exhibit A (which plots a group of prospective investments in risk/return space). Alternatively, a risk-adjusted hurdle-rate system is represented by line C-D. Under both systems, projects whose returns exceed the hurdle rate should be accepted.

The first insight from Exhibit A is that, over time, the use of a single corporatewide hurdle rate may alter the asset composition of the firm toward riskier projects, because, on average, those projects may move easily to clear the corporate hurdle rate. The second insight in Exhibit A stems from an analysis of the two regions of conflict between the two systems. In region I, the corporatewide hurdle rate would reject good projects (i.e., projects whose returns exceed a risk-adjusted hurdle). In region II, the corporatewide hurdle would accept bad projects. In theory, the corporatewide hurdle rate is useful for only one type of project: those that, from a risk standpoint, are clones of the entire firm.

One conclusion from this discussion is that corporatewide hurdle rates are easier to misuse than to use properly.

A common objection to the risk-adjusted hurdle-rate analysis is that, in using a risk-adjusted hurdle-rate system, low-absolute-return projects may get accepted by the firm, which would reduce the firm's total returns. The obvious reply is that investors value returns on a risk-adjusted basis; investing in low-absolute-return assets may indeed be the most value-creating thing managers can do for their shareholders.

The effect of the multiple-hurdle-rate system is illustrated in Exhibit B. Based on data given in the case text and case Exhibit 1, an appropriate weighted-average cost of capital (WACC) for the telecommunications division, appears to be 8.06 percent,[1] and for the computer software division, 19.5 percent--both considerably different from the current corporate hurdle rate of 13 percent. Assuming the EBIAT/capital ratios are good proxies for the division internal rates of return, under the divisional hurdle-rate system, the telecommunications division would apparently earn a positive return over cost of about 3.4 percent, while the computer software division would earn a *negative* return of about 4.7 percent. This result reverses the performance conclusions based on the 13 percent corporate hurdle rate. Clearly, the choice of hurdle rate is of immense importance to the managers of each division.

Exhibit B lends one other insight about corporatewide hurdle rates: they implicitly assume that all divisions have the same debt-bearing capacity. Compared on the basis of return on assets (ROA), the computer software division performance is better than the telecommunications division; yet this ranking reverses if return on equity (ROE) is used to compare the two divisions, mainly because of the use by the telecommunications division of more lower cost debt capital. The confusing reversal of rankings disappears if one focuses on spreads over funds costs (ROA − WACC, ROE − Ke); in that case, the telecommunications division is consistently superior.

Administrative Considerations

The introduction of divisional hurdle rates into a company can create sharp secondary effects in the form of unusual managerial behavior. Much of it springs from the difficult judgments analysts and general managers must make about capital costs, weights, tax rates, etc. In theory, most of this judgment would be left to a chief financial officer who, as an "umpire," would be left alone to determine the "correct" hurdle rate. In practice, however, firms are political systems in which advocates seek to sway the judgments of decision makers. The flavor of the advocacy is apparent in the commentaries by Aragon and Alegra. Barrymore should anticipate continuing argument and lobbying, even after a divisionalized system is imposed.

---

[1] In estimating the WACC for each division, the instructor must make a decision about the appropriate tax rate for software (.25 versus .34) and the appropriate capital structure for telecommunications (debt/total capital of 50.6 percent as presently versus 75 percent, which would be consistent with other telecommunications firms). The analysis here assumes the tax rate = .34 and debt to total capital = .506. The alternative assumptions do not alter the basic disparity between corporate and divisional hurdle rates revealed in Exhibit B.

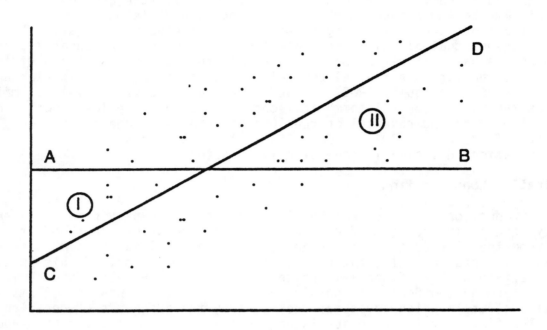

Line A-B: Single corporate-wide hurdle rate.
Line C-D: Risk-adjusted hurdle rate.

EXHIBIT B   Divisional Capital-Cost Comparison

	Telecommunications	Software
Total invested capital	$1,947	$304
Net assets ("equity")	$ 962	$292
Debt	$ 985	$ 12
Weight of equity	49.4%	96.1%
Weight of debt	50.6%	3.9%
EBIT	$ 338	$68
EBIAT (t = .34)	$ 223	$44.9
Net income	$ 166	$45
ROE (profit/equity)	17.3%	15.4%
ROA (EBIAT/capital)	11.5%	14.8%
Divisional WACC	8.06%*	19.50%**
Divisional equity cost (Ke)	14.00%	20.00%
Performance Measures		
ROA – WACC	+3.44%	-4.7%
ROE – Ke	+3.3%	-4.6%

*Given in the case.

**Derived from the weights presented here and the costs of debt (7.58%) and equity (20%) given in the case.

General Motors Corporation, 1988

SYNOPSIS AND OBJECTIVES

In the spring of 1988, closely following the announcement of strategic initiatives designed to address an evident inability to control costs and halt a decline in market share, General Motors was being criticized in the business press for poor financial performance. Students must evaluate GM's performance and identify the business units that are underperforming. Historical and expected returns are presented straightforwardly in the case. The task is to develop target rates of return on equity.

The case is intended to exercise a wide range of equity-pricing models: the capital-asset-pricing model (CAPM), dividend growth, risk premium, and earnings/price. It affords an opportunity for discussing the mechanical challenges in deriving an equity cost and the aspects of tradecraft in current use. The case can be suitably taught following the "Teletech Corporation" case, which treats cost of capital at a conceptual level.

STUDY QUESTIONS

1. Please estimate GM's cost of equity using data in the case. Specifically, you should draw on available approaches for estimating this cost, including: (a) earnings capitalization, (b) constant dividend growth, (c) risk premium, and (d) the CAPM. What might account for the differences among the estimated costs of capital yielded by these approaches? What are the relative strengths and weaknesses of each approach? What should be the equity hurdle rate for the entire firm?

2. Please estimate the cost of equity for: (a) the automotive division, (b) General Motors Acceptance Corporation, (c) Hughes Aircraft (GMHE), and (d) Electronic Data Systems. Use the five approaches cited in question 1. Please recommend an equity hurdle rate for each division.

3. In principle, *should* a divisional hurdle rate be different from a corporate-level hurdle rate? Why? If you think that it should, what administrative problems might multiple hurdle rates create? If you think that it should not, what are the implications for corporate resource allocation over the long run?

4. What is the interdivisional effect of GM's decision to offer 2.9 percent automobile loans instead of cutting unit prices? What are the possible benefits of such a policy? Will equity investors value these benefits (i.e., bid up the share price)?

Teaching note written by Robert F. Bruner. Copyright (c) 1988 by the Darden Graduate Business School Sponsors, Charlottesville, VA.

N.B.   Thorough preparation for this class would include a review of historical and future equity costs, an extrapolation of equity costs from comparable firms, and an adjustment for any qualitative effects you think are material.

TEACHING PLAN

A general strategy for covering this case in an 80-minute session is to deal with the practical aspects of estimating equity costs first, and then turn to the policy implications of so-called value-shifting among GM's divisions. Such a discussion sequence allows the instructor to end the class on the larger "forest" of policy issues, rather than on the "trees" of computational minutiae.

(30 minutes) What is your estimate of GM's (i.e., corporate) cost of equity? The ensuing discussion should cover the four principal approaches, with the instructor providing guidance if necessary on the accepted current tradecraft on the application of each approach. This part of the discussion must cover the principal strengths and weaknesses of each approach.

(5 minutes) What is your recommendation for a target equity hurdle rate for GM at the corporate level? The purpose of this question is to attempt to provide some closure to the opening discussion of tradecraft. Moreover, it sets the stage for contrasting the corporate and divisional equity hurdles. If necessary, the instructor can take a vote to finish the initial topic.

(20 minutes) What are your estimates of the divisional costs of capital under the various approaches? What do you recommend as the divisional equity hurdles? The emphasis during this segment of the discussion should be on "getting the numbers up" on the blackboard more straightforwardly than following question 1. At this stage, the instructor should begin to build contrasts among the divisional equity costs and between the divisions and the corporate level.

(10 minutes) Should divisional hurdle rates differ from the corporate rate? Pro and con arguments should be offered. Having seen while discussing question 3 that divisional and corporate rates can differ materially, the students are now asked, in effect, "Which one is right?" The objective of this question is to apply practically the concept of the risk-adjusted discount rate to large corporate divisions. If necessary, the instructor can take a vote to finish the discussion.

(15 minutes) Do you buy the argument that a dollar of loss in the automotive division is more costly to shareholders than a dollar of loss in GMAC? The proposition is fallacious. The purpose of the question is to test students' commitment to the divisional-hurdle-rate concept. Shareholders will capitalize a dollar of profit or loss at the corporatewide hurdle rate regardless of where in the firm the profit or loss is realized. The only way such value-shifting can affect shareholders' wealth is if, at the same time, it causes the weighted average of the divisional betas to change so that the corporatewide hurdle rate changes. This discussion should re-emphasize the point that the firm's asset beta is simply a weighted average of the betas of individual assets (or even of divisions). There is a wider business issue here. Are GM and GMAC really separate companies? If 3/4 of GMAC's business is with GM, then (1) the health of the 2 units is inseparable, (2) you couldn't spin off GMAC because of the control issue,

(3) operationally, GM dealers are agents for GMAC as well as GM, and (4) the market is really valuing the consolidated entity (i.e., if anything, GMAC trades at a discount because it is taking finance-company risk and auto-business risk.

ANALYSIS

A Note on GM's Equity Structure

GM has a complex equity structure which requires some clarification. Properly speaking, there are three classes of common stock of General Motors Corporation: $1 2/3 par value common stock, commonly called "GM Common" or, on the floor of the New York Stock Exchange, "Motors," Class E common stock, and Class H common stock. These classes of stock have distinct voting rights. ($1 2/3 par value stocks have 1 vote each, E shares have 1/4 vote, and H shares have 1/4 vote) and liquidation rights (a $1 2/3 share was worth roughly 3.9 E shares and 4.0 H shares at the end of 1987). Voting rights were fixed at the time of the issue of the E and H stocks in 1984 and 1985, respectively, but liquidation rights change over time based on changes in the retained earnings of EDS, GMHE and GM.

Reported earnings for E and H shares reflect the net income of EDS (for E) and GMHE (for H) adjusted to exclude the amortization of intangibles created by GM's acquisition of the two companies. The net incomes are apportioned on the basis of "dividend base shares" (121.9 million E, 400 million H). This apportionment does not affect the fact that GM (and not E and H shareholders) owns and controls EDS and GMHE; E and H shareholders do not elect the Boards of Directors of EDS and GMHE but only have a "claim" on EDS's and GMHE's earnings through dividends and increases in liquidation rights. Since GM (and therefore $1 2/3 shareholders) own roughly 2/3 of the dividend base E and H shares, 2/3 of EDS's and GMHE's earnings flow through to $1 2/3 shares (and all of EDS's and GMHE's earnings flow through to GM consolidated net income, though due to intercompany eliminations only about 50 percent of EDS's and GMHE's net is GM net). Similarly, 2/3 of the E and H dividends flow through to GM and are a component of cash available to $1 2/3 stockholders.

Estimates of Cost of Equity

Exhibit A presents a summary of the calculations of Ke for GM and its four divisions. The estimation approaches include CAPM, earnings capitalization, and the constant dividend growth model, using both the historical self-sustainable growth rate, and the forecasted dividend growth rate. The risk-premium approach was ignored for lack of supporting data. The Exhibit gives an average of the estimates as well as an "inferred" estimate, which gives greater weight to the approaches using expectational data and risk adjustment.

GM corporate. The estimates vary between 12.5 and 15.1 percent, and average 14 percent. GM's return on book equity for 1987 is significantly lower than the estimated equity costs, an insight which sets the stage for an inquiry into the areas of performance weakness.

GMAC. This is an unconsolidated subsidiary on which incomplete information is available. The two estimates are 16.1 and 12.7 percent. The CAPM estimate (16.1 percent) is based on a beta of 1.15, which is calculated by unlevering the betas of the comparable firms and relevering to reflect GMAC's capital structure, and then averaging. The wide disparity between the two estimates for

GMAC affords the instructor an opportunity to discuss the relative merits of the CAPM and the Gordon Growth Model. Under either estimate, GMAC appears to be performing reasonably well; its return on equity is comfortably above either estimate.

EDS. The estimates for EDS show an enormous range: 8.1 to 26 percent, with an average of 17 percent. The outliers here arise from the earnings-capitalization estimate and the constant-dividend-growth estimate using sustainable growth. The high estimate is attributable to EDS's high return on equity. The low estimate is simply the inverse of the price/earnings ratio. Choosing a Ke in the midrange suggests that EDS is the standout performer in GM's portfolio with an ROE of 30 percent.

GMHE. Here, too, the range of estimates is large: 5.3 to 11.8 percent. The average is 9.2 percent. Giving somewhat greater weight to the CAPM approach, GMHE appears to have earned a return on equity (9.5 percent) at, or just a little below, its inferred cost.

Automotive division. Data on this division are insufficient for using the earnings-capitalization and dividend-growth approaches. The CAPM approach is based on an average beta of other auto manufacturers and yields an estimate of 16.4 percent. General Motors reports no return on equity for this division, but by a process of elimination, automobile manufacturing is the source of GM's failing performance.

Most of the discussion of each method will focus on *which* assumption to use for the parameters of each model. The arbitrariness implicit in each approach will create a fair degree of frustration in students, so it is important for the instructor to emphasize that certain generally accepted assumptions about these parameters form the tradecraft of Ke estimation (e.g., an assumption for Rm – Rf). Wrestling with the computational issues gives students (1) a sense of the relative strengths and weaknesses of the classic approaches, (2) a healthy skepticism about the exactness of any given estimate, and yet (3) respect for the assistance that the various approaches can provide.

A Note on Using the CAPM

One of the details that students will debate is the choice of which risk-free rate and which market premium to use in the CAPM. Case Exhibits 9 and 11 present data on U.S. Treasury instrument yields, while case Exhibit 10 provides the basis for estimating a market premium. Students should be reminded that the purpose of the calculation is to arrive at an estimate of the *expected* required return on equity. But since, in the case of equities, an expected return is not directly measurable (as it is with bonds), we must use the CAPM to approximate it.

Two approaches generally are favored. The first uses the short term (e.g., 30-day) Treasury rate in combination with the arithmetic average market premium (i.e., 8.6 percent, calculated from case Exhibit 10 as the difference between 12.1 and 3.5 percent). The second approach uses the long-term (e.g., 10-, 20-, or 30-year) Treasury rate in combination with the geometric mean market premium (i.e., 5.6 percent, calculated as the difference between 10 and 4.4 percent). The superiority of one approach over another is often vigorously debated, although both are used in practice.

Divisional versus Corporate Equity Costs

That equity costs vary among the divisions and in comparison with the corporate cost reinforces the lessons of the "Teletech" case about how required returns must be determined by the economic fundamentals of different assets and businesses. The instructor may choose to dwell on those fundamentals and to abstract from them some inferences about risk and other determinants of equity costs. A sample board layout for this aspect of the discussion is presented in Exhibit B.

Value Shifting: Automotive to GMAC

The case indicates that new auto loans for 1986 amounted to $47 billion. Assuming that these were spread evenly over the year, and that the 2.9 percent financing was introduced on September 1 of 1986, approximately $15.7 billion of these loans were accepted in 1986. To determine the wealth loss to GM in that year requires the assumption of a target rate of interest, for which one might use the BBB industrial bond rate in 1986 of about 10.5 percent (the range given in case Exhibit 9 was 9.81 to 11.26 percent). Assuming that the life of these loans was 4 years, that GMAC bought them on September 1, 1986, and sold them on September 1, 1990, yields a value equal to 75.6 percent of face value, or $11.84 billion. The value loss was in the neighborhood of $3.82 billion.[1] In short, the losses under consideration were probably not trivial.

The instructor can probe the students on the issue of whether it matters where this loss was taken. The economic alternatives to the low-interest-rate loans would be (1) cash rebates and (2) product price cuts. Under these alternatives, the automotive division would have sustained the loss. GMAC, however, would bear the loss of the cut-rate loans.

First, from the summary calculations given in Exhibit A, the equity costs for GMAC and the automotive division are not materially different; thus it is hard to say that a dollar of loss is worth less in one division than another. But second, and more importantly, the value shift is simply a financial cosmetic: because GMAC is an unconsolidated subsidiary (accounted for on the equity method), losses taken in GMAC do not affect the operating profit margins reported in GM's (the parent's) financial statements. GM management may have wanted to improve the operating picture of GM's automotive business. The evidence is, however, that the security analysts knew what was happening at the time:

> These programs have the same effect on the parents' earnings as cash rebate programs, except that they promote the service of the credit subsidiaries over commercial banks and credit unions.... Although reduced-rate financing programs will eventually lose their effectiveness, as cash rebates did, we believe they will be replaced with other finance-oriented programs, such as balloon payment financing.[2]

Thus, the value shift was unlikely to have succeeded in boosting GM's share price.

---

[1] $47 billion x (4/12) x .244 = $3.82 billion.

[2] Jean-Claude Gruet, Salomon Brothers, Inc., *Automotive Credit Subsidiaries*, September 1986, p. 10.

EXHIBIT A   Summary of Cost-of-Equity Calculations for GM Corporate and Four Divisions

Generic Assumptions:
Rf (case Exhibit 11)   6.1%*
Rm   8.60% (see arithmetic mean returns: common stock minus T-bills)

Entity Assumptions	Corporate	GMAC	EDS	GMHE	Automotive	
Beta	0.95	1.15	1.15	0.65	1.19 (Auto = avg)	
Expected earnings per share	$10.75	$54.75	$3.10	$1.80		(case Exhibit 8)
Present stock price	$71.375	NA	$38.500	$34.250		(case Exhibit 7)
Expected dividend yield	7.1%	4.6%	1.3%	1.6%		(case Exhibit 4)
Expected dividend payout	49.7%	61.0%	19.6%	21.6%		(case Exhibit 4)
Return on equity	10.7%	20.8%	30.7	9.5%	NAv	(case Exhibit 4)
Forecasted growth rates	7.0%	NA	17.0%	9.0%		(case text)
Sustainable growth rates	5.4%	8.1%	24.7%	7.4%		(case Appendix formula)
Costs of Equity						
1. CAPM	14.3%	16.1%	16.1%	11.8%	16.4%	
2. Earnings capitalization	15.1%	NAv	8.1%	5.3%	NAv	
3. Constant dividend growth**	12.5%	12.7%	26.0%	9.0%	NAv**	
4. Constant dividend growth forecasted	14.1%	NAv	18.3%	10.6%	NAv†	
Average cost of equity†	14.0%	14.4%	17.1%	9.2%	16.4%	
Inferred cost of equity††	14.0%	14.5%	16.0%	10.5%	16.0%††	
Return on equity	10.7%	20.8%	30.7%	9.5%	NAv (case Exhibit 6)	

*Rate as of 4/11/88 (case Exhibit 11). Monthly rates given in case Exhibit 9 are average
of business-day data; the rate given in case Exhibit 11 is specific to the day.

**Based on sustainable dividend growth rate.

†Based on forecasted dividend growth rate.

††The author's inference of cost of equity, giving greater weight to estimates 1 and 4 and less to 2
and 3.

EXHIBIT B   Sample Board Layout for Discussion of Entity Fundamentals

Criterion	Corporate	EDS	GMAC	GMHE	Automotive
Industry	Diversified	Computers	Finance	Defense	Auto
Growth	Mature	High	High	Moderate	Negative
Cyclical	Yes	No	Mixed	No	Yes
Barriers	Medium	High	High	High	Medium
Degree of competition	High	Low	Medium	Medium	High
Risks	Technology		Cycle	Technology Cycle	Technology Foreign comp.
Profitability	Low	High	High	Medium	Low

The Investment Detective

SYNOPSIS AND OBJECTIVES

The case presents the cash flows of eight unidentified investments, all of equal initial investment size. The task of the student is to rank the projects. The first objective of the case is to motivate a critical examination of the principal capital-budgeting criteria. A second objective is to consider the problem that arises when net present value (NPV) and internal rate of return (IRR) disagree as to the ranking of two mutually exclusive projects. Third, the case is a vehicle for introducing the problem created in attempting to rank projects of unequal life and its solution--the equivalent annuity criterion.

STUDY QUESTIONS

The case is self-explanatory and can be used without the benefit of supplementary readings.

TEACHING PLAN

The following is a plan for an 80-minute class:

(10 minutes) Before doing any calculations, can't we rank the projects simply by inspecting the cash flows?

(10 minutes) What analytical criteria could we use to rank the projects? How do you define each? Let's get the numbers up on the board.

(20 minutes) Which of the two projects, 7 and 8, is more attractive?
• How sensitive is our ranking to the use of higher discount rates?
• Why do NPV and IRR disagree?

(15 minutes) What rank should we assign to each project?
• Why don't payback and NPV agree completely?
• Why don't average return on investment and NPV agree completely?
• What criterion is best?

(15 minutes) Are these projects really comparable on the basis of NPV? Because of the different lives, are we really measuring the "net present" value of the shorter lived projects?

The instructor may choose to close the class with some comments summarizing the key insights raised during class.

Teaching note written by Robert F. Bruner. Copyright (c) 1989 by the Darden Graduate Business School Sponsors, Charlottesville, VA

ANALYSIS

Simple Ranking of Projects

Exhibit A presents a summary of the NPVs, IRRs, accounting returns on investment (ROIs), payback, present value (PV) index, and equivalent annuity. (The exhibit identifies the method of computing ROI, PV index, and equivalent annuity.) Because the result is a blizzard of numbers, the instructor will want to narrow down the choice of method early in the class by reviewing the weaknesses of each analytical alternative. Key points should be:

IRR: Possibly incorrect opportunity-cost assumption. Violates value additivity. Multiple IRRs are possible.

NPV: May be difficult to explain.

ROI: Often computed on profits, not cash flow. Ignores time profile of flows and, therefore, time value of money.

Payback: Ignores time value of money, although it is a proxy for the liquidity or duration of an investment and is sometimes used in conjunction with NPV.

After a review such as this, students lose allegiance to ROI and payback, which makes the ranking by time-value criteria easier to accomplish.

The Mutually Exclusive Ranking: Projects 7 and 8

The place to begin the ranking of all projects is to settle the choice between the mutually exclusive projects. Unfortunately, as Exhibit A shows, IRR and NPV (at the 10 percent hurdle rate) disagree on the ranking of projects 7 and 8. At higher discount rates, however, IRR and NPV rank the projects consistently.

Exhibit B shows graphically what is happening. The value functions of the two projects cross over; hence, the rankings change as the discount rate varies from one side to the other of the crossover point.

The reason the value functions cross over is that the time profiles of the two projects are very different. Project 7 (see case Exhibit 1) offers large cash flows early, which dwindle to nothing as time passes—like a mine in which the miners extract the easiest and richest ore first. Project 8 requires continuing investment in the early years and then offers rising positive cash flows—rather like an orchard or a consumer brand name. At high discount rates, project 8's large future cash flows have a relatively smaller present value than they do at low discount rates. Project 7 is much less affected by higher discount rates, because its most significant cash flows appear early in its life.

The standard approach to the appearance of a crossover problem is to rely on the ranking by NPV, because one holds constant the discount rate across both projects. If the discount rate is reasonably chosen, then presumably, the implicit reinvestment-rate assumption is also reasonable. Ranking by IRR invites errors to the extent that the reinvestment-rate assumption is not reasonable. The NPV criterion makes the correct assumption that projects of equal risk should be discounted at the same rate.

The Problem of Unequal Scale

Superficially, all eight projects are of equal size; that is, the initial outlay in all cases is $2,000. Observant students will point out that, in the cases of projects 3 and 8, however, the outlays extend farther out in time. How one views these outlays is a matter of debate, but from one perspective, they represent continuing investment. According to this view, projects 3 and 8 are of larger scale than the other projects. The PV index adjusts for scale differences by showing the present value of benefits per dollar of outlay.

The Problem of Unequal Lives

Comparisons based on standard NPV ignore the inequality of project lives such as those in the case. Simply put, shorter lived projects could be replicated within the life of the longest project (e.g., project 6 could be replicated 15 times within the life of project 3), thus producing very different time profiles of cash flows for the projects. One solution to this problem is the so-called "replacement-chain" approach, in which shorter lived projects are replicated out to a horizon common with the longer lived projects, and the NPV on the entire chain is then calculated and compared with the NPV of the other chain. This approach can be cumbersome, however, in problems with many alternative investments. For instance, in this case, the common horizon for all eight projects is 840 years (we have projects of 1, 3, 5, 7, 8, and 10 years, so the common horizon is equal to 1 x 3 x 5 x 7 x 8 x 10).

An easier, and intuitively appealing, approach is to compare the "equivalent annuity" among all the projects. The equivalent annuity is the level payment across a project's specific life that has a present value equal to that of another cash-flow stream. Projects of equal size (such as those in this case) can be ranked directly by their equivalent annuity.

The lower panel of Exhibit A presents the equivalent annuities for the eight projects. Here we observe another ranking change. On a standard NPV ranking, project 3 is more attractive than project 8. Yet on the basis of equivalent annuities, project 8 is more attractive. The ranking changes because the simple NPV calculation ignores the unequal lives of the two projects; one could replicate project 8 almost twice within the lifespan of project 3, thus delivering twice the absolute (undiscounted) cash flow as valued in the initial analyis.

Ranking the Projects

After the students wrestle with the full range of ranking criteria, the equivalent-annuity criterion will probably gain the greatest acceptance (as it should). Based on equivalent annuities, we would rank the projects as follows:

1st	#8
2nd	3
3rd	4
4th	5
5th	1
6th	6
7th	2

There is no eighth project, because the only remaining project (number 7) was eliminated in the mutually exclusive choice between it and 8.

173

Naming the Projects

The case questions invite the students to imagine what kinds of real investment projects have cash flows similar to those in the case. The suggestion adds realism to the discussion, but it should be saved until the end of class, because the projects students mention often have widely varying risk levels. Thus, such discussion can go astray, as it often prompts students to apply different discount rates to the various projects in the case. Here is a sampling of project types:

Project Number	Type
1	Partially amortizing bond
2	Advertising campaign
3	Zero-coupon bond
4	Nuclear power plant, pesticide factory
5	Home mortgage
6	1-year bond
7	Mine
8	Orchard

EXHIBIT A Comparative Analysis of Investments

1. Project Free Cash Flows (in thousands of dollars)

Project number	1	2	3	4	5	6	7	8
Initial investment	($2,000)	($2,000)	($2,000)	($2,000)	($2,000)	($2,000)	($2,000)	($2,000)
Year 1	$330	$1,666		$160	280	$2,200*	$1,200	($350)
2	330	334*		200	280		900*	(60)
3	330	165		350	280		300	60
4	330			395	280		90	350
5	330			432	280		70	700
6	330			440*	280			1,200
7	330*			442	280			2,400*
8	1,000			444	280*			
9				446	280			
10				448	280			
11				450	280			
12				451	280			
13				451	280			
14				452	280			
15			10,000*	(2,000)	280			
Sum of cash flow benefits	$3,310	$2,165	$10,000	$3,561	$4,200	$2,200	$2,560	$4,300
Excess of cash flow over initial investment	$1,310	$165	$8,000	$1,561	$2,200	$200	$560	$2,300

175

EXHIBIT A (continued)

2. Analysis

Total life of investment	8	3	15	15	15	1	5	7
Payback (years)	7	2	15	6	8	1	2	7
Average ROI**	20.7%	36.1%	33.3%	11.9%	14.0%	110.0%	25.6%	30.7%
Net present value at:								
10%	$73	($85)	$394	$228	$130	($0)	$165	$260
11%	(11)	(107)	90	127	13	(18)	132	123
12%	(90)	(129)	(173)	30	(93)	(36)	99	(4)
14%	(234)	(170)	(599)	(146)	(280)	(70)	37	(236)
Internal rate of return	10.9%	6.3%	11.3%	12.3%	11.1%	10.0%	15.3%	12.0%
PV Index†	1.037	0.957	1.197	0.706	1.065	1.000	1.083	1.610
Equivalent annuity††	$13.7	($34.4)	$51.8	$30.0	$17.1	($0.0)	$43.5	$53.4
Equiv. annuity (to infinity)	$137.0	($343.6)	$517.9	$300.1	$170.5	($0.0)	$435.4	$534.0

*Indicates year in which payback is accomplished.

**Average return on investment is calculated as the average of the cash flows over the life of the project divided by the $2,000 investment up front.

†The PV index is calculated as the present value of all inflows (at a 10 percent discount rate) divided by the present value of all outflows. Ordinarily, it will rank projects identically to the standard NPV except where there are outflows in later years, as in projects 4 and 8; in these cases, it changes the ranking significantly.

††The equivalent annuity is that level annual payment over the life of the investment that yields a present value (at 10 percent) just equal to the net present value of the entire cash-flow stream. The annuity is determined by solving for A in

$$A = NPV/([1+(1.1)/(-n)]/.1)$$

176

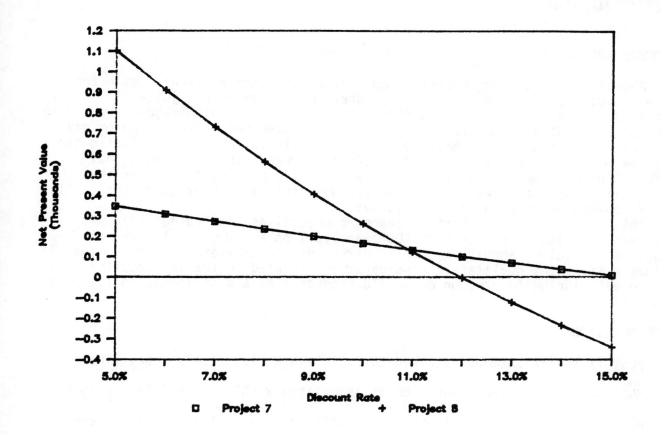

Westfield, Inc.

SYNOPSIS AND OBJECTIVES

A project manager for Westfield must assess the attractiveness of offering a new product, plastic cans, to manufacturers of frozen orange juice concentrate. Westfield is a producer of industrial and consumer-goods packaging material, including composite (i.e., paper) cans used for packaging motor oil and frozen orange juice. Competitors have recently introduced the plastic can into the motor-oil market, spurring Westfield to reexamine its traditional product line of composite cans. The essence of the problem is whether the all-plastic can, Plastitek, should replace Westfield's current composite can in the frozen-concentrate juice (FCJ) market.

This case can support various teaching objectives, including, (1) performing a discounted cash flow (DCF) analysis on a new product line, (2) using the equivalent annuity method to determine a breakeven unit price, and (3) reviewing important qualitative considerations related to the introduction of a new product, including erosion of an old product line and strategic positioning of the firm.

STUDY QUESTIONS

1. What is the investment required to establish a Plastitek product line?

2. What are the relevant annual costs associated with the Plastitek project?

3. What unit price is consistent with Westfield earning its target 15 percent rate of return on the project?

4. At the target price you determined, is the product viable? Do you anticipate that the product will sell in sufficient quantity at this target price? Why?

5. What considerations, if any, might justify Westfield charging a lower price (and earning a lower return)?

TEACHING PLAN

(20 minutes) Why is Westfield considering introducing a plastic can into the FCJ market? This opening should establish that the introduction is motivated by Westfield's strategic concerns rather than the physical appeal of the product itself.

(35 minutes) What price should Westfield establish on the plastic can in order to earn its 15 percent target return? Assume in your analysis that

---

Teaching note written by Robert F. Bruner, drawing on notes written for the case by Carrie Coker under the direction of John L. Colley, Jr. Copyright (c) 1989 by the Darden Graduate Business School Sponsors, Charlottesville, VA.

the old composite-can equipment would be diverted to alternative uses. This segment of the discussion lays out DCF analysis, which solves effectively in reverse for that unit price which gives a 15 percent return.

(15 minutes) Are there any qualitative factors that might justify a higher price? This segment should compare and contrast the composite and plastic cans.

(10 minutes) Can we justify changes in assumptions that might result in a lower price? The instructor can invite a review of key assumptions and a test of their sensitivity: discount rate, costs, investment amount, life.

The instructor can close the discussion with a vote by the class and a review of the key points of contention in the discussion.

ANALYSIS

Strategic Setting

The conversion in 1984 of the motor-oil can market from composite to plastic cans made Westfield reexamine its traditional product line of composite cans. The motor oil market was the Consumer Packaging Division's largest business segment (as a percentage of sales). Westfield was not a leader in this conversion; it *reacted* to the changes, which resulted in lost sales and low capacity-utilization rates. Westfield began to focus its attention on other key composite-can segments. The objective was to be proactive in any future conversions rather than reactive. The FCJ market, which represented 19 percent of the division's sales, was the focus of attention. Westfield had a 23 percent unit market share and was one of the largest providers of cans to FCJ producers.

Licensing the Plastitek thermoforming process would provide three strategic advantages: (1) a technological advantage (key benefits were the in-line forming process and control of thickness uniformity), (2) a proprietary position (competitors would be blockaded from this technology), and (3) first-mover status in the FCJ market.

Although the FCJ market was significant for Westfield, students might debate the basic attractiveness of this market. The case suggests that there is little loyalty on the part of juice producers, and unit growth is low (less than 5 percent) because of the consumer trend toward buying chilled ready-to-serve juice.

Discounted Cash Flow Analysis

Superficially, the case problem involves product pricing, but more careful examination reveals that the case requires a DCF analysis where the target rate of return is given and the breakeven unit price is to be determined.

Exhibit A presents a summary of the assumptions necessary to develop the financial forecast. One important aspect of the assumptions may merit discussion and analytical attention: the assumptions ignore erosion of the old FCJ composite-can product line and potential displacement of equipment. The assignment questions encourage students to ignore these effects and, therefore, may produce an overly optimistic estimate of breakeven unit price. On the other hand, the case is ambiguous on the necessity of equipment displacement; Westfield is a significant producer of composite packaging products and might be able to divert the equipment to other composite products.

The analysis begins as an equivalent-annuity problem. The net investment is $2,568,000.[1] At the end of the project's life, receivables and inventory are assumed to be liquidated at book value, $637,000, which has a present value of $176,000 at 15 percent. At a discount rate of 15 percent and a project life of 8 years, the annual cash flow from operations is found by determining the equivalent 8-year annuity that has a present value just equal to $2,392,000.[2] The solution is $533,000. (If the life of the equipment is 10 years, the equivalent annuity is $476,000.)

When we know the required "bottom line" and have assumptions for the interim-line items, we need only solve for the unit price. Exhibit B shows the breakeven unit price to be $45.68 ($44.52 if the equipment lasts 10 years).

Comparison: Composite and Plastic Cans

With breakeven unit pricing in mind, the tradeoffs involved in this new product introduction emerge more clearly than before. The all-plastic can is 11.5 percent more expensive than the composite can (cost of $40.96). The relatively higher price of the plastic can reflects the recovery of the $2.1 million capital expenditure. The price difference may be a fatal flaw. FCJ is a commodity product; presumably the FCJ producers are highly cost sensitive and will strongly resist the higher price can unless the can will differentiate the FCJ product. The ability to differentiate depends on the novelty of the plastic itself, since there remain some questions about the quality of the graphics on the plastic can.

On the other hand, the plastic can has a lower variable cost ($28.06) than the composite can ($33.30); the higher dollar contribution of the plastic can suggests higher operating leverage in this product line, and higher profitability at higher volumes, although, unfortunately, the breakeven was calculated assuming production at maximum capacity (three shifts, seven days per week).

Strategic Decision

The economic unattractiveness of this project will motivate many students to reject it. Yet some strategic considerations may mitigate this conclusion. First, Westfield is relatively new to the production of plastic cans. Adoption of this project might stimulate the transformation of Westfield toward a multi-material base of products. Diversifying the productive base of the business away from wood-based materials could have a long-run advantage. Second, licensing the Plastitek technology would pre-empt competitors from this cost-advantaged production process. Finally, entry into plastic cans at this early date might enable Westfield to define the competitive terrain for years to come.

---

[1] Consisting of fixed capital investment (-$2,099,000), investment in accounts receivable (-$240,000), and inventory (-$397,000) and an investment tax credit (+168,000).

[2] This amount is equal to the initial investment of $2,568,000 less the present value, $176,000, of the liquidation of receivables and inventory.

Item	Assumption
Annual volume (thousands of units)	81,000
Target return on investment	15%
Sales deductions (percentage of sales)	3.5%
($ thousands)	$129*
Variable mfg. costs (1,000 units)	$28.06
Plant costs ($ thousands)	$330
Book depreciation (straight-line years)	8 years
(percent of sales)	5%
($ thousands)	$175*
Fixed capital ($ thousands)	$2,099
Accounts receivable (days sales)	25
($ thousands)	$240*
Inventories (days inventories)	50
($ thousands)	$397**
Life of investment	8 years
Tax rate .49	

Assumptions Ignored in Basic Analysis

Annual inflation	5%
Life of investment	10 Years
Displacement of old equipment	$500,000
Erosion of composite can line	NAv

*Any assumption based on a percentage of sales introduces simultaneity into the computations: one is solving for sales and costs simultaneously. A simple solution is to estimate a dollar figure for the costs based on a moderate sales level, such as $3,500,000.

**Estimated assuming cost of goods at $2,900,000 per year.

EXHIBIT B Solving for Breakeven Product Price

Item	8-Year Scenario	10-Year Scenario
Unit price (thousands)	$ 45.68	$ 44.52
Volume	81,000	81,000
Gross sales	$3,700,000	$3,606,000
Sales deductions	129,000	129,000
Net sales	3,571,000	3,477,000
Variable costs	(2,273,000)	(2,273,000)
Gross profit	1,298,000	1,204,000
Plant costs	(330,000)	(330,000)
Depreciation	(262,000)	(262,000)
Mktg., tech., and admin. allocation	(175,000)	(175,000)
Pretax profit	531,000	437,000
Tax expense	(260,000)	223,000
Net profit	271,000	214,000
Depreciation	262,000	262,000
Cash flow, ops.	$ 533,000	$ 476,000

Boggs Mineral Company

SYNOPSIS AND OBJECTIVES

This producer of magnetite is considering which of four capacity-expansion alternatives to pursue. One possibility is to expand the existing facilities; the other three involve building new plants at locations closer to customers. The four alternatives illustrate tradeoffs between fixed and variable costs. The task of the student is to determine the relevant incremental costs associated with each alternative and determine their present value.

The primary objective of this case is to exercise the concept of relevant costs in project evaluation. In addition, the case is a useful vehicle for illustrating the cost (and value) tradeoffs implied by different marketing and production strategies. The case provides a good opportunity to exercise simple computer spreadsheet skills.

STUDY QUESTIONS

1. What are the cash flows for each alternative?

2. What tradeoffs determine the relative attractiveness of each alternative?

3. What should Stiffler do?

TEACHING PLAN

(10 minutes) Why is Boggs considering expanding its capacity? This discussion should develop the basic structure of the problem and motivate the analysis.

(50 minutes) What is the present value of cash flows associated with each alternative? The discount rate is given, so most of the discussion will center on the identification of relevant costs.

(10 minutes) What accounts for the difference in value among the alternatives? This discussion should highlight the different mixes of fixed and variable costs and the different incremental magnitudes by location.

(10 minutes) What should Stiffler do? The closing segment should integrate the quantitative analysis with strategic considerations.

ANALYSIS

Students often confuse standard and variable costs. A review of standard costing may be helpful for the students.

Teaching note prepared by Robert R. Fair and James R. Freeland. Copyright (c) 1989, by the Darden Graduate Business School Sponsors, Charlottesville, VA.

Boggs Mineral Company is faced with a facilities-planning decision. Although a number of qualitative factors are mentioned in the case, none will dominate the decision. Stiffler must perform a cash-flow analysis to determine the economic benefit of each alternative.

The first step is to determine contribution per ton for each alternative, which is done here in Exhibit A. Variable manufacturing costs can be derived from standard and fixed costs given in the case. Variable manufacturing costs apparently differ for each location (see also Exhibit B.)

Students are often confused about what additional fixed overhead is relevant and should be assigned to each alternative. Alternatives 2 and 3 require no additional fixed costs of overhead, despite the fact that, in alternative 3, the case says that 25 percent of the existing $540,000 of overhead will be assigned to Magsuspend operation. Such a cost is *not* relevant, because the fixed overhead will be a cost regardless of whether Magsuspend is produced at Middletown. On the other hand, the Hillside location (alternative 4) will incur an additional overhead cost of $135,000. This cost is relevant.

Exhibit C compares alternative 1 (no expansion) with alternative 2 (expansion at Adams site). Alternative 2 generates cash flows by expanding capacity, so that both the West Virginia and Pennsylvania markets can be served, and by generating depreciation tax savings on the investment. Ten years was chosen as the economic life of the investment because it corresponds to the tax life. This analysis is quite conservative for three reasons. First, the productive life of the Magsuspend plant should be longer than ten years. Second, Magsuspend demand is assumed to level off in 1989. This assumption is quite conservative, considering the growth in demand for coal that has already been experienced. Finally, the plant is assumed to have no terminal value, that, in fact, book value will approximate real value. Given the nature of the investment, to assume that it will be valueless after only ten years is conservative. These conservative influences are offset, however, by the case fact that, after five years, prices charged to West Virginia distributors will be forced lower as distribution costs rise. The analysis in Exhibit C considers this potential change in price.

The hurdle rate suggested by the case is 10 percent. As shown in Exhibit C, the net present value (NPV) at 10 percent of a $1,500,000 investment is $981,000. The internal rate of return is 20.31 percent, and payback occurs within 6 1/4 years.

Alternative 3 is to build a plant in Middletown, Virginia. Cash flows will come from four sources: additional contribution from Pennsylvania sales, additional contribution from West Virginia sales, contribution from new sales, and depreciation tax savings. These amounts are totaled in Exhibit D, which compares alternative 1 to alternative 3.

Using the 10 percent hurdle rate, the NPV of this investment is $1,992,000. The internal rate of return is 24.39 percent, and payback is within 5 1/2 years. Despite its larger initial outlay, alternative 3 is preferable to alternatives 1 or 2 on an economic basis.

Alternative 4 was not considered. As shown in Exhibits A and B, contribution per ton is less than alternative 3 for West Virginia sales, and the initial investment is higher. There is also the problem of additional fixed expense for overhead at Hillsdale.

Certain qualitative factors seem to favor the Middletown location. Middletown offers greater flexibility than other alternatives, since West Virginia is the most rapidly growing coal area. A plant at Middletown can offer better customer service and has less chance of being caught in a margin squeeze if distributor freight rates increase. Boggs will be matching moves of competitors who have already built plants to serve West Virginia. In the event

184

of a price war, Boggs can absorb price cuts without losing market share. A Pennsylvania location could not absorb price cuts because of the higher freight costs.

The Adams location is favored only by manpower considerations. Boggs wants to avoid cutbacks that would occur if production were halved at Adams, but there are a number of ways to avoid cutbacks. First, the Middletown plant can be phased in gradually as demand increases. Adams produced only 28,000 tons in 1983, so an immediate hiring freeze might reduce the need for hiring extra men and then firing them when Middletown opens. Overtime could be used to handle Adams' demand until the Middletown plant opens. Employees can be retrained or moved to the Middletown plant. If necessary, the Middletown assignment can be treated as temporary, and employees can be returned as demand at Adams increases.

An alternative not specifically listed but of some importance is the procurement of the mine in North Carolina. Some students will pick this up. If not, their attention should be directed to it. For an investment of $3.75 million, Boggs can save $44 − $10 = $34 for each ton. Thus, if Boggs were to use more than ($3,750,000)/($34) = 110,294 tons, this alternative would appear to be worthwhile.

RECOMMENDATION

Locate the new plant at Middletown. Investigate developing Boggs's own source for Magnetite. The rough figures provided in the case for the North Carolina source indicate the investment may satisfy Boggs's rate-of-return criterion, especially with savings in freight costs to the Middletown plant and increased production.

EXHIBIT A Comparison of Contribution/Ton for Alternatives 1 Through 4

	Do Nothing 1	Expand Adams 2	New Mill at Middletown 3		New Mill at Hillsdale 4	
			West Virginia	Pennsylvania	West Virginia	Pennsylvania
Selling price	$145.85	$145.85	$178.00	$153.50	$175.25	$153.50
Materials cost	44.00	44.00	44.00	44.00	44.00	44.00
Freight	19.15	19.15	36.10	19.15	38.75	19.15
Variable manufacturing cost*	42.55	42.55	45.40	42.55	42.85	42.55
Contribution	40.15	40.15	52.50	47.80	46.65	47.80
After-tax contribution**	$ 21.68	$ 21.68	$ 28.35	$ 25.81	$ 25.19	$ 25.81

*Variable cost/Ton = $\dfrac{\text{Standard manufacturing cost}}{\text{Ton}} - \dfrac{\text{(Overhead fixed costs)}}{\text{(Tons produced)}}$;

e.g., for Adams Plant: $42.55 = $\dfrac{\$51.85}{\text{Ton}} - \dfrac{(\$260,000)}{(28,000 \text{ tons})}$.

**Tax rate = 46%.

EXHIBIT B Factors Involved in Boggs's Alternatives

	Alternatives			
	2	3		4
	Adams	Middletown	Adams	Hillsdale
Investment	$1,500K	$2,250K	–	$3.090K
Installation period (months)	3	6		8
"Per Ton" Data				
Selling price	$145.85	$178.00	$153.50	$172.25
Material cost	44.00	44.00	44.00	44.00
Freight	19.15	36.10	19.15	38.75
Standard cost	51.85	50.90	51.85	48.25
Absorbed fixed cost*	9.30	5.50	9.29	5.50
Variable manufacturing cost	42.55	45.40	42.55	42.75
Contribution before tax**	40.15	52.50	47.80	46.75
Contribution after tax†	$ 21.68	$ 28.35	$ 25.81	$ 25.25
Add capacity	yes	yes	yes	yes

*$\dfrac{\text{Fixed costs}}{\text{Volume}} = \dfrac{\$260,000}{28,000 \text{ tons}} = \dfrac{\$9.30}{\text{Ton}}$.

**Contribution before tax = Selling price – (Material, Freight, Variable manufacturing costs).

†Contribution after tax = (1 – 46%) x Contribution before tax.

EXHIBIT C Incremental Benefit of Alternative 2 (Expansion at Adams Location) over Alternative 1 (No Growth): Net Present Value @ 10% Rate (dollars in thousands)

Year	Additional Sales (thousand tons)	Additional Contribution* (thousand tons x $21.68)	Depreciation** Tax Shield	Cash Inflow	PV Factor @ 10%	PV Amount	Cumulative
83	0			($1,500.00)	1.0	($1,500.00)	($1,500.00)
84	2	$ 43.36	$69	112.36	.909	102.14	(1,397.86)
85	6	130.00	69	199.00	.826	164.37	(1,233.49)
86	11	238.48	69	307.48	.751	230.92	(1,002.57)
87	16	346.88	69	415.88	.683	284.05	(718.52)
88	20	433.60	69	502.60	.621	312.12	(406.40)
89	24	520.32	69	589.32	.564	332.38	(74.02)
90	24	520.32	69	589.32	.513	302.32	228.30†
91	24	520.32	69	589.32	.467	275.21	503.51
92	24	520.32	69	589.32	.424	249.87	753.38
93	24	$520.32	$69	$589.32	.386	227.48	$ 980.86

*Contribution/ton equal to price less raw-material cost, freight, variable cost, and taxes, or (145.85 – 44 – 19.15 – 42.55) x .54. Depreciation not considered in calculation.

**($1,500 initial investment – 10-year life) x .46 tax rate.

†Payback = 6 1/4 years @ 10% rate. Rate of return = 20.31%.

138

EXHIBIT D Alternative 3 versus Alternative 1 (Expansion at Middletown versus No Growth): Net Present Value @ 10% Rate (dollars in thousands)

Year	Contribution from Adams*	Contribution from Middletown**	Contribution under Alternative 1†	Net Contribution††
83				($2,250.00)
84	$361.34	$510.30	$650.40	$ 221.24
85	412.96	567.00	650.40	329.56
86	464.58	652.05	650.40	466.23
87	516.20	737.10	650.40	602.90
88	567.82	793.90	650.40	711.22
89	619.44	850.50	650.40	819.54
90	619.44	850.50	650.40	819.54
91	619.44	850.50	650.40	819.54
92	619.44	850.50	650.40	819.54
93	$619.44	$850.50	$650.40	$ 819.54

Depreciation Tax Shield#	Cash Inflow	PV Factor @ 10%	PV Amount	Cumulative
	($2,250.00)	1.0	($2,250.00)	($2,250.00)
103.50	324.74	.909	295.19	(1954.81)
103.50	433.06	.826	357.71	(1597.10)
103.50	569.73	.751	427.87	(1169.23)
103.50	706.40	.683	482.47	(686.76)
103.50	814.72	.621	505.94	(180.82)
103.50	923.04	.564	520.59	339.77##
103.50	923.04	.513	473.52	813.29
103.50	923.04	.467	431.06	1244.35
103.50	923.04	.424	391.37	1635.72
103.50	923.04	.386	356.29	1992.01

*Tons/Year x $25.81/Ton.

**Tons/Year x $28.35/Ton.

†30,000 Tons x $21.68/Ton.

††(Contribution from Adams + Contribution from Middletown) – Contribution. under alternative 1.   Note: Depreciation not considered in this calculation.

#($2250 initial investment – 10-year life) x .46 tax rate.

##Payback = 5 1/2 Years.   Rate of return = 24.39%.

Sandbridge Company (A)

SYNOPSIS AND OBJECTIVES

The manager of planning and development of this engineering firm is wrestling with how rapidly to introduce a new computer-aided design (CAD) system into the firm. The system would quadruple the productivity of the average worker, reduce turnaround time on customer requests, and possibly permit Sandbridge to enter new markets. Complicating this decision are the facts that the system would justify elimination of redundant workers and that the firm is wholly owned by 400 of the firm's 600 employees.

This case is an excellent vehicle for considering the tradeoffs associated with the introduction of new, labor-saving technology. The task of the student is to recommend the *rate* of new-technology introduction. This decision involves integrating operational, financial, organizational, and strategic considerations.

STUDY QUESTIONS

1. What are the pros and cons of acquiring CAD systems?

2. Compare the effects on Sandbridge of (a) acquiring four systems per year over the next five years, (b) acquiring enough systems to keep employment steady, and (c) acquiring no CAD systems.

3. How many CAD systems should Sandbridge buy in the next five years?

TEACHING PLAN

(10 minutes) What is Sandbridge's business? Its strategy? How well has it performed under this strategy? The strategy of rapid growth is associated with volatile margins. Improving labor productivity emerges as a strategic imperative.

(10 minutes) Why is Sandbridge considering introducing interactive graphic design systems (IGDS)? This discussion will be a review of the major advantages of CAD.

(10 minutes) Why not convert completely and immediately to IGDS? This straw man is designed to elicit the adverse consequences of rapid introduction.

(40 minutes) How much of an effect do different rates of CAD investment have on Sandbridge? This question should elicit a comparison of project financial results under the three alternative assumptions of assignment question 2.

Teaching note prepared by Robert F. Bruner and John L. Colley, Jr. Copyright (c) 1989 by the Darden Graduate Business School Sponsors, Charlottesville, VA.

(10 minutes) What rate of CAD introduction should Robert Lane recommend? What should he say to sell his recommendation to senior management and the firm's employee-owners?

ANALYSIS

Sandbridge's performance during the past three years has been characterized by substantial swings in earnings, as can be seen in the following table of revenues, net income, return on net assets (RONA), return on equity (ROE) and return on sales (ROS):

	Base - 2	Base - 1	Base Year
Revenues (000s)	$30,943	$41,893	$46,488
Net income	$ 937	$ 2,126	$ 1,480
RONA	10.7%	18.5%	10.9%
ROE	14.5	25.9	14.1
ROS	3.0	5.1	3.2
Operating exp./ Total revenue	45.2%	41.3%	46%

The major cause of these swings in performance was variation in operating expenses relative to revenues. The variation in gross margin could be from variations in the billing multiplier, in the volume of billable hours, and in labor productivity. The multiplier and volume are primarily determined by the market for Sandbridge's services. As stated in the case, Sandbridge faces competition in the paper and pulp market, and presumably in its other markets. The competition probably reduces Sandbridge's pricing power. Thus, to maintain a consistent level of profitability or to increase it, Sandbridge has to control its expenses. Improving labor productivity, therefore, is an important means of improving financial performance.

Assuming that the billable hours of technical employees constitute the direct-cost portion of the income statement, that cost can be considered analogous to the cost of goods sold for a manufacturer. With the company operating without CAD, that cost would vary in direct proportion to the level of billable hours sold. Any hours that were nonbillable would, therefore, be included in the operating expenses. For example, if an engineer were paid for 8 hours of work but was able to bill only 6.8 hours to specific jobs, the 1.2 hours of time would become an operating expense. Therefore, an increase in the productivity of technical employees has a dramatic effect on profitability because of the impact of the multiplier. As productivity increases, operating expenses as a percentage of revenue decrease, and overall profitability rises. On this basis, and with all other relationships remaining constant, one could assume that productivity is lowest during periods when profitability is lowest.

While the firm has outperformed the Fortune 500 in ROE and RONA over the five-year period, "Base-4" through "Base," improved labor productivity could apparently yield even better performance than presently exhibited. The implementation of CAD could thus be very beneficial to Sandbridge's future.

191

Performance Indicators

For this note, the case data on expected cost and expected changes in cost were used to examine CAD acquisition at three levels and three utilization rates. The first level specified no CAD acquisition. The second was a moderate strategy with four CAD purchases per year. Last was the "big buy" strategy, with purchases offsetting the need to hire new technical personnel.

Starting with the expected growth rate in billable hours, two variables (gross fixed assets purchased and the change in labor required) were altered to develop scenarios to be studied. All other variables affecting the firm's performance were assumed to remain constant under each of the cases being examined. The impact of increased CAD conversion on Sandbridge as a result of the increased productivity of the technical labor could then be assessed.

If Sandbridge were to purchase enough systems to keep employment steady over the next 5 years, the firm would need 13, 5, 7, 8, and 6 systems in years 1-5, respectively. Exhibit A shows how these figures were calculated, and Exhibit B shows how the labor savings of each strategy were developed. A more moderate approach would be to purchase 4 systems per year. Exhibits C, D, and E present the company's projected financial statements in years 1 through 5 that would result from each of the three acquisition strategies. These exhibits assume a depreciation life of 5 years on newly purchased fixed assets. Depreciation on existing fixed assets was assumed to be $1 million each in years 1-3. All excess cash was distributed as dividends once debt was repaid.

Exhibit F presents a summary of financial ratios over the 5 years for the three strategies. The "buy big" strategy shows better performance in year 5, with an ROS of 23.2 percent and an ROE of 56.1 percent. The 4-per-year strategy has results that are almost as good, ROS of 18.1 percent and ROE of 54.1 percent. These performance figures are significantly better than those for a no-buy strategy.

CAD Tradeoffs

The attractiveness of the CAD conversion suggested by the forecasts discussed in the last section is balanced by other considerations: (1) the rate of technological innovation in CAD equipment, (2) the effect on employee morale, and (3) the effect on the operating leverage of the firm.

First, CAD systems with superior operating features and lower cost will probably be introduced in the future, granting a competitive advantage to those firms buying the newest systems. Jumping wholesale into CAD systems currently available thus involves a gamble that no better systems will be introduced *soon*. CAD conversion today would create some technological inflexibility, at least temporarily, as Sandbridge sought to earn a payback on its equipment investment.

Second, the new CAD technology would have an imponderable effect on employee morale. There would be a difficult training transition, and younger employees might grasp CAD more readily than older employees. In addition, whether or not CAD was popular, the choice of which employees were to receive the new equipment first might cause friction. On the other hand, if it eliminated the need to hire and lay off technical people as volume increased or decreased, CAD could result in a more stable work force. It could also expand the opportunity to increase wages for deserving technical employees.

Third, the substitution from labor into capital equipment is bound to increase the operating leverage of Sandbridge. The effects of this capital-for-labor substitution are illustrated in Exhibits G, H, and I, which present breakeven graphs under the three strategic alternatives. The instructor can prepare overhead transparencies of these graphs and overlay the "buy big" graph on top of the "buy none" graph to show the effects of the substitution. One can make several observations: with the "buy big" commitment to CAD, (1) the base of fixed costs rises, (2) the slope of the total cost line falls (i.e., variable cost falls because of increases in efficiencies), (3) the breakeven volume falls, and (4) operating leverage increases. (These effects are imperceptible in comparing the "buy four" and "buy none" graphs.) With higher operating leverage comes dramatic gains in profit from volume growth, but the most important implication of these effects regards the competitive posture of the firm. A lower volume breakeven would give Sandbridge greater pricing flexibility, which in a recession could be a decisive advantage.

Recommendation

The strategic and financial attractions of the CAD conversion outweigh the possible negative considerations. The decision is "how fast?" rather than "whether." While the major purchase strategy would be better from a purely quantitative standpoint, qualitative factors point toward a slower approach. If the company budgeted for 4 CAD systems per year, but market changes dictated that it buy more, it could easily adjust. If, on the other hand, it bought 13 the first year and a new system at a much lower price became available, Sandbridge might have incurred unnecessary cost and reduced its flexibility. As the industry leader, Sandbridge has less incentive to move quickly into a new technology than competitors do, but it must watch developments carefully and be flexible enough to respond to changes.

EXHIBIT A Calculation of CAD-System Purchases to Maintain Present Level of
          Technical Employees

Year Base + 1

    1,660   (total employees)
    –236   (nontechnical)

    1,424   (technical)

    1,424 x 0.225 (projected growth in billable hours)
          = 320.4 new technical employees required

    320.4/24 (productivity improvement/system) = 13.35 systems

      13 CAD systems

Year Base + 2

    1,744 x 0.0666 = 115.1
    115.1/24   = 4.80 systems

        5 CAD systems

Year Base + 3

    1,859 x 0.087 = 161.7
    161.7/24   = 6.74

        7 CAD systems

Year Base + 4

    2,021 x 0.096 = 194.0
    194.0/24   = 8.08

    8 CAD systems

Year Base + 5

    2,215 x 0.067 = 148.4
    148.4/24   = 6.18

        6 CAD systems

EXHIBIT B Calculation of Labor Savings with Purchase of CAD Systems: Major
          Purchase Scenario

Year Base + 1

$$\frac{1.205 \text{ (present labor hours/billable hour)}}{1,744 \text{ (employees required w/o CAD systems)}} = \frac{X}{1,424 \text{ (employees with}}$$
$$\text{13 CAD systems).}$$

X = 0.984 (labor hours/billable hour with 13 CAD systems).
Change from 1.205 to 0.984 = −18.34% (reduction in labor
      hours/billable hours = productivity improvement)

Year Base + 2

$$\frac{0.984}{1859} = \frac{X}{1,744}$$

$$X = 0.923$$

Change = −6.19%

Year Base + 3

$$\frac{0.923}{2021} = \frac{X}{1,859}$$

$$X = 0.849$$

Change = −8.01%

Year Base + 4

$$\frac{0.849}{2215} = \frac{X}{2,021}$$

$$X = 0.775$$

Change = −8.77%

Year Base + 5

$$\frac{0.775}{2363} = \frac{X}{2,215}$$

$$X = 0.726$$

Change = −6.25%

EXHIBIT C Buy None (thousands except per share data)

Income Statements

	Base	1	2	3	4	5
Professional fees	$46,488	$64,346	$74,697	$88,585	$105,924	$123,080
Direct costs						
Technical salaries	21,952	41,464	47,737	56,041	66,335	76,442
Nontechnical salaries	5,486	6,185	7,001	8,317	9,451	10,542
Depreciation		1,000	1,200	1,500	900	1,400
Total	27,438	48,650	55,938	65,859	76,686	88,383
Gross margin	19,050	15,696	18,759	22,726	29,238	34,696
General and admin. expenses	5,856	7,174	7,647	8,312	9,110	9,721
Income before income taxes	13,194	8,522	11,112	14,414	20,127	24,975
Provision for income taxes	(1,100)	(3,665)	(4,778)	(6,198)	(8,655)	(10,739)
Net income	$12,094	$4,858	$6,334	$8,216	$11,473	$14,236
Earnings per share	$3.02					
Dividends/common share	1.18	1.42	1.70	3.74	8.22	18.09
Retained earnings at beginning						
of year	12,094	5,966	8,899	11,211	20,518	23,963
Net income		4,858	6,334	8,216	11,473	14,236
Cash dividends paid	(579)	(1,925)	(4,021)	1,091	(8,027)	(10,941)
Capital stock purchased						
and retired	(5)	0	0	0	0	0
Balance at end of year	$5,966	$8,899	$11,211	$20,518	$23,963	$27,258

EXHIBIT C (continued)

Balance Sheets

	Base	1	2	3	4	5
ASSETS						
Current assets						
Cash	$ 764	$ 1,000	$ 2,000	$ 9,500	$ 9,500	$ 9,500
Accts. rec.	8,632	12,340	14,325	16,989	20,314	23,604
Prepaid expenses	132	0	0	0	0	0
Total current assets	9,528	13,340	16,325	26,489	29,814	33,104
Other assets	1,141	1,255	1,381	1,519	1,671	1,838
Fixed assets						
Cost	14,092	15,092	16,592	18,592	21,092	24,092
Less accum. deprec.	(3,235)	(4,235)	(5,435)	(6,935)	(7,835)	(9,235)
Net fixed assets	10,857	10,857	11,157	11,657	13,257	14,857
Total assets	$21,526	$25,452	$28,863	$39,664	$44,742	$49,799
LIABILITIES						
Current liabilities						
Notes payable	$ 2,725	$ 0	$ 0	$ 0	$ 0	$ 0
Current portion of long-term debt	301	0	0	0	0	0
Accts. pay.	1,733	7,331	8,429	9,924	11,555	13,318
Current inc. tax	25	25	25	25	25	25
Dividends payable	154	154	154	154	154	154
Other current liabilities	2,975	2,975	2,975	2,975	2,975	2,975
Total current liabilities	7,913	10,485	11,583	13,078	14,709	16,472
Long-term debt	2,260	0	0	0	0	0
Deferred Exec. Compensation	859	0	0	0	0	0
Total liabilities	11,032	10,485	11,583	13,078	14,709	16,472

197

EXHIBIT C (continued)

Balance Sheets

	Base	1	2	3	4	5
STOCKHOLDERS' EQUITY						
Capital stock	555	555	555	555	555	555
Capital in excess of par	3,973	5,514	5,514	5,514	5,514	5,514
Retained earnings	5,966	8,899	11,211	20,518	23,963	27,258
Total stockholders' equity	10,494	14,968	17,280	26,587	30,032	33,327
Total liabilities and equity	$21,526	$25,452	$28,863	$39,664	$44,742	$49,799

EXHIBIT D Buy Four per Year (thousands except per share data)

Income Statements

	Base	1	2	3	4	5
Revenues	$46,488	$64,346	$74,697	$88,585	$105,924	$123,080
Direct costs						
Technical salaries	21,952	39,182	42,781	47,838	54,171	59,889
Nontechnical salaries	5,486	6,185	7,001	8,317	9,451	10,542
Depreciation		1,800	2,700	3,700	3,800	5,000
Total	27,438	47,168	52,482	59,855	67,422	75,431
Gross margin	19,050	17,178	22,215	28,729	38,502	47,649
General and admin. expenses	5,856	7,174	7,647	8,312	9,110	9,721
Income before income taxes	13,194	10,004	14,568	20,417	29,391	37,928
Provision for income taxes	(1,100)	(4,302)	(6,264)	(8,779)	(12,638)	(16,309)
Net income	$12,094	$ 5,702	$ 8,304	$11,638	$ 16,753	$ 21,619
Earnings per share	$3.02					
Dividends/common share	1.18	1.42	1.70	3.74	8.22	18.09
Retained earnings at beginning of year						
Net income	12,094	5,966	10,975	15,432	25,922	29,959
		5,702	8,304	11,638	16,753	21,619
Cash dividends paid	(579)	(694)	(3,847)	(1,147)	(12,716)	(18,369)
Capital stock purchased and retired	(5)	0	0	0	0	0
Balance at end of year	$ 5,966	$10,975	$15,432	$25,922	$ 29,959	$ 33,210

Balance Sheets

	Base	1	2	3	4	5
ASSETS						
Current assets						
Cash	$ 764	$ 1,000	$ 2,000	$ 9,500	$ 9,500	$ 9,500
Accts. rec.	8,632	12,340	14,325	16,989	20,314	23,604
Prepaid expenses	132	0	0	0	0	0
Total current assets	9,528	13,340	16,325	26,489	29,814	33,104
Other assets	1,141	1,255	1,381	1,519	1,671	1,838
Fixed assets						
Cost	14,092	18,092	22,592	27,592	33,092	39,092
Less accum. deprec.	(3,235)	(5,035)	(7,735)	(11,435)	(15,235)	(20,235)
Net fixed assets	10,857	13,057	14,857	16,157	17,857	18,857
Total assets	$21,526	$27,652	$32,563	$44,164	$49,342	$53,799
LIABILITIES						
Current liabilities						
Notes payable	$ 2,725	$ 2,725	$ 0	$ 0	$ 0	$ 0
Current portion of long-term debt	301	0	0	0	0	0
Accts. pay.	1,733	7,107	7,908	9,019	10,159	11,366
Current inc. tax	25	25	25	25	25	25
Dividends payable	154	154	154	154	154	154
Other current liabilities	2,975	2,975	2,975	2,975	2,975	2,975
Total current liabilities	7,913	12,986	11,062	12,173	13,313	14,520
Long-term debt	2,260	0	0	0	0	0
Deferred Exec. Compensation	859	0	0	0	0	0
Total liabilities	11,032	12,986	11,062	12,173	13,313	14,520

EXHIBIT D (continued)

Balance Sheets

	Base	1	2	3	4	5
STOCKHOLDERS' EQUITY						
Capital stock	555	555	555	555	555	555
Capital in excess of par	3,973	5,514	5,514	5,514	5,514	5,514
Retained earnings	5,966	10,975	15,432	25,922	29,959	33,210
Total stockholders' equity	10,494	17,044	21,501	31,991	36,028	39,279
Total liabilities and equity	$21,526	$27,652	$32,563	$44,164	$49,342	$53,799

EXHIBIT E Buy Big (thousands except per share data)

Income Statements

	Base	1	2	3	4	5
Professional Fees	$46,488	$64,346	$74,697	$88,585	$105,924	$123,080
Direct costs						
Technical salaries	21,952	33,848	36,556	39,481	42,639	46,050
Nontechnical salaries	5,486	6,185	7,001	8,317	9,451	10,542
Depreciation		3,150	4,200	5,650	6,350	7,850
Total	27,438	43,184	47,757	53,448	58,440	64,442
Gross margin	19,050	21,162	26,940	35,137	47,484	58,638
General and admin. expenses	5,856	7,174	7,647	8,312	9,110	9,721
Income before income taxes	13,194	13,988	19,293	26,824	38,373	48,917
Provision for income taxes	(1,100)	(6,015)	(8,296)	(11,534)	(16,500)	(21,034)
Net income	$12,094	$7,973	$10,997	$15,290	$21,873	$27,883
Earnings per share	$3.02					
Dividends/common share	1.18	1.42	1.70	3.74	8.22	18.09
Retained earnings at beginning of year		5,966	13,246	20,794	31,838	36,713
Net income	12,094	7,973	10,997	15,290	21,873	27,883
Cash dividends paid	(579)	(694)	(3,449)	(4,246)	(16,998)	(25,680)
Capital stock purchased and retired	(5)	0	0	0	0	0
Balance at end of year	$5,966	$13,246	$20,794	$31,838	$36,713	$38,915

EXHIBIT E (continued)

Balance Sheets

	Base	1	2	3	4	5
ASSETS						
Current assets						
Cash	$ 764	$ 1,000	$ 2,000	$ 9,500	$ 9,500	$ 9,500
Accts. rec.	8,632	12,340	14,325	16,989	20,314	23,604
Prepaid expenses	132	0	0	0	0	0
Total current assets	9,528	13,340	16,325	26,489	29,814	33,104
Other assets	1,141	1,255	1,381	1,519	1,671	1,838
Fixed assets						
Cost	14,092	24,842	30,092	37,342	45,842	53,342
Less accum. deprec.	(3,235)	(6,385)	(10,585)	(16,235)	(22,585)	(30,435)
Net fixed assets	10,857	18,457	19,507	21,107	23,257	22,907
Total assets	$21,526	$33,052	$37,213	$49,114	$54,742	$57,849
LIABILITIES						
Current liabilities						
Notes payable	$ 2,725	$ 2,725	$ 0	$ 0	$ 0	$ 0
Current portion of long-term debt	301	0	0	0	0	0
Accts. pay.	1,733	6,507	7,196	8,054	8,806	9,710
Current inc. tax	25	25	25	25	25	25
Dividends payable	154	154	154	154	154	154
Other current liabilities	2,975	2,975	2,975	2,975	2,975	2,975
Total current liabilities	7,913	12,386	10,350	11,208	11,960	12,864
Long-term debt	2,260	1,352	0	0	0	0
Deferred Exec. Compensation	859	0	0	0	0	0
Total liabilities	11,032	13,738	10,350	11,208	11,960	12,864

EXHIBIT E (continued)

Balance Sheets

	Base	1	2	3	4	5
STOCKHOLDERS' EQUITY						
Capital stock	555	555	555	555	555	555
Capital in excess of par	3,973	5,514	5,514	5,514	5,514	5,514
Retained earnings	5,966	13,246	20,794	31,838	36,713	38,915
Total stockholders' equity	10,494	19,351	26,863	37,907	42,782	44,984
Total liabilities and equity	$21,526	$33,052	$37,213	$49,114	$54,742	$57,849

EXHIBIT F Comparative Income Statements: All Three Strategies

	Year				
Buy None	1	2	3	4	5
ROS	7.5%	8.5%	9.3%	10.8%	11.6%
ROA	20.7	23.3	25.7	29.5	30.8
ROE	38.2%	39.3%	41.7%	45.8%	46.4%
No. of technical employees	1,744	1,860	2,021	2,215	2,364
Buy 4/Year					
ROS	9.6%	11.8%	13.8%	16.4%	18.1%
ROA	24.6	28.1	31.8	37.2	40.6
ROE	45.3%	44.1%	45.4%	50.9%	54.1%
No. of technical employees	1,648	1,764	1,925	2,119	2,268
Buy Big					
ROS	14.3%	15.5%	18.2%	21.6%	23.3%
ROA	32.4	30.6	34.2	39.8	45.3
ROE	59.3%	45.7%	44.1%	49.6%	56.1%
No. of technical employees	1,424	1,424	1,424	1,424	1,424

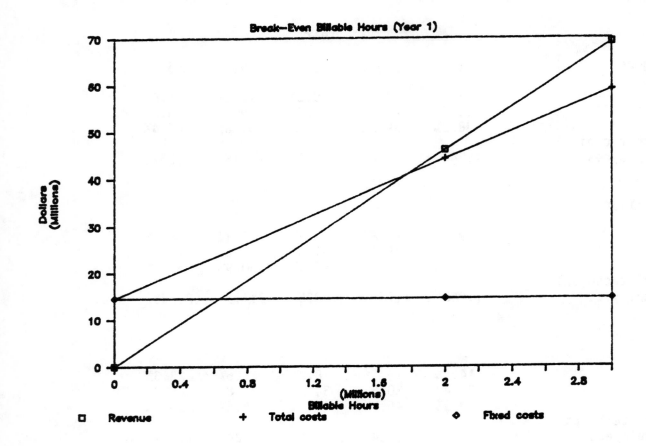

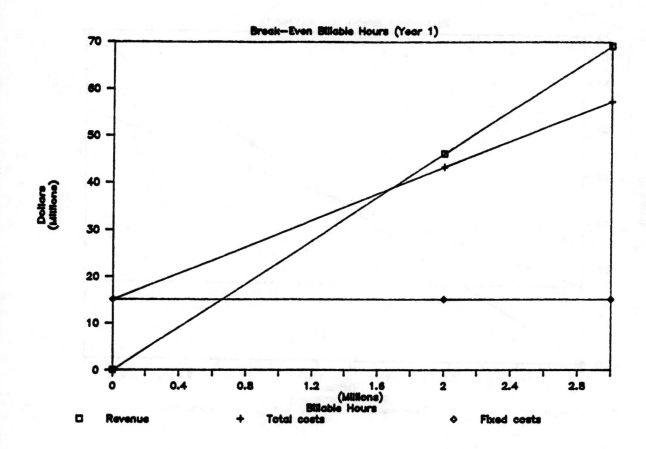

EXHIBIT I Buy Big

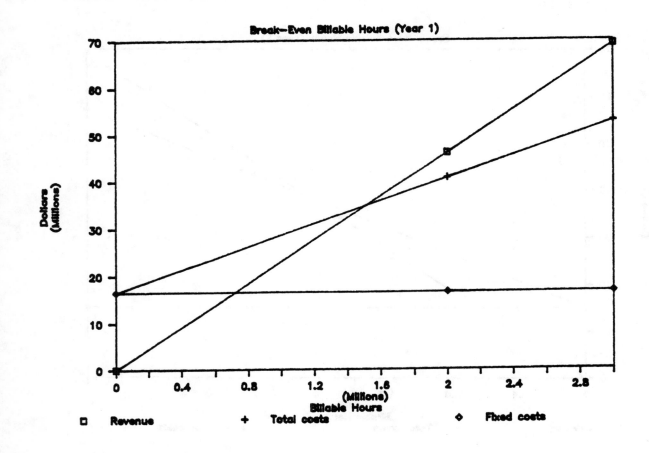

Palmetto Shipping & Stevedoring Co., Inc.

SYNOPSIS AND OBJECTIVES

Palmetto's executive vice president must resolve the issue of whether to rent or own a fleet of tractors. The analysis requires an assessment of tractor usage and calculation of the present value of costs under strategies of renting and owning. The rent/own decision also influences a related decision of whether to merge Palmetto's maintenance shop with those of its competitors in order to reduce costs.

The objective of the case is to introduce rental as one avenue of capital-equipment acquisition and an application of the discounted cash flow framework to the analysis of the rent-versus-own decision. Under consideration are both individual units of equipment as well as entire operating strategies. Ultimately, the case helps illustrate many of the subtle tradeoffs involved in making a decision to rent equipment.

STUDY QUESTIONS

1. What cash flows are associated with the alternative strategies of owning and leasing the tractors? What is the breakeven number of monthly rental hours, above which it makes more sense to own rather than rent a tractor?

2. If William Gibbs should decide to pursue the strategy of owning an optimal number of tractors, how many should Palmetto own?

3. What is the cash flow associated with the strategies of (a) owning 19 tractors, (b) owning the optimal number (i.e., the number you recommended in response to question 2), and (c) renting all tractors?

4. Which strategy should Gibbs recommend?

5. Should Palmetto merge its maintenance shop with those of its competitors?

TEACHING PLAN

(10 minutes) Why is Palmetto considering a strategy of renting its tractors? The purpose of this opening is to frame the general characteristics of renting and the qualitative aspects of renting versus owning. The instructor might prepare to give comments on the generic advantages of leasing.

(15 minutes) What is the optimum number of tractors for Palmetto to own? This addresses the question of the breakeven hours.

Teaching note written by Robert F. Bruner, drawing on some analysis by John L. Colley, Jr. Copyright (c) 1989 by the Darden Graduate Business School Sponsors, Charlottesville, VA.

(25 minutes) How costly is each strategy? This segment should be oriented toward laying out the cash flows associated with the three strategies and calculating their present values (PVs).

(15 minutes) What qualitative considerations might influence the choice between renting, status quo, and optimal owning strategies? Here the class should consider exposure to inflation, technological change, uncertainty about residual value, and other risks.

(15 minutes) What strategy should Gibbs recommend? How many tractors should Palmetto seek to own? Should Palmetto merge its maintenance shop with its competitors?

ANALYSIS

Nature of the Problem

At the start, it is worth highlighting that this case is about an operating strategy based on short-term rentals. This distinction is important, because the general subject of leasing can be decomposed into various types of leases, including financial and operating leases. This perspective is underscored by the fact that the case takes the perspective of the *user* of the equipment, rather than the lessor.

To cast the analytical problem in these terms, in essence, dictates that the analysis focus on the entire *operating strategy* associated with short-term rentals, rather than on the narrower valuation of a stream of rental payments. Other case studies and textbook problems are concerned with valuing a lease as a financial security; this case has a wider scope. More accurately, this case concerns the acquisition of capital equipment (hence its inclusion in the capital-budgeting module of the case book).

This orientation toward operating strategy has a significant influence on the structure of the analysis. The prospective free cash flows will be based on more than just financing flows and tax shields. Also, the appropriate discount rate will be the corporate hurdle rate[1] rather than the after-tax cost of debt. Presumably the risk of the cash flows associated with each operating strategy are more consistent with the corporate hurdle rate than the cost of debt.

Benefits of Renting

The instructor will have the opportunity to highlight some of the generic benefits of renting/leasing during the course of the case discussion. Renting or leasing will be attractive where

• the user's marginal tax rate is less than the lessor's marginal tax rate (i.e., the lessor obtains a larger benefit from a tax writeoff than the lessee);

---

[1] The case is ambiguous on the origin of the 15 percent hurdle rate. Presumably, this is Palmetto's estimated weighted-average cost of capital. In any event, the exact origin of this discount rate is something we wish to skirt in order not to divert the discussion from the more significant teaching points of the case.

- the user does not have a large enough taxable income to take advantage of tax shields such as depreciation or investment tax credits;

- there is a significant risk of technological change, rapid obsolescence, or other effects that would create uncertainty about residual values. Leases shift these risks from the user of the equipment to the lessor;

- the lessor is more skilled at reallocating equipment to higher valued uses than is the user, particularly as the user's need for the equipment wanes;

- lease financing may be more flexible (i.e., in terms of covenants) than borrowing associated with owning;

- the cost of lease financing may be lower than debt financing.

This case is only an indirect illustration of the purely financing benefits, because the nature of the case problem is to value the operating strategy associated with renting, rather than to value the rental stream *per se*.

Breakeven Hours per Tractor

One approach to assessing the attractiveness of renting is to estimate the number of hours of tractor use above which it would be less costly to own than rent. Exhibit A presents the calculation determining the breakeven rental hours per month: it is 47 hours. Exhibit B presents the average hourly use for Palmetto's tractor fleet drawn from case Exhibit 3. Based on that average, owning an additional 7 tractors would be economical.[2]

Present Values of Strategic Alternatives

One can estimate the relative economic attractiveness of the three strategic alternatives (i.e., renting, optimal owning, and status quo) by forecasting the relevant cash flows associated with each strategy, computing the incremental flows between pairs of strategies, and discounting the increments. The pairwise comparison reveals the dominant strategy.

Exhibits C, D, and E present the forecasts of relevant cash flows for each strategy. Note that variations among the forecasts are induced mainly by the number of tractors owned, the timing of tractor acquisitions and dispositions, the hourly tractor rental rate, and the magnitude of mechanics' salaries. For instance, if the rental strategy is adopted, hourly rental expense will fall from $18 to $16.50, and mechanics' salaries will decline by two-fifths (two of five mechanics can be laid off).

Exhibit F discounts the incremental flows. It appears that the rental strategy is the least attractive alternative and that optimal owning is the most attractive. Optimal owning dominates rental by about $1.3 million and dominates the status quo strategy of 19 tractors by $737 thousand.

Sensitivity analysis reveals that the discounted values of the incremental cash flows are sensitive to a few variables, including salvage values of the tractors, utilization hours, and the timing of equipment sales and purchases.

---

[2]The case mentions that Palmetto owns 20 fork lifts. These are to be distinguished from the 19 tractors.

Practically, the implication is that a strategy of optimal ownership of tractors is a gamble on asset values, obtaining enough business to use the tractors fully, and perhaps the ability to extend the life of the tractors beyond nine years.

Qualitative Issues and Recommendation

Plainly, the ultimate recommendation will hinge on factors not easily captured in the simple PV calculations. A list of factors might include uncertainty about maintenance expense, tax exposure, equipment costs and residual values, and perhaps most importantly, the operating implications of renting. Another element is the certainty with which Gibbs can anticipate a fixed rental rate of $16.50 over the nine-year horizon. And finally, Gibbs might worry about the ability of Terminal Services to accommodate any growth in Palmetto's equipment requirements over time.

Ultimately, the decision probably hinges on the desire of management to limit its exposure to costs in the maintenance and equipment department. Repair costs on the fleet of tractors are now beginning to rise as the fleet approaches the average age of five years. By undertaking the renting strategy, Palmetto essentially transfers this cost exposure to Terminal Services.

The use of rental arrangements to transfer benefits to their highest bidder and risks to firms that are able to shoulder them more easily is one of the most important teaching points in the subject area of leasing.

EXHIBIT A Determining Breakeven Hours of Tractor Use

Year	0	1	2	3	4	5	6	7	8	9
Cash flow of owning 1 tractor (@47 hours/month)										
Purchase price	$39,000									
Salvage										$7,800
Repairs		($2,000)	($2,100)	($2,205)	($2,315)	($2,431)	($2,553)	($2,680)	($2,814)	($2,955)
Property tax		(180)	(189)	(198)	(208)	(219)	(230)	(241)	(253)	(266)
Insurance cost		(320)	(336)	(353)	(370)	(389)	(408)	(429)	(450)	(473)
Depreciation		(7,800)	(7,800)	(7,800)	(7,800)	(7,800)	0	0	0	0
Subtotal		(10,300)	(10,425)	(10,556)	(10,694)	(10,839)	(3,191)	(3,350)	(3,518)	4,106
Tax (expense) savings		3,090	3,128	3,167	3,208	3,252	957	1,005	1,055	(1,232)
Add: Depreciation		7,800	7,800	7,800	7,800	7,800	0	0	0	0
Free cash flow from owning	(39,000)	590	503	411	314	213	(2,233)	(2,345)	(2,462)	2,874
Cash flow of leasing 1 tractor (@ 47 hours/month)										
Lease cost/hour		18	19	20	21	22	23	24	25	27
Annual cost		(10,152)	(10,660)	(11,193)	(11,752)	(12,340)	(12,957)	(13,605)	(14,285)	(14,999)
Tax savings		3,046	3,198	3,358	3,526	3,702	3,887	4,081	4,285	4,500
Free cash flow from leasing		(7,106)	(7,462)	(7,835)	(8,227)	(8,638)	(9,070)	(9,523)	(9,999)	(10,499)
Incremental free cash flows	($39,000)	$7,696	$7,964	$8,245	$8,541	$8,851	$6,836	$7,178	$7,537	$13,374

Net PV = $339

Monthly Usage Hours	Net PV of Incremental Free Cash Flow (@15%)	Monthly Usage Hours	Net PV of Incremental Free Cash Flow (@15%)
35	(9,804)	47	339
40	(5,577)	48	1,184
44	(2,196)	49	2,030
45	(1,351)	50	2,875
46	(506)	55	7,101

Rental Tractor	April	May	June	One-Month Average
1	92	127	95	105
2	86	127	91	101
3	67	9	69	77
4	67	74	43	61
5	67	61	43	57
6	63	50	28	47
7	63	50	28	47
8	50	38	28	39
9	43	39	28	37
10	31	32	28	30
11	18	21	28	22
12	18	21	23	21
13	9	19	23	17
14	4	10	23	12
15	4	4	8	5
16		4	8	4
17		4	8	4
18			4	1
19			4	1
20			4	1
21			4	1
22			4	1
23			4	1
24			4	1

EXHIBIT C Cash Flows of Status Quo Strategy

	1987	1988	1989	1990	1991	1992	1993	1994	1995
Equipment purchase*	$ 0	$122,850	$ 0	$541,769	$ 0	$ 0	$209,055	$ 0	$ 0
Equipment sales*	0	36,000	0	168,000	0	0	64,000	0	132,924
Suppl. rental expense**	150,264	157,777	165,666	173,949	182,647	191,779	201,368	211,437	222,008
Tractor repairs, prop. tax, and insurance	47,500	49,875	52,369	54,987	57,737	60,623	63,655	66,837	70,179
Tractor fuel and parts	64,686	67,920	71,316	74,882	78,626	82,558	86,685	91,020	95,571
Shop overhead	324,390	340,610	357,640	375,522	394,298	414,013	434,714	456,449	479,272
Depreciation†	29,600	54,170	24,570	132,924	132,924	132,924	150,165	150,165	41,811
Taxable cash flows	(616,440)	(757,202)	(671,561)	(1,186,033)	(846,231)	(881,897)	(1,081,641)	(975,907)	(775,917)
Tax savings	184,932	227,161	201,468	355,810	253,869	264,569	324,492	292,772	232,775
Add: Depreciation	29,600	54,170	24,570	132,924	132,924	132,924	150,165	150,165	41,811
Add: Nontaxable equip. sales*	0	0	0	0	0	0	0	0	83,622
Total cash flow	($401,908)	($475,871)	($445,523)	($697,299)	($459,438)	($484,404)	($606,984)	($532,971)	($417,709)

215

EXHIBIT C (continued)

*Equipment schedule:

	1987	1988	1989	1990	1991	1992	1993	1994	1995
Number of Years Old									
1									
2							4		
3			3		12		12	4	
4	4			3	3		3	12	4
5	12	4				12		3	12
6		12				3			3
7			4						
8	3	3	12	4	4	4			
9				12					
Total	19	19	19	19	19	19	19	19	19
Less: Tractors disposed	0	3	0	12	0	4	4	0	0
Plus: Tractors acquired	0	3	0	12	0	4	4	0	0
Total	19	19	19	19	19	19	19	19	19
Unit acquisition price	$39,000	$40,950	$42,998	$45,147	$47,405	$49,775	$52,264	$54,877	$57,621
Unit disposition price		12,000		14,000			16,000		
Total acquisition outlays	0	122,850	0	541,769	0	0	209,055	0	132,924
Taxable disposition receipts	0	$ 36,000	0	$168,000	0	0	$ 64,000	0	0
[sale of current equipment assumed to occur at "negotiated value" (see case Exhibit 1)]									
Nontaxable disposition receipts									$ 83,622
[sale of 1993 equipment assumed to take place at book value.]									

216

EXHIBIT C (continued)

**Supplemental rental expense:

	1987	1988	1989	1990	1991	1992	1993	1994	1995
Rental cost/hour	$18.00	$18.90	$19.85	$20.84	$21.88	$22.97	$24.12	$25.33	$26.59
Yearly rental hrs. (estimated by annualizing the tractor use given in case Exhibit 3)	8,348	8,348	8,348	8,348	8,348	8,348	8,348	8,348	8,348
Total rental cost	$150,264	$157,777	$165,666	$173,949	$182,647	$191,779	$201,368	$211,437	$222,008

†Depreciation schedule:

	1987	1988	1989	1990	1991	1992	1993	1994	1995
Tractors purchased in 1984	$ 29,600	$ 29,600							
Tractors purchased in 1988		24,570	$ 24,570	$ 24,570	$ 24,570	$ 24,570			
Tractors purchased in 1990				108,354	108,354	108,354	$108,354	$108,354	
Tractors purchased in 1993							41,811	41,811	41,811
Total depreciation expense	$ 29,600	$ 54,170	$ 24,570	$132,924	$132,924	$132,924	$150,165	$150,165	$ 41,811

EXHIBIT D Cash Flows of Pure Rental Strategy

	1987	1988	1989	1990	1991	1992	1993	1994	1995
Equipment purchase	$ 0	$ 0	$ 0	0	$ 0	$ 0	$ 0	$ 0	$ 0
Equipment sales*	208,800	0	0	0	0	0	0	0	0
Suppl. rental expense**	(535,161)	(561,919)	(590,015)	(619,516)	(650,492)	(683,016)	(717,167)	(753,025)	(790,677)
Tractor repairs, prop. tax, and insurance	0	0	0	0	0	0	0	0	0
Tractor fuel and parts	0	0	0	0	0	0	0	0	0
Shop overhead	(238,212)	(250,123)	(262,629)	(275,760)	(289,548)	(304,026)	(319,227)	(335,188)	(351,948)
Depreciation	0	0	0	0	0	0	0	0	0
Taxable cash flows	(564,573)	(812,042)	(852,644)	(895,276)	(940,040)	(987,042)	(1,036,394)	(1,088,213)	(1,142,624)
Tax savings	169,372	243,612	255,793	268,583	282,012	296,113	310,918	326,464	342,787
Add: Depreciation	0	0	0	0	0	0	0	0	0
Add: Nontaxable equip. sales	59,200	0	0	0	0	0	0	0	0
Total cash flow	($336,001)	($568,429)	($596,851)	($626,693)	($658,028)	($690,929)	($725,476)	($761,749)	($799,837)

*Taxable and nontaxable proceeds of equipment sales:

Negotiated value of equipment	$268,000	
Book value of equipment	59,200	(nontaxable proceeds)
Taxable gain on sale of equipment	208,800	(taxable proceeds)
Tax expense	(62,640)	
Plus: Gross proceeds	268,000	
Net sale proceeds	$205,360	

218

EXHIBIT D (continued)

**Rental expense:	1987	1988	1989	1990	1991	1992	1993	1994	1995
Rental cost/hour	$16.50	$17.33	$18.19	$19.10	$20.06	$21.06	$22.11	$23.22	$24.38
Yearly rental hrs.	32,434	32,434	32,434	32,434	32,434	32,434	32,434	32,434	32,434
Total rental cost	$535,161	$561,919	$590,015	$619,516	$650,492	$683,016	$717,167	$753,025	$790,677

Annualized total owned hours from case Exhibit 1: 24,086
Annualized total rental hours from case Exhibit 3: 8,348
Total annual hours of required use: 32,434

219

EXHIBIT E Cash Flows of Optimal Owning Strategy (tractor fleet Increased from 19 to 26)

	1987	1988	1989	1990	1991	1992	1993	1994	1995
Equipment purchase*	$273,000	$122,850	0	$541,769	0	0	$209,055	0	0
Equipment sales*	0	36,000	0	168,000	0	0	64,000	0	187,524
Suppl. rental expense**	43,200	45,360	47,628	50,009	52,510	55,135	57,892	60,787	63,826
Tractor repairs, prop. tax, and insurance	65,000	68,250	71,663	75,246	79,008	82,958	87,106	91,462	96,035
Tractor fuel and parts	88,504	92,929	97,576	102,454	107,577	112,956	118,604	124,534	130,761
Shop overhead	324,390	340,610	357,640	375,522	394,298	414,013	434,714	456,449	479,272
Depreciation	56,900	108,770	79,170	187,524	187,524	160,224	150,165	150,165	41,811
Taxable cash Flows	(850,994)	(742,769)	(653,676)	(1,164,524)	(820,917)	(825,286)	(993,535)	(883,396)	(624,180)
Tax savings	255,298	222,831	196,103	349,357	246,275	247,586	298,061	265,019	187,254
Add: Depreciation	56,900	108,770	79,170	187,524	187,524	160,224	150,165	150,165	41,811
Add: Nontaxable equip. sales*	0	0	0	0	0	0	0	0	83,622
Total cash flow	($538,796)	($411,168)	($378,403)	($627,643)	($387,118)	($417,477)	($545,310)	($468,213)	($311,493)

220

EXHIBIT E (continued)

*Equipment schedule:

Number of Years Old	1987	1988	1989	1990	1991	1992	1993	1994	1995
0									
1	7						4		
2		7	3		12			4	
3			7	3		12			4
4	4			7	3		12		
5	12	4			7	3		12	
6		12	4			7	3		12
7	3		12	4			7	3	
8		3		12	4			7	3
9						4			7
Total	19	26	26	26	26	26	26	26	26
Less: Tractors disposed	0	3		12			4		0
Plus: Tractors acquired	7	3		12			4		
Total	26	26	26	26	26	26	26	26	26

	1987	1988	1989	1990	1991	1992	1993	1994	1995
Unit acquisition price	$ 39,000	$ 40,950	$42,998	$ 45,147	$47,405	$49,775	$ 52,264	$54,877	$ 57,621
Unit disposition price		12,000		14,000			16,000		
Total acquisition outlays	273,000	122,850	0	541,769	0	0	209,055	0	187,524
Taxable disposition receipts		$ 36,000	0	$168,000	0	0	$ 64,000	0	
Nontaxable disposition receipts									83,622

[Sale of current equipment assumed to occur at "negotiated value" (see case Exhibit 1)]

(sale of 1993 equipment assumed to take place at book value.)

EXHIBIT E (continued)

*Supplemental rental expense:

	1987	1988	1989	1990	1991	1992	1993	1994	1995
Rental cost/hour	$18.00	$18.90	$19.85	$20.84	$21.88	$22.97	$24.12	$25.33	$26.59
Yearly rental hrs.	2,400	2,400	2,400	2,400	2,400	2,400	2,400	2,400	2,400
Total rental cost	$43,200	$45,360	$47,628	$50,009	$52,510	$55,135	$57,892	$60,787	$63,826

Yearly rental hours represents rentals for peak load handling).
The average of peak load requirements (i.e., for tractors 8 and higher
in case Exhibit 3) is 200 hours per month.

†Depreciation schedule:

	1987	1988	1989	1990	1991	1992	1993	1994	1995
Tractors purchased in 1984	$29,600	$29,600							
Tractors purchased in 1987	27,300	54,600	$ 54,600	$ 54,600	$ 54,600	$ 27,300			
Tractors purchased in 1988		24,570	24,570	24,570	24,570	24,570			
Tractors purchased in 1990				108,354	108,354	108,354	$108,354	$108,354	
Tractors purchased in 1993							41,811	41,811	41,811
Total depreciation expense	$56,900	$108,770	$79,170	$187,524	$187,524	$160,224	$150,165	$150,165	$41,811

222

EXHIBIT F Discounted Value of Incremental Cash Flows Among Operating Strategies

	1987	1988	1989	1990	1991	1992	1993	1994	1995
Strategy's free cash flows									
Status quo	($401,908)	($475,871)	($445,523)	($697,299)	($459,438)	($484,404)	($606,984)	($532,971)	($417,709)
Rental	(336,001)	(568,429)	(596,851)	(626,693)	(658,028)	(690,929)	(725,476)	(761,749)	(799,837)
Optimal owning	(538,796)	(411,168)	(378,403)	(627,643)	(387,118)	(417,477)	(545,310)	(468,213)	(311,493)
Incremental cash flows									
Rental, status	65,907	(92,558)	(151,328)	70,606	(198,590)	(206,525)	(118,491)	(228,779)	(382,128)
Optimal, status	(136,888)	64,703	67,119	69,656	72,320	66,927	61,674	64,758	106,216
Optimal, rental	($202,795)	$157,261	$218,447	($ 950)	$270,910	$273,452	$180,166	$293,537	$488,344

Net PVs (at 15%)

Rental, status: ($560,955)
Optimal, status: $176,283
Optimal, rental: $737,237

223

Sprigg Lane (A)

SYNOPSIS AND OBJECTIVES

The president of a natural-resource exploration company has to decide whether to invest in a new drilling opportunity. He already has a Lotus spreadsheet that projects the most likely scenario for the well and calculates the net present value (NPV) and internal rate of return (IRR); however, there are six uncertainties discussed by the president and another potential investor. He has also prepared a spreadsheet for a couple of downside scenarios--one in which gas is not able to be produced after the well has been drilled and a second in which gas is produced but all other uncertainties are at their 1 percent worst possible values.

The case is intended as a first opportunity for students to carry out a risk analysis through Monte Carlo simulation. The case would follow one or more days of introduction to Monte Carlo simulation, and it assumes that the student can use the electronic spreadsheet for pro forma analysis. The case offers an opportunity to meet joint finance/quantitative analysis (QA) objectives in the classroom. It may be co-taught by faculty from both areas.

The student is expected to do the following:

- choose the probability distribution for the uncertainties in the case

- use add-in software to place the uncertainty into the spreadsheet

- run the Monte Carlo simulation

- interpret the resulting probability distribution of NPV and cash-flow time pattern

- answer the question relating to the probability of a positive NPV

- decide go/no go on the project

The analysis described here uses the @RISK software; other software products can be used for the same purposes.

STUDY QUESTIONS

Students are given the case along with an introductory guide to @RISK software. The students are told that, to simplify the analysis, they may assume Sprigg Lane Natural Resources (SLNR) will retain 100 percent ownership, and they are given the following questions:

Teaching note prepared by Professor Samuel E. Bodily, Larry Weatherford, Research Assistant, and Robert F. Bruner. Copyright (c) 1988 by the Darden Graduate Business School Sponsors, Charlottesville, VA.

1. Based on the base-case scenario and the two alternative down side possibilities, is this investment economically attractive?

2. What benefit can Monte Carlo simulation add to Tom Dingledine's understanding of the economic benefits of the Bailey Prospect?

3. Incorporate uncertainties into the spreadsheet using @RISK. What do the Monte Carlo results reveal? What is the probability that the NPV will be greater than zero? Should Dingledine invest?

ANALYSIS

Initially, the students will look at Exhibit 1 of the case and think that this is a great deal based on an IRR greater than 40 percent and an NPV of $110.26 thousand at 15 percent interest. The stream of cash flows shows that over 80 percent of the NPV is returned by year 10, making the actual duration of the project much less than the 25 years that it appears to be on the surface.

After looking at case Exhibits 5 and 6, the student should become a little concerned at the potential down side. The real issue then becomes how likely the down side outcomes are, which is where Monte Carlo simulation comes into play. Monte Carlo is a powerful tool to analyze multiple levels of uncertainty that would otherwise be too cumbersome to evaluate (even with bracket medians or Pearson-Tukey approximations).

The results of 10,000 Monte Carlo simulation trials show that, using a discount rate of 9.3 percent (a reasonable risk-free rate from case Exhibit 3), the expected NPV equals $138,718 with a standard deviation of $108,082. There's an 89.85 percent chance that the actual NPV would be positive. Exhibit A presents the graph of the risk profile of the NPV and its associated statistics. Exhibit B shows the NPV up through any year of the project. Note that the Monte Carlo expected NPV is higher than the NPV from Dingledine's original scenario because of moving from a risk-adjusted discount rate of 15 percent to the risk-free rate of 9.3 percent. In fact, a Monte Carlo run with a discount rate of 15 percent yields an expected NPV of $83,244 (Exhibit C), $27,016 less than Dingledine's base-case result.

Exhibit D is a graph of the simulated levels of the six uncertain quantities extracted from the case. Students may have used slightly different assumptions in their analyses.

Unless Dingledine is risk averse, this investment appears to be a super opportunity. The proper discount rate to use is a subtle point, however, because in the initial deterministic spreadsheet, Dingledine used a value of 15 percent to incorporate the high level of risk that the project entailed. Now that the spreadsheet is probabilistic, the discount rate must be a risk-free rate, but of what duration? To be exact, the duration could be calculated as the weighted average of the time value maturities of the cash flows, and then this value would be used to find the risk-free rate of the corresponding duration. Because of its subtlety and the small difference in the rates for durations between 7 and 30 years, a rate of 9.3 percent was used.

TEACHING PLAN

Class Discussion

In the class outline of this section, the assumption is that this case will go in the quantitative analysis course, but that it will be jointly taught by QA and finance. QA can start by announcing that a finance colleague has come along to help in the discussion and that the finance colleague will start the discussion off. The QA faculty member may then be seated for the time being, perhaps by the computer in case running any spreadsheet what-ifs with video projection becomes appropriate.

(20-25 minutes) What analysis has Dingledine done so far? The finance faculty member can now talk about the income statement in Exhibit 1 of the base case: What assumptions are made, what financial measures are important?

Based on this analysis, what do you think of the project? Typically, students respond that it satisfies all of Dingledine's three criteria; go for it.

At this point, the QA faculty member may interject, "Wait a minute; you run one case and you think you're done. What about the assumptions you've tidily kicked under the rug?"
Finance reluctantly responds, "OK, we'll look at a down side scenario."
They then look at one or more scenarios on the pessimistic side. The students may turn to the two in case Exhibits 5 and 6, or they may suggest their own what-if case to be run in real time on the computer. The discussion should uncover at least one bad situation where the project loses a lot of money.

(65-70 minutes) Now what are we going to do? The down-side cases don't look good. Thomas wants to know how likely the down side is? Students will suggest simulation as a reasonable approach to finding the probability that NPV>0. The more astute may also recognize that E(NPV) from Monte Carlo is not equal to the NPV calculated from the means of the uncertain quantities. The finance professor will feign ignorance and defer to QA.

What uncertainties are we going to simulate? What do you know about these uncertainties? How do you model them?

- Will gas be produced? The case twice gives this as a discrete probability distribution with a 90 percent chance of success (1) and 10 percent chance of failure (0).

- How much gas is there? Again the students are told that this is a log-normal distribution with a mean of 33,000 million cubic feet (mcf) and standard deviation of 4,930 mcf. All they have to do is convert from 33 mcf to 33,000 mcf, etc.

- What is the total well cost? The case says the "average" cost (mean) is $160,000 and that there's a 95 percent chance that actual cost will be within $5,400 of the average. This information implies a normal distribution with mean = 160,000 and two standard deviations = 5,400, therefore, one standard deviation = 2,700.

- What is the BTU content? The case gives the lowest possible (1,055), most likely (1,160) and highest values (1,250). The student then models these three values with a triangular distribution.

- How will production decline? Students are given the most likely decline factors with the suggestion that all of these be multiplied by the same uncertain quantity each trial. In some other cell of the worksheet, a triangular probability distribution with low value of .5, most likely value of 1.0 and high value of 1.75 is entered. This value is then multiplied by each of the production decline factors given.

What is the proper inflation value to use? Dingledine is currently using his best guess of 3.5 percent. If you calculate the arithmetic average of the three forecasts given in case Exhibit 4, you get 3.73 percent, compared with an historical 4.91 percent average inflation rate over the 25-year period since 1953. No one forecasts inflation for the next 25 years, so you're left with a choice between historical performance or a 3-year forecast as a proxy for a 25-year forecast.

The issue here is whether to use historical values or not. Do you believe inflation is going to be as high as it has been recently? If you look at the 1953-87 period and compare the last 35 years' average inflation (4.5 percent) with the last 25 years' (5.39 percent) average with the last 16 years' average, (6.31 percent), you find a trend toward increasing inflation. This outcome tends to argue for using a *forecast* for the next 25 years. The odd thing is that the forecast (3.73 percent) is lower than the last 25 years of inflation, which defies the increasing trend. The lower inflation value was used in this note, because it is the more conservative (gives a lower NPV).

The analysis reported uses a normal distribution with a mean of 3.73 percent (forecast) and a standard deviation of 0.46 percent (historical). The difference in the expected NPVs is only $11,400 if a 4.9 percent rate is used (Exhibit E). It would be more realistic, though probably not worth the effort, to model inflation on a year-by-year basis and incorporate the roughly 2 1/2 percent standard deviation of year-to-year variations.

How does the simulation work? Students will describe what happens in the worksheet for each trial, which they should know from a previous class. The process makes objective selection of scenarios based on the probability inputs above and progresses through many trials.

What are our results? The expected value of NPV and the prob(NPV>0) is identified. The students may have only run 100 or so trials. Thus, there may be discussion of sampling error and whether enough trials have been run. They will be aware that the sampling error of the mean is the standard deviation reported by the simulation divided by the square root of n.

Some students may have looked at how the distribution of the average NPV per well varies when you invest in a package of 10 wells as opposed to a single well. The case mentions that this is what SLNR actually does, but the assignment allows them to simplify the analysis by looking at a single well. Of course, the package concept allows one to diversify away much of the dry-hole risk, with the result being a much tighter standard deviation of $34,736 and 99.99 percent chance of the average NPV being greater than 0 (see Exhibit F).

Now finance can re-enter the discussion, and both faculty then deal with questions about the treatment of risk. If risk is handled by adjusting the expected NPV for the spread in the NPV distribution, should one then use a discount rate that is already risk adjusted?

Does this project look too good to be true? Note that all of the input numbers came from Dingledine, who is also selling this project to investors. He has a major stake in this business working out well and may be optimistic. (In actuality, SLNR takes a 25 percent reversionary royalty out of net revenues once the well reaches payout; that is, when cumulative after-tax cash flow = initial investment). What would be your model if you were putting your own money into this? This question should result in what might be called a skeptical risk analysis.

If you widen and shift the uncertainties in the following way:

- well cost: mean 165,000, std. dev. 5,000

- enough to produce: probability .85

- production decline multiplier: triangular (1,1.2,2)

- GNP deflator: normal (2%,1.5%)

and add these uncertainties:

- federal tax rate: triangular (34%,38%,48%)

- annual lease expense: triangular (1,000,4,000,10,000)

and make the well-expense inflation factor equal to the GNP deflator, rather than one-half of it, you obtain the results in Exhibit F. The project has a 77.8 percent chance of a positive NPV and an expected value of $42,000 at a 9.3 percent discount rate; it still looks good enough for a go.
The value of this project comes largely from the federal tax credit, which expires in the year 2000. A Monte Carlo simulation was run with no tax credit, and the expected NPV decreased $72,000 to a value of -$30,000.
What is your decision? Students will probably conclude this is a go.

EXHIBIT A Risk Profile of NPV at 9.3 Percent Discount Rate

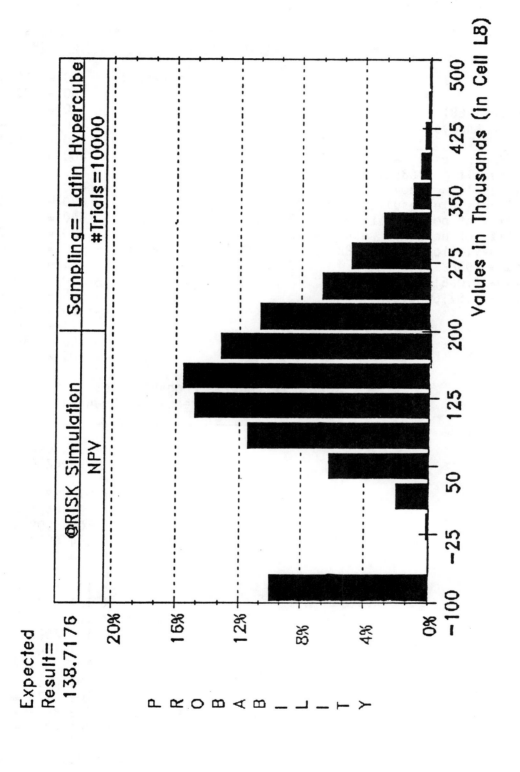

Statistics for NPV Risk Profile

Probabilities for Selected Values:
(values in thousands; in cell L8)

	Probability of result	>	0 =	89.99%
		>	60 =	87.26%
NPV (in cell L8)		>	120 =	67.19%
@RISK Risk Analysis		>	180 =	33.42%
		>	240 =	10.27%
		>	800 =	2.32%
Expected/mean result = 138453.7		>	860 =	.4%
Maximum result = 576855.8		>	420 =	.02%
Minimum result = 95304		>	480 =	.01%
Range of possible results = 672159.8		>	540 =	.01%
Probability of positive result = 89.99%		>	600 =	0.0%
Probability of negative result = 10.01%	Probability of result	<=	0 =	10.01%
Standard deviation = 97834.88		<-	15 =	10.%
Skewness = .9382299		<-	30 =	10.%
Kurtosis = 4.05614		<-	45 =	10.%
Variance = 9.571663E+09		<-	60 =	10.%
		<-	75 =	10.%
		<-	90 =	10.%
		<-	105 =	0.%

Percentile Probabilities:
(chance of result < shown value)

<- 95.304 =	0%
<- 93.6236 =	5%
<- 91.9432 =	10%
< 73.2961 =	15%
< 91.6441 =	20%
< 104.5009 =	25%
< 114.6554 =	30%
< 124.3352 =	35%
< 133.4844 =	40%
< 142.6541 =	45%
< 151.6075 =	50%
< 160.0164 =	55%
< 168.2988 =	60%
< 177.1543 =	65%
< 186.2902 =	70%
< 197.0632 =	75%
< 209.2775 =	80%
< 223.4677 =	85%
< 241.4396 =	90%
< 272.4324 =	95%
< 576.8558 =	100%

EXHIBIT B   Year-by-Year Analysis of NPV at 9.3 Percent Discount Rate

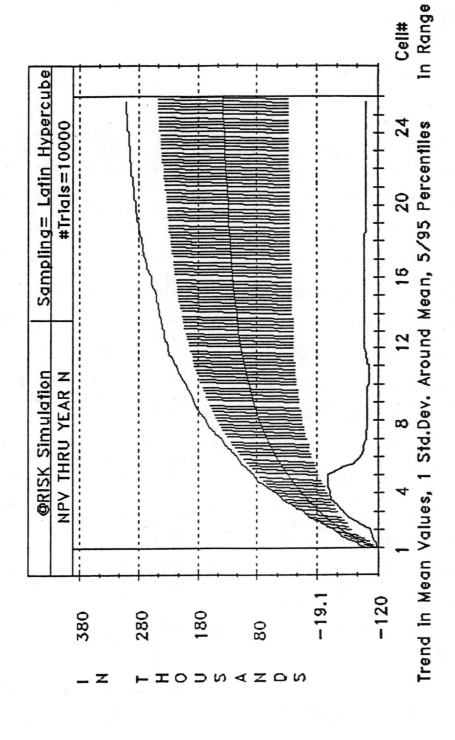

Statistics for Year-by-Year NPVs:

Simulation Summary:
   B:/SPRADV2.REV
   07 July 1988
   Iterations = 10,000
   Sampling = Latin Hypercube

Year

1)   NPV (in cell L8)
     Mean = 138456.7   SD = 97834.88
     Min = 95304   Max = 576855.8

2)   NPV thru year N (in cell C40)
     Mean = 57547.97   SD = 15510.28
     Min = 95304   Max = 581.4282

3)   NPV thru year N (in cell D40)
     Mean = 19847.64   SD = 29490.59
     Min = 95304   Max = 87197.2

4)   NPV thru year N (in cell E40)
     Mean = 8496.354   SD = 40229.82
     Min = 95304   Max = 156460

5)   NPV thru year N (in cell F40)
     Mean = 31233.39   SD = 48998.02
     Min = 95304   Max = 214417.3

6)   NPV thru year N (in cell G40)
     Mean = 49835.68   SD = 56316.13
     Min = 95304   Max = 263900

7)   NPV thru year N (in cell H40)
     Mean = 65025.32   SD = 62438.91
     Min = 95304   Max = 306136.4

8)   NPV thru year N (in cell I40)
     Mean = 77803.32   SD = 67712.95
     Min = 95304   Max = 342986.4

9)   NPV thru year N (in cell J40)
     Mean = 87515.56   SD = 71910.02
     Min = 95304   Max = 373884.4

10) NPV thru year N (in cell K40)
     Mean = 95617.14   SD = 75506.59
     Min = 95304   Max = 400777.9

11) NPV thru year N (in cell L40)
     Mean = 102359.7   SD = 78589.04
     Min = 95304   Max = 424178.1

12) NPV thru year N (in cell M40)
     Mean = 107954.8   SD = 81233.97
     Min = 95304   Max = 444531.5

13) NPV thru year N (in cell N40)
     Mean = 112580.6   SD = 83502.34
     Min = 95304   Max = 462227.9

14) NPV thru year N (in cell O40)
     Mean 116387.8   SD = 85448.73
     Min = 95304   Max = 477607.8

15) NPV thru year N (in cell P40)
     Mean = 119504.1   SD = 87117.27
     Min = 95304   Max = 490968.3

16) NPV thru year N (in cell Q40)
     Mean = 122038   SD = 88546.14
     Min = 95304   Max = 502569

17) NPV thru year N (in cell R40)
     Mean = 124300   SD = 89848.27
     Min = 95304   Max = 513143.5

18) NPV thru year N (in cell S40)
     Mean = 126319.1   SD = 91033.38
     Min = 95304   Max = 522782.5

19) NPV thru year N (in cell T40)
     Mean = 128121.2   SD = 92113.91
     Min = 95304   Max = 581568.9

20) NPV thru year N (in cell U40)
     Mean = 129729.3   SD = 93096.91
     Min = 95304   Max = 539577.9

21) NPV thru year N (in cell V40)
     Mean = 131598.4   SD = 94083.66
     Min = 95304   Max = 547309.1

22) NPV thru year N (in cell W40)
     Mean = 133277.6   SD = 94982.7
     Min = 95304   Max = 554357.9

23) NPV thru year N (in cell X40)
     Mean = 134786.3   SD = 95799.36
     Min = 95304   Max = 560784.4

24) NPV thru year N (in cell Y40)
     Mean = 136141.7   SD = 96543.32
     Min = 95304   Max = 566643.5

25) NPV thru year N (in cell Z40)
     Mean = 137359.5   SD = 97219.23
     Min = 95304   Max = 571985.4

26) NPV thru year N (in cell AA40)
     Mean = 138453.7   SD = 97834.88
     Min = 95304   Max = 576855.8

EXHIBIT C Risk Profile for NPV at 15 Percent Discount Rate

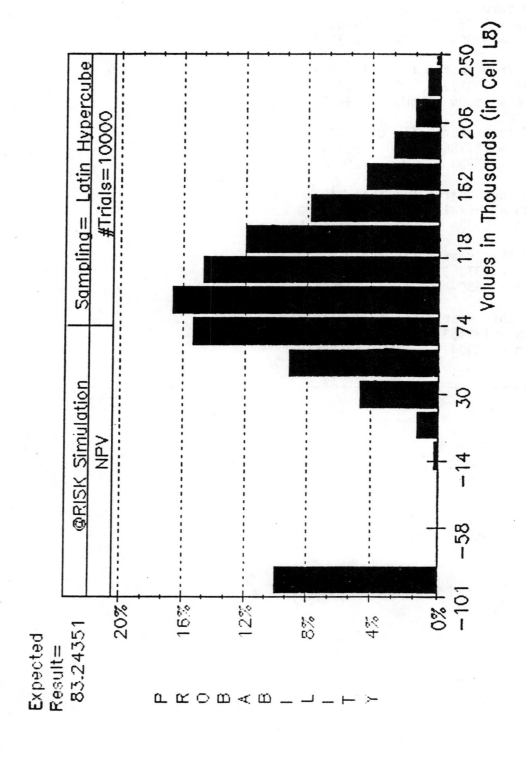

EXHIBIT C (continued)

Statistics for NPV at 15 percent:

Probabilities for Selected Values:
(values in thousands; in cell L8)

NPV at 15% (in cell L8)
@RISK Risk Analysis

Expected/mean result = 83243.51
Maximum result = 302381.8
Minimum result = 100563.1
Range of possible results = 402944.9
Probability of positive result = 89.89%
Probability of negative result = 10.11%
Standard deviation = 73008.98
Skewness = 1.069333
Kurtosis = 4.276597
Variance = 5.330311E+09

Probability of result	>	0	=	89.89%
	>	40	=	84.38%
	>	80	=	60.66%
	>	120	=	29.51%
	>	160	=	9.44%
	>	200	=	2.4%
	>	240	=	.86%
	>	280	=	.09%
	>	320	=	.0%

Probability of result	<=	0	=	10.11%
	<-	20	=	10.01%
	<-	40	=	10.%
	<-	60	=	10.%
	<-	80	=	10.%
	<-	100	=	.04%
	<-	120	=	0.%

Percentile Probabilities:
(chance of result < shown value)

<-	100.5631	=	0%
<-	95.4077	=	5%
<-	90.4895	=	10%
<	37.7555	=	15%
<	51.0837	=	20%
<	60.8796	=	25%
<	68.5433	=	30%
<	74.5613	=	35%
<	80.727	=	40%
<	86.9995	=	45%
<	93.3745	=	50%
<	99.2094	=	55%
<	105.1509	=	60%
<	112.2762	=	65%
<	119.2123	=	70%
<	126.6798	=	75%
<	134.7759	=	80%
<	145.3676	=	85%
<	158.2053	=	90%
<	180.2894	=	95%
<	302.3818	=	100%

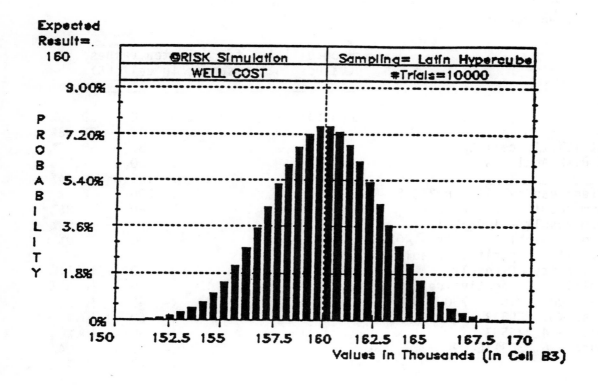

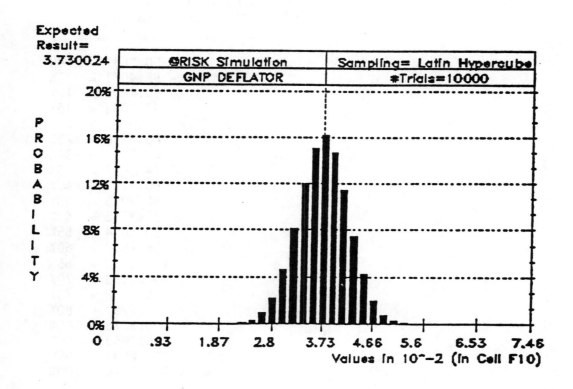

EXHIBIT D (continued)

Statistics for Well Cost Gross National Product (GNP) Deflator:

Well Cost (in cell B3)
@RISK Risk analysis

Expected/mean result = 160000
Maximum result = 170161.3
Minimum result = 149830.5
Range of possible results = 20330.86
Probability of positive result = 100%
Probability of negative result = 0%
Standard deviation = 2699.46
Skewness = 6.805427E-04
Kurtosis = 2.991001
Variance = 7287083

Probabilities for selected values:
(values in thousands (in cell B3))

```
Probability of result >   0 = 100%
                      > 110 = 100%
                      > 120 = 100%
                      > 130 = 100%
                      > 140 = 100%
                      > 150 =  99.99%
                      > 160 =  50%
                      > 170 =  .01%
                      > 180 =   0%
Probability of result <=0   =   0%
```

Percentile probabilities:
(chance of result < shown value)

```
                      < 149.8305 =   0%
                      < 155.5587 =   5%
                      < 156.5396 =  10%
                      < 157.201  =  15%
                      < 157.7275 =  20%
                      < 158.1788 =  25%
                      < 158.5836 =  30%
                      < 158.9596 =  35%
                      < 159.3158 =  40%
                      < 159.6604 =  45%
                      < 159.9999 =  50%
                      < 160.3397 =  55%
```

GNP Deflator (in cell F10)
@RISK Risk Analysis

Expected/mean result = 3.730011E-02
Maximum result = 5.520037E-02
Minimum result = 1.986256E-02
Range of possible results = 3.533781E-02
Probability of positive result = 100%
Probability of negative result = 0%
Standard deviation = 4.599575E-03
Skewness = 7.950235E-04
Kurtosis = 2.995622
Variance = 2.115609E-05

Probabilities for selected values:
(values in thousands (in cell F10))

```
Probability of result > 0    = 100%
                      > 1.95 = 100%
                      > 2.4  =  99.81%
                      > 2.85 =  97.21%
                      > 3.3  =  82.51%
                      > 3.75 =  48.27%
                      > 4.2  =  15.35%
                      > 4.65 =   2.28%
                      > 5.1  =   .15%
                      > 5.55 =    0%
Probability of result <=  0  =    0%
```

Percentile probabilities:
(chance of result < shown value)

```
                      < 1.9863 =   0%
                      < 2.9735 =   5%
                      < 3.1405 =  10%
                      < 3.2531 =  15%
                      < 3.3428 =  20%
                      < 3.4197 =  25%
                      < 3.4888 =  30%
                      < 3.5527 =  35%
                      < 3.6135 =  40%
                      < 3.6722 =  45%
                      < 3.73   =  50%
```

Percentile probabilities:
(chance of result < shown value)

Percentile probabilities:
(chance of result < shown value)

< 160.6838 =	60%
< 161.0404 =	65%
< 161.4159 =	70%
< 161.3214 =	75%
< 162.2729 =	80%
< 162.7983 =	85%
< 163.4601 =	90%
< 164.4426 =	95%
< 170.1613 =	100%

< 3.7878 =	55%
< 3.8465 =	60%
< 3.9072 =	65%
< 3.9713 =	70%
< 4.0403 =	75%
< 4.1172 =	80%
< 4.2068 =	85%
< 4.3196 =	90%
< 4.4868 =	95%
< 5.52 =	100%

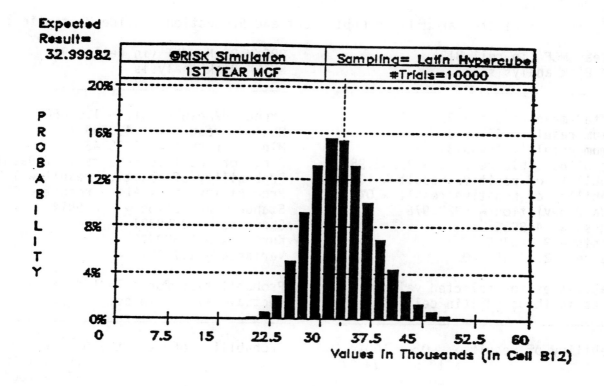

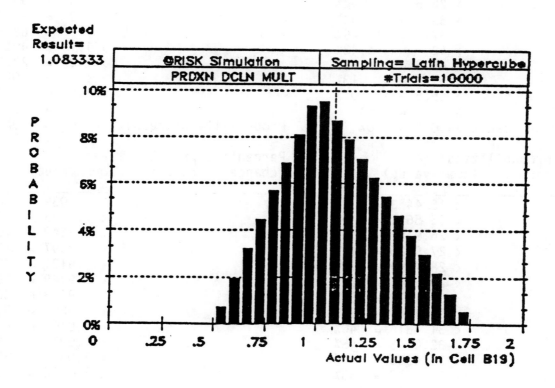

239

Statistics for First-Year Million Cubic Feet and Production-Decline Multiplier:

1st Year MCF (in cell B12) @RISK Risk analysis	PROXN DCLN MULT (in cell B19) @RISK Risk Analysis
Expected/mean result = 32999.8	Expected/mean result = 1.066667
Maximum result = 57739.3	Maximum result = 1.493798
Minimum result = 18445.31	Minimum result = .7038743
Range of possible results = 39293.98	Range of possible results = .7899238
Probability of positive result = 100%	Probability of positive result = 100%
Probability of negative result = 0%	Probability of negative result = 0%
Standard deviation = 4928.976	Standard deviation = .1649914
Skewness = .448936	Skewness = .2358321
Kurtosis = 3.346705	Kurtosis = 2.399979
Variance = 2.429481E+07	Variance = 2.722216E-02

Probabilities for selected values: (values in thousands (in cell B12))	Probabilities for selected values: (actual values (in cell B19))

Probability of result	>	0	=	100%	Probability of result	>	0	=	100%
	>	19.5	=	99.97%		>	.6	=	100%
	>	24	=	98.07%		>	.7	=	100%
	>	28.5	=	81.92%		>	.8	=	95.83%
	>	33	=	47.04%		>	.9	=	83.33%
	>	37.5	=	17.49%		>	1	=	62.5%
	>	42	=	4.48%		>	1.1	=	40%
	>	46.5	=	.86%		>	1.2	=	22.5%
	>	51	=	.13%		>	1.3	=	10%
	>	55.5	=	.01%		>	1.4	=	2.5%
	>	60	=	0%		>	1.5	=	0%
Probability of result	>=	0	=	0%	Probability of result	>=	0	=	0%

Percentile probabilities: (chance of result < shown value)	Percentile probabilities: (chance of result < shown value)

<	18.4453	=	0%	<	.7039	=	0%
<	25.5619	=	5%	<	.8095	=	5%
<	26.9781	=	10%	<	.8549	=	10%
<	27.9786	=	15%	<	.8897	=	15%
<	28.7999	=	20%	<	.9191	=	20%
<	29.5246	=	25%	<	.9449	=	25%
<	30.1919	=	30%	<	.9683	=	30%
<	30.8217	=	35%	<	.9898	=	35%
<	31.4316	=	40%	<	1.0101	=	40%
<	32.0343	=	45%	<	1.031	=	45%
<	32.6385	=	50%	<	1.0528	=	50%
<	33.2527	=	55%	<	1.0758	=	55%

Percentile probabilities:
(chance of result < shown value)

<	33.8905	=	60%
<	34.5601	=	65%
<	35.2822	=	70%
<	36.0789	=	75%
<	36.9849	=	80%
<	38.0707	=	85%
<	39.4814	=	90%
<	41.6717	=	95%
<	57.7393	=	100%

Percentile probabilities:
(chance of result < shown value)

<	1.1	=	60%
<	1.1258	=	65%
<	1.1536	=	70%
<	1.1838	=	75%
<	1.2171	=	80%
<	1.2551	=	85%
<	1.3001	=	90%
<	1.3587	=	95%
<	1.4938	=	100%

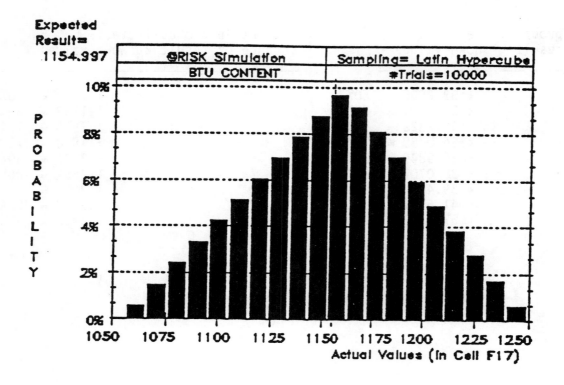

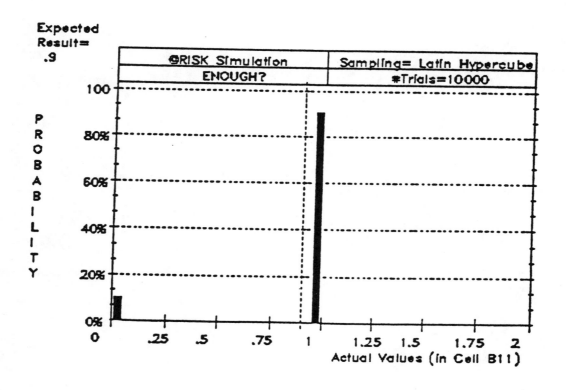

242

Statistics for BTU Content, Enough Gas to Produce:

BTU CONTENT (in cell F17)
@RISK Risk analysis

Expected/mean result = 1155.005
Maximum result = 1249.233
Minimum result = 1055.505
Range of possible results = 193.7284
Probability of positive result = 100%
Probability of negative result = 0%
Standard deviation = 39.85039
Skewness = 7.470662E-02
Kurtosis = 2.400349
Variance = 1588.053

Probabilities for selected values:
(values in thousands (in cell F17))

Probability of result > 0   = 100%
                      > 1050 = 100%
                      > 1100 = 90.11%
                      > 1150 = 55.92%
                      > 1200 = 14.25%
                      > 1250 = 0%
Probability of result <=0   = 0%

Percentile probabilities:
(chance of result < shown value)

< 1055.505 =   0%
< 1086.985 =   5%
< 1100.26 = 10%
< 1110.406 = 15%
< 1118.991 = 20%
< 1126.542 = 25%
< 1133.375 = 30%
< 1139.642 = 35%
< 1145.496 = 40%
< 1150.984 = 45%
< 1156.181 = 50%
< 1161.135 = 55%

ENOUGH? (in cell B11)
@RISK Risk Analysis

Expected/mean result = .9
Maximum result = 1
Minimum result = 0
Range of possible results = 1
Probability of positive result = 100%
Probability of negative result = 0%
Standard deviation = .3000091
Skewness = 2.666533
Kurtosis = 8.110501
Variance = 9.000544E-02

Probabilities for selected values:
(actual values (in cell B11))

Probability of result > 0   = 100%
                      > .15 = 90%
                      > .3   = 90%
                      > .45 = 90%
                      > .6   = 90%
                      > .75 = 90%
                      > .9   = 90%
                      >1.05 =   0%
Probability of result <= 0   =   0%
Percentile probabilities:
(chance of result < shown value)

< 0   =   0%
< .0025 =   5%
< .005 = 10%
< .9953 = 15%
< .9956 = 20%
< .9958 = 25%
< .9961 = 30%
< .9964 = 35%
< .9967 = 40%
< .9969 = 45%
< .9972 = 50%
< .9975 = 55%

Percentile probabilities:
(chance of result < shown value)

Percentile probabilities:
(chance of result < shown value)

< 1166.22	=	60%
< 1171.629	=	65%
< 1177.455	=	70%
< 1183.762	=	75%
< 1190.76	=	80%
< 1198.695	=	85%
< 1208.127	=	90%
< 1220.406	=	95%
< 1249.233	=	100%

< .9978	=	60%
< .9981	=	65%
< .9983	=	70%
< .9986	=	75%
< .9989	=	80%
< .9992	=	85%
< .9994	=	90%
< .9997	=	95%
< 1	=	100%

EXHIBIT E Risk Profile of NPV at 9.3 Percent Discount Rate but 4.91 Percent Inflation Rate

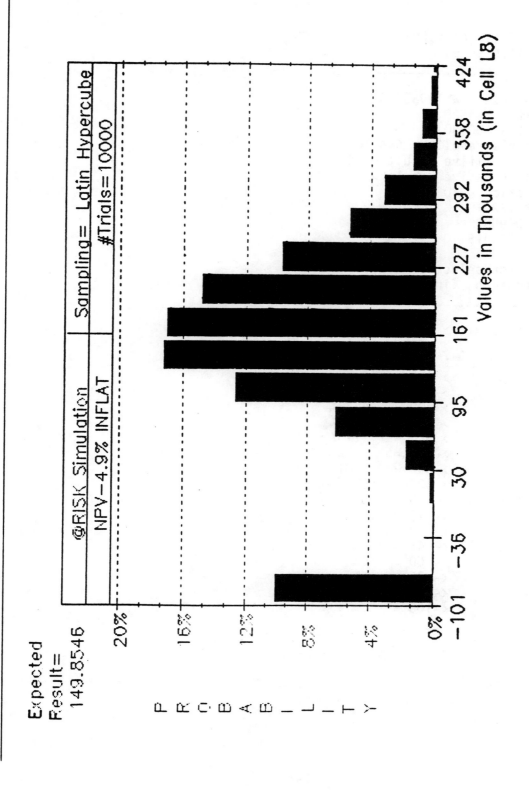

Statistics for NPV at 4.91 Percent Inflation:

NPV-4.9% INFLAT (in cell L8)
@RISK Risk analysis

Expected/mean result = 149854.6
Maximum result = 544529.9
Minimum result = 100380.1
Range of possible results = 644910
Probability of positive result = 90%
Probability of negative result = 10%
Standard deviation = 103510.4
Skewness = .8773201
Kurtosis = 4.009587
Variance = 1.071441E+10

Probabilities for selected values:
(values in thousands (in cell L8))

```
Probability of result >    0 =   90%
                      >   60 =   88.21%
                      >  120 =   71.94%
                      >  180 =   40.4%
                      >  240 =   14.94%
                      >  300 =    4.23%
                      >  360 =     .96%
                      >  420 =     .15%
                      >  480 =     .02%
                      >  540 =     .01%
                      >  600 =    0%
Probability of result <=   0 =   10%
                      <-  15 =   10%
                      <-  30 =   10%
                      <-  45 =   10%
                      <-  60 =   10%
                      <-  75 =   10%
                      <-  90 =   10%
                      <-105 =    0%
```

Percentile probabilities:
(chance of result < shown value)

```
            <-100.3801  =    0%
            < -95.3729  =    5%
            <   2.8057  =   10%
            <  80.1947  =   15%
            <  99.7988  =   20%
            < 113.0335  =   25%
            < 123.9004  =   30%
            < 134.8132  =   35%
            < 144.2948  =   40%
            < 152.7555  =   45%
            < 161.5229  =   50%
            < 171.4388  =   55%
            < 180,7535  =   60%
            < 190.3475  =   65%
            < 200.1293  =   70%
            < 211.7421  =   75%
            < 223.9351  =   80%
            < 239.7578  =   85%
            < 260.5678  =   90%
            < 292.6118  =   95%
            < 544.53    =  100%
```

EXHIBIT F Risk Profile for NPV with Skeptical Assumptions

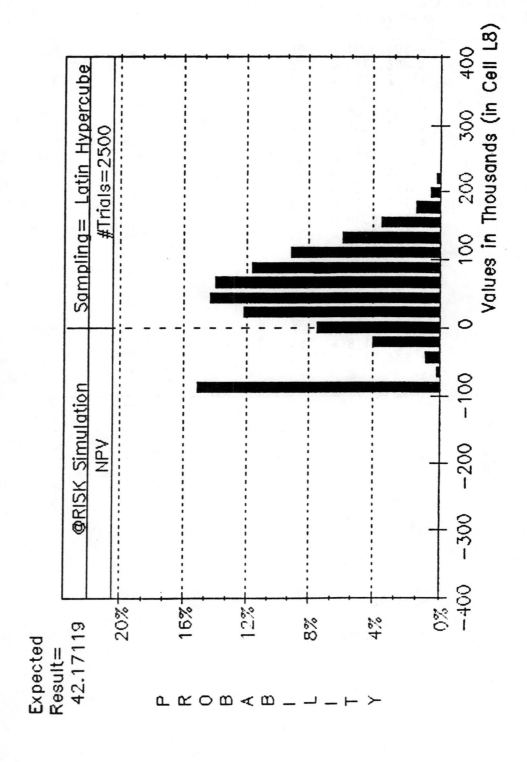

Statistics for NPV With Skeptical Assumptions:

NPV (in cell L8) 2500 trials Latin Hyper
@RISK Risk analysis

Expected/mean result = 42171.18
Maximum result = 342695.2
Minimum result = -97685.92
Range of possible results = 440381.1
Probability of positive result = 77.84%
Probability of negative result = 22.16%
Standard deviation = 72209.09
Skewness = .3632288
Kurtosis = 2.764142
Variance = 5.214152E+09

Probabilities for selected values:
(values in thousands (in cell L8))

Probability of result >   0 =   77.84%
                      >   40 =   56.84%
                      >   80 =   31%
                      > 120 =   12.4%
                      > 160 =   3.08%
                      > 200 =   .4%
                      > 240 =   .2%
                      > 280 =   .08%
                      > 320 =   .04%
                      > 360 =   0%
Probability of result <=   0 =   22.16%
                      <- 10 =   19.92%
                      <- 20 =   17.8%
                      <- 30 =   16.08%
                      <- 40 =   15.64%
                      <- 50 =   15.32%
                      <- 60 =   15.12%
                      <- 70 =   15.04%
                      <- 80 =   14.72%
                      <- 90 =   7.2%

Percentile probabilities:
(chance of result < shown value)

< -97.6859	=	0%
< -91.6613	=	5%
< -87.5939	=	10%
< -75.6668	=	15%
< - 9.6097	=	20%
< 7.9007	=	25%
< 18.4145	=	30%
< 26.7551	=	35%
< 34.9526	=	40%
< 43.4145	=	45%
< 50.2921	=	50%
< 58.16	=	55%
< 66.228	=	60%
< 74.1191	=	65%
< 81.7425	=	70%
< 90.577	=	75%
< 101.6866	=	80%
< 113.697	=	85%
< 126.6494	=	90%
< 148.377	=	95%
< 342.6952	=	100%

Enercon Corporation

SYNOPSIS AND OBJECTIVES

In 1988, the chief financial officer of this privately held investment company is considering the question of whether to invest in natural-gas drilling opportunities in western Virginia. Attendant on this decision is the question of how to market the gas. Indeed, the marketing decision greatly influences the economic attractiveness of the gas properties.

The marketing decision involves a choice of whether to build connecting pipelines to one or two national pipeline systems. Two pipelines require greater capital investment, but result in higher revenues per million cubic feet (MCF) because they create greater bargaining power for Enercon. The tasks for the student are (1) to review the discounted cash flow (DCF) model given in the case, (2) to determine whether the gains from redundant investment in pipelines offset the additional cost, and (3) to identify the highest value system of pipelines for Enercon.

The prime teaching objective of the case is to illustrate project interdependencies (i.e., between gas-field development and pipeline investment) and the potential creation of value through strategic positioning vis-a-vis customers. If the computer model is used, the principal challenges posed by the case are careful problem definition and interpretation of results.

STUDY QUESTIONS

The student may find helpful standard background readings in capital budgeting and discount-rate determination, but because of the structured valuation already existing in the case, such reading is not mandatory.

1. What decisions must Harrison make? Can the decision of whether to invest in the Buchanan and/or Leigh properties be made separately from the choice of pipelines? Why?

2. What are Harrison's alternatives for investment?

3. Which alternative is the most economically attractive? How does the pipeline decision affect the economic attractiveness of the drilling investments?

TEACHING PLAN

The following questions serve as a discussion outline intended for an 80-minute class session.

(40 minutes) What is the problem here? What are the decisions we have to make? What are the alternatives? As discussed later, the greatest task for

---

Teaching note written by Robert F. Bruner. Copyright (c) 1988 by the Darden Graduate Business School Sponsors, Charlottesville, VA.

the student is to structure the problem. Before getting into the numbers, it makes sense to lay out the various alternatives in decision-tree format. Begin by developing the simpler Leigh branch first in order to develop the structuring pattern, and then Buchanan and "both."

(15 minutes) Let's make sure we understand the valuation model being used in case Exhibits 4 and 5:

• What is the Devonian Shale tax credit? Is it material?   Case Exhibits 4 and 5 show that the Devonian easily offsets the federal and state tax expense for the Leigh field and somewhat offsets it for the Buchanan field.

• What is intangible drilling cost?

• What is gathering cost, and where is it reflected?

• Where in these two exhibits are pipeline costs, shipping costs, and the effect of changes in prices? Although the model can accommodate them, they are not reflected in case Exhibits 4 and 5; this task is left to the student.

• Is a hurdle rate of 10 percent appropriate?

(15 minutes) What are the internal rates of return (IRRs) and net present values (NPVs) associated with the various alternatives? Which pipeline and marketing strategy should Enercon adopt?

(10 minutes) About how much value does redundant pipeline investment add to the value of the gas fields? Why is it that, in this case, value is created by overinvesting?

ANALYSIS

Problem Definition

In the author's experience, simply parsing out the decision and alternatives will take at least half the class period. There are several elements that make this exercise complicated and interesting.

Multiple pipeline routes. As the map in case Exhibit 3 indicates, Enercon has six possible pipeline segments to choose among. The numerous combinations and permutations of these six segments force the student to eliminate superfluous subsets, such as simultaneous investment in segments 4 and 6.

Revenue considerations. In essence, connection to both Gulf Transmission and Kentucky Natural Gas (KNG) pipeline systems will afford Enercon greater bargaining power with KNG and, thus, a higher price per MCF:

	$/MCF
Shipment via Gulf:	$2.25 (equal to $2.80 – 0.41 – 0.14)
Sale to KNG:	2.10 (if no Gulf connection)
Sale to KNG:	$2.51 (if Gulf connection)

Clarence compressor. If Enercon ships via the Gulf system, it can connect at two possible points: (1) Walton and (2) Clarence (via the Olim pipeline). If Enercon chooses to ship via Clarence, it must pay Gulf $2 million to increase compression in the system; this is a one-time charge, but it obviously will

252

impair the economic attractiveness of the projects.[1] No compression investment is required at Walton.

A sensible approach to these and other complications is to make simplifying assumptions wherever possible. For instance:

1. If a redundant pipeline system is contemplated, the relevant contract price per MCF should be $2.51, since a rational manager would not choose to sell the product at a lower price. Also, if the contract price is $2.51, then one is implicitly assuming sale to KNG. It is sensible to assume that Enercon will only connect to the Gulf system and not actually ship that way—thus eliminating the expense of the Clarence compressor.

2. The case indicates that "back pumping" is not allowed and that the Buchanan-Olim pipeline (route 3 on the map in case Exhibit 3) runs in only one direction, as the arrow indicates. To "back pump" would enable the Leigh field to connect to Leona or Boswell, perhaps enhancing the operating flexibility of Enercon. Because Gulf has a partial ownership interest in the McCarin-Olim pipeline (route 3) and it would not be in Gulf's interest to enhance Enercon's bargaining power, we can assume that Gulf would prevent "back pumping" of the Buchanan-Olim pipeline. This assumption eliminates numerous pipeline/marketing alternatives.

Eliminating the superfluous alternatives still leaves 11 principal investment possibilities. Exhibit A presents the structure of these alternatives along with the NPVs, IRRs, and switches that must be thrown on the model. While the tree is largely self-explanatory, the instructor can observe that each main branch (i.e., Buchanan only, Leigh only, both) is further extended by building/shipping alternatives (i.e., Gulf, KNG, both) and complicated by the choice of specific routes. The instructor should anticipate that some students may want to extend the tree by another layer indicating to whom Enercon will sell its gas, but the first simplifying assumption in this section eliminates this complication. There may be other schemes for organizing the decision problem, but the author has found the decision tree to be most useful.

Valuation of Alternatives

After the specific alternatives to be valued have been identified, the quantitative analysis is a straightforward task of exercising the model. It is accomplished by varying the assumptions in the upper left-hand corner of each spreadsheet model. Because the two models treat Leigh and Buchanan independently, students may initially balk at how to value the alternatives where *both* fields are developed. Because the fields are independent of each other, however, valuing them jointly is simply a matter of adding their NPVs (obtaining an IRR for the joint case is more complicated and is not addressed here).[2]

---

[1]The model shows a deduction for the Clarence compressor as an after-tax cash outlay.

[2]A subtle error some students will make is to assume connection of both gas fields to the Olim pipeline and throw the switch to "yes" for the Clarence compressor in *both* spreadsheets. This error double-counts the expense of the compressor.

Cursory inspection of the model often raises questions about why Ben Harrison adds back intangible drilling expenses to get cash flow. The reason is that he deducts the *full* drilling expense in the cash-flow calculation: adding back intangible costs prevents them from being double-counted.

Students may use a range of discount rates for these projects. Harrison simply uses 10 percent, because Enercon is a private company and has not estimated its weighted-average cost of capital. Through the use of data on comparable companies in the case, however, students may estimate the cost of capital. Enercon has little debt in its capital structure, which prompts many students to wonder whether the assumption of higher leverage might not be more "typical" for projects like these and/or more consistent with Enercon's long-term financing targets. Exhibit B estimates a hurdle rate for this project based on assumptions of Enercon's current capital structure and of the average industry capital structure. The differing assumptions necessitates relevering beta and adjusting the weights in the weighted-average formula. The resulting weighted-average costs are 10.22 and 10.96 percent. In the analysis that follows, a 10 percent discount rate is used (to use the higher, risk-adjusted rates does not alter the ranking of the alternatives).

Exhibit A listed the IRRs and NPVs associated with the investment strategies. No matter whether one focuses on Leigh, Buchanan, or both, the value of hooking up to two pipelines is clear:

Net Present Values
(millions)

Gas Field	Customer		
	Gulf	KNG	Both
Buchanan	$1.1	$2.0	$2.8
Leigh	$6.8	$8.3	$11.3
Both	$7.9	$10.3	$14.1

Note: Each cell in this table assumes that the highest value pipeline route is adopted.

Developing both fields creates the most value for Enercon. "Overinvesting" in pipelines to both fields adds about $3.8 million ($14.1 - $10.3) in value to the project. This result illustrates how value can be created by *strategic positioning*, which, in this case, reduces buyer power.

Issue of Risk

If time permits, the instructor may choose to dwell on the qualitative differences in the two potential customer bases. The customer base available via Gulf consists of industrial, cyclical, and relatively short-term buyers. KNG is willing to commit to a longer term contract, and its demand for Enercon's gas is much more stable across the economic cycle. The KNG alternative is probably safer for Enercon. This factor raises the question of whether one should apply the same discount rate to valuing the two pipeline strategies. Such an adjustment is superfluous, since KNG, the less risky alternative, already dominates the Gulf alternative.

Sources of Value

As a closing discussion, the instructor can press students to identify the sources of the positive NPVs in this case. The first response of many students is that management has created value by finding potentially valuable deposits of natural gas. A second source of value is the benefit of pipeline redundancy in the form of enhanced bargaining power. And third, the Devonian shale tax credit contributes significantly to the cash flows. Without the second and third effects, the gas-well drilling project at either field is much less economically attractive. These latter two sources illustrate two of the most important ways in which general managers create value for their investors: through finding and exploiting unusual investment incentives (e.g., created by the Devonian shale tax credit) and then strategically positioning the firm to greatest advantage.

EXHIBIT A Structure of Alternatives for Investment Analysis

		$2MM compressor at Clarence?	Miles	Contract Price $2.80	Transport Cost $0.55	WACC = 10% NPV 6.768	Pre-Tax IRR 13.95	After-Tax IRR 21.89	K=11.6% NPV $5.356	K=13.9% NPV $3.677
LEIGH ONLY To Gulf only	via Olim	Y	22	$2.80	$0.55	6.768	13.95	21.89	$5.356	$3.677
To Kentucky only	via Stanleyville	N	27	2.10	0	8.315	16.25	27.37	6.887	5.186
To Both but sell to Kentucky	via Olim & S'ville	N	49	2.51	0	11.335	21.71	31.89	9.579	7.461
To Gulf only	via Olim (McLarin)	Y	0	2.80	0.55	1.121M	10.56	15.38	0.722	0.252M
	via Leona to Walton	N	27	2.80	0.41	0.299	3.59	11.87	0.044	(0.265)
BUCHANAN ONLY To Kentucky only	via Leona	N	11	2.10	0	1.784	9.40	23.35	1.435	1.019
	via Boswell	N	18	2.10	0	2.007	11.45	25.47	1.643	1.209
To both but sell to Kentucky	via Olim & Leona	N	11	2.51	0	2.590	15.82	29.07	2.165	1.656
	via Olim & Boswell	N	18(9)	2.51	0	2.813	17.97	31.41	2.373	1.847
	via Leona to Walton and Boswell	N	27	2.51	0	0.808	0.84	14.94	0.501	0.138
To Gulf only	both via Olim	Y	22	2.80	0.55	7.889			6.078	3.929
	Leigh to Olim and Buchanan to Leona-Walton	Y	49	2.80	0.55 0.41	7.067			5.400	3.412
BOTH LEIGH AND BUCHANAN To Kentucky only	Leigh to Stanleyville & Buchanan to Leona	N	38	2.10	0	10.099			8.322	6.205
	Leigh to Stanleyville & Buchanan to Boswell	N	27 + 9	2.10	0	10.322			8.530	6.395
To both pipelines	Leigh to Olim & S'ville Buchanan via Olim & Leona	N	60	2.51	0	13.925			11.744	9.137
	Leigh to Olim & S'ville Buchanan via Leona, Walton, & Boswell	N	76	2.51	0	12.143			10.080	7.619
	Leigh via Olim & S'ville Buchanan via Olim & Boswell	N	49 +9	2.51	0	14.148			11.952	9.328

Note: this assumes that the Buchanan-to-Olim pipeline will not reverse direction since the line is partially owned by Gulf & Gulf would probably resist actions enhancing Enercon's bargaining position.

EXHIBIT B   Estimate of Project Risk-Adjusted Discount Rates

	Based on Enercon's Capital Structure	Based on Industry Average Debt/Equity Ratio
ß (unlevered)[1]	.58	.58
Debt/equity	0	1.244[2]
ß (relevered)	.58	1.06
Risk-free rate[3]	.0597	.0597
$R_m - R_f$[4]	.086	.086
Cost of equity	.1096	.1509
i [Prime + 1%][5]	.095	.095
$K_d = i [1+t]$[6]	.063	.063
Debt/total capital	0	.554
Equity/total capital	1.0	.446
Weighted-average cost of capital	.1096	.1022

Notes:

1. Average for unlevered betas computed from the sample of diversified natural gas companies, case Exhibit 7.

2. Average debt/equity ratio for diversified natural gas companies, case Exhibit 7.

3. Annualized 30-day Treasury bill yield, case Exhibit 6.

4. Arithmetic mean of premium return, stocks over T-bills, case Exhibit 6.

5. Prime rate of 8.5 percent indicated in case Exhibit 6.

6. Marginal tax rate (t) assumed equal to .34.

Iskall Arno (Abridged)

SYNOPSIS AND OBJECTIVES

This manufacturer of ice cream, yogurt, and other consumer packaged foods is facing an unprecedented number of opportunities for expansion. Yet for policy reasons, the board of directors has decided to limit the firm's capital budget to an amount smaller than the sum of the available investments. The task of the Capital Budgeting Committee is to decide how to allocate the firm's capital among the various opportunities.

Presented in the case are cash flows, net present values (NPVs), internal rates of returns (IRRs), paybacks, and strategic concerns on a dozen potential investments. The case also presents information on the interdependencies or synergies among the various projects, which when taken into account, alter the ranking of feasible "baskets" of projects. The simple task is to choose the best set of investments based on financial and strategic criteria.

The main objective of this case is to exercise students' skills in corporatewide resource allocation. Specific issues to be raised are:

- choice of measure(s) for evaluating projects (i.e., relative strengths of IRR, NPV, payback);

- adjusting for possible biases because of differences among the projects in size and life;

- how strategic and other qualitative considerations intervene in what appears to be a quantitative form of analysis;

- how to adjust the analysis for synergies among the projects.

STUDY QUESTIONS

1. What are the major techniques for comparing and ranking capital expenditures? Prepare to discuss the strengths and weakness of each technique. Will all techniques give the same ranking? Why or why not?

2. Please rank the 11 proposals on the basis of any criteria you feel are important. How sensitive is your ranking to changes in the assumptions underlying the analysis presented in case Exhibit 5. Under what circumstances would you change your ranking?

3. Case Exhibit 7 summarizes the evaluation of bundles of projects. Why is this information important? How, if at all, does Exhibit 7 change your ranking based on case Exhibit 5?

Teaching note written by Robert F. Bruner. Copyright (c) 1988 by the Darden Graduate Business School Sponsors, Charlottesville, VA.

4. Which set of projects should the committee recommend to the board of directors?

In some class settings, discussion of this case will be enhanced by assigning background readings on the actual resource-allocation practices of managers. Two useful readings are: L. J. Gitman and V. A. Mercurio, "Cost of Capital Techniques Used by Major U.S. Firms: Survey and Analysis of Fortune's 1000," *Financial Management*, Winter 1982, pp. 21-29, and M. Ross, "Capital Budgeting Practices of Twelve Large Manufacturers," *Financial Management*, Winter 1986, pp. 15-22.

The practices revealed in these articles contrast sharply with recommended procedures discussed in finance textbooks. These articles reveal the prevalence of capital rationing, the widespread use of the payback criterion, the predominance of project size in assessing risk, and the use of unusual risk-adjustment techniques.

TEACHING PLAN

A good general teaching strategy for this case is to dispense with the analytical questions and issues first before pushing for a resource-allocation decision.

(10 minutes) Do we really need to look at the returns, paybacks, and NPVs? Can't we just "eyeball" the list of proposals and choose those that are most attractive?

(10 minutes) How was case Exhibit 5 prepared? How were the project criteria calculated?

(15 minutes) What are "synergies"? How do you value them? Are synergies in general a material concern in capital budgeting?

(10 minutes) How was case Exhibit 7 prepared? The instructor must ensure that students understand the development of case Exhibits 6 and 7 before proceeding.

(10 minutes) What does case Exhibit 7 reveal? How does this explicit treatment
   of project interdependencies affect our evaluation of the 11 projects?

(25 minutes) Which set of projects would you, as a member of the Capital Budgeting Committee, advocate? What would your recommendation be as a paid outside consultant?

The instructor might choose to end the discussion with a vote of the class.

ANALYSIS

The teaching plan requires considerable emphasis on a discussion of mechanical techniques. Because that subject is well covered by finance textbooks, the focus of the analysis here will be on the preliminary comparison of the specific projects.

Exhibit 5 of the case presents estimates of the weighted-average costs of capital (WACCs) for the various projects under three sets of assumptions. The panel in the exhibit that assumes a corporate debt/equity ratio of 0.31/0.69

shows resulting WACCs ranging from 10.8 percent for the plant expansion to 14.7 percent for the theme park. The next panel assumes debt/equity ratios based on the projects' industry averages. The WACCs range from 10.7 percent (Expand Plant) to 14.2 percent (R&D Project). The third panel is based on a maximum debt/equity ratio of 0.50/0.50 for all projects. By any method, the project-specific WACCs vary widely among themselves and, more importantly, depart materially from the corporatewide hurdle rate of 10.6 percent. The WACC calculations in case Exhibit 5 underline the inappropriateness of using a single corporate hurdle rate in making complex resource-allocation choices. All NPVs given in this note are based on project-specific WACCs calculated using industry average debt/equity ratios.

Because the 11 projects in case Exhibit 5 vary in life and scale, one could adjust for the possible distortion resulting from those differences. The appendix to this note discusses one approach (the approach used in the following analysis). The final panel of case Exhibit 5 presents the resulting NPVs, adjusted for (1) 10.6 percent hurdle rate, (2) corporate WACC, and (3) project-specific (industry) WACC. Exhibit A of this note presents the project-specific NPVs adjusted for (panel I) replacement to infinity [indicated by (n, ∞)], (panel II) scale only, and (panel III) both effects. These figures are presented here for comparative purposes in the event that students raise questions about the materiality of any of the adjustments.

The results of most interest are presented in panel III of Exhibit A. We observe that the rankings change little from the unadjusted base case taken from case Exhibit 5. (Expand Market South and New Product Line exchange places in the ranking, as do New Plant and Expand Plant, although the difference in NPV between them is not large.) The NPVs, however, change materially. Specifically, the effect of the adjustments is to amplify the NPVs: positive and negative NPVs get larger.

The case also introduces incremental cash flows arising from interdependencies among the projects--synergies. The quantitative analysis provides an objective examination of the elusive concept of synergy.

The project interdependencies makes consideration of the projects on an individual basis not appropriate. Instead, the analyst must evaluate bundles of projects. In fact, all reasonable combinations of the projects must be considered. Case Exhibit 7 presents the feasible bundles, although the instructor might want to dwell on why other sets weren't selected for analysis. (The chief reason is that interdependencies do not exist in other bundles.)

Case Exhibit 7 also presents the comparative measures for the relevant project bundles. Exhibit B presents the NPVs in summary, assuming adjustments for risk, scale, and life.

Although the quantitative analysis affords a straightforward ranking of the projects, other issues intervene. For instance, the Theme Park creates the most value, but many students question about the strategic fit between this project and the firm's core business. The Theme Park is viewed as the most risky project, with the NPV heavily dependent on the terminal value realized in year 10. The summary in Exhibit B, combined with a natural strategic bias against the Theme Park proposal, often pushes students toward favoring two bundles of projects: 2-7-9, (New Plant-Expand Eastward-New Product) and 2-7-10 (New Plant-Expand Eastward-Ad Campaign). Other students emphasize possible qualitative benefits from southward expansion or other projects.

Some students will emphasize the "social responsibility" of the firm to invest in the pollution-control project (not included in case Exhibits 5 and 7). The case contains enough information to price the cost of delaying this project: assuming that the pollution trap must be installed eventually, the cost of delay is at least the implicit compound rate of interest necessary to grow $4 million to $10 million over four years, or 26 percent. In fact, this cost could be higher if the government were to impose penalties on the firm. The pollution trap has an implicit IRR that ranks second of all 11 projects.

In closing the discussion, the instructor can return to the question of why we cannot just "eyeball" the projects and decide. The answer is that careful resource allocation depends on proper control for possible confounding effects and on careful weighing of qualitative considerations.

EXHIBIT A   Evaluation of Individual Projects

	(1) Expand Truck Fleet	(2) New Plant	(3) Expand Plant	(4) R&D Project	(5) Conveyer Systems	(7) Expand Market Eastward	(8) Expand Market Southward	(9) New Product Line	(10) Ad Campaign	(11) Theme Park
Total Investments										
Property	$20.00	$25.00	$10.00	$15.00	$14.00		20.00	$15.00	$15.00	$30.00
Working capital	2.00	5.00	10.00			20.00	20.00	3.00		10.00
Years	7	10	10	10	7	10	10	10	3	10
Project-specific WACCs	12.6%	11.0%	10.7%	14.2%	11.0%	11.2%	11.0%	11.5%	13.3%	14.0%
NPVs using WACCs	($3.12)	$0.43	$0.23	$2.07	($1.04)	$11.07	$8.43	$7.88	$0.58	$33.30
Rank	10	7	8	5	9	2	3	4	6	1
I. NPV(n,∞)*	($5.53)	$0.66	$0.36	$2.82	($2.01)	$16.92	$13.01	$11.88	$1.86	$45.60
Rank	10	7	8	5	9	2	3	4	6	1
II. NPV adjusted for scale**	($5.67)	$0.57	$0.92	$5.52	($2.97)	$22.14	$16.86	$17.51	$1.55	$33.30
Rank	10	8	7	5	9	2	4	3	6	1
III. NPV(n,∞) adjusted for scale	($10.05)	$0.89	$1.44	$7.51	($5.73)	$33.85	$26.03	$26.40	$4.95	$45.60
Rank	10	8	7	5	9	2	4	3	6	1

*NPV(n, ∞) = NPV(n)$[(1+k)^n/(1+k)^n-1]$.

**NPV adjusted for scale = ($40/Total investment) x NPV.

Note: All NPVs estimated in this note are based on project-specific WACCs calculated using industry average debt/equity ratios.

EXHIBIT B Ranking of Project Groups

	Synergy		Synergy Time Adjusted		Synergy Time and Scale Adjusted	
	Group	NPV	Group	NPV	Group	NPV
1	7,10,11	$55.87	7,10,11	$86.43	7,10,11	$133.40
2	8,10,11	$51.64	8,10,11	$80.43	8,10,11	$121.77
3	2,7,9	$34.36	2,7,10	$55.34	2,7,10	$115.74
4	2,8,9	$31.75	2,7,9	$52.41	2,8,10	$108.28
5	2,7,10	$30.37	2,8,10	$51.61	2,7,9	$100.33
6	2,8,10	$27.77	2,8,9	$48.61	2,3,7,10	$93.10
7	2,3,7,10	$26.49	2,3,7,10	$46.00	2,8,9	$92.72
8	2,3,8,10	$23.87	2,3,8,10	$42.20	2,3,8,10	$85.50
9	1,2,7	$23.62	1,2,7	$36.23	1,2,7	$66.66
10	1,2,8	$21.02	1,2,8	$32.48	1,2,8	$59.17
11	1,2,3,9	$18.55	1,2,3,9	$27.78	1,2,3,9	$57.67
12	1,2,9	$16.48	1,2,9	$24.49	1,2,9	$47.42
13	1,2,3,10	$4.67	1,2,3,10	$10.83	1,2,3,10	$26.31
14	1,2,10	$2.35	1,2,10	$6.01	1,2,10	$13.57
15	1,2,3	$0.52	1,2,3	$0.40	1,2,3	$1.92

Adjusting for time rearranges the relative values of the project groups that rank 3rd through 6th. Adjusting for scale after adjusting for time flips 4th and 5th places and 6th and 7th places.

Note that, if the Theme Park (project 11) is considered out of the question, adjusting for scale makes project group 2-7-10 relatively more attractive.

APPENDIX Adjusting for Life and Scale

Some students may note that differences in the projects' lives and scales make analytical comparison complicated if not impossible. To adjust for these differences requires two steps. First, to adjust for differences in life, one must assume that each project could be repeated for as long as necessary to equate their lives. In this case, that would mean running each project for 3 x 7 x 10 = 210 years. This span would be impractical, but a formula exists that allows for analysis assuming an infinite number of years (see Weston & Copeland, Eighth Edition, pp. 125-29, for its derivation):

$$NPV(n,\infty) = NPV(n)[(1+k)^n/(1+k)^n-1].$$

where

k = cost of capital
n = life of the project
$NPV(n)$ = net present value of the project over its expected life

Second, to adjust for scale, divide the largest capital outlay (in this case, $40 million for the Theme Park) by each project's capital requirement and multiply each project's NPV by the dividend. For example, the scale-adjusted NPV for expanding the plant would be ($40/$10) x $0.25 = $1.00.

Brown-Forman Distillers Corporation

SYNOPSIS AND OBJECTIVES

The chief executive officer of this producer of branded liquors must decide whether to acquire Southern Comfort Corporation for $94.6 million. Southern Comfort produces a liqueur with the same name, although curiously, consumers tend to view the drink as a whiskey. On the ambiguity of product positioning hangs one of the important judgment issues of the case, for whether Southern Comfort is (or will be) a whiskey or a liqueur affects the forecast assumptions and valuation of the company. Hence, although nominally this case is an exercise in discounted cash flow (DCF) valuation of an acquisition target, the student's analysis should also draw on the analysis of consumer demand and competitive trends.

This case affords a straightforward introduction to corporate valuation using DCF and to the general field of mergers and acquisitions. The case is also a useful problem in the valuation of intangible assets, the main focus being the value of a brand name that has relatively few hard assets associated with it.

STUDY QUESTIONS

Depending on the instructor's teaching goals and the students' skill level, one could distribute to the students before class the gross profit forecast given in Exhibit A.

1. Should Brown-Forman buy Southern Comfort Corporation at the asking price of $94.6 million?

2. On what key assumptions does your answer to the first question depend? How robust is the purchase decision to variations in those key assumptions?

3. If Brown agrees to acquire Southern Comfort, to what key considerations should he devote his attention in order to make the acquisition an economic success?

4. Apart from the possible acquisition, how appropriate is Brown-Forman's hurdle rate of 12 percent for projects in place?

TEACHING PLAN

An instructor may follow any of several teaching strategies with this case, including: (1) group or team presentations, (2) presentation by one individual followed by contrasting comments from other students, or (3) discussion of aspects of the analysis, leading to a recommendation at the end of class. The following plan corresponds to the third alternative.

Teaching note written by Robert F. Bruner. Copyright (c) 1989 by the Darden Graduate Business School Sponsors, Charlottesville, VA.

(20 minutes) Why is Brown-Forman considering buying Southern Comfort? The
purpose of opening the discussion this way is to uncover the strategic
motives of Brown and the various pros and cons of the acquisition.

(30 minutes) What is Southern Comfort worth? The discussion of DCF valuation
can be broken down into estimates of annual free cash flow, terminal value,
and discount rate.

(20 minutes) To which assumptions is the valuation most sensitive? The
purpose of this segment of the discussion is to build students' appreciation
for key value drivers. Growth rate will emerge as the key assumption,
spurring a discussion of whether Southern Comfort is a liqueur or whiskey.

(10 minutes) What should Brown do? The strategic review and valuation
should provide a springboard for action, including how to run Southern
Comfort if it is to be acquired. To get closure, the instructor may need to
take a vote.

The epilogue provides a dramatic counterpoint to the ambiguous outcome
suggested by the valuation. If time permits, the instructor might present the
epilogue and explore with students the possible explanations for the market
reaction.

ANALYSIS

Brown-Forman's Strategy

The distilling industry is dominated by firms more than four times the size
of Brown-Forman. Competition in the very high-volume, popular-price segments is
intense. In any event, entry to these segments is barred to all except those
firms that can afford the huge investment necessary to establish a brand name.

Facing this environment, Brown-Forman's strategy has been to find and
exploit profitable niches, particularly in the high-price/high-quality segment
of the product market. The company invests heavily in "advertising support in
order to build brands which have long life-cycles with generally higher margins."

Indeed, brands prove to be the key assets in the instances of Brown-Forman
and Southern Comfort. Thus, this case affords the opportunity to discuss the
valuation of intangible assets such as brands, patents, and specialized
know-how. In particular, one can draw the distinction between their treatment
under Generally Accepted Accounting Principles, and their likely values from a
DCF analysis.

Based on historical performance, Brown-Forman's strategy appears to be
working well. In 1978, the firm earned a return on net assets[1] of 12.75
percent, hurdling its target 12 percent rate of return on projects in place. As
the text and case Exhibit 1 note, Brown-Forman showed higher margins, higher
growth rates, and a stronger balance sheet than its major competitors.

---

[1]Return on net assets is calculated as

$$\frac{EBIT(1-t)}{(Assets - Current\ liabilities)} = \frac{69.15(.5)}{271.12}$$

266

If Brown-Forman hopes to maintain its above-average performance in the long run, it needs to invest in or acquire brands early in their life cycles, to supplant the performance of its older brands as they mature. Brown-Forman's challenge is to find new opportunities in order to maintain its corporate growth rate. Exhibit 5 shows that demand is shifting away from "brown goods" toward "white goods," wines, and specialty drinks. Among these, the liqueurs category stands out.

Southern Comfort

The acquisition target fits Brown-Forman's needs in several ways. First, Southern Comfort competes in the attractive liqueurs segment and is a good performer within that segment. Its long-run growth rate in cases shipped is 13 percent (see case Exhibit 8); case sales in the liqueurs segment grew by a total of 45.5 percent (case Exhibit 5), or an annual 7.8 percent between 1971 and 1976. In volume, Southern Comfort has been outperforming its own high-performance segment.

Second, marketing synergy might spring from the combination of the two separate sales forces. This was a major consideration in the sales projections. Because Southern Comfort had a very small sales force, the acquisition team thought that the weight of Brown-Forman's sales force would help Southern Comfort's sales substantially. Also, Southern Comfort might provide expertise in foreign distribution and sales—just when Brown-Forman is seeking to expand foreign penetration by Jack Daniels.

Third, Southern Comfort has been highly profitable. In 1977, it had a 6.8 percent profit-to-sales ratio, exceeded only by Hiram Walker and Brown-Forman itself. In addition, its cash flow is strong enough to meet ordinary financing needs (see Exhibit A).

Fourth, there may be a fit between the two organizational cultures: both have been family run and still carry a Southern heritage.

Fifth, the Southern Comfort liqueur has never been sold at a discount, which is consistent with Brown-Forman's strategy of building full-price or premium-price brands.

One wonders, however, how many years of 13 percent compound growth are possible before demand is saturated. Case Exhibit 9 shows that Southern Comfort's domestic growth was slowing, but that foreign growth was rising rapidly enough to maintain the overall growth rate. In short, performance will depend increasingly on foreign distribution. Does this factor expose Brown-Forman to new worries and challenges? To some extent the answer to these questions lies in Brown's belief that Southern Comfort was not being aggressively marketed. Perhaps more active brand management would lengthen and heighten Southern Comfort brand's life cycle.

In short, the appeal of this acquisition depends on Brown-Forman's ability to manage an existing brand better than it was previously managed. Brown-Forman's experience with the Jack Daniels brand suggests that the company is especially skilled at niche brand development.

Valuation

Cost of capital. The case states that Brown-Forman applies a discount rate of 14 percent to the evaluation of new projects. To test the reasonableness of this rate, students might be encouraged to estimate the weighted-average cost of capital (WACC) for Southern Comfort.

As a first approximation, one can assume that the risk of Southern Comfort is the same as the risk of Brown-Forman, because the similarities between the two firms are more prominent than the differences. (The main difference is that Southern Comfort is a "pure play" in liqueurs, whereas Brown-Forman sells a broad product line of alcoholic beverages, although one can only speculate on whether this difference would bias the estimate upward or downward.)

From case Exhibit 1, one can draw the data necessary to estimate Brown-Forman's cost of equity using the capital-asset-pricing model. Beta is 1.1. The risk-free rate and market premium are .07 and .087, respectively. The resulting cost of equity is 16.65 percent.

Brown-Forman's stated marginal cost of debt is 8.75 percent. Accounting for 7 percent compensating balances, however, renders the effective cost 9.4 percent.

Case Exhibit 1 reveals that Brown-Forman's debt/equity ratio is .25. Supposing that Brown-Forman will impose this same capitalization on Southern Comfort, the percentage weights of debt and equity will be 20 and 80, respectively. (For simplicity, one can ignore the preferred stock; relative to the volume of debt and common stock, the preferred is insignificant. Including preferred in the equity weighting will bias the estimated WACC slightly upward.)

Folding all these elements together, we discover that the estimated WACC for valuing Southern Comfort is

$$WACC = .2(1-.5).094 + .8(.1665) = .1426$$

Thus, the corporate target of 14 percent appears to be a fair discount rate to use.

Cash-flow forecasts. An estimate of free cash flow (FCF) grows straightforwardly from the forecast assumptions given in case Exhibit 9 and Exhibit A. The formula for FCF includes

$$FCF = EBIT(1-t) + Depreciation - Capital Expenditures - Additions to Net working capital$$

In each forecast year, EBIT (earnings before interest and taxes) will equal gross profits given in Exhibit A less corporate expenses given in case Exhibit 9. Exhibit 9 also indicates that depreciation and capital expenditures are expected to net to zero. Additions to net working capital can be estimated by assuming that net working capital will grow at the same rate as gross profits. (Incidentally, it may make sense to assume that the acquisition will be consummated at the end of 1978, which makes 1979 the first year in which a cash flow occurs and eliminates the slight complication from estimating half-year cash flows and discount factors.)

Terminal value (TV). To estimate the residual value of Southern Comfort in 1988, one can use the Gordon growth model:

$$TV = FCF(1989)/(k-g)$$

FCF for 1989 would be equal to FCF for 1988 compounded at the assumed growth rate. The spreadsheet in Exhibit B assumes low perpetual growth, such as 1 percent, consistent with the change in case volumes in 1987 and 1988. Higher growth rates later could be justified by assuming more aggressive marketing efforts and inflation. Obviously, 1 percent growth in the presence of any inflation implies that the business of the firm is contracting in real terms.

The sensitivity of the valuation results to variations in assumed growth is presented below.

Initial investment. A detail that some students will miss is the fact that land worth $5.9 million is being sold back to the Fowlers at the time of the transaction. Thus, the true initial investment is not $94.6 million, but rather $88.7 million.

DCF calculations and sensitivity analysis. Exhibit B presents a completed valuation based on an assumption of 1 percent perpetual growth in the terminal value. The DCF value is $-10.9 million. Using these conservative assumptions (i.e., low perpetual growth), Southern Comfort appears to be overpriced. Many students will propose walking away from the merger negotiations at this point. It is useful to remind them that valuation analysis provides a *foundation* for negotiating. The sensible recommendation is "bring down the price" rather than abandon discussions.

A second important lesson in this analysis is that the DCF values depend importantly on key assumptions. Merger professionals rarely work with a single estimate of a firm's value; rather, they bound the range of possible outcomes through extensive sensitivity analysis. For instance, the growth rate assumed in the terminal value proves to be a key driver of the DCF value of Southern Comfort, as the following table indicates:

Growth Rate	Net Present Value (millions of dollars)
1%	−10.924
3	−5.398
5	2.583
7	15.125
10%	57.455

Plainly, the huge swing in DCF value warrants detailed discussion about the possible long-term rate of growth. Since the Gordon growth model assumes growth in perpetuity, it is best not to assume a very aggressive rate. Nevertheless, one can reasonably assume that case shipments might increase at the rate of population growth or growth in real gross national product (1 to 2.5 percent per year). In addition, one can reasonably assume that Brown-Forman will be able to maintain the growth rate in gross profits at least at the rate of inflation. Annual inflation over the long term in the United States might be expected to average 5 percent. In short, a reasonable growth-rate assumption would be in the neighborhood of 6 to 8 percent. At 7 percent growth, the acquisition is economically attractive.

One way to deal with the ambiguity of growth rates is to determine that rate at which the net present value (NPV) of the acquisition just equals zero and then consider the reasonableness of that rate. Using the model given in Exhibit B by trial and error gives a breakeven perpetual growth rate of 4.44 percent. This rate appears to be within a reasonable range of possible long-term growth rates.

The Decision

The economic analysis suggests that an investment in Southern Comfort would at least pay its own way. That result depends importantly, however, on Brown-Forman's strategy for the brand. Plainly, higher growth of this brand could be associated with its positioning in the rapidly growing liqueur segment, but many consumers view Southern Comfort as a whiskey—a negative-growth brown-goods product. In the long run, positioning as a brown good could be devastating to growth. On the other hand, repositioning the brand as a liqueur is also fraught with risk.

Students are usually quite divided on the investment decision. Many believe that the NPVs should be higher in order to motivate the investment. Others believe in the skills of Brown-Forman management to create value with this sleepy brand.

EPILOGUE

Brown-Forman did make this acquisition at the $94.6 million price. On July 21, 1978, CEO W. L. Lyons Brown announced that the firm had purchased an option to buy Southern Comfort and said, "If existing projections materialize, Brown-Forman's return on this investment will considerably exceed our minimum goal of 14 percent after taxes for new projects."[2]

The reaction of the market was to bid up Brown-Forman's share price by 14.1 percent *over and above* the return on the Standard & Poor's 500, for a increase in total market value of equity of $61.5 million. Exhibit C presents the cumulative excess returns for Brown-Forman's stock from 15 days before the announcement to 175 days after. The gain in share value on the date of announcement was not subsequently dissipated.

This actual gain in market value is huge relative to students' estimates of the NPV of Southern Comfort. The author's interview with Marty Romm of First Boston Corporation, one of the leading analysts of the distilled liquor industry, summoned up the following explanations for the market reaction:

1. Recognition that Brown-Forman was entering a new market segment, liqueurs, which had faster unit growth than brown goods.

2. Belief that Southern Comfort had a high internal rate of return.

3. Belief that Brown-Forman would exploit the Southern Comfort brand more fully than it had been, in a manner similar to Jack Daniels and other brands.

4. Recognition that the acquisition would use Brown-Forman's financial "slack," i.e., $20 million of the firm's excess cash and $68 million of the firm's unused debt capacity.

---

[2]*Wall Street Journal*, July 22, 1978.

EXHIBIT A Forecast of Gross Profits

	1978	1979	1980	1981	1982	1983	1984	1985	1986	1987	1988
Gross profit per case											
U.S.	$10.77	$11.59	$12.13	$12.73	$12.34	$12.48	$12.59	$12.62	$13.18	$13.30	$12.92
Export	$7.89	$8.48	$9.07	$9.35	$9.43	$9.28	$9.81	$9.92	$9.94	$9.89	$9.74
Canada	$5.03	$5.03	$5.03	$5.03	$5.03	$5.03	$5.55	$5.55	$5.55	$5.55	$5.55
Dollar gross profit ($/Case x Volume)											
U.S.	12,278	14,198	15,951	17,949	18,633	20,155	21,718	23,158	25,345	26,387	26,034
Export	2,564	2,969	3,447	3,787	4,007	4,128	4,544	4,760	4,868	4,944	4,872
Canada	578	629	694	755	805	855	999	1,055	1,110	1,166	1,221
Total gross profit	$15,420	$17,796	$20,092	$22,491	$23,445	$25,139	$27,261	$28,972	$31,323	$32,496	$32,127

EXHIBIT B DCF Valuation of Southern Comfort Corporation

Cash-Flow Forecast	1978	1979	1980	1981	1982	1983	1984	1985	1986	1987	1988
Gross Profit	$15,420	$17,796	$20,092	$22,491	$23,445	$25,139	$27,261	$28,972	$31,323	$32,496	$32,127
Less: Corporate expenses	(2,208)	(2,702)	(2,656)	(2,642)	(2,822)	(2,615)	(2,824)	(3,051)	(3,295)	(3,558)	(3,843)
EBIT	13,212	15,094	17,436	19,849	20,623	22,524	24,437	25,921	28,028	28,938	28,284
Taxes (@ 49%)	(6,474)	(7,396)	(8,544)	(9,726)	(10,105)	(11,037)	(11,974)	(12,701)	(13,734)	(14,180)	(13,859)
EBIAT	6,738	7,698	8,893	10,123	10,518	11,487	12,463	13,220	14,295	14,758	14,425
Depreciation = investment (see case Exhibit 10)	0	0	0	0	0	0	0	0	0	0	0
Additions to working capital (@ 60% of gross profit)	0	(1,425)	(1,378)	(1,439)	(572)	(1,016)	(1,273)	(1,027)	(1,411)	(704)	221
FREE CASH FLOW (FCF)	6,738	6,273	7,515	8,684	9,945	10,471	11,189	12,193	12,884	14,055	14,646
Terminal value (assumed growth rate = 1.00%)											113,791
FCF PLUS TERMINAL VALUE	6,738	6,273	7,515	8,684	9,945	10,471	11,189	12,193	12,884	14,055	128,437

($88,700)

Present value of FCF (@ WACC = 14%) $77,776

Investment: ($94,600)
Proceeds from sale of land: $5,900
Net present value: ($10,924)

Internal rate of return: 12.03%

272

EXHIBIT C   Cumulative Daily Excess Returns

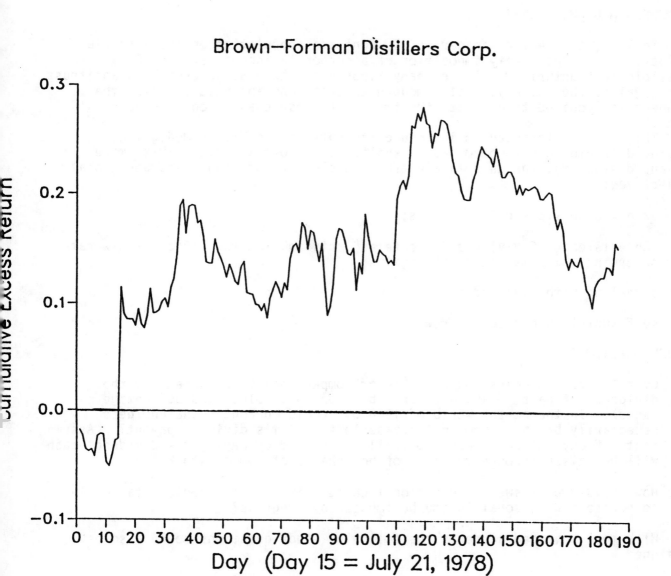

Brown–Forman Distillers Corp.

E. I. du Pont de Nemours Powder Company: 1909

SYNOPSIS AND OBJECTIVES

In 1909, the senior managers of Du Pont are speculating on the possible effects of (1) the likely imposition of a corporate income tax and (2) a possible restructuring of the company imposed by the U.S. government's antitrust suit against the company. Using modern theories and analytical tools, the student is required to evaluate the impact of these changes on shareholders' wealth.

This case is intended to introduce students to the Miller-Modigliani dividend-irrelevance theorem (as it applies in a no-tax world). With more advanced students, the case is a useful vehicle for pursuing these additional objectives:

- ex dividend stock price changes;

- the existence of dividend "clienteles" arising from the different tax rates on ordinary income and capital gains;

- signaling with dividends;

- self-sustainable rate of growth.

STUDY QUESTIONS

1. Over the recent years, Du Pont Powder Company has been increasing the dividends it pays to shareholders (both on an absolute and percentage basis). In the no-tax world of 1908-09, would Du Pont's shareholders necessarily benefit from an increase in the firm's dividend payout? (Assume that, if any internal cash shortfall is created by paying the dividend, cash will be raised through the sale of new shares of common stock.)

2. How would your answer to question 1 change, if at all, should a tax on corporate and personal income be imposed by Congress?

With more advanced students the following study questions could also be assigned.

3. At what percentage annual growth rate will Du Pont be able to increase its assets, assuming that it desires to sell no more common stock and desires to keep its present mix of debt and equity in: (a) the no-tax environment of 1908 and (b) an environment with a 1 percent tax on corporate income.

Teaching note written by Robert F. Bruner. Copyright (c) 1988 by the Darden Graduate Business School Sponsors, Charlottesville, VA.

4. On the day that Du Pont's shares go ex dividend (assuming a 1.75 percent quarterly dividend), how will Du Pont's share price respond: (a) in the no-tax environment of 1908; (b) in a taxable world with a 1 percent tax on all income (corporate and personal) and; (c) in a taxable world with a 1 percent tax on corporate and personal *ordinary* income and a .5 percent tax on *capital gains*.

5. The antitrust lawsuit threatens to split up the firm. What would be the effect of spinning off $5 million in assets to shareholders on: (a) the market value of Du Pont's equity, (b) the market value of Du Pont's debt, (c) Du Pont's equity beta, and (d) Du Pont's asset beta? How would these effects differ if the lawsuit required:

- a special $5 million dividend from cash;

- a special $5 million share repurchase from cash;

- an issue of $5 million in new equity and payment of a $5 million dividend;

- an issue of $2.5 million each in debt and equity and payment of a $5 million dividend.

TEACHING PLAN

The case is purposely abbreviated so that, when it is used as an introduction to the subject of dividend policy, the instructor will have time to dwell on ideas as well as their practical application. The following list of questions is offered as one possible discussion outline for an 80-minute class:

(35 minutes) In 1909, if Du Pont's investment needs are given and no new debt is to be issued, will the level of dividend payout have any effect on the wealth of the firm's shareholders?

(5 minutes) What do you suppose would be the shareholders' relative preferences for earnings retained versus dividends in the no-tax world?

(10 minutes) How, if at all, would Du Pont's share price change at the "exdividend" date?

(30 minutes) What would be the effect on Du Pont's debt and equity values of a split-up of the company? How would this effect compare with effects of a dividend, of a share repurchase, etc. (see assignment questions)?

ANALYSIS

Dividend Irrelevance

The first question invites a discussion of the Miller-Modigliani (M&M) dividend-irrelevance theorem. The theorem holds that, where there is a binding investment requirement, dividends must be offset by dilution in share value so that the investor will be indifferent to dividend policy. It may be illustrated either by an analysis of cash flows (M&M's classic sources-and-uses framework) or by an analysis of percentage returns. The basic scenario for this analysis is the assumption that Du Pont will raise its dividend from a payout of 7 percent to 7.75 percent.

The returns-based analysis is easily illustrated. On one hand, the stockholders' wealth is being increased by .75 percent over the previous payout. To finance this dividend increase, however, Du Pont must sell an additional interest in the company equal to .75 percent of its value. Because the asset portfolio of the company is unchanged by this transaction, the value of the company must be unchanged, and as a result, the value of old shareholders' wealth must have declined by .75 percent. The change in the dividend and the increased dilution offset one another, producing no change in shareholders' wealth. Another way for the instructor to exploit this insight is to observe that the dilution effect is equivalent to lost growth: it must be that earnings not retained penalize the expansion of the firm. Thus, higher dividends are achieved at the expense of lost capital gains.

The cash-flow-based illustration of dividend irrelevance can be drawn from facts in the case. Key assumptions are that (1) the market value per share is $95 (from case Exhibit 3); (2) earnings available to common shareholders increase to $3.4 million as mentioned in the case; (3) Du Pont does not borrow more or liquidate its investment portfolio; and (4) Du Pont's investment requirements are $1.45 or $3 million, as stated in the case. The basic comparison is presented in Exhibit A. Lines C through D reveal that gains to shareholders resulting from an increased dividend are offset by dilution losses, to produce a net effect of no change in shareholder wealth. This result hinges importantly on the assumption of no change in the total market value of equity (line 5) such as might arise from a signaling effect.

Having developed the basic irrelevance result, the instructor may wish to hint at the signaling and clientele effects (discussed in next section) by pointing out that this result hinges on two key assumptions: (1) that the value of the firm remains invariant to the change in dividend and (2) that shareholders are truly indifferent between a dollar received in the form of dividends versus a dollar received in capital gains.

Ex Dividend Stock Price Movements

If there are no taxes, Du Pont's share price must fall by the full amount of the dividend paid. This conclusion rests on the sources-and-uses logic of M&M. In a world of taxes, however, the effect of paying dividends will depend on whether or not ordinary income (i.e., dividends) is taxed differently from capital gains. If so, the different rates of taxation may cause investors to value taxable cash dividends differently from capital gains. For instance, the expected price change on exdividend day will be

$$\frac{P_{t-1} - P_t}{D_t} = \frac{1 - t_o}{1 - t_c}$$

276

That is, the change in stock price as a percentage of the dividend D will hold in the same proportion as 1 minus the ordinary income tax rate (t_o) divided by 1 minus the capital gains tax rate (t_c).[1]

To illustrate, suppose that the quarterly dividend is $1.75 per share (at a 7 percent of par value payout). The following should occur:

	Ex-Dividend Stock Price Change
No tax world	-$1.75
1% tax, income and gains	-$1.75
1% tax, income and .5% tax gains	-$1.74

The lower decline under differential taxation occurs because a dollar of capital gains is worth more after taxes than a dollar of dividends; to prevent arbitrage profits, the gain from selling early (taking a capital gain) must equal the gain from taking the dividend and then selling. So paradoxically, as the ex dividend change grows smaller, the more advantageous it is to take capital gains.

This ex-dividend-day effect has been shown to be associated with the level of dividend yield of the firm (see footnote 1) and is consistent with M&M's prediction that "a corporation would tend to attract to itself a 'clientele' consisting of those preferring its particular payout ratio." Whether one clientele is as good as another, as M&M claim, remains a matter of debate.

Clientele and Signaling Effects

As suggested in the preceding two sections, the classic results about irrelevance and ex dividend movements invite a discussion of two important effects of dividends that contribute extremely important practical ideas about dividend policy.

- *Signaling*. One of the important assumptions behind M&M's irrelevance result is that the value of the firm will remain invariant to what are viewed as purely financial rearrangements. Recent research suggests, however, that surprise changes in dividends may convey information to investors that may justify a revaluation of the firm. For instance, surprise dividend cancellations or reductions are usually met with substantial declines in share value. Similarly, surprise dividend initiations and increases are met with abnormal increases in share value. In essence, these revaluations of the firm are viewed as responses by investors to new information about the long-term prospects of the firm suggested by the surprise changes.

- *Clienteles*. The ex dividend result suggests that the magnitude of the difference in ordinary and capital-gains tax rates that an investor faces may affect the attractiveness of that investment to the shareholder. Wealthy investors in high tax brackets will have a preference for low-current-income/high-capital-gains stocks, whereas relatively poor

---

[1]This relationship was presented in Edwin Elton and Martin Gruber, "Marginal Stockholder Tax Rates and the Clientele Effect," *Review of Economics and Statistics*, 1970, pp. 68–74.

investors may have a preference for current income. In other words, taxes may create natural "clienteles" or investor segments for a firm's securities. Also, clienteles may form around gender, age groups, sociological segments, etc. The broader implication of the existence of clienteles is that the dividend-payout decision is actually a marketing decision: one should choose a dividend policy that will position the firm's securities within that clientele willing to pay the most for those securities.

In short, information asymmetries and capital-market segmentation may create circumstances in which careful dividend-policy design can result in higher share prices.

Retention of Earnings and Self-Sustainable Growth

The irrelevance result is important because it implies that the main consideration in setting dividend policy is the profitability of internal investment in the firm. That is, if the firm exhausts all possible profitable investments and there remains some excess cash in the company, the residual should be returned to shareholders for them to invest (or consume).

That a capital-intensive manufacturing firm would exhaust its queue of prospective projects using a 45 percent retention ratio seems unlikely, but appearances can be deceiving. The self-sustainable growth model [ROE x (1-payout ratio)] reveals that annual asset growth without further equity sales could advance at 3.65 percent per year. Assets have grown at a nominal 5.3 percent compound rate from 1904 to 1909.

Possible Restructuring

The final teaching question invites a comparison of the various vehicles for returning value to shareholders. Following is a prospective chalkboard diagram to help sort out the effects of each tactic:

	Equity Value	Debt Value	Asset Beta	Equity Beta
Dividend	down	down	up	up
Repurchase	down	down	up	up
Levered dividend	down	up	no change	up
Split-up: Du Pont	down	down	?	?
Shareholders	no change	no change	no change	no change

The point of this comparison is to show that the dividend and share repurchase are economically equivalent and that they both illustrate the M&M irrelevance proposition. The levered dividend is a useful foil for testing students' understanding of the irrelevance idea; it deviates from the basic case by holding constant the total value of assets and varying the capital structure. Finally, the split-up is shown for Du Pont, which loses assets, and for the shareholders who continue to hold a portfolio containing the same assets as before the split-up. Economically, the split-up should have no effect on shareholders' wealth.

EPILOGUE

Du Pont lost the antitrust lawsuit in 1911 and immediately began negotiating a plan of disintegration with the U.S. Attorney General. In 1912, the court approved a plan whereby the assets of Du Pont would be split into Hercules Powder Company, Atlas Powder Company, and Du Pont.

A federal excise tax on corporate income was enacted in 1909, as was an amendment to the Constitution allowing a federal income tax. This amendment was finally ratified in February 1913. A tax rate of 1 percent was imposed on the income of every individual and corporation, with graduated rates levied on incomes in excess of $20,000 per year (roughly $200,000 in 1980s' dollars).

EXHIBIT A Test of Effect of Dividend Increase on Shareholders' Wealth

	$1.45 Million		$3.0 Million	
	7% Dividend	7.75% Dividend	7% Dividend	7.75% Dividend
A. Estimate of capital required:				
1. Earnings available to common (Case)	$3.40	$3.40	$3.40	$3.40
2. Investment (Case)	(1.45)	(1.45)	(3.00)	(3.00)
3. Dividend*	(1.95)	(2.16)	(1.95)	(2.16)
4. Requirement	.00	(.21)	(1.55)	(1.76)
B. Estimate of stock price exdividend:				
5. Total market value of equity**	$26.475	$26.475	$26.475	$26.475
6. Market value of equity to be raised (line 4 above)	.000	.210	1.550	1.760
7. Ex dividend stock price†	$95.00	$94.25	$89.43	$88.68
C. Loss in stock price		($.75)	($.75)	
D. Dividend		.75	.75	
E. Change in shareholder wealth		$.00	$.00	

*Equal to percentage dividend times par value of common stock ($100), times number of shares (278,685).

**Equal to stock price ($95) times number of shares (278,686).

†Value of old equity (line 5) less value of new equity raised (line 6) divided by number of shares.

280

Cleveland-Cliffs Iron Company

SYNOPSIS AND OBJECTIVES

This case considers the tender offer by Cleveland-Cliffs for Detroit Steel Corporation. The unusual feature of this tender offer is that Cleveland- Cliffs simultaneously agreed to sell the operating assets of Detroit to Cyclops Corporation, leaving Cleveland-Cliffs with Detroit's remaining assets, 1,130,150 shares of Cleveland-Cliffs common (27 percent of shares outstanding). In short this move is a share repurchase cloaked as an acquisition. Whether and why these simultaneous transactions create value for shareholders of the three firms is the subject of the case.

The case can be a vehicle for discussing:

• the financial and signaling effects of share repurchases;

• the concept of the economic or market-value balance sheet and the practical application of market values of assets to the analysis of corporate restructurings;

• the principle of the conservation of value--that dividing the claims more or less finely will not change the total value of those claims;

• the effects of decomposing a firm to unlock latent value; and

• financial restructuring.

STUDY QUESTIONS

Please give your recommendations about the proposed transaction from the standpoints of three parties:

1. Detroit shareholders: Should they accept Cleveland-Cliffs' offer? At that offering price, is Detroit fairly valued?

2. Cleveland-Cliffs: Will this deal create value for Cleveland-Cliffs' shareholders? What justifies the purchase premium for Detroit shares? Should Cleveland-Cliffs proceed with the offer?

3. Cyclops Corporation: Why is this transaction more attractive than a direct tender for Detroit? Should Cyclops proceed with this transaction?

Teaching note written by Robert F. Bruner. Copyright (c) 1986 by the Darden Graduate Business School Sponsors, Charlottesville, VA.

TEACHING PLAN

The following list of questions affords an outline for a case discussion in 80 minutes:

(10 minutes) What was the structure of the proposed transaction? Who would give what to get what?

(5 minutes) What was Cleveland-Cliffs' tender premium for Detroit Steel?

(25 minutes) What is the value of Detroit Steel? To Cyclops? To Cleveland-Cliffs? To Detroit shareholders?

(5 minutes) Why would Cleveland-Cliffs be willing to settle for a transaction that merely breaks even?

(5 minutes) Should Detroit shareholders sell?

(15 minutes) Why did Cyclops agree to cooperate with Cleveland-Cliffs?

(15 minutes) Who won? Who lost?

The discussion can be closed with a presentation of the resulting stock prices and some summary comments on value conservation.

ANALYSIS

Conservation of Value

In the absence of capital-market imperfections, the value of an asset should be unaffected by the structuring of the security claims against that asset. In other words, the value of a pie should be determined by its size, not how you slice its pieces. The instructor can easily demonstrate this concept in connection with the share-repurchase decision. Unless the repurchased shares are undervalued in the market, a share repurchase should create no value if there are no leverage changes or signaling effects from the repurchase: it simply results in the pie being sliced less finely than before.

Cleveland-Cliffs' Purchase Premium

Cleveland-Cliffs' tender premium of 85.9 percent (based on Detroit's closing price on May 26) is exceptionally large.[1] The size of this premium is made possible by four conditions: (1) Detroit's extraordinarily deep discount from the market value of its investment portfolio, (2) the large number of Cleveland-Cliffs' shares in Detroit's portfolio, (3) the standard effect of a share repurchase on Cleveland-Cliffs' stock, and (4) the swap of Cyclops' holdings of Detroit for Detroit's operating assets. Consider each of these conditions in turn.

---

[1]In comparison, one academic researcher, Michael Bradley, found an average risk-adjusted tender premium of about 40 percent.

Deep discount. On May 26, Detroit was selling so cheaply that its shares were priced *below* the market value per share of Detroit's portfolio of marketable securities:

Detroit's book value per share (12/31/69)	$21.17
Detroit's market value per share (5/26/70)	$ 8.875
Market-to-book-value ratio	.419
Cleveland-Cliffs' bid per share	$16.50
Market value of Detroit's investment portfolio (5/26/70) per share[2]	$ 9.77

Therefore, against the market value of Detroit's portfolio, Cleveland-Cliffs' bid offered a 69.0 percent premium (rather than an 85.9 percent premium against Detroit's stock price).

Share repurchase effect. Second, Detroit's portfolio of securities consisted mainly[3] of Cleveland-Cliffs' stock--a fact of some relevance to Cleveland-Cliffs. It is the value of Detroit's portfolio on which the attractive economics of this transaction hinge. The fact that much of the portfolio is committed to Cleveland-Cliffs' common stock is revealed only in the footnote to Detroit Steel's balance sheet (case Exhibit 5).

The apparently large tender premium is reduced further by the predictable effects of a share repurchase on the value of Cleveland-Cliffs' stock. In buying Detroit (i.e., acquiring Detroit and canceling the Cleveland-Cliffs' stock), the relevant share price is *not* the price before the announcement (May 26, 1970), but rather, the expected share price *after repurchase*. Data on price/earnings ratios (P/Es) and earnings per share (EPS) can be used to adjust Cleveland-Cliffs' share price as follows:

$$\text{New price} = \text{Old price (May 26, 1970)} \times \text{Adjustment}$$

$$\text{Adjustment} = \frac{\text{Price (after)}}{\text{Price (before)}} = \frac{\text{P/E (after)} \times \text{EPS (after)}}{\text{P/E (before)} \times \text{EPS (before)}}$$

If P/E and net income remain constant across the repurchase, then

$$\text{Adjustment} = \frac{\text{Shares (before)}}{\text{Shares (after)}} = \frac{4.166}{3.036} = 1.372$$

So

$$\text{New price} = 33.75 \times 1.372 = \$46.305$$

The analysis based on P/E ratios is a useful teaching tool for employing the value-conservation logic. Cleveland-Cliffs' value will increase modestly, however, as a result of the asset swap with Cyclops. Exhibit A presents the calculation of Cleveland-Cliffs' expected price per share based on all flows of assets in the deal; the estimated value is $46.77 per share.

At a post-repurchase price of $46.77 per Cleveland-Cliffs' share, Detroit's investment portfolio had a value of $13.50 per share of Detroit common. In this light, Cleveland-Cliffs is really just paying a 22.0 percent premium relative to Detroit's expected portfolio value.

---

[2]The market value of the portfolio equals $38,481,127/3,940,000 shares.

[3]In addition to the Cleveland-Cliffs' stock, the portfolio contained 120,571 shares of Steep Rock Mines, Ltd., a small Ontario iron-ore company. The market value of these shares was $343,627.

The swap with Cyclops. The purchase premium dwindles further in view of the fact that Cyclops was exchanging its 19.3 percent interest in Detroit and a $1.4 million note (payable to Cleveland- Cliffs) for Detroit's operating assets. In other words, Cleveland-Cliffs would pay $51,063,070 ([(1−.193) x 3.94 m shares x $16.50] − $1.4m) for securities having a market value on May 26 of $38,481,127,[4] but after repurchase, having a market value of $53,200,743. In this light, Cleveland-Cliffs is buying at a 4 percent *discount* rather than an 86 percent premium.

Even at the expected price of $46.77, the pro forma book value of Cleveland-Cliffs is $49.92 [($189.991−51.063)/2.783]. Therefore, Cleveland-Cliffs is effectively "buying" its own assets at a 6.3 percent discount from book value.[5]

Note that the repurchase will alter Cleveland-Cliffs' capital structure very little on a book basis (debt/capital = .038 before, .05 after). On the basis of market value, the capital-structure change is also immaterial.

Corporate Control

If the transaction is basically a breakeven proposition for Cleveland-Cliffs, why would the company bother to complete it? One hypothesis is that the company is carrying excess cash, which management has decided to give to shareholders. The problem with this hypothesis is that, whether or not Cleveland-Cliffs' level of cash is presently excessive, the company is facing an unprecedented level of capital investment as it strives to meet the rising demand for iron ore. Ignoring the effects of dividends and investment in working capital, cash flows calculated from Exhibit 3 of the case suggest these financing needs:

Year	Incremental Need	Cumulative Need
1970	$−26.0 million	$−26.0 million
1971	+ 3.3	−22.7
1972	+11.6	−11.1
1973	+14.9	+ 3.8
1974	−16.3	−12.5
1975	$ −1.2 million	$−13.7 million

---

[4]Market value of securities:

	Before Repurchase	After Repurchase
Cleveland	$38,137,500	$52,857,116
Steep Rock	343,627	343,627
Total	$38,481,127	$53,200,743

[5]One should be reluctant to carry this latter line of reasoning very far, because it ignores the economic earning power of the assets purchased. Nevertheless, it does suggest the bargain nature of Cleveland-Cliffs' purchase. Furthermore, should the instructor wish to discuss the correctness of Cleveland-Cliffs' pricing at the $46.77 level, comparative financial data are provided in the case.

At first glance, reinvesting the cash would seem to be more consistent with the operating strategy than using it to repurchase shares. Yet in light of the firm's $77.5 million in marketable securities, Cleveland-Cliffs seems capable of covering the $26 million shortfall in 1970 *and* repurchasing shares for $51 million. Therefore, reinvesting the cash would be more consistent with the demands on the company than distributing.

The second hypothesis is that management feels threatened by the possibility of a quarter of Cleveland-Cliffs' equity falling into hostile hands. Consider the list of companies expressing a strong interest in buying Detroit; arguably all are natural-resources companies who have some affinity to mining. Although their interest in a failing steelmaker is probably nil, their interest in the leading firm in the booming iron-ore industry is probably high. In short, the repurchase makes sense (from management's standpoint) as a defensive move.

Detroit Shareholders' View

Recipients of Cleveland-Cliffs' tender offer must decide whether it reflects the intrinsic economic value of the equity. Ordinarily, this question would require students to project Detroit's cash flows and discount them to the present. Notwithstanding the heroic assumptions this task would require, a *prima facie* case can be made that Detroit's shares aren't worth much more than the underlying value of Detroit's investment portfolio:

- Detroit's earnings had deteriorated significantly over the preceding five years. The downturn was attributed variously to Detroit's weak competitive position, the inefficiency of its plants, and the current softness in the industry. The company's default under the loan agreement is another warning flag about Detroit's financial health.

- Detroit's book value was diminished by its pension liability:

Book value (12/31/69)	$83.419 million
Pension liability	36.256
Net	$47.163
Per 3.94 m shares	$11.97/share

- Additional investment of $15 million is required to allow Detroit's operations to carry on *just at the present level*. The likelihood of a positive return on this investment seems small.

In view of these facts, Cleveland-Cliffs' offer of $16.50 per share seems adequate, if not generous.

Cyclops' Perspective

Why did Cyclops cancel its tender offer and agree to buy the assets from Cleveland-Cliffs? The reason was to be able to purchase at lower cost. Compare Cyclops' total payment under both deals:

	Cyclops' Tender	Cleveland-Cliffs' Tender
Amer. Export shrs.	$17.00 million	$17.00 million
$15/shr. to others (15 x 3.1795)	47.69	
Subtotal of cost	64.69	17.00
Sells C-C shrs. (1.13 x 33.75)[6]	38.14	Gives note 1.414
Cyclops pays net	$26.55 million	$18.414 million

In other words, Cyclops gets control of the same assets for 70 percent of the cost under its proposed tender offer. Moreover, the transaction resolves some uncertainty: Cyclops no longer has to guess about the price Cleveland-Cliffs will pay. Furthermore, the price it is paying comes closer to the true book value of Detroit's operating assets:

Gross book value	$83.419 million
Pension liability	(36.256)
Mkt. value, C-C shrs.	(38.140)
Net book value	$ 9.023 million

Finally, by paying $18.9 million for assets with a book value of $64.326 million [$83.419 (gross book value) less $19.093 (market value of securities)], Cyclops stands to enjoy a large negative amortization.

Economics of Transaction: Summary

The case illustrates well the benefits of decomposing a firm (Detroit Steel) and selling its pieces to buyers with higher valued uses. Detroit Steel could actually be viewed as two entities: (1) an operating company and (2) an investment portfolio. As the section "Deep Discount" implies, the operating entity was in effect accorded a *negative* value, of which the sale at any positive price would create value. The operating assets were evidently worth more to Cyclops than to Detroit's shareholders. Moreover, the analysis explicitly shows that Cleveland-Cliffs' shares were worth as much as 37 percent more to Cleveland-Cliffs than to other potential buyers of those shares. The chief beneficiaries of the transaction were the stockholders of Detroit Steel, who received an 86 percent bonus as the result of the decomposition.

EPILOGUE

The transaction was completed as outlined in the case. The consequences were: (1) Detroit's shareholders were paid a large premium for their shares; (2) Cyclops bought Detroit's operating assets at a substantial discount from its own

---

[6]Astute students may suggest that $33.75 is the current depressed price of Cleveland-Cliffs' shares and that $40 is more consistent with the value of the firm before the political events of late May.

proposed terms; and (3) Cleveland-Cliffs' shareholders received a large capital gain, while management saved a large block of its equity from falling into unfriendly hands. The immediate effect on share prices was as follows:

Changes in Stock Prices

	May 26	June 1	% Change
Detroit	8.875	16.50	+ 85.9%
Cleveland-Cliffs	33.75	42.875	+ 27%
Cyclops	23.875	28.50	+ 19%
Standard & Poor's 500	70.25	77.84	+ 10.8%

The transaction appeared to create value for the shareholders of each of the participating firms. Exhibit B shows that, viewed over a long period, Cleveland-Cliffs' shares rose by about 30 percent more than the market. As the analysis here shows, however, a simple repurchase of the same number of shares should have caused the share price to rise by 39 percent above the market (from $33.75 to $46.77 as given in Exhibit A).

One can only speculate why the actual gain did not equal the theoretical gain. First, the repurchase may have signaled greater management entrenchment. It certainly took the company somewhat farther "out of play" and thus may have discouraged takeover speculators from continued investment. Second, the repurchase may have signaled that the firm had fewer profitable investment opportunities for its cash and unused debt capacity.

EXHIBIT A Market Value Balance Sheets for Cleveland-Cliffs

	Before Transaction (May 26, 1970)	Adjustments	After Transaction
Net assets[1]	$165.3 million	-52.47^4 $+65.03^6$ -12.56^7 $+1.4^5$	$166.7 million
Debt[2]	7.5		7.5
Preferred stock[2]	17.2		17.2
Equity[3]	140.6	-52.47^4 $+65.03^6$ -12.56^7 $+1.4^5$	142.0
Total capital	$165.3 million		$166.7 million

$$\text{Price per share after should be:} \quad \frac{\text{Market value of Equity(MV)}}{\text{Number of shares}} = \frac{142.0}{3.036} = \$46.77$$

---

[1]Total assets less current liabilities, equal to the market value of debt plus equity.

[2]Market values of debt and preferred stock are assumed to equal book values.

[3]Before the transaction, equity equals $33.75 times 4.166 million shares.

[4]Cash purchase of Detroit's shares except for those held by Cyclops (3.941 m – .761) x 16.50 = 52.47.

[5]Promissory note from Detroit Steel (Cyclops) to Cleveland-Cliffs.

[6]Increase in assets equal to purchase price of Detroit's assets worth $16.50 x 3.941 million.

[7]Transfer assets to Cyclops worth $16.50 x .761 million.

EXHIBIT B Market-Adjusted Change in Cleveland-Cliffs' Stock Price

	Share Price	S&P 500	Percentage Change in Stock Price from May 26	Percentage Change in Stock Price Less Percentage Change in S&P 500
May 15, 1970	39 2/8	76.90	--	
May 22, 1970	35 6/8	72.25	--	
May 26, 1970	33 6/8	69.29	--	
May 29, 1970 Tender offer announced	42 7/8	76.55	27	+16.5
June 1, 1970	43 7/8	77.84	30	17.7
June 15, 1970	40 5/8	74.58	20.4	12.8
July 1, 1970 Has 80% of Detroit Steel stock	40 7/8	72.92	21.1	15.9
August 3, 1970	45 7/8	77.02	35.9	24.7
September 10, 1970 Merger consummated	49 1/8	82.30	45.6	26.8
November 13, 1970 Operating assets sold to Cyclops	50	83.37	48.1	27.8
December 3, 1970 Detroit Steel delisted	50 7/8	88.90	56.7	28.4

Southboro Corporation

SYNOPSIS AND OBJECTIVES

In mid-1988, the chief financial officer of this large CAD/CAM (computer-aided design and manufacturing) equipment manufacturer must decide on the magnitude of the firm's dividend payout. The case serves as an omnibus review of the many practical aspects of the dividend decision, including: (1) signaling effects, (2) clientele effects, and (3) financing and investment implications of increasing dividend payout. This case can follow a treatment of the Miller-Modigliani dividend-irrelevance theorem and serves to highlight practical considerations in setting dividend policy.

STUDY QUESTIONS

The case is rich enough to be used over two successive class periods. The following assignment questions suggest how the case discussion could be focused on the two days. If the case is to be treated in one day, the instructor should choose a subset of questions and review the analysis in case Exhibit 8 in summary fashion. The case is also useful for student team presentations, in which instance the instructor may wish to provide the entire set of questions. (See the bibliography for a list of collateral readings the instructor may wish to assign.)

Day 1 Study Questions

1. In theory, to fund an increased dividend payout, a firm might invest less, borrow more, or issue more stock. Which of these three elements is Southboro management willing to vary, and which elements remain fixed as a matter of policy?

2. What happens to Southboro's financing need and unused debt capacity if:

    a. no dividends are paid;
    b. there is a 20 percent payout;
    c. there is a 40 percent payout.

    Note that case Exhibit 8 presents an estimate of borrowing needed. Assume that maximum debt capacity is, as a matter of policy, 40 percent of equity.

3. What risks does Southboro face? How robust are the estimated financing side effects of the various dividend-payout levels?

4. How much additional cash will Southboro have to pay out in total over the 1988-94 period in order to increase the percentage payout by 1 percent? How

---

Teaching note written by Robert F. Bruner. Copyright (c) 1989 by the Darden Graduate Business School Sponsors, Charlottesville, VA.

much will this payout amount to per share? What will be the effect of this payout on the company's earnings per share?

Day 2 Study Questions

On day two, one could assign a supplemental reading on equity signaling such as the Asquith and Mullins article listed in the bibliography.

1. How will Southboro's various providers of capital, such as stockholders and bankers, react to declaration of a dividend in 1988? Over what ranges of payout will these reactions persist?

2. Many companies, like Southboro, pay dividends while simultaneously increasing debt. Is this wise? Under what conditions? If not, why is it done?

3. What should Kyle Tucker recommend to the board of directors regarding a long-run dividend policy for Southboro Corporation?

TEACHING PLAN

Day 1

(30 minutes) What determines Southboro's asset needs? Discussion following this question should address the nature of the industry, the strategy of the firm, and its performance. This discussion will lay the groundwork for the later review of strategic considerations that bear on the dividend decision.

(40 minutes) What are the implications of different payout levels for Southboro's capital structure, and unused debt capacity? The discussion here must present the financial implications of higher dividend payouts, particularly the consumption of unused debt capacity. Some attention might be given to a sensitivity analysis over the entire 1988-94 period, given cyclicality of demand or overruns in investment spending.

(15 minutes) Based on this inside-oriented view of dividend payout, what policy should Tucker recommend? Frequently students recommend zero payout. Getting closure, even on such an extreme recommendation, sets the stage for a turnabout the next day as the class reviews signaling implications.

Day 2

(40 minutes) What is the nature of the dividend decision Tucker must make, and what are the pros and cons of the alternative positions? (Or alternatively, "Why pay any dividends?") How will Southboro's various providers of capital, such as stockholders and bankers, react to declaration of no dividend? A positive dividend? Here the instructor needs to elicit the notions that the dividend-payout announcement may affect stock price and that at least some stockholders have a preference for dividends. The signaling and clientele considerations must be raised here.

(20 minutes) Does the stock market appear to reward high dividend payout? Low dividend payout? The data can be manipulated to support either view. The point is to show that simple extrapolations from stock market data are

untrustworthy, largely because of econometric problems associated with size and omitted variables (see Black and Scholes, 1974.)

(20 minutes) What should Tucker recommend? Students must synthesize a course of action from the many facts and considerations raised. The instructor may choose to stimulate the discussion by using an organizing framework such as FRICT (Flexibility, Risk, Income, Control, and Timing).

The class discussion can be ended with a vote on the alternatives, followed by a summary of key points.

ANALYSIS

Relationship between Dividends and Stock Price

Some of the advocates of a higher dividend payout suggest that higher stock prices are associated with higher payouts. Students will attempt to abstract proof of this point from the evidence in case Exhibit 7. As we know from academic research (such as Friend and Puckett, 1964), proving such an association in any scientific way is extremely difficult. The reason is, in simple terms, because price/earnings (P/E) ratios are probably associated with many factors for which dividend payout may be proxying in any regression model. The most important of these possibly missing variables is the firm's investment strategy; indeed, the whole point of Miller and Modigliani's dividend-irrelevance theorem is that the investments a firm makes (not the dividends it pays) determine stock prices.

Plots of some of the data in case Exhibit 7 are given in Exhibit A of this note. There is no visible association between P/E and payout, or between yield and payout for the sample of rapidly growing firms.

Financial Side–Effects

The instructor can guide the students through the financial implications of varying dividend–payout levels either in abbreviated form (for a one–period class) or in detail (for a two–period class). The abbreviated approach simply uses the total cash-flow figures (i.e., for 1988-94) found in the right-hand column of case Exhibit 8. In essence, the approach uses the basic sources-and-uses of funds identity:

$$\text{Asset change} = \text{New debt} + (\text{Profits} - \text{Dividends}).$$

With asset additions fixed largely by the firm's competitive strategy, and with profits determined largely by the firm's operating strategy and the environment, the large remaining decision variables are (1) changes in debt and (2) dividend payout. Even here, however, additions to debt are constrained by the firm's maximum leverage target, a debt/equity ratio of .40. This framework can be spelled out for the students as a means of helping them see the larger financial context.

Exhibit B presents an analysis of the effect of payout on unused debt capacity based on the projection in case Exhibit 8. The top panel summarizes the firm's investment program over the forecast period, as well as the financing provided from internal sources. The bottom panel summarizes the effect of higher payouts on the firm's financing and unused debt capacity. The principal insight this analysis affords is the rapidity with which the firm's unused debt capacity disappears, and maximum leverage is achieved, as the payout increases.

292

To go from 20 to 40 percent dividend payout (an increase in cash flow to shareholders of $41 million)[1] consumes $56 million in unused debt capacity. Evidently there is a multiplier relationship between payout and unused debt capacity--every dollar of dividends paid consumes about $1.40[2] of debt capacity. The multiplier exists because a dollar must be borrowed to replace each dollar of equity paid out in dividends, and each dollar of equity lost sacrifices $.40 of debt capacity that it would have carried.

Where the abbreviated approach considered the total of 1988-94 cash flows, the detailed approach considers the pattern of the individual annual cash flows. Exhibit C reveals that, although the debt/equity ratio in 1994 (associated with a 40 percent payout) is well under the maximum of .4, during the intervening years this maximum is exceeded. This result is consistent with Bud Valdosta's rough calculation in the case that the debt/equity ratio would rise to 41 percent.[3] Exhibit D shows that, under the 20 percent payout policy, the debt policy maximum is respected in the intervening years.

Exhibits C and D also reveal some of the financial-reporting and valuation implications of the two policies. Earnings per share (line 31) and the implied stock price (line 32) for instance, will decline because of the greater interest expense associated with higher leverage. Return on book equity (line 30) rises with higher leverage, however, as the equity base contracts. And discounted cash flow (line 37) reflecting the benefits of leverage and the time value of money, is marginally higher at higher dividend payouts.

Company Strategy and Risks

Neither the abbreviated nor detailed forecasts consider adverse deviations from plan. Case Exhibit 8 assumes no cyclical downturn over the 7-year forecast period. Moreover, it assumes that net margin doubles to 5 percent and then increases to 8 percent. And finally, working-capital requirements are projected at 1.5 percent of sales, whereas in the past they averaged 2.6 percent of sales. Additions of only $10 million per year seem optimistic during a period of 15 percent growth. The company may be able to rationalize these optimistic assumptions on the basis of its restructuring and growth of the Artificial Workforce; yet such a material discontinuity in the firm's performance will warrant careful scrutiny. Moreover, continued growth may required new-product development after 1989, possibly incurring significant R&D expenses, and reducing net margin.

Students will point out that, so far, the company's restructuring strategy is associated with losses (in 1985 and 1987) rather than gains. Although these restructurings appear to have been necessary, the credibility of the forecasts

---

[1]The change in cash flow to shareholders is equal to the difference between dividends paid under the 40 percent policy ($143 million) and the dividends ($71.6) and stock buy-back ($30.4) under the 20 percent policy.

[2]Equal to $56/$41 or about 1.4. In theory, the resulting ratio will be exactly 1.4; in this instance, rounding in the model reduces it to 1.37.

[3]Note that the computer model accompanying this note calculates profits based on the profit/sales ratio assumption. As a result, net income in the model is slightly different from case Exhibit 8. The differences are not material, however, and produce no qualitative change in the results.

depends on the assessment of management's ability to begin harvesting potential profits. Plainly, the Artificial Workforce has the competitive advantage at the moment, but the volatility of the firm's performance in the current period is significant: cost of goods sold to sales rose from 61 percent in 1986 to 65.9 percent in 1987. Meanwhile, selling, general, and administrative expense to sales is projected to fall from 30.5 percent in 1987 to 24.3 percent in 1988. Admittedly, some of this volatility is from the restructurings, but the case suggests several sources of volatility that are external to the company: recession, currency, new-competitor entry, new-product foul-ups, cost overruns, and surprise acquisition opportunities.

A brief survey of risks invites a sensitivity analysis of the firm's debt/equity ratio under a reasonable downside scenario. Exhibit E reveals that, with a slightly lower net margin (by .5 percent) a 0 percent dividend-payout policy is necessary to preserve the debt policy in the first two years. Thereafter, the dividend payout can rise. The general insight remains that the unused debt capacity of Southboro is relatively fragile and easily exhausted.

Clientele Considerations

The profile of Southboro's equity owners may also influence the choice of dividend policy. Reginald Peterboro, the chairman of the board and scion of the founders' families and management (who collectively own about 30 percent of the stock) seeks to maximize growth in the market value of the company's stock over time. This forces the analysis into the arena of valuation, although the instructor might point out that, as the population of diverse and disinterested heirs to Southwinn and Peterboro grows, the demands for current income might rise.

Signaling Considerations

The case indicates that the board committed itself to resuming a dividend as early as possible-- "ideally in 1988." The board's letter has the effect of charging this dividend decision with some heavy signaling implications. If the board declares no dividend--even when it previously stated its own desire to do so--investors are bound to take the declaration as an indication of adversity. One is reminded of *The Memoirs of Sherlock Holmes*, in which Dr. Watson asks where to look for a clue:

> 'To the curious incident of the dog in the night-time.'
> 'The dog did nothing in the night-time.'
> 'That was the curious incident,' remarked Sherlock Holmes.[4]

A failure to signal a recovery might reverse or interrupt the trend in average share prices (see case Exhibit 5), which has been rising since 1985. In this context, a dividend--almost *any* dividend--might indicate to investors that the firm's prosperity is returning, more or less according to plan.

Astute students will observe that there is an even deeper signaling problem in this case: what kind of firm does Southboro want to signal that it is? Case Exhibit 6 shows that CAD/CAM equipment and software companies pay low or no dividends, in contrast to the electrical machinery manufacturers, who pay out a third to a half of their earnings. One can argue that, as a result of its

---

[4]From "The Silver Streak," by Sir Arthur Conan Doyle.

restructuring, Southboro is making a transition from the latter to the former. If so, then the deeper issue is how to tell investors.

The article by Asquith and Mullins suggests that the most credible signal about corporate prospects is cash, either in the form of dividends or capital gains. Until the Artificial Workforce product line begins to deliver significant flows of cash, the share price is not likely to respond significantly. In addition, any decline in cash flow, caused by the risks listed earlier, would worsen the anticipated gain in share price.

Decision

The decision at hand is whether to declare a dividend in the third quarter, although for practicality, students will find themselves deciding for all of 1988. As the analysis so far suggests, the case draws students into a fundamental tug of war between financial considerations (which tend to reject dividends, at least in the near term) and signaling considerations (which call for the resumption of dividends at some level, however small). Students will tend to cluster around three proposed policies: (1) zero payout, (2) low payout (1-10 percent), and (3) a residual payout scheme calling for dividends when cash is available.

The arguments in favor of zero payout are that (1) the firm is making the transition into the CAD/CAM industry where zero payout is the mode; (2) one should not ignore the financial statements and act like a Blue Chip firm; Southboro's risks are large enough without compounding them by disgorging cash; and (3) the signaling damage has already occurred, when the directors suspended the dividend in 1988.

The arguments in favor of a low payout are usually based on optimism about the firm's prospects, and beliefs that Southboro has sufficient debt capacity, that Southboro is not exactly a CAD/CAM firm, and that any dividend that does not restrict growth will enhance share prices. Usually, the signaling argument is most significant for the proponents of this policy.

The residual policy is a convenient alternative, although it resolves none of the thorny policy issues in this case. Pursuit of a residual dividend policy is bound to create significant signaling problems as the firm's dividend waxes and wanes.

Inexperienced students tend to dismiss the signaling considerations quite readily; senior executives and seasoned financial executives on the other hand take them quite seriously. If the class votes to declare no dividend in 1988, it might be useful to ask some of the students to dictate a letter to shareholders explaining the board's decision. The difficult issues of credibility will emerge in a critique of this letter.

If the class does vote to declare a dividend, the instructor can challenge the students to identify on which operating policies their decision is a gamble. Indeed, the deeper question is whether, if adversity is encountered, the operating, debt, or dividend policies will be the first to be sacrificed.

Dividend policy is, to use Fischer Black's term, "puzzling," largely because of its interaction with other corporate policies and its signaling content. Decisions about the firm's dividend policy are perhaps the best to illustrate the significant role of managerial judgment in corporate finance. Whichever way the class votes, one of the ultimate teaching points is that managers must make difficult, even high-stakes, policy choices on the basis of incomplete information and uncertain prospects--but that is what managers are paid for.

BIBLIOGRAPHY

Asquith, Paul, and Mullins, David, W. Jr. "Signalling with Dividends, Stock Repurchases, and Equity Issues." *Financial Management*, Autumn 1986, pp. 27-44.

Black, Fisher. "The Dividend Puzzle." *Journal of Portfolio Management*, Winter 1976, pp. 5-8.

Black, Fisher, and Scholes, Myron. "The Effects of Dividend Yield and Dividend Policy on Common Stock Prices and Returns." *Journal of Financial Economics*, vol. 1, 1974, pp. 1-22.

Friend, Irwin and Puckett, M. "Dividends and Stock Prices." *American Economic Review*, vol. 54, September 1964, pp. 656-82.

Miller, Merton, and Modigliani, Franco. "Dividend Policy, Growth and the Valuation of Shares." *Journal of Business*, vol. 34, October 1961, pp. 411-33.

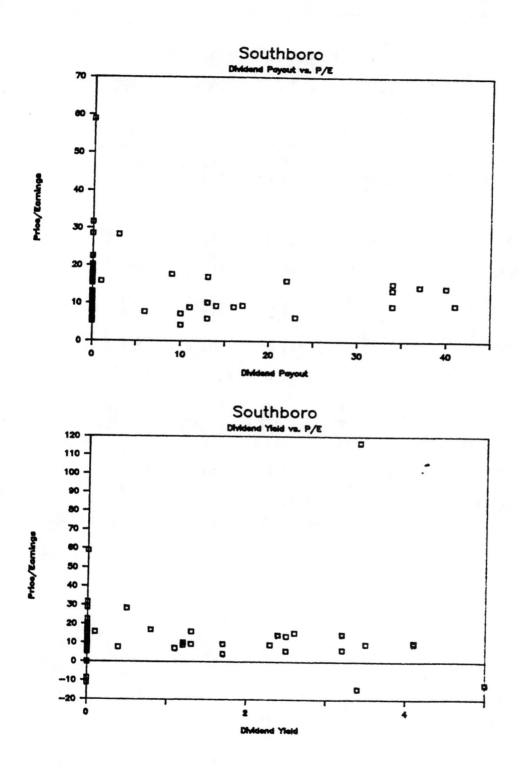

EXHIBIT B Impact of Dividend Payout on Need for External Funds by 1994
          (millions of dollars)

	Targeted Dividend Payout			
	0%	20%	40%	50%
Net profit	$358	$358	$358	$358
Less dividends	0	71.6	143	179
Earnings retained	358	285.4	215	179
New debt (stock buy-back)	(103)	(30.4)	40	76
Depreciation	168	168	168	168
Increase in assets	423	423	423	423
Initial debt (1987)	53.5	53.5	53.5	53.5
Plus new debt	0	0	40	76
Ending debt (1994)	53.5	53.5	93.5	129.5
Initial equity (1987)	188.4	188.4	188.4	188.4
Earnings retained	358	285.4	215	179
Stock buy-back	(103)	(30.4)	0	0
Ending equity (1994)	443.4	443.4	403.4	367.4
Total capital	$496.9	$496.9	$496.9	$496.9
Debt/total capital	11%	11%	19%	26%
Debt/equity	12%	12%	23%	35%
Debt capacity (@ .4 debt/equity)	$ 77.4	$177.6	$161.4	$147.0
Debt capacity used	53.5	53.5	93.5	129.5
Unused debt capacity	$123.9	$123.9	$ 67.9	$ 17.5

EXHIBIT C Forecast of Financing Need Assuming 40 Percent Payout (dollars in millions)

Common Assumptions

1 Sales growth	15.00%						
2 Net income margin	2.1%	4.0%	5.0%	5.6%	6.0%	5.6%	8.0%
3 Dividend payout	40.0%	40.0%	40.0%	40.0%	40.0%	40.0%	40.0%
4 Beginning debt	53.4						
5 Beginning equity	200.1						
6 Shares outstanding	12.31						
7 Price earnings ratio	16						
8 Current market price	$32.00						
9 Debt/equity maximum	40.00%						
10 Borrowing rate	11.00%						
11 Tax rate	34.00%						

	1988	1989	1990	1991	1992	1993	1994
13 Sales	$580.0	$667.0	$767.1	$882.1	$1,014.4	$1,166.6	$1,341.6
Sources:							
14 Net income	12.2	26.7	38.4	49.4	60.9	65.3	107.3
15 Depreciation	15.0	17.0	20.0	23.0	27.0	31.0	35.0
16 Total sources	27.2	43.7	58.4	72.4	87.9	96.3	142.3
Uses:							
17 Capital expenditures	35.0	40.0	45.0	50.0	55.0	60.0	65.0
18 Working capital	13.0	10.0	10.0	10.0	10.0	10.0	10.0
19 Total uses	48.0	50.0	55.0	60.0	65.0	70.0	75.0
20 Excess cash (borrowings)	(20.8)	(6.3)	3.4	12.4	22.9	26.3	67.3
21 Dividends	4.9	10.7	15.3	19.8	24.3	26.1	42.9
22 Net	(25.7)	(17.0)	(12.0)	(7.4)	(1.5)	0.2	24.4
23 Cumulative source (need)	(25.7)	(42.7)	(54.7)	(62.0)	(63.5)	(63.3)	(38.9)
24 After-tax int. cost new debt	(1.9)	(3.1)	(4.0)	(4.5)	(4.6)	(4.6)	(2.8)
25 Net net source (need)	(27.6)	(45.8)	(58.6)	(66.5)	(68.1)	(67.9)	(41.7)

EXHIBIT C (continued)

	1988	1989	1990	1991	1992	1993	1994
26 Debt (excess)	81.0	101.0	117.0	128.9	135.0	139.4	117.8
27 Equity	$205.5	$218.5	$237.5	$262.6	$294.5	$329.1	$390.7
28 Debt/equity	39.4%	46.3%	49.3%	49.1%	45.8%	42.3%	30.1%
29 Unused debt capacity	$ 1.3	-13.7	$-22.0	$-23.8	$-17.1	$-7.7	$ 38.5
30 Return on avg. equity	5.1%	11.1%	15.1%	18.0%	20.2%	19.5%	29.0%
31 EPS	$ 0.84	$ 1.92	$ 2.79	$ 3.65	$ 4.57	$ 4.93	$ 8.49
32 Implied stock price*	$ 13.41	$ 30.65	$ 44.69	$ 58.35	$ 73.12	$ 78.94	$135.82
33 Dividends per share	$ 0.40	$ 0.87	$ 1.25	$ 1.61	$ 1.98	$ 2.12	$ 3.49
Return to investor:							
34 Stock value (terminal)	$ 0.00	$ 0.00	$ 0.00	$ 0.00	$ 0.00	$ 0.00	$135.82
35 Dividend received	$ 0.40	$ 0.87	$ 1.25	$ 1.61	$ 1.98	$ 2.12	$ 3.49
36 Total cap. apprec. and divs.	$ 0.40	$ 0.87	$ 1.25	$ 1.61	$ 1.98	$ 2.12	$139.31
37 Total PV (@ 15%)	$ 57.01						
38 Current market price	$ 32.00						
39 Return (IRR)	25.34%						

*EPS times assumed P/E.

Note: The model adds any excess cash flow (which results in negative debt) to the base to calculate unused debt capacity—in this case, at a maximum debt/equity ratio of 40%.

EXHIBIT D Forecast of Financing Need Assuming 20 Percent Payout (dollars in millions)

Common Assumptions

1 Sales growth	15.00%
2 Net income margin	2.1%
3 Dividend payout	20.0%
4 Beginning debt	53.4
5 Beginning equity	200.1
6 Shares outstanding	12.31
7 Price earnings ratio	16
8 Current market price	$32.00
9 Debt/equity maximum	40.00%
10 Borrowing rate	11.00%
11 Tax rate	34.00%

	1989	1990	1991	1992	1993	1994
	4.0%	5.0%	5.6%	6.0%	5.6%	8.0%
	20.0%	20.0%	20.0%	20.0%	20.0%	20.0%

	1988	1989	1990	1991	1992	1993	1994
13 Sales	$580.0	$667.0	$767.1	$882.1	$1,014.4	$1,166.6	$1,341.6
Sources:							
14 Net income	12.2	26.7	38.4	49.4	60.9	65.3	107.3
15 Depreciation	15.0	17.0	20.0	23.0	27.0	31.0	35.0
16 Total sources	27.2	43.7	58.4	72.4	87.9	96.3	142.3
Uses:							
17 Capital expenditures	35.0	40.0	45.0	50.0	55.0	60.0	65.0
18 Working capital	13.0	10.0	10.0	10.0	10.0	10.0	10.0
19 Total uses	48.0	50.0	55.0	60.0	65.0	70.0	75.0
20 Excess cash (borrowings)	(20.8)	(6.3)	3.4	12.4	22.9	26.3	67.3
21 Dividends	2.4	5.3	7.7	9.9	12.2	13.1	21.5
22 Net	(23.3)	(11.7)	(4.3)	2.5	10.7	13.3	45.9
23 Cumulative source (need)	(23.3)	(34.9)	(39.2)	(36.7)	(26.0)	(12.8)	33.1
24 After-tax int. cost debt	(1.7)	(2.5)	(2.8)	(2.7)	(1.9)	(0.9)	2.4
25 Net net source (need)	(24.9)	(37.4)	(42.1)	(39.4)	(27.9)	(13.7)	35.5

EXHIBIT D (continued)

	1988	1989	1990	1991	1992	1993	1994
26 Debt (excess)	78.3	92.5	99.7	99.8	91.0	78.7	30.4
27 Equity	$208.2	$227.0	$254.8	$291.7	$338.5	$389.8	478.1
28 Debt/equity	37.6%	40.8%	39.1%	34.2%	26.9%	20.2%	6.4%
29 Unused debt capacity	$ 4.9	$ -1.7	$ 2.2	$ 16.8	$ 44.3	$ 77.2	$160.8
30 Return on avg. equity	5.1%	11.1%	14.7%	17.1%	18.7%	17.7%	25.3%
31 EPS	$ 0.85	$ 1.96	$ 2.88	$ 3.80	$ 4.79	$ 5.23	$ 8.91
32 Implied stock price*	$13.64	$31.38	$46.15	$60.74	$76.65	$83.71	$142.62
33 Dividends per share	$ 0.20	$ 0.43	$ 0.62	$ 0.80	$ 0.99	$ 1.06	$ 1.74
Return to investor:							
34 Stock value (terminal)	$ 0.00	$ 0.00	$ 0.00	$ 0.00	$ 0.00	$ 0.00	$142.62
35 Dividend received	$ 0.20	$ 0.43	$ 0.62	$ 0.80	$ 0.99	$ 1.06	$ 1.74
36 Total cap. apprec. and divs.	$ 0.20	$ 0.43	$ 0.62	$ 0.80	$ 0.99	$ 1.06	$144.37
37 Total PV (@ 15%)	$56.59						
38 Current market price	$32.00						
39 Return (IRR)	24.98%						

*EPS times assumed P/E.

Note: The model adds any excess cash flow (which results in negative debt) to the base to calculate unused debt capacity--in this case, at a maximum debt/equity ratio of 20%.

302

EXHIBIT E Forecast of Financing Need Assuming Residual Dividend Policy (dollars in millions)

Common Assumptions

1 Sales growth	12.00%
2 Net income margin	1.6%
3 Dividend payout	0.0%
4 Beginning debt	53.4
5 Beginning equity	200.1
6 Shares outstanding	12.31
7 Price earnings ratio	16
8 Current market price	$32.00
9 Debt/equity maximum	40.00%
10 Borrowing rate	11.00%
11 Tax rate	34.00%

	1988	1989	1990	1991	1992	1993	1994
		3.5%	4.5%	5.1%	5.5%	5.1%	7.5%
		0.0%	10.0%	30.0%	38.0%	38.0%	61.0%
13 Sales	$580.0	$649.6	$727.6	$814.9	$912.6	$1,022.2	$1,144.8
Sources:							
14 Net income	9.3	22.7	32.7	41.6	50.2	52.1	85.9
15 Depreciation	15.0	17.0	20.0	23.0	27.0	31.0	35.0
16 Total sources	24.3	39.7	52.7	64.6	77.2	83.1	120.9
Uses:							
17 Capital expenditures	35.0	40.0	45.0	50.0	55.0	60.0	65.0
18 Working capital	13.0	10.0	10.0	10.0	10.0	10.0	10.0
19 Total uses	48.0	50.0	55.0	60.0	65.0	70.0	75.0
20 Excess cash (borrowings)	(23.7)	(10.3)	(2.3)	4.6	12.2	13.1	45.9
21 Dividends	0.0	0.0	3.3	12.5	19.1	19.8	52.4
22 Net	(23.7)	(10.3)	(5.5)	(7.9)	(6.9)	(6.7)	(6.5)
23 Cumulative source (need)	(23.7)	(34.0)	(39.5)	(47.4)	(54.3)	(61.0)	(67.5)
24 After-tax int. cost new debt	(1.7)	(2.5)	(2.9)	(3.4)	(3.9)	(4.4)	(4.9)
25 Net net source (need)	(25.4)	(36.5)	(42.4)	(50.9)	(58.2)	(65.4)	(72.4)

EXHIBIT E (continued)

	1988	1989	1990	1991	1992	1993	1994
26 Debt (excess)	78.8	91.6	100.0	111.3	122.2	133.3	144.7
27 Equity	$207.7	$227.9	$254.5	$280.2	$307.3	$335.2	$363.8
28 Debt/equity	38.0%	40.2%	39.3%	39.7%	39.7%	39.7%	39.8%
29 Unused debt capacity	$ 4.2	$ -0.4	$ 1.8	$ 0.7	$ 0.8	$ 0.8	$ 0.9
30 Return on avg. equity	5.2%	11.1%	14.4%	16.4%	17.6%	16.3%	22.6%
31 EPS	$ 0.87	$ 2.01	$ 2.98	$ 3.95	$ 5.01	$ 5.53	$ 9.34
32 Implied stock price*	$13.87	$32.12	$47.60	$63.13	$80.19	$88.48	$149.42
33 Dividends per share	$ 0.00	$ 0.00	$ 0.00	$ 0.00	$ 0.00	$ 0.00	$ 0.00
Return to Investor:							
34 Stock value (terminal)	$ 0.00	$ 0.00	$ 0.00	$ 0.00	$ 0.00	$ 0.00	$149.42
35 Dividend received	$ 0.00	$ 0.00	$ 0.00	$ 0.00	$ 0.00	$ 0.00	$ 0.00
36 Total cap. apprec. and divs.	$ 0.00	$ 0.00	$ 0.00	$ 0.00	$ 0.00	$ 0.00	$149.42
37 Total PV (@ 15%)	$56.17						
38 Current market price	$32.00						
39 Return (IRR)	24.63%						

*EPS times assumed P/E.

Note: The model adds any excess cash flow (which results in negative debt) to the base to calculate unused debt capacity--in this case, at the annual maximum debt/equity ratio assumed.

Morgan Stanley Group, Inc.: Initial Public Offering

SYNOPSIS AND OBJECTIVES

This case affords students an opportunity to evaluate Morgan Stanley's decision to go public from strategic and financial points of view. The appraisal hinges on the analysis of two kinds of restructuring: (1) the restructuring of an entire industry and the forces that motivate it and (2) the restructuring of an individual firm's residual ownership interest, or equity restructuring.

The case is a useful medium for addressing several topics:

* initial public offerings (IPOs)--why firms go public and how the offering price can be evaluated;

* industry restructuring--why profitable and successful firms merge into bigger firms; the relative merits of merger versus its alternatives; and

* equity restructuring--the redesign of the firm's equity claims with emphasis on changes in clientele, in the ability of investors to enter or exit the clientele group, in voting control, in allocation of value, and in the potentially conflicting interests of the public versus insiders, and junior versus senior insiders.

STUDY QUESTIONS

1. Why is Morgan Stanley going public? How does this course of action compare to decisions by Goldman Sachs and Kidder Peabody/Dillon Read?

2. Is the offering price of $42-$46 reasonable?

3. Before the IPO, how was the residual ownership in the company structured? Please be prepared to demonstrate with a numerical example how Morgan Stanley's promise to repurchase shares from its partners may interrupt the growth of the firm and create subclienteles of relatively junior and senior partners. On an economic balance sheet, what would be the effect of the promise to repurchase shares?

4. How, if at all, will the IPO change the residual ownership claim in the company?

Teaching note written by Robert F. Bruner. The author gratefully acknowledges a number of insights provided by Judson P. Reis, Morris Visiting Professor of Business Administration. Copyright (c) 1987 by the Darden Graduate Business School Sponsors, Charlottesville, VA.

5. How are the potential benefits of this transaction allocated among (a) the new public investor, (b) Morgan Stanley's older managing directors (with, say, 5-10 years of service left), and (c) Morgan Stanley's younger managing directors (say, with 25 years of service left)?

To emphasize the strategic dynamics of setting the price for an IPO, the instructor can divide the class into three groups and assign the following question for advance preparation:

6. You have been assigned to one of the following groups and should determine the number of shares your clientele would demand at the following per share offering prices: $35, $40, $45, $50, $55, $60, $65, $70, $75, $80, and $85. Each group should assume that the maximum number of shares available at any price would be 4,500,000.

Group A: Arbitrageurs/speculative investors.
Group B: "Market risk" investors: willing to accept the risk
           inherent in the common stocks of the typical firm
           listed on the New York Stock Exchange.
Group C: Conservative, retirement-oriented investors for whom
           preservation of capital is primary.

TEACHING PLAN

The instructor can take numerous paths in this case. One strategy that has worked well for the author is to address the industry and IPO aspects early and dispense with them rather quickly in order to leave time for thoughtful development of the equity-restructuring aspect. The following plan for an 80-minute class reflects this approach.

•   One can begin the case by laying the groundwork for a later role-play: designate three students to be 60-year-old managing directors of Morgan Stanley and three others to be 40-year-old managing directors. Tell them you will call on them in an hour or so to evaluate the merits of the IPO.

•   Then one can take a vote of all the students on the question of whether Morgan Stanley should go public. That the IPO is heavily, if not unanimously, favored will stand in stark contrast to the later divergence of opinion when the class addresses the allocational issues raised by the equity restructuring.

•   What are the pros and cons of Morgan's decision to go public? What are the alternatives, and how does the IPO compare?

•   What is going on in the industry to prompt this rash of restructurings?

•   As a public investor, would you buy at $42-$46 per share? If question 6 of the preceding section is assigned, this point would be the juncture for presenting the demand curves of the three clienteles, and then aggregating them.

•   How will the IPO change the nature of Morgan's residual ownership? What was it like before? After?

- Why does this equity restructuring make sense in light of recent changes in the industry?

- (To the 60- and 40-year-old managing directors, respectively) In debating the IPO decision inside the company, what concerns would you have voiced? How does the IPO change your view of your equity interest in the firm?

The discussion can be drawn to a close with a presentation of the epilogue and a summary of the equity-restructuring framework.

ANALYSIS

Equity Restructuring

Before an analysis of the case, a framework for the analysis of equity restructurings is worth developing as the conceptual focus for leading the discussion. Equity restructuring is simply the redesign of a firm's residual ownership interest in an effort to relieve various possible constraints on the firm. One analogy is debt restructuring, in which the fixed claims on the firm are renegotiated or substituted for other claims that better fit the firm's strategy and expected performance. As the analogy implies, there is a negotiating element in an equity restructuring. Thus, considering the possible tradeoffs underlying any proposal is a useful method of assessing the entire proposal.

The tradeoffs may become apparent in considering the various "levers" that management can use to restructure equity:

- *Choice of Clienteles*: Who owns the equity can have an enormous influence on the behavior and value of the equity layer. Elsewhere it has been argued that, in a segmented capital market, stock prices may be affected by the choice of a target market for those shares [see Harvard Business School, "Note on Capital Market Inefficiency" (9-282-048)]. Clienteles can be formed on many bases: individuals versus institutions, managers versus outsiders, growth-oriented versus income-oriented investors. The purpose of estimating the demand curves for each clientele is to show that the choice of an offering price will significantly influence the mix of equity clients the firm initially attracts.[1]

- *Distribution of Voting Control*: Although "one share, one vote" is the general rule in most corporations, managers can influence the outcomes of contests for corporate control by many means. These are embedded in the design of the equity claim and include multiple classes of common stock (voting and nonvoting), a commitment to rights offerings, use of employee stock-ownership plans, and cumulative election of directors. Most takeover defenses are elements in the distribution of voting control.

---

[1]Obviously, the initial shareholders may not be the long-term shareholders. The demand curve ultimately shows the price at which the market clears 4.5 million shares. If the equilibrium share price is greater than that offered by a clientele, one would expect that clientele to sell its investment in Morgan Stanley shares to a higher bidder.

- *Value Allocation*: The allocation of the firm's residual cash flow is more than just dividend policy (i.e., paying dividends to the entire class of common shareholders). Firms often implicitly or explicitly make decisions about the distribution of value among various equity clienteles of the firm. For instance, in leveraged recapitalizations, public shareholders receive large dividends while managers receive more common shares. For another example, nonvoting common stock sometimes carries a larger dividend than does the voting class of shares.

- *Barring or Easing Investor Entry and Exit*: Firms can also restructure the means of entry and exit for their equity clients. At one extreme, a firm can raise barriers to entry by means of partnership election, family ties, or wealth requirements. Barriers to exit may take the form of trusts, as in the case of the Rockefeller family, which can be created to perpetuate shareholding by a particular clientele. Other exit barriers may offer enormous incentives for staying with the investor group; for example, *tontines* (a form of group insurance) allocated all wealth to the last surviving member of the investor group. At the opposite extreme, firms can ease entry and exit by choosing to list their shares for trading on a major stock exchange.

The existence of these levers suggests that the challenge of equity restructuring is first to choose one or more equity clienteles and then to cut bargains with them (in terms of voting control, value allocation, and entry/exit barriers) in ways that maximize the value of the firm's shares and enhance managerial flexibility.

The IPO Decision and Industry Setting

Early in the discussion, several strategic issues need to emerge in order to motivate the later discussion of equity restructuring.

Morgan, like other leading investment banks, faces the prospect of enormous capital requirements if it is to maintain or improve its share of market. New capital is required by (1) globalization of capital markets, (2) advances in information technology, (3) the importance of a "full-service" product line, and (4) recent and prospective regulatory changes (such as Rule 415), which place a competitive premium on a firm's ability to commit large amounts of capital on short notice.

By any standard, Morgan is not undercapitalized now; nor is it clear that the firm will need a large infusion of new equity capital in the future. With a return on equity in the range of 18-20 percent and a dividend payout of zero, Morgan can self-sustain fairly high rates of growth indefinitely. The compound annual growth rate in assets from 1981 to 1985 was 22 percent. However, the growth in assets may not be smooth (one can speculate on the types of capital requirements that would be large and sudden, such as a new technological advance in worldwide communications or a sudden bear market). The $189-$207 million in new equity capital will be more useful for a cushion against unexpected demands on capital than for immediate use in the expansion.

One sign of a new, destabilizing environment is the volatility of the firm's pretax net margin. Exhibit A reveals a drop from 14.1 percent in 1981 to 7.9 percent in 1984. This swing in profitability is significant, but it obscures even greater volatility, which may be seen by eliminating from the analysis that part of Morgan's activities that is basically banking (i.e., borrowing and lending): a low-margin, high-volume business. This elimination leaves a pretax margin for Morgan's trading and advisory activities. Exhibit A shows that, between 1981 and 1984, Morgan's margin in these activities dropped by *13* percentage points--a volatility nothing less than breathtaking. The decline was mainly caused by increases in overhead expense and the falling profitability of trading. The increase by 6 percentage points in 1985 was attributable to merger advisory fees. Increasing volatility in the markets required increasing specialization within segments of the firm, which itself increased risk because shifting people and assets in response to the changing profitability of different business activities then became more difficult. In this environment, the expansion of the equity reservoir would be rational.

Another important reason for going public is the impermanence of equity capital cited in footnote 1 of the case. Exhibit B illustrates the impermanence problem and shows that it is not simply the loss of partners that threatens the equity base, but the loss of *senior* partners who have a significant cumulative interest in the retained earnings of the firm. First, as the sudden drops in equity around years 11 and 32 show, the departure of long-tenured executives can have a destabilizing effect on the firm. Second, a comparison of the share values of old and new partners suggests that the cumulative nature of the claim on retained earnings may serve to create subclienteles rather than to unify the equity investors. The ratio of old and new partners' value per share is initially quite wide, although the disparity narrows over time, as indicated by the parity ratio (ratio of old and new shareholders' value per share).

Introducing the impermanence problem early in the case discussion lays the foundation for addressing equity restructuring later in the class period. One can reasonably assume that much of the industry restructuring is being driven by a desire to resolve equity-size and -impermanence problems.

Problem of Share Valuation

The analysis of the appropriateness of Morgan Stanley's offering price range serves to highlight the difficulty of assessing *any* IPO price. In most valuation problems, evidence can be obtained about the capital market's assessment of the company itself. In the case of IPOs, however, no current share price or other basis of assessment is available. Moreover, securities regulations prevent dissemination of cash-flow forecasts, and although internal forecasts exist, they often fall wide of the mark because of market cyclicality.

One good approach in a situation like this is to test the reasonableness of assumptions implicit in the offering range. Exhibit C presents the calculation of market-to-book multiples implicit in Morgan's offering range. These multiples are comparable to the 2.2 multiple for which Goldman sold an equity interest to Sumitomo.[2] The multiples of 2.6 for Kidder and 3.0 for Dillon, Read are justifiably higher, since the buyers in those transactions obtained control.

Exhibit D uses the constant-growth valuation model to identify the rate of growth implicit in the stock price. The resulting growth rates of 4.7-7.3 percent are modest in light of the fundamental rates of profitability and growth in the industry.

---

[2]Goldman's new capital base will be $1.8 billion, one-eighth of which is $225 million. Sumitomo's investment of $500 million is 2.22 times this 12.5 percent book interest.

Changes in Residual Ownership

The case affords two avenues for developing the equity-restructuring framework. The first is a before-and-after comparison of the design of Morgan's equity claim. The second is a comparison of Morgan's equity claim *ex post* with those of Goldman Sachs and Kidder Peabody/Dillon Read.

Before-and-after comparison. After the IPO, Morgan's equity claim would be a standard, "plain vanilla" public common stock, in contrast to the claim *ex ante*: private, puttable common stock. As case footnote 1 indicates, the firm guaranteed the repurchase of shares at book value. No doubt the put option was necessary to provide some liquidity for partners in a way that did not threaten the stability of the firm. Note that, under the theoretical condition known as put/call parity, stock with a put affords investors the same payoff as a bond with a conversion option into stock. The instructor can probe the students on why puttable stock is more desirable for the firm than convertible debt, although the reason is obvious: the firm needs some kind of pure equity layer in its capital structure.

A second observation on puttable stock is that the effect of the put option on the economic balance sheet is to reduce the market value of equity. The put option given to its stockholders is much the same as a financial guarantee issued by the firm or an unfunded pension liability: all are contingent liabilities, and the existence of contingent liabilities must reduce the residual value of the firm. Moreover, the put option may reduce the debt capacity of the firm, to the extent that creditors lend against the market value of equity.

As a result of this transaction, the residual ownership claim in Morgan Stanley would change dramatically, in ways indicated by a comparison based on the equity-restructuring framework (see Exhibit E). This comparison suggests that the greatest changes were in entry/exit and the value claim. The change in clientele was modest, and the effective change in voting control was small, given that the insiders would vote as a bloc.

What are the different effects of this change on younger and older partners? Partners nearing retirement probably have a large amount of their wealth tied up in the firm and may prefer the certainty of book valuation as opposed to market valuation. What could induce them to accept a security whose value will fluctuate more and in which liquidity is somewhat limited? One important inducement at Morgan was that current market values exceeded book values by two or three to one.

Younger partners might have taken the longer view and not been as influenced by the exit restrictions. However, they might have worried about the eventual loss of control. Here the voting restrictions could motivate them to accept the equity restructuring.

Morgan versus others. The other way of appraising the equity restructuring is in comparison with the chief alternatives evidenced by the other investment banks. The alternatives were private transactions, and few of the restructuring details were made public, yet the students can usefully speculate on the differences among the approaches, some of which are suggested in Exhibit F.

This comparison shows very different results from the three types of restructurings. The first (outright sale) leaves the least equity flexibility: insiders lose control, and barriers to entry are raised; new investors must buy the parent's shares. The second and third also involve some loss of inside control, although it is relatively small. The difference between these two and the first restructuring is in the resulting entry-and-exit flexibility for the equity clients. Given the virtues of the IPO alternative, Goldman's partial sale to Sumitomo is difficult to rationalize. Indeed, in early 1987, rumors were published that Goldman would somehow unwind its partial sale and then go public.

EPILOGUE

On March 21, 1986, Morgan Stanley Group offered its shares at $56.50 in an offering that was heavily oversubscribed and immediately traded at $70 per share, which reflected, in part, investor enthusiasm for IPOs (i.e., a temporary "window" for IPOs) and the fact that stock prices of securities firms had risen during the offering period. It also reflected the fact that the investment banking industry was in the midst of the largest underwriting boom in its history. In the first half of 1986, underwriters raised as much capital as they did in all of 1985--which itself was not a bad year for underwriting. On April 29, Morgan Stanley reported that its first-quarter earnings had tripled from a year earlier. Second- and third-quarter profits were up 59 and 53 percent, respectively, and Morgan closed 1986 with net income of $201 million, twice 1985's net income. Morgan Stanley appears to have timed its IPO extraordinarily well.

EXHIBIT A   Analysis of Pretax Profit Margin

	1981	1982	1983	1984	1985
Pretax profit margin [from case Exhibit 7]	14.1%	12.8%	10.0%	7.9%	10.2%
Analysis of pretax margins in the firm's "banking" (i.e., borrowing and lending) segment:					
Interest income ($ mm)	342.3	362.7	415.	794.9	938.
Interest expense ($ mm)	323.2	335.5	390.9	747.9	900.2
Net interest income	19.1	27.2	24.1	47.0	37.8
Pretax margin	5.6%	7.5%	5.8%	5.9%	4.0%
Analysis of pretax margins in the firm's trading and financial advisory segments:					
Adjusted revenues (without interest) ($ mm)	291.8	362.8	444.6	545.6	856.9
Adjusted pretax income (without interest) ($ mm)	69.5	65.6	62.1	58.8	145.5
Adjusted pretax profit margin	23.8%	18.1%	14.0%	10.8%	17.0%

EXHIBIT B Example of the Capital-Impermanence Problem

Assumptions:

1. The firm earns a return on equity of 20%.
2. Original partners invest $1,000.
3. Partners claim cumulative pro rata interest in retained earnings.
4. Half the original partners withdraw their capital at the very end of year 11.
5. At the end of year 11, new partners replace the lost capital by buying the 50% interest for $500 (i.e., par value).
6. The other half of the original partners withdraw their capital at the end of year 31.

Year	Beginning Equity	Net Income	Additions/ Withdrawals	Ending Equity	Ending Percentage Claim	Value Total	Value per Share	Ending Percentage Claim	Value Total	Value per Share	Old/New Parity
	Equity T-Accounts				Original Shareholders			New Shareholders			
1	$ 1000	$ 200	0	$ 1200	100	$ 1200	$ 12.00	0	0	0	--
2	1200	240	0	1440	100	1440	14.40	0	0	0	--
3	1440	288	0	1728	100	1728	17.28	0	0	0	--
4	1728	346	0	2074	100	2074	20.74	0	0	0	--
5	2074	415	0	2488	100	2488	24.88	0	0	0	--
6	2488	498	0	2986	100	2986	29.86	0	0	0	--
7	2986	597	0	3583	100	3583	35.83	0	0	0	--
8	3583	717	0	4300	100	4300	43.00	0	0	0	--
9	4300	860	0	5160	100	5160	51.60	0	0	0	--
10	5160	1032	0	6192	100	6192	61.92	0	0	0	--
11	6192	1238	-3215	4215	50	3715	37.15	50	500	$ 10.00	--
12	4215	843	0	5058	50	4137	82.73	50	922	18.43	4.5
13	5058	1012	0	6070	50	4642	92.85	50	1427	28.55	3.3
14	6070	1214	0	7284	50	5249	104.99	50	2034	40.69	2.6
15	7284	1457	0	8740	50	5978	119.55	50	2763	55.25	2.2
16	8740	1748	0	10488	50	6852	137.03	50	3637	72.73	1.9

313

EXHIBIT B (continued)

	Equity T-Accounts				Original Shareholders			New Shareholders			Old/New
Year	Beginning Equity	Net Income	Additions/ Withdrawals	Ending Equity	Ending Percentage Claim	Value Total	Value per Share	Ending Percentage Claim	Value Total	Value per Share	Parity
17	10488	2098	0	12586	50	7901	158.01	50	4686	93.71	1.7
18	12586	2517	0	15103	50	9159	183.18	50	5944	118.88	1.5
19	15103	3021	0	18124	50	10669	213.39	50	7454	149.09	1.4
20	18124	3625	0	21749	50	12482	249.64	50	9267	185.34	1.3
21	21749	4350	0	26098	50	14657	293.13	50	11442	228.83	1.3
22	26098	5220	0	31318	50	17267	345.33	50	14052	281.03	1.2
23	31318	6264	0	37582	50	20398	407.97	50	17183	343.67	1.2
24	37582	7516	0	45098	50	24157	483.13	50	20942	418.83	1.2
25	45098	9020	0	54118	50	28666	573.33	50	25451	509.03	1.1
26	54118	10824	0	64941	50	34078	681.56	50	30863	617.26	1.1
27	64941	12988	0	77929	50	40572	811.45	50	37357	747.14	1.1
28	77929	15586	0	93515	50	48365	967.30	50	45150	903.00	1.1
29	93515	18703	0	112218	50	57717	1154.34	50	54502	1090.03	1.1
30	112218	22444	0	134662	50	68939	1378.77	50	65724	1314.47	1.0
31	134662	26932	0	161595	50	82405	1648.10	50	79190	1583.80	1.0
32	161595	32319	-98564	95349	0	0	0.00	100	95349	1906.98	---
33	95349	19070	0	114419	0	0	0.00	100	114419	2288.38	---
34	$114419	$22884	0	$137303	0	0	0.00	100	$137303	$2746.06	---

Note: "Old/New Parity" is the ratio of the original shareholders' value per share to the new shareholders' value per share.

314

EXHIBIT C Implicit Market-to-Book Multiples

$/Share	Shares Offered	Proceeds	Total Value of Equity (Proceeds/.19)	Adjusted Book Value	Market-to-Book Multiple
42.00	4.5 m	$189.00 m	$ 995 m	$503 m	1.97x
46.00	4.5	207.00	1,089	521	2.09
56.50	4.5 m	$254.25 m	$1,337 m	$568 m	2.35x

Note: Adjusted book value is equal to [$314 m + ($/Sh. x 4.5 m)].

One way to evaluate the initial offering price (estimated to be between $42
and $46 per share) is to solve the constant dividend growth model:

$$\text{Value} = \frac{\text{Cash flow to equity}}{K_e - g}$$

Suppose: Value = $44/sh. x 24.2 million shares = $1,064.8 million;
         cash flow to equity = Net income last year = $106 million;
              $K_e = .20;$*

Then: g = .10.

However, this simple analysis ignores the productivity of the new capital
raised, $198 million (4.5 million shares times $44 per share). The survey of
industry fundamentals should afford a range of internal rates of return (IRR) on
equity. The following table presents a sensitivity analysis assuming a share
price of $44:

IRR New Equity	Adjusted Cash Flow to Equity	Implicit Growth Rate in $44 Share Price
30%	$165.4 m	4.5%
25	155.5	5.4
20	145.6	6.3
15%	$135.7 m	7.3%

Even at the relatively low rate of return of 15%, the implicit growth rate is
modest compared with recent and expected industry growth rates. Morgan Stanley
appears to be fairly priced (or even underpriced) in the offering.

---

*Using the data in Exhibit 1 of the case, one can calculate the average
unlevered beta for the three firms with significant underwriting
franchises--Salomon, First Boston, and Bear Stearns. Their average unlevered
beta is 1.2, which is used here:

	Long-Term Debt to Total Capital	Debt to Equity	B_L	B_U
Salomon	.50	1.00	1.95	1.300
First Boston	.25	.33	1.40	1.202
Bear Stearns	.24	.355	1.30	1.104
Average				1.202
Morgan	.24	.316	1.40	

Footnote (continued)

This unlevered beta is then relevered to reflect Morgan Stanley's ratio of long-term debt to equity (calculated from case Exhibit 1) of .30, which gives a levered beta of 1.4. For the risk-free rate, one can use the 30-year Treasury bond rate in case Exhibit 3 of 7.96% and the average market premium of 8.6%. When these figures are inserted into the capital-asset-pricing model, the cost of equity is estimated to be 20%.

EXHIBIT E   Comparison of Equity Claim in Morgan Stanley

	Before	After
Clienteles	100% partners.	19% outsiders (probably institutions). 81% insiders (nonpartners allowed to invest).
Voting control	Pro rata by shares. Noncumulative election. Four officers control 14.6%.	Pro rata by shares. Noncumulative election. Controlled by former insiders. Four officers control 11.9%. Insiders must vote their shares in accord with the vote of the majority of inside shares.
Value claim	By shares and length of tenure.	Pro rata by shares.
Entry/exit	Entry: by election and purchase. Exit: sale by put to firm for cumulative book value.	Entry: by purchase. Exit: sale on the New York Stock Exchange for market value. Firm has right of first refusal to purchase at book value shares sold by insiders who were fired. New shares freely traded. Sales by insiders forbidden for two years and limited thereafter.

EXHIBIT F Comparison of Equity Restructuring

	Outright Sale (Dillon/ Kidder)	Sale of Quasi-Equity (Goldman Sachs)	IPO (Morgan Stanley)
Clientele	Public via large corp. management	87.5% partners; 12.5% Sumitomo	81% partners 19% outsiders
Voting control	External.	Mainly internal but Sumitomo may have special monitoring rights; Sumitomo's active control limited by the Fed.	Mainly internal but laws and regulations give outsiders special monitoring rights.
Value claim	All to owner.	Pro rata by shares and tenure.	Pro rata by shares.
Entry/ exit	Entry: barred Exit: by divestiture.	Entry: by election. Exit: by put to firm.	Entry: by open-market purchase (market is NYSE). Exit: sale on open market at market value.

Spiegel, Inc. (Abridged)

SYNOPSIS AND OBJECTIVES

In early October 1987, the executives of this large catalog retailer must decide on the pricing and timing of their initial public offering (IPO). The weakening conditions of the stock market calls for prompt action. The task of the student is to recommend a course of action—particularly, a price at which Spiegel's shares should be offered.

The challenging market conditions and dramatic epilogue make this case a useful vehicle for

- illustrating the equity underwriting process in general and the IPO process in particular. The unusual conditions of this case underscore the risks of the investment banker and the difficult decisions to be made by the issuer and underwriter;

- exercising students' valuation skills and learning to integrate capital-market assessments into the valuation process;

- motivating a discussion of equity management, including (1) the strategic issues involved in the decision to go public and (2) the decision to issue two classes of common stock, voting and nonvoting.

STUDY QUESTIONS

1. Why is Spiegel proposing to go public? What motivates its decision to issue nonvoting shares?

2. What is the process for initially issuing common stock? What role does an investment banker play? What risks does the investment banker assume? Are the motives and interests of the issuer and investment banker the same?

3. At what price should Spiegel issue its shares?

TEACHING PLAN

(15 minutes) Why is Spiegel considering going public? What are the pros and cons of going public? The purpose of this opening is to discuss the strategic motives for the IPO.

(10 minutes) In the abstract, would Spiegel be an attractive company to invest in? Yes. Spiegel, and generally all catalog retailers, recently established new peaks of financial performance.

Teaching note written by Robert F. Bruner with the assistance of analysis by Kathryn Coffey. Copyright (c) 1989 by the Darden Graduate Business School Sponsors, Charlottesville, VA.

(10 minutes) Is this a good time to go public? The purpose of this question is to motivate a discussion of IPO "windows." In light of subsequent events, the IPO window was about to slam shut.

(25 minutes) At what price should Alton Withers seek to issue the shares? Here one should deal with the pricing and valuation problem.

(20 minutes) Will Merrill Lynch automatically accept Withers' target price? No. Merrill wants a price that will clear the shares from its inventory. In this segment of the discussion, the class should review the underwriter's risks and goals.

The class discussion can be closed with a vote of the students on a "fair price" followed by a discussion of the epilogue. An alternative approach to this case would be to use the bidding framework suggested in the teaching note of the "Morgan Stanley Group" case, where the class is divided into clienteles and requested to indicate the number of shares each would be willing to buy at varying price levels.

ANALYSIS

Some Lessons About Underwriting

At first glance, the process of underwriting seems benign and uncomplicated: shares are bought and sold within a short space of time, leaving the underwriter with what appears to be a relatively riskless profit. Students should understand that the process is more complicated and the risks more significant than the first glance reveals.

Underwriting is risky, as the "British Petroleum Company, Ltd." case in this book and other[1] cases show. The risks are essentially related to the marketing of the issue: designing and pricing the "product." Design issues include where to list the stock, the contemplated dividend, and the decision whether to restrict voting. The design choices must be driven by the needs of the issuer as well as the needs of the target equity clientele (e.g., institutional versus retail).

The pricing of an equity issue is much more the result of bargaining than is issuing bonds, a mortgage against real estate, or a term loan secured by a machine tool. Fixed-income securities are more easily priced with reference to comparable issues in the capital market. Stocks are less easily compared. In addition, there is no current quoted price for Spiegel's shares, as there would be for a secondary equity issue. Finally, differing expectations about company performance or capital-market conditions could lead to widely differing required prices. As a result, expert judgment influences the outcome significantly. The price-bargaining negotiations often pit the chief financial officer of the issuer against the lead underwriter.

For these reasons, the IPO is one of the more challenging events in corporate finance, both to evaluate and to manage.

---

[1]Weston and Copeland in their eighth edition of *Managerial Finance* (pp. 731-32) describe in detail IBM's debt offering in October 1979. The members of the underwriting syndicate sustained losses estimated to be $15 million when, shortly after the offering began, the Fed announced a significant increase in its discount rate, thus depressing the market value of the bonds.

Company and Strategy

The catalog segment of the retailing industry grew at 12-15 percent per year between 1982 and 1986, more than twice as fast as the retailing industry at large. Advances in computer technology and an increased number of women working outside the home were indications that the exceptional growth enjoyed by mail-order retailers would continue for at least another five years. Spiegel had just automated its distribution and customer ordering systems, and had repositioned its merchandise and presentation to compete with specialty retailers. Therefore, the firm was well positioned to exploit the exceptional growth expected for catalog companies.

The challenges to Spiegel's growth, as for any retailer, were management of margins and the decreasing opportunities for specialty chain retailers to sustain the high growth rates of the past five years. Computerized inventory management and the general shift toward higher margin soft goods were important tools for Spiegel and its competitors to apply in improving profitability. Traditional retailers faced decreasing options for location expansion, while Spiegel built its growth on new catalog formats, upgraded merchandise, and exceptional service. Essentially, Spiegel capitalized on the fundamental shifts in the way people valued their spare time and shopped, shifts favoring strategies based on service.

Given a conservative industry growth rate of 12 percent, compounded annually from the 1984 base of industry sales of $44.4 billion, catalog sales were expected to reach $62.4 billion in 1987 and $70 billion in 1988. Using the most recent growth figures of 15 percent, these amounts would be $67.5 billion and $77.7 billion, respectively. Spiegel's catalog sales of $882.2 million in 1986 suggest a small current market share of 1.6 percent. The rapid growth in the industry, combined with Spiegel's strength as a catalog retailer, indicated a good opportunity for exceptional growth, perhaps in excess of the 15 percent estimates for the industry.

High rates of industry growth often attract new competitors (Speigel's specialty chain competitors would be naturally drawn to the catalog segment). But barring the entry of these new competitors were (1) huge capital investment and expertise needed to establish dedicated computer-automated warehousing, (2) distribution and order-taking facilities, and (3) proven mailing lists.

Spiegel's candidacy for an IPO was assisted by strong financial performance in recent years, including (1) a compound sales-growth rate of 19.9 percent from 1982 to 1986, (2) a compound growth rate in net earnings of 62.2 percent for the same period, and (3) dramatic improvements in gross margin, operating margin, and net margin. The seasonality of Spiegel's sales accounts for the fact that margins for the first six months of the year were consistently below those for year-end.

Two salient features appear in Spiegel's balance sheet. First, with a year-end at December 31, most of Spiegel's assets are in the form of accounts receivable, as is to be expected from a retailer with heavy commitment to the Christmas selling season. Second, Spiegel is significantly dependent on debt financing, with debt/total capital at 78 percent as of June 1987. The company's debt consisted almost entirely of commercial paper supported by bank letters of credit. This source of financing creates risks from interest-rate increases and from continuous refinancing.

Economic Conditions

Retailers are acutely sensitive to changes in consumer spending power. The economic data provided in the case suggest that the economy was strong ans still

322

on an upward trend. Consumer confidence was at an all-time high—suggesting at least a strong Christmas season 1987 and spring season 1988. Inflation, unemployment, and interest rates all seemed to be holding at comfortable levels. The percentage of the population in the high-spending 25 to 44 year-old age group was increasing (from 28 percent in 1980 to 31 percent in 1985). Careful analysts would find some causes for concern, however, including (1) faltering housing starts, (2) plateauing disposable personal income (adjusted for inflation), (3) high level of installment debt as a percentage of disposable personal income, (4) the phase-out of the tax deduction of consumer interest expense included in the Tax Reform Act of 1986, and (5) wide attention given to the macroeconomic problem of the twin deficits.

Motives for Going Public

The case does not state explicitly why Spiegel's managment and owners were seeking to take the company public. One can speculate on the following reasons: (1) a desire to add stability and permanence to a highly levered capital structure, (2) a desire to exploit price/earnings (P/E) multiples that were at historical highs,[2] (3) a desire to create an acquisition currency should Spiegel want to participate in the current trend of consolidation in the retailing industry, (4) to create a standard for defining value and arriving at a selling price should Otto-Versand want to sell Spiegel, (5) to exploit its own strong financial performance in recent years including impressive growth and repositioning. In short, the offering was probably entertained for market timing and flexibility reasons.

Effects of the Proposed Equity Issue

The proposed equity financing would have the effect of improving the capital structure, diluting projected earnings per share (EPS), and reducing the volatility of projected net income. Exhibits A and B present projected income statements and balance sheets, respectively, assuming an equity issue occurred at $18 per share.

First, the debt-to-capital ratio would decline from 76 percent at the end of 1986 to 53 percent in 1987. Assuming a target debt/capital ratio of 75 percent and proceeds from the offering of $101.82 million ($18 per share, less the 5.75 percent underwriting discount), Spiegel could support a year-end debt level of $659 million—$241 million above the debt outstanding at June 30, 1987.

EPS would be diluted by 13.3 percent.[3] Given Spiegel's high expected growth rate, however, this dilution does little to kink the ramp of steadily growing EPS. For the full year of 1988, EPS is projected to be $1.52, a 16 percent gain over the preceding year.

Discounted Cash Flow Valuation

A test of the reasonableness of the $18.00–$16.00 offering price range is the DCF estimate of the per share value. Exhibits C and D provide the analysis.

---

[2]In July 1987, comparable firms on average were selling at P/E ratios 1.46 times their historical five-year average P/Es.

[3]Dilution estimated by the formula:

$$DIL = - [Old shares/(Old shares + New shares)]$$

Cash flows. Exhibit C presents a forecast of free cash flows abstracting somewhat from the financial statements in Exhibits A and B. EBIAT[4] and changes in net working capital are drawn from the financial statements. Because of Spiegel's strategy of self-financing its receivables, the increases in net working capital during the period of high growth are quite significant. For simplicity, the modest additions to fixed assets are assumed to net out against depreciation expense.

Discount rate. The cost of equity is based on a beta of 1.91.[5] The average market premium used is 8.6 percent; the short-term risk-free rate is 6.22 percent, the 90-day T-bill rate. Applying these factors to the capital-asset-pricing model produces a cost of equity of 22.7 percent. The pretax cost of debt was assumed to be 8.75 percent, as suggested in the case. When adjusted for an assumed 34 percent tax rate, the cost of debt was 5.8 percent. The capital structure over the forecast period was assumed to unlever gradually, although it remains in the area of 50 percent. The average weighted-average cost of capital used in the analysis was 13.37 percent. (This WACC assumption is conservative: if Spiegel is assumed to lever up to a 75 percent debt-to-capital ratio, its WACC would be about 10 percent.)

Terminal value. The value of the firm in 1992 was estimated by capitalizing the estimated EBIAT (net of a corresponding increase in net working capital) at various perpetual WACCs and growth rates. The data table in Exhibit D presents the *share value* consistent with various perpetual WACCs and growth rates. The analysis reveals that an $18.00 share price requires a very high perpetual growth rate (i.e., greater than 10 percent) if one assumes a WACC in the area of 13.5 percent. Under these base-case assumptions, an offering price of $18.00 seems too high.

Viewed from another perspective, Exhibit D suggests that, if Spiegel were to grow in perpetuity at 5 percent, a rate slightly above inflation, an $18.00 share price would require a WACC of about 10 percent. The great sensitivity of Spiegel's share value to growth and WACC focuses attention on management's future financial policies: if they intend to return to a debt-to-capital ratio of 75 percent, then an $18.00 share price might be justified.

Market Multiples

Assuming an offering price of $18 per share, the P/E multiple to 1986 earnings would barely fail to meet the target of "at least 20 times"; the implied P/E multiple would be 19.56x. Given the declining market conditions in September, Spiegel management should consider this implicit multiple within grasp of their goal. Data on other industrial IPOs for 1987 are also consistent with a 20x multiple.

---

[4]Earnings before interest and after taxes.

[5]The average levered beta for the industry was 1.54. Adjusting for the debt of the industry, the average unlevered beta is 1.17. Using the projected debt/equity ratio of 1.22 following the offering produces an estimated levered beta for Spiegel of 1.91.

Recommendation

The strategic question for Spiegel is how investors would perceive the company: (1) as a specialty retailer (with extremely volatile stock price, currently entering a period of difficulty) or (2) as a mail-order retailer (with relatively stable stock prices that held their value during the recent down market days in August and September). One can argue that Spiegel is more properly perceived as a mail-order retailer, whose key assets are its proven mailing lists and know-how in efficient marketing and order fulfillment. Much of this stability is attributable to the fact that Spiegel was, to a significant degree, a bank: the credit operation was much more profitable a product line than was the catalog operation. By design, the firm carried a high level of accounts receivable; 73 percent of sales were financed by Spiegel; and the company charged an average of 20 percent on outstanding balances.

The nonvoting feature of the shares would dictate that they would trade at a discount to voting shares; the text of the case suggests 3.89 percent was the average discount for nonvoting shares at the time. Another depressing factor for Spiegel's shares would be the high leverage for the company relative to its peers. Finally, there is the general practice of pricing share issues 15–20 percent below the expected market-equilibrium price to generate a strong investor response. All these factors suggest a share offering price toward the low end of the discussed offering range, (i.e., around $16 per share).

EPILOGUE

Given the rapidly deteriorating market conditions, the offering was almost canceled on October 6, 1987. The Germans, unfamiliar with the dynamics and volatility of the equity markets and with the process of pricing securities in the U.S. market, were extremely frustrated and felt they were virtually giving away 13 percent of Spiegel. Not really needing the money made them even more reluctant to go ahead with the offering. They eventually decided to price at around 4 a.m. Eastern Standard Time on October 6, 1987. This allowed for an offering Tuesday morning in both Europe (Luxembourg Exchange) and New York. The issue was priced at $16 per share. The Dow fell 91.55 (3.47 percent) that Tuesday, and the shares traded in the $14.50–$15.00 range until October 19–20, when the price fell to $10.75 and $8.00, respectively. Six months later, the shares were trading at about $11.00.

As an illustration of the magnitude of the exposure the underwriters experienced in this episode, one can calculate their hypothetical maximum loss over the ensuing days. Based on their cost of $15.08 per share,[6] the effects would be:

Holding Period	Share Price	$ Loss	Simple Loss	Annualized Loss
1 Day	$14.50	$3.48 m	3.8%	1387.0%
2 Weeks	8.00	42.50	46.9	1219.0
6 Months	11.00	24.50 m	27.1%	54.2%

The extent of the losses sustained by the underwriting syndicate is not publicly known. However, these hypothetical estimates serve to underscore the inherent riskiness of the securities underwriting business.

---

[6]($16 per share) x (1 – .0575) = $15.08.

EXHIBIT A   Projected Spiegel Income Statements (dollars in thousands except per share data)

Forecast Assumptions

Pre-IPO shares outst.: 39,000
Dividend payout: 10.0%
IPO offering price: $18.00
Underwriting fee: 5.75%
Interest rate: 8.75%

	Actual 1986		1987	1988	1989	1990	1991	1992
Sales growth:			8.0%	15.0%	15.0%	15.0%	15.0%	15.0%
Net sales	$ 882,169	88.0%	952,743	$1,095,654	$1,260,002	$1,449,002	$1,666,353	$1,916,306
Finance revenue	102,698	10.2	110,914	127,551	146,684	168,686	193,989	223,087
Other revenue	17,363	1.7	18,752	21,565	24,800	28,520	32,797	37,717
Gross margin	1,002,230	100.0	1,082,408	1,244,770	1,431,485	1,646,208	1,893,139	2,177,110
Cost of sales	599,483	59.8	647,442	744,558	856,242	984,678	1,132,379	1,302,236
SG&A	294,726	29.4	318,304	366,050	420,957	484,101	556,716	640,223
Operating income	$ 108,021	10.8	116,663	134,162	154,286	177,429	204,044	234,650
Interest	36,492	3.6	27,644	30,699	34,301	38,387	43,025	48,295
EBT	71,529	7.1	89,019	103,463	119,985	139,042	161,019	186,355
Taxes	35,320	3.5	30,266	35,178	40,795	47,274	54,746	63,361
Net income	$ 36,209	3.6	$ 58,752	$ 68,286	$ 79,190	$ 91,768	$ 106,272	$ 122,995
EPS	$0.93		$1.31	$1.52	$1.76	$2.04	$2.36	$2.73
Dividends			$ 11,880	$ 5,400	$ 7,919	$ 9,177	$ 10,627	$ 12,299

EXHIBIT B   Projected Spiegel Balance Sheets (dollars in thousands)

	Actual 1986		1987	1988	1989	1990	1991	1992
Cash	$ 4,400	0.4%	$ 4,620	$ 4,851	$ 5,094	$ 5,348	$ 5,616	$ 5,896
Receivables	552,688	55.1	596,903	686,438	789,404	907,815	1,043,987	1,200,585
Refund taxes	4,000	0.4	4,320	4,968	5,713	6,570	7,556	8,689
Inventories	119,406	11.9	128,958	148,302	170,548	196,130	225,549	259,382
Prepaids	24,608	2.5	26,577	30,563	35,148	40,420	46,483	53,455
Current assets	705,102	70.4	761,378	875,123	1,005,906	1,156,283	1,329,190	1,528,007
Net PP&P	38,652	3.9	39,000	39,000	39,000	39,000	39,000	39,000
Other assets	926	0.1	1,000	1,150	1,323	1,521	1,749	2,012
Total assets	$ 744,680	74.3	$ 801,378	$ 915,273	$1,046,229	$1,196,804	$1,369,940	$1,569,019
Current long-term debt	$ 660	0.1	$ 50	$ 50	$ 50	$ 50	$ 50	$ 50
Payables	69,368	6.9	74,917	86,155	99,078	113,940	131,031	150,686
Accrueds								
Salaries	13,569	1.4	14,655	16,853	19,381	22,288	25,631	29,475
Other	16,419	1.6	17,733	20,392	23,451	26,969	31,014	35,666
Taxes payable	16	0.0	17	20	23	26	30	35
Deferred taxes	99,739	10.0%	99,739	99,739	99,739	99,739	99,739	99,739

EXHIBIT B (continued)

	Actual 1986		1987	1988	1989	1990	1991	1992
Current liabs.	$ 199,771	19.9%	$ 207,111	$ 223,209	$ 241,722	$ 263,012	$ 287,495	$ 315,651
Long-term debt	414,000	41.3	315,881	350,792	391,963	438,657	491,664	551,893
Total liabs.	613,771	61.2	522,992	574,001	633,685	701,669	779,160	867,544
		0.0						
Preferred	1,570	0.2	0	0	0	0	0	0
Class B	39,000	3.9	39,000	39,000	39,000	39,000	39,000	39,000
Class A	0	0.0	6,000	6,000	6,000	6,000	6,000	6,000
Add. paid in	3,003	0.3	99,138	99,138	99,138	99,138	99,138	99,138
Retained earnings	87,376	8.7	134,248	197,134	268,405	350,997	446,642	557,337
Total equity	130,949	13.1%	278,386	341,272	412,543	495,135	590,780	701,475
Liabs. and equity	$ 744,720		$ 801,378	$ 915,273	$1,046,229	$1,196,804	$1,369,940	$1,569,019
Debt/(debt+equity)			0.532	0.507	0.487	0.470	0.454	0.440

328

EXHIBIT C Spiegel Cash-Flow Projections
(dollars in thousands except per share data)

	1987	1988	1989	1990	1991	1992
EBIAT	$76,997	$88,547	$101,829	$117,103	$134,669	$154,869
Deprec., addns. to fixed assets	0	0	0	0	0	0
Change in net working capital	(48,716)	(97,415)	(112,028)	(128,832)	(148,157)	(170,380)
Free cash flow	$28,281	($8,868)	($10,199)	($11,729)	($13,488)	($15,511)
						$2,202,165

Unlevered beta	1.17
Levered beta	1.89
Risk-free rate	6.22%
Cost of equity	22.45%
Cost of debt	8.75%
WACC (5 year)	13.58%
WACC (perpetual)	10.00%
Perpetual cash flow	106,805
Growth rate	5.15%
Terminal value	2,202,165
Present value, assets	1,124,759
Present value, debt	315,931
Present value, equity	808,828
Value per share	$17.97

EXHIBIT D   Share Values by Perpetual WACC and Perpetual Growth Rate

Perpetual WACC

		8.0%	8.5%	9.0%	9.5%	10.0%	10.5%	11.0%	11.5%	12.0%	12.5%	13.0%	13.5%	14.0%
	4.0%	$26.63	$22.79	$19.72	$17.21	$15.12	$13.34	$11.83	$10.51	$9.36	$8.34	$7.44	$6.63	$5.91
	4.5%	30.00	25.26	21.57	18.62	16.21	14.20	12.50	11.04	9.78	8.67	7.70	6.83	6.05
	5.0%	34.48	28.43	23.89	20.35	17.53	15.21	13.29	11.66	10.26	9.05	7.99	7.05	6.22
	5.5%	40.77	32.66	26.86	22.51	19.13	16.43	14.22	12.37	10.81	9.48	8.32	7.30	6.41
	6.0%	50.20	38.58	30.83	25.29	21.14	17.92	15.33	13.22	11.46	9.97	8.69	7.59	6.62
Perpetual	6.5%	65.91	47.45	36.38	29.00	23.73	19.77	16.70	14.24	12.22	10.54	9.13	7.91	6.85
Growth	7.0%	97.33	62.25	44.71	34.19	27.17	22.16	18.40	15.48	13.14	11.23	9.63	8.28	7.12
Rate	7.5%	191.61	91.85	58.60	41.97	31.99	25.34	20.59	17.03	14.26	12.04	10.23	8.72	7.44
	8.0%	NMF	180.64	86.36	54.94	39.23	29.80	23.51	19.03	15.66	13.04	10.94	9.23	7.80
	8.5%	NMF	NMF	169.67	80.88	51.28	36.48	27.61	21.69	17.46	14.29	11.82	9.85	8.23
	9.0%	NMF	NMF	NMF	158.70	75.39	47.63	33.74	25.41	19.86	15.89	12.92	10.60	8.75
	9.5%	NMF	NMF	NMF	NMF	147.73	69.91	43.97	31.00	23.22	18.03	14.32	11.54	9.38
	10.0%	NMF	NMF	NMF	NMF	NMF	136.76	64.42	40.31	28.26	21.02	16.20	12.76	10.17

An Introduction to Debt Policy and Value

SYNOPSIS AND OBJECTIVES

This case consists of a set of incomplete worksheets with which the student must calculate the effect of hypothetical changes in capital structure on firm value, and the effect of a major recapitalization on the share price of Koppers Company. After completing the worksheets, the student's task is to compare results among the problems.

The purpose of this exercise is to illustrate Modigliani and Miller's theory about the relationship between debt and firm value in a taxable world. In particular, the case illustrates the effect of debt tax shields. For clarity of focus, other considerations, such as default risk or signaling, are skirted.

STUDY QUESTIONS

The case is self-explanatory and requires no particular direction from the instructor. Moreover, the case can be assigned with or without the benefit of supplemental readings on M&M. If no supplemental readings are assigned, the instructor should plan to allocate some time to presenting the theory in class.

TEACHING PLAN

The plan for this class can be simple: the instructor can make transparencies of the worksheets and fill in the blanks based on contributions from the students. The *execution* of this plan, however, can be challenging. One needs to pause at points along the way to make sure that all students are keeping up with where the numbers come from. At other points, one should pause to discuss the substantive insights arising from the numbers, particularly the comparison of the results in problems 1, 2, and 3. This can easily take a full 80-minute class and still leave some students asking questions afterward. I recommend allocating no more than one class period to this case, however, for once the students get the mechanics, they are ready to move on.

ANALYSIS

Solutions to the first three problems are given in Exhibits A, B, and C. They explain the source of the M&M result, illustrated by the equation given at the end of problem 3. The gains in the value of the firm are attributable to savings in tax expense.

In working through these problems, the instructor needs to make sure students understand the type of capital-structure change contemplated. Because EBIT (earnings before interest and taxes) and the book value of the firm remain constant across capital structures, it must be that the funds from borrowing are used to repurchase shares rather than to invest in assets.

Teaching note written by Robert F. Bruner. Copyright (c) 1989 by the Darden Graduate Business School Sponsors, Charlottesville, VA.

The M&M result obtains only if market-value weights are used in the calculation of levered betas and the weighted-average cost of capital (WACC). The notion of market-value balance sheets may be novel to students. In addition, M&M assume default-risk-free debt; thus, the result holds only if one assumes the firm's pretax cost of debt is equal to the risk-free rate.

Exhibit D presents an answer key to problem 4. The purpose of the problem is to show that, even though total market value of equity declines with increases in leverage, on a *per share* basis, the shareholders are better off.

Questions 5 and 6 seek to broaden the discussion of debt tax shields. In essence, prudent additions to leverage appear to benefit shareholders. To the extent that shareholders can lever on their own, however, they should pay no premium to a manager or entrepreneur for doing that for them. This is M&M's debt-irrelevance result based on "homemade leverage," but M&M assumed a perfect world. To the extent that imperfections and frictions creep into the picture (e.g., information asymmetries, transaction costs, differing personal and corporate tax rates or interest rates), shareholders may benefit if firms do the levering.

Question 6 seeks to disabuse students of the notion that the gains from debt tax shields are in any sense a societal money pump. Debt tax-shield benefits of leverage arise from a wealth transfer from the public sector to the private sector. Society is truly better off only if the levering or unlevering of the firm makes other things happen--for example, motivates managers, bonds the firm to disgorge cash, generally resolves agency problems, or signals expectations about the firm's future performance.

Question 7 requires the students to project the effects of a leveraged recapitalization; Exhibit E presents the completed worksheet. The main hurdle for students is calculating the present value of the perpetual debt tax shield as the product of the marginal tax rate (t) and the amount of debt (B). Consistent with problem 4, the value per share after relevering is higher than before, and is higher than the raider's offer. This analysis takes into account no default-risk discount. It does suggest, however, why raiders often drive their targets into strategies of dramatic relevering.

EXHIBIT A   Solution to Problem 1

	0% Debt/ 100% Equity	25% Debt/ 75% Equity	50% Debt/ 50% Equity
Book value: Debt	0	$ 2,500.00	$ 5,000.00
Book value: Equity	$10,000.00	$ 7,500.00	$ 5,000.00
Market value: Debt		$ 2,500.00	$ 5,000.00
Market value: Equity	$10,000.00	$ 8,350.00	$ 6,700.00
Pretax cost of debt	0.07	0.07	0.07
After-tax cost of debt	0.0462	0.0462	0.0462
Unlevered beta	0.8	0.8	0.8
Levered beta	0.8	0.958083	1.194029
Risk-free rate	0.07	0.07	0.07
Market premium	0.086	0.086	0.086
Cost of equity	0.1388	0.152395	0.172686
WACC	0.1388	0.127926	0.118632
EBIT	$ 2,103.00	$ 2,103.00	$ 2,103.00
– Taxes (@ .34)	715.02	715.00	715.00
EBIAT	1,388.00	1,388.00	1,388.00
+ Depreciation	500.00	500.00	500.00
– Capital expend.	–500.00	–500.00	–500.00
Free cash flow (FCF)	1,388.00	1,388.00	1,388.00
Value of assets (FCF/WACC)	$10,000.00	$10,850.00	$11,700.00

	0% Debt/ 100% Equity	25% Debt/ 75% Equity	50% Debt/ 50% Equity
Cash flow to creditors (CF)	0	$ 175.00	$ 350.00
Pretax cost of debt (rd)	$ 0.07	0.07	0.07
Value of debt (CF/rd)	0	$ 2,500.00	$ 5,000.00
Cash flow to shareholders			
EBIT	$ 2,103.00	$ 2,103.00	$ 2,103.00
– Interest	0	–175.00	–350.00
Pretax profit	2,103.00	1,928.00	1,753.00
– Taxes (@ .34)	715.02	655.52	596.02
Net income	1,387.98	1,272.48	1,156.98
+ Depreciation	500.00	500.00	500.00
– Capital expend.	–500.00	–500.00	–500.00
– Debt amortization	0	0	0
Residual cash flow	$ 1,387.98	$ 1,272.48	$ 1,156.98
Cost of equity	0.1388	0.152395	0.172686
Value of equity	$10,000.00	$ 8,350.00	$ 6,700.00
Value of assets (value of debt + equity)	$10,000.00	$10,850.00	$11,700.00

EXHIBIT C   Solution to Problem 3

	0% Debt/ 100% Equity	25% Debt/ 75% Equity	50% Debt/ 50% Equity
Pure business cash flows			
EBIT	$ 2,103.00	$ 2,103.00	$ 2,103.00
- Taxes (@ .34)	715.02	715.00	715.00
EBIAT	1,388.00	1,388.00	1,388.00
+ Depreciation	500.00	500.00	500.00
- Capital expend.	−500.00	−500.00	−500.00
Free cash flow	$ 1,388.00	$ 1,388.00	$ 1,388.00
Unlevered beta	0.8	0.8	0.8
Risk-free rate	0.07	0.07	0.07
Market premium	0.086	0.086	0.086
Unlevered WACC	0.1388	0.1388	0.1388
Value of pure business flows			
(CF/Unlevered WACC)	$10,000.00	$10,000.00	$10,000.00
Financing cash flows			
Interest expense	0	175.00	350.00
Tax reduction (@ .34)	0	59.50	119.00
Pretax cost of debt (rd)	0.07	0.07	0.07
Value of financing effect			
(Tax reduct./rd)	0	850.00	1,700.00
Total value (sum of values of pure business flows and financing effects)	$10,000.00	$10,850.00	$11,700.00

EXHIBIT D Solution to Problem 4

	0% Debt/ 100% Equity	25% Debt/ 75% Equity	50% Debt/ 50% Equity
Total market value of equity	$10,000.00	$8,350.00	$6,700.00
Cash paid out	0	$2,500.00	$5,000.00
Original shares (#)	1,000.00	1,000.00	1,000.00
Stock price	$10.00	$10.85	$11.70

	Before Recapitalization	After Recapitalization
Book-Value Balance Sheets		
Net working capital	$ 212,453	$ 212,453
Fixed assets	601,446	601,446
Total assets	813,899	813,899
Long-term debt	172,409	1,738,096
Deferred taxes, etc.	195,616	195,616
Preferred stock	15,000	15,000
Common equity	430,874	(1,134,813)
Total capital	$ 813,899	$ 813,899
Market-Value Balance Sheets		
Net working capital	$ 212,453	$ 212,453
Fixed assets	1,618,081	1,618,081
Present value of debt tax shield	58,619	590,953
Total assets	$1,889,153	$2,421,487
Long-term debt	172,409	1,738,096
Deferred taxes, etc.	0	0
Preferred stock	15,000	15,000
Common equity	1,701,744	668,391
Total capital	$1,889,153	$2,421,487
Number of shares	28,128	28,128
Price per share	$60.50	$23.76
Value to Public Shareholders		
Cash received	$ 0	$1,565,687
Value of shares	1,701,744	668,391
Total	$1,701,744	$2,234,078
Total per share	$60.50	$79.43

Tonka Corporation

SYNOPSIS AND OBJECTIVES

The case presents the financial and strategic positions of the sixth largest U.S. toy manufacturer, Tonka, as of early 1987. At this time, Tonka carried virtually no debt on its balance sheet, in sharp contrast to the other major toy manufacturers. Based on competitive and financial considerations, the student is challenged to recommend a capital-structure policy for the firm.

The case was developed to motivate a discussion of the determinants of corporate debt policy. Of a possibly long list of determinants, this case highlights two: (1) the value-creating benefits of debt tax shields and (2) the need for financial slack as dictated by the firm's competitive position. The case is usefully paired with "Coleco Industries, Inc." (Case 30), which also considers debt policy and illustrates the costs of financial distress.

STUDY QUESTIONS

A useful supplementary reading for this case is "How Much Debt is Right for your Company?" by T. R. Piper and W. A. Weinhold, *Harvard Business Review,* July–August 1982, pp. 106–14 (Reprint No. 82413). Because an important issue in this case is the desired level of financial flexibility, Gordon Donaldson's "Strategy for Financial Emergencies," *Harvard Business Review,* November–December 1969, Reprint No. 69604, is also a helpful background reading.

1. How much business risk does Tonka face?

2. How much potential value, if any, can Tonka create for its shareholders at each of the proposed levels of debt? How would leveraging up affect the company's taxes?

3. How much financial risk would Tonka face at each of the proposed levels of debt shown in Exhibit 12 of the case? How would the capital markets react to a decision by the company to increase the use of debt in its capital structure?

4. What capital structure would you recommend as appropriate for Tonka?

5. How might Tonka implement a more aggressive capital-structure policy? What are the alternative tactics for leveraging up?

6. What arguments would you advance to persuade Tonka's management to adopt your recommendation?

Teaching note written by Robert F. Bruner. Copyright (c) 1989 by the Darden Graduate Business School Sponsors, Charlottesville, VA.

TEACHING PLAN

If this case is paired with "Coleco Industries, Inc.," the teaching focus of the "Tonka" case can be usefully narrowed to consider two general determinants of a firm's capital structure: the benefits of exploiting debt tax shields and industry economics. In the next class, "Coleco" can introduce default risk as a determinant. The following outline assumes this scheme.

The strategy of the outline is to test student sentiments twice during the discussion: at the beginning and again near the end of class. Students often initially support high levels of debt simply on the basis of case Exhibit 12, but upon considering the competitive situation in toy manufacturing, they tend to scale down their targets. This shift in sentiment can leave a large impression.

(10 minutes) How much leverage, if any, would you recommend that Tonka assume? One can invite specific recommendations from two or three students and then take a vote of the students supporting various debt levels.

(10 minutes) Is the toy industry competitive? Why? This segment of the discussion should address ease of entry, barriers, risks, and the jockeying among the dominant manufacturers.

(20 minutes) What is Tonka's strategy? How effectively has this strategy mitigated any of the toy-industry risks? How well has Tonka performed under this strategy? These questions return the discussion to Tonka with a view toward profiling its competitive strengths and weaknesses.

(20 minutes) How was case Exhibit 12 derived? What's the *quid pro quo* for these gains in value? The purpose of this question is to identify tax shields as the source and then extend the analysis beyond the simple linearity of the Miller/Modigliani theory.

(5 minutes) Where do we come out on this? Vote again.

(15 minutes) How would you try to convince Tonka's management to adopt our recommended policy? Here the challenge for the student is to put into plain language the concepts applied and developed earlier in the discussion. This is also an opportunity for the instructor to check on the comprehension of the students.

The instructor can close the discussion with a presentation of the epilogue and perhaps some preparatory comments about the "Coleco" case.

ANALYSIS

Economics of Toy Manufacturing

Toy manufacturing is dominated by a few major players. In the abstract, market dominance should yield high returns and even stability, but unlike many oligopolies, the positioning of the players is subject to surprise and large change. The reasons are:

* short product life cycles. Increasingly, toys are fad products, a result of fickle tastes of children compounded by the effectiveness of television marketing in stimulating demand and then switching demand to newer products;

- design risks and significant new-product costs;

- sudden new entry of competitors or significant new products (e.g., GoBots, Transformers, foreign competitors);

- demographic changes;

- government regulation based on safety (Consumer Products Safety Commission) and advertising (Federal Trade Commission, Federal Communications Commission);

- mergers and consolidations;

- cyclicality and seasonality of demand.

Tonka's Strategy and Performance

Within this dynamic environment, Tonka has adopted a strategy characterized by a few key elements:

- business-portfolio concept. Tonka's product line consists of a mature, stable product segment (e.g., trucks) and a more volatile fad segment (e.g., Pound Puppies). Exhibit A contrasts these segments based on case facts and general knowledge. Of concern is the fact that half of Tonka's revenues derive from the risky plush-toy segment. Only 25 percent of revenues is derived from the stable toy-truck line;

- product-line strategy of extension of product lives with add-ons (e.g., Pound Puppy dog houses) and diversification of the product portfolio (seeking to limit dependence on any individual product to a maximum of 25 percent of sales);

- distribution strategy seeking international diversification and the purchase, rather than internal development, of new channels (e.g., the purchase of the Bandai distributor in Australia);

- conservative financial policies reflected in low leverage, low dividend payout, and relatively liquid asset mix.

Judged by some standard measures, this strategy has succeeded. Compound sales growth has been 37 percent annually. Market share has risen from 1.2 to 3.5 percent, growing at a compound rate of 31 percent. Return on equity has ranged between 16 and 29 percent, while return on assets has ranged between 6.9 and 14.1 percent. These ranges are the highest of the big five toy manufacturers.

The main inconsistency with this success story is the failure of Tonka's stock price to respond. Its price/earnings ratio, 8.1, is about half that of its larger competitors. Students can speculate on the reasons; the firm's conservative financial policies usually figure prominently in any list.

Tax Benefits

Case Exhibit 12 sheds light on the possible lost opportunity resulting from a low-debt policy. This table was derived by estimating the market value of the entire firm and solving for value of equity (essentially, the same procedure as developed in "An Introduction to Debt Policy and Value" (Case 28)). The analysis ignores possible default-risk discounts, so the estimated stock prices are not exact. One of the significant judgment calls in the case is the change in default risk as the firm levers up. Often, naive students will ignore default risk and advocate the 60 percent debt level (or even higher).

To illustrate the mechanics of case Exhibit 12, one can examine the development of one leverage scenario. For instance, at the 20 percent debt level, one solves first for the present value of the perpetual annual tax savings (t x B, or .45 x 22.7). Adjusting the value of the tax shield causes the value of assets to rise to $174.9 million. The resulting total value of equity is $152.2 million, and price per share is equal to that value plus cash paid out ($6 million, the new borrowings), divided by number of pre-existing shares (7.67 million), or $20.62 per share—an increase of 2 percent.

Risk

The increase in share price could be viewed as originating from the more efficient use of corporate resources (i.e., debt capacity, a resource like manufacturing capacity or depth of managerial talent in an organization), a redeployment of resources that might generate no added risk for the firm's shareholders. Whether or not the relevering adds risk cannot be resolved conclusively from case facts, which affords the opportunity for a rich airing in class of student analysis and judgment.

Sensitivity analysis of case Exhibit 12 can lend some insight into the potential risk/return tradeoffs associated with higher degrees of leverage. For instance, one can apply the traditional *EBIT/EPS analysis* (earnings before interest and taxes to earnings per share), for which brief explanations are given in many corporate finance texts. In essence, this analysis would substitute varying EBIT levels into the top panel of case Exhibit 12 to determine the associated EPS.

Exhibit B presents a graph of the EBIT/EPS results yielding at least two important insights. First, the EPS function associated with the 20 percent debt/capital ratio is virtually indistinguishable from that associated with the firm's current debt/equity ratio. In other words, Tonka's EPS would be immaterially different if the firm levered to 20 percent. At higher EBIT levels, the functions fan out, creating a difference of about $1.00 in EPS between the highest and lowest leverage scenarios when EBIT reaches $50 million.

Second, the EPS functions cross over at an EBIT level of about $21 million. This indifference point compares with EBIT levels of $44 million in 1986 and $39.8 million in 1985. What might drive the recent EBIT levels down lower than the indifference point? In one possible scenario, all plush toys might decline simultaneously, with no new plush-toy product introductions. With plush toys at 50 percent of revenues, EBIT could fall toward the indifference level. More significantly, it takes an EBIT of about $9 million to produce negative earnings per share, under the assumption of the 60 percent debt/capital policy.

The relative imperviousness of Tonka's financial performance to variations in EBIT may be attributed to its toy trucks, a stable "cash cow." At 25 percent of revenues, the truck line may well account for about $10 million in EBIT, ensuring the operating earnings necessary to service even a 60 percent debt/capital policy. Based on an analysis of predictable adversity in Tonka's environment, the firm could apparently satisfactorily bear a much higher debt level.

Flexibility

If maintaining high financial slack is necessary, it must be because of the "unknown unknowns" in Tonka's environment that could create sudden and large demands on cash. Examples would be the opportunity to acquire a major competitor, successful competitor entry into the toy-trucks market, or a government ban on television advertising followed by a depression in demand.

Setting a target for reserves is difficult because of the indefiniteness of the potential crisis the reserve is meant to meet. The major determinants are the magnitude of the potential demand and the degree of risk aversion of the policy-makers. Suffice it to say that the wisdom of maintaining a large reserve is proved, like a large insurance policy, in its ultimate use.

EPILOGUE

Quite unexpectedly, Tonka exhausted its entire unused debt capacity in one move. On September 8, 1987, the firm, acting as a White Knight against a hostile tender offer from New World Entertainment, Inc., announced it had agreed to acquire Kenner-Parker for $628 million. To make the move, Tonka increased its own debt from $8 million to $360 million, producing a debt-to-capital ratio of 85 percent. The acquisition more than doubled Tonka's sales.

As luck would have it, however, the same day Tonka announced it had successfully acquired 95 percent of Kenner-Parker's shares, the stock market crashed. The timing couldn't have been worse for the two cycle-sensitive toy manufacturers. In the final three months of 1987, shipments of Tonka's Pound Puppies fell 50 percent--perhaps signaling the end of the life cycle for that product line. Analysts worried whether Tonka would be able to fill the gap in its product line. More generally, the crash created fears of consumers retreating from the forthcoming Christmas selling season. Retailers slashed inventories and purchase orders. In an effort to trim expenses, toy manufacturers reduced advertising. As predicted, toy sales slumped.

As Exhibit C reveals, the new Tonka reported net losses in 1987 and 1988. The already small dividend was eliminated entirely in the third quarter of 1987. Analysts had expected the higher interest expense and various transaction costs to penalize Tonka's performance for 1987, but no one anticipated a shock to the firm's operating performance. The operational restructuring that Tonka imposed on Kenner-Parker hurt productivity and morale. Moreover, expected economies in advertising evaporated as analysts realized that promotional toys, which formed the core of Kenner-Parker's product line, required higher and dedicated levels of advertising expenditure. *Value Line* concluded:

> The balance sheet remains a concern. The toymaker's strained finances...afford little cushion in the event that its products fail to excite young consumers. To its credit, however, Tonka has entered many toy categories, thereby providing greater balance to its portfolio. Still, given the company's erratic operating performance, we think this volatile stock is best suited for risk-tolerant accounts only.[1]

---

[1] *Value Line Investment Survey*, May 26, 1989, p. 1556.

EXHIBIT A   Comparison of Tonka's Two Main Product Segments

	Trucks	Plush Toys
	25% of revenues	50% of revenues
	Low advertising expense	High advertising expense
	High margin	Very high margin
	Stable demand	Volatile demand (faddish)
	Low growth rate	Temporary explosive growth
	Very long life cycle	Short life cycle
	Universal appeal	Appeals to segments
	Long lasting	Worn out relatively quickly

EXHIBIT B   EBIT/EPS Graph

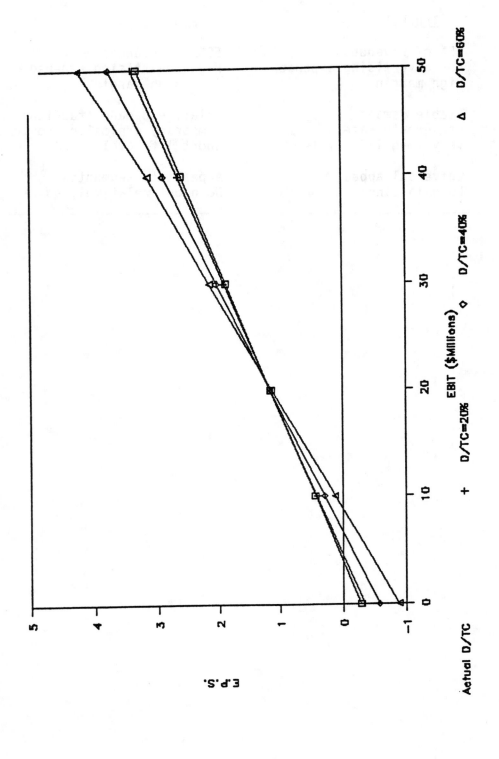

344

EXHIBIT C   Tonka's Financial Performance, 1985-88

	Fiscal Year			
	1985	1986	1987	1988
Sales (millions)	$244.4	$293.4	$382.6	$907.7
Operating margin	19.2%	17.7%	2.9%	14.9%
Net profit (millions)	$19.5	$22.3	($7.5)	($5.8)
EPS	$2.99	$3.04	($0.97)	($0.75)
Dividends per share	$0.07	$0.07	$0.06	$0.00
Long-term debt (millions)	$8.1	$8.1	$526.2	$503.9
Net worth (millions)	$51.3	$96.3	$95.8	$87.6
LTD/NW	15.8%	8.4%	549.3%	575.3%
Stock price				
High	$22.00	$32.375	$25.00	$13.375
Low	6.875	15.875	4.375	8.00

Coleco Industries, Inc.

SYNOPSIS AND OBJECTIVES

In March 1988, this large toy manufacturer is facing the consequences of bearing too much debt in a volatile competitive environment. The task of the student is to recommend a response to the worsening situation by which the firm can be returned to financial health. At the date of the case, the company is not under protection of the court, although bankruptcy looms as a distinct possibility if negotiations with lenders summon forth no mutually agreeable solution.

The case was developed to motivate a discussion of the determinants of corporate debt policy, as part of a pair of cases set in the toy industry (see "Tonka Corporation"). In sharp contrast to the Tonka case, this case raises the costs of financial distress as a constraint on the use of debt. The case discussion can also sharpen students' thinking on the exact nature of financial distress and how it differs from the special case of bankruptcy. Moreover, the case can be used to illustrate the allocative issues that arise in working out a satisfactory financial plan for recovery. And finally, the case affords the opportunity to compare the equity in a distressed firm with an out-of-the-money option on the firm's assets.

STUDY QUESTIONS

1. Assess the product-market strategy and financial strategy Coleco pursued through 1987. Compare Coleco's strategy with that of Tonka in early 1987.

2. What went wrong? How did Coleco respond?

3. Assess various alternatives at this stage of Coleco's difficulties. What sort of refinancing plan would alleviate Coleco's financial difficulties?

4. What should Paul Meyer do now? Consider this question from the perspective of:

   - Coleco management,
   - its lenders,
   - its shareholders.

TEACHING PLAN

(30 minutes) What is Coleco's financial condition, and how did it come about? This segment of the discussion might review many of the same industry and strategic considerations brought up in the Tonka case discussion. A comparison with Tonka can be an important teaching avenue of the case.

Teaching note written by Robert F. Bruner. Copyright (c) 1989, by the Darden Graduate Business School Sponsors, Charlottesville, VA.

Identifying the origins of Coleco's financial distress will also be useful to the analysis.

(30 minutes) At this point, who are the significant players in any potential outcome? What are each of their motivations? A review of the goals and comparative strengths of management, creditors, and shareholders develops the allocational theme of the case and can motivate a discussion of the agency conflicts that arise in financial distress.

(20 minutes) What are management's alternative courses of action? How does each work? The chief alternatives worthy of discussion are: issuing equity, selling the company, recapitalizing the firm outside of bankruptcy, recapitalizing the firm in bankruptcy, liquidating the firm. At the end of this discussion, the instructor can observe that all the alternatives are variations on the theme of restructuring.

(10 minutes) What should Meyer do? How should he persuade his colleagues and board of directors of the effectiveness of this course of action? The case discussion can be closed with a vote by the class on the most popular alternatives, followed by a presentation of the epilogue.

ANALYSIS

What Happened?

This is a case of dramatic adversity. As recently as 1985, Coleco reported sizable net earnings and offered promising prospects for the future. Understanding the turn for the worse is one of the important learning vehicles for the students. The record suggests that Coleco's decline resulted from its strategy of financing its way out of adversity, instead of making operational changes to "bootstrap" its way out.

Exhibit A gives a summary of the sources and uses of funds for the company for two time periods: the 1980–85 period of the firm's explosive growth, and 1986–87, the period of the firm's aggressive acquisition strategy and large losses. The exhibit shows that, in the first period, uses were primarily in the form of additions to current assets. These were financed by subordinated debentures, additions to current liabilities, and profits. In contrast, the large use of funds in the 1986–87 period was to cover operating losses. These were financed by more subordinated debentures and current liabilities. Coleco displayed an ability to stretch its current creditors, adding $289 million in current liabilities versus $278 million in current assets over the entire 1980–87 period.

The sources of Coleco's adversity were the very shocks against which Tonka's conservative debt policy was designed to guard:

- external shocks such as the contraction in consumer toy spending following the stock market crash of October 1987;

- the foreshortened life cycle of a key product (i.e., Cabbage Patch);[1]

---

[1]The product life-cycle problem, and the extent to which the company's recovery is a bet on new products, is apparent in case Exhibit 4, which shows that three products (Furskins, Wrinkles, and Rambo) were expected to decline

- the failure to develop new high-demand products to replace waning older products;

- the constriction of financial flexibility (evident in the wariness of lenders to finance ongoing operations);

- adverse settlement of lawsuits against the company related to alleged infringement of trademarks and designs (i.e., MCA and "Donkey Kong" and the Adam computer).

The combination of these shocks produced various danger signals about the company's financial health: (1) Coleco's debt rated CCC+ by Standard & Poor's (2) steep losses for the fourth quarter and year of 1987 ($-99 and $-105 million, respectively), (3) negative net worth ($-84 million), (4) high debt level ($460 million), and (5) falling stock price to a quarter of what it had been a year earlier. Another index of the firm's health at the date of the case is provided by the yields of the firm's subordinated bonds: they are yielding about 40 percent to maturity.[2] This high yield compares to yields of 12-19 percent on other CCC-rated issues listed in case Exhibit 11. Plainly, investors are demanding a huge default-risk premium.

Coleco's Strategy

Many of the specific causes of Coleco's financial distress can be traced to a mismatch between the financial policies of the firm and the degree of risk created by its operating strategy. Indeed, what is remarkable about Coleco's experience in toy manufacturing is that it seemed to have no product-market strategy at all. The firm lurched from fad to fad, betting that it could play the product life cycle effectively (e.g., Adam computer, Colecovision, and the Cabbage Patch doll line). The search for new products appeared to be completely opportunistic. Because Coleco had no enduring core products, a growth-oriented strategy depended upon large successes based on significant investments. Coleco's active acquisition program (evidenced in purchases of Selchow and Righter, Tomy Kogyo) was an expansion, rather than diversification, program. The need for diversity was manifest. Colecovision and Adam, huge temporary successes, ultimately threatened the life of the firm as they wound down. Like a bicycle, Coleco had stability only when its products generated velocity.

Coleco's financial policy showed no consistency with the huge risks associated with its operating strategy. The company relied on substantial amounts of debt financing—especially to finance product development and introduction—but this financing assumed product success and longevity, enough

---

entirely, only two years after introduction. Furthermore, the exhibit reveals that $300 million of sales was expected to come from products introduced before 1987, $200 million from products introduced in 1987, and $125 million from products introduced in 1988; in other words, the prevention of decline in revenues depends entirely on the success of new products.

[2]This rough estimate understates the true yield to maturity by ignoring the effect of sinking-fund payments, on which there is incomplete information in case Exhibit 8. Including these payments would increase the yield to maturity. The basic point remains: the market is applying a huge default-risk premium to Coleco's debt securities.

to repay the principal. Senior lenders, at least, were not persuaded that the debt could be easily serviced; Coleco resorted to financing itself with subordinated convertible securities. The heavy reliance on debt financing restricted the firm's flexibility to respond to shocks. The issuance of shares of stock to satisfy lawsuits implies that management was even willing to dilute the old shareholders' interest to remain in operation.

The dark side of Coleco's strategy is that it sharpened some classic agency conflicts between stockholders and creditors. These conflicts emerge most clearly in financial distress, although they are always present, regardless of the health of the firm. In particular, distress invites behavior that buys time for the residual investors and/or shifts risks from the junior to the senior claimants.

Illustration of Creditor–Shareholder Conflicts[3]

Exhibit B gives the details for a discussion of risk shifting by creditors and shareholders. To begin with, assume a one-period model, in which everything is liquidated a year later (except in the final case, when liquidation is immediate). The required return on assets (WACC) is 10 percent in the initial example.

Panel 1 of Exhibit B illustrates the base case, before distress. Here, the firm has five equally likely values at the end of the year; the expected value is $110. The debt has a required return of 5 percent and a face value of $90, but because there is default risk, it has an expected value of only $84. Finally, the future expected value of the stock is $26, and its present value is $20. The implied return to shareholders is 30 percent.

Now, suppose the market learns that the firm has no new toys as originally thought. The payoffs on the value of the firm shift downward, but the risks (i.e., variance) remain the same; so the required return on assets is still 10 percent. As can be seen from the debt-payoff column, the creditors bear higher default risk; so suppose that the required return on debt rises to 8 percent. As a result of this shift, the present values of the firm, the debt, and the equity fall to $63.64, $59.26, and $4.38, respectively. Value is destroyed by this development.

In the second case, shareholders have only a 20 percent chance of getting anything, versus a 60 percent chance before. The bondholder has an 80 percent chance of being the residual owner (i.e., of getting all the firm value at liquidation). Bondholders basically own the firm now, and stockholders own the "outside chance" of survival (i.e., an out-of-the-money call option on the assets, where exercise price is $90, and the current asset value is $70).

Next, consider a new possibility: an investment opportunity arises in which the company could spend $20 more to produce a Cabbage Patch "follow-up" product that will either fail (i.e., lose the $20) or pay off handsomely, generating a value of the firm of $200 at the maximum, rather than $120. The range of outcomes shows that this new project has the effect of widening the variance: the up-side payoff rises considerably, while the payoff in the other four states falls by $20. Assume that because of this higher variance, WACC rises to 18 percent, and the cost of debt rises to 10 percent. Here, the value of the firm and the value of debt fall (they are $59.32 and $43.64, respectively), while the value of equity *rises* (to $15.68). The net effect of the risky project is to create value for shareholders and destroy value for creditors. Intuitively,

---

[3]Ken Eades developed this illustration.

349

this outcome is consistent with viewing common stock as a call option on the assets of the firm: the option should be more valuable as variance increases.

Faced with the prospect of behavior like this, the bondholder at this point could attempt to (1) raise all expected payoffs so that everyone wins or (2) lower the risk, even if stockholders lose. In panel 4 of Exhibit B, bondholders "throw away" the up-side potential in favor of a more certain liquidation value, which is assumed to be received immediately. The variance of payoffs on the assets is narrowed considerably. The present expected value of payoffs to bondholders ($68) is higher under liquidation, however, than it is under the shareholders' new investment plan ($43.64).

To summarize, shareholders fare as follows:

Stock Price

Base case	$20.00
No new products	4.38
High-flyer project	15.38
Liquidation	$ 2.00

The naturally conflicting interests of creditors and shareholders tends to obscure the overriding possibility that both parties might be better off if they were to cooperate. One of the arts of restructuring a distressed firm is determining solutions in which the wealth of creditors and shareholders is jointly enhanced and in (re)gaining cooperation among them.

Valuing Coleco Stock as an Option

Viewing Coleco's situation with the aid of option-pricing theory (OPT) yields some rich insights into Meyer's predicament. Specifically, one can use OPT to determine the time horizon implicit in Coleco's stock price.

Exhibit C provides a summary of the parameters assumed in the analysis. The exercise price is straightforward: it is the par value of liabilities. The market value of assets must be approximated by summing the market value of liabilities and equity; these results are less sensitive to variations in asset value, so that estimation errors here do not dramatically affect the ultimate insights about time and risk. Asset volatility is assumed equal to 40 percent, the approximate volatilities of Coleco's subordinated debentures given in case footnote 6. However, the assumption of 40 percent is extremely high. To test the sensitivity-to-the-risk assumption, an asset volatility of 20 percent is also used.

At $2.50 per share, and 17.33 million shares outstanding, the total market value of equity is $43.33 million. What is the term of the option implied in this stock price?

Assume: Asset value = $446.21 mm
         Exercise price = $619.80 mm

Term	Risk-Free Rate	Volatility	
		.40	.20
1 yr.	6.21%	$ 30.3 mm	$ 4.39 mm
2 yrs.	7.0%[4]	69.4 mm	40.70 mm
3 yrs.	7.38%	$104.0 mm	$42.84 mm

The analysis suggests that the term of the option on the value of the assets (i.e., 1.5 to 3 years) is considerably *less* than the term to maturity of Coleco's debt, 13 years. Indeed, the expected life of the equity is probably overstated in this analysis, since the analysis ignores the effect of funds flows out of the company (i.e., to pay creditors and suppliers). Regardless of the exact number, the insight from this analysis is that *the market* considers the equity to be a rather short-lived option. Paul Meyer does not have the luxury of ample time to develop a restructuring plan.

Strategic Alternatives

As is typical of firms in financial distress, Coleco's management has little flexibility in responding to its deteriorating financial condition. The main task is to reschedule the service of liabilities, which will require a reallocation of the security interests in the firm in a way consistent with economic reality: that the assets of the firm are worth less than the par value of its old liabilities and equity. This reallocation can occur in a number of ways:

Negotiated financial restructuring: In this approach, the senior creditors are induced to reschedule the service on their credits in return for an equity interest (i.e., a "kicker" that would increase the rate of return to the lenders). The stockholders and subordinated creditors are washed away in the resulting dilution.

Sale of new equity: New investors are induced to take an equity interest in the company, in return for control. Old equity investors are washed away in the resulting dilution. The feasibility of this alternative is doubtful.

Bankruptcy: In this case, the business is restructured, and security interests reallocated under the umbrella of the courts. Creditors may be averse to this alternative, because outcomes rarely conform to strict, absolute priority, and the process takes a long time. Ultimately, stockholders and subordinated creditors are liable to be washed away. In addition to bankruptcy being time consuming and expensive, management and shareholders lose bargaining power. (In Chapter XI, creditors can seek a court-ordered liquidation to protect their investments.) A final disadvantage of bankruptcy is publicity: the negotiations to restructure are conducted in an essentially open court, signaling in detail the firm's difficulties to suppliers, customers, and competitors.

Liquidation: The firm is dismembered voluntarily in an effort to obtain the highest immediate value of wasting assets. The odds are that the liquidation value of assets will be less than their value in an ongoing firm.

---

[4]This rate was extrapolated from data in case Exhibit 10.

As the list of alternatives suggests, a negotiated financial restructuring may be the superior alternative for creditors. The success of this restructuring will depend, however, on the willingness of stockholders and junior creditors to succumb and on successful management of what is likely to be an extremely complicated negotiating process. Case Exhibit 9 reveals that seven banks are the principal holders of secured debt, 650 investors hold the subordinated and convertible subordinated issues, and 1,200-plus are trade creditors. This last group is liable to be especially contentious and difficult to manage, given the small sizes and international distribution of the participants.

Recommendation

Seasoned turnaround consultants and work-out lenders recommend a pro-active approach. Rather than waiting for things to turn better (or for the other shoe to drop), management should organize the process of negotiating a financial restructuring immediately. The goal should be to determine the terms of exchange under which the existing creditors would swap their claims for a new package of rescheduled debt and equity. At the same time, management should continue to monitor ongoing operations and the value of the firm. Should the negotiations become disorderly and/or the value decline steeply, management should seek the protection of the courts via bankruptcy.

EPILOGUE

In early 1988, the Cabbage Patch product line, the mainstay of Coleco's sales, waned more rapidly than anyone expected. Cabbage Patch sales for all of 1988 amounted to only $58 million, as against the $125 million forecasted for 1988 in case Exhibit 4. The operating decline precipitated a cash crisis.

In the first quarter of 1988, Coleco attempted to restructure its financial obligations. The company offered to exchange common stock and $119 million of debentures, paying less than 5 percent for the $335 million (face value) of debentures outstanding in the spring. In consequence, annual cash interest expense would decline to $12 million from $40 million on the old debentures. The offer would have diluted current shareholders by 50 percent. In addition to cutting the principal amount and interest the firm would have had to pay, the exchange would also have extended the maturity of the debt.

At the same time, Coleco began to negotiate with its short-term creditors. The working-capital credit line, secured by substantially all of the company's assets, was set to expire in the second quarter of 1988.

The attempt to restructure failed. The company could not obtain approval from debenture holders for the stock-for-debt exchange; the exchange offer was extended until July 1, when the company reported that it would rescind the offer.

On July 12, 1988, Coleco filed for bankruptcy. Coleco's stock price closed at $1.375 per share. Evidently, the forces triggering the bankruptcy filing were the firm's slow strangulation by suppliers, whose payables were severely stretched, and the unwillingness of the firm's working-capital lenders to finance the firm's inventory build-up for the 1988 Christmas selling season. Three private investment partnerships purchased the $86 million of bank debt outstanding at a 50 percent discount. Two asset-based lenders agreed to provide $50 million of secured working-capital loans.

On the operational side, Coleco's management undertook a restructuring that included the following steps:

- retained a crisis management firm to organize an "office of the chief executive";

- sold its headquarters building for $13.2 million;

- laid off 13 percent of its headquarters staff and a "substantial portion" of its work force;

- sold certain product lines and the plants where they were manufactured to Hasbro for $27 million. The products accounted for $77 million of 1987 sales;

- implemented a bonus payment plan to get its Hong Kong suppliers to accelerate production and shipping to allow Coleco to retain customers for the 1988 Christmas selling season. Under the bonus payment plan, Coleco paid $0.22 to suppliers on its past-due accounts for every $1.00 of new product shipped to Coleco on time; and

- entered a joint marketing agreement with Mattel, whereby Mattel would distribute the company's products in Western Europe, the Middle East, and Africa.

On January 27, 1989, Coleco filed its reorganization plan with the Federal Bankruptcy Court in New York. The plan had several features: (1) repaying secured creditors 100 percent of face value of debt as soon as possible; (2) giving senior unsecured creditors ($80 million face value claim) a note for $40 million and preferred stock convertible into 43 percent of fully diluted common shares; (3) giving unsecured creditors ($417 million face value of debt) stock and warrants that would bring fully diluted ownership to 49 percent; and (4) giving existing common and preferred shareholders 5 percent of the new common stock.

A liquidation analysis submitted by the company to the court revealed that senior secured creditors would receive 100 percent of their claim, and senior unsecured creditors would receive 79 percent of their claim, under conservative assumptions. Subordinated creditors and equity investors would receive nothing in liquidation. The cost of administering the liquidation would be about $25 million.

In June 1989, Coleco agreed to sell most of its remaining assets to Hasbro for $85 million plus warrants for one million shares of Hasbro stock, pending Bankruptcy Court approval. The assets included the Cabbage Patch line and the Scrabble board game. After the sale, Coleco became a shell company with more than $100 million available in tax-loss carryforwards that could be used to shelter income of a profitable operation.

As one analyst said,

> The fate of Coleco is now in the hands of the court. It's going to take an awful lot of homework to work out what each class of [debentures] may or may not be entitled to...[5]

---

[5]C. J. Chipello and J. Pereira, "Coleco Seeks Creditor Shield of Chapter 11," *Wall Street Journal*, July 13, 1988, p. 4.

EXHIBIT A   Sources and Uses of Funds

	1980-85	1986-87
SOURCES		
Increases in current liabilities	$ 96,483	$193,117
Additions to long-term debt	4,171	--
Additions to deferred liabilities	26,279	--
Additions to preferred stock	--	22
Increases in subordinated debs.	52,445	162,914
Increases in convert. sub. debs.	75,777	4,172
Increases in common stock	19,359	27,067
Profits	64,920	--
Total sources	$339,434	$387,292
USES		
Increases in current assets	$247,407	$29,229
Dividends	21,110	--
Increases in net plant and equip.	33,043	10,465
Increases in other assets	37,874	98,322
Decreases in long-term debt	--	12,085
Decreases in deferred liabilities	--	23,479
Losses	--	213,712
Total uses	$339,434	$387,292

EXHIBIT B An Illustration of Stockholder-Bondholder Risk-Shifting Games In
Financial Distress

1. Before Financial Distress:

Probability	Value of Firm	Payoff on Debt	Payoff on Stock
.2	$160	$90	$70
.2	130	90	40
.2	110	90	20
.2	90	90	0
.2	60	60	0
Expected value	$110	$84	$26
Discount rate	.10	.05	.3
Present value	$100	$80	$20

2. Firm Announces It Has No New Toys:

Probability	Value of Firm	Value of Debt	Value of Stock
.2	$120	$90	$30
.2	90	90	0
.2	70	70	0
.2	50	50	0
.2	20	20	0
Expected value	$ 70	$64	$ 6
Discount rate	.10	.08	.371
Present value	$ 63.64	$59.26	$ 4.377

3. Firm could spend $20 to produce a Cabbage Patch follow-up that will either do nothing (i.e., lose the $20) or produce a huge payoff (i.e., firm value rises to $200 not 120):

Probability	Value of Firm	Value of Debt	Value of Stock
.2	$200	$90	$110
.2	70	70	0
.2	50	50	0
.2	30	30	0
.2	0	0	0
Expected value	$ 70	$48	$ 22
Discount rate	.18	.10	.403
Present value	$ 59.32	$43.64	$ 15.68

4. Immediate Liquidation:

Probability	Value of Firm	Value of Debt	Value of Stock
.2	$80	$70	$10
.2	70	70	0
.2	70	70	0
.2	70	70	0
.2	60	60	0
Expected value	$70	$68	$ 2
Discount rate	1.0	1.0	1.0
Present value	$70	$68	$ 2

EXHIBIT C Illustration of Valuing Coleco Common Stock with OPT

1. Volatility of Assets   .40

    Secured-debt volatility: probably low
    Subordinated-debt volatility: .411, .431
    Equity volatility: .647

2. Exercise Price

    Face value of liabilities, 12/31/87 $619.8 mm

3. Value of Assets

    Mkt. value of current liabilities $311.4
    Mkt. value of senior debt   9.6
    Mkt. value of sub. debt
        .27 x 163   44.0
        .34 x 52.7   17.9
    Mkt. value of conv. sub. debt,
        assume price = $25
        .25 x 79.9   19.98
    Mkt. value of equity
        17.33 x $2.5 $ 43.33 $446.21 mm

4. Term   To be solved

5. Risk-Free Rate (10-yr. Treasury, case Exhibit 10): 8.21%

Design Technologies, Inc.

SYNOPSIS AND OBJECTIVES

The Bank of Boston's newly formed Corporate Finance division is asked to help arrange financing for a management buyout of a struggling integrated-circuit manufacturer. The bank must consider making both a bridge loan and an equity investment. Students must value the firm, estimate the risk of the transaction, and structure the debt and equity investment to compensate the bank properly for the risk incurred.

At an introductory level, this case can be used to exercise the basic discounted-cash-flow (DCF) valuation technique applied to firms. With some direction, the case can also illustrate the creation of value through levering a firm. In addition, the case is effective as an introduction to merchant banking: the banker's task in this case is to use standard credit-analysis and equity-valuation skills to assess the total package of debt and equity. Finally, the case can be used to motivate a discussion of equity kickers and potential cross-subsidization between loans and kickers.

STUDY QUESTIONS

1.   Is Design Technologies the kind of potential bank customer to which Bill Stern should devote much effort?

2.   Is the loan an attractive business proposition for the bank?

3.   What explains Consolidated Can's interest in taking 50,000 shares of Design Technologies' stock? Is this really an equity investment?

4.   Is the equity investment attractive for Frank Harrison and the bank? How much of the $1 million in new outside equity would you propose that the bank buy?

TEACHING PLAN

A general useful strategy is to heighten the natural tension in this case between the firm's mediocre past and its potentially glowing future. Students and seasoned lenders are often quite skeptical of this business relationship until the potentially high returns from the equity investment become apparent in the latter part of the discussion. Frequently, this reversal in attitude makes a large impression on those discussing the case.

(10 minutes) Is a relationship with Design Technologies one we should go to any trouble to obtain? What kind of company is it?

(10 minutes) On its own merits, is the loan attractive?

Teaching note written by Robert F. Bruner. Copyright (c) 1989 by the Darden Graduate Business School Sponsors, Charlottesville, VA.

(10 minutes)   What explains Consolidated Can's equity position in Design Technologies after the buyout?

(40 minutes)   On its own merits, is an equity investment by Bank of Boston attractive?

(10 minutes)   How much of an equity position is needed to raise the return on the relationship to an acceptable level?

The discussion can be closed with a brief presentation of the epilogue and some comments on the similarities and differences between the merchant banking and commercial banking points of view.

ANALYSIS

Credit Analysis

If the relationship were to be judged strictly on the basis of the loan, the assessment would be straightforwardly negative. While Harrison is an effective manager with a good record in achieving turnarounds, and while the company is well positioned to exploit the demand for semicustomized chips, the negative aspects are intimidating. First, the track record for the company itself is unfavorable. Second, the bank's auditors have recommended against the loan. Third, the backlogs may mean little, because purchasers are obligated to buy only 25 percent of the contracted amount. Most importantly, however, the proposed interest rate on the loan (base plus 1.0 percent) is plainly below the going rate on credits of similar risk (i.e., base plus 2.5 percent). Exhibit A reveals that, if the Bank of Boston were to sell its loan at a present value based on the going rate, the bank would sustain a loss of $313,000.

Seasoned lenders often point out that, while the bank has no relationship with Design Technologies, it has a considerable relationship with Harrison. The strong and successful character of the leading individual in this company will, to many students, mitigate the demerits of the loan.

An interesting point to develop with some audiences is that Design Technologies does not conform to the usual profile of a leveraged-buyout candidate: low growth, mature market position, established strength of cash flow, established management team, low technological change, and good asset values. From this perspective, one can understand the bank's initial reluctance to participate in this deal: it fails to meet the profile of traditional targets of highly leveraged transactions.

Consolidated Can's Equity Position

An important first step in the analysis of this case is to view Consolidated Can's "equity" investment as debt. Consolidated Can probably had to take a deferred payment in order to sell the division at the desired total price. Calling this interest "equity" rather than "debt" seems like a cosmetic effort to comfort a potential lender. One can make a strong case that Consolidated Can's interest is nothing more than a zero-coupon subordinated seller's note.

The mandatory retirement[1] in two years differentiates Consolidated's "equity" from the equity investment of Harrison and the bank.

Viewing Consolidated Can's interest as debt has some important implications for the analysis. Mainly, it suggests that a DCF analysis of equity should actually focus only on the equity investment of Harrison and the bank, and that in an economic balance sheet, Consolidated Can's interest would show up in the debt balance rather than in equity. Case Exhibit 4 forecasts the future in these terms.

Despite the directiveness of the case on this point, a discussion about the nature of Consolidated Can's interest is an important learning opportunity for students. Viewing securities and the structure of a transaction uncritically is a mistake. Not infrequently in highly leveraged transactions does the *economic* character of a security differ materially from its legal or accounting character.

Valuing the Equity of Design Technologies

The economic attractiveness of the equity investment by the bank and Harrison can be assessed using the DCF valuation approach. The inappropriateness of other valuation approaches (such as book value or price/ earnings multiples) is especially clear in restructuring cases such as this where history is a poor indicator of the future and where no sample of comparable companies is likely to be a reliable measure of Design Technologies' worth.

Cash Flow. The residual cash-flow projection is given in Exhibit 5 of the case. Two features should be highlighted. First, it assumes that the company will repurchase the shares held by Consolidated Can at the end of year 2 and will borrow to the extent that profits do not cover the repurchase. Second, while the loan terms call for scheduled repayments of $300,000 per year, the forecast assumes that the company will prepay to the extent that funds allow.[2] This factor greatly simplifies the DCF analysis, because there is only one flow, the terminal value, to discount.

---

[1] Some students will object to this view, saying that Consolidated Can's equity is to be repurchased only if profits permit it, and that Design Technologies' earnings are yet too uncertain to view the repurchase as a sure thing. The response is that the "profits permitting" mainly affords Harrison and the bank some flexibility, and that Harrison and the bank will have a large incentive to repurchase the shares (i.e., to minimize dilution). The analysis here assumes that the bank will extend credit to the extent that profits do not cover the repurchase.

[2] The incentive to prepay is probably enormous. Loan covenants in highly leveraged transactions usually prohibit the payment of dividends until the debt is substantially reduced. In addition, any exit strategy for the equity investors (e.g., by initial public offering) probably includes presenting a fairly conventional balance sheet to prospective investors. Prepayment essentially accelerates realization of the investment's terminal value, the basis for the equity investors' return.

[3] The present value of this figure (at the geometric mean cost of equity of 35.9 percent) is $1.335 million.

Terminal Value. Students might use the projected accumulated value of equity in 1989, $6.189 million, as the basis for a terminal-value estimate.[3] The analysis in Exhibit B uses the constant growth model and estimates a terminal value of $10.38 million.

Discount Factors. The discount rate to be used in this analysis can be determined with the aid of the capital asset pricing model. A special feature of this case is that the capital structure will unlever over the next five years. These changes in financial risk need to be reflected in the estimated cost of equity. Exhibit 3 of the case gives the firm's unlevered beta, 1.45. Exhibit B here relevers the beta using the average debt/equity ratio for each year and computes the cost of equity for each year. Equity cost varies from 50 percent (in the first year) to 27 percent (in 1989). The nonconstant cost of equity violates the usual DCF convention--that the discount factor for the cash flow in any year is simply the product of the discount factors. That is, for year 2,

$$DF_2 = 1/[(1+K_1)(1+K_2)] = 1/(1+K)^2$$

Because K_1 does not equal K_2, squaring 1+K is inappropriate. The solution is to calculate a separate discount factor for each year, based on the different discount rates for the years. Exhibit B calculates this cumulative discount factor based on the annual equity costs.

Discounting and Sensitivity Analysis. Exhibit B reveals that the present value of this terminal value using the cumulative discount factor is about $2.24 million, which compares favorably with the invested value of $1 million. The forecast may be varied in numerous ways to test the sensitivity of this result. For instance, varying the perpetual growth rate embedded in the terminal value produces these present values:

Growth Rate	Present Value
10%	$2.236 million
8	1.961
5	1.644
3	1.477
1	1.355
0%	$1.273 million

The present value of equity appears to be reasonably robust to variations in the perpetual-growth-rate assumption. The reasons are that most of the value is created by growth in the 1985-89 period and that the cost of equity in 1989 is still very high, 26.7 percent,[4] relative to which, little variation in perpetual growth produces a small effect.

Market-Value Debt/Equity Ratios. Much of the methodology of discount-rate estimation used here assumes the use of market value, rather than book value, debt/equity ratios. Stern believed he had approximated a forecast of market

---

[4]The cost of equity for 1989 given in Exhibit B is not to be confused with the cumulative discount factor for that year, 0.215. The latter is simply the compound product of one plus the varying K_e, then inverted.

value balance sheets in case Exhibit 5. In making that exhibit, he assumed that the market values of debt and equity were exactly equal to what the providers of capital were willing to contribute. The present-value analysis in Exhibit C reveals, however, that the equity is worth more than the investors' outlay.[5] Exhibit C presents a revised DCF analysis of equity in which the present value of equity is used as the initial amount invested. This estimate is produced by a process of iteration. The revised analysis estimates the present value of equity to be $2.86 million.

Bank's Percentage Ownership

The percentage equity participation by the bank remains to be determined. One could approach this question in various ways, but the most useful is to view it in the context of overall account profitability. For instance, the analysis in Exhibit A revealed that the loan *per se* would destroy value. The question is then: How much equity is necessary for the equity gains to just offset the loan unprofitability? This is a breakeven problem--the percentage of equity, X, needed to subsidize the loan shortfall:

$$\$313 = X(\$2,236 - 1,000)$$

The solution is that the bank should acquire at least 25.3 percent of all the shares owned by other than Consolidated Can, or 12.7 percent of the entire capitalization of 100,000 shares.

Seasoned lending officers often object vociferously to the cross-subsidy that this analysis implies. They argue that the loan should stand on its own merits or else not be made. To take this attitude suggests, however, that one should be willing to pass up a profitable total relationship because one component is unprofitable. On closer questioning, one can establish that banks offer many "loss leaders" in hopes of building the profitability of entire relationships. This at least is one hallmark of the merchant banking point of view.

EPILOGUE

The Bank of Boston concluded the debt-and-equity transaction in May of 1984. The bank acquired 12.5 percent of total equity (5 percent voting and 7.5 percent nonvoting stock) in return for an investment of $125,000.

Within the first quarter after the acquisition, Frank Harrison managed to achieve Design Technologies' first monthly profit. Thereafter, performance exceeded Stern's projection. In 1988, the firm's sales were $37.3 million, compared with a projection of $14.95 million (this growth was accomplished completely internally).

During the summer of 1985, Harrison took the company public. The total market value of the equity based on the offering price was approximately $20 million, making the bank's initial $125,000 equity investment worth about $2.5

---

[5]Also, the debt is worth less than the investors' outlay. The bank is lending at a below-market interest rate, and the initial value of a zero-coupon bond (i.e., Consolidated Can's "equity") will be less than par. For simplicity, the revised analysis in Exhibit C ignores this adjustment and, therefore, underestimates the present value of equity.

million, a gain of about 2,000 percent. (Prior to making the public offering, the company management arranged to repurchase the shares held by Consolidated Can.) The bank retained its equity interest in Design Technologies; by 1989, the value of its investment had risen to $5.625 million.

EXHIBIT A   Net Present Value of the Loan

		1985	1986	1987	1988	1989
Balance of Bank Debt (case Exhibit 4):						
Debt, beginning		$2,677.0	$2,503.3	$3,951.7	$3,393.3	$2,198.3
Changes		(173.7)	1,448.4	(558.4)	(1,195.0)	(1,603.0)
Debt, ending		2,503.3	3,951.7	3,393.3	2,198.3	595.3
Debt, average		2,590.2	3,227.5	3,672.5	2,795.8	1,396.8
Cash Flow to Bank:						
Interest		361.4	317.4	550.9	447.3	223.5
Principal	($2,677.0)	173.7	(1,448.4)	558.4	1,195.0	2,198.3*
Total	($2,677.0)	535.1	(1,131.0)	1,109.3	1,642.3	2,421.8
Required Return:						
Base rate		12.50%	13.25%	14.00%	15.00%	15.00%
Base + 2.5%		15.00%	15.75%	16.50%	17.50%	17.50%
Discount factor		0.870	0.751	0.645	0.549	0.467
Present values	($2,677.00)	$ 465.3	($ 849.6)	$ 715.3	$ 901.3	$1,131.1
Net present value	($313.6)					

---

*Assumes bank debt is repaid in full at end of 1989.

EXHIBIT B DCF Analysis Using $1 million as the Initial Equity Balance

	1985	1986	1987	1988	1989
Average debt/equity ratio	3.910	2.422	1.355	0.743	0.287
Levered beta	4.398	3.277	2.472	2.010	1.666
Cost of equity	0.502	0.406	0.337	0.297	0.267
Cumulative					
Discount factor	0.666	0.473	0.354	0.273	0.215
Geometric mean K_e					0.359
Residual cash flows	0	0	0	0	0
Terminal value					$10,381*
Present value	$2,236				

*Assumes no more debt is repaid. The terminal value for 1989 was calculated as the residual cash flow in 1990 capitalized at $K_e - g$. The residual cash flow in 1990 was assumed equal to the net income in 1989 times $(1+g)$ (or 1580.5 x 1.10). Other assumptions were g = 10%, K_e = 26.7%.

EXHIBIT C DCF Analysis Using Present Value of Equity As the Initial Equity Balance

Forecast of Economic Balance Sheet and Capital Accounts

	@ Closing	1985	1986	1987	1988	1989
Cash	$ 0.0	$ 180.0	$ 220.0	$ 260.0	$ 298.9	$ 343.7
Other net working cap.	1,347	2,290.0	2,749.2	3,208.4	3,656.1	4,170.7
Net fixed assets	2,330	1,640.0	1,690.0	1,927.0	1,777.0	1,527.0
Goodwill	3,857	3,770.2	3,746.8	3,499.3	3,529.0	3,401.2
Total assets	7,534	7,880.1	8,405.9	8,894.6	9,261.1	9,442.6
Debt	4,677	4,503.3	3,951.7	3,393.3	2,198.3	595.3
Equity	2,857	3,290.0	4,178.4	5,222.1	6,465.3	8,045.8
Debt and equity	7,534	7,880.1	8,405.9	8,894.6	9,261.1	9,442.6

Memo: Debt Balances

	@ Closing	1985	1986	1987	1988	1989
Debt, beginning	4,677	4,677.0	4,503.3	3,951.7	3,393.3	2,198.3
Changes		(173.7)	(551.6)	(558.4)	(1,195.0)	(1,603.0)
Debt, ending		4,503.3	3,951.7	3,393.3	2,198.3	595.3
Debt, average		4,590.2	4,227.5	3,672.5	2,795.8	1,396.8

Memo: Equity Balances

	@ Closing	1985	1986	1987	1988	1989
Equity, beginning	$2,857	2,857.0	3,290.0	4,178.4	5,222.1	6,465.3
Changes		433.0	888.5	1,043.7	1,243.1	1,580.5
Ending		$3,290.0	$4,178.4	$5,222.1	$6,465.3	$8,045.8
Average D/E ratio		1.503	1.157	0.798	0.495	0.207
Levered beta		2.583	2.323	2.052	1.823	1.606
Cost of equity		0.346	0.324	0.301	0.281	0.262
Cumulative Discount factor		0.743	0.561	0.431	0.337	0.267
Geometric mean K_e						0.303
Residual cash flows		0	0	0	0	0
Terminal value*						$ 10,711
Present value		$ 2,857				

---

*Assumes no more debt is repaid. The terminal value for 1989 was calculated as the residual cash flow in 1990 capitalized at K_e – g. The residual cash flow in 1990 was assumed equal to the net income in 1989 times (1+g) (or 1580.5 x 1.10). Other assumptions were g = 10%, K_e = 26.2%.

Delta and Eastern Airlines

SYNOPSIS AND OBJECTIVES

This case projects the student into the strategic settings of these two direct competitors in air transportation in early 1981. The industry is in turmoil, having been deregulated in 1978, shocked by dramatic fuel price increases in 1979, and rocked by recession in 1980. While Delta and Eastern share some of the same geographic markets, their abilities to withstand these shocks differs substantially--stemming largely from differing operating and financial strategies and route structures. The task of the student is to assess these differences in strategy and competitive position, and then to recommend adjustments in policies to position each firm better for the future. This case is well suited for team presentations.

The main objective of the case is to motivate a discussion of financial strategy. Such a discussion would recognize the interdependence of operating performance, debt policy, dividend policy, and investment targets (i.e., self-sustainable growth targets). Moreover, the case suggests how fundamental choices about product-market positioning (i.e., choice of route structure) can heavily influence the selection of financial policies. Finally, the comparison of two close competitors with dramatically different policies is intended to illustrate the use of financial policy as a competitive instrument.

STUDY QUESTIONS

Whether or not the instructor chooses to organize the case discussion on the basis of team presentations, the following questions are useful in motivating preparation of the case.

1. What drives the profitability of the air transport industry? Which variables can individual carriers control or influence most in the market environment of early 1981?

2. Given your understanding of industry economics, in what ways would an airline respond to (a) entry by a competitor into its route system or (b) an increase in equipment capacity by an existing competitor? What are the possible implications of these responses when generalized to the industry level?

3. How vulnerable are Eastern and Delta to changes in competition? Be prepared to discuss the apparent business strategy of each. What role does finance play? What apparent tradeoffs in goals have the senior managers of Eastern and Delta made?

4. What are the financial requirements of each carrier for the next few years? How should each line meet those requirments?

Teaching note written by Robert F. Bruner. Copyright (c) 1989 by the Darden Graduate Business School Sponsors, Charlottesville, VA.

5. Compare and contrast the competitive and financial positions of Eastern and Delta. Based on this comparison, would you say that corporate financial policy determines or is determined by competition?

A worthy supporting reading in the area of financial strategy and self-sustainable growth is "Managing Growth," Chapter 5 in *Analysis for Financial Management* by Robert C. Higgin (Homewood, Ill.: Dow Jones-Irwin, 1983).

TEACHING PLAN

One way to organize the discussion is to appoint two teams of students (four teams in total) to analyze each airline and to give oral presentations summarizing their "client's" operating and financial strategy and recommending changes. If restricted to 10 minutes each, this approach consumes half an 80-minute class period, leaving the remainder for questions and general discussion.

Alternatively, the instructor can lead a standard case discussion, along the following lines:

(30 minutes) What are the competitive positions of Delta and Eastern? How are they similar and different? How do their strategies differ? The purpose of this line of questioning is to establish the basic comparison that underlies later insights about financial strategy.

(15 minutes) How well have the two airlines performed? Why, if Eastern's breakeven load factor is declining, does it continue to lose money? These questions prompt a discussion of the determinants of airline profitability, outlined in case Appendix A. The objective is to show that capital spending is the lever over which management has the most control.

(20 minutes) Can either airline sustain its recent rate of asset growth? Here the discussion enters an analysis of the self-sustainable growth rate of each airline and, ultimately, a discussion of the interdependence of financial policies.

(15 minutes) Assuming the forecast number in the case, what will be the external-capital requirements of each airline? What effect might this have on each line's competitive operating strategy? The implication of the numbers is that Delta will be largely self-sufficient, while Eastern will have a huge external requirement. The competitive implication for Delta is positive; for Eastern, it is negative.

The instructor can close the discussion with a brief review of the histories of the two airlines since 1981 and with summary comments about financial strategy.

ANALYSIS

Competitive Positions, Strategies, and Performance

Superficially, the similarities between these two companies are more apparent than the differences. In terms of operations, Eastern and Delta are about the same scale ($3.5 and $3.0 billion in revenues, respectively). Also, they overlap significantly in geographic markets served, as case Exhibit 1 reveals.

However, closer inspection of case Exhibit 1 reveals some important differences. First, Eastern's route structure is heavily North-South oriented along the eastern coast of the United States—easily the most heavily competitive set of routes in the country.[1] Delta, on the other hand, shares both a North-South *and* East-West configuration, freeing it from the confines of the heavy Eastern Seaboard competition as well as from the vagaries of regional weather (e.g., a frosty Florida winter that would discourage vacation travel on the New York-Florida routes).

Second, Delta's route structure corresponds more directly to a *hub*, linking Atlanta to other cities in the structure. Delta was the originator of the hub concept, a route structure yielding benefits in traffic retention and lower operating costs. The origin of Delta's hub is useful to raise in class: it developed from a virtual monopoly for the southeastern United States the government regulators granted to Delta in return for servicing many smaller cities there.

To some extent, the route-structure "endowment" of each firm may explain the historical origins of each's financial policies. Exhibit A suggests how the comparison of the the competitors might be set up on a chalkboard. In profile, Eastern appears to value growth and investment at the expense of financial flexibility. In contrast, Delta seems to value financial strength and flexibility above growth. One can argue that Eastern had no choice but to invest its way out of an aging fleet and highly competitive route structure. Eastern's thinner net margins on its route structure meant that it would have to rely to a greater extent on external capital to finance its investment.

Delta, because of its more sheltered competitive position, was able to generate more cash internally, invest in new equipment in more timely fashion, and invest where it wanted rather than where and when it had to. In other words, Delta dealt from strength; Eastern from weakness.

The performance of the respective airlines is consistent with the competitive positions and strategies of each. The Du Pont ratio analysis given in case Exhibit 13 and other performance indicators given in case Exhibits 7 and 12 provide a revealing assessment of the two firms' approaches. In essence, Delta is more profitable because of its higher margin and faster asset turnover, which, in turn, are attributable to key differences in operating effectiveness. Exhibit B summarizes these differences and shows that Delta uses its planes longer each day, has a lower breakeven load factor, operates at a positive load factor above breakeven, and yields less per revenue passenger mile (RPM), but has lower unit cost per available seat mile (ASM) and, therefore, produces a higher profit per seat.

There is another competitive difference. Using the betas, the return on the 30-year Treasury bond as the risk-free rate, and the geometric mean market premium, it appears that Delta has a lower required return on equity (18.41 percent) than does Eastern (20.41 percent), probably because of its lower risk.[2]

---

[1]This conclusion is drawn from general knowledge, but it can be developed in the classroom by inviting students to describe the competition in flying out of LaGuardia field (in New York).

[2]Using the alternative capital-asset-pricing-model approach, (i.e., the 90-day T-bill rate and arithmetic mean market premium) gives estimated equity costs for Delta and Eastern of 24.48 and 27.49 percent, respectively.

Importance of Capital Investment

Because investment and asset growth are important to understanding the key differences between the two firms, it might be appropriate for the instructor to dwell on the relative significance of capital spending in the general framework of airline economics. The case Appendix A suggests four determinants of airline profitability:

Revenues   = Yield x Revenue passenger mile
                (Price)   (Quantity demanded)

Costs   = Unit cost x Available seat–miles
                (Cost)   (Capacity)

In the newly deregulated environment, *yield* will be determined by fare competition among the airlines--no longer set by government regulators. *RPMs* will be determined by a combination of pricing, advertising, positioning, competition, etc. *Unit costs* are substantially driven by the configuration of fleet equipment, negotiations with labor unions, and suppliers of fuel. The fact is that these first three determinants give management little leverage in delivering profits to investors. Only through the fourth item, *available seat-miles*, can management significantly influence the profitability of the firm. ASMs are determined by choice of equipment and route structure. Broadly speaking, capital investment is the strategic key to higher airline performance.

The Self–Sustainable Growth Problem

As the previous sections suggest, active and aggressive capital spending was warranted by the emerging strategic situation in early 1981. The large question was the extent to which Delta and Eastern could sustain the investment necessary to maintain or improve their competitive positions. A rough answer is provided by the self–sustainable growth model (a more detailed answer is provided through forecasting in the next section).

Dwelling on self–sustainable growth has a pedagogical advantage in that it reveals the interdependence among financial policies when firms pursue a policy of issuing no new equity.[3] Under the assumption of no issues of new equity, the assets of the firm can grow only as fast as it retains earnings, unless it increases its percentage of leverage. Thus, the formula,

$$G = (1- Payout) \times ROE$$

where: ROE = Profit/Sales x Sales/Assets x Assets/Equity unites dividend policy (i.e., payout), debt policy (i.e., assets/equity), investment policy (i.e., the percentage growth rate of assets, G), and operating policies (i.e., in profit/sales, sales/assets).

Exhibit C summarizes the actual recent growth rates, the self–sustainable growth rates, and the determinants of self–sustainable growth for the two

---

[3]One can argue that this is a reasonable assumption in the cases of Delta and Eastern. Delta issued equity very rarely, and in practical terms, Eastern could not issue equity.

airlines, computed from data for 1980 alone and from average data for the 1976-80 period. The exhibit reveals that Delta has the higher self-sustainable growth rate of the two airlines, 7.3 percent measured in 1980 and 12.3 percent measured over the five years. Eastern's is negative for 1980 and +8.3 percent over the five-year period. This difference is a dramatic source of competitive advantage and investment flexibility for Delta--and persists even though Delta pays a dividend and maintains lower leverage than Eastern. The key to Delta's growth advantage is the fundamental profitability of its operations: Delta's five-year average profit/sales ratio is almost four times higher than Eastern's.

Exhibit C also gives a clue to the difficulty (even, impossibility) of Eastern's ambitious growth goals. Over the five-year period, Eastern's assets grew at a compound rate of 21 percent, while the self-sustainable model would justify a growth rate of 8.3 percent on average. The higher asset growth was accomplished with increasing amounts of leverage. The issue in early 1981 was how long Eastern could continue adding liabilities at this pace. A quick inspection of the firm's capitalization and coverage ratios would suggest that even higher leverage was not in prospect for Eastern--unless the profitability of the firm improved dramatically.

Future Financing Need

A more detailed perspective on Delta's advantage and Eastern's predicament is apparent in a forecast of financing needs prepared from assumptions in the case, as given in Exhibit D. The first panel of the exhibit suggests that Eastern requires external financing of $553 million. Assuming this is accomplished by issuing more debt, Eastern's capitalization ratio will remain static, as suggested by the second panel of the exhibit.

A forecast for Delta suggests that it might sustain a financing surplus while investing $1.7 billion in new aircraft, a computer system, and the Dallas hub facilities. In comparison, Eastern is expected to sustain a significant external need while investing only $687 million. Eastern's inability to invest at a rate consistent with its principal competitor must, in the long run, spell its defeat.

EPILOGUE

Over the 1981-89 period, Delta executed an aggressive capital-spending program consistent with the magnitudes expressed in the case. As a measure of its serious commitment to the program, Delta even cut its dividend in the summer of 1983, in reaction to a bitter fare war, rather than lever up or reduce its capital spending. Eighteen months later, the dividend was restored. In 1986, Delta purchased Western Airlines to fill the gap in the northwest corner of Delta's route map. An analyst called this "unequivocally the most successsful merger since deregulation."[4] Delta successfully expanded its Dallas hub and established a new hub at Cincinnati. In 1988, Delta became the offical airline of Disney World, grabbing the franchise from Eastern. In the late 1980s, Delta's fleet continued to be the most fuel-efficient in the nation. One writer summarized Delta's competitive position as follows:

---

[4]Timothy Pettee of Bear, Stearns & Co., quoted in Paulette Thomas, "Playing it Safe Has Made Delta a Winner," *Wall Street Journal*, July 25, 1988.

While Texas Air and Pan Am went deeply into hock to expand, Delta remains the least-leveraged airline in the industry. While United battles its pilots and Eastern wars with its machinists, Delta maintains the most loyal work force in the skies. Its profit margins are the industry's fattest and its stock has been the industry's highest-flier this year.

Now, Delta is finally shedding some of the stodginess that sheltered it through the tumult of deregulation. Roughly $1.4 billion in new aircraft are coming in, and hundreds of additional flights, including a number overseas, are being planned.

"We've gained momentum as we've grown, and now we're like a freight train coming down the track," says W. Whitely Hawkins, senior vice president of marketing.[5]

In contrast, from 1981 onward, Eastern lurched slowly toward collapse, nearly defaulting on a major credit agreement in 1982, passing a preferred dividend in 1983, technically defaulting on $2.5 billion in debt in 1985, and finally agreeing to an acquisition by Texas Air in February 1986. Through this period, Eastern experienced severe price competition in its markets, which it sought to mitigate through layoffs and wage concessions from its unions. By early 1986, Eastern's relations with its unions had become so poisonous that the Machinists' Union announced it was considering making a hostile tender offer for the company.

The merger with Texas Air was consistent with a wave of consolidation among major air transportation companies. However, the merger did little to resolve Eastern's financial and operational difficulties. Eastern lost $300 million in fiscal 1988 (versus a loss of $181 million in 1987). Frank Lorenzo, the chairman of Texas Air, sought wage concessions from Eastern's unions, including a five-year waiver of payments to the pension plan. In reply, the Machinists' Union struck Eastern on March 4, 1989. Six days later, Eastern Air Lines filed for bankruptcy. In May 1989, Lorenzo sold the Eastern Shuttle to Donald Trump for $353 million and had under consideration offers for the rest of the airline.

---

[5]"Playing it Safe Has Made Delta a Winner."

EXHIBIT A Comparison of Financial Policies

	Delta	Eastern
Dividends	Payout is low but steady (Divs./profits = .20)	Payout is zero
Debt	Low leverage (Debt/capital = .20) Avge. maturity < 4 yrs. Mostly fixed rate Standard securities	High leverage (Debt/capital = .77) Maturity 5–15 yrs. Floating and fixed rate More exotic securities • sub. converts • preferred stock • equip. leasing
	No fancy recapitalizations	1980 debenture exchange gave $25 mm gain
Issues equity?	No	Yes, if able
Investment: Compound asset growth	g = .14	g = .15
Focus	Cost efficiency Careful route growth	Cost efficiency Aggressive route growth

EXHIBIT B   Comparison of Operating Statistics, 1980 Data

	Delta	Eastern
Utilization hours	10.46	9.33
Load factor:		
Realized	60.5%	61.33%
Breakeven	58.5%	62.2%
Cents/RPM	10.45	11.15
Cents/ASM	6.6	7.5
Profit/seat-mile	3.85	3.65

EXHIBIT C   Comparison of Self-Sustainable Growth, 1980 Data

	Delta		Eastern	
	1980	1976–80	1980	1976–80
Profit/sales	.031	.0508	(.012)	.016
Sales/assets	1.45	1.249	1.22	1.25
Assets/equity	2.21	2.33	6.47	4.18
Return on equity	.099	.1478	(.073)	.0836
Dividend payout	.26	.1675	0	0
Self-sustainable growth rate	.073	.123	(.073)	.0836
Compound growth rates:				
Sales	.179		.1727	
Assets	.086		.213	
ASMs	.092		.074	
RPMs	.104		.0966	

EXHIBIT D Projected Financial Needs

1. Eastern, through 1982

Capital investments	$ 687 mm
Debt amortization and leases	382
Dividends	0
Additions to working capital*	20
Total uses of funds	$1,089 mm
Net profit	$ 60 mm
Depreciation and amortization	476 mm
Total sources of funds	$ 536
Cumulative external financing need	$ 553 mm

2. Effect on Eastern's Capital Structure

	1980	Changes	1982
Long-term debt	$1,460	−151 Amort +553 Debt	$1,861
Pfd. and common	435	+60 Profits	495
Total capital	$1,895		$2,356
Debt/capital	.77		.79

3. Delta, through 1985

Equipment additions	$1,200 mm
Dallas hub	356
Computer system	150
Debt amortization and additional leases	129
Dividends	200
Additions to working capital*	0
Total uses of funds	$2,035
Net profits	$1,258
Depreciation and amortization	1,194
Total sources of funds	$2,452
Net surplus of funds	$ 417 mm

*Additions to working capital for both Eastern and Delta were assumed to be largely financed by "Air Traffic Liability," an account payable to suppliers and other airlines on which Delta and Eastern had booked tickets for its passengers.

Johnstown Corporation

SYNOPSIS AND OBJECTIVES

In the spring of 1988, the chairman of this small steel mill is pondering how to finance the growth of his firm: either with an initial public offering of equity or a private placement of 10-year senior notes with warrants. The task for the student is to sort out the comparative advantages and disadvantages of each alternative--including valuing the possible securities--and recommend a course of action.

This case is intended to be a vehicle for discussing the basic choice between debt and equity financing. It allows an application of the classic "FRICT" framework, as well as an opportunity for students to exercise their valuation skills. In addition, the case illustrates the decision to go public and the role of private-placement financing.

STUDY QUESTIONS

1. Why is Jack Sheehan considering obtaining long-term capital?

2. Can Johnstown Corporation successfully service the senior notes? Please prepare a forecast of the firm's financing needs.

3. What are the principal risks the firm faces? Under some reasonable down-side scenario, could Johnstown continue to service the debt?

4. From an investor's standpoint, are the terms of the notes-and-warrants package attractive? (To value the warrants, note that all the parameters of the option-pricing model are available in the case, except for volatility. Over a recent five-year period, steel manufacturers experienced volatilities in the neighborhood of .35.)

5. As for the possible equity issue, would an offering price of $9.00 per share be fair?

6. Which course of action should Sheehan adopt?

TEACHING PLAN

(10 minutes) How well has Johnstown done? Will the firm require external financing? Why?

(10 minutes) What are the comparative advantages and disadvantages of the two financing alternatives?

Teaching note written by Robert F. Bruner. Copyright (c) 1988 by the Darden Graduate Business School Sponsors, Charlottesville, VA.

(30 minutes) Do you think Johnstown Corporation will be able to issue new shares of common stock at $9.00 per share or more?

(25 minutes) What are the units of notes and warrants worth?

(5 minutes) What should Sheehan do? The instructor can close the discussion with a vote of the students.

ANALYSIS

Pro Forma Financial Statements

Exhibits A and B present *pro forma* forecasts of balance sheets and income statements for the 1988-93 period. These forecasts use a revenue growth rate of 10.3 percent and historical percentage-of-sales figures for expenses and most balance-sheet accounts. The 10.3 percent rate of growth is drawn from the case and is consistent with that of similar companies and with trends in the steel industry.[1] Other assumptions are summarized in the exhibits.

The notes-payable balances in Exhibits A and B reveal that either financing alternative will satisfy the firm's funds requirements, at least through 1990. Indeed, the first question is why Sheehan feels he *needs* $7.5 million in new capital. For instance, it appears that $6.2 million would suffice for equity financing, and $6.7 million for debt financing. The answer probably has to do with Sheehan's desire to build some financial slack as a hedge against future adversity. Sensitivity analysis of the forecasts reveals that slight deterioration in gross margin, or slight increases in the ratio of gross fixed assets to sales, will induce significant increases in external financing requirements.

The instructor can probe the students for circumstances that might cause an adverse change in the fundamental assumptions: (1) increased price competition (resulting in lower margins and/or higher accounts receivable); (2) introduction of new technology; (3) labor difficulties resulting in higher wages or adverse work rules; (4) a strengthening dollar, making foreign steel cheaper; (5) an acquisition binge; (6) a sudden rise in scrap-metal prices.[2] Unfortunately, it is harder to imagine circumstances under which the external financing requirement would be lower than forecasted (the two obvious sources are higher productivity and self-imposed capital-spending restraints). Many of the

---

[1]Observant students will note that the projected growth rate given in the case under "Johnstown Corporation's Outlook" will be affected by the product mix. If one calculates an average projected growth rate weighted by the percentage of 1987 sales in each product, the result is 9.43 percent rather than 10.3. Weighted by the projected 1988 sales mix, the total growth rate is 11.2 percent. Using this higher rate produces a marginally greater financing need in the future.

[2]The case indicates that direct materials, including scrap metal, accounted for 26 percent of cost of goods sold (COGS) in 1987. Analysis of case Exhibit 2 reveals some breathtaking swings in scrap-metal prices over the preceding 13 months. From April 1987 to November 1987, scrap prices rose 72 percent. Then, in the following two months, they fell 12.5 percent. Over the entire period, the mean scrap price was $120.50/ton, with a standard deviation of $23.00.

productivity improvements possible in this situation are probably already in place, however, and management probably invests conservatively as it is.

The comparative projections in Exhibits A and B suggest some important differences between the two financing alternatives. First, the interest-coverage and capitalization ratios associated with debt financing (Exhibit A) are significantly lower than those associated with equity financing (Exhibit B). Moreover, the fixed-charges coverage ratio for the debt alternative drops below 2x in 1990, a level that would leave bankers and financial analysts uncomfortable. The second important difference between the projected results is in return on equity: debt financing is associated with returns that are materially higher than those in the equity case.
Finally, the results differ in the obvious effects of dilution: the earnings-per-share figure (EPS) is lower by more than half under equity financing than under debt financing. Also, under equity financing, EPS does not recover to its 1987 level during the forecast period.

In sum, the projections frame the terms of the classic "eat well versus sleep well" tradeoff. Debt financing is associated with higher returns and EPS than equity financing, and affords less financial flexibility and cash-flow coverage in the event of adversity.

Valuation of Johnstown's Equity

One important question is the possible price at which Johnstown could issue its shares of stock. In the case, Sheehan expresses the wish that the shares would float above $9.00, the price at which employees had most recently been offered an opportunity to buy. Is $9.00 an appropriate price, or could Johnstown sell its shares at an even higher price?

Exhibit C presents a valuation of Johnstown's shares using some of the informal rules of thumb suggested in the case to generate terminal values for use in a discounted cash flow (DCF) analysis. The analysis supposes that no cash will flow to equity-holders until the terminus in 1993 and reveals that share values associated with debt financing are significantly higher than with equity financing; even at the low end, a share price of $9.00 is conservative.

Value of the Notes-and-Warrants Units

The units may be valued by valuing the components separately and then summing. In valuing the notes, the chief issue is whether the coupon of 13 percent is fair. To decide requires some judgment on the yields on competitive issues and on how risky Johnstown is. Case Exhibit 9 presents yields to maturity on BBB and CCC debt securities and over a range of maturities. A coupon of 13 percent falls in the mid-range of these issues and seems roughly consistent with a credit rating in the neighborhood of B or BB. If a 13 percent coupon is reasonable for the note component of these units, then market value equals par value.

The warrants are more difficult to value, although it is possible to develop a value range. The known parameters of the Black-Scholes option-pricing model are:

Volatility = .35 (assignment question)

Risk-free rate[3] = .0837 (case Exhibit 8)

Maturity = 10 years (case Exhibit 5)

Exercise price = $1.00 (case Exhibit 5)

Warrant dilution factor[4] = .784, .872

The remaining parameters are dividend payout (which is assumed to remain at zero) and today's stock price. Since a $9.00 share value represents a focal point for Sheehan, that value will be used in this analysis, although an investor would take into account his/her own estimate.

Assuming the $9.00 stock price, the value of the warrant per share is $8.33 before any adjustment for dilution. As case Exhibit 5 shows, the warrant entitles the holder to purchase between 40,000 and 75,000 shares, depending on the future performance of the firm. This translates to a total value of the warrant ranging between $290,550 and $489,804.

Adding the two components together indicates that Johnstown would be selling a claim for $7,500,000 that is actually worth between $7,790,550 and $8,789,804.

FRICT Analysis

A more traditional EBIT/EPS analysis can illuminate other differences between the two financing alternatives. Exhibit D assumes new shares are sold at $9.00 each and compares the resulting EPS under two different EBIT levels to the EPS available under the debt financing.

Exhibit D reveals that, within a range of reasonable EBITs, the debt alternative dominates the equity alternative in terms of higher EPS. The point of indifference between the two financing alternatives is at an EBIT of $1.947 million, well below the 1987 EBIT of $4 million. If the firm continues to grow, the debt alternative is favored.

There are a range of concerns that might weigh against the debt-financing alternative; these emerge in a standard FRICT analysis:

Flexibility: Johnstown's work force is unionized and employed under a contract set to expire in June 1989. Given the company's low wage base and the strong union sentiment in the western Pennsylvania area, the company could be faced with a strike at that time. This could be offset by the all-too-clear memory of U.S. Steel's intention to shut down the plant because it had uncompetitively high costs. Other threats to flexibility would include loss of a major account (together, USX and Bethlehem Steel accounted for 42 percent of

---

[3]This is the 10-year Treasury bond yield. Some students may use the 3-month Treasury rate, which is also given in case Exhibit 8. One should choose a rate contemporaneous with the life of the option being valued.

[4]This figure reduces the value of the warrant by the extent of the dilution in share price imposed by the warrant's exercise. If warrants are exercised for 75,000 shares, the division factor is .784; for 40,000 shares, it is .872.

Johnstown's revenues in 1987) and product obsolescence. Sensitivity analyses of the financial forecasts reveal that, under realistic assumptions, Johnstown approaches but does not violate its covenant ratios under the new debt issue.

Risk: A predictable downturn in the economy would reduce Johnstown's cash flow from operations. As long as capital spending is reduced, however, and receivables and inventory are managed tightly, the firm should be able to weather the storm.

Income: As detailed in the EBIT/EPS analysis, the debt alternative is favored.

Control: An issue of common stock will dilute the current owners' interest significantly.[5] But under debt financing, absolute control is maintained until the warrants are exercised, and then diluted comparatively slightly.[6]

Timing: It may be unrealistic to consider issuing stock so soon after the crash of October 1987. The size of the issue and negative history would affect adversely the ability to sell the shares. On the other hand, the rate of interest on the private placement is relatively high compared to the rates presented in case Exhibit 8, though not out of line with "junk bond" yields at the time.

Summary and Recommendation

Neither of the two alternatives stands out as a clear independent choice, although between the two, the equity alternative is plainly less attractive from the standpoint of Sheehan. The private placement is the preferred approach, since Sheehan wants to fix his interest-rate exposure, provide a long-term capital base for growth in the future, and avoid severe dilution. The unspoken alternatives in this case include sale of the company (although one wonders whether the firm is very marketable at this time) and simply slowing the firm's growth. In addition, the firm could temporize and continue to fund its growth with short-term debt until a more favorable capital-market environment arose.

---

[5]To raise $7,500,000 at $9.00 per share necessitates an offering of 833,333 shares, which will reduce the previous equity owners from a 100 percent interest in the company to 21.9 percent (233,000/(233,000+833,333)).

[6]New shares issued under exercise of the warrant would vary between 40,000 and 75,000. Thus, the original equity-owners' interest would fall from 100 percent to between 85.3 and 75.6 percent.

EXHIBIT A   Forecast of Financial Statements: Growth Financed with Debt (dollars in thousands except per share data)

Common Assumptions

Revenue growth rate	10.30%	Inventory/revenues	13.00%
COGS/revenues	78.00	Other curr. assets/revenues	1.00
SG&A/revenues	13.00	Gross fixed assets/revenues	48.00
Profit sharing	25.00	Accts. payable/revenues	14.00
Tax rate	34.00	Other curr. liabs./revenue	7.00
Depreciation/gross fixed assets	5.60	Interest rate	10.00
Cash/revenues	0.70	Change in def'd tax/taxes	25.00%
Accts. receivable/revenues	20.00	Primary shares	233,000
Prime rate	8.50%		

Income Statements

	Actual			Projected			
	1987	1988	1989	1990	1991	1992	1993
Revenues	$34.8	$38.4	$42.3	$46.7	$51.5	$56.8	$62.7
COGS	(27.7)	(29.9)	(33.0)	(36.4)	(40.2)	(44.3)	(48.9)
Selling, general, and admin.	(4.0)	(5.0)	(5.5)	(6.1)	(6.7)	(7.4)	(8.1)
Interest (notes, old loans)*	(1.1)	(0.4)	(0.4)	(0.6)	(0.6)	(0.6)	(0.6)
Interest (new loan @ 13%)		(0.98)	(0.98)	(0.98)	(0.98)	(0.98)	(0.98)
Profit before profit sharing	2.1	2.1	2.5	2.6	3.0	3.5	4.1
Profit sharing	(0.5)	(0.5)	(0.6)	(0.6)	(0.8)	(0.9)	(1.0)
Profit before taxes	1.6	1.6	1.9	1.9	2.3	2.6	3.0
Taxes	0.0	(0.5)	(0.6)	(0.7)	(0.8)	(0.9)	(1.0)
Profit after taxes	$1.6	$1.0	$1.2	$1.3	$1.5	$1.7	$2.0
Profit with extraord. item	1.8						
Earnings per share	$7.57	$4.50	$5.27	$5.48	$6.41	$7.45	$8.63

EXHIBIT A (continued)

	Actual 1987	Projected					
		1988	1989	1990	1991	1992	1993
Balance Sheets							
Cash	$0.2	$0.3	$0.3	$0.3	$0.4	$0.4	$0.4
Accounts receivable	6.8	7.7	8.5	9.3	10.3	11.4	12.5
Inventory	4.7	5.0	5.5	6.1	6.7	7.4	8.1
Other current assets	0.4	0.4	0.4	0.5	0.5	0.6	0.6
Total current assets	12.1	13.3	14.7	16.2	17.9	19.7	21.7
Gross fixed assets	16.7	18.4	20.3	22.4	24.7	27.3	30.1
Accumulated depreciation	(2.5)	(3.5)	(4.7)	(5.9)	(7.3)	(8.8)	(10.5)
Net fixed assets	14.2	14.9	15.7	16.5	17.4	18.4	19.6
Other assets	0.1	0.1	0.1	0.1	0.1	0.1	0.1
Total assets	$26.4	$28.3	$30.4	$32.8	$35.4	$38.2	$41.4
Notes payable (plug figure)	$(4.8)	$(0.8)	$(0.6)	$(0.1)	$ 0.2	$ 0.5	$ 0.7
Accounts payable	4.6	5.4	5.9	6.5	7.2	8.0	8.8
Other current liabilities	2.3	2.7	3.0	3.3	3.6	4.0	4.4
Total current liabilities	11.7	7.3	8.2	9.7	11.1	12.5	13.9
Old long term debt (Note 1)	9.8	7.4	7.2	6.7	6.2	5.7	5.2
New long term debt		7.5	7.5	7.5	7.5	7.5	7.5
Deferred taxes	1.3	1.4	1.6	1.8	1.9	2.2	2.4
Total liabilities	22.8	23.7	24.6	25.6	26.7	27.9	29.0
Common stock	0.2	0.2	0.2	0.2	0.2	0.2	0.2
Paid-in surplus	0.2	0.2	0.2	0.2	0.2	0.2	0.2
Retained earnings	3.2	4.2	5.5	6.8	8.2	10.0	12.0
Total liabilities and equity	$26.4	$28.3	$30.4	$32.8	$35.4	$38.2	$41.4

EXHIBIT A (continued)

	Actual 1987	Projected						
		1988	1989	1990	1991	1992	1993
Comparative ratios							
EBIT/interest	2.90	2.58	2.87	2.59	2.86	3.18	3.57
EBIT/(interest + amort.)	1.93	NMF	2.49	1.98	2.19	2.43	2.71
Liabilities/equity	6.33	5.09	4.18	3.58	3.09	2.68	2.34
(Debt+notes)/equity	4.06	3.05	2.40	1.97	1.62	1.33	1.08
Profit/revenues	5.1%	2.7%	2.9%	2.7%	2.9%	3.1%	3.2%
Profit/equity	49.0%	22.5%	20.9%	17.9%	17.3%	16.7%	16.2%

*Interest expense and balances on existing loans are taken from case Exhibit 6 and are adjusted for repayment of subordinated notes ($975,000) and of $4.8 million of the working-capital line. The firm is assumed to borrow at prime plus 2% and lend at prime less 2%.

EXHIBIT B Forecast of Financial Statements: Growth Financed with Equity, Shares
Sold at $9.00 Each (dollars in thousands except per share data)

Common Assumptions

Revenue growth rate	10.30%	Inventory/revenues	13.00%
COGS/revenues	78.00	Other curr. assets/revenues	1.00
SG&A/revenues	13.00	Gross fixed assets/revenues	48.00
Profit sharing	25.00	Accts. payable/revenues	14.00
Tax rate	34.00	Other curr. liabs./revenue	7.00
Depreciation/gross fixed as.	5.60	Interest rate	10.00
Cash/revenues	0.70	Change in def'd tax/taxes	25.00%
Accts. receivable/revenues	20.00	1987 primary shares	233,000
Prime rate	8.50%	1988+ primary shares	1,066,333

Income Statements

	Actual 1987	Projected 1988	1989	1990	1991	1992	1993
Revenues	$34.8	$38.4	$42.3	$46.7	$51.5	$56.8	$62.7
COGS	(27.7)	(29.9)	(33.0)	(36.4)	(40.2)	(44.3)	(48.9)
Selling, general, and admin.	(4.0)	(5.0)	(5.5)	(6.1)	(6.7)	(7.4)	(8.1)
Interest (notes, old loans)*	(1.1)	(0.3)	(0.3)	(0.5)	(0.5)	(0.4)	(0.3)
Interest (new loan @ 13%)		0.00	0.00	0.00	0.00	0.00	0.00
Profit before profit sharing	2.1	3.1	3.5	3.7	4.2	4.7	5.3
Profit sharing	(0.5)	(0.8)	(0.9)	(0.9)	(1.0)	(1.2)	(1.3)
Profit before taxes	1.6	2.3	2.6	2.8	3.1	3.5	4.0
Taxes	0.0	(0.8)	(0.9)	(0.9)	(1.1)	(1.2)	(1.4)
Profit after taxes	$1.6	$1.5	$1.7	$1.8	$2.1	$2.3	$2.6
Profit with extraord. item	$1.8						
Earnings per share	$7.57	$1.45	$1.64	$1.70	$1.93	$2.18	$2.46

EXHIBIT B (continued)

Balance Sheets

	Actual 1987	Projected 1988	1989	1990	1991	1992	1993
Cash	$0.2	$0.3	$0.3	$0.3	$0.4	$0.4	$0.4
Accounts receivable	6.8	7.7	8.5	9.3	10.3	11.4	12.5
Inventory	4.7	5.0	5.5	6.1	6.7	7.4	8.1
Other current assets	0.4	0.4	0.4	0.5	0.5	0.6	0.6
Total current assets	12.1	13.3	14.7	16.2	17.9	19.7	21.7
Gross fixed assets	16.7	18.4	20.3	22.4	24.7	27.3	30.1
Accumulated depreciation	(2.5)	(3.5)	(4.7)	(5.9)	(7.3)	(8.8)	(10.5)
Net fixed assets	14.2	14.9	15.7	16.5	17.4	18.4	19.6
Other assets	0.1	0.1	0.1	0.1	0.1	0.1	0.1
Total assets	$26.4	$28.3	$30.4	$32.8	$35.4	$38.2	$41.4
Notes payable (plug figure)	$ 4.8	$(1.3)	$(1.8)	$(1.9)	$(2.1)	$(2.5)	$(3.1)
Accounts payable	4.6	5.4	5.9	6.5	7.2	8.0	8.8
Other current liabilities	2.3	2.7	3.0	3.3	3.6	4.0	4.4
Total current liabilities	11.7	6.7	7.1	7.9	8.7	9.4	10.1
Old long term debt (Note 1)	9.8	7.4	7.2	6.7	6.2	5.7	5.2
New long term debt		0	0	0	0	0	0
Deferred taxes	1.3	1.5	1.7	2.0	2.2	2.5	2.9
Total liabilities	22.8	15.7	16.0	16.6	17.1	17.6	18.2
Common stock	0.2	1.0	1.0	1.0	1.0	1.0	1.0
Paid-in surplus	0.2	6.9	6.9	6.9	6.9	6.9	6.9
Retained earnings	3.2	4.7	6.5	8.3	10.4	12.7	15.3
Total liabilities and equity	$26.4	$28.3	$30.4	$32.8	$35.4	$38.2	$41.4

EXHIBIT B (continued)

	Actual 1987	Projected					
		1988	1989	1990	1991	1992	1993
Comparative ratios							
EBIT/interest	2.90	10.59	13.69	7.89	9.69	12.46	17.02
EBIT/(interest + amort.)	1.93	NMF	7.97	4.07	4.74	5.62	6.78
Liabilities/equity	6.33	1.24	1.11	1.02	0.94	0.86	0.78
(Debt+notes)/equity	4.06	0.48	0.38	0.30	0.22	0.16	0.09
Profit/revenues	5.1%	4.0%	4.1%	3.9%	4.0%	4.1%	4.2%
Profit/equity	49.0%	12.2%	12.1%	11.2%	11.3%	11.3%	11.3%

EXHIBIT C   Valuation of Equity

	Debt Financing	Equity Financing
Assumptions:		
Cash flow to equity	Zero: 1988-92	Zero: 1988-92
Terminal values, 1993		
1. Book value	$12.39 (million)	$23.23 (million)
2. 1.5 x book value	$18.59	$34.84
3. 4 x EBIT less debt	$9.14	$20.41
4. 12 x earnings (case Ex. 7)	$24.12	$31.53
5. 18 x earnings	$36.19	$47.30
6. 21 x earnings	$42.22	$55.18
Cost of equity		
Unlevered beta	0.35	0.35
Beta (case Ex. 7)	1.3	0.47
Risk-free rate (case Ex. 8)	0.057	
Market risk premium	0.086 (Ibbotson and Sinquefield estimate, 1926-86)	
Ke = .057 + ß(.086)	16.9%	9.7%
Present total values of equity		
Book value	$4.86 (million)	$13.32 (million)
1.5 x book value	$7.29	$19.98
EBIT multiple	$3.59	$11.70
Price/earnings (12x)	$9.46	$18.08
(18x)	$14.19	$27.13
(21x)	$16.56	$31.65
Present values of equity per share		
Book value	$20.86 ($/share)	$12.49 ($/share)
1.5 x book value	$31.30	$18.74
EBIT multiple	$15.39	$10.97
Price/earnings (12x)	$40.61	$16.96
(18x)	$60.92	$25.44
(21x)	$71.07	$29.68
Number of shares used (million)	0.233	1.066

EXHIBIT D EBIT/EPS Analysis

	Debt		Equity	
EBIT (1988 level)	$2.7 m	$4.0 m	$2.7 m	$4.0 m
Interest				
(old: $7.1M @ 10%)	.7	.7	.7	.7
(new: $7.5M @ 13%)	.975	.975	0	0
Profit before profit sharing	1.025	2.325	2.0	3.3
Profit sharing	.256	.581	.5	.825
Profit before taxes	.769	1.744	1.5	2.475
Taxes (@ .34)	.262	.593	.51	.842
Net income	$ .507 m	$1.151 m	$ .990 m	$1.633 m
Number of shares	.233 m	.233 m	1.066 m*	1.066 m
Earnings per share	$2.18	$4.94	$.93	$1.53

$$\frac{(EBIT - 1.675) \times .75 \times .66}{.233} = \frac{(EBIT - .7) \times .75 \times .66}{1.066}$$

$$(EBIT - 1.675) \times .5277 = (EBIT - .7) \times .1153$$

$$(EBIT \times .5277) - .8838 = (EBIT \times .1153) - .087$$

$$EBIT (.5277 - .1153) = .8031$$

$$Breakeven\ EBIT = 1.947\ million$$

*Assumes new shares are sold at $9.00 each.

Merit Marine Corporation

SYNOPSIS AND OBJECTIVES

A lending officer for Omni Bank has positioned the bank as a financial advisor to an existing credit customer. With the aid of the bank's corporate finance department, the lending officer is faced with restructuring a customer's balance sheet to extend the maturity of debt and to fix a larger portion of the firm's interest payments. The student must first determine the borrower's credit needs and then evaluate the relative costs and benefits--to both the customer as well as the bank--of using a private placement and/or an interest-rate swap. Through analysis of the funding source of the swap and the flexibility offered by the private placement, the placement emerges as the best alternative.

The case shows a lending officer in the role of corporate financial advisor. The alternatives suggested introduce the student to interest-rate swaps and private placements that fix a borrower's interest payments. The case also reveals how the earnings a bank generates from an existing credit relationship can be affected when alternatives to traditional bank debt are used.

STUDY QUESTIONS

1. What is Merit's external funds requirement for the years 1985-88?

2. How well do each of the three financing alternatives meet the requirement? How do they differ? What are the comparative strengths and weaknesses?

3. What is the least costly alternative? Over what years?

4. Which alternative would be most profitable for Omni Bank?

5. Which alternative should Jeff Finch and Ginny Shields recommend?

TEACHING PLAN

The questions that follow form a path for guiding the case discussion that emphasizes problem definition and discussion of the financing alternatives:

(15 minutes) Why, if at all, does Merit need to restructure its debt?

(15 minutes) Is Merit a creditworthy customer? Is it a relationship Omni would like to keep?

(45 minutes) Let's understand the relative merits of the financing alternatives:

Teaching note written by Robert F. Bruner and Peter R. Hennessy, Research Assistant. Copyright (c) 1985 by the Darden Graduate Business School Sponsors, Charlottesville, VA.

- What are the details of each? How does a swap work? Why a private placement (as opposed to a public placement)? Why the unusual prepayment and fixing provisions on the placements?

- What is the cost of each?

- Any other pros or cons?

Following is a question the author sometimes works in if time permits: Let's brainstorm for a minute. Are there other financing tactics not considered by Shields and Finch that might be appropriate for Merit?

The discussion can be closed with a vote of the class on what Omni should do, a presentation of the epilogue, and some closing comments on the emerging role of commercial bankers in corporate finance.

ANALYSIS

The case affords many opportunities for analysis, some highlights of which are presented in the following discussions.

Merit's Need to Restructure

The need to restructure Merit's capital base stems from the $27 million invested in capital improvements between 1980 and 1983. Despite the capital investment, Merit did not take on any appreciable long-term debt until 1983, and even then the term was far shorter than the life of the assets being financed.

The case mentions that the decision to restructure was an evident one. The balance sheet of first glance, however, looks appropriate--with $23 million in fixed assets and $28 million in long-term debt. The need to restructure becomes more obvious after examining case Exhibits 2 and 5. Exhibit A in this note shows Merit's historical performance indicators, and Exhibit B looks closely at Merit's capital structure. The analysis assumes that the $10 million in Olympus Credit Corporation funds would always be outstanding because of the preferential rate and thus should be considered part of the firm's capital structure. The term "total funds" is defined as total capital plus the Olympus funds. Merit is highly leveraged, with equity representing just 45.3 percent of its total funds. However, the firm is easily within the loan covenant of total liabilities/net worth of less than 3.00.

The term and rate of Merit's long-term debt can and should be addressed. Case Exhibit 2 indicates that fixed-rate debt accounts for only 2.4 percent of Merit's total funds. Case Exhibit 5 explains that the maturity on Merit's long-term revolving debt is either December 31, 1986, or 13 months after demand. Clearly a borrowing need exists past 1986 (Exhibit C), but to this point Merit has been unable to arrange longer term financing. The case tells of an aborted attempt to secure a private mortgage at a rate acceptable to Merit. The reader can only assume that the possibility of a mortgage in the future is a function of Merit agreeing to an interest rate in excess of 12 percent.

Many students miss the fact that Merit's basis risk is a significant motive for restructuring. This fact can be illustrated by calculating Merit's breakeven interest rate (i.e., that prime rate above which Merit is likely to default). A simplified cash-flow statement is

$$[\text{EBIT} - (\text{Interest rate} \times \text{Outstandings})](1 - \text{Tax rate})$$

$$+ \text{ Depreciation} - \text{Investment} - \text{Amortization} = \text{Cash flow}$$

Setting cash flow equal to zero and solving for interest rate (assuming that depreciation and investment cancel each other out and that debt is rolled over) yields the following breakeven rates:

EBIT	Breakeven Rate
$6.6 mm	13.2%
5.0	10.0
$4.0 mm	8.0%

Case Exhibit 7 shows that the current corporate borrowing rate (which approximates prime) is 10.5 percent and that the standard deviation of the prime rate over the past 10 years is 4.32 percent. Although not close to default currently, Merit could have great difficulty extricating itself if profitability or interest-rate conditions changed.[1]

Exhibit C displays Merit's external financing requirements through 1988 based on the projections given in the case text and in case Exhibit 10. The two most prominent financing needs arise in 1985, when the $31 million in short-term debt matures, and in 1986, when the $25 million revolver expires.

Even though debt can be reduced in 1987 and 1988, long-term needs still remain around $25 million. Unless Merit refinances or extends the $25 million revolver during 1985, the company will have to refinance a total of $55 million in short- and long-term debt in 1986. If Merit wishes to fund the firm's fixed assets with matching debt, such as a 20-year mortgage, then it must be willing to pay over 12 percent. The alternative is to lock into medium-term (i.e., 3 to 10 years) debt, with the hopes that interest rates will decline and Merit Marine's creditworthiness will improve. The big tradeoff remains getting reasonably priced medium-term debt now and risk refinancing versus paying a 1/2-1 1/2 percent premium to lock into long-term, fixed-rate debt.

Is Merit's the kind of relationship the bank would like to keep? John Merit shows no loyalty to Omni or any of the other banks. Indeed, he plays them off against one another. One wonders also about Merit's abilities and intentions. For instance, Merit's return on equity (ROE) for 1984 was 8 percent, well below the current returns on even risk-free securities. Moreover, John Merit seems to have far overinvested in the warehouse and service center constructed in 1982. The case notes that the facility will allow Merit to double sales, but at a 5 percent growth rate, 14 years will be needed to exhaust the excess capacity. These moves may not be evidence of poor management, however, if, as most entrepreneurs, John Merit minimizes profits to reduce tax expense (hence, the low ROE) and uses the warehouse as a personal real estate investment. The problem is that, *prima facie*, John Merit does not have a promising record that would motivate Omni to extend and nurture the relationship.

The account officer's decision to take the initiative to act as a financial advisor and devise nontraditional financing alternatives for a borrower of Merit's credit quality is a significant one. The account, which brought in $305,000 in net income in the first 11 months of 1984, will come under pressure in 1985 when an additional $10 million in commercial paper-based debt becomes

---

[1]This calculation ignores the benefit of interest income and the earned discount (which in 1984 was $5 million) on the grounds that these benefits may evaporate in a recession or in financial distress. However, if interest income and earned discount are included in the calculation, the breakeven interest rate at a $6.6 million EBIT is 23.2 percent.

available for Merit through Olympus Credit Corporation. The additional debt will probably reduce external short-term funding needs to $3-$4 million dollars. If the revolver is displaced, then Merit's banking needs will all but be eliminated. An interesting question arises: Did the competitive atmosphere of the lending group or the presence of a possible long-term lender dictate that the lending officer suggest alternatives that would displace existing bank debt? The impact of each alternative on Omni Bank's profitability is presented in case Exhibit 11 and discussed in the "Relationship Profitability" section of this note.

Interest-Rate Swaps versus Private Placements

While the swap and the private placement are completely different products, each is capable of fixing a portion of the user's interest payments. Exhibit D compares the key characteristics of private placements with interest-rate swaps. The most significant difference between the two involves pricing. The yield curve (Exhibit E) shows that, as the maturity on interest-rate swaps lengthens, the spread over Treasury bonds declines, with the seven- to ten-year maturities being the most attractive. Spreads over Treasuries for private placements, however, widen as the term increases, so that the three-year maturity is the most favorable.

Interest rate swap. The interest-rate swap funded with the commercial paper from Olympus Credit Corporation yields a fixed rate of 10.66 percent (Exhibit F), which is lower than the prime rate that Merit is now borrowing at and 1.34 percent lower than the fixed rate proposed in the private placement. Since Merit will be receiving the 6-month LIBOR (London Interbank Borrowing Rate) rate to cover its interest payments on its commercial paper-based debt, Merit incurs a basis risk equal to the variability of the spread between 6-month LIBOR and the A1-P1 commercial paper rate. Merit's effective interest rate will increase or decrease to the extent that the spread between LIBOR and commercial paper is less than or greater than the historical spread of 102 basis points.

What appears to be a great rate must be examined more closely, however. The market for interest-rate swaps relies on the borrower who desires fixed-rate financing being able to acquire inexpensive (usually commercial paper-based) variable-rate debt. Traditionally, the party providing the variable-rate financing in a swap can issue commercial paper above the company's existing short-term needs to fund the swap that can provide long-term, fixed-rate financing.

In Merit's situation, the commercial paper-based debt that makes the swap attractive is already being used to finance working-capital needs. If a swap is entered into to fix $10 million in debt designed to cover Merit's fixed assets, then the $10 million in working capital that was being covered by the commercial paper must be covered by prime-based debt. The transaction transforms the commercial paper debt (priced at 8.51 percent on January 23), into three-year, fixed-rate debt at 10.66 percent. But since as Merit grows, it will almost certainly have to increase its bank outstandings to replace the commercial paper line, the swap is in effect being funded with prime-based debt, which yields an effective interest rate of 12.65 percent (Exhibits G and H).

While the interest-rate swap manages to fix the interest payment on $10 million in debt, it does so at a rate that is not acceptable to management. The three-year swap becomes an attractive alternative only to the extent that the swap uses commercial paper-based debt that would otherwise go unused.

392

Private placement. The $10 million in 12 percent, fixed-rate, 3-year debt seems rather plain, but it emerges as part of the most attractive alternative. At the time of the placement, Omni Bank was unwilling to extend fixed-rate term debt to Merit at any price because of Merit's questionable credit quality. The memo in case Exhibit 6 that profiles a private-placement candidate indicates that Merit is a marginal candidate at best. The operating loss before LIFO liquidation of $743,000 in 1983 and the firm's leverage violate two of the five screening criteria listed in the memo. Add the industry that Merit is involved in and the company's reliance on the Olympus franchise, and one wonders that Finch could attract any institutional investors. Given these concerns, the 12 percent, fixed-rate debt looks attractive, relative to the historical and current interest-rate environment.

The second private placement offers Merit flexibility and below-prime-rate financing with the option to fix for 3 years. The option to fix up to $15 million just as the first $10 million is coming due is significant. Case Exhibit 7 shows that the five-year average spread between the prime rate and the 91-day Treasury rate is 3.849 percent. This spread, less the 2 percent that is added to the Treasury rate, leaves the debt priced at prime + 1.849 percent.

The case notes Finch's concern over committing Merit to debt that could not be prepaid if the company's cash flow were sufficient to do so, and Exhibit C indicated that a minimum of $25 million in long-term debt would be needed through 1988. If cash flow is stronger than anticipated, Merit can still reduce the $15 million variable-rate placement between June 30, 1986, and March 31, 1988—the later date being the maturity date of the first private placement. Assuming that the option to fix is not exercised, the second placement gives Merit much needed long-term debt. The option to fix could be invaluable if Merit's performance prohibits the company from entering into additional medium-term, fixed-rate debt when the first placement expires in March 1988. In short, the two private placements afford enormous flexibility and amount to fixed-rate funds extendible from 3 to 6 years and expandable at the third year from $10 to $15 million. Moreover, the entire arrangement would free Merit from annual negotiations with banks.

Valuing the option to fix. An interesting question is whether the insurance company considered the option to fix when determining the rate on the second private placement. The rate at which the $15 million would be fixed was 122 percent of 3-year Treasuries. In effect, Treasuries would have to be above 9.83 percent (12.0%/1.22%) for the rate to reflect any premium, because the insurance company required 12 percent on straight debt for this company. Since three-year Treasuries were yielding 10.10 percent, the premium for the option to fix would have been 32 basis points as of January 23 (10.10% x 122% = 12.32%). Option-pricing theory could give an indication of the value of the option to fix, but because the underlying volatility of the value of the firm's debt is unknown, that approach is not useful. It would be reasonable to say that the value of the option to fix for 3 years is worth more than 32 basis points.

Sensitivity analysis. The private placement provides $10 million in fixed-rate debt at 65 basis points less than a comparable interest-rate swap, yet the effective interest rate is still greater than the prevailing prime-based debt. Assuming the decision is made to do both private placements, the average prime rate would have to be greater than 12.44 percent over the 3-year life of the fixed-rate private placement for the net interest expense to be less under the private-placement alternative (Exhibit I). When the fees for floating the private placements and the cost of compensating balances under the revolving-debt agreement are considered, the average prime rate must be above

12.48 percent for the private placements to be the least expensive alternative (Exhibit J). Considering that the average prime rate over the last 10 years was 11.71 percent with a standard deviation of 4.32 percent, the chance of the private placement remaining the least expensive alternative is moderate.

Relationship Profitability

Account profitability is a function of net interest earned on outstanding loans, income earned on non-interest-bearing deposits, and any fee income generated. During 1984, Omni Bank's loan agreement provided for compensating balances of 5 percent of the total lines made available to Merit.

Any decision made by the relationship manager to alter the products offered a client should be done with an understanding of the impact the change might have on the account's profitability. Different scenarios depend on whether a private placement, an interest-rate swap, or some other private mortgage is pursued. Case Exhibit 11 shows the five most likely scenarios.

Assuming that the $25 million in private placements are completed, the anticipated annual earnings beginning in 1986 from the account are only $52,000. Unless additional fee-based products can be sold to Merit, the anticipated income may not justify servicing the account after the placement is concluded. The decision to reduce the compensating-balance agreement from 5 percent to 2 1/2 percent and to take on the role of Merit's financial advisor must be weighed against the probability of having existing loans to Merit displaced.

EPILOGUE

Omni Bank completed the $10 million, 12 percent fixed-rate, private placement and the $15 million, variable-rate private placement on March 8, 1985. The package originally started out as:

- $10 million private placement with a 7-year maturity and a 5-year average life and

- a $5 million interest-rate swap for 5 years.

The difference between the proposed structure and the actual structure was a function of the 12 percent interest-rate ceiling imposed by Merit's owner. The only maturity that provided for a 12 percent, fixed-rate private placement was 3 years. The swap proposal was dropped because of management's lack of familiarity with the product.

The entire transaction, from the time the relationship manager identified the prospect to the closing of the private placements, took 66 days. The $25 million in institutional debt displaced the entire revolver previously shared by the three banks in the credit group. On learning of the private placements from Merit's president, the other banks were outraged. Relationships between Omni Bank and Sun Coast have been strained ever since. In addition, John Merit sits on the board of directors for Ybor National Bank. The relationship between Sun Coast Bank and Omni Bank worsened as Finch went on to arrange a similar transaction for another customer, whose outstanding debt with Sun Coast Bank was significantly more than Merit's.

EXHIBIT A Merit Marine Historical Financial Indicators

	1980	1981	1982	1983	1984
Change in sales		0.1%	-31.5%	-4.1%	40.9%
Change in pretax profit		-77.0	44.8	NMF*	NMF
Change in total debt		-54.0%	28.6%	59.2%	-7.9%
Return on sales	1.6%	0.7%	0.9%	0.3%	2.2%
Return on assets	2.1	1.0	1.0	0.2	2.5
Return on equity	8.5%	3.0%	2.7%	0.8%	8.0%
Days in receivables	76	77	66	94	80
Days in inventory	121	98	121	142	82
Days in payables	14	11	27	25	18
Current ratio	1.27	1.46	1.29	1.78	1.95
Working capital	$20,062	$25,439	$13,185	$34,424	$39,353
Working capital/sales	0.15	0.20	0.15	0.40	0.33
Total liabilities/equity	3.13	1.98	1.62	2.42	2.17
Total debt/equity	2.81	1.74	1.35	2.14	1.85
Total debt/(debt + equity)	73.8%	63.5%	57.5%	68.2%	65.0%
Long-term debt/ (LTD + equity)	10.4%	11.0%	10.4%	48.2%	45.9%
Interest coverage (times)	1.48	1.09	1.27	0.90	1.78

*Not a meaningful figure.

EXHIBIT B Evaluation of Merit Marine Capital Structure

Capital Structure (12/31/84)		% of Capital	% of Total Funds
Long-term debt (less current portion)	$28,083	44.5%	38.5%
Deferred taxes	1,994	3.2	2.7
Stockholders' equity	33,059	52.3	45.3
Total capital	63,136	100.0%	
Olympus funds deemed to be permanent financing	9,866		13.5
Total funds	73,002		100.0%

Summary Ratios	
LTD/total capital	44.5%
LTD/total funds	38.5%
Total debt/total capital	60.4%
Total debt/total funds	52.0%
Floating-rate debt/total debt*	97.6%**

*Long-term debt plus Olympus funds deemed to permanent financing.

**Fixed-rate debt amounted to $921,000 at 12/31/84.

EXHIBIT C Merit Marine External Funds Requirements (in thousands)

	1983	1984	1985	1986	1987	1988
Net sales	$85,492	$120,472	$126,496	$132,820	$139,461	$146,434
Sources of funds						
Net income	248	2,659	3,036	3,188	3,347	3,514
Depreciation	1,388	1,650	1,700	1,734	1,847	1,755
Deferred taxes	504	672	1,022	805	704	592
Total	2,140	4,981	5,758	5,727	5,898	5,861
Uses of funds						
Net capital expenditures	4,984	289	3,000	3,000	3,000	3,000
Reduction in debt	77	77	77	77	77	77
Increase in	105	315	31,223	25,595	195	317
net working capital	21,239	4,929	222	633	597	558
Increase in other assets	735	(289)	300	300	300	300
Total	27,140	5,321	34,822	29,605	4,169	4,252
External funds	25,000	340	29,064	23,878	(1,729)	(1,609)
Capitalization						
Short-term debt	35,879	31,122	28,963	27,246	27,051	26,734
Long-term debt	28,495	28,184	28,184	28,284	26,455	24,846
Total debt	64,374	59,306	57,147	55,430	53,506	51,580
Shareholders' equity	30,477	33,059	36,018	39,129	42,399	45,836
Total	$94,851	$ 92,365	$ 93,165	$ 94,559	$ 95,905	$ 97,416
Short-term debt/capitalization	37.8%	33.7%	31.1%	28.8%	28.2%	27.4%
Total debt/capitalization	67.9%	64.2%	61.3%	58.6%	55.8%	52.9%
Net working capital/sales	40.3%	32.4%	31.0%	30.0%	29.0%	28.0%

397

Key Characteristics	Interest-Rate Swap	Private Placement
1. Pricing	More advantageous at 5- or 7-year maturities.	Most advantageous at 3-year maturity.
2. Basis risk	The LIBOR/commercial paper risk exists in swap.	There is no basis risk.
3. Covenants	The swap document is no more restrictive than the covenants in the former credit facility.	Financial covenants should not be more restrictive than those in the revolving-credit facility.
4. Balance-sheet treatment	The underlying commercial paper outstandings would appear on the balance sheet as short-term debt. A footnote would explain that the interest rate on the paper outstandings had been fixed through an interest-rate swap.	The private placement would appear on the balance sheet as long-term debt.
5. Flexibility in retiring the debt	Commercial paper can be retired, and the swap contract terminated. If interest rates have declined, the result will be an expense to Merit. If interest rates have increased, Merit can terminate at a profit.	The private placement cannot prepaid.
6. Timing	Swaps can be arranged in one or two business days.	Placements can be arranged in five to ten business days.
7. Access to capital markets	Access to public and private debt markets is maintained.	Access to public debt markets is maintained. Access to private markets would be enhanced.

EXHIBIT E Yield-Curve Information

Maturity	Treasuries	A-rated Private Placements	Baa-rated Private Placements	Merit's Private Placement	LIBOR-Funded Swaps	Commercial Paper-Funded Swaps	Prime-Funded Swaps
3	10.10%	10.80%	11.05%	12.00%	11.18%	10.66%	12.64%
5	10.61	11.36	11.61	12.51	11.41	10.94	12.92
7	10.88	11.68	11.93	12.68%	11.53	11.06	13.04
10	11.00%	11.90%	12.15%	NAp	11.60%	11.13%	13.11%

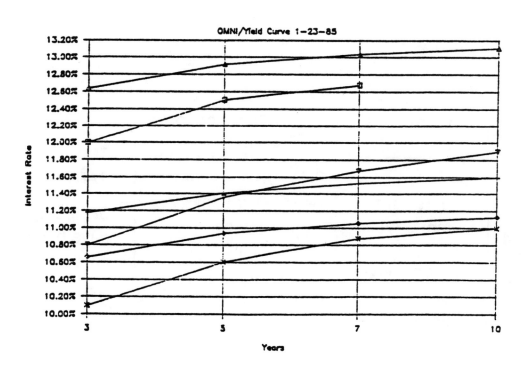

OMNI/Yield Curve 1-23-85

x Treasuries   ∇ A-Rated Private   □ Merit's Private

+ LIBOR Swaps   ◇ CP Swaps   △ Prime Swaps

Goal: To determine the effective interest rate of a three-year LIBOR swap
      funded with commercial paper.

Item	Rate
Fixed rate paid by Merit	Treasuries + 1.08%
Floating rate received in swap	LIBOR
Floating rate paid on underlying borrowing	LIBOR - .52%*
Effective Fixed Rate Cost =	= Treasuries + .56%
	= 10.10% + .56
	= 10.66%

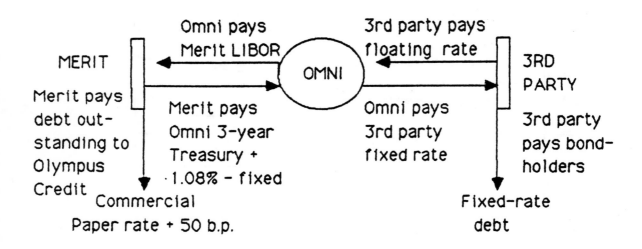

*The average spread between 6-month LIBOR and 30-day A1-P1 commercial paper on a
bond-equivalent basis was 1.02% [i.e., LIBOR = CP + 1.02%]. Subtracting the .5%
spread over the A1-P1 rate that Merit was paying Olympus Credit Corp. results in
a net adjustment to LIBOR of −.52% [Rate = LIBOR − 1.02 + .5].

EXHIBIT G Determining Interest Rate under a Prime-Based Swap

While the swap alternative allows for the lowest fixed-rate debt (10.66%), it also uses up the least expensive variable-rate financing that would be outstanding if not used for the swap. What if Olympus terminated the commercial paper financing? The resulting effective fixed-rate cost would be determined as follows:

Item		Rate
Fixed rate paid by Merit	=	Treasuries + 1.08%
Floating rate received in swap	=	LIBOR
Floating rate paid on underlying borrowing	=	LIBOR + 1.465%*
Effective fixed-rate cost =		= Treasuries + 2.545%
		= 10.10% + .56
		= 12.65%

*Case Exhibit 7 indicates that the average historical spread of prime rate over LIBOR was 1.465%.

EXHIBIT H Effect of Displacing Commercial-Paper Debt

A look at Merit's $10 million in commercial paper-based debt and $25 million revolver before any transaction yields an average interest rate of 9.932% on January 23, 1985.

Amount	Type	Rate	Weighted Cost
$10 mm	Revolver	10.5% (prime)	3.000%
$15 mm	Revolver	10.5 (prime)	4.500
$10 mm	Working cap.	8.51 (CP)	2.432
	Effective interest rate		9.932%

If the swap is concluded, then the working-capital line must be funded through prime-based debt:

Amount	Type	Rate	Weighted Cost
$10 mm	Revolver	10.66% (CP swap)	3.046%
$15 mm	Revolver	10.50% (prime)	4.500
$10 mm	Working cap.	10.50% (prime)	3.000
	Effective interest rate		10.546%

Because the swap displaces cheap working-capital (WC) financing, the real cost of the swap consists of the direct cost (calculated in Exhibit F) plus added costs resulting from the displacement:

Direct cost	10.66%	
Secondary cost		
New cost of WC line		10.50%
Old cost of WC line		8.51
Change in cost		1.99%
Adjusting for proportion		x 10/35
	.57	
Total cost	11.23%	

Note: the prime rate used here, 10.5%, is taken from case Exhibit 7, which gives the rate specific to Omni Bank. The prime rate given in case Exhibit 8, 11%, is an average for 10 banks.

EXHIBIT I   Sensitivity Analysis of Financing

Transaction completed: $10 million, fixed at 12.0%
                         $15 million, variable rate at 2.0% + 91-day
                               Treasury-bill rate

What would the prime rate have to increase to before the net interest expense of the proposed transaction would be exceeded by the current prime-based $25 million revolver?

Assumption: the spread between 91-day T-bills and prime remains constant at 2.68% (this is conservative, since the 5-year average spread is 3.849%)

Interest expense (fixed rate)   = $10 mm x 12%

Interest expense (variable rate) = $15 mm x (prime + .29)*

Interest expense (prime)   = $25 mm x prime

Breakeven Equation

Int. exp. (fixed rate) + Int. exp. (variable rate) = Int. exp. (loan at prime)

$1.2 mm + $15.0 mm (prime + .29%)   = $25.0 mm x prime

$25.0 mm (prime) - $15.0 mm (prime) = $1.2 mm + $.044 mm

$10.0 mm (prime) = $1.244 mm

Breakeven prime rate = 12.44%

The average prime rate over the period would have to be 1.94% higher for the $25.0 million private placement to cost Merit less in interest expense.

91-day T-bill rate =	8.79%
+ 200 basis points =	2.00
	10.79%
Prime	10.50
Spread	.29%

---

*The prime rate used here, 10.5%, is taken from case Exhibit 7, which gives the rate specific to Omni Bank. The prime rate given in case Exhibit 8, 11%, is an average for 10 banks.

The fees associated with the revolver and the private placement must also be considered.

Private Placement Fee

1.0% of first $10.0 million	= $100,000
.5% of remaining $15.0 million	= <u>75,000</u>
	$175,000

Revolver

Collected balances (2.5%)	$625,000
Times assumed interest rate	<u>x 10%</u>
	62,500
Times number of years	<u>x 3</u>
	$187,500

Net present value of the fee income generated from compensating balances = $162,830.

Including the additional $12,170 in fees ($175,000 - $162,830), the average prime rate that would have to prevail would be:

$$\$10 \text{ mm (prime)} = \$1.244 \text{ mm}^* + .0127 \text{ mm/3 years}$$
$$\text{prime} = 12.48\%$$

or 1.98% greater than the current prime of 10.5%.

---

*From the breakeven calculation in Exhibit I.

Chrysler's Warrants: September 1983

SYNOPSIS AND OBJECTIVES

This case is a vehicle for discussing the theory and practice of option pricing. The three opportunities for option-pricing analysis are (1) valuation of the warrants proposed as an equity kicker to the government's loan guarantee as of May 1980, (2) evaluation of the economic fairness of the loan guarantee itself, and (3) valuation of the warrants again in September 1983. The pedagogical issues in this case are to establish the determinants of an option's value, to see the correspondence of an option to loan guarantees and other financial phenomena, and to use the Black-Scholes option-pricing model.

STUDY QUESTIONS

1. Value the Chrysler warrants held by the government on five dates:

- September 14, 1979 (see case Exhibit 5 for calculation of standard deviation of stock returns).

- January 7, 1980 (see case Exhibit 6).

- April 8, 1980 (see case Exhibit 7).

- May 12, 1980, the day before the government guarantee agreement was signed (see case Exhibit 8).

- September 1, 1983 (see case Exhibit 4); on about this date, bids for the government's Chrysler warrants were due.

  Why did the warrants' value change over this time?

  To test the estimate of sigma given in case Exhibit 4, use the data in case Exhibit 9 on Chrysler's publicly traded warrants to solve for the sigma implied by the warrant's price.

2. Value the government's loan guarantee as of May 12, 1980. Remember that it amounts to a put option, which allows the banks to put their risky Chrysler loans to the government. The variance of returns on Chrysler debt is suggested by case Exhibit 10.

3. What is the prospective internal rate of return to the government on the loan guarantee as of May 12, 1980, taking into account the expected fees and current value of the warrants? How does this IRR compare with Chrysler-type risks priced in the open market?

Teaching note prepared by Robert F. Bruner from public information. Copyright (c) 1986 by the Darden Graduate Business School Sponsors, Charlottesville, VA.

4. What price should Chrysler bid for its warrants in September 1983?

5. Based on your bid price, what was the IRR on the government's liability after the fact?

6. Do you agree with Lee Iacocca that "The government's money was never at risk in the first place?" Was the government's "profit ... almost indecent?" Is "usury" an appropriate term for describing the government's pricing of its guarantee?

7. In the abstract, should an issuer of a financial guarantee charge a fee if the guarantee is not used? Why?

A knowledge of option-pricing theory is required to answer these questions. The case may also be supported by readings on options in any of the leading corporate finance texts.

Students will also probably require a way of deriving numerical solutions to the option-pricing problems. Several alternatives are available:

- By hand: Brealey and Myers (3rd ed., pp. 488, 489) greatly simplifies the calculations for put and call options.

- Program for the Hewlett-Packard 12C calculator: Harvard Business School Case Services has published "Black-Scholes Option Pricing Program for the HP 12C Calculator" (1-285-057). It gives call-option values only.

- Programs for personal computers: Cox and Rubinstein's *Options Markets* (footnote 1) presents programs in BASIC.

Experience shows that each of these alternatives gives slightly different option values--probably because of differences in the mathematical approximations of the normal curve. The instructor may want to specify only one alternative.

TEACHING PLAN

One approach to an 80-minute discussion would be as follows:

(30 minutes) What does the Black-Scholes option-pricing model tell us the warrants were worth at the five dates in question? Why did the warrants' value change? How close was the statistical estimate of sigma to the sigma implied in prices of Chrysler's publicly traded warrants?

(30 minutes) Was it reasonable for Chrysler to ask the government to return the warrants for free? What determines economic fairness? As of May 12, 1980, was the government to be fairly compensated? What was the value of the claim the government was giving up? What was the IRR on that claim if the guarantee was to be outstanding until 1990?

(20 minutes) The Shearson/American Express bid already appears to exceed the rational economic value of the warrants. Should Chrysler bid more? How much more?

ANALYSIS

The suggested flow of questions begins with a purely mechanical review of the use of the option-pricing model and the determinants of option values. A sensible approach is to deal with any uncertainty about this issue up front and to gain the resulting warrant values as a foundation for later discussion. Exhibit A, Panel I, provides the relevant analysis based on the Black-Scholes model programmed in Lotus. Many students will take the estimate from the Black-Scholes model to be the warrant value. This assumption ignores, however, the dilutive effect on Chrysler's stock price of issuing new shares under the warrant. To adjust for this dilution, one multiplies the Black-Scholes estimate by this factor:

$$1/(1 + (M/N)) = 1/(1 + (27.686/68.5)) = .71$$

Where M is the number of new shares to be issued, and N is the number of shares outstanding. Exhibit A presents the warrant values with and without the dilution adjustment. Reflecting either only the government warrants (14.4 million shares) or the combination of government and bank warrants (27.686 million shares). With these results on the chalkboard, the instructor can pause and explore the reasons for variations in warrant values: sigma and stock price (1/7/80), sigma and interest rates (4/8/80 and 5/12/80). This comparison motivates a discussion of the determinants of option values.

Panel II gives the estimate of the implied volatility. The sigma implied by the market price of Chrysler's publicly traded warrants is 1.36, which suggests that the sigma estimated in Exhibit 4 of the case is too low, or what is more likely, the public's warrants impound more volatility because trading in Chrysler's public warrants was comparatively thin. Different warrants on the same firm will *often* have different implied volatilities because of different warrant terms to expiration and/or differences in thinness of trading.[1]

The next appropriate step is to extend option pricing to the evaluation of financial guarantees. Whether the government's return is "fair" requires first an estimate of the value it gave up (i.e., the loan guarantee) using the Black-Scholes option-pricing model. Strictly speaking, this model will over-estimate the value of the put option because (1) the underlying asset (i.e., the loans) generates periodic interest and sinking-fund payments, whereas the Black-Scholes model assumes none, and (2) Chrysler can call the loan and/or the put can be exercised before maturity, which means that the appropriate analogy is an *American* option, not a European option as assumed in the Black-Scholes model. Models developed by Merton and others adjust for these variations, and if the instructor chooses to emphasize the theory of option pricing, these models may be applied here. Practically speaking, however, these refinements are moot, because they could only lower what is already a low estimated value. This estimate, $444 million, is derived in Exhibit A, Panel III.

Calculating the IRR on the loan guarantee (assignment question 3) is fairly straightforward. The estimate of $444 million becomes the initial outflow. Inflows come from the equity kicker and fees. Students may suggest that the flows include an annual charge representing the extinguishment of the option over its life. This charge should *not* be included, however, because it is not a genuine flow of value or cash. The entire cash-flow profile produces an IRR of

---

[1]John C. Cox and Mark Rubinstein, *Options Markets* (Englewood Cliffs, NJ: Prentice-Hall, 1985).

-13.9 percent (see Exhibit B). This result often sparks a lively debate over the proper role of government (i.e., to make a profit?) and whether the analysis accounts for massive potential social costs to the welfare system, Pension Benefits Guarantee Corp., etc.

Iacocca argued his position without benefit of quantitative analysis, but even if he had used it, his arguments might not have rendered up the warrants. By September 1983, the warrants were so far "in the money" that the analytical elegance of the Black-Scholes model is unnecessary. Here other considerations (e.g., voting control, shareholder dilution) prevail. The class can explore these strategic issues.

SOME CONCEPTUAL POINTS

This case is flexible enough to be used to focus on the mechanics of valuing an option and on the option-like characteristics of all types of corporate securities. Several conceptual points may be drawn out in the case discussion or in a mini-lecture:

- Common stock is an option on the assets of a levered firm. This point was originally made by Black and Scholes in their seminal article. The Chrysler case shows that, even though the market value of its liabilities may have exceeded the market value of its assets, Chrysler's common stock traded at a positive value. Specifically, Chrysler's common stock is an out-of-the-money option in a highly volatile business environment. Indeed, volatility enhances the value of distressed firms, because they are bound to have considerable upside potential.

- The value of a put option can be thought of as a default-risk discount applied to the current market value of a contemporaneous, riskless, zero-coupon bond. This view is suggested by put-call parity, which states that the combination of risky debt plus a put option must equal the value of a riskless zero-coupon bond.

- Because almost all industrial bonds have some default-risk discount (however small), bonds have option-like valuation features. Bond prices fall with increases in interest rates, with decreases in asset values, with lengthening of maturity, and with increases in the risk to the firm's assets--all because of the option-like qualities of the default-risk premium.

EPILOGUE

The sealed-bid auction occurred on September 12, 1983. Chrysler common was trading just under $30 per share. With the advice of Salomon Brothers, Chrysler won the bid for its warrants at $21.602, or a total of $311 million. Other bids were: First Boston ($15.559), Morgan Stanley ($17.541), and Goldman, Sachs/Prudential-Bache ($20.668).

EXHIBIT A Valuation Summary

Date	Stock Price	Exercise Price	Risk-Free Rate	Volatility	Time (Years)	Warrant Value	Dilution-Adjusted Warrant Value	
							With Govt., Without Banks (+14.4m shs)	With Govt. and Banks (+27.686m shs)
I. For Loan-Guarantee Warrants								
9/14/79	$ 7.875	$13	.0927	.523	10	$ 5.32	$ 4.396	$ 3.79
1/7/80	7.50	13	.1063	.803	10	6.33	5.23	4.59
4/8/80	6.625	13	.1103	.560	10	4.64	3.83	3.30
5/12/80	7.50	13	.1052	1.005	10	6.85	5.66	4.88
9/1/83	$28.375	$13	.1193	.653	6.66	$24.16	$19.96	$17.21
II. For Publicly Traded Warrants								
9/1/83	$28.375	$13	.0959	1.36*	.25	$16.38 (given)		

EXHIBIT A (continued)

III. For Loan Guarantee

5/12/80 $1.5 bn $1.5 bn   .1052   1.046   10 $1.42 bn (call)

Where: Call value   = $1.42 bn
        Asset value   = $1.5 bn
        Present value (exercise)   = 1.5 (e − (.1052)(10)) = $.524 bn
Then: Value of put**   = 1.42 − 1.5 + .524 = $.44 bn = Value of
                                                                   loan guarantee

*Found by trial and error.
**Put is valued assuming put-call parity.

EXHIBIT B   Estimate of IRR on Government Loan Guarantee: *Ex Ante* Analysis
(assumes immediate sale of warrants)

Years	Put Option	Warrants	Fees	Total
0	($444 m)	$69.98 m	--	($374 m)
1			$15 m	15
2			15	15
3			15	15
4			15	15
5			15	15
6			15	15
7			15	15
8			15	15
9			15	15
10			$15 m	$15 m

IRR = −13.9%

Flowers Industries, Inc. (Abridged)

SYNOPSIS AND OBJECTIVES

The chief financial officer of this $600 million (sales) producer of branded baked foods, snack foods, and convenience foods must decide whether to proceed with an issue of $50 million in convertible subordinated debentures, as opposed to an issue of common stock or straight debt. Figuring importantly in the decision is the company's strategy of growth by acquisition. The main teaching objective of this case is to introduce students to the subject of convertible securities and their advantages and disadvantages relative to "straight" securities. The case can also be used to develop students' mastery of option valuation and of EBIT/EPS analysis.

STUDY QUESTIONS

Two readings that summarize well the use of convertibles are (1) Brennan and Schwartz's "The Case for Convertibles," *Continental Bank Journal of Applied Corporate Finance*, Summer 1988, pp. 55–64, and (2) John Ritchie's "Convertible Securities and Warrants," *Handbook of Fixed-Income Securities*, second ed., Fabozzi and Pollack, eds. (Homewood, Ill.: Dow Jones-Irwin, Inc., 1987).

1. What is a "convertible"? What are its merits as opposed to straight debt or straight equity? Consider the effect on shareholders' income, the risks that each form of financing entails, whether the financing increases or reduces financial flexibility, the effect on voting control, and the timing of the financing.

2. Are the terms of the convertible subordinated debenture as outlined in case Exhibit 7 "fair"? Please value the convertible. (The standard practice is to view a convertible as having two components, a bond portion and an option, to value the components separately, and then to add the values. From the issuer's standpoint, a convert would be costly if its true value were above par value and cheap if its true value were below par value.)

3. Should Marty Wood go forward with the convertible issue?

TEACHING PLAN

This case can be the focus for either one or two class periods, depending on the depth of analysis the instructor seeks. The following teaching plan assumes only one period and that the students have been introduced to option valuation.

(10 minutes) Why is Flowers seeking new capital? Is $50 million sufficient? Some stage setting is necessary to lend relevance to the case. The key idea here is that, although there is no current financial shortfall, the

---

Teaching note written by Robert F. Bruner. Copyright (c) 1989 by the Darden Graduate Business School Sponsors, Charlottesville, VA.

corporate strategy of growth by acquisition dictates that the company build itsfinancial slack in anticipation of unexpected new acquisition opportunities.

(20 minutes) What are the features of the three alternatives? The point of the discussion here is to define convertibles through a process of comparison with straights. See Exhibit A for a sample board plan. Also, this is an opportunity to review the terminology specific to convertibles.

(10 minutes) When will investors likely convert? When could the firm force conversion? This is an opportunity for reviewing the incentives for investors to convert and the firm's strategy involved in the decision to force conversion. In this connection, it is necessary to elicit a forecast of earnings per share (EPS), dividend per share (DPS), and dividend yield--all of which can be derived from the forecast in case Exhibit 5. The conclusions here determine the practical term of the conversion option--a key assumption for use in valuing the option.

(20 minutes) At the terms outlined in case Exhibit 7, is the convertible fairly priced? As suggested in the assignment question, the approach is to value the components and sum the values. The instructor should expect some healthy debate over whether the life of the option is 20 years or more like 4 years.

(15 minutes) What is the effect of each financing alternative on the reported performance of the firm? This question invites a review of EBIT/EPS analysis.

(5 minutes) Should Wood go forward with the convertible issue? The instructor can close the discussion by taking a vote and presenting the epilogue and some summary comments.

ANALYSIS

Timing of the Conversion

The comparison of the three financing alternatives hinges importantly on when investors might "flip" (i.e., convert) their debt into equity. Conversion might occur in one of two ways:

Voluntary conversion: The rational investor would exchange his/her debt for shares if two conditions are met: (1) the stock price is higher than the conversion price, and (2) the dividend yield on the stock is higher than the coupon rate on the convertible bond.

Forced conversion: The redemption provision affords the company the right to retire the bonds at about par.[1] If the stock price is higher than the conversion price of the bonds, the rational investor will convert the bonds

---

[1]Actually, as case Exhibit 7 shows, Flowers will have to pay a premium to retire the bonds before 1989.

rather than cash in. In this circumstance, the company is said to "force" the conversion.[2]

While the likelihood of voluntary conversion or forced conversion depends on many things, one can get a sense of whether conversion might occur soon or late by examining the expected stock prices and dividends of the company. Exhibit B presents a forecast of the EPS, DPS, dividend yield, and the price/earnings ratio implied by a $24 share price. First, one observes that, by 1988, the $24 conversion price is consistent with a P/E of 14.2x; by 1989, the implied P/E is 12.6—within the P/E range for the last two years. One can assume that, other things being equal, the company's stock will trade above the conversion price by late 1988. The analysis that follows assumes that the debentures convert (voluntarily or forcibly) in 1988.

Exhibit B also gives evidence to suggest that, for the conversion to occur in 1988, it must be forced. By then, the dividend yield will be in the 2.6–3.0 percent range, hardly approaching the 8.25 percent coupon on the debentures.

Effects on Reported Earnings

Exhibit B shows that, on a fully diluted basis, the convertible debt alternative is associated with a uniformly higher EPS than the other alternatives, amounting to a $.17–.20 premium by 1989. The instructor can probe the students on why this is so: the convertible carries a lower coupon rate than the debt alternative and entails less dilution than equity financing.

Effects on Capital Structure and ROE

Exhibit C gives the projected capital structures under the three financing alternatives. The capitalization and interest-coverage ratios all clearly attest to reasonableness (if not conservatism); under the straight-debt alternative, the debt/capital ratio reaches a maximum in 1989 of 35.8 percent, slightly higher than its actual level for 1984. The managerial implication is that, even under the straight-debt alternative, the firm will probably not be especially highly levered.

A comparison of the return on equity shows the effects of dilution under the equity alternative. With equity financing, the firm will apparently not come close to meeting its target 20 percent ROE any time in the next five years. With straight debt, ROE rises to 18.3 percent in 1989, closer to the target. With the convertible, an ROE in the range of 17–18 percent is maintained even after conversion occurs.

The capitalization and ROE comparisons reveal most clearly the hybrid nature of the convertible: as debt, it enhances returns; as equity, it builds financial borrowing capacity.

Risk Analysis

The analysis so far has said nothing about possible variation in cash flows from those projected in case Exhibit 5. The company's industry is mature, and

---

[2]The convertible structure outlined in case Exhibit 7 also requires that, if the conversion is forced before March 1987, there is an added requirement that the common stock must be trading above 140 percent of conversion price. As discussed, Flowers is unlikely to force conversion before 1988, so this special requirement is not discussed further here.

the demand for baked goods is stable. Yet under the relatively calm surface of the industry exists some turmoil stemming from the consolidation occurring in the industry and from the keen competition for share of market among current players. Also, a wild card in the firm's performance might be adverse growing weather and the resultant effects on grain prices. This assessment allows one to speculate on at least three sources of risk in the firm's EBIT stream:

- periods of severe price competition,
- periods of higher raw materials prices, and
- a stumble on the acquisitions trail.[3]

A shorthand method of addressing the risk element is through EBIT/EPS analysis. The shortcoming of this approach is manifest: it focuses on accounting measures of performance rather than cash flow or investment measures. Nonetheless, this method can give some indication as to the vulnerability of the firm to variations in EBIT.

Exhibit D presents a summary of the EBIT/EPS analysis. Exhibit E graphs these results. In essence, the straight-debt alternative is associated with the highest EPS, the convertible is next, and the equity alternative last. More importantly, the graph shows that, at EBITs below about $50 million, Flowers suffers a decline in EPS relative to historical levels (i.e., EPS below $.94). Management's stated objective is to realize 15 percent compound EPS growth; therefore, the hurdle EPS for 1985 should be $1.104. Only in 1985 does the firm suffer a decline in EPS below the 15 percent growth target. Nowhere is it in danger of omitting a dividend.

A more sophisticated approach to risk analysis would be to run detailed scenario analyses of the financial forecasts. Exhibit F presents summary figures for two scenarios:

- Cost adversity: sales grow by 15 percent annually while EBIT grows by only 10 percent annually

- Sales adversity: sales and EBIT grow at only 10 percent annually

Under both scenarios, the firm's borrowing requirements rise because of the diminished internal financing capability of the firm. Borrowings increase also because it is assumed that acquisition spending is maintained (which is realistic, because growth through acquisition is at the core of the firm's strategy).

Under neither of the two scenarios, however, is the survival of the firm endangered, or a dividend omitted. Capitalization ratios rise and interest-coverage ratios decline, but this is to be expected during a period of adversity, and in any event, all balance-sheet ratios remain within a range of reasonableness. Predictably, ROE declines precipitously under the two adversity scenarios.

––––––––––––

[3]On this point, the company's strategy involves acquiring underperforming companies and turning them around. Although the acquisition strategy has worked well in the past, each acquisition must have an uncertain element: in 1980, for instance, the company wrote off about $1.5 million from the sale of discontinued operations related to its institutional beef- and chicken-processing business.

Is Equity—Linked Debt Appropriate for Flowers?

Somewhere in the midst of the analysis, the student should ask whether convertible debt is an appropriate financing vehicle for this company. Broadly speaking, there are two approaches to answering this question.

The traditional approach is founded on the assumptions that convertible financing is inherently cheap capital[4] and that management can influence the conversion of debt into equity. We can ignore the first assumption (the cost of convertible debt can be viewed as a weighted average of the cost of straight debt and the cost of equity) and focus mainly on the second aspect, capital-structure management.

Suppose that the world consists of two types of firms: Type A is that firm whose financing need is greatest when its stock price is relatively high; Type B is that firm whose financing need is greatest when its stock price is relatively low:

		Financing Need Is	
		High	Low
Stock price is relatively	High	Firm A	Firm B
	Low	Firm B	Firm A

If both firms are growing, convertible debt financing is less appropriate for firm B and more appropriate for firm A. For firm A, the convertible might flip exactly when the firm needs to build its borrowing base for expansion (northwest corner); conversely, when its needs are low, the convertible will not flip and impose dilution on the unfortunate shareholders. For firm B, just the reverse happens: when financing needs are high, the convertible does not flip; it remains as debt to consume borrowing capacity. When financing needs are low, the convertible flips, unlevering the firm and diluting the old shareholders' interest unnecessarily.

Companies do not fit the A/B mold easily, but one can make the case that Flowers is type B. Given a strategy of buying underperforming firms, it is likely to increase its volume of acquisitions during a recession exactly when stock prices are generally depressed—because Flowers' strategy is to buy underperforming companies. The counterargument is that Flowers is likely to acquire in *all* market environments, giving it a high financing need all the time. Moreover, the acquisition spending is discretionary: under onerous conditions, management could relieve a financing constraint by reducing or stopping its acquisition program. The purpose of the A/B framework is not to resolve the question, but rather to illustrate the capital-structure management issues embedded in a decision to finance with convertibles.

The second main approach to the question of "fit" suggests that convertibles are appropriate for companies about whose riskiness managers and outside investors disagree. Brennan and Schwartz (B&S) note that convertible securities are relatively insensitive to changes in the risk of the issuing company because

---

[4]The aforementioned article by Brennan and Schwartz presents an excellent refutation of the "cheap capital" argument for convertibles.

of the complementarity of their bond and option components: an increase in risk would cause a decrease in the value of the bond component and an offsetting increase in the value of the option component. B&S observe (in the article noted previously, p. 64),

> Companies issuing convertible bonds tend to be characterized by higher market and earnings variability, higher business and/or financial risk, stronger growth orientations, and shorter corporate histories than their straight debt counterparts.

Certainly the cash flows from Flowers' core businesses are as stable or more stable than other firms in its industry (an inference from its strong market and cost positions). The instability, if any, comes from the firm's aggressive acquisition program, particularly the rate of acquisition and success in achieving profitable results. The B&S rationale fits Flowers to the extent that management is more confident of its abilities to execute the acquisition program successfully than would-be investors are in straight-debt securities.

The B&S approach raises a valuable teaching point: hybrid securities may be a useful way to resolve agency problems related to risk shifting.

Valuing the Convertible Debenture

The task of valuing the convertible highlights the issues of riskiness and conversion horizon. The standard approach is to value the bond and option components separately and then sum the values.

The bond component is easily valued. Assuming a discount rate of 13.8 percent to value a 20-year coupon stream at 8.25 percent (there are no principal payments before maturity) yields a value per $100 of $62.57.

Valuing the conversion option involves more controversy. The first item of debate will be the life of the option. The terms (case Exhibit 7) indicate that it is a 20-year bond; yet analysis suggests that conversion could be forced in the fourth or fifth year. The life of the option affects not only the time assumption, but also the choice of risk-free rate (ideally the rate should be contemporaneous with the life of the option).

The second item of debate will be the risk assumption. Case Exhibit 12 computes in detail the standard deviation of stock returns for Flowers. In comparison, volatilities of other large food-processing companies are materially higher.

The Black-Scholes option-pricing model using a stock price of $20, an exercise price of $24, a dividend yield of 1.95 percent (a dividend of $0.39), and various assumptions about time, risk, and interest rate generates the following sensitivity table:

Sensitivity Analysis of Conversion Option Values

		No Dilution Adjustment		Adjusted for Dilution[5]	
		4 Years	20 Years	4 Years	20 Years
Interest rate	=	10.5%	11.57%	10.5%	11.57
	.16	$1.53	$12.30	$1.41	$11.30
Risk	.20	2.01	12.36	1.85	11.24
	.25	2.60	12.49	2.39	11.49

The time assumption affects both the value of the conversion option and the bond component. Value is destroyed on the bond component as the bond life is lengthened, since the coupon rate is less than the discount rate on the bond component. Assuming volatility at 16 percent, the economic value of a $1,000 (par value) convertible bond is as follows:

Sensitivity Analysis of Convertible Bond Values

	No Adjustment for Dilution		Adjusted for Dilution	
	4 Years	20 Years	4 Years	20 Years
Bond value	$833.65	$625.71	$833.65	$625.71
Option value[6]	$63.75	$512.50	$58.77	$470.99
Total value	$897.40	$1138.21	$892.42	$1096.70

From the standpoint of the pre-existing shareholders of the firm, the convertible debenture is an economically attractive vehicle only if it is really

---

[5]Depending on the goals of the course and the instructor's desired level of analytical detail, one could dwell on the dilution effect attendant on conversion of bonds. Generally, bond-conversion options issued by a corporation are worth less than call-option contracts of similar terms but written by individual investors, because new shares are issued in support of the exercise. The extent of the discount will be equal to $1/[1+(m/n)]$, where m is the number of shares to be issued upon conversion, and n is the number of common shares previously outstanding. In this case, m/n is 2.083/23.606, and the discount factor is .919.

[6]At a conversion price of $24, each $1,000 par value of debentures gives 41.667 shares.

a 4-year bond. On the other hand, investors will find the convertible attractive to the extent that they believe its life is 20 years. This disparity raises an interesting difference in perspectives: managers see the financial forecast and perhaps have strong faith in their own ability to execute the acquisition program successfully and force conversion in the near or medium term. In contrast, investors cannot see the forecast [under Securities and Exchange Commission (SEC) rules] and, in the absence of better information, may assume that the conversion option will be relatively longer lived. Perhaps this convertible debenture is a way of exploiting an information asymmetry.

The Managerial Decision

In gaining closure on what can be a complicated analysis, the instructor may choose to use some organizing framework such as the traditional "FRICT" scheme (flexibility, risk, income, control, timing).

Flexibility is lowest under the straight-debt alternative and highest under equity financing. The convertible provides a flexible middle path, assuming the firm performs as forecast and that management can force the conversion of the debentures.

Risk appears not to be a major consideration; under all three alternatives, the capitalization ratios and coverage ratios fall within a reasonable range. Moreover, the sensitivity analysis and EBIT/EPS analysis show no looming vulnerability under the debt-financing alternatives.

The *income* or value component is indicated by ROE and EPS. EPS is highest under the convertible-debt alternative, because the convertible minimizes the joint impact of interest expense and share dilution. ROE is highest under the convertible alternative until the convertible flips, after which straight debt affords the highest ROE. Finally, valuing the convertible bond reveals that shareholders' wealth may be enhanced to the extent that management succeeds in forcing conversion in the near-to-medium term.

Control by managers and the family investors is undoubtedly a concern. The issue of common equity (at $20) would result in higher dilution, 9.6 percent, than would the convertible (8.1 percent dilution). The straight-debt issue would impose no dilution of shareholders' control.

Regarding *timing*, the case suggests that interest rates are rising (case Exhibit 9) and that this may be an opportune moment to lock in long-term fixed-rate financing.

On balance, the convertible looks like a reasonable blend of advantages and a reasonable mitigation of disadvantages.

EPILOGUE

Flowers issued the convertible debentures, on terms as outlined in the case, in March 1985. The offering was oversubscribed, and the investment bankers exercised their overallotment option (or "Green Shoe"), causing the full amount of bonds issued to rise to $57.5 million.

With the exception of 1987, the firm has been successful in meeting its goals of 15 percent EPS growth and 20 percent return on beginning equity. Exhibit G summarizes aspects of the firm's financial performance from 1984 to 1988. Acquisitions over the period amounted to $48 million, in excess of the forecasted $43.5 million (case Exhibit 5). This was offset by lower-than-forecasted internal spending and by a total of $41.7 million of divestitures spread over 1987 and 1988. In short, the company has not encountered a financing constraint that would make it necessary to force conversion of the debentures.

In 1987 and 1988, the stock price traded above the conversion price.[7] However, the dividend yield over this period, 2.6 to 2.4 percent, hovered well below the coupon rate on the debt. As of early 1989, investors had converted none of the debentures.

---

[7]The firm's common stock split three-for-two in 1987, which reduced the conversion price from $24 to $16.

Straight Debt	Straight Equity	Convertible
Rating BBB-		Rating BBB-
Term: 20 years	Permanent	20 yrs./permanent
Coupon: 13.8%	Div. yld: 1.9%	Coupon: 8.25%
Uses debt capacity	Builds debt cap.	Builds debt cap.
No dilution	9.1% dilution	8.6% dilution

EXHIBIT B Projected EPS and Conversion Analysis

	Actual 1984	Projected				
		1985	1986	1987	1988	1989
Earnings-per-Share Summary						
EPS unadjusted for new interest	$0.94	$1.09	$1.28	$1.49	$1.73	$2.00
Fully diluted EPS adjusted for new interest*						
Debt financing	$0.94	$1.02	$1.17	$1.32	$1.50	$1.71
Equity financing	$0.94	$1.07	$1.22	$1.37	$1.54	$1.74
Convertibles financing (conversion in 1988)	$0.94	$1.09	$1.24	$1.41	$1.69	$1.91
Implied P/E Multiple (under convertibles financing; at conversion price of $24)	25.6	22.1	19.3	17.1	14.2	12.6
Dividend Summary						
Dividends/share (given)	$0.326	$0.390	$0.470	$0.550	$0.630	$0.710
Dividend yield (if stock price is $24)	1.4%	1.6%	2.0%	2.3%	2.6%	3.0%

*Equity was adjusted for the after-tax effect of additional interest income or expense. The assumed rates of interest for the various debt instruments were:

IRB	8.28%(.6 x 13.8%)
Straight debt	13.80%
Conv. debt	8.25%
Interest on net cash	8.70%

EXHIBIT C   Capital-Structure Forecast and Ratio Analysis

	Actual 1984	Projected				
		1985	1986	1987	1988	1989
Balance-Sheet Assets						
Net working capital	$ 29,537	$ 34,672	$ 39,873	$ 45,854	$ 52,732	$ 60,642
Net PP&E	154,654	169,910	187,454	207,630	230,832	257,514
Other assets	7,823	7,823	7,823	7,823	7,823	7,823
Goodwill	5,502	5,502	5,502	5,502	5,502	5,502
Acquisitions (accumulated)		8,753	18,818	30,394	43,705	59,014
Total assets	$197,516	$226,660	$259,470	$297,202	$340,594	$390,495
Balance-Sheet Capital						
1. Assuming straight-debt financing (@13.8%)						
Long-term notes	$ 30,131	$ (8,039)	$ 5,471	$ 21,642	$ 40,617	$ 62,543
New debt issued		50,000	50,000	50,000	50,000	50,000
Industrial Revenue Bond	27,263	27,263	27,263	27,263	27,263	27,263
Deferred income taxes	12,115	14,604	17,465	20,757	24,542	28,894
Preferred stock	1,349	1,349	1,349	1,349	1,349	1,349
Equity	126,658	143,283	162,323	184,421	210,321	240,876
Cum. interest*	0	(1,801)	(4,401)	(8,229)	(13,498)	(20,430)
Total capital	$197,516	$226,660	$259,470	$297,202	$340,594	$390,495
2. Assuming equity financing						
Long-term notes	$ 30,131	$(11,000)	$ (552)	$ 12,505	$ 28,327	$ 47,058
Industrial Revenue Bond	27,263	27,263	27,263	27,263	27,263	27,263
Deferred income taxes	12,115	14,604	17,465	20,757	24,542	28,894
Preferred stock	1,349	1,349	1,349	1,349	1,349	1,349
New equity issued		50,000	50,000	50,000	50,000	50,000
Equity (old and retained)	126,658	143,283	162,323	184,421	210,321	240,876
Cum. new dividends**		(975)	(2,150)	(3,525)	(5,100)	(6,875)
Cum. interest*	0	2,136	3,772	4,433	3,892	1,930
Total capital	$197,516	$226,660	$259,470	$297,202	$340,594	$390,495

EXHIBIT C (continued)

	Actual 1984	Projected				
		1985	1986	1987	1988	1989
3. Assuming convertible financing (conversion in 1988)						
Long-term notes	$ 30,131	$ (9,642)	$ 2,085	$ 16,326	$ 32,860	$ 51,642
Convertible debt		50,000	50,000	50,000	0	0
Industrial Revenue Bond	27,263	27,263	27,263	27,263	27,263	27,263
Deferred income taxes	12,115	14,604	17,465	20,757	24,542	28,894
Preferred stock	1,349	1,349	1,349	1,349	1,349	1,349
Equity upon conversion		0	0	0	50,000	50,000
Equity (old and retained)	126,658	143,283	162,323	184,421	210,321	240,876
Cum. new dividends		0	0	0	(1,942)	(3,421)
Cum. interest*	0	(198)	(1,015)	(2,913)	(3,798)	(6,108)
Total capital	$197,516	$226,660	$259,470	$297,202	$340,594	$390,495
Comparative Ratios:						
Debt to capital						
Debt financing	29.1%	30.5%	31.9%	33.3%	34.6%	35.8%
Equity financing	29.1%	7.2%	10.3%	13.4%	16.3%	19.0%
Convertibles financing	29.1%	29.8%	30.6%	31.5%	17.7%	20.2%
EBIT to interest						
Debt financing	8.75	6.48	6.05	5.68	5.37	5.13
Equity financing	8.75	70.02	27.43	17.29	12.85	10.42
Convertibles financing	8.75	6.66	6.35	6.04	11.67	9.71
Return on book equity						
Debt financing	17.5%	17.0%	17.4%	17.7%	18.0%	18.3%
Equity financing	17.5%	14.4%	14.8%	15.2%	15.5%	15.9%
Convertibles financing	17.5%	17.9%	18.2%	18.3%	17.1%	17.4%

*See footnote to Exhibit B.

**It was assumed that management would strive to maintain its record of 1/2 cent per share quarterly increase in dividends. Moreover, it was assumed that, in an equity-financing strategy, the firm would issue 2,500,000 shares at $20. Under the convertible-financing strategy, it was assumed that investors would convert in 1988, thus adding 2,083,000 shares (at $24) to the share base.

EXHIBIT D   EBIT–EPS Analysis (in millions)

| | Financing Alternatives | | | | | |
	Common Stock		Straight Debt		Convertible Debt	
EBIT	$40.0	$50.0	$40.0	$50.0	$40.0	$50.0
Interest						
Old*	5.18	5.18	5.18	5.18	5.18	5.18
New	0	0	6.9	6.9	4.38	4.38
Pretax profit	34.82	44.82	27.92	37.92	30.44	40.44
Tax (@.45)	15.67	20.17	12.56	17.06	13.70	18.20
Net income	19.15	24.65	15.36	20.86	16.74	22.24
Shares						
Primary	26.107		23.607		23.607	
Diluted	26.107		23.607		25.690	
EPS						
Primary	$0.73	$0.94	$0.65	$0.88	$0.71	$0.94
Diluted	0.73	0.94	0.65	0.88	0.75**	0.96**

*Assumes debt currently outstanding is not reduced by $5 million as the company plans.

**The fully diluted EPS in the case of convertible debt adjusts for the assumed conversion of the debt by adding back the after-tax cost of the debt.

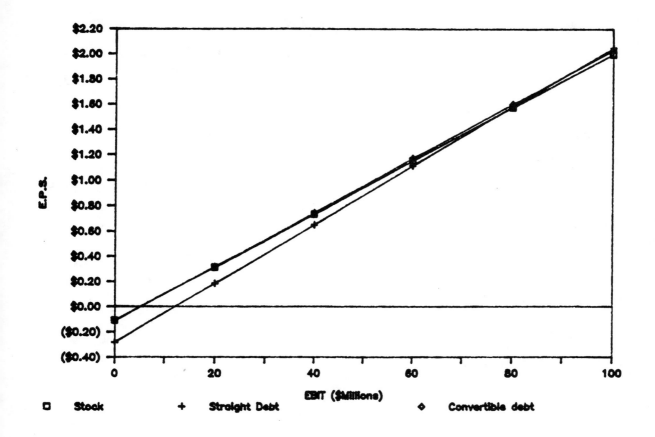

EXHIBIT F Analysis of Adversity Scenarios

1. Sales and EBIT Grow at 10%; Asset Additions Grow as Originally Projected

	Actual 1984	Projected 1985	1986	1987	1988	1989
Earnings-per-Share Summary:						
EPS unadjusted for new interest	$0.94	$1.04	$1.16	$1.29	$1.43	$1.58
Fully diluted EPS adjusted for new interest*						
Debt financing	$0.94	$0.97	$1.05	$1.13	$1.21	$1.29
Equity financing	$0.94	$1.03	$1.11	$1.19	$1.27	$1.36
Convertibles financing (conversion in 1988)	$0.94	$1.04	$1.13	$1.21	$1.39	$1.48
Implied P/E Multiple (under convertibles financing; at conversion price of $24):	25.6	23.2	21.3	19.8	17.2	16.2
DIVIDEND SUMMARY:						
Dividends/share (given)	$0.326	$0.390	$0.470	$0.550	$0.630	$0.710
Dividend yield (if stock price is $24)	1.4%	1.6%	2.0%	2.3%	2.6%	3.0%
Comparative Ratios:						
Debt to capital						
Debt financing	29.1%	30.4%	31.9%	33.8%	35.9%	38.2%
Equity financing	29.1%	6.8%	9.9%	13.2%	16.7%	20.3%
Convertibles financing	29.1%	29.7%	30.6%	32.0%	18.1%	21.5%
EBIT to interest						
Debt financing	8.75	6.30	5.66	5.08	4.56	4.12
Equity financing	8.75	81.65	27.95	16.18	11.14	8.39
Convertibles financing	8.75	6.48	5.95	5.41	10.09	7.83
Return on book equity						
Debt financing	17.5%	16.3%	16.1%	15.9%	15.7%	15.6%
Equity financing	17.5%	13.9%	13.8%	13.7%	13.6%	13.6%
Convertibles financing	17.5%	17.2%	16.9%	16.5%	15.0%	14.9%

2. Sales Grow at 15%; EBIT Grows at 10%

	Actual 1984	Projected 1985	1986	1987	1988	1989
Earnings-per-Share Summary:						
EPS unadjusted for new interest	$0.94	$0.94	$0.94	$0.94	$0.94	$0.94
Fully diluted EPS adjusted for new interest*						
Debt financing	$0.94	$0.86	$0.81	$0.73	$0.63	$0.49
Equity financing	$0.94	$0.92	$0.90	$0.83	$0.75	$0.63
Convertibles financing (conversion in 1988)	$0.94	$0.92	$0.89	$0.81	$0.81	$0.69
Implied P/E Multiple (under convertibles financing; at conversion price of $24):	25.6	26.0	27.0	29.5	29.6	35.0
Dividend Summary:						
Dividends/share (given)	$0.326	$0.390	$0.470	$0.550	$0.630	$0.710
Dividend yield (If stock price is $24)	1.4%	1.6%	2.0%	2.3%	2.6%	3.0%
Comparative Ratios:						
Debt to capital						
Debt financing	29.1%	30.4%	34.2%	39.1%	44.9%	51.3%
Equity financing	29.1%	8.0%	12.1%	18.5%	25.6%	33.4%
Convertibles financing	29.1%	30.9%	32.9%	37.3%	27.1%	34.6%
EBIT to interest						
Debt financing	8.75	5.73	4.33	3.25	2.45	1.87
Equity financing	8.75	46.64	16.46	7.79	4.56	2.96
Convertibles financing	8.75	5.63	4.53	3.42	4.29	2.85
Return on book equity						
Debt financing	17.5%	14.5%	12.9%	11.3%	9.7%	7.9%
Equity financing	17.5%	12.7%	11.5%	10.3%	9.1%	7.8%
Convertibles financing	17.5%	15.7%	13.8%	12.2%	9.9%	8.5%

*See footnote to Exhibit B.

EXHIBIT G   Financial Performance, 1984-88

| | Stock Price | | Purchase | | |
Year	High	Low	of PP&E	Acquisitions	Divestitures
1984	$11.750	$ 7.875	$30.3 m	$7.6 m	0
1985	15.750	10.875	24.1	4.6	0
1986	19.250	13.25	37.6	14.3	0
1987	20.625*	14.75*	30.4	28.7	$39.0 m
1988	R22.000	16.00	$29.4 m	$ .4 m	$ 2.7 m

*In 1987, the common stock was split 3-for-2. At that time, the conversion price of the convertibles financing dropped from $24 to $16.

British Petroleum Company, Ltd. (1987 Stock Offering)

SYNOPSIS AND OBJECTIVES

On October 30, 1987, the British government proceeded with the largest stock offering in history. Over 2 billion shares of British Petroleum (BP) Company, with an aggregate value of over $12 billion, were offered. The underwriters of the issue lost millions of dollars, because they agreed to the price of the firm-commitment offering before the stock market crash of October 19, 1987. These losses, however, were attenuated by a rescue plan in which the Bank of England would purchase shares at a floor price. The Bank of England repurchase offer is equivalent to a put option granted to the underwriters. Students are invited to value this put option and compare it with the change in market values of the U.S. underwriters.

This case provides an exercise in option valuation in a corporate finance context. The put option embedded in the Bank of England repurchase plan obviously is valuable; students should compute its value as well as determine who gained and who paid for the option. Tracking the transfer of wealth from the British government to the U.S. underwriters provides interesting insights into the geopolitical characteristics of international equity markets. The role of government in freely operating capital markets is brought into focus.

The British Petroleum case can be used in a corporate finance course to cover material on issuing securities and the undewriting process. It can be used in an investments course to present a practical application of option pricing as well as study the impact of the October 1987 market crash. It may be used in an international finance course to study international equity markets. Finally, the case can also be used to analyze the appropriate role of government in the capital market.

STUDY QUESTIONS

The *Note on the Valuation of Put Options* should be assigned to students who have insufficient option-pricing background.

1. What is the function of the underwriter in a stock offering?

2. Why were only four underwriters included in the U.S. syndicate?

3 How would the stock market crash affect the underwriters?

4. Why did the Bank of England provide the repurchase plan? What should be the role of the government in a freely operating capital market?

5. How much is the repurchase plan worth to the U.S. underwriters? Use the Black-Scholes options-pricing formula to value the repurchase plan to the U.S. underwriters.

Teaching note written by Chris J. Muscarella and Michael R. Vetsuypens
Copyright (c) 1988.

6. Compare your value for the repurchase plan with the total change in equity value for the U.S. underwriters on October 30, 1987.

CASE ANALYSIS

The repurchase plan announced by Nigel Lawson, the British Chancellor of the Exchequer, on the evening of October 29 was designed to provide underwriters with a safety mechanism that would limit their losses. Under the terms of the plan, the Bank of England would stand ready to purchase, for at least one and at the most two months (January 6, 1988, was the expiration date), any and all partly paid shares at a price of £0.70.

In the BP repurchase offer, Lawson had, in essence, given the U.S. underwriters a costless put option by granting them the right to sell their BP shares to the Bank of England at the floor price of £0.70. Clearly, this pseudo-put is valuable, because it protects the underwriters against further price declines in the value of BP stock.

The Black-Scholes put-option formula can be used to value the repurchase plan. The pseudo-put value can then be compared with the actual change in the market value of the equity of the U.S. underwriters on October 30, 1987. If the option has significant value, it ought to result in an increase in the stock prices of the U.S. underwriters. (Only Morgan Stanley, Salomon Brothers, and Shearson Lehman Brothers are included in this valuation. Goldman Sachs is privately held and was not included in the analysis.)

The Black-Scholes formula can be applied to the BP repurchase plan as follows.

Exercise Price

The determination of the true exercise price is somewhat obscured by the installment feature of the newly issued BP shares. Strictly speaking, the Bank of England repurchase offer of £0.70 per share only applies to the first installment of partly paid BP shares. As explained in the case, holders of partly paid BP shares commit themselves to make two future installment payments of £1.05, the first on August 30, 1988, and the second on April 27, 1989. Combined with the first installment of £1.20 due at issue, the total offering price is £3.30 per BP share.

Tendering partly paid shares to the Bank of England not only provides investors with a cash payment of £0.70 per share, but also relieves them of the obligation to make the final two installments. Thus, the total exercise price implicit in the BP buy-back offer is the sum of (1) the cash payment of £0.70, plus (2) the present value of the second and third installments; the first term is the cash *in*flow at exercise; the second term represents the reduction in future cash *out*flows. Using U.K. interest rates taken from the October 30, 1987, issue of the *Financial Times*, the total value of the exercise price is computed as £0.70 plus £0.975 (the present value of the second payment of £1.05 using an annualized 10-month interest rate of 9.25 percent) plus £0.92 (the present value of the third payment of £1.05 using an annualized 18-month interest rate of 9.25 percent), or a total of £2.595:

	Payment (in Pounds)	Present Value	
10/30/87	0.70	0.70	= .700
8/30/88	1.05	$1.05/(1.095)^{10/12}$	= .975
4/27/89	1.05	$1.05/(1.095)^{18/12}$	= .920
			2.595

Current Stock Price

For use in the formula, the closing bid price of BP shares on the London Stock Exchange on October 30, 1987, is £2.65.

Time to Maturity

The Bank of England repurchase offer was announced October 29, 1987, and expired on January 6, 1988. Hence, the time to maturity is 69 days. Expressed as a fraction of a year (as required in the Black-Scholes put formula), the time to maturity is 0.189.

Interest Rates

The Black-Scholes formula requires as an input variable the annualized risk-free interest rate for a maturity corresponding to that of the put option. From quotes in the *Financial Times* on October 30, 1987, the annualized two-month U.K. interest rate to use is 9.25 percent.

Volatility

By far the most difficult input variable to measure for use in the Black-Scholes formula is the volatility of BP shares. Unlike the other variables, it is not reported in the financial press. Volatilities can be computed by using several different methodologies, and option values tend to be very sensitive to the choice of the volatility estimate.

The most straightforward way to estimate a stock's volatility is to apply standard statistical techniques to historical stock price data. (This procedure assumes that historical volatilities accurately reflect expected future volatilities.)

Exhibit A lists closing BP stock prices on the London Stock Exchange and estimates the volatility of BP stock over the period 10/16/87 through 10/30/87. The last two weeks of October 1987 were one of the most volatile periods ever in U.S. and worldwide equity markets, and this unusually high volatility is reflected in the variance of BP.

BP volatility is computed by taking the standard deviation of the continuously compounded rate of return on BP stock. The price relative is computed as today's price divided by the previous day's price. Next, the natural logarithm of the price relatives is computed. The mean of the log of the price relatives is calculated to be -0.027247. The squared deviations from the mean of the log of the price relatives are summed and divided by 9 (10 - 1) to calculate a daily variance of 0.00285. This number is annualized by multiplying it by 253, and the square root is taken to compute the annual standard deviation, 0.849193.

This approach is only one of many possible calculations to determine the volatility of BP shares. Some students may suggest that a larger time series of BP stock prices should be used in the calculation, which would result in a somewhat lower figure for the standard deviation. Another method of determining volatility is to use the implied volatility found in BP options. Using traded BP options traded in either the U.S. and Britain, the calculations for implied volatility result in high estimates of the standard deviation, although not quite as high as the 0.849 calculated above. There obviously is no one "correct" measure of volatility, and the instructor is free to choose among the various methods.

All the inputs to the put-valuation model are now known. Exhibit B illustrates the computation of the put value. The cumulative normal probability density function may be either looked up in tables found in any statistical textbook or estimated using a polynomial approximation. The figures presented in Exhibit B use the latter technique.

The value of the put is calculated to be £0.3339 per partly paid BP share. Using the October 30, 1987, exchange rate of $1.722/£, each put option is worth $0.575. The three publicly traded U.S. underwriters collectively purchased 361.08 million partly paid BP shares. Thus, the Bank of England repurchase plan was worth $207.6 million to the U.S. underwriters.

The actual change in the market value of equity of the U.S. underwriters is entirely consistent with this put-value estimate. The announcement of the repurchase offer was made in London late in the evening of October 29, after U.S. equity markets had closed. (The announcement crossed the Dow Jones News Wire at 5:07 p.m. EST.) Thus, the effect would be reflected in stock prices during the next trading day, October 30. Exhibit C computes the unexpected change in market value for the underwriters on October 30, 1987. First, the total equity values for all three underwriters is computed for October 29 and 30. The expected return for the underwriters on October 30, 1987, is calculated as the average beta of the underwriters (.6733) times the market return on October 30, 1987, of 3.328 percent Thus the expected return of the underwriters on October 30 resulting from normal market fluctuations is 2.24 percent. The equity value of the underwriters increased by $367 million on October 30, 1987. Part, $120 million, can be explained by the general rise in the market on that day. The remaining $247 million increase in value for the underwriters can potentially be attributed to the impact of the BP repurchase plan. The previous estimate of the value of the repurchase plan ($207.6 million) is equivalent to 84 percent of the unexpected change in underwriter value ($247 million).

Thus, while publicly stating that the British government would not bail out the underwriters of the BP offering, the repurchase plan increased the value of the U.S. underwriters by a substantial amount. At this point in the class, the instructor may wish to foster a discussion of the role of the government in a freely operating capital market.

EPILOGUE

The offering of BP shares was massively undersubscribed on the offering day. The UK underwriters were able to sell only 6.1 percent of their 1.0946 billion shares, while the international underwriters sold only 4 million (.36 percent) of their 1.1 billion shares. Each of the four U.S. underwriters reported pretax accounting losses of between $75 and $80 million as a direct result of their participation in the BP offering.

The U.S. underwriters proceeded to alter the price of the shares to reflect current market conditions. Each American Depository Share was priced at $17.25, equivalent to £0.838 per ordinary share, which is considerably less than the £1.20 that the underwriters paid for them.

Wood Gundy Corporation, the lead Canadian underwriter, suffered after-tax losses equal to about 10 percent of its total capital. As a result, First Chicago Corporation, which had agreed in June to purchase a 35 percent equity stake in Wood Gundy, canceled its proposed $200 million investment.

The price of BP shares never fell below the £0.70 Bank of England support price. In early November, the Kuwait Investment Office began buying BP partly paid shares and had purchased almost 600 million of the shares by mid-November. By the January 6, 1988, expiration date of the Bank of England buy-back offer, Kuwait owned over a billion of the partly paid shares, representing approximately 18 percent of the total outstanding shares of BP. By March 1988, Kuwait owned 22.5 percent of BP shares.

The Bank of England did acquire abut 39 million BP shares at the buy-back price of £0.70, even though when the offer expired, the shares were trading on the London Stock Exchange at £0.80. Thus, the big winner in the BP offering was the British government (and, ultimately, British taxpayers), and the big losers were the worldwide underwriters (although the Bank of England and Kuwait reduced potential losses). The final result of Kuwait's huge investment in BP is yet to be determined.

The Bank of England repurchase plan was universally heralded when it was announced. The U.S. and Canadian underwriters received some of the support they had sought, and Lawson received widespread acclaim for his compromise solution. The following editorials were typical:

THE SKILL OF THE CHANCELLOR
The Times (of London) October 31, 1987

Mr. Nigel Lawson has pulled a political rabbit out of hat in his last-minute compromise on the Government's sale of BP shares. His own backbenchers, who must have awaited his statement on Thursday night with nervousness, emerged with more satisfaction than the Opposition.

Their relief will in no way have been dulled by events on the stock market yesterday, where the partly-paid BP shares stayed well above the level at which the Bank of England would be called upon to make good its confidence-boosting guarantee. Given that the Chancellor of the Exchequer was presiding over the biggest stock market flop in history, and the end of any ambition to use BP to spread share ownership, that showed great political skill.

Mr. Lawson's feel has been underestimated in the past. In this case he owes some debt to the Bank of England, which had memories of buying Burmah Oil's stake in BP at the bottom of a stock market slump in 1975 and making an enormous profit on the £180 million it paid to steady City nerves.

The potential for wider share ownership had been lost as soon as the stock market crashed. It would not have returned for many a moon. The Chancellor was still faced with two conflicting aims. The first was to proceed with

the issue at almost any--but, it was hoped, minimum--
cost. He wanted to secure important revenues, not so much
this year as in the following two financial years when tax
revenue may not be so buoyant.

There was a strong political imperative to maintain
the Government's reputation for strong nerves and for
sticking to its policies through thick and thin. Since the
resolute approach is credited--not least in industry--
with a strong role in boosting long-term business
confidence, it should evidently not be thrown away lightly
at a time when business confidence is inevitably being hit
by shrapnel from the crash of stock markets round the
world. There was an equally strong political imperative
for the Government not to bail out the underwriters, whose
insurance fees have been so heavily criticized in previous
privatization issues.

On the other side of the equation, any political
leader has an awesome responsibility at a time of crisis in
financial markets to avoid anything that might undermine
confidence further and hence add to the risk of trouble
spreading to the economy in general. Mr. Lawson is well
aware of this, though M. Jacques Delors, the President of
the European Commission, was evidently not when he did his
best to talk down a falling dollar.

In Britain, the risk to confidence stemmed from the
drain of cash to take up the BP shares rather than from the
risk of underwriting, which, under the City system of
sub-underwriting, is ultimately carried in tiny amounts by
millions of life assurance policyholders and pension fund
members. Abroad, where underwriting banks and securities
houses take the risk of issues themselves to maximize
profits, the consequential risk of potential losses of up
to £400 million is greater. Mr. Lawson chose to guarantee
liquidity but not offer much help on losses. He will not
thereby make friends in Canada or New York.

The package inevitably puts more emphasis on domestic
political imperatives than the world stock market problem.
The Chancellor calculated that withdrawing the sale would
do more harm than good. He will now want to turn away from
the domestic scene and take a lead in more positive
initiatives to restore confidence.

THE FLOOR UNDER THE MARKET
Financial Times (London) October 31, 1987

Few things more succintly encapsulate the dramatic
change in governmental attitudes to markets than the short
history of the British Petroleum share offer. At the
outset it was seen as the Thatcher Administration's most
determined effort yet to sell the merits of market
capitalism to the British people. Yet within the space of
a mere two weeks this £7.2bn issue has become the subject
of a highly unusual exercise in government intervention in
the capital markets.

At the behest of Mr. Nigel Lawson, the Chancellor, the Bank of England's role as lender of last resort to the banking system has been extended not only to British but to international investment institutions and securities firms. After the wild gyrations on the world's bourses over the past fortnight there are few takers for what President Reagan once called the magic of the markets; and some of the most ardent campaigners for deregulation were predictably enough among the more clamorous in their demands for a BP bailout.

Mr. Lawson can at least claim that this ideological about-turn is not a rescue for the underwriters. He has merely put a floor under the BP share price by arranging for the Bank of England to buy back shares over a limited period at a price that is in line with the closing price on Thursday. The underwriters will thus incur substantial losses while enjoying short-term protection from a further market slide. This has the merit of preserving the original point of the exercise, which was precisely to protect the Government and the taxpayer against market instability while ensuring that the market comes under less liquidity pressure.

Not everyone was entirely pleased with the repurchase plan, however. Some members of the financial community were able to see the repurchase plan for exactly what it was. The following letter to the editor appeared in *The Times* (of London) on October 31, 1987:

Sir, as a fund manager representing a sub-underwriter in the BP issue with a substantial foreign pension-fund interest, it was with considerable dismay that I learnt of the Chancellor's solution to the potential underwriting losses sustained in the issue (report, October 30). By bailing out US investment banks and similar institutions, at a support price, he succumbed to vested interests when a totally non-interventionist market approach was the only viable solution should he have decided not to pull the issue.

In the end he got the worst of both worlds, since he failed to uphold free market principles on which all past privatisations have been based and at the same time prejudiced the very people who (unlike the U.S. underwriters) had prepared to accept the losses, but had taken measures to protect their clients by buying put options (the right to sell shares at a certain price up to a given date) or by selling old shares in the account to prevent further underwriting losses.

By authorizing the Bank of England to issue free put options, the Chancellor has sustained further losses for such underwriters, who only yesterday had been paying massive sums of money for such options.

The sooner the so-called British share-buying public
realize they have had their savings cynically manipulated
and exploited, the better. The Government expect us to
play the game, but they do not play it themselves.

Yours Faithfully,
N.M.OSTRER, Director
Marathon Asset Management, Ltd.

EXHIBIT A Worksheet to Compute Volatility (σ)

Date	BP Price	Price Relative	Log of Price Relative	Log of Price Relative Less μ	Square of Previous Column
10/16/87	348				
10/19/87	314	0.90230	-0.10281	-0.07556	0.00571
10/20/87	283	0.90127	-0.10395	-0.07670	0.00588
10/21/87	295	1.04240	0.04153	0.06878	0.00473
10/22/87	282	0.95593	-0.04507	-0.01782	0.00032
10/23/87	285	1.01064	0.01058	0.03783	0.00143
10/26/87	265	0.92982	-0.07276	-0.04551	0.00207
10/27/87	258	0.97358	-0.02677	0.00048	0.00000
10/28/87	252	0.97674	-0.02353	0.00372	0.00001
10/29/87	258	1.02381	0.02353	0.05078	0.00258
10/30/87	265	1.02713	0.02677	0.05402	0.00292

Period: 10/16–10/30
Number of prices: 11
Number of price relatives: 10
Sum of log of price relatives: -0.272473
Average of log of price relatives (μ): -0.027247
Sum of (log price relatives – μ)^2 0.025653
Daily variance: 0.002850
Annual variance: 0.721128
Annual standard deviation: 0.849193

EXHIBIT B   Calculation of Put Value

K = 2.595

S = 2.650

r = 1.0925

t = 69/365 = .189

σ = 0.849

y = (ln[(2.595)(1.0925)$^{-.189}$]/2.65)/(0.849)(0.189)$^{.5}$ - (.5)(0.849)(0.189)$^{.5}$

  = -0.28683

N(-0.28683) = 0.38712

y + $\sigma\sqrt{t}$ = -0.28683 + (0.849)(0.189)$^{.5}$ = 0.08239

N(y+$\sigma\sqrt{t}$) = 0.53284

P = (2.595)(1.0925)$^{-.189}$(0.53284) - (2.65)(0.38712) = 0.3339

EXHIBIT C Calculation of Market Values

Underwriter	Number of Shares (000)	Share Price, 10/29/87	Equity Value, 10/29/87 ($M)	Share Price, 10/30/87	Equity Value, 10/30/87 ($M)
Morgan Stanley	24,864	$49.00	$1,218	53.375	$1,327
Salomon Brothers	152,000	18.875	2,869	20.00	3,040
Shearson Lehman	86,729	14.75	1,279	15.75	1,366
Total			$5,366		$5,733

$$\text{Average underwriter beta} = \frac{.39 + .86 + .77}{3} = .6733$$

$$\text{Market return on } 10/30/87 = \frac{251.79 - 243.68}{243.68} = 0.03328$$

Expected return on underwriters on 10/30/87 = (.6733)(0.03328) = 0.0224

Expected change in underwriter value on 10/30/87 = (0.0224)(5,366)

$$= \$120 \text{ million}$$

Total change in underwriter value on 10/30/87 = 5,733 − 5,366 = $367 million

Unexpected change in underwriter value on 10/30/87 = 367 − 120 = $247 million

Brunswick Federal Savings and Loan Association

SYNOPSIS AND OBJECTIVES

In July 1984, an investment banker is requested to develop and evaluate the terms of exchange with which Brunswick would offer to swap convertible debentures for convertible preferred stock. The task of the student is to recommend a coupon and conversion rate for the convertible debentures. This recommendation must hinge on an assessment of Brunswick's expected performance and on its vulnerability to macroeconomic adversity.

This case can be used to approach several objectives:

- develop the vocabulary and mechanics of convertible securities, as well as the logic of the voluntary conversion decision on the part of investors and the decision to force conversion by the issuer;

- introduce the logic and mechanics of exchange offers;

- apply option-valuation techniques to conversion rights;

- build students' appreciation of the operating economics of financial institutions, and of structural change in the savings and loan industry.

STUDY QUESTIONS

1. What would motivate Brunswick to consider an exchange offer for its convertible preferred stock?

2. Do you support Bob Roberts' recommendation on coupon and conversion premium for the new convertible debenture? Why? At these terms, what is the value of the new convertible bond? Are the holders of the convertible preferred likely to make the exchange? The yields on 2- and 20-year U.S. Treasury debt were 12.88 percent and 13.36 percent, respectively.

3. How would the exchange and future conversion affect current stockholders? What is the net present value of this exchange for them?

TEACHING PLAN

(20 minutes) Why is Brunswick considering a possible exchange? This segment of the discussion should review the strategic and financial issues motivating the exchange.

Teaching note written by Robert F. Bruner, with contributions from James G. Rose, Jr. Copyright (c) 1989 by the Darden Graduate Business School Sponsors, Charlottesville, VA.

(30 minutes)   What are the incremental cash flows resulting from this exchange? What is the time horizon (i.e., when can we force conversion)? At what discount rate should we value these incremental flows? What is the present value? This segment addresses the wealth gain or loss to current shareholders resulting from the exchange.

(15 minutes)   What is the value of the proposed convertible debenture? Will the preferred holders make the swap? This segment considers the exchange from the preferred investors' standpoint.

(15 minutes)   To variations in what assumptions is the analysis particularly sensitive? This final segment brings the discussion full circle, back to the strategic and environmental issues that motivate the exchange to begin with. Expected interest rates prove to be the major variable.

ANALYSIS

Expected Performance

Much of the analysis of the exchange offer depends on the forecasted earnings and share price of Brunswick, because these determine the expected conversion date of the securities, and hence the horizon for the analysis.

Forecasts from the case for net income, earnings per share, dividends per share and common stock prices are shown in case Exhibit 11. The time horizon has been limited to five years because of the inaccuracy and decreasing importance of cash flows beyond five years, and because both securities would probably convert into common within five years. The data have been calculated on six-month intervals to coincide with the payment dates of the preferred dividends and the bond interest. The dividend, net income, and earnings-per-share (EPS) figures represent amounts for the previous twelve months ending on June 30 and December 31 of each calendar year. Common stock prices assume a constant 3.2 price/earnings (P/E) multiple.

Discussion of Terms

Exhibit 10 of the case shows that the items to be recommended by Bob Roberts are coupon rate, conversion premium, and call protection. The text of the case indicates, however, that Roberts is considering recommending a coupon of 14.25 percent and a conversion price of $11.25 based on a conversion premium of 25 percent. The contemplated coupon is surprisingly high, given that straight bonds are trading to yield between 13.38 and 14.88 percent; convertible bonds usually offer a lower current yield, reflecting the value latent in the conversion option. One rule of thumb is that coupons for convertibles are set at 60 percent of the coupons of comparable straights. *A priori*, one would judge that Roberts is proposing to price the new convertible debenture too richly. Exhibit A gives a completed term sheet for the exchange, assuming an 80 percent exchange as opposed to the 100 percent implied in case Exhibit 10.

The difference between the face amount of the preferred stock retired, $50,800,000 (2,032,000 shares x $25 per share), and the new debt securities issued, $36,576,000 (2,032,000 x $18), represents a one-time gain of $14,224,000 to Brunswick. In 1984, this gain was nontaxable and would be added to retained earnings. Exhibit B presents Brunswick's liabilities and equity for December 31, 1983, restated to show the effect of the exchange. The primary capital-to-assets ratio is not affected by the exchange, since both preferred stock and subordinated debt are defined as primary capital by the regulatory authorities. If one classifies the new debt as strictly a liability rather than as a quasi-equity security, equity as a percentage of total assets declines from 3.77 percent to 3.23 percent.

The Cost of Calling the Preferred

The implicit alternative to making this exchange is simply to redeem the preferred issue and sell a new issue of convertible debentures. A rough calculation reveals that this strategy is expensive: Brunswick will be paying $27.10 per share (the redemption price given in case Exhibit 5) for securities that have a market value of $18.00--a 51 percent premium. The $2.10 premium over par value would be deductible for tax purposes, although the tax savings would have a relatively minor effect on the economic cost of this strategy. If an exchange can be designed effectively to substitute debt for the preferred, then exchange would be economically more attractive than redemption and issuance.

Evaluation of 80 Percent Exchange, at Proposed Terms

The incremental effect of the exchange offer from the common shareholders' point of view can be evaluated using discounted cash-flow (DCF) analysis. The point of departure for the analysis is to establish the conversion horizons for the preferred and debt securities. Drawing on the projection in case Exhibit 11, one might assume that the preferred stock would convert to common when the common stock price reaches the conversion price of $16.34. After the preferred conversion, the holders will realize an increase in income, because the dividends on the 1.53 shares of common they receive will exceed the $2.10 dividend per original preferred share. Conversion of the debt into common is assumed to take place in 1986 when the common stock price reaches the conversion price of $11.25. When the debt converts, the holders will suffer a temporary loss of current income: $2.56 in bond interest versus $1.20 in common dividends (1.60 shares x $0.75 per share). Should Brunswick be concerned about the unwillingness of debt-holders to convert, the company could include the right to force conversion into the bond indenture.

With the conversion horizons in hand, one can forecast the cash flows under the preferred and debt alternatives and determine the incremental cash flow. The preferred cash flow will consist of annual dividends ($2.667 million) until the conversion. Thereafter, dividends will be pegged to the common equity dividend rate. The cash flow under the debt alternative will be the sum of transaction costs ($1.016 million), interest, tax savings, preferred dividends on the remaining 20 percent of the issue still outstanding, and common dividends after the conversion date. The incremental cash flow will be the difference between the cash flows under these two alternatives.

The discount rate for the incremental cash flow is 11.70 percent (5.85 percent, semi-annually), the current yield on the preferred issue. The rationale for this discount rate is that the risk of the security in place is the risk of the incremental cash flow.

Exhibit C gives the DCF valuation of the incremental cash flows arising from this exchange. The net present value (NPV) of these flows is $1.312 million. The more attractive conversion rate of the new debt appears to be the major source of savings. By structuring the deal so that conversion of the debt securities occurs in 1986, rather than in 1989 with the preferred stock, Brunswick replaces the preferred dividends with common stock dividends. Even though the debt securities offer more common shares at conversion (1.60 shares versus 1.53), not until 1989 does Brunswick pay out more in common dividends under the debt alternative than is paid out in preferred dividends under the preferred scenario.

Note that the tax benefits of the new debt play a minor role, largely because the debentures convert into common stock the same year that Brunswick returns to tax-paying status. The transaction costs, on the other hand, have a significant effect on the cash flows.

More importantly, the operating performance of Brunswick and the market multiple of its earnings are the driving forces behind the common stock price, which, in turn, will determine when conversion of either security occurs.

In class, a useful contrast to point out is this $1.3 million NPV against the $14 million accounting gain described in the preceding section. In essence, it is the NPV rather than the accounting gain that measures the effect of this transaction on shareholder wealth.

Sensitivity Analysis: Key Assumptions

Students can test the robustness of the $1.3 million gain in shareholder wealth along a number of dimensions. The worksheets for various scenarios are not presented here, although their results are summarized in the following table:

Net Present Values of the Debt-for-Preferred
Exchange under Various Scenarios

Scenario	NPV
1. Base case: 14.25% coupon, 80% exchange	$1.312 million
2. Coupon is 15%, 80% exchange	.974
3. Coupon is 14.25%, 100% exchange	1.645
4. Coupon is 15%, 100% exchange	1.217
5. Bond par value is $20, 80% exchange	(.412)
6. Conversion premium raised to 39%	(1.509)
7. Lower EPS[1]	$ .060 million

In the first four scenarios, the benefits of the exchange appear to be relatively robust to variations in coupon and percentage exchanged. The significant variations in value in the last three scenarios are associated with the *timing* of the debt conversion into common and the *magnitude* of common stock dividends after conversion. For instance, a higher conversion premium (scenario 6) worsens the exchange, because it delays by two years the eventual conversion of the debt. Lower EPS (scenario 7) also delays the conversion and dissipates the benefit of the exchange. A higher bond par value (scenario 5) worsens the exchange because it results in larger interest payments and later, higher common dividends.

The implication of this sensitivity analysis is that Brunswick must structure its exchange terms so as to encourage early conversion and reduce annual interest expense. Brunswick faces a tradeoff here, however, for the lower the conversion premium, the sooner the debt securities convert. The lower the premium, however, the greater the number of common shares the debt issue will be converted into. Because an earlier conversion has a much more positive impact on the cash flows than the negative impact of additional common shares,

---

[1]EPS is projected to be $2.90 in 1984 and to grow at an annual rate of 8 percent through 1990. The P/E multiple is expected to remain constant at 3.2.

the primary objective of the pricing should be an early conversion into common stock. The dilutive effect of a greater number of shares is minor.[2]

Evaluation from Preferred Investor's Perspective

The investor holding the convertible preferred shares will choose to exchange if the new convertible debentures are worth more than the shares. Also influencing the decision would be questions about marketability, call protection, and absolute dollar yield--all of which will vary in importance according to the individual investor.

For simplicity, consider the narrow valuation question: each preferred share is trading at $18.00; how does the value of the proposed convertible debenture compare? The analytical procedure here is to estimate the value of the bond component and call option, and add them together.

The value of the bond component depends on assessing the appropriateness of the proposed 14.25 percent coupon. Case Exhibit 9 and the discussion in the text suggest that it falls within a reasonable range. For simplicity, one could assume that market value of the bond equals its par value, $18.00.

The value of the conversion option could be approximated using an option-pricing model and the following parameters:

Current stock price	$ 9.00 (an estimate based on trends)
Exercise price	$11.25
Risk-free rate	
2-year T-note	12.88% (in study question 2)
20-year T-bond	13.36% (in study question 2)
Term	2, 20 years
Volatility	28% (case Exhibit 8)

The term of the option is debatable. From management's standpoint, Brunswick will seek the conversion of the debentures as soon as possible, in the range of 2 to 3 years, and will obtain conversion by forcing the issue if necessary. The naive investor, on the other hand, may see the debenture as containing a 20-year option. In the analysis that follows, option values are estimated using both terms. Ignoring the payment of dividends on the common stock and interest on the debenture will slightly bias upward the value of the call option, but this bias does not change the qualitative conclusion of the analysis from the investor's point of view.

The Black-Scholes option-pricing model suggests that each 2-year option is worth $1.546 and each 20-year option, $8.25. Because each debenture contains

---

[2]The preferred issue converts into 3,886,200 common shares (1.53 x 2,540,000) and the new debt converts into 4,028,440 common shares (1.60 shares x 2,032,000 + 1.53 shares x 508,000) if the exchange is 80 percent successful and 4,064,000 shares (1.60 x 2,540,000) if the exchange is 100 percent success-ful. These differences in common shares between the preferred stock and the new debt, 142,240 and 177,800, respectively, represent a small fraction of the current total common shares outstanding. The exchange is marginally dilutive.

options on 1.60 shares, the option component is worth $2.47 or $13.20.[3]

Adding together the bond and option components of the convertible debenture indicates that the preferred holder is being offered a security with a value somewhere between $20.47 and $31.20 per current preferred share.[4] Ignoring any other considerations, one might expect the preferred holder to participate in the exchange, along the terms outlined in case Exhibit 10. If, however, Roberts set the coupon at 60 percent of the rate of comparable straight bonds (say, .60 x 14.25, or 8.55 percent), then the bond component would be worth about $10.80, and the whole security would be worth between $13.27 and $24.00.[5] In this instance, the decision of the preferred holder would be far more sensitive to the perceived value of the conversion option, which itself depends on the perceived term of the option. In essence, setting the coupon at the traditional 60 percent of straight bonds renders the preferred holder's decision more problematical.

In either instance, the preferred holder may be spurred to make the exchange out of one final consideration: the potential loss of liquidity of the investment. If 80 percent of investors swap their preferred for the debt, the remaining preferred holders could be stuck with a security that trades infrequently and is given to relatively large swings in price on small fluctuations in volume. Institutional investors, at least, would find this outcome unappetizing.

Conclusion

At Roberts' contemplated terms, high (if not complete) participation by the preferred holders is likely. If, as the case says, one should not strive for 100 percent exchange, then one would recommend a downward adjustment in the contemplated coupon rate.

From the standpoint of Brunswick's existing common shareholders, the exchange is modestly attractive, although the extent depends importantly on expected earnings and share price performance of the firm. Dilution and capital-structure effects are not material. The actual outcome of this exchange for shareholders will ultimately depend on operating policies and macroeconomic forces to which the savings and loan industry is so vulnerable.

One could challenge Roberts on the timing of the exchange. Why this exchange needs to take place in the near future is not clear. Brunswick won't pay taxes until 1986. Yields on subordinated debentures are at a 22-month high

---

[3]These estimated option values ignore the effect of dilution. Depending on the level of detail the instructor wishes to pursue, one could include the effect of dilution. Generally call-option contracts written by individual investors are worth more than bond-conversion options issued by a corporation, because new shares are issued in support of the exercise (i.e., conversion of the bond). The extent of the discount will be equal to $1/(1+(m/n))$, where m is the number of shares to be issued upon conversion, and n is the number of common shares previously outstanding. In this case, m/n is 4,028,440/13,191,275, and the dilution discount factor is .766. As a result, the adjusted option values are $1.89 and $10.11.

[4]Adjusting for dilution, the security values are $19.89 and $28.11.

[5]Adjusting for dilution, the respective security values are $12.69 and $20.91.

and on an upward trend. In a rising-interest-rate environment, Brunswick's balance sheet would appear marginally more conservative with the preferred than with the debt issue. Perhaps the proposed exchange is an idea whose time has yet to come.

If class time permits, the instructor might broaden the discussion to consider whether exchanges such as this merit much senior management attention. Some students will argue that, in the context of expected 1984 earnings of $65.8 million and market value of equity of $115.4 million, the NPV of $1.3 million is trifling, and that this sort of financial entrepreneurship diverts senior managers from more worthy problems. Other students will respond that $1.3 million isn't bad for a few days' work, and that the real motivating consideration for the exchange is the pursuit of financial strategy: shedding the hung convertible preferred and positioning the firm to exploit debt tax shields as it returns to tax-paying status in the near term. In other words, nursing financial strategy is always worth senior management time. A class exchange such as this helps build a broad appreciation for the benefits and limitations of purely financial tactics.

Proceeds of debt offering from exchange	$36,576,000
Number of securities issued	2,032,000
Par value	$18.00
Date of issuance	September 1, 1984
Annual interest payment per bond	$2.56 payable semi-annually
Total Interest Payable	$5,201,920 payable semi-annually
Interest yield	14.25%
Conversion price	Convertible into 1.60 shares of common stock (equivalent to a conversion price of $11.25 per share of common stock)
Common stock price at time of issuance	$9.00
Conversion premium	25%
Sinking fund	None
Maturity	August 31, 2004

Notes:

Face value of preferred stock equals $63,500,000 (2,540,000 shares x $25 par value).

Market value of preferred stock equals $45,720,000 (2,540,000 shares x $18 market price).

Market value of preferred stock to be exchanged equals $36,576,000 (2,032,000 shares x $18 market price).

EXHIBIT B   Brunswick's Liabilities and Equity Showing the Effect of the Exchange
Offer (as of December 31, 1983)

	1983 Restated	1983 Actual
Total retail funds	$4,349,834	$4,349,834
Total wholesale funds	1,814,753	1,814,753
Loans in process	211,915	211,915
Advance payments by borrowers	39,094	39,094
Accounts payable etc.	122,983	122,983
Long-term debt		
14.25% conv. sub. debt.	36,576	0
Total liabilities	$6,575,155	$6,538,579
Stockholders' Equity:		
$2.20 conv. preferred stock	$ 50,000	$ $50,000
$2.10 conv. preferred stock	12,700	63,500
Common stock	132	132
Additional paid-in capital	27,869	27,869
Retained earnings	$ 128,730	114,506
Total stockholders' equity	$ 219,431	$ 256,007
Total liabilities and stockholders' equity	$6,794,586	$6,794,586

EXHIBIT C DCF Analysis of Incremental Cash Flows ($36.6 million of 14.25% debentures due 8/31/04
for 80% of $63.5 million redemption value of $2.10 preferred stock; dollars in thousands)

	(A)	(B)	(C)	(D)	(E)	(F)	(G)	(H)	(I)	
	Existing Preferred Stock				New Debt					
Period Ending	Preferred Dividends	Common Dividends	Total Cash Flow (A+B)	Trans. Costs	Pretax Interest	Tax Benefits	Preferred Dividends	Common Dividends	Total Cash Flow (E+F+G+H)	Net Cash Flow (C+D+I)
08/31/84				(1,016)						(1,016)
12/31/84	2,667		2,667		(1,737)		(533)		(2,271)	396
06/30/85	2,667		2,667		(2,606)		(533)		(3,139)	(472)
12/31/85	2,667		2,667		(2,606)		(533)		(3,139)	(472)
06/30/86	2,667		2,667		(1,303)	391	(533)	(569)	(2,014)	653
12/31/86	2,667		2,667				(533)	(1,300)	(1,834)	833
06/30/87	2,667		2,667				(533)	(1,300)	(1,834)	833
12/31/87	2,667		2,667				(533)	(1,496)	(2,029)	638
06/30/88	2,667		2,667				(533)	(1,528)	(2,061)	606
12/31/88	2,667		2,667				(533)	(1,723)	(2,257)	410
06/30/89	2,667		2,667				(533)	(1,788)	(2,322)	345
12/31/89		2,332	2,332					(2,417)	(2,417)	(85)
06/30/90		2,487	2,487					(2,578)	(2,578)	(91)
12/31/90		2,681	2,681					(2,780)	(2,780)	(98)

Net Present Value discounted at
5.85% per semi-annual period
(equal to a pre-tax annual rate
of 11.70%):   22,253   (1,016)   (19,977)   1,316

EXHIBIT C (continued)

Column Notes:

(A) Dividends are $2.10 per share per year. Conversion into common stock is assumed to take place in the second half of 1989.

(B) Preferred stock converts into 3,886,200 shares (1.53 x 2,540,000) of common stock. Common stock dividends are $1.15 per share in 1989 and $1.33 in 1990.

(D) Transaction costs are assumed to be $0.50 for each new debt security issued.

(E) Interest is payable semi-annually at 14.25% of principal value of $36.6 million; 50% of debt converts in the first half of 1986 and 50% in the second half.

(F) Marginal tax rate of 30%, with the company not paying taxes until 06/30/86.

(G) Dividends are $2.10 per share for the 508,000 shares that did not accept the exchange offer. These shares convert in 1989.

(H) The debt securities convert into 3,251,200 shares (1.60 x 2,032,000) of common stock. The 508,000 preferred shares convert in 1989. Common stock dividends are drawn form the forecast in case Exhibit 11.

Emerson Electric Company

SYNOPSIS AND OBJECTIVES

In the spring of 1987, the chief financial officer of this diversified electric products company is considering three alternatives for raising US$65 million in new debt capital: (1) a U.S. dollar issue in the domestic U.S. capital market, (2) an issue of Swiss franc-denominated Eurobonds, or (3) an issue of New Zealand dollar-denominated Eurobonds. Despite the high nominal coupon rate and the lack of any material business activity there, the New Zealand issue appears to create the most value for Emerson's shareholders.

This case may be used to introduce and exercise the theory of interest-rate parity and to explore the macroeconomic reasons why forward currency-exchange rates vary from spot rates. In addition, the case affords a useful vehicle for exploring the characteristics of Eurobonds and rationalizing the existence of the Eurobond market.

STUDY QUESTIONS

1. What are the costs of the NZ$, Swiss franc, and US$ debt issues?

2. What economic scenarios explain the changing forward exchange rates of US$ for NZ$ and SF?

3. Which issue should W. F. Bousquette choose? Do any qualitative factors influence your recommendation?

TEACHING PLAN

(15 minutes) Isn't the Kiwi issue, at a coupon of 18.55 percent, a "non-starter"? Isn't the Swiss franc issue, at 4.58 percent, a "no-brainer"?

(35 minutes) What is the US$ cost of the NZ$ and SF issues?
- Why do the costs change so dramatically?
- What do the forward rates suggest will happen to the NZ$ and SF relative to the US$?
- What would be Bousquette's "bet" if he issues either the NZ$ or SF bonds instead of US$ bonds?
- Do the economic expectations about NZ$ or SF support these "bets"?

(30 minutes) Why does the Eurobond market exist? Isn't plentiful debt capital available domestically?

The instructor can close the discussion with a presentation of the epilogue and some summary points about the Eurobond market.

Teaching note written by Robert F. Bruner. Copyright (c) 1989 by the Darden Graduate Business School Sponsors, Charlottesville, VA.

ANALYSIS

Cost of the Three Alternatives

One of the important learning points of the case is that exchange-rate movements implicit in forward exchange rates can affect the nominal coupon rate of a bond denominated in a foreign currency. The interest-rate parity theorem explains this; depending on the student and the amount of collateral reading assigned, the instructor might prepare notes for comments on parity.

To determine the cost in U.S. dollars of the Swiss and New Zealand issues requires that the cash flows of each of these issues be translated into US$ flows using the forward rates given in case Exhibit 7. One of the more frequent errors is to translate the future flows at the spot rate. Another, more subtle, error is to attempt to use the interest-rate-parity theorem equation to solve for the US$ interest rate; the parity theorem assumes we are dealing with pure discount bonds, which is not an appropriate assumption in this case.

With cash flows translated into US$, one can determine either the percentage cost (IRR) or net present value. In computing the NPV, the relevant discount rate is the cost of US$ debt, 8.65 percent.

Exhibit A presents the IRR and NPV calculations. The Swiss franc issue carries a cost of 8.79 percent versus a Kiwi dollar issue cost of 7.28 percent. At this point in a discussion, the instructor can emphasize that, to Emerson, the nominal coupon rates mean little; without knowing the schedule of forward exchange rates, one cannot say whether a coupon of 18.55 percent is a "non-starter." The Kiwi dollar issue has an NPV of +$1.48 million, while the Swiss franc issue has an NPV of -$.172 million. Barring other considerations, the Kiwi dollar issue is materially preferable to the alternatives.

Sources of Value

It is worth exploring with students the possible sources of value in the Kiwi issue. In a perfect and efficient capital market, there should be no profitable arbitrage opportunities. Yet if Bousquette can hedge his Kiwi exposure in the forward market, Emerson can arbitrage profitably.

At the time of this case, observers saw a "window of opportunity" for arbitrage in Australian and New Zealand dollar issues. This stemmed from widely differing expectations about the firmness with which both governments would respond to high rates of inflation. For instance, the Fisher-effect equation (which theorizes that the ratio of interest rates in two currencies must equal the ratio of expected inflation rates) or interest-rate parity predict that inflation expected in New Zealand over the next two years will average 15.4 percent.[1] Whether this high rate of inflation would persist over

---

[1] Under interest-rate parity, the ratio of forward and spot rates must equal the ratio of expected inflation rates. Therefore, we can solve for expected New Zealand inflation as follows:

$$E(1+i_{NZ})^2 = E(1+i_{US})^2 \times [Fwd.(NZ/US)/Spot(NZ/US)]$$

$$1.33 = (1.041)^2 \times [2.166/1.762]$$

The square root of 1.33 suggests an implied annual inflation rate of 15.4 percent.

the two years was the central question. There were many arguments as to why it would not. New Zealand had an inverted yield curve and expected negative real growth in gross national product. The authorities had recently de-controlled interest and exchange rates. The leftist Labour Party, the party in power, had expressed a strong commitment to fighting inflation.

A second possible explanation for the window of arbitrage opportunity was a supply-demand imbalance. American mutual fund investors had awakened to the possibilities of international investing, particularly through regional mutual funds oriented to the Pacific basin. These funds were looking for Kiwi-denominated issues to fill and balance their portfolios, and they appeared to bid more (i.e., accept a lower interest rate) than would be rationally implied by the forward exchange rates.

EPILOGUE

Emerson issued the Kiwi-denominated debt and immediately swapped it for floating-rate U.S. dollar obligations. The tombstones accompanying these transactions are given in Exhibit B.

EXHIBIT A Evaluation of Cash Flows for the Three Debt Alternatives

Year	0	.5	1	1.5	2	Semi-Annual IRR	Ann'l IRR
Swiss Franc-Debt Cash Flows							
In Sf	99.45	-2.28	-2.28	-2.28	-101.73	2.29%	4.58%
Exchange rate	1.53	1.51	1.47	1.44	1.41		
In US$	65.00	-1.51	-1.55	-1.58	-72.15	4.39%	8.79%
New Zealand Dollar-Debt Cash Flows							
In NZ$	114.53	-10.62	-10.62	-10.62	-127.21	9.27%	18.55%
Exchange rate	1.762	1.905	1.992	2.079	2.166		
In US$	65.00	-5.57	-5.33	-5.11	-57.78	3.64%	7.28%
U.S. Dollar-Debt Cash Flows							
In US$	65.00	-2.81	-2.81	-2.81	-67.81	4.33%	8.65%

Net Present Values of Cash Flows
(at a discount rate of 8.65%/2)

	Present Value	Net Present Value
SF	-65.1722	-.1722
NZ$	-63.52	+1.48
US$	-65.00	0.0

454

This announcement appears as a matter of record only.

Emerson Electric Co.

NZ$100,000,000/US$56,550,000

Two-Year Currency Swap

The undersigned acted as principal in this transaction.

Prudential-Bache Capital Funding

March 19, 1987

New Issue

NZ$100,000,000

Emerson Electric Co.

18.55% New Zealand Dollar Notes Due 1989

Price 100%
(plus accrued interest, if any, from March 25, 1987)

Copies of the Prospectus Supplement and the related Prospectus describing these securities and the business of the Company may be obtained from any of the undersigned in States in which such underwriters may legally offer these securities. This announcement is neither an offer to sell nor a solicitation of an offer to buy these securities. The offer is made only by the Prospectus Supplement and the related Prospectus.

Prudential-Bache Capital Funding

Bear, Stearns & Co. Inc.	The First Boston Corporation
Merrill Lynch Capital Markets	Morgan Stanley & Co. Incorporated
Salomon Brothers Inc	Shearson Lehman Brothers Inc.
The Nikko Securities Co. International Inc	Yamaichi International (America), Inc.
Newhard, Cook & Co. Incorporated	Stifel, Nicolaus & Company Incorporated

March 19, 1987

Merchants Cotton Company

OBJECTIVES

"Merchants Cotton Company" is specifically designed to introduce the
students to the analysis, evaluation, and hedging of foreign exchange risk
associated with the financing of a fixed asset in a foreign country. The
student is asked to evaluate financing issues within the context of both
quantitative and qualitative constraints imposed by management and to respond to
such issues by using such hedging tools as forward exchange contracts in
conjunction with a U.S. dollar-denominated loan, or a "natural hedge" such as a
loan denominated in the domestic currency (Australian dollar).
Specific objectives of the case include:

- Forcing students to evaluate and to take a position as to what amount of
  unhedged adverse exchange risk (if any) they would be willing to accept,
  based on historical movements seen in the Australian dollar relative to the
  U.S. dollar, and what cash-flow consequences to the project would be
  associated with the degree of risk that is accepted. Although this is
  largely accomplished through quantitative analysis of the effect of exchange
  rate movements on cash flow, the case also clearly emphasizes decision
  making through analysis of historical exchange rate movements.

- Encouraging students to approach the evaluation of foreign exchange risk
  using sensitivity analysis based on various ranges for the Australian dollar.

- Acclimating students to reading and interpreting graphical data illustrating
  currency movements, both with regard to the U.S. dollar on a "global" basis
  (case Exhibit 7) and the Australian dollar on a "country-specific" basis
  (case Exhibit 6).

- Familiarizing students with the trade-weighted U.S.dollar index (both spot
  and futures) as one of the most prevalent measures of strength or weakness
  in the U.S. dollar relative to other major currencies.

- Encouraging students to differentiate the effects of currency conversion on
  cash flow from the profit-and-loss effects of currency translation on
  accounting earnings.

- Encouraging students to recognize the importance of proper timing when
  actual conversion of currency takes place, especially with an unhedged
  foreign exchange position.

- Familiarizing students with the concept and use of forward exchange
  contracts (both short- and long-term) and the theoretical derivation thereof.

Teaching note prepared by Richard L. Fisher, M.S., CPA, a vice president and
managing director of Dunavant Enterprises, Inc. Copyright (c) 1989 by Richard
L. Fisher.

- Familiarizing students with the concept of interest-rate differentials between two countries and the resulting effect on the derivation of forward exchange rates.

SUGGESTED QUESTIONS FOR ADVANCE ASSIGNMENT

1. What amount of total Australian dollars would be required to service the U.S. dollar debt as initially proposed by California National (see case Exhibit 2)?

2. After the Australian-dollar debt service is deducted from the operational projections presented in case Exhibit 3, does the project meet management's quantitative criteria, assuming a constant level of 80.00 cents on the Australian dollar?

3. How much would the total Australian-dollar debt-service requirements over the five-year repayment period change if the Australian dollar weakened to a level of, say, 65.00 cents? Based on the conclusions drawn from analysis of a 65.00 cent Australian dollar, would the project, after debt service, continue to meet management's quantitative criteria?

4. How, if at all, would use of the indicative foreign exchange contracts detailed in Exhibit 4 of the case affect the total Australian-dollar cash-flow requirements for debt service over the five-year repayment period, and does the use of such contracts provide an adequate hedge for the project to meet management's quantitative criteria?

5. Based on the total Australian dollars required for debt service relative to the scenarios postured in questions 1-4, what amount of total Australian dollars would be required if, instead of borrowing U.S. dollars, Australia National's 14 percent Australian-dollar proposal were accepted?

TEACHING PLAN

The following questions should be explored at the discussion level:

- Is Simmons' preliminary assessment of the (seemingly) cost-effective nature of the California National 10 percent U.S.-dollar proposal realistic and comprehensive? Would pursuit of that course of action constitute a hedged or unhedged strategy relative to financing of the facility?

- How realistic are the foreign exchange assumptions inherent in Simmons' analysis of the California National proposal, as exhibited in column two and the footnotes to case Exhibit 2?

- Has Simmons adequately considered sensitivity analysis of any possible deviations from the 80.00 cent exchange rate used in his projections and how such deviations would affect the Australian dollar cash-flow requirements for debt service?

- With respect to historical changes seen in the Australian dollar, both over a four-year period (as indicated in case Exhibit 6), as well as in recent years (as exhibited in case Exhibit 7), what degree of possible downside movement in

the Australian dollar should management consider risking so as not to
jeopardize the quantitative viability of the project with regard to
management's expressed criteria?

- Is consideration of a level of, say, 65.00 cents on the Australian dollar at
  some point in the future reasonable based on historical movements in the
  Australian dollar exhibited in either of the graphs presented in case
  Exhibits 6 or 7?

- Based on a quantitative comparison of the Australian dollar cash flow
  required to repay the California National Loan using five-year forward
  exchange contracts, versus borrowing the funds exclusively in Australian
  dollars, is the theory of interest-rate parity consistent with a 4 percent
  interest-rate differential between the two countries?

- Even though debt-service payments are required only once a year, has Simmons
  given proper attention to the intrayear trading ranges previously
  experienced in the Australian dollar, and is he cognizant that a given debt
  service payment could fall due at the bottom of a given exchange rate cycle
  (even if the overall trend in exchange rates is acceptable)?

- If the Australia National Australian-dollar proposal is accepted, need any
  additional hedging strategies be considered with respect to the
  Australian-dollar loan?

- Even if management has firm feelings about the overall direction of the U.S.
  dollar over the next several years, should management be comfortable that
  the Australian dollar will necessarily move *inversely* to how the U.S. dollar
  moves relative to that global basket of currencies detailed in case Exhibit
  7? Have "expected" inverse movements (i.e., a rising Aussie when the U.S.
  is falling versus other currencies, and vice versa) been consistently
  exhibited, and how should any inconsistent movements of the U.S. dollar
  globally (as opposed to movement in a "country-specific" currency such as
  the Australian dollar) affect Simmons' evaluation of exchange rate risk?

ANALYSIS

Financial Parameters

Bill Simmons finds himself facing management that is strategically motivated
to purchase a cotton-ginning facility, but a project whose cash flow is
extremely sensitive from both foreign exchange and financing standpoints, based
on its projected operational cash-flow performance as presented in case Exhibit
3.

Simmons also finds himself faced with a project that is subject to very
sensitive quantitative constraints imposed by senior management, as per the
following: Australian-dollar cash flow before income taxes must be sufficient to
meet annual principal and interest payments, with a positive residual annual
Australian-dollar cash flow.

The California National proposal (U.S. dollars). Obviously, before the
financial aspects of the California National proposal can be properly evaluated,
the debt-service projections (in Australian dollars, taken from Exhibit 2 of the
case) must be combined with the pre-debt-service Australian-dollar cash-flow
projections presented in case Exhibit 3; a comprehensive pro forma prepared on

this basis appears as case Exhibit A; note that no withholding taxes need be taken into account, as case Exhibit 2 indicates that they are not applicable.

Exhibit A indicates that the facility's projected cash-flow performance will satisfy management's criteria, but students must be careful to note that the projected debt service detailed in case Exhibit 2 *assumes a continued level in the Australian dollar of 80.00 cents*, presumably on an indefinite basis. Although the case specifically allows for a hedge of short-term exchange rate risk through closing of the purchase in December (resulting in an effective 80.00 cent exchange rate as of December 31, 1988), the assumption of an 80.00 cent Australian dollar beyond December 1988 is a speculative assumption, and one that Simmons seems to take for granted (rather than a variable to which he should be sensitive from a risk standpoint).

Note, however, that if Simmons did not enter into the six-month forward contract, he would have immediate exchange rate exposure for the next six months through closing of the purchase. With a seller apparently firm on the A\$8,625,000 price, Merchants would be exposed to whatever amount of U.S. dollars it would take to convert (at the *then*, December 31, 1988 exchange rate) into A\$8,625,000 at closing; if he does not use the six-month forward contract, the purchase price in U.S. dollars could increase if the Australian dollar strengthens relative to the U.S. dollar during the July-to-December period.

Furthermore, what Simmons appears not to realize is that, by initially favoring fixed-rate financing in U.S. dollars, he is actually postulating an unhedged foreign exchange risk, even though he believes that having such financing available at a palatable rate (10 percent) minimizes financing risk. In reality, the overall financing risk is far from minimized, because any significant drop in the Australian dollar will cause the Australian facility's principal and interest payments to be substantially more costly (in Australian-dollar terms), as actual conversion of Australian dollars takes place when required debt-service payments are made to California National in U.S. dollars.

What is critical to realize is that additional Australian-dollar cash outflow (beyond what would be required in an 80.00 cent Australian-dollar environment) will take place in *any* Australian-dollar environment weaker than 80.00 cents, as Australian dollars are annually exchanged for U.S. dollars at then prevailing exchange rates (presumed, for the sake of illustration, in column 3 of Exhibit B to be based on a weaker, 65.00 cent, Australian dollar).

With a 65.00 cent Australian dollar, first-year *interest* payments alone will require more total Australian dollars (A\$1,061,539) than originally projected at a level of 80.00 cents (A\$862,500), so that at a conversion rate of 65.00 cents, the conversion will still yield the requisite \$690,000 to be paid to California National, which U.S. dollars must be paid to California National *irrespective of movements in the exchange rate*. The revised projected cash flows associated with a 65.00 cent Australian dollar scenario are detailed in Exhibit C.

The same applies with regard to the first year's principal payment, which will require a total of A\$2,123,077 in order to make the required \$1,380,000 payment. The excess Australian dollars required for the first year can be summarized as follows:

	Year-1 U.S. Dollars Required[1]	Assumed Exchange Rate	Equivalent Actual Australian Dollars Required	Per 80.00 Cent Pro Forma	Excess Australian Dollars Required
Principal	$1,380,000	.65	A$2,123,077	A$1,725,000	A$398,077
Interest	690,000	.65	1,061,539	862,500	199,039
	$2,070,000		A$3,184,616	A$2,587,500	A$597,116

[1]These amounts are required to be remitted to California National totally irrespective of changes in exchange rates. In other words, California National is expecting a fixed amount of U.S. dollars for principal and interest (based on its proposal), and the bank is not concerned if more (or less) Australian dollars are actually required to be exchanged in order to provide the requisite amount of U.S. dollars.

Obviously, the need for the incremental Australian dollars arises because, based on an assumed decline in its level to 65.00 cents, a given Australian dollar will "buy" less U.S. dollars upon conversion, which conversion is *required* annually in order to meet the requisite debt service to California National. This conversion will require the Australian facility to suffer additional direct decreases in its projected Australian-dollar cash flow (including an incremental A$398,077 for principal repayment), all only with respect to year 1. As the third column of Exhibit B indicates, the cumulative excess Australian dollars required at a 65.00 cent Australian dollar versus the 80.00 cent assumption used in Simmons's projection amounts to A$2,587,500.

At a level of 65.00 cents on the Australian dollar, the additional financing costs cause the pro forma to fall short of the criteria expressed by management (Exhibit C). Under such circumstances, the pre-debt-service cash flow of the facility is insufficient to provide enough Australian dollars, upon actual conversion, to make 100 percent of the debt-service payments required in U.S. dollars.

The question then becomes: can the Australian dollar trade lower, to a level of, say, 65.00 cents, over the course of the first year of operations and possibly be at that low a level at the time any given principal and interest payment comes due? The answer to that question is very possibly "yes." Based on the historical trading range of the Australian dollar since 1984, one would generally surmise that a return to a weaker Australian-dollar environment is equally or more likely to occur than a sustained or stronger dollar, given its current level of 81.50 cents (the Australian dollar had not been at a level of 80.00 cents or more since December of 1984—see Exhibit 6 of the case). Because of the sensitivity of the cash flows projected for the facility, Simmons must allow for a weaker Australian dollar, as a decline to a level below 71.50 cents in the first three years would generally cause the project to fall short of management's primary criteria (see the "Strategic Consideration and Focus" section of this analysis for a discussion of forward exchange rates and their relationship to "break-even" debt-service exchange rates). A decline to the Australian dollar's mid-1986 level of 60.00 cents would have even more dramatic negative effects.

In contrast to the exchange rate *weakness* that Simmons must consider from a risk standpoint, note that subsequent to June 1988, the Australian dollar actually *strengthened* substantially against the U.S. dollar. As Exhibit D indicates, the Australian dollar rose dramatically through the balance of 1988 and remained at not less than 84.00 to 85.00 cents through the fall; shortly thereafter, on February 2, 1989, it reached a new five-year high of 89.63 cents. Such movements obviously require a new evaluation of the risk of various financing alternatives, as well as consideration of the increased probability of a weaker Australian dollar as it rises (which probability generally increases the higher the level reached; note from case Exhibit 6 that the Australian dollar had not been as high as 85.00 cents since the last quarter of 1984).

Also interesting is the retracement in the Australian dollar that occurred unexpectedly in the spring of 1989 and generally continued at least through May of 1989, when it reached 75.00 cents (see Exhibit D). The student must realize that, without a hedge, unexpected retracements could also affect any loan payback year. It is imperative that students consider what degree of risk they would be willing to take with respect to a weaker dollar environment, and to quantify their decisions by evaluating the effect of various exchange movements on the projected cash flows, with or without the use of hedges. The reasonableness of projections and the underlying legitimacy of inherent assumptions must be questioned any time significant changes in key parameters (such as the level of the Australian dollar) occur.

The risk of a weaker Australian dollar, and its financial consequences, is the primary quantitative risk that must be evaluated with respect to the obvious strategic and/or financial benefits of purchasing and operating the ginning facility. Weakness in the Australian dollar became a reality in 1989 when it depreciated some 14.00 cents (or approximately 16 percent) relative to its high point of some 89.63 cents in the spring.

The instructor may want to distribute a copy of Exhibit D after the discussion to give students a tangible feel for subsequent exchange rate events.

The Australia National proposal (Australian dollars). The question also becomes: what can Simmons do, or what alternatives can be presented to management, to reduce exchange risk on the financing side? One alternative, to hedge the exchange risk "naturally," is to finance the facility in Australian dollars, thereby eliminating the need for conversion of Australian dollars into U.S. dollars as annual debt-service payments come due. Using this strategy, $8,625,000 would be borrowed from Australia National, would be converted into $6,900,000 U.S. dollars, and would be repaid to the parent company immediately subsequent to closing; with an 80.00 cent exchange rate locked in via the six-month forward contract, repayment of the $6,900,000 to the parent company would be assured within the budgeted Australian-dollar purchase price of A$8,625,000.

Note, however, that the use of Australian-dollar 14 percent fixed-rate financing would carry a premium in terms of gross Australian-dollar interest cost. Case Exhibit 5 illustrates that an approximate 3-4 percent non-inflation-adjusted interest-rate differential (Australian over U.S. rates) currently existed, and the rates quoted in the case seem to reinforce this phenomenon. Such a differential causes the interest component of the Australian-dollar financing to be at a premium to what would be experienced with the 10 percent U.S.-dollar financing (assuming a constant 80.00 cent Australian dollar).

The use of Australian-dollar financing would, however, eliminate future exchange risk on payments of principal and interest, as such amounts would be payable in Australian dollars in Australia over the five year period, and no conversion of debt service into U.S. dollars would be required on an annual basis (unlike with the California National proposal). The comprehensive cash-flow effects of the 14 percent Australian-dollar loan alternative are explored in Exhibit E: the revised statement of projected cash flows indicates that, on this basis, the project will also satisfy management's criteria.

With respect to the interest-rate differential, note that the spread between Australian and U.S. bond rates is presumably reasonably indicative of five-year interest-rate spreads, which have been as high as 7 percent historically; if the Australian-dollar funding option is chosen, "locking in" a 14 percent rate is probably a prudent idea, since the quoted interest-rate differential appears to be reasonable when viewed from an historical perspective.

Use of multi-year forward exchange contracts. This discussion and exhibits address Exhibit 4 in the case, which details forward-exchange contract levels under the assumption that the company accepts the California National U.S.-dollar proposal and locks in the indicated forward exchange rates over the five-year repayment period. The effective forward rates are detailed in the right-hand column of case Exhibit 4, and it is at these exchange rates that the company would be locked in to exchange Australian dollars for U.S. dollars in order to meet the required U.S.-dollar debt service, if the company accepts that proposal and chooses to use forward contracts as a hedge. Assuming that the bank is able to put the supply and demand sides of the rates together, the Australian subsidiary would be assured of being able to exchange Australian dollars for U.S. dollars at those quoted levels, thereby eliminating any risk of adverse movements in the Australian dollar. In other words, the company would have contracted the level of its foreign exchange conversion on a defined basis, if it were willing to accept the discounted levels in the Australian dollar reflected in such rates.

However, by accepting such discounts and locking in the rates, the company could very possibly be accepting too low a level on the Australian dollar, depending on where the exchange rate ultimately goes. As one can tell from Exhibit 4 of the case, accepting the fifth year rate of 65.32 assumes that the company would not want to speculate that the Australian dollar could be any cheaper than 65.32 cents at the end of the five-year period. Conversely, if the company believed strongly that the Australian dollar was going to stay at any given level *higher* than the discounts reflected in the forward rates for any future points in time, the company would not be making a financially preferable decision, because the net result of locking in the forwards could cost the company more Australian dollars (in terms of the total Australian dollars needed to fund the U.S.-dollar denominated debt service).

In any event, use of the forwards does eliminate speculation risk, and it allows the company to define the future Australian dollars that will be needed to service each U.S.-dollar debt-service payment, as the middle column of Exhibit F indicates. Notice that when the Australian-dollar equivalents are incorporated into the original statement of projected cash flows, as presented in Exhibit G, the resulting cash flows for the facility are still positive, indicating that the facility will meet management's quantitative requirements.

Interest-rate-parity theory would indicate that the interest-rate differentials between the two countries (presumably reflected in the forward rates) would ultimately eliminate any cash-flow differentials between the combination of a U.S.-dollar loan with the use of forward contracts and a pure Australian-dollar loan.

Notwithstanding, reference to Exhibits E and G indicates that, although the annual net cash-flow residuals are both positive and are approximately the same, they are not exactly the same; it is useful for students to realize that the foreign exchange forward markets are often not totally efficient, as one might think, particularly if especially cheap money is available in the U.S. currency or if an Australian bank is particularly aggressive when quoting its Australian-denominated loan, even if the interest-rate differentials reflected in the indicative forward rates are comparable and competitive from institution to institution.

Financing-alternatives summary. From a risk standpoint, the company must evaluate what is the most preferable policy on which it would desire to proceed. If it chooses U.S.-dollar denominated debt and makes no provision for use of the forwards (or any other hedge), then the company will be subject to the existing levels in the Australian dollar at whatever point debt-service payments come due and conversion of Australian dollars into U.S. dollars takes place. This approach can, of course, work to the advantage or disadvantage of the company depending on whether the Australian dollar strengthens or weakens from the 80.00 cent level Simmons used in his projections. As Exhibit C indicates, a level of 65.00 cents on the Australian dollar would be problematic as far as management's quantitative criteria, all other things being equal.

However, use of forward exchange contracts in conjunction with U.S.-dollar denominated debt allows the company to quantify its exposure, and the resulting cash flows, after debt service, will still fall within management's quantitative requirements. Obviously, a negative to the use of forwards is a certain inflexibility and the fact that the company can no longer participate in any upside movement or speculation in the Australian dollar; although the company will essentially be tied to a fixed amortization at specified levels in the Australian dollar, its risk will have been quantified.

The third alternative presented in the case is to finance the facility with Australian-denominated debt; this option still appears to satisfy management's quantitative criteria, and such a natural hedge also allows the company to avoid speculation as far as the foreign exchange risk goes, as the company's ultimate risk is also quantified, albeit in a different fashion. However, its interest cost can be more expensive.

The net result of all the alternatives is to give the company a smorgasbord of alternatives that can hedge or eliminate the speculative risk, while accentuating the primary point of the case: a U.S. dollar denominated loan, even at a reasonable interest rate, still leaves the company exposed with respect to foreign exchange risk if the level of the Australian dollar falls. Certainly a level of 65.00 cents places the project in a problematic posture with respect to management's expressed criteria, which is something management should evaluate when it makes a decision on how low a level in the Australian dollar it will consider accepting from a risk standpoint.

Case Parameters

Note that exchange rates are obviously not static, and it is somewhat unrealistic to assume that an exchange rate would continue at a level of 80.00 cents or immediately drop to a level of 65.00 cents. The accompanying exhibits are designed, realizing that averages in these ranges are by far the more likely scenarios, simply to provide a snapshot of the conversions that would be experienced should exchange rates at the time of conversion be at the 65.00 or 80.00 cent levels.

Note also that the presentation here focuses on the cash-flow effects of only the *financing payments*, which focus (as the case states) contemplates no current plans to convert and repatriate any Australian dollars (other than for U.S.-dollar denominated debt service) to U.S. destinations; although the case specifically stipulates that only U.S.-dollar debt-service payments are to be repatriated to U.S. destinations (assuming, of course, that a U.S.-dollar financing package is selected), at the instructor's discretion, conversion and repatriation of additional Australian dollars could be assumed in order to evaluate the facility as to net present value or internal rate of return. On such a basis, assumptions about residual value would be required, which assumptions can easily be combined with the projected cash flows from operations in 1993.

Finally, the case has been written with a bias toward students accepting the projection parameters for the gin operation as presented in case Exhibit 3, where the ginning revenue rates represent the top of the current market. The writer did not think any time should be spent analyzing expenses, but, should students wish to vary those projections to see what the effect on projected cash flow would be from increased gin revenues, etc., they could do so, even though such is not a focal point of the case.

Accounting Issues

The case does not take into account any issues relating to depreciation charges. The purpose was to focus students' concentration on currency-conversion and cash-flow issues rather than accounting profit or loss (which requires an evaluation of depreciation charges) or tax-affected earnings. Note, however, that one problem in international financial reporting relates to the fact that movements in the exchange rate (and the application of specific exchange rates as of a given date to a company's balance sheet and results of operations) can result in aberrations in the timing of reported accounting profits and losses. Depending on movements in exchange rates, such aberrations may reverse or continue over the course of the various financial-reporting periods.

For example, a decline in the Australian dollar from, say, a level of 70.00 cents to a level of 65.00 cents as of a given financial-statement year-end may result in a P&L effect based on the application of current financial-reporting standards. Subsequent to year-end, however, if the exchange rate recovered to the 70.00 cent level, and *no physical conversion* (a cash-flow concept) of actual currency had taken place at the weaker rate, no economic or cash-flow effect would have resulted, although temporary reported P&L effects may have.[2] The evaluation of such translation effects is not required here, because the objective of the case is to evaluate what happens to the *cash flow* of the project rather than to its reported profit and loss.

Finally, comprehensive translation of financial statements into U.S. dollars is not highlighted or required by the case so as to keep students' focus strictly on the foreign exchange and financing issues and the resulting cash-flow effects, while not confusing the calculations by requiring the application of FASB or other standards to the Australian-dollar financial statements.

Strategic Considerations and Focus

From a strategy standpoint, the case has deliberately been written to highlight certain fallacies in the way Simmons is approaching the decisions in

---

[2]The distinction is drawn between foreign exchange *translation* (for accounting purposes) in accordance with accounting-profession standards and foreign exchange *conversion*, which involves an actual exchange of currency and a resulting realization of a permanent cash-flow economic benefit or detriment relative to original projected cash-flow performance.

question. As pointed out in the case, Simmons seems somewhat predisposed to accept and/or ignore long-term exchange rate risk rather than attempting to quantify its potential downside and to minimize its risk. In this regard, the following strategic errors should be considered for class discussion:

1. Because Simmons obviously does not fully appreciate the overall risk of a weaker Australian dollar over the five-year financing period, he appears to favor the California National alternative, as it is seemingly cheaper and easier to administer. Also, because of Simmons' artificial level of comfort over retracement of the exchange rate to 80.00 cents by *and beyond* the end of the year (he really has no basis for such an assumption), it is somewhat unclear whether he will seriously consider the use of long-term forward exchange contracts as a potential hedge for the U.S.-dollar denominated alternative, even though he apparently is aggressive enough to solicit indicative quotes for the five-year repayment period. Clearly he should consider their applicability, regardless of his "uninformed" position on potential movements in the Australian dollar.

2. Even if Simmons chooses not to hedge the U.S.-dollar exchange risk adequately, he should probably make some attempt to quantify any effect on the additional cotton-merchandising profit opportunities potentially arising in a weaker Australian-dollar environment, much as might be management's primary focus of cost/benefit. For example, very simplistically, the additional cost in Australian dollars under the 65.00 cent-dollar scenario for the first year is A$597,116, which equates to approximately A$9 per bale when spread over the probable increase in merchandising volume (A$597,116/65,000 bales).

   In essence then, at a 65.00 cent Australian dollar, the increased financing costs can potentially eradicate a large portion, if not all, of the annual profit per bale that the company would hope to generate on the additional cotton to which its merchandising arm will likely have access through the gin (a per bale profit of A$8 to A$10 per bale would be a desirable margin on the merchandising side).

   This type of cost/benefit analysis, albeit rudimentary, and only addressing the first year, would allow Simmons to realize that his inattention to exchange rate risk could neutralize one of the most important strategic and potentially profitable aspects of the project--notably, the cotton-merchandising opportunities. Although the gin must "stand alone" financially, sensitivity to other implications surrounding the gin decision is important, especially in light of cotton merchandising being the primary business and focus of the company and its management.

3. Simmons also appears not to be cognizant that, even if he is correct on the long-term trend or level of exchange rates, the relatively inflexible required annual debt-service payments still expose him to adverse consequences resulting from the *timing* of any exchange rate movements, which might come at any specific conversion date for debt service; in other words, even if the trend in exchange rates prior to a specific transaction date were to be acceptable, he could "get caught" with an adverse movement on the specific date of a particular currency conversion.

4. The instructor might ask students if they have examined any "break-even" levels in Australian-dollar exchange rates, found by dividing the total U.S. dollars required in any given year for debt service (case Exhibit 2) by the

corresponding projected Australian-dollar "pretax cash flow before debt service" for the corresponding period of time (case Exhibit 3). These calculations yield the following break-even rates:

1989	69.87	(i.e., $2,070,000 ÷ A$2,962,500)
1990	71.16	(i.e., $1,932,000 ÷ A$2,715,000)
1991	70.28	etc.
1992	64.94	etc.
1993	59.53	etc.

Notice that as the amount of annual debt service amortizes in each year, the break-even scenario changes dramatically, even though operational projections do not vary that much over the five-year period. The break-even rate hovers near 70.00 cents in the first three years and relaxes to below 65.00 cents thereafter.

The level of these break-even rates provides an interesting comparison with the indicative forward rates specified for each year in case Exhibit 4; the break-even rates also provide an interesting backdrop against which to evaluate how much retracement in the current exchange rate would have to occur before a given debt-service break-even rate or an indicative forward rate would be reached. Again, it is very important for students to have to set their own parameters regarding the maximum limits on downside exchange movements at which they would be willing to gamble by not hedging, or by using forward contracts at given levels; their "bottom-line" exchange rates set the standard for evaluating other case parameters.

In summary, these issues indicate a somewhat fundamental lack of focus on Simmons' part and some naivete over where he should be concentrating his primary risk analysis—particularly in light of the fact that so many dramatic movements in the Australian dollar have recently been witnessed; equally unpredictable and severe movements in the near future could be very adverse to a project requiring significant annual debt service.

EXHIBIT A California National Proposal Projected Cash Flows: Australian Dollar at 80.00 Cents (for the calendar years ended December 31)

	1989	1990	1991	1992	1993	Five-Year Total
Cotton ginning revenues	A$ 3,500,000	A$ 3,500,000	A$ 3,500,000	A$ 3,500,000	A$ 3,500,000	A$ 17,500,000
Miscellaneous revenues	662,500	415,000	252,500	250,000	250,000	1,830,000
TOTAL REVENUES	A$ 4,162,500	A$ 3,915,000	A$ 3,752,500	A$ 3,750,000	A$ 3,750,000	A$ 19,330,000
Ginning expenses	1,200,000	1,200,000	1,200,000	1,200,000	1,200,000	6,000,000
Pretax cash flow before debt service	A$ 2,962,500	A$ 2,715,000	A$ 2,552,500	A$ 2,550,000	A$ 2,550,000	A$ 13,330,000
Interest expense*	(862,500)	(690,000)	(517,500)	(345,000)	(172,500)	(2,587,500)
Cash flow required to meet principal payments*	(1,725,000)	(1,725,000)	(1,725,000)	(1,725,000)	(1,725,000)	(8,625,000)
Residual pretax cash flow (deficit)	A$ 375,000	A$ 300,000	A$ 310,000	A$ 480,000	A$ 652,500	A$ 2,117,500

*Calculations assume that principal and interest payments reflect the Australian-dollar equivalents needed to fund the California National 10 percent proposal, at a constant Australian-dollar level of 80.00 cents. Principal and interest calculations taken from case Exhibit 2.

Conclusion: Results acceptable (residual pretax cash flows positive)

EXHIBIT B Analysis of Financing Costs If U.S. Dollars Are Borrowed from California National

Payment Due Date	U.S. Dollars Due to California National (Note 1)	Australian Dollars Required to Service U.S.-Dollar Debt at an Exchange Rate of	
		80.00 cents (Notes 5,6)	65.00 cents (Note 6)
12/31/89			
Principal	$1,380,000 (Notes 2,3)	A$ 1,725,000 (Note 3)	A$ 2,123,077 (Note 3)
Interest	690,000 (Note 4)	862,500	1,061,539
Total	$2,070,000	A$ 2,587,500	A$ 3,184,616
12/31/90			
Principal	$1,380,000	A$ 1,725,000	A$ 2,123,077
Interest	552,000	690,000	849,231
Total	$1,932,000	A$ 2,415,000	A$ 2,972,308
12/31/91			
Principal	$1,380,000	A$ 1,725,500	A$ 2,123,077
Interest	414,000	517,500	636,923
Total	$1,794,000	A$ 2,242,000	A$ 2,760,000
12/31/92			
Principal	$1,380,000	A$ 1,725,000	A$ 2,123,077
Interest	276,000	345,000	424,615
Total	$1,656,000	A$ 2,070,000	A$ 2,547,692
12/31/93			
Principal	$1,380,000	A$ 1,725,000	A$ 2,123,077
Interest	138,000	172,500	212,307
Total	$1,518,000	A$ 1,897,500	A$ 2,335,384
Total principal payments	$6,900,000	A$ 8,625,000	A$10,615,385
Total interest payments	2,070,000	2,587,500	3,184,615
Total payments over five years	$8,970,000	A$11,212,500	A$13,800,000
Greater (fewer) Australian dollars required based on deviations from exchange rate of 80.00 cents	N/Ap	A$ -0-	A$ 2,587,500

---

(1) All payments of principal and interest payable in U.S. dollars at a U.S. branch in San Francisco.

(2) Principal to be retired at a straight-line rate of 20% per year over a five-year period.

(3) For example, this calculation is made as follows for a 80.00 cent Australian dollar: Funds required are $1,380,000 U.S. dollars, which when divided by .80 results in A$1,725,000 Australian dollars being required. For a 65.00 cent Australian dollar, the required conversion would yield A$2,123,077. Comparable mechanics apply to all other conversions of U.S. dollars into Australian dollars.

(4) Calculated at a rate of 10% on the outstanding balance of the proposed debt to California National used to reimburse the parent company for bridge financing of $6,900,000 U.S. dollars.

(5) Rate of exchange assumed as of the date of permanent financing being drawn down on January 1, 1989.

(6) Assumes no use of forward exchange contracts during the loan repayment period.

Source: California National Bank financing proposal and Merchants Cotton Company internal analyses.

EXHIBIT C California National Proposal Projected Cash Flows: Australian Dollar at 65.00 Cents (for the calendar years ended December 31)

	1989	1990	1991	1992	1993	Five-Year Total
Cotton ginning revenues	A$ 3,500,000	A$ 3,500,000	A$ 3,500,000	A$ 3,500,000	A$ 3,500,000	A$ 17,500,000
Miscellaneous revenues	662,500	415,000	252,500	250,000	250,000	1,830,000
TOTAL REVENUES	A$ 4,162,500	A$ 3,915,000	A$ 3,752,500	A$ 3,750,000	A$ 3,750,000	A$ 19,330,000
Ginning expenses	1,200,000	1,200,000	1,200,000	1,200,000	1,200,000	6,000,000
Pretax cash flow before debt service	A$ 2,962,500	A$ 2,715,000	A$ 2,552,500	A$ 2,550,000	A$ 2,550,000	A$ 13,330,000
Interest expense*	(1,061,539)	(849,231)	(636,923)	(424,615)	(212,307)	(3,184,615)
Cash flow required to meet principal payments*	(2,123,077)	(2,123,077)	(2,123,077)	(2,123,077)	(2,123,077)	(10,615,385)
Residual pretax cash flow (deficit)	A$ (222,116)	A$ (257,308)	A$ (207,500)	A$ 2,308	A$ 214,616	A$ (470,000)

*Calculations assume that principal and interest payments reflect the Australian-dollar equivalents needed to fund the California National 10% proposal, at a constant Australian-dollar level of 65.00 cents. Principal and interest payments calculated in column three of Exhibit B.

Conclusion: Results unacceptable (certain residual pretax cash flows negative)

EXHIBIT D   Recent Movements in the U.S. Dollar Index* and the Australian Dollar**

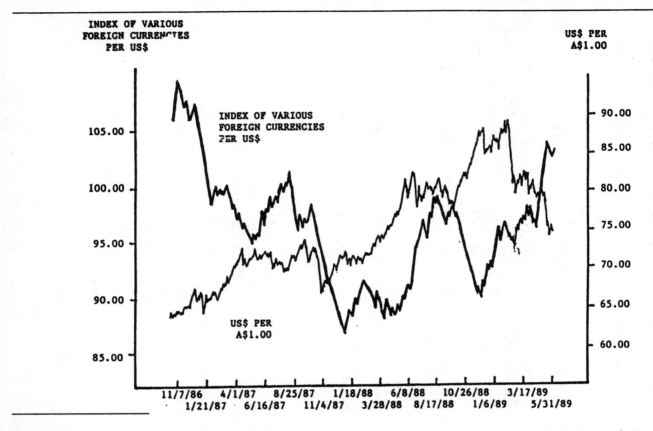

*Index represents the U.S. dollar measured against a trade-weighted index of ten other currencies, including those of (percentage weighting in the index): West Germany (mark, 20.8%), Japan (yen, 13.6%), France (franc, 13.1%), United Kingdom (pound, 11.9%), Canada (dollar, 9.1%), Italy (lira, 9.0%), Netherlands (guilder, 8.3%), Belgium (franc, 6.4%), Sweden (krona, 4.2%), and Switzerland (franc, 3.6%). An upward movement in the index signifies a strengthening U.S. dollar relative to the other currencies in the index.

This index reflects the spot (or cash) index for the described basket of currencies. A similarly structured futures index trades on the New York Stock Exchange's FINEX under the symbol "USDX"; on March 31, 1988, the futures index closed at 88.47 versus a cash-index close of 88.30 at that time.

Quotes for the U.S.-dollar futures contract and the spot index may be found in the Currency Trading section of the *Wall Street Journal*

**Scale of this graph varies slightly from that of case Exhibit 7.

Source: Knight-Ridder Financial Information Group.
        Copyright (c) Knight-Ridder Tradecenter.

EXHIBIT E Australia National Proposal Projected Cash Flows (for the calendar years ended December 31)

	1989	1990	1991	1992	1993	Five-Year Total
Cotton ginning revenues	A$ 3,500,000	A$ 3,500,000	A$ 3,500,000	A$ 3,500,000	A$ 3,500,000	A$ 17,500,000
Miscellaneous revenues	662,500	415,000	252,500	250,000	250,000	1,830,000
TOTAL REVENUES	A$ 4,162,500	A$ 3,915,000	A$ 3,752,500	A$ 3,750,000	A$ 3,750,000	A$ 19,330,000
Ginning expenses	1,200,000	1,200,000	1,200,000	1,200,000	1,200,000	6,000,000
Pretax cash flow before debt service	A$ 2,962,500	A$ 2,715,000	A$ 2,552,500	A$ 2,550,000	A$ 2,550,000	A$ 13,330,000
Interest expense*	(1,207,500)	(966,000)	(724,500)	(483,000)	(241,500)	(3,622,500)
Cash flow required to meet principal payments*	(1,725,000)	(1,725,000)	(1,725,000)	(1,725,000)	(1,725,000)	(8,625,000)
Residual pretax cash flow (deficit)	A$ 30,000	A$ 24,000	A$ 103,000	A$ 342,000	A$ 583,500	A$ 1,082,500

*Calculations assume that principal and interest payments reflect the Australian dollars needed to fund the Australia National 14% proposal. Principal and interest payments taken from Exhibit H.

Conclusion: Results acceptable (residual pretax cash flows positive)

EXHIBIT F Analysis of Financing Costs if U.S. dollars are borrowed from California National and Forward Contracts are used

Payment Due Date	Proposed U.S.- Dollar Debt Service	Australian Dollars Required to Service U.S.-Dollar Debt at Exchange Rates Specified for Forward Contracts	
		Australian Dollars	Forward Rates (case Exhibit 4)
12/31/89			
Principal	$1,380,000 (Notes 1,2,3)	A$ 1,794,072 (Note 3)	
Interest	690,000 (Notes 2,4)	897,036	
Total	$2,070,000	A$ 2,691,108	76.92 (Note 3)
12/31/90			
Principal	$1,380,000	A$ 1,869,412	
Interest	552,000	747,765	
Total	$1,932,000	A$ 2,617,177	73.82
12/31/91			
Principal	$1,380,000	A$ 1,940,383	
Interest	414,000	582,115	
Total	$1,794,000	A$ 2,522,498	71.12
12/31/92			
Principal	$1,380,000	A$ 2,025,837	
Interest	276,000	405,168	
Total	$1,656,000	A$ 2,431,005	68.12
12/31/93			
Principal	$1,380,000	A$ 2,112,676	
Interest	138,000	211,269	
Total	$1,518,000	A$ 2,323,945	65.32
Total principal payments	$6,900,000	A$ 9,742,380	
Total interest payments	2,070,000	2,843,353	
Total payments over five years	$8,970,000	A$12,585,733	
Greater (fewer) Australian dollars required based on deviations from constant exchange rate of 80.00 cents	NAp	A$1,373,233	

(1) Principal to be retired at a straight-line rate of 20% per year over a five-year period.

(2) All payments of principal and interest payable in U.S. dollars at a California National branch in San Francisco.

(3) For example, this calculation is made as follows for a 76.92 cent forward exchange rate: Funds required are $1,380,000 U.S. dollars, which when divided by .7692 results in A$1,794,072 Australian dollars being required. Comparable mechanics apply to all other conversions of U.S. dollars into Australian dollars, at the indicated forward exchange rates.

(4) Calculated at a rate of 10% on the outstanding balance of the proposed debt to California National used to reimburse the parent company for estimated bridge capital of $6,900,000 U.S. dollars.

Source: California National Bank financing proposal and Merchants Cotton Company internal analyses.

EXHIBIT G   California National Proposal Projected Cash Flows Using Five-Year Forward Exchange Contracts
(for the calendar years ended December 31)

	1989	1990	1991	1992	1993	Five-Year Total
Cotton ginning revenues	A$ 3,500,000	A$ 3,500,000	A$ 3,500,000	A$ 3,500,000	A$ 3,500,000	A$ 17,500,000
Miscellaneous revenues	662,500	415,000	252,500	250,000	250,000	1,830,000
TOTAL REVENUES	A$ 4,162,500	A$ 3,915,000	A$ 3,752,500	A$ 3,750,000	A$ 3,750,000	A$ 19,330,000
Ginning expenses	1,200,000	1,200,000	1,200,000	1,200,000	1,200,000	6,000,000
Pretax cash flow before debt service	A$ 2,962,500	A$ 2,715,000	A$ 2,552,500	A$ 2,550,000	A$ 2,550,000	A$ 13,330,000
Interest expense*	(897,036)	(747,765)	(582,115)	(405,168)	(211,269)	(2,843,353)
Cash flow required to meet principal payments*	(1,794,072)	(1,869,412)	(1,940,383)	(2,025,837)	(2,112,676)	(9,742,380)
Residual pretax cash flow (deficit)	A$ 271,392	A$ 97,823	A$ 30,002	A$ 118,995	A$ 226,055	A$ 744,267

*Calculations assume that principal and interest payments reflect the Australian-dollars
needed to fund the California National 10% proposal, assuming that five-year forward exchange
contracts are used. Principal and interest payments taken from middle column of Exhibit F.

Conclusion: Results acceptable (residual pretax cash flows positive)

Payment Due Date	Debt Service in Australian Dollars to Australia National at 14% Interest (Note 1)
12/31/89	
Principal	A$ 1,725,000 (Notes 1,2)
Interest	1,207,500 (Note 3)
Total	A$ 2,932,500
12/31/90	
Principal	A$ 1,725,000
Interest	966,000
Total	A$ 2,691,000
12/31/91	
Principal	A$ 1,725,000
Interest	724,500
Total	A$ 2,449,500
12/31/92	
Principal	A$ 1,725,000
Interest	483,000
Total	A$ 2,208,000
12/31/93	
Principal	A$ 1,725,000
Interest	241,500
Total	A$ 1,966,500
Total principal payments	A$ 8,625,000
Total interest payments	3,622,500
Total payments over five years	A$12,247,500

(1) All payments of principal and interest payable in Australian dollars at an Australian branch to be designated by Australia National. Debt service based on an A$8,625,000 loan, which is the Australian-dollar equivalent of $6,900,00 assuming the loan is made with the Australian dollar at an effective level of 80.00 cents, via use of the 6-month forward contract.

(2) Principal to be retired at a straight-line rate of 20% per year over a 5-year period.

(3) Calculated at a rate of 14% on the outstanding balance of the A$8,625,000 projected debt to Australia National used to reimburse the parent company for bridge capital of $6,900,000, assuming an effective Australian-dollar level of 80.00 cents when the funds are borrowed and converted in order to repay the parent company (see Note 1).

Gifford Bunsen & Company

SYNOPSIS AND OBJECTIVES

A director of research for a large, fixed-income portfolio management company must assess the potential returns and interest-rate risk associated with six investment alternatives. The case is intended to be an omnibus introduction to fixed-income investments. The instructor should consider allocating two class periods to a full discussion of it.

The case was developed to achieve the following objectives:

1. Exercise formulas and techniques in bond mathematics such as yield to maturity, yield curves, the relationship between forward and spot rates, and duration.

2. Introduce students to bonds and preferred stock as investment vehicles. In particular, one goal is to suggest the mechanics for pricing fixed-income securities (i.e., on the basis of expected yield, maturity, and risk).

3. Introduce the concept of interest-rate risk and the use of duration to measure that risk.

4. Develop students' knowledge of capital-market institutions and some of the decision processes by which money managers allocate capital.

STUDY QUESTIONS

1. Compute the yields to maturity and the duration of the four bonds. What are the duration and expected internal rate of return of the preferred stocks? Which offers the highest return? The lowest risk?

2. Graph the Treasury yield curves as of August 24, 1987, and November 2, 1987, using final maturity as the measure of time. Why did the yield curve shift? Was the shift proportional across all maturities?

3. Compare the prices of the 10.125s of February 1988 and the 9.875s of November 2015 on August 24 and November 2. Why were the price changes of the two bonds not the same? How can duration explain this effect?

4. Assuming the economists' interest-rate forecast comes true, what will the market value of the six potential investments be at the end of 1988? Which, if any, of these issues should Gifford Bunsen recommend to the two clients?

Teaching note written by Robert F. Bruner. Copyright (c) 1988 by the Darden Graduate Business School Sponsors, Charlottesville, VA.

TEACHING PLAN

The rationale for the following teaching outline is that the case calls for substantial figure work and a two-period commitment--a heavy burden without the motivation of the decision facing the manager in this case. Therefore, the first portion of the first class period is devoted to constructing a view of what pension managers do, how they make investment decisions, and the consequences to them of making poor decisions. With the setting in mind, the plan proceeds through the figure work and then obtains closure in the discussion of a possible recommendation by the students.

The following sequence of questions covers the main issues of the case within two class periods:

The First Period

(15 minutes) What is the problem in this case? What does Gifford Bunsen do? How have the six investment alternatives arisen? What are the clients looking for?

(40 minutes) What are the six investment alternatives? How do they compare on the basis of sinking fund, rating, coupon, yield to maturity, maturity, and duration? How does a "Pay-in-Kind" preferred work? How do you compute internal rate of return on a PIK?

(15 minutes) What is duration, and what does it tell us about these investments? How does the duration of an instrument vary as the following parameters vary: (1) maturity, (2) coupon (in dollars), (3) yield to maturity, (4) sinking fund, (5) total cash flow, and (6) par value?

The Second Period

(10 minutes) What is a yield curve? How has it varied over the past few months?

(25 minutes) Is a little shift of 1 percent in bond yields something you, as an investment manager, would lose sleep over? In what way can duration tell us whether a 1 percent shift in rates is material?

(25 minutes) How do the six investment alternatives compare on the basis of exposure to interest-rate change? Suppose the average forecast of the economists comes true; what will happen to the value of the six instruments?

(20 minutes) Which of the six instruments would you recommend that Gifford Bunsen's clients invest in? Why?

ANALYSIS

The Administrative Setting

In the course of developing the case discussion, the quantitative analysis should be motivated by laying out the administrative setting in which the decision-maker is working. The essential points are these:

- The protagonist is the director of research of the firm and is therefore required to "get the numbers right" as well as to make a wise recommendation. In this situation, simply reviewing either the qualitative or the quantitative aspects is insufficient.

- Two clients are demanding higher returns from their investment manager. The simple solution would be to give them the returns they ask for by ignoring risk considerations, but this response is neither ethical nor professional. The situation calls for wise judgment rather than quick action.

- The consequences of making a bad recommendation are probably the loss of clients and, more importantly, the loss of reputation.

In short, considerable pressure on the director of research is implied by the setting. Careful quantitative analysis is imperative.

Assessment of Returns

Given that returns figure so prominently in the recommendation, it is worthwhile to work carefully through the yields to maturity of the bonds and the internal rates of return (IRRs) on the preferred PIKs (assuming they are redeemed in 1991). Simple analysis of the cash flows reveals the yields to maturity to be 14.1 percent (Athlone), 13.37 percent (Conair), 15.7 percent (Ramada), and 18.2 percent (Turner).

The IRRs on the PIK preferreds can be computed straightforwardly from the cash flows given in the case, although a review of how those cash flows were estimated may be helpful. In essence, each year's dividend is assumed to be a constant percentage of the par value of PIK preferreds outstanding at the beginning of the period. The value accumulates until the assumed redemption date, when the original preferred shares are redeemed for $25 each, and the dividend shares are redeemed for accumulated value. The cash-flow analysis in Exhibit A reveals that the Fruehauf issue has a geometric IRR of 56.13 percent and the SPI issue an IRR of 28.13 percent. Students may ask why we should not use the simple annual IRRs as shown in Exhibit A; one would be indifferent as long as one is comparing them to other simple IRRs. Another question that arises in whether we should not focus on the "pays in cash" case. The answer to this is that, since it is cheaper for SPI and Fruehauf to pay in kind, the cash alternative is not realistic. In light of these extraordinarily high returns, dwelling on the implicit risks may be worthwhile.

Duration Analysis of the Alternatives

The purpose of including a duration aspect to this case is to impress on students the superiority of duration (as opposed to final maturity) as a measure of economic exposure. Assuming this case to be the students' first exposure to the concept of duration, the instructor should be prepared to walk through the mechanics of computing duration.

One way to enhance an intuitive grasp of duration is to show that the duration of a zero-coupon bond (e.g., the Conair issue) is equal to its term to maturity. Then one can address the duration of the two preferred issues and show that they are equivalent, in profile of cash flows, to a zero-coupon bond (assuming all dividends are paid in kind). Discussion of the zero-coupon case dispatches three of the six investment alternatives.

479

As for the other three, Exhibit B shows durations of 2.98 years for Ramada, 3.53 years for Athlone, and 4.23 years for Turner. One way of probing the students' grasp of durations is to ask why the duration of the issues vary; the reply should cite the differences in coupon and amortization.

Yield–Curve Shifts and Duration

Yield curves for the two dates in question can be plotted directly from case Exhibit 6. Exhibit C presents the plots and shows that, superficially at least, the yield curve has shifted little. Closer inspection shows, however, that rates in the four–year (duration) range have apparently risen about 50 basis points. At durations of four years (and required rates of 14.5 percent), a 1 percent change in interest rates produces a 3.5 percent change in the value of bonds. A 35–basis–point shift will change value by about 1.22 percent, a seemingly small figure but large if it means the difference between mediocre and good investment performance. With grumpy clients, Gifford Bunsen may care greatly about such small margins of performance.

This yield–curve analysis illustrates the interpretation of duration as an elasticity. An alternative route to this insight is to consider the economists' interest-rate forecasts given in case Exhibit 7. Long-term rates will apparently fluctuate down and then up again by 50 basis points over the next year, which naturally invites a discussion of how Bunsen might exploit these swings on behalf of its clients. (The solution would be to take long-duration positions while rates are falling and short-duration positions while rates are rising.)

Recommendation

Ultimately, the decision rests on a careful tradeoff of returns, on the one hand, and two types of risk, on the other: (1) market or interest-rate risk and (2) credit or default risk. Market risk is summarized by the duration of the instruments. Default risk is summarized by the credit ratings of the instruments. Plainly, the attractiveness of the high–return PIK preferreds is offset by the higher likelihood of default and by the other possibility, early redemption. Students tend to reject the PIKs because of these risks. The decision as to which bond(s) to recommend will tend to divide the class into the somewhat more aggressive and the less aggressive students, which can be resolved by a vote.

EXHIBIT A Internal Rates of Return on PIKs

		SPI PIK		FRUEHAUF PIK	
		Pays in Cash	Pays in Kind	Pays in Cash	Pays in Kind
Cash flows at quarter =	0	−17.375	−17.375*	−7.5	−7.5*
	1	1	0	0.92	0
	2	1	0	0.92	0
	3	1	0	0.92	0
	4	1	0	0.92	0
	5	1	0	0.92	0
	6	1	0	0.92	0
	7	1	0	0.92	0
	8	1	0	0.92	0
	9	1	0	0.92	0
	10	1	0	0.92	0
	11	1	0	0.92	0
	12	1	0	0.92	0
	13	1	0	0.92	0
	14	1	0	0.92	0
	15	1	0	0.92	0
	16	26	46.82453**	25.92	44.57176**
Quarterly IRR		7.29%	6.39%	16.07%	11.78%
Geometric IRR		32.51%	28.13%†	81.51%	56.13%†
Simple annual IRR		29.16%	25.57%††	64.29%	47.13%††

---

*Initial outflow is equal to the market value per share.

**Final inflow for the "Pay-in-Cash" alternatives is equal to the redemption value per share ($25.00) plus the dividend for that quarter. Final inflow for the "Pay-in-Kind" alternatives is equal to ($25 x $(1.04)^{16}$ − 1) for SPI and ($25 x $(1.0368)^{16}$ − 1) for the Fruehauf issue. Note that this assumes the PIK will pay a steady percentage dividend on par value (not market value).

†Equal to $(1 + \text{Quarterly IRR})^4$ − 1.

††Equal to (4 x Quarterly IRR).

EXHIBIT B   Duration Calculations (assumed annual required rate of return is 14.50%)

		Years	Athlone		Ramada		Turner	
			Cash		Cash		Cash	
Year	Period	Elapsed	Flow	TPV*	Flow	TPV*	Flow	TPV*
1988	1	0.5	0.198	0.092	3.352	1.563	7	3.263
1988	2	1.0	0.559	0.486	13.352	11.608	7	6.086
1989	3	1.5	0.179	0.218	2.852	3.468	7	8.511
1989	4	2.0	0.504	0.762	12.852	19.427	7	10.581
1990	5	2.5	0.161	0.284	2.352	4.144	7	12.333
1990	6	3.0	0.453	0.893	12.352	24.349	7	13.799
1991	7	3.5	0.145	0.311	1.852	3.971	7	15.010
1991	8	4.0	0.408	0.932	11.852	27.082	7	15.995
1992	9	4.5	0.130	0.312	1.352	3.241	7	16.778
1992	10	5.0	0.367	0.911	11.352	28.188	7	17.827
1993	11	5.5	0.117	0.298	0.852	2.170	7	17.827
1993	12	6.0	2.248	5.823	17.899	46.367	107	277.184
Present value			3.206		58.918		98.0405	
Sum				11.322		175.577		414.748
Duration				3.532		2.980		4.230

*T = years elapsed; PV = present value.

EXHIBIT C   Treasury Yield Curves, August and November, 1987

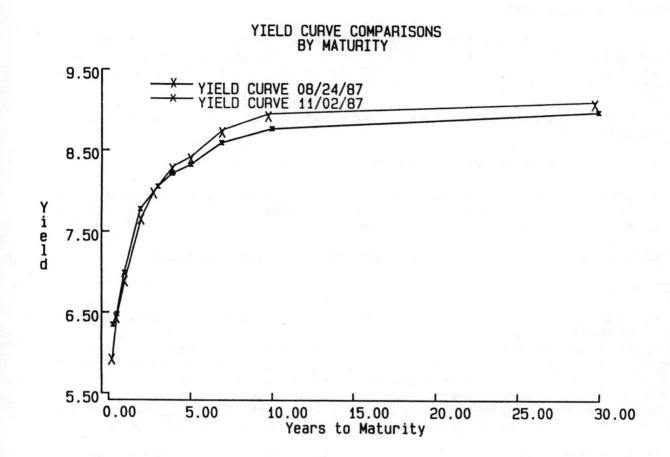

Boston Celtics Limited Partnership

SYNOPSIS AND OBJECTIVES

This case requires the student to analyze a partnership-based corporate restructuring. The analytical tasks are to assess the appropriateness of the transaction, to value it, and to identify the underlying source of value. Case objectives include:

• describing the partnership form of organization and contrasting it with the corporate form;

• introducing an agency explanation for partnership restructurings;

• identifying the economic features of targets of Master Limited Partnerships (MLP) restructurings and the cash-flow consequences of the MLP both for the parent company and for the outside investor;

• determining the allocation of the potential restructuring benefits.

STUDY QUESTIONS

A useful review of the economics of MLPs is found in J. M. Collins and R. P. Bey, "The Master Limited Partnership: An Alternative to the Corporation," *Financial Management*, Winter 1986, pp. 5-14. Also see J. W. Kensinger and J. D. Martin, "Royalty Trusts, Master Partnerships, and Other Organizational Means of "Unfirming" the Firm," *Midland Corporate Finance Journal*, Summer 1986, pp. 72-79. If the instructor chooses to emphasize the agency aspects in the case discussion, Michael Jensen's "Agency Costs of Free Cash Flow, Corporate Finance, and Takeovers," *American Economic Review*, May 1986, pp. 323-29 may also be assigned.

Students should be reminded that, before 1987, the maximum corporate income tax rate was .46, the maximum personal income tax rate was .50, and the capital gains tax rate was .21. Beginning in 1987, the maximum rates would be .28 and .34 for persons and corporations, respectively (the schedules did not differentiate between income and capital gains).

1. What is a Master Limited Partnership, and how does it differ from a corporation?

2. Please evaluate the Boston Celtics limited partnership proposal.

    • Does this company fit the profile of a candidate for MLP restructuring?

    • Why would Don Gaston, Paul Dupee, and Alan Cohen seek to restructure the company in this fashion? What are the benefits to them?

Teaching note written by Robert F. Bruner. Copyright (c) 1987 by the Darden Graduate Business School Sponsors, Charlottesville, VA.

- Will investors buy these units at the proposed offering price? On what critical economic factors does the attractiveness of this investment depend?

3. What, if anything, creates value in this restructuring?

TEACHING PLAN

This case poses a strong pedagogical challenge. Given the dynamic nature of the tax code, to pitch this as a tax case would be a mistake. Although the tax effects are dominant and must be addressed, the tax code will continue to change in specific ways, while the basic economic insights afforded by studying the economics of partnerships probably will not change. Therefore, the author suggests that the instructor focus on the basic economic logic of the proposal and the motives of the real managers.

The assignment questions form a useful outline for the class discussion. The discussion can be closed with a brief presentation of the epilogue.

ANALYSIS

Is it a Logical Candidate?

Breakeven test of tax efficiency. The profile of the ideal target for MLP restructuring includes high profitability, low reinvestment rates, high marginal corporate tax rates, and/or low marginal personal tax rates among the equity clientele. These criteria can be summarized in terms of a formula[1] indicating the conditions under which cash flows to shareholders in an MLP will be larger than those in a corporation:

$$\frac{\text{Cash reinvested (CR)}}{\text{Earnings before tax (EBT)}} < \frac{t_c \, (1 - t_p)}{t_p}$$

where t_c is the marginal corporate tax rate, and t_p is the marginal personal tax rate on ordinary income.

For the Boston Celtics, cash reinvested/earnings before taxes was 0.01 and the marginal-rates formula yielded a figure of 0.874. For the Boston Celtics, one could argue that CR/EBT will be nil, because it is a service business and there are no long-lived physical assets. For the sake of detail, however, one can note that the statement of cash flow shows purchases of equipment and improvements amounting to $63,877 in 1986, against pretax income in that year of $4,830,993. One would conclude that the franchise is a sensible candidate; the low rate of reinvestment relative to profits for the firm is consistent with the profile of a partnership candidate.

The setting for the Boston Celtics includes the team's remarkably successful record and the open window for initial public offerings (IPOs) in the capital markets. This restructuring is motivated by capital-market opportunity rather than product-market strategy.

---

[1] This test was presented in Collins and Bey's article.

Risks. The attractivness of the deal to investors depends importantly on there being no adverse changes in the tax code. As the breakeven analysis suggested, decreases in the corporate tax rate, increases in the personal tax rate, and changes in allowances for noncash charges (depreciation, amortization, and depletion) would reduce the attractiveness of a partnership/trust restructuring in comparison with leaving those assets in a corporation.

The attractiveness of the Boston Celtics deal depends on a continuation of the team's winning performance. The returns to investors are not "sure things." A cynical interpretation of the timing of the restructuring is that it represents an exit by the investors at the market top, but this view is inconsistent with the continuing large holdings by Gaston, DuPee, and Cohen in the Celtics.

Insiders' Evaluation

The assignment question asks the students to evaluate the Boston Celtics deal from the standpoint of the insiders—Gaston, DuPee, and Cohen. Exhibit A presents an estimate of the increase in the insiders' wealth as a result of this restructuring. Based on some simple assumptions, the value of insiders' wealth increases by about half.

The exhibit's columnar comparison of a subchapter-S corporation versus a limited partnership lends some insight into the sources of increase in value. The management fee proves to be a material source of value, but the bulk of new value derives from the valuation of the basic cash flows in the market. The fact that the same cash flow is worth more to outsiders than insiders may reflect the unusual franchise of the Celtics and the desire of fans to own a piece of the team. In addition, it reflects the general appetite of the stock market for IPOs.

Finally, the increase in value of the holdings could reflect the increase in tax shields as a result of the restructuring. The case says that the transaction would increase the cost basis of amortizable assets—particularly the franchise, player contracts, and broadcasting contracts. The cost basis will be equal to the value of assets contributed by the insiders ($19 million) plus the purchase price paid by the public to acquire the units ($48.1 million), or $67.1 million. If all of this money is allocated to amortizable assets, the transaction would at least quadruple the size of the tax shield.

Valuing the Units

The unit offering price was $18.50. The expected dividend in the next 12 months was $1.95. To the dividend should be added the pretax value of the tax shield. For conservatism, one could assume that deductible expenses flowing to investors would equal the franchise amortization charge in 1986 of $3.086 million (or $.48 per unit). The pretax equivalent of the dividend and tax shield will be $2.137 per unit.[2] Assuming a 5 percent growth rate and a 15 percent cost of equity, the unit will be worth (according to the dividend-growth model) $21.37.

---

[2]The calculation involves computing the after-personal-tax cash flow per unit and then grossing up that flow to a pretax equivalent. In other words, $[(1.95(1-.28) +.48 \times .28]/(1-.28)$.

Because the amortization shield will probably be much higher, the price at first glance seems attractive. The amortization tax shield and the growth rate of the cash flows, however, remain quite uncertain. In fact, the latter may be close to zero or even negative if the team's fortunes wane. In the history of professional sports, teams tend to go through life cycles: a period of growth followed by league leadership and then by atrophy. That the team's winning streak can be maintained forever seems inconceivable . Assuming zero growth, the capitalized value of pretax equivalent cash flows is $14.25. Cast in this light, the offering is rather richly priced at $18.50.

EPILOGUE

The restructuring occurred as proposed. The price of Boston Celtics units fell steadily in the nine weeks after the offering (see Exhibit B). The team did not make it into the championship finals that year (one factor being the loss of Bill Walton, the team's center, as a result of ankle surgery). At least one skeptical analyst claimed that the units sold only because they were bought by fans—an unusual equity clientele.

Effect of the Boston Celtics Reorganization on Gaston, DuPee, and
Cohen (in millions)

Item	Sub.-S Corp.	Limited Partnership	Notes
Set-up costs	0	($2.734)	1
Recapture tax	0	0	2
Capital-gains tax	0	0	2
Present value mgt. fee	0	8.360	3
Value of securities	$ 50.00	72.150	4
			Change
Total	$ 50.00	$77.776	$27.776

Notes:

1. Equal to the insiders' share (60%) times total setup costs of $4.549.

2. Since Gaston, DuPee, and Cohen will receive securities in exchange for their interest in the franchise, there is no immediate tax liability. For simplicity, this analysis assumes that the securities are held in perpetuity. If the instructor chooses to drill the students in the mechanics of calculating capital gains and recapture taxes, the following would be the calculation for the limited partership:

Capital Gains Tax		Recapture Tax	
Sold for	$72.150 (= .6 x $120.25)	Amort. and	
Bought for	$15.000	depreciation	$6.200
Gain	$57.150	Tax rate	.500
Tax rate	.210	Tax	$3.100
Tax	$12.002		

In essence, Gaston, DuPee, and Cohen deferred personal tax expense of about $15 million by structuring the transaction as an exchange rather than a cash sale.

3. Annual fees in the first year will be $.75 plus 1 percent of cash flows (or $.836). This figure was capitalized at 15% less a 5% growth rate to get a present value of $8.36 million.

4. The value of the interest in the limited partnership is .6 x $120.25 (the value of the firm implicit in the offering). The value of the subchapter-S corporation is assumed to be equal to the 1986 net cash flows from operating activities, about $7.5 million, capitalized at 15 percent. This latter estimate assumes no growth (the team is at its peak) and no amortization of debt.

EXHIBIT B Unit Prices of Boston Celtics Limited Partnership

Date	Boston Celtics	S&P 500
12/01/86	--	$249.05
12/04/86	$18.375	253.04
12/12/86	17.250	247.35
12/19/86	16.000	249.73
12/26/86	16.000	246.92
01/05/87	15.750	252.19
01/12/87	15.375	260.30
01/19/87	15.750	269.34
01/26/87	14.750	269.61
02/02/87	14.750	276.45
03/31/87	14.250	291.70
06/30/87	13.250	304.00
09/30/87	13.125	321.83
12/31/87	11.500	247.08
03/31/88	13.125	258.89
06/30/88	$13.000	$273.50

Societe Generale de Belgique (A)

SYNOPSIS AND OBJECTIVES

This case places the student midway through a bidding contest for control of this Belgian holding company in 1988. The student is asked to consider whether and how a large French holding company, Companie Financiere de Suez ("Suez"), should enter the bidding. To resolve this issue, the student is required to sort out the complicated situation, assess the motives of the various players, evaluate various share prices, and develop a bidding strategy for Suez.

The purpose of the case is to develop a broad perspective on hostile takeovers, rather than a detailed quantitative analysis. In contrast to American takeovers, the hostile takeover in Europe is less fettered by disclosure requirements, waiting periods, and fair-price rules. Therefore, a case such as this provides a more pure view of the dynamics of an auction for corporate control than a U.S. situation. The tale of Societe Generale de Belgique (SGB) is also noteworthy as the first large intra-Europe hostile takeover attempt.

As an issues case, "Societe Generale" complements "Brown-Forman Distillers Corporation" (Case 22) and "Hybritech, Inc." (A)/"Eli Lilly and Company" (Cases 47 and 51), which require detailed quantitative analysis. This case also complements "Walt Disney Productions, June 1984" (Case 1), a hostile takeover set in the United States.

STUDY QUESTIONS

1. What is the situation that Suez faces on February 3? How did it develop? Who are the various players? What are their goals?

2. Suppose that Societe Generale is worth 87.5 billion Belgian francs. Would bidding upwards of 4,000 BeF per share be rational? Under what circumstances?

3. What should Suez do?

TEACHING PLAN

(30 minutes) Who is Suez and what is its problem? I favor a directive opening such as this in order to focus the discussion initially on sorting out the situation. Supporting questions should develop the perspectives of De Benedetti, Leyson, and the *noyau dur* (hard core) group.

(20 minutes) Why is SGB under attack? Here, the discussion should turn to SGB's underperformance, the environmental pressures, and the strategic motives of the players.

(30 minutes) Should Suez bid for SGB? At what price? Students need to perceive the difference between marginal and average values, to distinguish

---

Teaching note written by Robert F. Bruner. Copyright (c) 1988 by the Darden Graduate Business School Sponsors, Charlottesville, VA.

among the various degrees of control, and to anticipate the outcomes of various scenarios.

One way to close the class discussion would be to distribute the (B) case (Case 49) which describes the outcome of the bidding. The epilogue contained in this note summarizes events since the completion of the takeover. Either ending can be used to stimulate a summary discussion of the dynamics of hostile takeovers and their effects.

ANALYSIS

Motives for the Takeover

At first glance, SGB's story would seem an incongruous beginning to the wave of European hostile takeovers. The firm is a hodge-podge of interests in financial, industrial, and service firms. Belgium, its headquarters country, is a relatively small component of the European Economic Community. The firm itself manifestly does not want to be taken over: it has barricaded itself with a hard core of equity-holders, presumably committed to defending the firm to the last.

Closer inspection of the situation, however, suggests several attractions to a raider. First, the firm is huge. Although Belgium is diminutive, SGB accounts for about 30 percent of its gross national product, which probably ranks the firm among the more significant in Europe.

Second, the firm is underperforming and is ripe for restructuring. The nickname "old lady" is evocative of these facts. Its recent annual returns on equity of 5.5, 8.2, and 3.9 percent were well below the average industry returns of 12 percent for that period and the risk-adjusted return of 10.54 percent[1] computed from the capital-asset-pricing model.

Third, there may easily be hidden values in SGB or opportunities to eliminate managerial inefficiencies. The nickname "octopus" is consistent with SGB's many investment interests diagrammed in case Exhibit 3. Some of the investments are beyond the borders of Belgium (e.g., Suez). Some are indirect holdings; some are unconsolidated. The many acronymns make it difficult to tell just what the investments are. To the uninitiated observer, SGB is virtually opaque. A setting like this could contain many information asymmetries, yielding significant gains to the diligent analyst. That there are such hidden values is suggested by the estimate of Dewaay that SGB is worth 87.5 billion BeF, or 3,108 BeF per share, a 38 percent premium over the price of 2,250 that prevailed two weeks before De Benedetti announced his bid.

The case suggests that De Benedetti might be able to sell one-third of SGB's assets at book value and earn a return on equity of 12 percent on the remaining two-thirds. This suggests sale proceeds of 30.3 billion BeF in the near future. Some portion of this could be dividended to shareholders. Exhibit A presents the analysis. Keeping the capital structure in constant proportion (with debt/equity equal to .357) by repaying liabilities would result in an extraordinary dividend of 22.32 billion BeF. The resulting book equity would be 45.236 billion BeF. If SGB earned 12 percent, the cash flow would be 5.428 billion BeF. Capitalizing this at the firm's cost of equity, 10.5 percent, less

---

[1]Case Exhibit 6 indicates a Belgian equity-market risk premium of 4 percent and a beta of .597 for SGB. Case Exhibit 9 gives a long-term Belgian government bond yield of 8.15 percent.

a growth rate just marginally above the rate of inflation, 6.4 percent,[2] results in a value of equity of 65.32 billion BeF.

In sum, this rough calculation suggests that SGB could be restructured to deliver a value of about 5,494 BeF per share to current shareholders. This estimate ignores any other benefits, such as from strategic synergies between Olivetti and SGB or Suez and SGB, and from possible capital-structure changes. It also ignores changes in the firm's risk profile that might cause a change in cost of equity. In any event, the potential benefit from restructuring is likely to be large.

A fourth potential motive for the raid would be to exploit a temporary depression in the price of the firm's shares following the market crash the previous October. This motive presumes the existence of a market inefficiency, which is difficult to accept for a firm whose shares are so significant in the Belgian stock market.

Finally, SGB may have a far higher value in post-1992 Europe, where cross-border trade and management will be easier, than it does in the current environment. This value can only be considered in qualitative terms, for it is unclear what the magnitude of the benefits will be. However the 1992 issue raises an important strategic issue of positioning: a raider could desire to obtain a strong commercial stance in Belgium and, in the process, pre-empt a competitor from exploiting that opportunity. This issue proved to be highly relevant in the SGB takeover conflict and continues to be significant in the ensuing merger wave in Europe.

Control and Efficacy of SGB's Defenses

There are at least two levels at which a raider might be thought to have some control over SBG: (1) owning 25 percent of shares, at which the raider can block the raising of capital and prevent any changes in the company's structure, and (2) owning 50 percent, which allows the raider to assume absolute control and wield day-to-day management authority.

SGB management sought to defend its control by two means. First, in October 1987, it undertook several transactions that would have the effect of actually or potentially diluting a raider. Specifically, it issued 1.5 million shares (at a price of 3,942 BeF each).[3] It also issued bonds with warrants (exercise price unknown) and sold shares in a rights offering at 3,350 each. Another 16 million shares were authorized but not issued, forming a huge (57 percent of currently outstanding shares) implicit Poison Pill for a raider, because management could choose to issue these shares at will. Second, management formed a *noyau dur* of loyal shareholders equal to 25 percent of shares.

---

[2]This note is the lowest money-market rate of return for Belgium in January 1988, given in case Exhibit 9. It is assumd to represent the expected rate of inflation plus a small risk premium.

[3]Whoever bought these shares must have been a friend indeed. In the month and a half following the crash, SGB's share price hovered around 2,200 BeF.

With the defection of De Benedetti and Dumenil Leble, SBG's *noyau dur* declined to 19.5 percent.[4] Indeed, at the time of De Benedetti's surprise announcement over dinner, the voting strength of raider and target were approximately equal: 18.6 percent versus 19.5 percent. From case Exhibit 2, which lists major institutional holdings in SGB, one infers that the balance of SGB's shares, about 61.1 percent, are available for purchase through the hostile tender offer auction.

Upon De Benedetti's public announcement of his tender offer, SGB's management triggered its Poison Pill: management announced the sale of the 16 million authorized but unissued shares. Later, this was reduced to 12 million. Ultimately, this defense failed, because the entire block represented a controlling position equal to 29.9 percent of shares. In its haste to evade De Benedetti, SGB gave an option to purchase 10 million of these new shares (24.9 percent of the new total) to Andre Leyson.

Leyson's entry marked a turning point in the contest for control. Nominally, Leyson appeared to be a defender of SGB: he was a Belgian and held interests in many of the same companies forming SGB's remaining *noyau dur*. But given Leyson's subsequent desire to cut a deal with De Benedetti during the week of January 25, Leyson can hardly be characterized as a defender.

Because Leyson already controlled 4 percent, the option agreement signaled that SGB management was willing to sell control and that the attempt to retain managerial control through the Poison Pill had collapsed.

Leyson's entry changed the contest in another dimension as well. He was backed significantly by Paribas, the large French financial institution and bitter rival of Suez. A successful takeover of SGB by Leyson would in effect mean that Paribas indirectly controlled the largest Belgian financial institution. Suez was concerned about the strategic implications of this. Denying Paribas the ability to control SGB was of special significance, because the "low countries" (i.e., Belgium and Holland) were one of Paribas's primary markets. SGB represented an opportunity to penetrate Paribas's market and challenge its rival in its inner sanctum.

It might be useful to discuss with students why SGB's defenses collapsed and why the contest turned into an auction. The general conclusion of takeover studies in the United States is that takeover defenses merely buy time; rarely do they repel a raid and allow a company to continue as before. The answer must lie in the strength of the motives enumerated here; there is too much to be gained from change. A return to the *status quo ante* serves no one well who might adequately defend SGB.

The Role of Government Regulation

As mentioned earlier, takeovers in Belgium at this time were significantly less regulated than in the United States. Nonetheless, the government intervened at three points in the process:

---

[4]Case Exhibit 2 indicates that Cerus (controlled by de Benedetti) and Dumenil Leble owned 18.6 percent of SGB. The text suggests that the two firms owned 5.5 percent. The former represents the shareholdings *after* De Benedetti's surprise announcement; the latter gives the known (to management) shareholdings *before* the announcement.

- The Belgian Banking Commission required that it be notified 15 days in advance of a tender offer, and it had the power to penalize the offeror for improper filing by delaying the offer. The commission also had to approve SGB's defensive stock issue, and it declared a policy against such issues.

- In Tribunal de Commerce, the commercial court of Brussels, De Bendetti sued SGB to block the defensive stock issue.

- The Belgian Finance Minister extracted assurances from De Benedetti that absolute control of SGB would not reside outside Belgium, representing a nativist concern.

The theory of government intervention in takeovers is that intervention is necessary to ensure an orderly process wherein the small and uninformed investors will not be harmed. As illustrated here, however (and in many other takeover cases), government intervention actually becomes an instrument of the defender or attacker. Regulation stimulates the control contest into new levels of complexity and more arcane strategems of attack and defense.

The Marginal Value of SGB Shares

How high could the bidding go? At what height does the bidding become detached from reality? On January 22, De Benedetti offers 3,400 BeF per share; is his group likely to bid more to gain control? The answer depends on several factors: (1) the intrinsic value of SGB if restructured, (2) the number of remaining shares necessary to gain control, and (3) the cost of De Benedetti's existing share position in SGB. At the margin, the bidding for a few remaining shares necessary to gain control could go quite high and still be economically rational.

To illustrate, assume that the intrinsic value of SGB if restructured is 154.71 billion BeF, or 5,494 BeF per share, and that the average cost per share in De Benedetti's opening position of 18.6 percent was 3,000 BeF. To obtain another 31.4 percent of shares (8.84 million) necessary to gain absolute control, De Benedetti would be willing to pay no more than 6,973 per share.[5] If De Benedetti keeps his costs per share relatively low (i.e., in the range of 3,400), the marginal maximum bid price rises exponentially as he approaches 50 percent of shares.

The purpose of this illustration is merely to show that Suez could observe apparently wild bidding for SGB's shares that was, in fact, economically rational in light of the expected restructuring gains and the fact that De Benedetti is paying for shares at the *margin* and not on the average. This illustration also yields one other important insight: De Benedetti's accumulated pool of shares gives him an enormous tactical advantage in the bidding, to the extent that these shares were acquired at lower cost. Competing bidders who enter later in the process are forced to buy at higher prices, which reduces their maximum marginal bid prices.

---

[5]With an interest of 50 percent, De Benedetti's market value of shares would be 77.36 billion BeF. He has already spent 15.712 billion (3,000 x 5.2374 million shares) to obtain his 18.6 percent interest. Thus, he would rationally be willing to spend no more than the balance, 61.64 billion, to acquire the remaining shares necessary for control, or 8.84 million shares. For the balance, he would pay no more than 6,973 BeF per share (61.64/.00884).

Recommendation

Suez should enter the bidding in a serious and determined way. The incentives are substantial, including (1) the prospect of real economic gains, (2) the intangible benefit of pre-empting Paribas in its own market, and (3) positioning Suez as a pan-European firm after 1992. Bidding, however, needs to be guided by a careful assessment of SGB's value upon restructuring and the investment cost bases of itself and its competing bidders. Suez might explore the possibility of joint control with De Benedetti, although the possibility that he would accept a co-equal in running SGB is doubtful.

EPILOGUE

The (B) case describes Suez' entry into the bidding and its eventual success in gaining control with 50.7 percent of shares. De Benedetti emerged with 48.9 percent of shares. Consistent with the analysis of marginal share prices above, De Benedetti's bidding for SGB peaked at 8,000 BeF per share.

Six months after gaining control of the firm, Suez announced a reorganization of SGB and declared that SGB would double its profits to 3.61 billion BeF by 1989. The reorganization involved selling assets of minority interests, reorganizing the existing portfolio of 1,300 businesses into 13 units, bringing in hard-nosed managers, and simplifying the chain of command. The operating results for 1988 were negative because of large restructuring charges.

In May of 1989, SGB shares were trading around 4,700 BeF. SGB sought to exploit the bouyant market and issued common shares equal to 11 percent of its equity base. In anticipation of this offer, SGB shares rose to 5,060 BeF.

EXHIBIT A Analysis of Restructuring

Pro Forma Balance Sheets, 1987 (BeF in millions)

	Before Restructuring		After Restructuring
Assets	91.708	−30.30	61.408
Liabilities	24.152	−7.98	16.172
Capital and reserves	67.556	−22.32	45.236
Total liabilities, capital, and reserves	91.708	−30.30	61.408
Liabilities/capital	.3575		.3575

Analysis of Gains to Shareholders (billion of BeF except per share data)

Extraordinary dividend		22.32
Resulting equity value:		
Returns (.12 x 45.236)	5.428	
Required return on equity	10.5%	
Expected perpetual growth rate	6.4%	
Total value of equity		132.39
Total restructuring value		154.71
Value per share (28.158 million shares)		5,494 BeF

Societe Generale de Belgique (B): The Outcome

WEDNESDAY, FEBRUARY 3, – FRIDAY, FEBRUARY 5

Through its affiliate, Banque Indosuez, Financiere de Suez changed 2.5 billion French francs into Belgian francs in Brussels and entered the takeover battle for Societe Generale de Belgique. The trading in SGB stock became frenzied. Two million shares were traded on the floor, and it was reported that just as many may have been traded off the floor at prices reaching 4,000 BeF. The Suez group, before accounting for possible allies such as CGE, Lazard, and Lyonnaise des Eaux, held 10 percent of SGB and was reputedly striving for a minority blocking control of 25 percent. At the time, analysts viewed Suez's entry as a defensive measure, since it was also a potential takeover target. They claimed that, by stopping De Benedetti's attempt, Suez was discouraging potential suitors.

As the week ended, Suez claimed it was willing to cooperate with the other SGB suitors and actually began talks with the Leyson group. Meanwhile, De Benedetti and Leyson continued their discussions as Cerus announced a new tender offer price of 4000 BeF/share for 15 percent of SGB. By Friday, the SGB holdings were as follows:

Suez	More than 10%, maybe up to 15%.
CGE	Its 2.5% stake increased to 4%.
Lazard	Still with 4%.
Gevaert	As much as 4.5%.
De Benedetti	Held 18.6% but had friends buying for him.

Supposedly, the friends of SGB, including Leyson, held up to 41 percent of the stock.

MONDAY, FEBRUARY 8 – FRIDAY, FEBRUARY 12

Leyson claimed leadership of a group of 20 companies, mainly Belgian, which combined had a 27.5 percent holding in SGB without the shares from the new issue. The group included one "foreigner"; it was speculated to be Lazard. A debate developed within the group whether an agreement should be reached with Suez or with De Benedetti. Leyson continued discussions with both parties.

De Benedetti was reputed to control almost 30 percent of SGB through his own and the holdings of friends. The latter were reputed to be First Boston, Credit Suisse, and Stern (a French bank). Toward the end of the week, he claimed to hold 38 percent.

On Tuesday, the court stripped the voting rights of the new SGB shares. SGB stated it would appeal the decision to a higher court on February 19. The

---

Case prepared by Robert Reton under the direction of Robert F. Bruner. Copyright (c) 1989 by the Darden Graduate Business School Sponsors, Charlottesville, VA.

commission gave the go ahead on De Benedetti's tender offer for 15 percent of the outstanding SGB shares; the offer would run from February 15 to March 4.

On Wednesday night, Leyson and Suez signed an accord to control SGB with their mutual holdings of 43 percent.

Friday morning, an announcement was made that Leyson's group had broken up and that Leyson had given up his leadership position. Paribas was identified as the cause of the break-up; it claimed it had not been properly consulted about the Suez accord. SGB's stock price tumbled. Suez was now said to control 20 percent of SGB by itself.

MONDAY, FEBRUARY 15 – FRIDAY, FEBRUARY 19

As the tender offer commenced, De Benedetti maintained his 4,000 BeF/share price even though the current market price was higher.

SGB continued to look towards Suez and Paribas to determine the outcome against De Benedetti. Both French banks were trying to shore up a new Belgian group with which to oppose him. The opponents realized that the Belgian companies' holdings would be critical to a victory and were working to get them.

Meanwhile, SGB's stock continued to change hands. On the De Benedetti side, Cerus bought Dumenil Leble's SGB shares, by exercising a call option, after Suez started buying up Dumenil Leble's stock. Royale Belge sold its 3.75 percent holdings to Banque Generale du Luxembourg. Generale du Banque, SGB's Belgian banking affiliate, held 44 percent of Banque Generale du Luxembourg. The players were beginning to face cash problems, so they used friends to buy SGB shares for them with guarantees to cover a price drop.

On Friday, SGB announced a victory. Suez and its allies claimed to hold more than 50 percent as follows:

Suez	20%
Indosuez	5
Lyonnaise des Eaux	2
CGE	>5
Lazard	4
Artois	3
AG Groupe and others	13%

MONDAY, FEBRUARY 22 – FRIDAY, FEBRUARY 26

A media battle continued, with both sides disclaiming the other's SGB holdings. De Benedetti said he controlled 43 percent, while the Franco-Belgian coalition grouped around Suez claimed to have about 52 percent in a solid alliance with signed agreements.

On Thursday, De Benedetti offered a tender price of 8,000 BeF/share for 7 percent of SGB's stock. The premium price was an attempt to get the shares he needed for control of SGB from the Belgians in the Suez group who might be sorely tempted to cash in.

MONDAY, FEBRUARY 29 – FRIDAY, MARCH 4

The creation of Europe 1992 was announced. The new company, with the distinct purpose of holding SGB shares, was held 55 percent by De Benedetti along with Cobepa and Gevaert, each with 22.5 percent. Leyson sold his remaining 2 percent stake in SGB to a friend of De Benedetti. The new alliance called for De Benedetti to place a portion of his SGB holdings in Europe 1992, while Cobepa and Gevaert supplied the capital for future SGB stock purchases. The deal was viewed as a move by Paribas to head off Suez while creating a business association with the Italian financier. Later, Shearson Lehman and Cie. de Banque et d'Investissements (a Swiss financial firm) joined Europe 1992 with about 200,000 shares each.

On Tuesday, the Court of Appeals approved the new SGB shares and their voting rights. Originally, the 12 million-share issue had been fully subscribed by Sodecom, an affiliate of SGB, which intended to place them with Leyson. Since then, Sodecom had been sold off and was now owned by the Franco-Belgian coalition with a 73 percent stake, of which Suez held 34 percent. Leyson claimed to still hold an option on 10 million of the shares, whereas the coalition claimed that it was up to Sodecom to decide who to place the shares with. Either way, it would have probably taken months before all the legal alternatives had been exhausted and a final court ruling made, so it was considered preferable for all the parties if the new shares were forgotten.

Since Friday was the last day for the tender offer, De Benedetti requested an extension from the commission. It agreed to extend the offer until March 18 if De Benedetti would disclose the identities and SGB holdings of his allies. He agreed and provided the following:

Cie. de Banque et d'Investissements	(Swiss)	11.72%
FAI Insurances	(Australian)	3.24
Banque Financiere de la Cite	(Swiss)	3.24
Odyssey Partners	(USA)	.97
Other (demanded anonymity)		2.92
Cerus and Europe 1992	(French)	25.10
Total		47.01%

MONDAY, MARCH 7 - FRIDAY, MARCH 11

Phillips and Nestle announced they might support De Benedetti by joining Europe 1992 and contributing capital for stock purchases.

On Thursday, De Benedetti called for an extraordinary general meeting of the SGB shareholders in April to conclude the issue of control.

MONDAY, MARCH 14 - APRIL 15

SGB called the extraordinary general meeting for April 14. The tender offer failed to get De Benedetti the shares needed for control. If all warrants were to be exercised, the groups would hold as follows: De Benedetti, 48.9 percent; Suez, 50.7 percent.

Cash was tight as De Benedetti sold his Buitoni food company for $1.45 billion, and Suez made a bond issue of 4.8 billion francs to cover its costs.

The two groups were negotiating in an attempt to reach an agreement on the control of SGB, and thus avoid both losing their investments through paralyzed management because both held a blocking control. On April 14, the SGB board nominations made by De Benedetti were rejected by a majority at the extraordinary general meeting held in Brussels.

Carlo De Benedetti had lost the battle, but he still had the power to continue the war with his large minority stake. As he said prior to the vote, "No one can think that the board that will be elected will be definitive and representative. Sooner or later--in a week, in a month, six months, or a year--my associates and I will play a major role in this company."

Bumble Bee Seafoods, Inc.

SYNOPSIS AND OBJECTIVES

Bank of Boston is offered an opportunity to finance the leveraged buyout of this tuna-canning company. The case invites students to evaluate the transaction from the standpoints of the bank, the mezzanine investor, and the equity investor. The analysis serves to (1) survey techniques of valuing debt and equity securities, (2) illustrate the use of tax shields in creating shareholder value, (3) demonstrate the challenges of deal structuring or financial engineering, and (4) highlight the economic incentives for banks to participate in various ways in leveraged buyouts (LBOs).

STUDY QUESTIONS

To sharpen some of the analytical insights in the case, and reduce the workload to a level manageable for one class meeting, one can divide the class into teams charged with evaluating the transaction from the standpoint of one of three groups: bankers, mezzanine investors, and equity investors. In addition, all students should address certain questions:

1. (To the bankers) What are the credit risks inherent in this loan, and what, if anything, mitigates those risks? Should Bank of Boston participate in the senior debt layer? Including fees, what will be the bank's return on assets for this loan? Is the return on assets appropriate for the risks?

2. (To the mezzanine investors) What is the prospective return to investors who buy the package of senior subordinated notes plus common stock? Is this sufficient inducement to invest? Will Castle & Cooke be fairly compensated for its investment in the junior subordinated notes? What is the net present value of the junior notes?

3. (To the equity investors) Given the projections, what is the economic value of the equity in Bumble Bee at date of closing? Is the return on equity fair? Please remember to relever the beta in determining the discount rate for equity.

4. (To all students) What creates value in this transaction?

5. (To all students) Why is the structure of the financing so complicated? For instance, why isn't the transaction financed with equal amounts of bank credit and equity?

If the instructor chooses to teach this case over two class periods, additional work can be assigned in the form of sensitivity analyses to determine

---

Teaching note written by Robert F. Bruner. Copyright (c) 1987 by the Darden Graduate Business School Sponsors, Charlottesville, VA.

how robust Bumble Bee and the investors' returns are to a decline in sales, a decline in gross margin, loss of Puerto Rican tax status, etc.

TEACHING PLAN

What follows is a series of questions and comments designed to motivate and direct the discussion. The author usually begins with the structure of the financing on the blackboard at the start of class (for example, see Exhibit A).

(20 minutes) Why does this deal have such a complicated structure?

- Why the Puerto Rican aspect?

- Why so many layers? Why do the mezzanine layers exist?

- Regarding the junior subordinated notes, what would explain the schedule of amortization and the below-market coupon? Why would Castle & Cooke take back any notes?

- Why is the senior subordinated debt packaged with equity?

(20 minutes) How attractive is this deal from the standpoint of the bank lender? Should Bank of Boston lend?

(20 minutes) What is the economic value of the equity layer? Are the pure-equity investors fairly compensated?

(10 minutes) What is the economic value of the senior subordinated debt layer?

(5 minutes) What creates the value in this deal?

(5 minutes) Who are the big winners here? The relatively small winners? Why are the winnings distributed as they are?

One of the tricks in teaching this case is to value the equity before valuing the mezzanine play, because the equity valuation is a component of the mezzanine valuation. The discussion can be closed with a presentation of the epilogue and a summary of insights that this case presents regarding financial engineering.

ANALYSIS

Of the many analytical opportunities in this case, four are presented in the following sections: analysis of structure, credit analysis of the bank loan opportunity, equity valuation, and valuation of the senior mezzanine strip.

Analysis of Structure

Discussion of the deal structure provides some insights that are useful to introduce early in the discussion. In response to the first discussion question, students should note that the deal structure is complicated by several things:

1. The desire to exploit the value-creating effects of leverage.

2. The need of bank lenders for "cushion" or, to say the same thing, their unwillingness to lend $59.2 million on an equity base of $3.3 million. To the senior lenders, the mezzanine layers look like equity; to the equity layer, the mezzanine looks like debt.

3. Application of all available cash flow to the reduction of the debt. Converting the income statements in case Exhibit 8 into a statement of cash flow (i.e., profits plus depreciation, less investment and debt amortization) reveals little or no cash flow to equity-holders. The rapid amortization of debt is necessary to induce lenders to lend and, in large part, is the source of gains to equity-holders.

4. Tailoring: the exploitation of unusual opportunities or of requirements of lenders and investors. For instance:

   • The use of lower-cost Puerto Rican debt is made possible by Bumble Bee's operations there.

   • The coupon on the junior subordinated debt is plainly below-market (compared with the coupon of the senior subordinated debt). Castle & Cooke would be just as well off taking $13.8 million in notes with a 16 percent coupon as taking $15 million with a 12 percent coupon. To design the junior layer this way implies that C&C wants to avoid more writeoffs in the midst of its battle for corporate control. The rapid amortization of the junior layer also may be explained by C&C's distress.

   • Packaging the senior subordinated note with common stock reflects the reality that the typical mezzanine investor will probably want a higher return on investment than 16 percent, but that the annual cash flows are not large enough to provide that return in the form of interest payments. Most likely, the senior subordinated note is the "plug" security in the transaction—designed to supply the financing, meet investors' required returns, and yet not overburden the firm financially.

Credit Analysis

The standard evaluation of the deal from the standpoint of the bank lender should highlight a few points:

1. Under the projections given in case Exhibits 7 and 8, the covenants proposed in case Exhibit 9 are covered. See Exhibit B for a presentation of various ratios.

2. The ability of Bumble Bee to service its scheduled obligations depends importantly on:

   • $9.6 million of anticipated annual cost savings from reduced overhead ($3 mm), foreign sourcing ($3.6 mm), and reduced advertising ($3 mm);

   • no changes in the tax treatment of borrowings under Section 936 (as footnote 1 in the case indicates, Congress is contemplating changes);

   • No large increases in floating interest rates.

3. Assuming a base borrowing formula of 50 percent of inventories and 75 percent of accounts receivable, there is insufficient security for a loan of $40 million.[1]. A large question is whether Bumble Bee's trademarks constitute much, if any, security. The Figaro pet food brand recently fetched an offer of $11 million. Since Figaro accounts for 20 percent of Bumble Bee's business, one might speculate that all the trademarks might be worth $55 million (i.e., $11/.20). Most asset-based lenders are quick to point out, however, that the trademarks could be worth considerably less in a fire sale. Moreover, even on an ongoing basis, one could worry about the effect of reduced advertising expenditures on the value of the brands.

The author was told that the terms of the loan were fairly typical of those offered to Bank of Boston in early 1985. Plainly, a decision to lend is not straightforward. If time permits, the instructor can invite students to suggest how they might redesign the terms of the loan to satisfy their qualms, if any.

Valuing the Equity Layer

This task is the chief analytical hurdle in the case. The price/earnings approach is useless here, given the peculiarities of an LBO. The discounted cash flow (DCF) approach more effectively captures this transaction's restructuring aspects.

A good way to begin this part of the discussion is to ask what the time horizon should be in setting up the discounting exercise; for instance, should it be year 2000 when the senior subordinated note is completely amortized? Here it is useful to discuss the similarity between leveraged buyouts and real property investments. Owners sell real properties when tax shields run out (i.e., when properties are largely depreciated and the debt is largely repaid) because, thereafter, the annual gain in the value of equity tends to be small. So it is with leveraged buyouts: the life of a deal is typically five years.

Case Exhibit 7 shows that the senior debt and junior subordinated debt are repaid by the end of 1992, which the author chose as a logical investment horizon. Next, a simplifying assumption is important: that the equity-holders receive no cash until the debt is amortized or the company is sold, whichever happens first. Such a policy is consistent with the natural conservatism of lenders in a highly leveraged deal such as this. In effect, all spare cash is funneled to the lenders. Therefore, the valuation problem for equity-holders is to discount the terminal value of equity at the end of 1992 back to 1985.

The discount factor for the equity cash flows must reflect the initially high leverage of the company. The capital structure will unlever in a predictable way over time. Equity-holders assume enormous financial risk in the early years and relatively less in the later years, which means that the levered beta of Bumble Bee will be high, initially, and decline toward the unlevered level in the later years. Under the following assumptions, Exhibit C shows the effect of unlevering over time:

- unlevered beta = .57, the average of the unlevered betas of the four companies listed in case Exhibit 10;

---

[1]For instance, using the projected balance sheet for 1985 (case Exhibit 7), permitted advances would be $28 million:

$$(.5 \times 54.9) + (.75 \times 1.1) = \$28 \text{ mm}$$

- marginal tax rate is 15 percent because of various tax efficiencies (e.g., Puerto Rican operations);

- debt/equity ratios are based on the average pro forma debt and equity in case Exhibit 7 for each year. "Debt" is defined as total liabilities less accruals and payables;

- risk-free and market rates are as given in case Exhibit 10.

A frequent mistake of students is to take the equity cost of the first year (67 percent) as the cost for the entire holding period. This approach is incorrect, because the equity cost declines as the firm unlevers and the equity risk declines. The correct response is to use the product of the various costs as the discount factor:

$$(1.67)(1.37)(1.27)(1.22)(1.19)(1.18)(1.16) = 5.77$$

This method accounts for the fact that equity-holders bear great financial risk initially and relatively less later on. It may be useful to note for the students that the geometric mean-equity cost implicit in the cumulative discount factor is $(5.77)^{1/7} - 1 = .285$. Casual conversations with investors in LBOs suggest that a 28.5 percent target rate of return is toward the low end of the reasonable range of desired equity returns.

The cash flow to investors at the end of 1992/beginning of 1993 must include the terminal value (i.e., the present value of cash flow occurring *after* 1991), that is estimated here using the constant-growth model. The long-term growth rate is assumed to be 5 percent; the cost of equity at the end of 1992, as calculated previously, is 16 percent. The cash flows to equity in 1993 are estimated by growing the cash flow for 1992 at 2.5 percent, the long-term growth rate of gross profits. The "cash flow" for 1992 must assume that the company is mature and stable: specifically that depreciation, and asset additions net to zero and that future debt repayments on the senior subordinated notes are rolled over. A reasonable proxy for this steady-state equity cash flow in 1992 is net income.

$$CF_e \ (1993) = CF_e \ (1992) \times 1.025 = \$14.00 \ mm \times 1.025 = \$14.33 \ mm$$

Accordingly, the value of the equity of Bumble Bee at the end of 1992 would be

$$V_e \ = \ CF_e(1993)/K_e - g \ = 14.33/(.16 - .05) \ = \ \$106.14 \ mm$$

Subtracted from the value of equity is the accumulated cash deficit in the firm of \$2.819 million, which one can assume to have been funded by a line of credit to be repaid at the terminus. The total terminal value in 1992 is \$103.4 million.

The present value is

$$PV_e = 103.4/5.77 = \$17.91 \ mm$$

which compares with total equity invested of \$3.3 million. The internal rate of return on this investment is 63.7 percent.

Valuing the Senior Mezzanine Participation

With the equity valuation completed, assessing the mezzanine play is straightforward. There are two approaches to making the assessment. The first is to value the two components separately ($7 million note and 20 percent of equity), then sum the parts. Given that the interest and amortization are scheduled, the value of the notes depends mainly on the choice of discount rate. Case Exhibit 11 provides interest rates against which to evaluate the offered coupon of 16 percent. Assuming that 16 percent is the appropriate rate, the net present value of the notes will be zero. This method thus implies that the NPV of the "strip" will equal 20 percent of the NPV of the equity layer, or $6.9 million.

The second approach is useful to illustrate the DCF method. Here the procedure is to lay out the expected cash flows of interest, principal, and equity, as in Exhibit D, and determine the internal rate of return. As Exhibit D shows, the IRR is 27 percent. One can develop a "hurdle rate" against which to compare this IRR by taking a weighted average of the geometric mean cost of equity, 28.5 percent, and the required return on the notes (assume 16 percent) weighted according to their proportion in the strip (i.e., 1/8 for equity and 7/8 for notes). The hurdle rate is 17.6 percent. In comparison, the IRR on the strip is larger by about 10 percent.

EPILOGUE

The transaction was successfully completed in May 1985. Bank of Boston extended the $40 million revolving-term debt and $20 million working-capital line as outlined in the case. Furthermore, the bank bought the entire senior mezzanine participation, the only modification being that the senior subordinated debt would amortize with the bank debt.

Bumble Bee exceeded budgeted revenue and operating income over the next nine months. It successfully realized the anticipated savings from decreases in overhead and advertising expenses. Ironically, in the face of these cuts, Bumble Bee actually gained 2-3 percent in market share and tied for second in the market with Chicken-of-the-Sea. As a result of this performance, Bumble Bee amortized $15 million of the acquisition debt within nine months of closing (only $600,000 in amortization had been scheduled).

Castle & Cooke was taken over by David Murdoch of Flexi-Van, who proceeded to liquidate all unnecessary assets. In October 1985, Bank of Boston allowed Bumble Bee to draw down $15 million under the acquisition facility to buy the junior note and the Puerto Rican canning plant.

In February 1988, Heinz offered $235 million in cash for Bumble Bee, which would result in proceeds of $220 million after repayment of certain loans. The IRR to all equity holders would be 185 percent.

Students can be reminded, the positive results notwithstanding, how different the epilogue would have been under different conditions. A sensitivity analysis of the deal would provide a useful focus for a second day's discussion and could be motivated with scenarios of higher interest rates, higher tax rates, lower gross margins, etc. Such an analysis will show that Bumble Bee could sustain some financial adversity without danger of immediate collapse.

The question of flexibility is a useful springboard to some closing observations on financial engineering. The challenge is to create value through financial leverage while avoiding financial collapse. This feat is achieved by a careful financial design covering all aspects of financial policy: mix of debt and equity, maturity structure, basis (fixed versus floating rates), clienteles, and the use of exotic securities. In this case, the high leverage was ameliorated by

- a maturity structure featuring the aggressive amortization of debt and full employment of pre-equity cash flows;

- a balance of fixed- and floating-rate securities as a hedge against interest-rate movements;

- the attraction of a clientele of players who either had self-interest in the success of the transaction (Castle & Cooke) or had the sophistication to appraise the economic potential of the deal;

- the use of nonstandard features in designing the participations to lower costs or tailor cash flows to the needs of the players (strips, discount notes, Puerto Rican debt, etc.).

In a real sense, it is successful financial engineering rather than any of the usual explanations (tax shields, market inefficiencies, etc.) that has created the value in this transaction.

EXHIBIT A   Proposed Financial Structure of the Acquisition

$62.5 mm	Purchase Price
	<u>Financing</u>
27.2	Revolving-term debt originating in the United States. Cost = Prime + 1.5% = 16%. Amortizes 1987-1992.
10.0	Revolving-term debt orginating in Puerto Rico under Section 936 of the IRC. Cost = Cost of funds + 3% = 12%. Amortizes 1987-1992.
7.0	Senior subordinated notes, amortizing 1997-2000. Coupon = 16%. Packaged in a "strip" of securities including $1 million of common stock.
15.0	Junior subordinated notes, amortizing 1986-90, to be held by Castle & Cooke. Coupon = 12%.

3.3	Common equity, held by:
	    senior subordinated investor ($1 mm
	       buys 20%)
	    First Boston ($2 mm buys 40%)
	    management ($0.3 mm buys 40%)

$62.5 mm	Total

EXHIBIT B Covenant and Ratio Analysis for the Year Ended June 30 (dollars in millions)

	@ Closing	1986	1987	1988	1989	1990	1991	1992
Covenant Ratios								
Total liabs.-sub. debt/equity + sub. debt		3.07	2.47	1.87	1.54	0.97	0.53	0.22
Interest coverage		1.74	1.88	2.07	2.56	3.54	4.24	7.47
Working capital		$61.0	$61.3	$60.5	$58.1	$67.6	$67.6	$70.0
Net worth		$ 8.6	$14.8	$21.8	$30.4	$42.0	$54.3	$68.3
Profitability Indicators								
Net profit/sales		2.5%	2.9%	3.3%	4.1%	5.1%	5.5%	6.2%
Net profit/ending equity		61.7%	41.7%	32.1%	28.5%	27.5%	22.7%	20.4%
Net profit/ending assets		7.0%	8.0%	9.1%	11.2%	13.9%	14.8%	16.3%
Liquidity Indicators								
Current ratio	20.00	6.25	6.00	6.00	4.97	7.51	7.51	7.74
Quick ratio	18.30	5.81	5.59	5.57	4.62	7.02	7.02	7.25
Solvency Indicators								
Total debt/net worth	17.94	6.69	3.57	2.08	1.22	0.73	0.34	0.07
Debt/total capital	0.95	0.87	0.78	0.68	0.55	0.42	0.25	0.06
Cash-flow interest coverage		1.78	1.94	2.15	2.65	3.67	4.42	7.78
Debt-service coverage		1.39	1.43	1.56	1.40	3.67	4.42	7.78
Net worth	$ 3.3	$ 8.6	$14.8	$21.8	$30.4	$42.0	$54.3	$68.3
Total debt	$59.2	$57.6	$52.8	$45.3	$37.3	$30.4	$18.4	$ 4.6
Covenants								
Working capital (minimum)	$47	$47	$47	$47	$47	$47	$47	$47
Total liabs.-sub. debt/equity+ sub. deb. (maximum)	4.0	4.0	2.5	2.0	2.0	2.0	2.0	2.0
Interest coverage (minimum)	1.33x	1.33x	1.7x	2.0x	2.0x	2.0x	2.0x	2.0x
Net worth (minimum)	$3.3	$3.3	$9.5	$16.0	$23.0	$31.0	$31.0	$31.0

508

EXHIBIT C DCF Valuation of Equity

	For the Year Ended June 30,						
	1986	1987	1988	1989	1990	1991	1992
Cost of Equity Using Average D/E Ratio							
Beginning D/E ratio	17.9	6.6	3.6	2.1	1.2	0.7	0.3
Ending D/E ratio	6.6	3.6	2.1	1.2	0.7	0.3	0.1
Average D/E	12.3	5.1	2.8	1.6	1.0	0.5	0.2
Levered beta	6.5	3.0	1.9	1.4	1.0	0.8	0.7
Cost of equity	0.67	0.37	0.27	0.22	0.19	0.18	0.16
Discount factor for 1992 CFs							5.771306
Geometric mean Cost of equity							0.285
Calculation of Cash Flows to Equity							
Net income	$5.3	$6.2	$7.0	$8.7	$11.6	$12.3	$14.0
Plus depreciation	0.3	0.5	0.6	0.6	0.7	0.8	0.8
Less capital expenditures	−1.0	−1.0	−1.0	−1.0	−1.0	−1.0	−1.0
Less additions to working capital	−4.0	−0.3	0.8	2.3	−9.4	0.0	−2.4
Less debt amortization	−1.6	−4.8	−7.5	−8.0	−6.9	−12.1	−11.3
Cash flow to equity	($1.0)	$0.6	($0.1)	$2.6	($5.0)	$0.0	$0.1**

Steady-state CF = $14.33†
Terminal value of equity $106.14††
Accumulated cash deficit ($2.82)**
Total terminal value $103.33

PV cash flows to equity $17.90
COMPARE THIS TO A $3.3 MM OUTLAY*,**

---

*This is the present value of the total terminal value, discounted using the varying-rate discount factor computed in the preceding panel.

**Leveraged buyouts are usually designed so that debt service absorbs virtually all the cash flow of the firm. In this specific case, the firm will apparently run a small cash deficit, which would presumably be funded by a line of credit, to be repaid at terminus. None of the interim cash flows (1986-91) are reflected in the DCF.

†Assumes net income is a good proxy (i.e. asset additions and depreciation net out, as do increases and decreases of debt). This is net income for 1992, grown at 2.5 percent (which is the 5-year growth rate of gross profit).

††Steady-state CFe capitalized at Ke − g where Ke = 16%, and g = 2.56%, the 5-year growth rate of gross profit.

EXHIBIT D DCF Valuation of Mezzanine Participation (notes and stock; dollars
           in millions)

Year	Equity	Principal	Interest	Total Cash Flow
1985	-1	-7		-8
1986			1.12	1.12
1987			1.12	1.12
1988			1.12	1.12
1989			1.12	1.12
1990			1.12	1.12
1991			1.12	1.12
1992	20.67751		1.12	21.79751
1993			1.12	1.12
1994			1.12	1.12
1995			1.12	1.12
1996		1.4	1.12	2.52
1997		1.4	0.896	2.296
1998		1.4	0.672	2.072
1999		1.4	0.448	1.848
2000		1.4	0.224	1.624

Internal rate of return   0.27

Benchmark for evaluating IRR   Cost   Weight
  Do a weighted average of: K_e =   28.5%   0.125
                          i(debt) =   16.0%   0.875
                  Weighted average =   7.6%

IRR minus K = 0.10

Aqua Company (A) and (B)

SYNOPSIS AND OBJECTIVES

"Aqua Company" (A) is a leveraged-buyout (LBO) case that requires students to act as the financial advisor to the acquirer, a group of managers. Students must value the company, analyze the assumptions behind the company's projected growth rates, and evaluate the proposed financing package.

"Aqua Company" (B) is a follow-up case that asks students to reevaluate the company, from the perspective of the acquirer's financial advisor, to determine whether a bridge loan should be granted to speed up the settlement process. Students must determine, assuming their company would now be a creditor, whether Aqua is a viable LBO candidate. The case also asks students to evaluate the terms of the proposed bridge loan and determine how rapidly the company could amortize its debt.

DISK FILES

The student disk contains the case exhibits in usual fashion. If it would fit the goals of the class session, students can be provided the finished Lotus program from the instructor's disk, which allows them to run sensitivity analyses on Aqua's projected growth and value. The appendix at the end of this teaching note describes the structure of the finished model.

STUDY QUESTIONS--(A) CASE

1. Does Aqua Company conform to the profile of a good LBO candidate?

2. How conservative would you consider the projections for Aqua?

3. What would Aqua be worth if it were not acquired but were left to continue operating as it is?

4. What is a fair value for Aqua Company, assuming a leveraged buyout?

5. What did Merrill Lynch have to gain from the acquisition?

STUDY QUESTIONS--(B) CASE

1. Could Aqua Company service the proposed bridge loan and the other debt under the LBO?

2. Are the terms of the proposed bridge loan competitive?

3. What are the major credit risks?

Teaching note written by Robert F. Bruner. Copyright (c) 1988 by the Darden Graduate Business School Sponsors, Charlottesville, VA.

4. How sensitive is the value of Aqua to small variations in assumptions; that is, how likely is default?

5. What would be a reasonable set of amortization schedules, assuming all free cash flow were used to pay interest and principal?

TEACHING PLAN

The following outline of questions assumes that two 80-minute class periods are available to cover the (A) and (B) cases. While "Aqua" (A) may reasonably be taught as a stand-alone case, to teach "Aqua" (B) alone is difficult, because much of the information in the (B) case depends on understanding the events and analysis in the (A) case.

Day 1: Aqua (A)

(10 minutes) (The structure of financing from the case "Proposal" is listed on a chalkboard.) Why is the structure of this deal so complicated?

(5 minutes) What does Aqua do? What is its strategy?

(5 minutes) How well has it done in the past?

(5 minutes) Is Aqua a typical LBO target?

(20 minutes) What is Aqua worth on a "steady-as-she-goes" basis (i.e., with no LBO)?

(20 minutes) What is Aqua worth *with* the LBO?

(10 minutes) What has created the increase in value here?

(5 minutes) Do you support the buyout of Aqua for $257 (plus $28 million of refinancing and $30 million of transaction expenses for a total of $323 million)? Vote.

Day 2: Aqua (B)

How has Ray Minella's problem changed since the (A) case?

What is a "bridge loan"?

What are the risks?

What incentives do the terms of the bridge loan create for all the players in this deal? What does Merrill Lynch stand to gain? What creates these high returns?

What is Merrill Lynch's "bet" if it does this deal?

The discussion of the second day can be closed by a brief review of the epilogue and summary comments about the teaching points in the case.

AQUA COMPANY (A)—ANALYSIS

Aqua is an almost ideal LBO candidate: it has a well-defined and -defended market niche; entry barriers are high because of high initial capital-expenditure requirements, and growth is slow, which has freed cash to service debt. The company's core business unit, however, the Water and Gas Products Division (W&GPD), is highly dependent on the housing industry. W&GPD manufactures fire hydrants and, together with its Canadian arm, Aqua Canada, was responsible for 76 percent of corporate sales in 1985.

Aqua acquired five small divisions between 1982 and 1984 in an attempt to expand its product line and make it more recession proof. Through 1985, the new divisions, all of which manufactured valves or other fluid- or gas-control devices, had been unprofitable (case Exhibit 1). Aqua management believed, however, that the company's real growth would come largely from these divisions. Marginally improved performance was projected for each division in 1986 (case Exhibit 1).

Case Exhibits 9 and 10 provide some guidelines for valuing the firm. Two comparable companies were trading in the market at between 2 and 4 times book value and 18 to 22 times earnings. The average price/earnings ratio of other publicly traded valve companies (excluding one at 48) was 21. At 18 to 22 times 1985 earnings, Aqua would have been worth between $338 million to $413 million, if left to continue operating as it was.

At issue for Merrill and FinanceCorp is how much Aqua is worth and how much leverage the company could handle, assuming reasonable growth rates for the company's divisions.

The present-value table given in Exhibit A is based on the forecasted financial statements for Aqua provided in case Exhibits 7, 8, and 9. Working capital was calculated assuming cash to be an historical average of 13 percent of noncash assets, or $46 million, from 1988 through 1995 (over that period, cash and equivalents were projected to be less than $46 million on the balance sheet provided in the case).

To determine the discount rate, case Exhibit 9 provides betas of comparable companies (average .39 up and .92 down) and case Exhibit 11 provides comparative return data for stocks and Treasuries. The parameters for estimating the return factors for the capital-asset-pricing model were as follows: (1) R_m was estimated to be equal to the 20-year Treasury bond yield (7.5 percent) *plus* the difference (7.4 percent) between the arithmetic mean return on stocks and on long-term government bonds; (2) R_F was estimated to be equal to the 20-year Treasury-bond yield (7.5 percent) *less* the difference (1.2 percent) between the arithmetic mean return on long-term government bonds and on Treasury bills. Exhibit B presents estimates of Aqua's beta, which range from 4.25 initially to 1.22 in 1995. The costs of equity consistent with these betas are:

(May 1986) $K_e = 0.63 + 4.25(0.149 - 0.087) = 43$ percent
(1995) $K_e = 0.63 + 1.22(0.149 - 0.087) = 17$ percent

Assuming an average pretax cost of debt of 13 percent[1] and after-tax cost of debt of 9 percent, and assuming debt/capital ratios varying from 91 percent at

---

[1] The pretax interest rate was estimated by dividing 1987 interest expense ($37 million) by 1987 ending long-term debt of $282 million.

May 1986 to 53 percent at 1995, Aqua's weighted-average cost of capital ranges from 12.5 percent (May 1986) to 12.9 percent (1995).[2]

As Exhibit A reveals, a total purchase price of $323 million falls toward the upper end of a reasonable range of values consistent with conservative growth rates. Assuming a cost of capital of 13 percent, the purchase price is consistent with a perpetual growth rate of about 7.5 percent.

Exhibit C details the cash available for amortization after interest expenses are paid out of projected free cash flow and the flows of excess cash on the projected balance sheet. Note that, in 1986 and 1988, the figures are negative.

AQUA COMPANY (B)—ANLAYSIS

Aqua Company accepted FinanceCorp's bid of $257 million ($323 million including debt refinancing and transaction costs), but the acquisition was threatened by a family member, Harvey Murphy (owner of 10 percent of the company's stock), who wanted to find a buyer that would allow family members to manage the company. The case mentions that Mr. Murphy was spreading the rumor that FinanceCorp would not be able to arrange sufficient financing. That eventuality would mean that a "yes" vote on the part of shareholders would simply be a waste of time. It was, therefore, imperative that FinanceCorp prove it could raise the necessary funds.

Merrill, FinanceCorp, and Morgan Stanley (Aqua's advisor) called the other 137 shareholders, and all agreed to vote in FinanceCorp's favor—provided they could be paid out by May 30 instead of July 31. To accommodate their demands, the shareholder meeting was moved up a month to May 2. General Electric Credit Corp (GECC) agreed to provide $53 million of senior secured debt at that time, the investor in the $36 million of junior subordinated debentures was also prepared to act, and FinanceCorp could provide the $30 million of equity. That left the $60 million of senior notes and the $125 million of senior subordinated debentures to be registered by Merrill.

The registration could not be completed in time, so Ray Minella, managing director of Merrill's leveraged-acquisitions group, was considering the viability of a $185 million bridge loan. The terms he was considering were 500 basis points over the floating 30-day A1P1 paper rate (about 11.8 percent) on a 6-month maturity, payable on demand when the securities' registrations were completed. In addition, the debt would have a 2 percent commitment and funding fee. (As shown in case Exhibit 1, three past Merrill Lynch bridge financings were, respectively, at prime + 200 b.p., T-bill + 500 b.p., and an issue at 89.25 percent of par. Case Exhibit 3 indicates that yields on recent junk-bond issues averaged about 11.5 percent and ranged from a low of 6.88 percent for a convertible subordinated debenture to 14.69 percent for senior subordinated notes.)

If the securities were successfully placed, Merrill had much to gain—$14.48 million in fees and interest over a very short period, specifically:

---

[2]Strictly speaking, where discount rates vary, the analyst should discount each cash flow by the product of the individual years' cash flows. For simplicity, this approach is not presented here. However, the instructor can consult teaching notes for "Design Technologies" (Case 31) and "Bumble Bee Seafoods" (Case 44) for discussions of this approach.

	2-Month Loan	6-Month Loan
Fee, "highly confident letter"	$0.15 million	$0.15 million
Fee, "firm forward underwriting commitment"	1.25	1.25
Bond-underwriting commission	7.40	7.40
Bridge-loan commitment fee	1.85	1.85
Bridge-loan advisory fee	1.85	1.85
Bridge-loan net interest income	1.54	4.63
Merger advisory fee	3.00	3.00
gross proceeds	$17.04 million	$20.13 million
Bridge-loan (Merrill Lynch asset)	$185 million	$185 million
Term	2 months	6 months
Annualized gross return on assets	55.2%	21.8%

The large prospective returns reveal the large incentive to make the bridge loan and save the deal. Moreover, the steep decline in returns as the loan term lengthens creates a huge incentive for Merrill to place the securities and fund out its own bridge loan as soon as possible.

If, however, FinanceCorp fails to pay off the bridge loan within 6 months and it becomes a long-term loan that Merrill retains on its books, Merrill would earn interest at the rate of 800 basis points over the 30-day floating AIPI rate. At this point, the current yield would be about 14.8 percent.

At the time, Merrill Lynch was the lead underwriter of about 10 percent of all offerings with BB ratings or below. *The risks to Merrill Lynch* in this case were (1) they would not sell the junk bonds in the market, and (2) Aqua would underperform, leading to default. The company's largest divisions relied greatly on the housing industry, which was projected to remain strong over the near term, but a quarter of the company's sales came from the small, as yet unprofitable, divisions that Aqua considered to be the primary source of future growth and principal repayment. Exhibit D provides Merrill's earnings projections for Aqua under a moderate-recession scenario and resulting cash-flow projections similar to those in Exhibit A.

Exhibit D's projections are also based on the following amortization assumptions:

* assumed debt of $10.9 million in the form of an 8 percent industrial revenue bond amortizes gradually through 1995;

* the $53 million senior secured debt is paid off by 1990 (the exhibit assumes Aqua borrows $65 million; they actually borrowed only $53 million ultimately);

* the $60 million senior notes' sinking fund begins in 1991 at $12 million per year;

* the $125 million senior subordinated debentures and the $36 million junior subordinated debentures do not amortize through 1995.

Based on Exhibit D, the bridge loan appears to be a reasonable investment decision. The company would be able to service its debt and meet the proposed amortization schedule. In 1988, however, projected EBIT fails to cover interest payments, although it recovers the following year. Aqua is not completely robust to reasonable adversity.

The situation in the (B) case occurred in early 1986, just prior to the upsurge in bridge lending. At this time, Merrill was the only major provider of bridge financing. The company had just completed its largest one, for $106 million--just under half of the total acquisition price (compared with 70 percent in this case). Merrill had arranged one for $250 million dollars in October 1985 (18 percent of the acquisition price), but the securities were registered early enough to obviate the need for the bridge financing (see case Exhibit 1).

At issue for Merrill, given that it would now be a creditor and that GECC would only be providing $53 million (not the $65 million built into the original projections), was whether Aqua was still a good risk. The case asks students to determine for Merrill how rapidly Aqua could be expected to amortize its debt, so the terms of the loans could be negotiated with creditors.

EPILOGUE

Two years after the LBO, FinanceCorp sold Aqua to a company with other divisions in the fluid-control business for $90 million plus the assumed debt. The equity investors realized a 44 percent return on equity. The acquiring company planned to keep Aqua intact and maintain it as a wholly owned subsidiary.

EXHIBIT A Aqua Company Net Present Value (assumes scheduled payments of interest and principal; dollars in millions)

	6 Mo. 86	87	88	89	90	91	92	93	94	95
EBIT	$28	$48	$51	$54	$57	$63	$67	$73	$78	$84
Taxed EBIT (46%)	15	26	28	29	31	34	36	39	42	45
Plus:										
Depreciation	4	9	9	11	12	14	15	16	18	19
Amortization	2	3	4	4	4	4	4	3	4	4
Deferred tax	2	3	2	2	3	3	3	2	2	2
Cash flow from opers.	23	41	43	46	50	55	58	60	66	70
Less:										
Capital expenditure	15	15	10	15	15	15	20	25	30	35
Change in work. cap.*	3	−10	40	−2	0	−11	6	6	4	2
Free cash flow (FCF)	$ 5	$36	($ 7)	$33	$35	$51	$32	$29	$32	$33
Cash flow @ 11%	4.853	30.67	−5.73	22.98	21.71	28.69	16.30	13.43	13.21	12.36
12%	4.830	30.25	−5.61	22.26	20.85	27.31	15.38	12.55	12.23	11.34
13%	4.807	29.84	−5.48	21.57	20.02	26.00	14.51	11.74	11.34	10.42
14%	4.785	29.44	−5.36	20.91	19.24	24.76	13.70	10.98	10.52	9.587
15%	4.762	29.05	−5.24	20.28	18.49	23.59	12.94	10.28	9.767	8.821
16%	4.740	28.67	−5.13	19.67	17.78	22.49	12.22	9.638	9.071	8.122

Terminal value at Dec. 1994 discounted at cost of capital

TV95 = (FCF95/(K−g))		Cost of Capital					
		11%	12%	13%	14%	15%	16%
	2%	137	113	95	80	68	58
	3%	155	126	104	87	74	62
Perpetual	4%	177	142	116	96	80	68
growth	5%	206	162	130	107	88	74
rate	6%	247	189	149	120	98	81
	7%	309	227	174	137	110	90
	8%	412	284	209	160	126	102

*Change in working capital assumes minimum cash required to operate business is 13% of noncash assets (generally $46). Excess used to service and amortize debt [see (A) case Exhibit 2].

		Cost of Capital					
		11%	12%	13%	14%	15%	16%
Present value of free cash flows (1986–1994)	2%	$283	$254	$229	$209	$192	$177
	3%	$301	$266	$239	$216	$197	$182
Perpetual	4%	$323	$282	$250	$225	$204	$187
growth	5%	$352	$302	$265	$236	$212	$193
rate	6%	$393	$329	$283	$249	$222	$200
	7%	$455	$367	$308	$266	$234	$209
	8%	$558	$424	$343	$289	$250	$221

EXHIBIT B Aqua Company Levered and Unlevered Betas (dollars in millions)

	86	87	88	89	90	91	92	93	94	95
Long-term debt	294	282	270	258	246	236	214	197	185	173
Shareholders' invest.	34	38	44	52	63	76	93	114	140	170
Beginning debt/ equity	37%	865%	742%	614%	496%	390%	311%	230%	173%	132%
Ending debt/ equity	865	742	614	496	390	311	230	173	132	102
Average debt/ equity	451%	803%	678%	555%	443%	351%	270%	201%	152%	117%
Unlevered beta	0.75									
Levered beta	4.25	4.00	3.50	3.00	2.55	2.17	1.84	1.57	1.37	1.22
K_e [6.3% + (B x 8.6)]	43%	41%	36%	32%	28%	25%	22%	20%	18%	17%
Debt/capital	90%	88%	86%	83%	80%	76%	70%	63%	57%	50%
Equity/capital	10	12	14	17	20	24	30	37	43	50
Weighted after-tax cost of debt (9%)	8.1	7.9	7.7	7.5	7.2	6.8	6.3	5.7	5.1	4.5
Weighted-average cost of equity	4.4	4.8	5.1	5.4	5.7	6.1	6.7	7.2	7.8	8.3
Weighted-average cost of capital	12.5%	12.8%	12.8%	12.9%	12.9%	12.9%	13.0%	12.9%	12.9%	12.9%

EXHIBIT C   Aqua Company Cash Remaining for Amortization of Debt (dollars in millions)

Free cash flow	$ 5	$36	($7)	$33	$35	$51	$32	$29	$32	$33
Excess cash*	0	0	0	0	0	0	0	1	3	5
Available cash for interest and amort.	5	36	-7	33	35	51	32	30	35	38
Interest	18	35	34	33	32	31	28	26	23	20
Cash available for amortization	($13)	$ 1	($41)	$ 0	$ 3	$20	$ 4	$ 4	$12	$18

*Excess cash = cash and equivalents given on projected balance sheets minus $46 million required operating cash (13% of noncash assets).

EXHIBIT D   Aqua Company Forecast: Moderate Recession (assumes scheduled payments of interest and principal; dollars in millions)

	6 Mo. 86	87	88	89	90	91	92	93	94	95
EBIT	$28	$48	$34	$41	$50	$55	$65	$73	$78	$84
Taxed EBIT (46%)	15	26	18	22	27	30	35	39	42	45
Plus:										
Depreciation	4	9	9	11	12	14	15	16	18	19
Amortization	2	3	4	4	4	4	4	3	4	4
Deferred tax	2	3	2	2	3	3	3	2	2	2
Cash flow from opers.	23	41	33	39	46	51	57	60	66	70
Less:										
Capital expenditure	15	15	10	15	15	15	20	25	30	35
Change in work. cap.*	3	–10	40	–2	0	–11	6	6	4	2
Free cash flow (FCF)	$ 5	$36	($17)	$26	$31	$47	$31	$29	$32	$33
Excess cash**	0	0	0	0	0	0	0	1	3	5
Available cash for interest and amort.	5	36	–17	26	31	47	31	28	29	28
Interest	18	35	34	33	32	31	28	26	42	45
Cash available for amortization†	($13)	$ 1	($51)	($ 7)	($ 1)	$16	$ 3	$ 2	($13)	($17)

*Change in working capital assumes minimum cash required to operate business is 13% of noncash assets (generally $46).

**Excess cash = cash and equivalents given on projected balance sheets minus $46 million required operating cash.

†Negative quantities imply assets will have to be sold or other external funding obtained.

521

James Rose reviewed the results of his projections to ensure their accuracy. The historic and projected portions of the model provided in the text are as follows:

__Exhibit Title__	__Lotus Cell Range__
Historical and Projected Statements of Income	A78--U129
Historical and Projected Balance Sheets	A157--U218
Historical and Projected Cash Flows	A348--U412

The file also contains the following sections that are not provided in the text:

__Data Given__	__Lotus Cell Range__
Hypothetical Transaction Structure	A15--J52
Key Financial Relationships	A242--U310
Calculation of Pro Forma Opening Balance Sheet	A430--M491
Selected Summary Statistics	H513--U566
Hypothetical Rates or Return to Investors	H593--U707
Tax-Loss Carryforward Calculation	I131--U154
Principal Assumptions	X44--AL97

Spreadsheet Layout

Hypothetical Transaction Structure		Principal Assumptions
Historical and Projected Statements of Income		
	Tax Loss Carryforward Calculation	
Historical and Projected Balance Sheets		
Key Financial Relationships		
Historical and Projected Cash Flows		
Calculation of Pro Forma Opening Balance Sheet		
	Selected Summary Statistics	
	Hypothetical Rates of Return to Investors	

Aqua Company (B)

Aqua Company had just agreed to be acquired through a leveraged buyout by FinanceCorp for $257 million.[1] In late April 1986, James Rose, an associate with Merrill Lynch Capital Markets (Merrill Lynch or Merrill) High Yield Strategic Financing Group working on behalf of FinanceCorp, had been in the process of writing the registration statements to sell $60 million of senior notes and $125 million of senior subordinated debentures to help finance the acquisition. General Electric Credit Corporation (GECC) had already agreed to provide $53 million of senior secured debt. Another source had agreed to issue $36 million of junior subordinated debt, and FinanceCorp was going to provide $30 million of equity. The excess proceeds from the loans ($47 million) would be used to refinance existing debt and pay related expenses. The shareholder meeting at which the proposed acquisition was expected to be approved was scheduled for early June, and the merger and closing were expected to be consummated simultaneously on July 31. Three days ago, however, Raymond Minella, managing director of Merrill Lynch's High Yield Strategic Financing Group, had received a phone call that threw a spanner in the works.

An executive director of FinanceCorp told Mr. Minella that Edward Strong, Aqua's chairman and chief executive officer, had just told *him* that Harvey Murphy, a dissident member of the family that owned Aqua, who himself held 10 percent (13,600 shares) of Aqua's stock, disapproved of the acquisition. Mr. Murphy was angry that FinanceCorp had not planned to include Murphy family members in management, and he wanted to find a buyer that would allow the family to maintain an ownership interest. The acquisition proposal submitted by FinanceCorp had already been approved by Aqua's board, but it needed 80 percent shareholder approval to pass (each of the 136,000 shares represented one vote). Mr. Murphy was trying to muster enough support to block the acquisition by alleging that FinanceCorp would not be able to arrange sufficient financing.

The four members of the Murphy family who were on the eight-member board of directors owned 43 percent of the outstanding shares. Directors who were not members of the Murphy family, including Mr. Strong, owned stock appreciation rights (SARs), the value of which was based on the earnings per share of the company but which carried no voting rights.

Over the last couple of days, FinanceCorp, Merrill Lynch, and Morgan Stanley, Aqua's financial advisor, had called the other 137 shareholders--all members of the Murphy family--and all agreed to vote in FinanceCorp's favor, provided they could be paid out by May 30, not July 31. There were indications that some shareholders would vote with Harvey Murphy if this deadline were not met.

---

[1] The total payment would amount to $323 million, including debt refinancing ($36 million) and fees ($30 million).

Case written by Casey S. Opitz under the direction of Robert F. Bruner and with the assistance of management at Aqua Company, FinanceCorp, and Merrill Lynch Capital Markets. Copyright (c) 1988 by the Darden Graduate Business School Sponsors, Charlottesville, VA.

To accommodate their request, the shareholder meeting was moved up to May 2. GECC agreed to issue $53 million of senior secured debt before all the necessary paperwork could be completed ($12 million less than Merrill Lynch had used in its earlier projections, because further analysis revealed that more debt could be assumed rather than refinanced); FinanceCorp could provide the $30 million of equity; and the investor in the $36 million of junior subordinated debt was also prepared. That left the $185 ($60 million + $125 million--the Securities) of debt to be registered and sold through Merrill Lynch. There was insufficient time to finalize and file the registration statements and wait the four to six weeks for the Securities and Exchange Commission to review the registration and return it with amendments before initiating two weeks of marketing using the red herring, so Merrill had to arrange financing that would be available by May 30 to effect the merger.

Mr. Minella and Mr. Rose were trying to piece together a package that made sense for all parties. They were considering a $185 million bridge loan from Merrill Lynch to provide the necessary proceeds to close the merger by May 30, bridging the proceeds of the public offering of the Securities. In other words, Merrill would extend a brige loan for 6 months to close the merger and, subsequently, would complete the registration of the Securities and sell them in order to repay the bridge loan.

Mr. Minella had been confident that the registered senior notes and senior subordinated debentures could be sold and had thus offered FinanceCorp a "highly confident letter"[2] on the $60 million and a "firm forward underwriting commitment"[3] on the $125 million. Providing bridge loans, however, which required the investment bank to take on marketing as well as capital risk, was an uncommon new phenomenon. It stemmed from the blurring of the distinctions between commercial banks and investment banks. Merrill Lynch was the leading provider of bridge loans among both investment banks and commercial banks, and even it had provided only a few. Exhibit 1 presents information about its three largest previous deals.

Typically, Merrill would offer the bridge loan at 300 to 500 basis points over floating commercial-paper rates, which tended to be lower than the rates on the long-term fixed securities yet to be registered and sold. In Merrill's view, the justification behind a bridge loan was to facilitate transactions for its clients. In this case, FinanceCorp risked losing the deal if it could not come up with the full amount of the purchase price in cash by May 2. As one investment banker later stated about bridge loans and junk bonds, "It's one thing to offer the bridge, and another to get out of it. Firms will have to look to their capability in high-yield securities, which Drexel has dominated, to take out these loans."[4]

---

[2]The letter stated that Merrill Lynch was sure of its ability to underwrite the Securities, given no adverse change in the markets, at then current rates.

[3]Stronger than a "highly confident letter," the commitment stated that, subsequent to the registration of the Securities, Merrill Lynch would provide all the proceeds to the borrower even if Merrill was unable to sell or place all the Securities covered by the commitments.

[4]"This and subsequent quote from "View from Bridge Makes Bankers' Heads Spin," *Euromoney*, May 1987, p. 66.

In early 1986, Drexel Burnham Lambert was the lead underwriter of 45 percent of all public debt offerings rated BB or below. Merrill Lynch came in second as lead underwriter with 10 percent of the market; Salomon Brothers held 8 percent, and Morgan Stanley 7 percent.

Bridge loans were risky but potentially very profitable:

> The firms clean up on refinancing operations as well. Standard underwriting commissions on junk bonds are 3.25% or 3.5% [of the proceeds underwritten in the public offering]. Add to that a substantial advisory fee, and it's not surprising that bankers, used to lower brokerage commissions and tight returns on conventional corporate finance, find their heads spinning.

Based on their past deals, Mr. Minella and Mr. Rose thought a reasonable price and structure on the bridge loan would be 500 basis points over the floating 30-day A1/P1 commercial paper rate and a 6-month maturity--the bridge loan being payable on demand upon issuance of the Securities. In addition to the underwriting commission of 4 percent of the proceeds of the Securities ($7.4 million), Merrill would charge 1 percent of the amount of the bridge loan as a commitment fee and 1 percent as an advisory fee. Because the bridge loan would have an initial rate lower than the 14 percent subordinated notes (although Merrill could not guarantee that rate in the future), as incentive for FinanceCorp to use the bridge financing for as short a period as possible, after 6 months the bridge loan would convert to a 15-year subordinated debt security at a rate floating at 800 basis points over the 30-day A1/P1 commercial paper rate. This higher interest rate was also structured to be higher than Merrill had forecast the rates on the senior notes and senior subordinated debentures to be. (Current market interest rates and interest rates on comparable high-yield securities are provided in Exhibits 2 and 3.) In addition to these other sources of income, Merrill Lynch anticipated receiving a merger advisory fee of $3.0 million.

Mr. Minella and Mr. Rose had been confident of Aqua's ability to service its debt obligations under the financing plan that included the senior notes and senior subordinated debentures. At issue now was whether Merrill was willing to take the credit risk of being a subordinated creditor to Aqua and was confident of its ability to underwrite and distribute the Securities at interest rates favorable to Aqua. If Merrill could not place the Securities during the initial 6 months, then Merrill would own a 15-year subordinated debt obligation (bridge debenture) of Aqua's. The risk to Merrill was that it would become a long-term creditor of Aqua--a business that Merrill did not want to be in--although the bridge debenture could be registered and placed privately in order for Merrill to liquidate its position. (Merrill Lynch's financial statements are provided in Exhibits 4 and 5. Exhibit 6 gives comparative financial data for other investment banks and commercial banks.)

As part of their review, Mr. Minella and Mr. Rose reevaluated their forecasts for Aqua, provided in Exhibits 7, 8, and 9. The performance of the company's core division (76 percent of sales in 1985) depended on the housing industry, which economists were expecting to be strong because of the recent decline in interest rates. One economist, Lacy H. Hunt of Carroll, McEntee & McGinley Inc had noted,

...housing starts averaged an annual 2.02 million-unit rate in
January and February, compared with a 1.77 million-unit rate in
the fourth quarter of last year, and he believes that starts
may well exceed that pace through the year. If his projections
are accurate, real residential expenditures will rise more than
10 percent this year, compared with 1.7 percent last year....[5]

In their previous forecasts, Mr. Minella and Mr. Rose had assumed housing starts
would remain steady at 1.7 million a year.

Aqua's other divisions were comparatively small and unprofitable. How
quickly would they grow and to what extent should Aqua rely on them to service
its debts? What would be the impact of the $12 million decrease in the secured
loan from the previous projections? Merrill Lynch also had to negotiate the
terms of the loans with creditors; how rapidly could Aqua amortize its debt?
Could the company prosper if it decreased its working capital and used all free
cash flow to pay off debt?

Given the nature of the transaction and the time pressure, if the bridge
loan was the best possible plan, Mr. Minella and Mr. Rose would have to have it
approved this weekend by the Leveraged Transaction Committee. The committee
included the heads of investment banking, junk-bond sales, and trading, mergers
and acquisitions; the Merrill Lynch and Company chief financial officer; and two
senior-level investment bankers who were not involved in the deal. Would this
committee and FinanceCorp find this plan acceptable?

Mr. Minella and Mr. Rose wanted to spend some time considering the
alternatives--perhaps a different financing package, or a recommendation that
FinanceCorp take its chances or increase its offer and wait until the Securities
were registered, or a suggestion that FinanceCorp withdraw its offer--before
settling on a bridge loan that would be risky for Merrill.

---

[5]"Car Sales May Idle, But Housing Will Have Power to Spare," *Business Week*,
April 14, 1986, p. 26.

EXHIBIT 1 Merrill Lynch Bridge Loans (dollars in millions)

Acquirer	Acquiree	Date	Price	Bridge Amount	Bridge Structure	Fees
Merrill Lynch Capital Partners and management*	Hastings Drug	10/85	$1,356	$250	$290.5 subordinated debt due 2001 at 11 1/8% and 89.25% of par	1% commit 1% fund
Alpha Partners and management	Circle Atlantic	4/86	$226.4	$106	$106 6 month at 90-day T-bill equivalent yield + 500 basis points	1% commit 1% fund
Management	Division of Ole Swenson Textiles	1/86	$104.6	$40	Secured senior floating-rate note, maturity 9 months at prime + 200 basis points or 11%; next 6 months at prime + 250 basis points	1% commit 1% fund

*Bridge never took place; securities sold in time.

EXHIBIT 2 Current Market Yields

| | Bond Yields | | | | Commercial Paper* | | | |
	Aaa	Aa	A	Baa	1-Mo.	2-Mo.	3-Mo.	Prime
1985--Dec 13	10.26%	10.73%	11.25%	11.70%	7.85%	7.76%	7.65%	9.50%
20	10.05	10.50	10.09	11.43	7.79	7.67	7.52	
27	9.97	10.43	11.05	11.36	7.86	7.73	7.58	
1986---Jan 3	9.92	10.40	11.04	11.36	7.89	7.73	7.59	
10	9.95	10.37	11.00	11.37	7.75	7.68	7.58	
17	10.18	10.56	11.11	11.48	7.84	7.78	7.71	9.50
24	10.13	10.49	11.07	11.49	7.77	7.71	7.64	
31	10.00	10.43	10.96	11.43	7.72	7.66	7.59	
Feb 7	9.90	10.35	10.87	11.29	7.70	7.63	7.55	
14	9.84	10.29	10.80	11.25	7.73	7.67	7.60	9.00
21	9.64	10.07	10.60	11.10	7.69	7.63	7.52	
28	9.29	9.81	10.40	10.82	7.66	7.59	7.48	
Mar 7	9.08	9.59	10.29	10.59	7.52	7.40	7.27	
14	8.98	9.48	10.15	10.52	7.20	7.13	7.04	9.00
21	9.03	9.52	10.14	10.50	7.22	7.13	7.01	
28	8.94	9.43	10.04	10.42	7.25	7.13	7.00	
Apr 4	8.74	9.24	9.89	10.28	7.22	7.02	6.82	
11	8.75%	9.23%	9.87%	10.24%	6.83%	6.66%	6.53%	9.00%

| | Treasuries | | | | | | | |
	3-Mo.	6-Mo.	1-Yr.	3-Yr.	5-Yr.	10-Yr.	20-Yr.	30-Yr.
1985--Dec 13	7.10%	7.12%	7.65%	8.41%	8.76%	9.31%	9.81%	9.61%
1986--Jan 17	7.17	7.26	7.86	8.57	8.86	9.35	9.70	9.49
Feb 14	7.11	7.18	7.69	8.17	8.44	8.87	9.30	9.11
Mar 14	6.59	6.58	7.03	7.26	7.40	7.72	8.09	7.85
Apr 11	6.07	6.08	6.41	6.82	7.04	7.31	7.50	7.39

*Unweighted average of offering rates on issues of firms with Aa bond ratings or equivalent on bank-discount basis, not higher investment-yield basis.

Source: *Federal Reserve Bulletin*.

EXHIBIT 3   Yields on Junk Bonds, April 1986

1986 Issue Date	Company	Form of Debt	Maturity	Rating	Yield to Maturity
3/3	AmBrit Inc.	Senior sub. notes	1996	CCC	14.69%
3/4	Geothermal Resources	Subordinated notes	1996	B−	13.75
3/4	Great Lakes Fed S&L	Conv. sub. debent.	2011	B	7.25
3/4	Navistar Int'l	Subord. debent.	2011	CCC	13.25
3/4	Ungerman-Bass	Conv. sub. debent.	2011	B−	6.88
3/5	Vestron Inc.	Conv. sub. debent.	2011	B+	9.00
3/6	Banner Industries	Senior sub. notes	1996	B−	13.00
3/6	Banner Industries	Subord. debent.	2006	B−	13.75
3/6	Homestead Savings	Subord. debent.	1996	B	13.38
3/13	Coleco Industries	Sub. sink. fund deb.	2001	B−	12.63
3/18	Turner Broadcasting	Senior sub. deb.	2011	CCC	14.25
3/19	America West Airline	Conv. sub. debent.	2011	B−	7.50
4/8	Cannon Group	Senior sub. debent.	2001	B	8.88
4/10	BCI Holdings	Senior notes	1996	BB−	11.00
4/10	BCI Holdings	Senior sub. debent.	1998	B	12.50
4/10	BCI Holdings	Subord. debent.	2001	B	12.75%

Source: *Moody's Bond Record*.

EXHIBIT 4 Merrill Lynch Consolidated Statements of Income (dollars in thousands)

Revenues	1984	1985
Commissions	$1,217,233	$1,573,341
Interest	2,451,660	2,590,365
Investment banking	582,333	720,340
Principal transactions	560,980	882,018
Real estate	461,769	574,651
Asset management and custodial	237,170	298,384
Insurance	i71,201	194,130
Other	228,206	283,746
Gain on sale of headquarters	127,250	0
Total revenues	$6,037,802	$7,116,975

Expenses		
Compensation and benefits	$2,266,441	$2,746,189
Interest	2,109,110	2,218,075
Communications and equipment rental	359,509	376,473
Occupancy	236,900	264,758
Advertising and marketing	170,414	217,007
Brokerage, clearing, and exchange fees	142,866	167,438
Depreciation and amortization	88,860	160,480
Professional fees	144,171	147,751
Office supplies and postage	113,605	119,113
Insurance policyholder benefits	98,404	97,207
Other	237,230	238,179
Total expenses	5,967,510	6,752,670
Earnings before taxes	70,292	364,305
Income tax expense (benefit)	(25,056)	140,018
Net earnings	$ 95,348	$ 224,287

EXHIBIT 5   Merrill Lynch Consolidated Balance Sheets (dollars in thousands)

	1984	1985
ASSETS		
Cash and securities on deposit	$ 1,013,754	$ 1,354,216
Receivables:		
Customers	6,263,789	9,319,497
Brokers and dealers	675,541	2,935,320
Securities borrowed	957,131	2,828,798
Loans	1,708,049	2,594,789
Resale agreements	7,379,411	8,932,271
Other	1,705,644	1,978,363
	18,689,565	28,589,038
Securities inventory, market value	8,521,394	15,396,923
Investment securities	600,613	436,853
Property, net	738,267	892,256
Equity advances for properties	304,995	302,278
Deferred acquisition costs	971,343	1,145,468
Total assets	$30,839,931	$48,117,032
LIABILITIES AND STOCKHOLDERS' EQUITY		
Bank loans	$ 1,430,387	$ 561,495
Commercial paper	5,127,811	8,704,237
Repurchase agreements	9,707,076	14,372,449
Demand and time deposits	883,564	1,027,241
Securities loaned	584,795	1,682,192
Total current liabilities	17,733,633	26,347,614
Long-term borrowings	2,163,102	3,722,041
Securities sold but not yet purchased	2,350,336	3,285,213
Other liabilities	6,514,148	12,420,819
Total liabilities	28,761,219	45,775,687
Common stock	129,225	137,596
Paid-in capital	604,235	745,611
Foreign currency translation adjust.	(10,650)	(22,082)
Retained earnings	1,412,718	1,558,095
Less: Treasury stock	20,793	20,824
Unamort. stock grants expense	36,023	39,664
Notes receivable on stock sale	0	17,387
Total equity	2,078,712	2,341,345
Total liabilities and equity	$30,839,931	$48,117,032

EXHIBIT 6   Comparative Data, 1985 (dollars in millions)

Investment Banks

	Revenues	Net Profit Margin	Current Ratio	Long-Term Debt	Equity
Advest Group	$ 146.6	3.6%	114.3%	$ 36	$ 61
Bear Stearns	2,163.9	6.1	102.9	298	651
Drexel	2,000.0*	N.A.	101.0	230	719
E. F. Hutton	3,139.0	0.4	103.5	333	825
First Boston	888.3	14.7	101.4	338	704
Goldman	NAv	NAv	104.4	781	868
Legg Mason, Inc.	111.5	7.4	136.7	2	55
Morgan Stanley	1,794.9	5.9	101.6	358	314
PaineWebber	1,885.1	1.8	94.8	291	431
Salomon	27,896.0	2.0	103.8	917	2,954
Shearson	3,246.0	6.2	97.1	1,319	1,177
MERRILL LYNCH	$ 7,117.0	3.2%	108.5%	$3,722	$2,341

Commercial Banks

	Net Interest Income	Net Profit	Total Assets	Long-Term Debt	Equity	Return on Assets
BankAmerica	$4,042	($577)	$118,541	$ 5,388	$4,547	NMf
Bankers Trust	852	371	50,581	1,638	2,495	0.7%
Chase Manhattan	2,749	565	87,685	3,807	4,459	0.6
Chemical	1,572	390	56,990	1,622	2,820	0.7
Citicorp	5,446	998	173,597	18,215	7,805	0.6
J. P. Morgan	$1,418	$705	$ 69,375	$ 1,400	$4,392	1.0%

NMF = no meaningful figure.

*Approximate.

Source: *Value Line Investment Survey*.

532

EXHIBIT 7 Aqua Company Historical and Projected Statements of Income (dollars in millions)*

	Fiscal Year Ended November 30		6 Months Ended 11/30/86	Projected Fiscal Years Ended November 30								
	1984	1985	1987	1988	1989	1990	1991	1992	1993	1994	1995
Sales	$212	$277	$168	$329	$346	$368	$391	$418	$448	$479	$513	$548
Cost of sales	142	188	110	216	225	239	254	270	290	311	333	356
Depreciation and amortization	7	9	4	8	10	11	12	14	15	16	17	19
Gross profit	63	80	55	105	111	118	125	134	143	152	163	173
Selling, general, and admin. exp.	30	43	23	48	50	54	57	60	64	68	72	76
Operating income	32	37	32	57	60	64	68	74	79	85	91	97
Other nonoperating income (expense)	(3)	(5)	(4)	(8)	(9)	(9)	(10)	(10)	(10)	(11)	(11)	(12)
Amortization of trans. expenses	0	0	0	(1)	(1)	(1)	(1)	(1)	(1)	(1)	(1)	(1)
Earnings before interest and taxes	$29	$32	$28	$48	$51	$54	$57	$63	$67	$73	$78	$84
Interest expense:												
Existing debt	1	3	0	1	0	0	0	0	0	0	0	0
Senior secured credit	0	0	4	7	6	4	3	2	1	0	0	0
Senior loan	0	0	4	8	8	8	8	8	7	5	4	2
Senior subordinated debt	0	0	9	18	18	18	18	18	18	18	18	18
Junior subordinated notes	0	0	3	5	5	5	5	5	5	5	5	5
Discount debentures	0	0	0	0	0	0	0	0	0	0	0	0
Interest income	(1)	(1)	(1)	0	(1)	(1)	(1)	(2)	(1)	(1)	(2)	(2)
Total interest expense (income)	(0)	2	19	37	36	34	33	31	29	27	24	23
Earnings before taxes	29	30	10	11	15	20	25	32	38	46	54	62
Provision for income taxes:												
Current income taxes	13	14	5	6	9	11	13	17	21	24	28	32
Deferred income taxes	0	0	2	3	2	2	3	3	3	2	2	2
Total provision for income taxes	13	14	7	9	11	13	16	20	23	26	30	33
Net income	$16	$16	$3	$2	$4	$6	$9	$11	$15	$19	$24	$28

*Figures may not add because of rounding.

533

EXHIBIT 8 Aqua Company Historical and Projected Balance Sheets (dollars in millions)*

	Fiscal Year Ended November 30		Pro Forma	Projected Fiscal Years Ended November 30									
	1984	1985	5/31/86	1986	1987	1988	1989	1990	1991	1992	1993	1994	1995
ASSETS													
Cash and equivalents	$ 15	$ 25	$ 5	$ 14	$ 5	$ 8	$ 8	$ 13	$ 21	$ 17	$ 18	$ 22	$ 29
Receivables	28	40	53	45	45	45	45	47	48	49	51	53	55
Inventories	43	43	65	67	67	67	68	68	71	73	75	79	81
Other current assets	8	10	5	7	6	5	5	4	3	4	3	4	5
Total current assets	93	117	128	132	123	125	126	132	143	142	146	158	170
Property, plant, and equip.	126	133	92	107	122	132	147	162	177	197	222	252	287
Accumulated depreciation	(67)	(72)	0	(4)	(13)	(22)	(33)	(45)	(59)	(74)	(90)	(108)	(127)
Net property, plant, and equip.	59	62	92	103	109	110	114	116	118	123	132	144	160
Other assets	10	1	16	15	14	12	11	10	8	7	6	6	5
Purchase price premium	0	10	124	121	118	113	110	106	102	98	95	91	87
Total assets	$162	$189	$360	$371	$364	$360	$360	$364	$371	$371	$379	$399	$422
LIABILITIES AND SHAREHOLDERS' EQUITY													
Notes payable and current portion LTD	$6	$9	$0	$0	$0	$0	$0	$0	$0	$0	$0	$0	$0
Accounts payable	34	16	17	20	20	21	23	25	27	28	30	32	34
Accrued liabilities	0	17	18	24	22	23	23	23	23	25	26	28	30
Other current liabilities	0	4	3	3	3	3	4	5	5	6	6	7	8
Total current liabilities	40	46	38	47	45	47	49	53	55	59	62	67	72
Existing long-term debt	29	36	10	8	6	4	2	0	0	0	0	0	0
Acquisition financing:													
Senior secured credit	--	--	65	65	55	45	35	25	15	5	0	0	0
Senior loan	--	--	60	60	60	60	60	60	60	48	36	24	12
Senior subordinated notes	--	--	125	125	125	125	125	125	125	125	125	125	125
Junior subordinated notes	--	--	36	36	36	36	36	36	36	36	36	36	36
Total long-term debt	29	36	296	294	282	270	258	246	236	214	197	185	173

EXHIBIT 8 (continued)

	Fiscal Year Ended November 30		Pro Forma 5/31/86	Projected Fiscal Years Ended November 30									
	1984	1985		1986	1987	1988	1989	1990	1991	1992	1993	1994	1995
Unamortized debt discount	0	0	(8)	(8)	(7)	(7)	(6)	(6)	(5)	(5)	(4)	(3)	(3)
Other noncurrent liabilities	10	10	4	5	8	11	13	16	19	22	25	27	28
Total liabilities	79	92	330	338	329	321	315	310	306	291	280	275	271
Common stock and surplus	1	0	0	0	0	0	0	0	0	0	0	0	0
NEWCO common	0	0	30	30	30	30	30	30	30	30	30	30	30
Retained earnings	82	97	0	3	5	9	15	24	35	50	70	93	122
Total equity	83	97	30	33	35	39	45	54	65	80	100	123	152
Total liabilities & equity	$162	$189	$360	$371	$364	$360	$360	$364	$371	$371	$379	$399	$422

*Figures may not add because of rounding.

EXHIBIT 9 Historical and Projected Cash Flows (dollars in millions)*

	Fiscal Year Ended November 30		6 Months Ended 11/30/86	Projected Fiscal Years Ended November 30								
	1984	1985		1987	1988	1989	1990	1991	1992	1993	1994	1995
Operating income	$32	$37	$32	$57	$60	$64	$68	$74	$79	$85	$91	$97
Other nonoperating income (expense)	(3)	(5)	(4)	(8)	(9)	(9)	(10)	(10)	(11)	(11)	(12)	(12)
Amortization of trans. exp.	0	0	0	(1)	(1)	(1)	(1)	(1)	(1)	(1)	(1)	(1)
Cash earnings before interest and taxes	29	32	28	48	51	54	57	63	67	73	78	84
Depreciation/amortization	7	9	6	12	14	15	16	18	19	20	21	23
Cash flow before interest expense	36	41	34	60	65	69	73	81	86	92	99	107
Interest expense:												
Existing debt	1	3	0	1	0	0	0	0	0	0	0	0
Senior secured credit	0	0	4	7	6	4	3	2	1	0	0	0
Senior loan	0	0	4	8	8	8	8	8	7	5	4	2
Senior subordinated debt	0	0	9	18	18	18	18	18	18	18	18	18
Junior subordinated notes	0	0	3	5	5	5	5	5	5	5	5	5
Interest income	(1)	(1)	(1)	0	(1)	(1)	(1)	(2)	(1)	(1)	(2)	(2)
Total interest expense (income)	0	2	19	37	36	34	33	31	29	27	25	23
Cash flow before income tax	37	39	16	23	29	35	41	50	57	65	74	84
Current income tax expense	13	14	5	6	9	11	13	17	21	24	28	32
Cash flow before mandatory debt service	23	25	11	17	20	24	28	33	36	41	47	53
Debt-service requirements:												
Senior secured credit	--	--	0	10	10	10	10	10	10	5	0	0
Senior loan	--	--	0	0	0	0	0	0	12	12	12	12
Senior subordinated debt	--	--	0	0	0	0	0	0	0	0	0	0
Junior subordinated notes	--	--	0	0	0	0	0	0	0	0	0	0
Existing debt	--	--	2	2	2	2	2	0	0	0	0	0

EXHIBIT 9 (continued)

	Fiscal Year Ended November 30		6 Months Ended	Projected Fiscal Years Ended November 30								
	1984	1985	11/30/86	1987	1988	1989	1990	1991	1992	1993	1994	1995
Cash flow before discretionary items	23	25	8	3	7	12	16	23	14	24	35	41
Discretionary items:												
Capital expenditures	7	10	15	15	10	15	15	15	20	25	30	35
Increase in noncash working cap.	14	8	(14)	1	(2)	(2)	(2)	1	(1)	1	2	0
Increase in other assets	2	(9)	(1)	(1)	(2)	(1)	(1)	(1)	(1)	(1)	(1)	(1)
Amort. of trans. exp.	0	0	0	(1)	(1)	(1)	(1)	(1)	(1)	(1)	(1)	(1)
Preferred stock dividends	4	4	0	0	0	0	0	0	0	0	0	0
Total discretionary items	27	13	0	14	5	11	11	14	18	24	31	34
Cash flow	$(4)	$12	$ 8	$(9)	$ 3	$ 0	$ 4	$ 8	$(3)	$ 0	$ 4	$ 7

*Figures may not add because of rounding.

Sybron Corporation

SYNOPSIS AND OBJECTIVES

In early 1986, the leveraged-buyout (LBO) firm of Forstmann Little & Co. is reviewing the opportunity to take private Sybron Corporation, a manufacturer of low- to medium-technology medical, laboratory, and chemical supplies. The central task for the student is to value Sybron and recommend an offering price. The case has been used to (1) exercise students' valuation skills, (2) illustrate a "bust-up" leveraged buyout, and (3) convey the unusual perspective of a prominent pure-equity investor in LBOs.

Sybron is a good example of a second-generation LBO, i.e., one in which value is maximized by a significant restructuring of the target company. The instructor may want to use this case as a contrast following a traditional LBO case such as "Bumble Bee Seafoods, Inc." (Case 44), in which a company's unused debt capacity is used by the LBO group to effect the purchase of the company at a significant premium to market, after which value is created through exploiting debt and depreciation tax shields, cost reductions from reverting to private-company status, and successful anticipation of future interest-rate movements.

STUDY QUESTIONS

The instructor may choose simply to let the students deal with the questions contained at the end of the case. If a more directive teaching strategy is required, the instructor may want to give the students this fuller list:

1. Is Sybron a suitable target for a leveraged buyout?

2. How much is Sybron worth now (i.e., before a buyout)?

3. Given its forecasted operating cash flows, how much debt can Sybron bear?

4. How much would Sybron be worth if it were taken private and recapitalized as outlined near the end of the case?

    Note: Case Exhibits 9 and 10 present information relevant to the choice of a discount rate. Case Exhibits 6 and 7 provide information necessary to forecast cash flows.

5. What must happen in order for Sybron to service the buyout debt? How robust is Sybron's debt-servicing ability to possible environmental and operating risks?

6. How much should Forstmann Little offer?

Teaching note prepared by Judson P. Reis and Robert F. Bruner. Copyright (c) 1988 by the Darden Graduate Business School Sponsors, Charlottesville, VA.

An added teaching device in this case is to divide the students into teams and ask each team to submit bids--with the highest bidder obtaining Sybron. This competitive dimension often motivates students to scrutinize the opportunity very carefully and lends even more impact than otherwise to the epilogue.

TEACHING PLAN

If the students have been required to submit competitive bids, the instructor can collect the written bids at the start of class (no bids allowed to change thereafter) and then invite the respective teams to present their analyses in 10-minute talks. Closure is gained by comparing the various analyses, discussing errors or inappropriate methodologies, and then presenting the epilogue.

Under a more traditional discussion-leadership approach, the instructor may find the following outline to be a useful organizing scheme for an 80-minute class:

(10 minutes) Is Sybron a reasonable LBO target?

(15 minutes) What is Sybron worth, assuming no LBO?

(15 minutes) What operating and asset changes could Forstmann Little make that would unlock new value?

(20 minutes) Assuming these changes are made, and a purchase is financed as suggested late in the case, what would be the value of Sybron? What should Forstmann Little bid?

(10 minutes) What justifies the large premium price? What are the sources of new value?

For the final 10 minutes of class, the instructor can present the epilogue and possibly general comments on the role of LBOs as corporate restructuring devices.

ANALYSIS

Sybron as an LBO Target

Several aspects of Sybron Corporation make it an ideal candidate for restructuring upon purchase:

- Sybron is nothing more than a group of discreet businesses that in no way rely upon one another or need to belong together.

- The public historical record of Sybron is poor, which has led to possible undervaluation by the marketplace. Much of the poor performance is the result of a series of nonrecurring items related to Sybron's unsuccessful attempt to restructure itself.

- There are legitimate questions as to the value added or created by corporate headquarters.

- One could logically assume that some of Sybron's disparate businesses contribute little in terms of cash flow compared with their asset values. Thus, there may be sources of cash for debt reduction (stemming from selective divestitures) that would not significantly affect operating cash flow. For instance, Sybron could sell (1) small units that appear unlikely to have the scale in their competitive markets for exceptional performance, (2) units with high risk in cash flows, and/or (3) units that are poor performers.

- The operating cash flows of the remaining core businesses appear to be strong and relatively predictable due to (1) good competitive positions, (2) low rates of market growth, (3) low rates of technological change, and (4) good management at the divisional levels.

Valuation:

The case makes clear that a winning bid would have to top the $25.95 already bid by Kelso. One way to approach the analysis is to examine whether prices in the area of $26-$30 per share might make sense.

One obvious benchmark for comparison is a discounted cash-flow valuation based on current conditions. A DCF analysis assuming no buyout is presented in Exhibit A based on the data in case Exhibits 6 and 7. The top panel of Exhibit A presents the estimation of residual cash flows, starting with the divisional operating cash flows given in the case. The middle panel estimates the terminal value of the firm, based on the constant-growth model and varying growth rates and equity costs. The bottom pannel of Exhibit A gives the present value of annual and terminal cash flows under various growth-rate and equity-cost assumptions.

Exhjbit A reveals that Sybron's historical equity values of $224 to $182 million[1] are consistent with moderate growth rates (of around 5 percent) and low equity costs (10-12 percent). The firm appears to be reasonably valued by investors on the basis of its current strategy and management.

Exhibit B recasts the valuation assuming (1) no asset sales, (2) the reversion of excess pension assets, (3) the virtual elimination of corporate overhead, (4) the write-up of asset values (and subsequent depreciation), and (5) massive releveraging of the firm. First, the firm would apparently generate annual operating cash flows after tax in the neighborhood of $40 million per year, which would be adequate to cover debt service on a substantial volume of debt. Second, the resulting present value of equity (e.g., $122 million) is well in excess of the amount to be invested ($25 million). A restructuring of Sybron could make Forstmann Little a substantial profit.

Restructuring Actions

The case contains clues as to what Forstmann Little plans to do if it acquires Sybron. First, given the disparate and independent nature of Sybron's Forstmann operating units (and their divisions) and the clear antagonisms between operating and corporate management, one should question the need for $14 million of corporate overhead. Drastic cuts should be possible that would create pretax savings in the area of $10 million or more.

---

[1] 9.92 million shares times the range of stock prices for the fourth quarter of 1985, listed in case Exhibit 1 ($22.625 to $18.375).

Second, Forstmann Little's bank financing requires heavy repayments in the first two years. Thus, cash clearly has to be raised quickly from the sale of Forstmann certain Sybron assets and from recapture of the $43 million pension fund surplus. An analyst who sets up the following criteria could come up with a sensible divestiture plan.

- Sell any small businesses that do not appear to have the scale needed for exceptional performance. Candidates could be Thermoline, Analytical Products, Mediatech, and Cryogenics.

- Sell businesses that seem to have the highest risk. Candidates would include Brinkmann (dependence on foreign sourcing, subject to currency fluctuations, no manufacturing or proprietary products) and, possibly, Sybron Chemicals if it is more cyclical than other Sybron businesses, is subject to greater competition, or exhibits liability risks inherent in the chemical business (pollution, product liability, etc.).

- Sell relatively poor performers, e.g., all the Medical Products group and the Midwest Division of the Dental Products Group.

Depending on assumptions made, and assuming the artful use of mirror subsidiaries in the acquisition to eliminate taxes on the sale of assets, a student should be able to down-size Sybron along the following lines:

	Proceeds ($ millions)
Pension fund surplus	$43
Brinkmann (3–5 x 1986 EBIT)	23–38
4 Medical Divisions	
a. (3–4 x 1986 EBIT)	23–30
b. (3–4 x 1987 EBIT)	37–50
Small laboratory: Thermoline, Analytical Products, Mediatech	
a. (4–6 x 1986 EBIT)	15–22
b. (4–6 x 1987 EBIT)	19–29
Sybron Chemical	
a. (5–6 x 1986 EBIT)	43–52
b. (5–6 x 1987 EBIT)	49–59
Midwest Division of Dental Products	$ 5–10

"Average" proceeds from this table would yield $183 million.

Assuming pay-down of $183 million of debt immediately and purchase at $26 per share, the LBO company would have the following capitalization:

	Predivestiture Capitalization	Post-divestiture Capitalization
Debt	$310	$127
Equity	25	25
	$335	$152

Obviously, this divestiture strategy creates an added dimension for exploiting the latent value in Sybron.

EPILOGUE

Forstmann Little bought Sybron for $335 million, equivalent to $30.33 per share, or a 47 percent premium over the mean stock price in the fourth quarter of 1985. The sources of financing are summarized in Exhibit C; in general, the acquisition occurred in the proportions outlined near the end of the case. Shortly thereafter, Forstmann Little undertook the restructuring of Sybron. First, more than $10 million of corporate overhead was cut. Second, various divisions were put up for sale (see Exhibit D for a summary of the divestiture program). The proceeds were consistent with expectations. Third, the remaining operations were managed more closely, resulting in 1987 in material favorable variances from budget in both net sales and operating profits (see Exhibit E for a summary). In short, Forstmann Little repaid $257 million in debt within the first 18 months after the acquisition, and it also realized operating profits on the remaining business (approximately one-half of the former firm) that exceeded the former firm's operating profits.

Then, just after the stock market crash (October 22, 1987), Forstmann Little sold the remaining assets to one buyer for $380 million gross, or $305 million (after deducting remaining debt of $68 million and closing expenses of $7 million). The rates of return for 20 months of holding were 260 percent to the equity investors (net of carried interest; 350 percent before) and 70 percent to the subordinated debt investors who also had a 37.5 percent equity interest (see Exhibit F).

	1986	1987	1988

Cash-Flow Forecast

	1986	1987	1988
Divisional operating cash flow (case Exhibit 7)	$78.10	$92.86	$100.75
Less: Corporate overhead (Note 1)	$14.00	$14.50	$15.00
Interest expense (Note 2)	$14.00	$14.00	$14.00
Pretax income	$50.10	$64.36	$71.75
Taxes (46%; see "Memo" below)	($11.56)	($17.65)	($20.02)
After-tax operating cash flow	$38.54	$46.71	$51.73
Less: Capital expenditures (Note 3)	($20.00)	($22.00)	($24.00)
Additions to working capital (Note 4)	($11.40)	($13.50)	($13.00)
Debt amortization (Note 2)	$0.00	$0.00	$0.00
Residual cash flow	$7.14	$11.21	$14.73

Memo: Tax-expense computation

	1986	1987	1988
Divisional operating profits	$53.12	$66.87	$72.52
Less: Corporate overhead (Note 1)	($14.00)	($14.50)	($15.00)
Interest expense (Note 2)	($14.00)	($14.00)	($14.00)
Pretax income	$25.12	$38.37	$43.52
Tax expense (@ 46%)	$11.56	$17.65	$20.02

Estimates of Terminal Value

Terminal values = CF(1+g)/K-g
   Where CF = 1988 residual cash flow

		Equity Costs		
		10%	15%	18%
Growth	3%	$216.8	$126.4	$101.2
Rates	5%	$309.3	$154.7	$119.0
	7%	$525.4	$197.0	$143.3

Present-Value Calculation

Present values of residual cash flows and terminal value

		Equity Costs		
		10%	15%	18%
Growth	3%	$189.7	$107.5	$84.6
Rates	5%	$259.2	$126.1	$95.5
	7%	$421.6	$153.9	$110.3

543

Notes:

1. The case indicates that corporate headquarters overhead was $14 million in 1985. This was grown modestly in 1987 and 1988.

2. Assumes debt is maintained at the 1984 level. Some students will note the high level of interest income for 1984 and seek to net that against interest expense, but the large cash balances that generated this income had disappeared by the end of 1984.

3. Case Exhibit 8 shows capital spending to be no less than $17 million but spiking up to $24 million in 1984. The trend assumed in this forecast begins at about the midpoint between the high and low ($20 million) and then grows at $2 million per year.

4. Working capital/sales was 48.3% in 1982, 40.8% in 1983, and 39.7% in 1984 (see case Exhibit 4). Using $124,292 as year-end working capital (from Exhibit 4) yields a working capital as a percentage of combined divisional sales ($515.2 million in 1984) of 33.8%.

    Each dollar of sales forecast in case Exhibit 5 is assumed to require 33.8 cents of working capital.

EXHIBIT B   Valuation of Sybron Corporation as if Buyout (dollars in millions)

Cash-Flow Forecast	1986	1987	1988
Divisional operating cash flow (case Exhibit 7)	$78.10	$92.86	$100.75
Less: Corporate overhead (Note 1)	$0.00	$0.00	$0.00
Reversion of excess pension assets (Note 2)	$43.00		
Interest expense (see "Memo")	($24.54)	($20.34)	($16.13)
Taxes (see "Memo")	($27.94)	($16.42)	($20.95)
After-tax operating cash flow	$68.62	$56.11	$63.67
Less: Capital expenditures (Note 3)	($20.00)	($22.00)	($24.00)
Additions to working capital (Note 4)	($11.40)	($13.50)	($13.00)
Debt amortization (see "Memo")	($42.07)	($42.08)	($8.92)
Residual cash flow	($4.86)	($21.47)	$17.74

Memo: Interest expense and debt amortization computations

Amortization	Day 0	1986	1987	1988
Revolving credit (.15 x $255)	$38.25	$38.25	$38.25	$38.25
Senior term loan (.5 x $255)	$127.50	$85.43	$43.35	$34.43
Subordinated debs. (.25 x $255)	$63.75	$63.75	$63.75	$63.75
Total	$229.50	$187.43	$145.35	$136.43
Debt amortized		$42.07	$42.08	$8.92
Interest (prime rate = 8.50%)				
Revolver (P+1.5%)		$3.83	$3.83	$3.83
Senior term (P+1.5%)		$12.75	$8.54	$4.34
Sub debs. (@ 12.5%)		$7.97	$7.97	$7.97
Total interest expense		$24.54	$20.34	$16.13

Memo: Tax-expense computation

	1986	1987	1988
Divisional operating profits (case Exhibit 6)	$53.12	$66.87	$72.52
Less: Corporate overhead (Note 1)	$0.00	$0.00	$0.00
Additional patent amortization (Note 6)	($6.00)	($6.00)	($6.00)
Additional depreciation (Note 6)	($4.84)	($4.84)	($4.84)
Reversion of excess pension assets	$43.00		
Interest expense (see "Memo")	($24.54)	($20.34)	($16.13)
Pretax income	$60.73	$35.69	$45.55
Tax expense (@ 46%)	$27.94	$16.42	$20.95

Estimates of Terminal Value

Terminal values = CF(1+g)/K-g
  Where CF = residual cash flow for 1988

		Equity Costs		
		10%	15%	18%
Growth	3%	$261.08	$152.30	$121.84
Rates	5%	$372.61	$186.30	$143.31
	7%	$632.84	$237.32	$172.59

Present-Value Calculation

Present values of residual cash flows and
  terminal value (see Note 5)

		Equity Costs		
		10%	15%	18%
Growth	3%	$196.15	$100.14	$74.15
Rates	5%	$279.95	$122.50	$87.22
	7%	$475.46	$156.04	$105.05

Notes:

1. Reflects closing the corporate headquarters entirely. This is consistent with the view that Sybron's management strength was at the division level and that headquarters management was comparatively weak.

2. Reversion of excess pension funds mentioned in the case was assumed to be fully taxable.

3. Case Exhibit 8 shows capital spending to be no less than $17.3 million but spiking up to $24 million in 1984. The trend assumed in this forecast begins at about the midpoint between the high and low ($20 million) and then grows at $2 million per year.

4. Working capital/sales was 48.3% in 1982, 40.8% in 1983, and 39.7% in 1984 (see case Exhibit 4). Using $124,292 as year-end working capital (from Exhibit 4) yields a working capital as a percentage of combined divisional sales (of $515.2 million in 1984) of 33.8%.

    Each dollar of sales forecast in case Exhibit 5 is assumed to require 33.8 cents of working capital.

5. Unlike Exhibit A of this note, the present-value calculation in this exhibit assumes that negative residual cash flows are funded by additional borrowings, while positive cash flows are used to prepay debt.

6. Because this would be a purchase transaction, the property could be written up for tax purposes. The additional depreciation was computed from the information given in the case: ($10/18 + $30/7). Amortization of goodwill and patents is carried separately in the analysis at $6 million per year.

Exhibit C Summary of Actual Terms of Investment and Financing (dollars in millions)

Initial investment (February 1986)		$335.0
Bank loan	$225	
Forstmann Little sub. debs.		
(10 1/2%)	100	
Equity	25	
	$350	
Less divestitures, etc.		257.2
		$ 77.8*

_____

*Debt reduced to $68 at time of sale.

EXHIBIT D   Summary of Units Divested in the Forstmann Little-Led Restructuring
(dollars in millions)

Units Divested	As Estimated in January 1986	As Actually Realized
Brinkmann	$ 33–45	$ 33.0
Mediatech	2–4	5.3
Denco*	2	7.1
Baisch*	--	.5
Cryogenics	8–14	7.0
Liebel–Flarsheim	14	14.0
Taylor/Tycos*	15	20.0
Midwest	14	9.0
Servomex*	9–10	11.3
Sybron Chemical	40–60	51.5
Castle	20	30
	$157–198	$188.7

Other Cash Flows

Pension reversion	43	43
Misc. real estate	12.5	12.5
U.K. lawsuit	--	13
Total gross restructuring	$ 55.5	68.5
Cash flows	$212.5–253.5	$257.2

*Some of the units divested are not identified in the case. These were small units of the four operating segments.

EXHIBIT E 1984-87 Sales and Operating Profits by Division (dollars in millions)

Net Sales	1984	1985	1986	1987 Budget	1987 Forecast
Kerr	$ 61.9	$ 63.4	$ 69.1	$ 71.8	$ 80.4
Ormco	34.4	36.1	38.5	40.2	41.5
Barnstead/Thermolyne	24.6	26.2	26.0	30.1	30.2
Erie	23.1	27.3	37.5	40.9	42.2
Nalge	37.6	41.0	44.8	48.5	50.8
Total net sales	$181.6	$194.0	$215.9	$231.5	$245.1

Operating Profits

	1984	1985	1986	1987 Budget	1987 Forecast
Kerr	$ 9.1	$ 9.6	$ 11.4	$ 13.0	$ 16.3
Ormco	6.5	7.2	7.5	8.2	9.5
Barnstead/Thermolyne	3.6	4.2	4.3	6.5	6.7
Erie	3.4	4.4	5.1	7.1	7.3
Nalge	8.5	9.1	8.7	11.0	12.8
Total operating	$ 31.1	$ 34.5	$ 37.0	$ 45.8	$ 52.6

January 1986
   estimates for
   total company $ 39.1 $ 52.9

EXHIBIT F Summary of Sale of Remaining Assets (October 20, 1987; dollars in millions)

Business Units Sold	Jan. 1986 Estimate		Actual Realized
Nalge	$ 52 --	$ 70	
Erie	26 --	30	
Barnstead	7 --	9	
Thermolyne	9 --	11	
Laboratory Products Group total	94 --	120	
Kerr/Beaver	35 --	40	
Ormco	40 --	50	
Dental Products Group total	75 --	90	
Total sale proceeds	$169 --	$210	$380*
Less outstanding bank debt			(68)
Less closing expenses			(7)
Proceeds to shareholders			$305
Multiple of original equity			12.2

*$365 cash and $15 pay-in-kind bonds; revised from agreed price of $390 of $375 cash, $15 pay-in-kind bonds after October 19, 1987, market crash.

Closing on 10/22/87

Returns over 20 months of holding were:
   Equity investors: 260% (net of carried interest of 20% of profit to Forstmann Little)
   Forstmann Little
     sub. deb.
     investors   70%

Hybritech Incorporated (A) and Eli Lilly and Company

SYNOPSIS AND OBJECTIVES

Eli Lilly, one of the largest U.S. pharmaceuticals company, and Hybritech, the leader in the new and promising field of monoclonal antibodies research, are discussing a possible merger. The two cases present information pertaining to the two sides in the negotiation. The students' tasks are to value Hybritech, based on the information privy to each side, and then negotiate the price and terms.

The "Lilly"/"Hybritech" module presents the instructor with a wide variety of teaching opportunities.

- The model exercises students' *valuation skills*. Under the competitive pressure of negotiation, students are motivated to value Hybritech carefully, typically by conducting sensitivity tests of key assumptions. They confront the inherent ambiguity of valuation analysis and are forced to decide and act despite that ambiguity.

- Students must exercise their *bargaining skills*. The data provided to each side of the negotiation do not point naturally to a common outcome or settlement price. Whether and where the teams settle is heavily influenced by the seriousness and skillfulness of negotiation.

- The apparently "financial" outcome rests heavily on making wise *general-management judgments*, such as assessing strategy and synthesizing concepts and knowledge from other functional areas—including marketing, production, research, and accounting. Hybritech's worth is fundamentally a bet on the ability of Hybritech and Lilly to invent and commercialize products that as yet do not exist. This exercise helps students recognize the important link between financial analysis and general-management judgment.

- When used in conjunction with "Hybritech Incorporated" (B), which follows with its teaching note (Case 52) in this manual, the module of cases illustrates the *usefulness of contingent earn-outs* in striking mutually agreeable merger terms.

- The exercise requires students to analyze a variety of motives, benefits, and risks in the merger (ranging from finance to strategy to organization) and thus affords the instructor excellent *closure* in an instructional module on mergers.

Teaching note written by Robert F. Bruner. Copyright (c) 1988 by the Darden Graduate Business School Sponsors, Charlottesville, VA.

STUDY QUESTIONS

Students are assigned to sides of the negotiation (usually in small, 1-3 person, groups). Both sides can be given the following questions to stimulate their preparation.

1. What do you believe Hybritech is worth?

2. What are the advantages and disadvantages of a combination of Lilly and Hybritech?

3. From your perspective as a manager, what are your goals in this negotiation? What do you expect are the goals of the other side?

4. Develop a negotiating strategy, including identification of your opening and walk-away bid (ask) prices and an estimate of Hybritech's best alternative to a negotiated agreement with Lilly. What key financial assumptions determine the range of high and low values for Hybritech?

ADMINISTRATION OF THE EXERCISE

After studying the case, each side meets separately with the instructor for 30-80 minutes to help develop the point of view unique to that side. The topics covered in that briefing could include: goals, strengths and weaknesses, corporate culture, valuation issues, and negotiation issues (see Analysis section of this note for a discussion of these items.) Before leaving this meeting, each team is asked to give the instructor (privately) its planned opening bid (ask) price and its walk-away bid (ask) price. The students are then dismissed to negotiate an agreement.

While the students are negotiating, the instructor can prepare a table or figure like Exhibit A summarizing the negotiating positions of the teams.

After a reasonable (pre-announced) time period (at least two and one-half hours), the teams are asked to return and report the results of their efforts. In this debriefing session, the instructor can present the negotiating range (i.e., opening prices and walk-away prices) for each side and then ask the outcome. This approach creates a sense of drama and stimulates a discussion of the negotiation process and valuation analyses. If time permits, the instructor can conclude the debriefing with a summary valuation of Hybritech or a review of the actual terms of merger.

ANALYSIS

The Issue of "Fit"

The success of the exercise depends in part on the extent to which both sides believe that a combination of Lilly and Hybritech makes sense, for if either side believes that the price is the only dimension that matters, then the negotiators are bound to press for consummation somewhat less intently. To help develop an awareness of the strategic fit between the two companies, the instructor can ask the following questions in the prenegotiation team briefings:

• What are the goals of Lilly/Hybritech?

• How does the "culture" of your company differ from the other company?

552

- What are the strengths and weaknesses of your company and the other company?

- Why bother to discuss merger; why not go it alone?

- What is your next best alternative to a negotiated agreement?

What emerges from a discussion such as this is a multidimensional comparison of the two companies. A representative board layout of such a discussion is given in Exhibit B.

Any study of the fit of the two companies boils down to a conclusion that each side has something valuable that the other side wants. Lilly has ample financial resources[1] and solid expertise in marketing and production,[2] but needs major new products in order to regain earnings momentum after a less-than-successful experiment with diversification. Hybritech seems to be on the verge of major research breakthroughs, but it has little experience with product commercialization and has a rapid rate of cash consumption.[3]

The combination of Lilly and Hybritech is not flawless. The cultural profiles of the two firms differ: Lilly is large, conservative, and perhaps bureaucratic; Hybritech is small, "scientific," and entrepreneurial. Also, one can imagine a difference based on regional location: Southern California versus Central Indiana.

Despite the apparent fit between the two companies, this merger is not the only means by which each company could achieve its goals. Lilly could acquire other MoAb research firms. Hybritech could merge with Merck or Abbott Labs. Or Lilly and Hybritech could go forward together on a joint-venture basis.

Nevertheless, weighed in the balance, a merger of the two firms dominates other alternatives. Hybritech is entertaining no other suitors. Lilly and Hybritech already work jointly in some areas; the negotiations imply that merger is attractive. The cultural differences between the firms are mitigated by Lilly's history of leaving its new acquisitions alone.

At some point, students will observe that the powerful figures on both sides of the transaction probably *want* the merger: Lilly's CEO and Henry Hillman, a major investor in Hybritech, initiated the discussions. The venture-capital investors may desire to "flip" their investment in the face of future huge external financings that threaten to dilute their equity position. Ted Greene, Hybritech's CEO, stands to gain from the sale of his own shares in the company.

Valuation

A quick examination of the cases reveals large differences in the cash flows forecasted by the two sides. Hybritech's management expects revenues to grow to $1 billion by 1992. Lilly, on the other hand, forecasts Hybritech's revenues to grow to only $344 million by that year. This disparity stems mainly from

---

[1]A triple-A bond rating and a cash balance of almost half a billion dollars.

[2]Lilly has distinguished itself in the commercialization of biotechnology breakthroughs in its hugely successful production and marketing of human insulin based on technology licensed from Genentech.

[3]Hybritech's latest balance sheet shows a cash balance of $21.8 million, but based on Hybritech's own cash-flow forecast, the company will exhaust its cash in less than three years.

different expectations about whether Hybritech will discover a major breakthrough product over the next 10 years (e.g., cancer or AIDS therapy), as is evident in the therapy category [Line 4, Exhibit 5 in "Lilly" case, and Exhibit 4 in "Hybritech" (A)]. A second difference is that Lilly has assessed much larger R&D and SG&A expenses as a percentage of sales through 1992, probably associated with introduction of the new product.

A terminal value summarizing the cash flows after 1996 is especially problematic. One must wrestle here with the long-term expected growth rates--which are bound to vary quite substantially because of the optimism of the Hybritech side and the conservative realism of the Lilly side.

A discount rate for Hybritech may be calculated using a beta extrapolated from Exhibits 7 of each case and the capital-asset-pricing model. Representative valuations of the free cash flows estimated by the two sides are given in Exhibits C and D. They suggest the essential negotiating problem: the very wide difference in valuation of Hybritech must be bridged if the strategic benefits of the merger are to be realized.

Negotiation Issues

Because each side comes to the negotiations with private information, the talks may be characterized as a *process* of persuasion and release of new information. Issues that the instructor may wish to highlight (either before or after the talks) include (1) who quotes a value first, (2) the justification of each side's growth expectations, and (3) the strategic benefit of opening the discussion with an excessively high (low) price.

The use of special terms of payment--specifically an "earn-out"--is one way of breaking an impasse in the negotiation process. Under the terms of an earn-out, Lilly would pay the departing shareholders an extra amount if Hybritech's optimistic forecasts are achieved. Although Hybritech costs more, presumably Lilly also benefits from superior performance. Thus, the earn-out is a way of resolving the large differences in expectations. Whether the instructor should explicitly present the earn-out as a way to resolve this issue before the negotiations begin will depend on the relative sophistication of the students.

EPILOGUE

As the "Hybritech Incorporated" (B) case will indicate, Lilly and Hybritech did reach a tentative merger agreement based on a complicated package of cash, convertible debentures, warrants, and an innovative "contingent payment unit," the value of which was estimated by the Lilly negotiators to be $32 per Hybritech share, or $418 million on a fully diluted basis. After the merger, Hybritech performed at a level consistent with Lilly's more conservative forecasts. Nevertheless, Hybritech's shareholders fared well in the ensuing years, because the Lilly warrants and convertible bonds they received were buoyed by Lilly's surging stock price.

Negotiating Teams	Opening Offer	Walk-Away Offer	Final Offer	Closing Terms
1. Lilly	$275 m	$350 m		$360 m (outsiders get
1. Hybritech	618	335		cash, insiders get cash and warrants
2. Lilly	250	300	$300	No close
2. Hybritech	399	320	$320	
3. Lilly	280	375		360 (cash and
3. Hybritech	400	300		management)
4. Lilly	330	500		358 (320 cash,
4. Hybritech	400	250		365 15 stock market earn-out, options 30
5. Lilly	200	350		350 (300 cash, 50
5. Hybritech	469	285		warrants, ex. now)
6. Lilly	350	555		430 (376 cash,
6. Hybritech	320	500		54 warrants
7. Lilly	321	386.25		325 (192 cash,
7. Hybritech	473	215		133 warrants or stock)
8. Lilly	270	300 warrants and earn-out		$350 m (150 cash,
8. Hybritech	$322 m	$475 m		200 warrants, ex. @ $85 for 6 yrs.)

(See graph on following page.)

Graphic Depiction of Opening Negotiating
Ranges of Lilly and Hybritech Teams

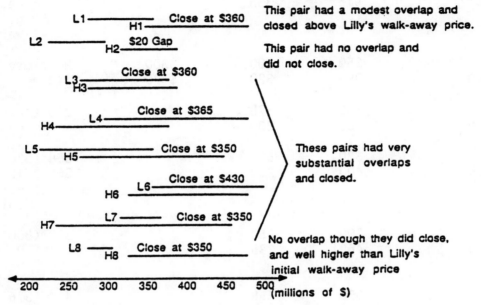

Observations

This pair had a modest overlap and closed above Lilly's walk-away price.

This pair had no overlap and did not close.

These pairs had very substantial overlaps and closed.

No overlap though they did close, and well higher than Lilly's initial walk-away price

Note: L1, H1 designate team 1 of the Lilly & Hybritech sides, respectively.

BOARD 1

	Hybritech	Lilly
Goals	Money Exit for venture capitalists Manufacturing capacity Marketing skills Autonomy Skills in commercialization	Another big product Skills in MoAb research Pre-empt competitors

Strengths	$29 million cash
	Unused debt capacity
	R&D skills
		$500 million cash
		Strong cash flow
		AAA bond rating
		Huge unused debt capacity
		Experience with
		  commercialization
		Marketing and production
		  skills

Weaknesses	Rapid "burn rate" on cash	Big Slow Conservative

BOARD 2

Cultural Fit
R&D vs. marketing/production

Small vs. big

California vs. Indiana

Aggressive vs. conservative

Hybritech's BATNA
(i.e., Best Alternative to a Negotiated Agreement)

1. "Go it alone"
2. Sell to Merck

3. Joint venture

Valuation Issues
1. Cash flows: huge increases from big new products. How certain?
2. Redeployment opportunities: cash, plant
3. Tax-loss carryforward of $15.2 million
4. Which beta?
5. What growth rate?
6. Lack of capital-structure data forces the use of "free cash flow" valuation approach

Negotiation Issues

Negotiating momentum--been at it for months
Style differences
Justifying rapid (slow) revenue growth
Open with outrageously high (low) price?

EXHIBIT C Lilly Forecast of Hybritech Financial Statements (dollars in millions except per share data)

Income Statements	Actual 1984	1985	1986	1987	1988	1989	1990	1991	1992	1993	1994	1995
Sales												
Cancer diagnostics	0	0	4	8	15	20	31	45	61	72	77	81
Other diagnostics	15	32	40	60	90	120	150	170	175	180	185	190
Imaging	0	0	1	2	7	15	25	50	60	75	91	95
Therapy	0	0	0	0	0	0	0	8	48	80	100	120
Total sales	15	32	45	70	112	155	206	273	344	407	453	486
Cost of sales	7	17	20	25	39	54	72	96	124	142	154	160
% of sales	46%	53%	44%	35%	35%	35%	35%	35%	36%	35%	34%	33%
Gross profits	8	15	25	46	73	101	134	177	220	265	299	326
% of sales	54%	47%	56%	65%	65%	65%	65%	65%	64%	65%	66%	67%
Contract revenue	16	22	22	15	12	4	4	4	4	4	4	4
Operating expenses												
R&D	14	23	25	27	29	33	37	44	52	53	54	58
% of sales	91%	73%	56%	38%	26%	21%	18%	16%	15%	13%	12%	12%
SG&A	12	21	25	32	44	64	87	104	127	138	136	136
% of sales	81%	65%	55%	45%	39%	41%	42%	38%	37%	34%	30%	28%
Total expenses	26	44	50	59	73	96	124	147	179	191	191	194
Other income	3	0	0	1	-1	-2	-2	-3	-2	0	0	3
Income before taxes	1	-7	-3	2	11	7	12	31	43	77	113	138
Taxes	0	0	0	1	4	2	4	11	15	27	39	48
Tax rate (%)	4%	8%	10%	35%	35%	35%	35%	35%	35%	35%	35%	35%
Net income	1	-7	-3	1	7	4	8	20	28	50	73	90

EXHIBIT C (continued)

	Actual 1984	1985	1986	1987	1988	1989	1990	1991	1992	1993	1994	1995
Net income	1	-7	-3	1	7	4	8	20	28	50	73	90
Add:												
After-tax depreciation	2	3	3	2	2	3	4	5	6	7	7	8
Deferred taxes	0	0	0	1	2	3	4	5	8	11	13	15
Less:												
Working capital	4	6	6	7	14	17	19	20	28	16	6	6
Capital expenditures (6% of sales)	15	9	9	9	10	11	15	18	24	27	28	30
Other	2	0	0	0	0	0	0	0	0	0	0	0
Cash flow	-18	-19	-15	-12	-13	-18	-18	-8	-10	25	59	77
Average shares outstanding (mm)	10.28	10.28	10.28	10.50	10.50	10.50	10.50	10.50	10.50	10.50	10.50	10.50
Earnings/share	0.09	-0.69	-0.34	0.14	0.69	0.41	0.76	1.92	2.68	4.78	6.98	8.56
Balance Sheets												
Net working capital	27	33	38.6	45.2	58.8	76.2	95.2	115.2	143.2	159.2	164.8	170.8
Net fixed assets	20	26	32	39	47	55	66	79	97	117	138.4	160.8
Other assets	6.3	6.3	6.3	6.3	6.3	6.3	6.3	6.3	6.3	6.3	6.3	6.3
Total assets	53.3	65.3	76.9	90.5	112.1	137.5	167.5	200.5	246.5	282.5	309.5	337.9
Long-term debt	5.2	24.6	39.4	52.1	67	87.915	109.815	122.815	140.815	126.615	80.365	18.665
Equity	48.1	40.7	37.5	38.4	45.1	49.585	57.685	77.685	105.685	155.885	229.135	319.235
Total capital	53.3	65.3	76.9	90.5	112.1	137.5	167.5	200.5	246.5	282.5	309.5	337.9
Debt/equity ratio	10.81%	60.44%	105.07%	135.68%	148.56%	177.30%	190.37%	158.09%	133.24%	81.22%	35.07%	5.85%
Levered beta (assuming Bu = 1.6)	1.71	2.23	2.69	3.01	3.15	3.44	3.58	3.24	2.99	2.44	1.96	1.66
Cost of equity (Rf = .1052, Premium = .056)	0.20	0.23	0.26	0.27	0.28	0.30	0.31	0.29	0.27	0.24	0.22	0.20
Weighted-average cost of cap. (Kd = .09)	0.19	0.18	0.17	0.17	0.17	0.17	0.16	0.17	0.17	0.17	0.18	0.19

559

EXHIBIT C (continued)

DCF Analysis

DCF Analysis	Actual 1984	1985	1986	1987	1988	1989	1990	1991	1992	1993	1994	1995
Pretax income as given	1	-7	-3	2	11	7	12	31	43	77	113	138
Add back financing items ("other income")	3	3	3	3	3	3	3	3	3	3	3	3
EBIT	4	-4	0	5	14	10	15	34	46	80	116	141
EBIT x (1-t); (tax rate = 35%)	2.6	-2.6	0	3.25	9.1	6.5	9.75	22.1	29.9	52	75.4	91.65
Plus noncash items	2	3	3	3	4	6	8	10	14	18	20	22.6
Less: Additions to working capital	-4	-6	-5.6	-6.6	-13.6	-17.4	-19	-20	-28	-16	-5.6	-6
Less: capital expenditures	-15	-9	-9	-9	-10	-11	-15	-18	-24	-27	-28.4	-30
Free cash flow	-14.4	-14.6	-11.6	-9.35	-10.5	-15.9	-16.25	-5.9	-8.1	27	61.4	78.25
Residual value (Ko = .18, g = .10)												978.125
Total free cash flow (FCF)	-14.4	-14.6	-11.6	-9.35	-10.5	-15.9	-16.25	-5.9	-8.1	27	61.4	1056.375

PV of FCF (Ko = .18, g = .10)   140.08
Less: Current debt   -14.20
Value of equity ($ mm)   125.88
Price per share (12.94 mm shares) fully diluted)   9.73
Implicit P/E (EPS = $.04)   243.20
Implicit market/book (book = $49.5 mm)   2.54

Sensitivity Analysis

Value of Equity (in millions)

K = -g Spread		0.06	0.08	0.1	0.12
Term. Value		1300	975	780	650
Range of	0.19	$146.7	$98.7	$69.9	$50.8
Capital Costs	0.18	165.3	112.7	81.1	60.1
	0.17	186.0	128.3	93.6	70.5
	0.165	197.3	136.7	100.3	76.1
	0.16	209.1	145.6	107.4	82.0
	0.15	234.7	164.8	122.9	95.0
	0.14	263.1	186.2	140.1	109.3
	0.13	294.9	210.1	159.3	125.4
	0	1,282.0	957.0	762.0	632.0

EXHIBIT D Greene's Forecast of Hybritech Income Statements and Cash Flows (dollars in millions)

Income Statements	Actual 1984	1985	1986	1987	1988	1989	1990	1991	1992	1993	1994
Sales											
Cancer diagnostics	0	5	23	56	107	181	249	274	282	281	268
Other diagnostics	15	23	32	45	75	110	135	165	190	210	225
Imaging	0	0	2	13	52	106	146	166	174	186	184
Therapy	0	0	0	0	8	57	171	307	400	375	305
Total sales	15	28	57	114	242	454	701	912	1046	1052	982
Cost of sales	7	10	21	41	84	159	224	294	332	336	322
% of sales	48%	36%	37%	36%	35%	35%	32%	32%	32%	32%	33%
Gross profits	8	18	36	73	158	295	477	618	714	716	660
% of sales	52%	64%	63%	64%	65%	65%	68%	68%	68%	68%	67%
Contract revenue	16	21	23	15	12	4	3	3	3	3	3
Operating expenses											
R&D	14	20	24	18	21	21	32	43	51	52	50
% of sales	96%	71%	42%	16%	9%	5%	5%	5%	5%	5%	5%
SG&A	12	15	24	45	93	176	259	323	369	372	349
% of sales	82%	54%	42%	39%	38%	39%	37%	35%	35%	35%	36%
Total expenses	26	35	48	63	114	197	291	366	420	424	399
Other income	3	2	2	0	-3	-10	-25	-38	-43	-37	-20
Income before taxes	1	6	13	25	53	92	164	217	254	258	244
Taxes	0	0	5	9	19	32	57	76	89	90	85
Tax rate (%)	0.35	0.35	0.35	0.35	0.35	0.35	0.35	0.35	0.35	0.35	0.35
Net income	1	6	8	16	35	60	107	141	165	168	159

EXHIBIT D (continued)

Cash Flow	Actual 1984	1985	1986	1987	1988	1989	1990	1991	1992	1993	1994
Net income	1	6	8	16	35	60	107	141	165	168	159
Noncash items	0	1	2	2	6	10	18	19	15	8	-1
Working capital	-4	-8	-12	-22	-63	-101	-118	-100	-61	1	39
Capital expenditures	-15	-6	-5	-23	-53	-93	-111	-98	-66	-10	-10
Cash flow	-18	-7	-7	-27	-76	-124	-104	-38	53	167	187

Balance Sheets

	Actual 1984	1985	1986	1987	1988	1989	1990	1991	1992	1993	1994
Net working capital	27	35	47	69	132	233	351	451	512	511	472
Net fixed assets	20	27	34	59	118	221	350	467	548	566	575
Other assets	6.3	6.3	6.3	6.3	6.3	6.3	6.3	6.3	6.3	6.3	6.3
Total assets	53.3	68.3	87.3	134.3	256.3	460.3	707.3	924.3	1066.3	1083.3	1053.3
Long-term debt	5.2	14.2	24.8	55.6	143.1	287.3	427.7	503.6	480.5	329.8	141.2
Equity	48.1	54.1	62.5	78.7	113.2	173	279.6	420.7	585.8	753.5	912.1
Total capital	53.3	68.3	87.3	134.3	256.3	460.3	707.3	924.3	1066.3	1083.3	1053.3
Debt/equity ratio	10.81%	26.25%	39.68%	70.65%	126.41%	166.07%	152.97%	119.71%	82.02%	43.77%	15.48%
Levered beta (assuming Bu = 1.6)	1.72	1.88	2.02	2.35	2.93	3.35	3.22	2.86	2.47	2.06	1.76
Cost of equity (Rf = .1052, Premium = .056)	0.20	0.21	0.22	0.24	0.27	0.29	0.29	0.27	0.24	0.22	0.20
Weighted-average cost of capital (Kd = .09)	0.19	0.19	0.18	0.18	0.17	0.17	0.17	0.17	0.17	0.18	0.19

EXHIBIT D (continued)

DCF Analysis

	Actual 1984	1985	1986	1987	1988	1989	1990	1991	1992	1993	1994
Pretax income as given	0.6	6	13	25	53	92	164	217	254	258	244
Add back financing items ("other income")	3	2	2	0	-3	-10	-25	-38	-43	-37	-20
EBIT	-2.4	4	11	25	56	102	189	255	297	295	264
EBIT x (1-t); (tax rate = 35%)	-1.56	2.6	7.15	16.25	36.4	66.3	122.85	165.75	193.05	191.75	171.6
Plus noncash items	0	1	2	2	6	10	18	19	15	8	-1
Less Additions to working capital	-4	-8	-12	-22	-63	-101	-118	-100	-61	1	39
Less capital expenditures	-15	-6	-5	-23	-53	-93	-111	-98	-66	-10	-10
Free cash flow	-20.56	-10.4	-7.85	-26.75	-73.6	-117.7	-88.15	-13.25	81.05	190.75	199.6
Residual value (Ko = .18, g = .10)											2495
Total free cash flow	-20.56	-10.4	-7.85	-26.75	-73.6	-117.7	-88.15	-13.25	81.05	190.75	2694.6

PV of FCF (Ko = .18, horizon = 1985–1994) 422.46
Less: Current debt -14.20
Value of equity ($ mm) 408.26
Price per share (12.94 mm shares fully diluted) 31.55
Implicit P/E (EPS = $.04) 788.75
Implicit market/book (book = $49.5 mm) 8.25

Sensitivity Analysis

Value of Equity (in millions)

		K-g Spread			
		0.06	0.08	0.1	0.12
	Term. Value	3000	2500	2000	1650
Range of Capital Costs	0.19	456.5	368.7	280.9	219.5
	0.18	504.7	409.2	313.7	246.8
	0.17	557.9	453.9	349.8	277.0
	0.165	586.5	477.9	369.3	293.3
	0.16	616.5	503.1	389.8	310.5
	0.15	681.2	557.6	434.0	347.5
	0.14	752.6	617.7	482.8	388.4
	0.13	831.5	684.2	536.9	433.8

Eli Lilly and Company

In September 1985, Ron Henriksen, director of financial development at Eli Lilly and Company, was preparing for final negotiations between his company and Hybritech, Inc., a biotechnology firm specializing in monoclonal antibody (MoAb) research. Lilly was already carrying out some of its own biotechnology research, but management wanted the company to become more involved in the field and believed purchasing the talent was faster than developing it internally. Lilly and Hybritech had been in and out of acquisition negotiations for about a year, but agreement appeared to be near; price and form of payment were the only remaining issues to be resolved.

Negotiations had been carried on in secret among only four people in addition to Henriksen and each company's counsel: Jim Cornelius, Lilly vice president and chief financial officer; Gene Step, president of the Lilly pharmaceutical division; Ted Greene, Hybritech chairman and chief executive officer; and Tim Wollaeger, Hybritech senior vice president and CFO. Greene also maintained close communications with Henry Hillman and Tom Perkins throughout the negotiating process. These two men represented Wilmington Investments (a 26 percent owner of Hybritech stock) and Kleiner, Perkins, Caufield & Byers, which, together with six other investors, owned 23 percent of the company (see Exhibit 1).

ELI LILLY AND COMPANY

Eli Lilly, a leading therapeutics and pharmaceuticals firm headquartered in Indianapolis, Indiana, was founded in 1876 and incorporated in 1901. Until the 1970s, the company had been closely managed by members of the Lilly family. Its hallmark conservative management style continued to be reflected by its Aaa and AAA bond ratings--one of only 18 companies with the highest quality rating from both Moody's and Standard & Poors. The company had 28,000 employees--4,500 were involved in R&D, 1,240 marketed pharmaceuticals in the United States, and 1,300 marketed them in Europe. Summary financial data for Lilly are provided in Exhibit 2.

In 1984, human health products were responsible for two-thirds of Lilly's $3.1 billion in sales, and the remainder was from sales of agricultural chemicals, animal health products, and cosmetics (primarily the Elizabeth Arden brand). Lilly's pharmaceuticals included pain relievers, an antiarthritis agent, antibiotics, antidiabetic agents, cardiovascular drugs, hormones, sedatives, and vitamins. The company also had developed and manufactured a variety of medical instruments, including patient vital-signs measurement and

---

Case written by Casey S. Opitz under the direction of Robert F. Bruner at the Darden Graduate School of Business Administration, with the assistance of Eli Lilly and Company management. Copyright (c) 1988 by the Darden Graduate Business School Sponsors, Charlottesville, VA.

monitoring systems, intravenous-fluid delivery and control systems, pacemakers and defibrillators[1] and coronary angioplasty[2] catheter systems.

Lilly had long manufactured and marketed injectable antibiotics to hospitals, but this market was on the decline for Lilly because of patent expirations and increased competition. The company also marketed a number of oral antibiotics, two of which were expected to provide sales of between $500 million and $600 million in 1985. The patent for one, Keflex® would expire in 1987, but a research report of Bear, Stearns & Company said that Ceclor®'s sales were expected to show a compound growth rate of 15 percent a year through 1990. If this forecast proved true, Ceclor would be the largest selling oral antibiotic ever.

By the early 1980s, spurred primarily by recent changes in Medicare rules, hospitals were beginning to institute serious cost-containment programs, which were expected to have some negative effect on pharmaceutical and medical supply companies' margins. An even greater threat to Lilly and other research-based pharmaceutical companies came from the growing use of generic pharmaceuticals. Some insurance companies required that generics be used to fill prescriptions, and some states allowed pharmacists to substitute a generic even when a name brand was specified by the physician. Pharmacists often favored generics because their lower prices meant higher possible margins for them. To counter the negative effects of generic drugs on its own sales and margins, Lilly was focusing its marketing efforts on Ceclor, Humulin®, Dobutrex®, and its other proprietary products. Lilly was also expanding into additional chronic-use drugs, beyond human insulin and into antidepressant and antiulcer markets.

Another factor affecting the pharmaceuticals industry was a drug-discovery drought that had lasted throughout much of the 1970s. To sustain their growth rates, many drug companies had somewhat forsaken their commitment to research and development in favor of expanding into cosmetics, confectioneries, and medical equipment. As Lilly moved into cosmetics and medical equipment, its R&D expenditures reached a low of 7.8 percent of sales in 1980 before rebounding to 11.0 percent in 1984.

One of Lilly's most successful ventures into the high-technology medical-equipment market was its 1984 purchase of Advanced Cardiovascular Systems (ACS), a manufacturer of coronary angioplasty catheters. Through this acquisition, Lilly purchased the trademark to one of only two such devices in the United States (C. R. Bard had the other). On an annualized basis, ACS's sales rose from $19 million to $45 million between 1984 and 1985--from 20 percent of all such devices to almost 50 percent. This highly regarded acquisition had been accomplished through the use of an earn-out. The earn-out allowed for additional payment over the initial purchase price to be made to the original handful of shareholders (primarily ACS management and venture capitalists). These payments in Lilly stock were based on ACS exceeding certain sales and earnings projections. Bear, Stearns expected Lilly's total medical instruments sales to increase at a compound annual rate of 21 percent a year, from an expected $350 million in 1985 to between $900 million and $1 billion by 1990.

Lilly also had a monoclonal antibody research group involved in the same sort of work as Hybritech (described later). Bear, Stearns stated, "The most

---

[1]Devices that stimulate an arrested heart by providing an electric shock.

[2]Balloon catheters used to dilate narrowed coronary arteries. This procedure often replaced heart bypass surgery.

exciting products may ultimately emanate from the company's use of MoAb to treat cancer...."[3] This relatively new area of biotechnology research could open a broad range of scientific possibilities to Lilly, in terms of both therapeutics and diagnostics--an area the company had not been involved in previously.

Overall, Bear, Stearns expected Lilly's human health products and medical instruments sales to lead the company, while its agricultural chemicals and animal health products would decline. Corporate sales were expected to be $3.2 billion in 1985 and $3.4 billion in 1986.

Similarly, *Value Line Investment Survey* stated that Lilly had

> ...healthy sales of its new health care products, with very high price tags.... In light of the company's strong earnings prospects, high returns on investment, and relatively low P/E multiple, even the most conservative investor would do well to consider these shares...[4]

... at the current price of $45. *Value Line* projected sales of $3.5 billion and a net profit margin of 16 percent for the company in 1986.

THE BIOTECHNOLOGY INDUSTRY AND MONOCLONAL ANTIBODY RESEARCH

Lilly had a strategic interest in gaining a position in Hybritech's field of monoclonal antibody research. Lilly had several in-house research labs working on the therapeutic use of monoclonal antibodies, but unlike Lilly, Hybritech's research effort was totally focused on MoAb technology.

Broadly, at this time, biotechnology included two fields. The first, genetic engineering, involved manufacturing proteins by splicing and recombining DNA (deoxyribonucleic acid--the genetic material in every cell). This recombinant DNA (rDNA) technology has allowed scientists to manufacture large quantities of very pure proteins by using the cell's natural protein-replicating characteristics.

The second field, hybridoma or cellular engineering, was best described from page one of the 1984 Hybritech Incorporated annual report:

> Monoclonal antibody technology is only ten years old. Yet, it has already been acknowledged as an achievement worthy of a Nobel Prize. In 1984 Cesar Milstein and George J. F. Kohler, the developers of the technique that provided the first ready source of monoclonal antibodies, shared the Nobel Prize in Medicine with Niels K. Jerne, another renowned immunologist. Working at Cambridge in 1975, Milstein and Kohler achieved the first successful fusion of a special form of myeloma cells with antibody-producing cells to form hybridoma cells. The laboratory-made hybrid cells combine specific antibody-making ability with vigorous growth. Hybridoma cells are programmed to produce one and only one type of antibody. For the first time

---

[3]Bear, Stearns & Company Investment Research, Joseph P. Ricardo and Barbara A. Ryan, August 20, 1985.

[4]*Value Line Investment Survey*, November 15, 1985.

scientists and physicians had at their disposal unlimited sources of antibodies of purity and consistency comparable to that of pharmaceutical compounds or synthetic chemicals.

Antibodies, the body's own disease fighters, have long been used in medicine. But antibodies from the blood of rabbits, goats, sheep, horses and even humans--the only sources before hybridoma technology--are obtained as an impure mixture of antibody types.

These blood-derived antibodies also have variable properties from animal to animal and from day to day. Researchers and doctors could never exploit the full potential of antibodies until sufficient amounts of antibodies with uniform, consistent properties could be produced. Monoclonal antibodies are meeting this need.

In 1980, Genentech became the first biotechnology firm to go public. The price of its stock went from $35 to $89 per share in the first 20 minutes of the offering. By late 1981, the first MoAb diagnostic application, developed by Hybritech, had been approved by the Food and Drug Administration (FDA). In 1982, the first rDNA therapeutic product, human insulin, was approved. Human insulin's gene-expression system was developed by Genentech, while the scale-up, clinical work, and marketing of the product was done by Lilly. Diagnostic applications were responsible for far more product introductions than were therapeutics. By the end of that same year, 23 new MoAb diagnostic products had reached the market; there were 45 on the market by June 1983. In 1985, the FDA approved the second rDNA therapeutic product, human growth hormone, which was researched, developed, and marketed by Genentech. In that same year, the pharmaceutical firm of Bristol-Myers acquired a one-third interest in a joint subsidiary of Genetic Systems and Syntex. The new biotechnology firms were attracting a good deal of well-deserved attention.

By 1985, new applications for genetic and cellular engineering were being discovered at a rapid pace, and competition to apply rDNA and MoAb (themselves competing technologies for certain clinical conditions) was heating up. Biotechnology companies were pouring money into research and development (equal to 41 percent of total sales for Hybritech by September 1985), and the effort was beginning to pay off as research led to application. MoAb research had been most widely applied to diagnostics. The most important developments had been tests for pregnancy, allergies, prostate cancer, and anemia. The biotechnologies also had applications for livestock and crops, such as the development of growth hormones and hardier plants. By the year 2000, biotechnology industry sales were expected to be between $15 and $40 billion, according to the Office of Technology Assessment. Other estimates placed sales as high as $100 billion by the end of the century.

Producing a single gram of MoAb for research purposes cost about $2,000 in 1985. However, long-term commercial product costs needed to be in the $100-$200 per gram range. Monoclonal antibody production could only be cost effective when manufactured on a large scale, but large-scale production could not be carried out in laboratory culture dishes or mice. Equipment for mass production had been developed by 1985, but scale-up was difficult and outside the experience of most biotechnology companies, including Hybritech. Clinical trials for *in vitro* diagnostics were not particularly expensive; however, product development requiring human clinical trials could run $50-$100 million per product. These costs were the most prohibitive investment facing all the biotechnology companies.

The ability to patent MoAb products and the value of doing so depended on the market (diagnostics, imaging, or therapeutics) and the aspect to be patented (antibody, process, or test format). Within the area of diagnostics, the most important and easily policed aspect would be the design and format of the test. Within the imaging and therapeutics areas, the final product--the antibody and the imaging agent or other therapeutic substance--was probably most patentable. The real value of any such patents was undetermined by the courts. Technological advances were considered likely to move faster than the issuance of patents, particularly in the diagnostics business.

HYBRITECH INCORPORATED

Hybritech, founded in 1978, was one of the first biotechnology companies, and went public in late 1981. By year-end 1983, it had the largest equity base of any MoAb company. The company was located in San Diego, California, biotechnology's answer to Silicon Valley. Lilly had facilities in nearby La Jolla, and the scientists at the two companies knew each other well. Hybritech was the first firm to develop, produce, and market MoAb products, and it remained the industry leader. Under the leadership of Ted Greene, Hybritech was considered the MoAb flagship, from the quality of its venture capitalists to its R&D team.

By 1985, the company had developed a line of 21 low-cost, simple-to-use diagnostic tests known as Tandem® and Icon® tests. Tandem tests gave a quantitative measurement of a substance associated with a disease or condition. Icon tests indicated qualitatively if a substance was present at all. By September 1985, the most important uses of Tandem and Icon tests were for pregnancy, thyroid disorders, allergies, heart attacks, colon cancer, anemia, and dwarfism.

Most Tandem and Icon tests had a competitive advantage in that they were both cheaper and faster than other tests; in addition, because the tests were easy to use, they could be carried out in a doctor's office, rather than in laboratories. They were also as reliable as traditional lab tests. Given the cost-cutting trend in the health care field, the tests were expected to be very popular. The question that remained was how to sell these tests cost-effectively to individual practitioners.

On average, each office visit by a sales representative cost a pharmaceutical company $75, and a typical visit lasted only a few minutes as the doctor moved from one patient to another. Marketing high-margin drugs this way was profitable, but not low-margin tests. Most standard medical tests were marketed to clinical labs that served a large number of doctors, and at this time, Tandem and Icon tests were being marketed to labs with some success; however, individual physicians were believed to be the real market. There were approximately 300,000 office-based physicians serviced by less than 10,000 clinical laboratories in the United States. For this clinical laboratory segment, Hybritech was also developing improved instrumentation systems (four were on the market) for automating and reading test results. Few other MoAb companies were taking this systems approach to product development.

In addition, Hybritech was developing a process called *imaging*, whereby monoclonal antibodies would be coupled to radioactive isotopes. These conjugated antibody-isotopes ("magic bullets") would seek out and accumulate in tumors, where their radioactivity would then be detected. The hope was that this approach would provide greater accuracy than currently possible in the detection of cancers and, eventually, that imaging could be used to monitor the treatment of cancer by monoclonals linked to cancer drugs or other, stronger radioactive isotopes. This approach could be used to kill cancer cells selectively. One such radioisotope was in the clinical-testing stage at Johns Hopkins University and, if successful, would be Hybritech's first entry into the therapeutics market. This therapeutic was truly novel and could represent a significant entry into a market that was very unsatisfied. Hybritech was working in the early stages of many other promising therapeutic concepts.

Hybritech had grown from a 19-person company in 1978 to 800 employees in 1984, more than 200 of whom were directly involved in MoAb research. In addition to its corporate headquarters in San Diego, the company had just purchased a facility in Liege, Belgium, for its European headquarters. Some 41 percent of the company's employees and 36 percent of its facilities were devoted to R&D; 34 percent of employees and 41 percent of facilities were involved in manufacturing. The remainder were in marketing and administration. At 42, Greene was older than most of the other executive officers.

Unlike most biotechnology companies, Hybritech had a successful direct sales force--particularly in marketing to labs. It employed 40 diagnostic salespersons in the United States and also had direct sales forces in West Germany, Belgium, and the United Kingdom.

HYBRITECH'S FINANCIAL PAST AND FUTURE

Historical financial statements for Hybritech are provided in Exhibits 3 and 4. Sales grew rapidly in 1984 and early 1985 from sales of pregnancy tests to clinical labs and hospitals (25 percent of these markets). Contract revenues were from R&D funding from the two Hybritech limited partnerships, which were formed to undertake R&D for selected MoAb-based product technology. In the case of Hybritech Clinical Partners, these contracts were to provide revenues of $63 million through 1989; $9 million had been recognized as of 1984. Hybrigenetics Cancer Research Limited, an early R&D limited partnership, had nearly completed its research contracts. Hybrigenetics had provided $7 million in funding from 1982 through 1985. Other revenue stemmed from payments under R&D agreements with nearly a dozen other major pharmaceutical companies; an additional $6 million was to be realized under the present agreements. These contracts offered Hybritech some flexibility in generating revenues. The existing agreements could be expanded to cover other areas of research interest or additional firms could be added as revenue sources. By 1985, Hybritech's senior vice president of finance, Tim Wollaeger, had raised a significant war chest for research through the use of this complex and creative array of financing.

The decline in the company's gross margin on product sales was the result of start-up expenses for a new plant in San Diego that represented about one-third of the company's total floor space. Economies of scale were beginning to be noticed in the areas of selling, general, and administrative expenses, marketing, and R&D. The 75 percent tax rate in 1984 resulted from nondeductible losses on foreign operations; actual federal taxes were 46 percent. At this point, the company had $15.2 million in available tax-loss carryforwards and $1.1 million of unused investment and R&D tax-credit carryforwards.

The nature of Hybritech's products made projecting future sales difficult. What would result from MoAb research and how soon? Applications of the technology were growing rapidly. However, regulatory approvals and the results of broad-based use were always uncertain in health care markets. As a result, Henriksen believed Hybritech management faced many different options for use of MoAb technology. He knew that employees of Hybritech, many of whom had large personal investments in the company, believed the cure for cancer was at hand—certainly within the next 5 to 10 years. Henriksen, however, believed that the prudent course would be not to assume anything quite so grandiose when determining the current value of the company.

In contrast to his thinking, Hambrecht and Quist, an institutional research firm that maintained a market in Hybritech's stock, believed that the company's sales over the next few years would be fueled by *in vitro* diagnostic tests in the clinical and hospital lab segments, the introduction of an over-the-counter pregnancy test in 1986, the increasing importance of the company's diagnostic instrument line, and the possible introduction in 1988 of a hybridoma cancer therapeutic. On the down side, they expected contract revenue to level off and other revenue from R&D agreements to dwindle.

Greene told Henriksen and Cornelius that Hybritech could be a $1 billion company by 1992. Lilly, based on the information it had available, thought a more likely scenario was that Hybritech would be only about half that size by 1995. One of Lilly's scenarios of Hybritech's sales and cash flows is provided in Exhibit 5. Henriksen believed it was one reasonable projection of the possible outcome.

Although Henriksen thought Hybritech was financially stronger than many of its biotechnology competitors (Wollaeger and Greene had just raised $70 million through the latest tax-advantaged partnership arrangement), he believed the company would probably have a long-term need for cash that it could not meet on its own. Major MoAb research, development, and large-scale production programs were expensive. The company's major diagnostics competitor—Abbot Labs—had greater financial resources than Hybritech to support research, clinical trials, large-scale production, and finally direct marketing. "In the diagnostics business, "Henriksen remembered Greene saying, "it is Abbott and the seven dwarfs."

Henriksen told Cornelius,

> Small start-up companies won't be able to afford the
> necessary major investments in product development, human
> clinical trials, and production scale-up. Right now,
> Hybritech is a window of opportunity for us. An argument
> could be made that they need us, and at the same time, the
> acquisition would take us a step beyond traditional
> pharmaceutical technology.

Cornelius agreed and added,

> The investment decision to move on this technology has been
> made based on scientific strategy. At this stage, the
> science is always high risk. We need to think creatively
> about how to finance this strategic move in a manner that
> is fair to both Lilly and Hybritech and can be accomplished
> at a reasonable cost. We could pay more if we were more
> certain of the return.

Henriksen interjected,

> Valuing this deal is a real problem. Earnings multiples
> and asset values are dead ends, even multiples of sales are
> meaningless. Their cash, the partnership income, the NOLs
> [net operating losses], and the tax credits all help reduce

the real cost to acquire, but there must be two dozen legal
agreements, including noncompete, product license, and
research contracts, out there confusing the situation.

Cornelius concluded, "We need to reexamine the whole biotech group and give some
thought to a creative Hybritech deal structure."

RECENT NEGOTIATIONS

Initial conversations about a combination of Lilly and Hybritech began in
June 1984. The negotiations were discontinued for a time, but resumed in the
summer of 1985. Hybritech's major investor, Henry Hillman, and Richard Wood,
chairman and CEO of Lilly, had known each other for a long time (they both
served on the board of Chemical Bank) and had discussed the possibility of an
acquisition, as had Cornelius, Step, Greene, and Wollaeger. Wood and Hillman
provided the leadership and a vision of the two companies working together.
However, the deal had to be fair and equitable to both sides.

In October 1984, when the first in-depth discussions were held, Hybritech's
management believed their company's sales potential was generally unrecognized
by the market and thus their company was undervalued (in 1984, its stock traded
for between $11 and $22.75 per share). Then, throughout the first eight months
of 1985, Hybritech's stock price rose steadily (as did the prices of most
biotechnology and pharmaceutical companies' stocks) from $20 to $24.75 per
share. Hybritech's, Lilly's, and their competitors' recent stock prices are
provided in Exhibit 6. Biotechnology companies' financial data are given in
Exhibit 7.

Over the spring of 1985, Lilly studied the major biotechnology companies as
possible acquisition candidates. A select group of closely tracked biotech
companies became known as the "sweet 16." Careful review of this group
confirmed that Hybritech was the premier MoAb company. Hybritech, however, was
in no hurry to be acquired; the marriage had to be a "good fit" at the right
price. Cornelius had made it clear to Greene and Wollaeger that a company like
Lilly had a lot to offer, including money to support R&D, medical and clinical
experience, a scientific base, an infrastructure for bringing products to
market, and manufacturing scale-up know-how. Hybritech could develop the
product, but Lilly could scale up to production quantities and market it. In
addition, Lilly was already in the unique position of being able to produce
large quantities of MoAbs for research and clinical trial use.

In May, contact was reestablished, and both firms were ready to talk again.
By the end of the summer, the secret negotiations had become serious, but they
remained highly confidential to avoid speculation as well as any possible
negative discussions within either company. Several questions posed by Lilly's
corporate culture would still have to be answered: "We don't need them; we
already have our own biotech area." "It would be our biggest acquisition ever
and yet it has the shortest track record." "We're a therapeutics company, so
why are we getting into diagnostics?" "We're offending our own scientists by
buying others." "Can you patent genes?"

The price Lilly could justify paying for the company depended in part on the
cost of financing the acquisition. Henricksen therefore studied the interest-
rate and yield information provided in Exhibit 8. Price was the first order of
business; he would not concern himself with the form of payment until the time
came. So far, he and Cornelius were assuming a cash payment, but they were

willing to consider other alternatives. This deal would involve valuing three
separate concerns--the diagnostics, imaging, and therapeutics opportunities
embodied in the synergy with Hybritech.

EXHIBIT 1 Hybritech Stock Ownership as of September 13, 1985

	Shares	Percentage
Wilmington Investments, Inc.	2,677,001	26.0%
Kleiner, Perkins and six major investors	2,346,540	22.9
Other institutions (total of 24)	1,473,640	14.3
Total institutions	6,497,181	63.2
Officers and directors	640,585	6.2
Other insiders	318,725	3.1
Total insiders	959,310	9.3
All other investors	2,823,937	27.5
Total shares outstanding	10,280,428	100.0%
Also outstanding:		
Series C stock*	489,162	
Warrants**	1,401,500	
Options†	766,396	
	12,937,486	

---

*Each share of Series C common stock would convert into one share of common stock upon the merger or acquisition of the company.

**The company issued warrants to the limited partners of Hybritech Clinical Partners, Ltd., to purchase a total of 1,401,500 shares of the company's common stock. These warrants were exercisable between March 31, 1987, and March 31, 1989, at $17.09 per share; on April 1, 1989, the exercise price would increase to $22.09 per share. The warrants expired on March 31, 1992.

†Options were granted to employees, consultants, and advisors, with exercise prices ranging between $2.85 and $26.43 per share.

EXHIBIT 2   Eli Lilly and Company and Subsidiaries Selected Financial Data
            (dollars in millions except per share data)

	Year Ended December 31		
	1982	1983	1984
Net sales	$2,962.7	$3,033.7	$3,109.2
Operating costs and expenses	2,291.8	2,308.8	2,364.9
Other income, net	13.3	29.9	26.4
Net income	$411.8	$457.4	$490.3
Earnings per common share	$2.71	$3.07	$3.36
Dividends paid per common share	1.30	1.375	1.4875
Average common shares outstanding (thousands)*	151,868	149,248	145,710
Cash and marketable securities	$303.8	$491.0	$445.3
Current assets	1,680.5	1,830.1	1,827.5
Current liabilities	873.6	988.3	1,067.2
Property and equipment	1,135.6	1,212.6	1,280.4
Total assets	3,155.1	3,413.8	3,643.9
Long-term obligations	49.4	90.7	116.6
Shareholders' equity	$2,055.5	$2,121.0	$2,221.2
Return on average assets	13.6%	13.9%	13.9%
Return on shareholders' equity	20.9%	21.9%	22.6%
Number of employees	29,300	29,200	28,700
Research and development	$267.4	$293.6	$341.3
Capital expenditures	236.6	199.9	205.3
Depreciation and amortization	$ 83.1	$ 98.3	$120.7

*Adjusted for 2-for-1 stock split 12/31/85.

EXHIBIT 3 Hybritech Incorporated Consolidated Income Statements
(dollars in thousands except per share data)

| | Year Ended December 31 | | | Through |
	1982	1983	1984	June 30, 1985
Operating revenues				
Product sales	$1,841	$6,859	$14,599	$14,524
Contract revenues	1,297	5,735	16,227	11,736
Total operating revenues	3,138	12,594	30,826	26,260
Operating costs and expenses				
Cost of sales	1,741	2,660	6,881	6,569
Research and development	4,987	6,293	13,700	10,983
Marketing	3,348	4,947	8,067	5,500
General and administrative	1,918	2,466	3,891	2,447
Other	9	29	120	60
Total operating expense	12,003	16,395	32,659	25,559
Operating income (loss)	(8,865)	(3,801)	(1,833)	701
Other income (expense)				
Interest income	1,618	3,371	3,107	699
Foreign exchange loss	0	(37)	(121)	(60)
Other loss	(21)	(7)	(35)	(20)
Total other income, net	1,597	3,327	2,951	619
Income (loss) before income				
taxes and extraordinary item	(7,268)	(474)	1,118	1,320
Provision for income taxes	0	0	750	647
Income (loss) before				
extraordinary item	(7,268)	(474)	368	673
Extraordinary item—use of				
operating-loss carryforward	0	0	708	0
Net income	($7,268)	($474)	$1,076	$673
Per share of common stock:				
Net income (loss) before				
extraordinary item	($0.82)	($0.05)	$0.04	$0.06
Net income (loss)	($0.82)	($0.05)	$0.10	$0.06

EXHIBIT 4 Hybritech Incorporated Consolidated Balance Sheets
            (dollars in thousands)

| | Year Ended December 31 | |
	1983	1984
Current assets		
Cash and cash investments	$32,884	$21,792
Accounts receivable	1,815	3,772
Inventories, at cost	3,077	5,891
Other current assets	1,830	3,201
Total current assets	39,606	34,656
Equipment at cost		
Leasehold improvements	2,449	5,931
Equipment and furniture	5,174	17,039
Total equipment	7,623	22,970
Depreciation and amortization	(1,151)	(2,918)
Net equipment	6,472	20,052
Investments	44	3,019
Other assets	1,944	3,354
Total assets	$48,066	$61,081
Current liabilities		
Accounts payable	$959	$2,605
Accrued liabilities	1,008	2,204
Deferred revenue	670	46
Notes payable to bank	0	949
Current portion of long-term debt	36	1,847
Total current liabilities	2,673	7,651
Long-term debt	666	5,231
Total liabilities	3,339	12,882
Common stock, 1984: 10.25MM shares outstanding	59,470	59,858
Series B common, 1984: 0 shares outstanding*	392	0
Series C common, 1984: 0.49MM shares outstanding*	1,178	1,472
Common stock warrants	0	2,453
Accumulated deficit	(14,807)	(13,731)
Foreign currency adjustment	(25)	(119)
Notes receivable: sale of stock	(1,481)	(1,734)
Total shareholders' equity	44,727	48,199
Total liabilities and equity	$48,066	$61,081

*Series B and Series C common stock were sold to employees, directors,
and consultants; a maximum of 250,000 and 500,000 shares, respectively, could be
sold. No dividends could be paid on Series B, and dividends of one-twentieth
the amount paid on common stock could be paid on Series C.

EXHIBIT 5 One Lilly Forecast* of Hybritech Income Statements and Cash Flows (dollars in millions except per share data)

	Actual 1984	1985	1986	1987	1988	1989	1990	1991	1992	1993	1994	1995
Sales												
Cancer diagnostics	0	0	4	8	15	20	31	45	61	72	77	81
Other diagnostics	15	32	40	60	90	120	150	170	175	180	185	190
Imaging	0	0	1	2	7	15	25	50	60	75	91	95
Therapy	0	0	0	0	0	0	0	8	48	80	100	120
Total sales	15	32	45	70	112	155	206	273	344	407	453	486
Cost of sales	7	17	20	25	39	54	72	96	124	142	154	160
% of sales	47%	53%	44%	36%	35%	35%	35%	35%	36%	35%	34%	33%
Gross profits	8	15	25	45	73	101	134	177	220	265	299	326
% of sales	53%	47%	56%	64%	65%	65%	65%	65%	64%	65%	66%	67%
Contract revenue	16	22	22	15	12	4	4	4	4	4	4	4
Operating expenses:												
R&D	14	23	25	27	29	33	37	44	52	53	54	55
% of sales	93%	72%	62%	39%	26%	21%	18%	16%	15%	13%	12%	11%
SG&A	12	21	25	32	44	64	87	104	127	138	136	136
% of sales	80%	66%	56%	46%	39%	41%	42%	38%	37%	34%	30%	28%
Total expenses	26	44	50	59	73	97	124	148	179	191	190	191
Other income	3	0	0	1	(1)	(2)	(2)	(3)	(2)	0	0	3
Income before taxes	1	(7)	(3)	2	11	6	12	31	43	77	113	142
Taxes	0	0	0	1	4	2	4	11	15	27	40	49
Tax rate	4%	8%	10%	35%	35%	35%	35%	35%	35%	35%	35%	35%
Net income	1	(7)	(3)	1	7	4	8	20	28	50	74	92
Avg. primary shares outstanding (millions)	10.28	10.28	10.28	10.50	10.50	10.50	10.50	10.50	10.50	10.50	10.50	10.50
Earnings per share	0.09	-0.69	-0.34	0.14	0.69	0.41	0.76	1.92	2.68	4.78	6.98	8.56

577

EXHIBIT 5 (continued)

	Actual 1984	1985	1986	1987	1988	1989	1990	1991	1992	1993	1994	1995
Gross profits and contract revenue	24	37	47	61	85	105	138	181	224	269	303	330
Less: Total expenses	(26)	(44)	(50)	(59)	(73)	(97)	(124)	(147)	(179)	(191)	(190)	(191)
EBIT	(2)	(7)	(3)	2	12	8	14	34	45	77	113	139
EBIT: (1-taxes)	(2)	(7)	(3)	1	8	6	9	22	29	50	73	88
Plus: Noncash items	2	3	3	3	4	6	8	10	14	18	20	23
Less: Working capital add.	(4)	(6)	(6)	(7)	(14)	(17)	(19)	(20)	(28)	(16)	(6)	(6)
Less: Capital expenditures	(15)	(9)	(9)	(9)	(10)	(11)	(15)	(18)	(24)	(27)	(28)	(30)
Free cash flow	(19)	(19)	(15)	(12)	(12)	(16)	(17)	(6)	(9)	25	59	75

*These numbers do not represent Lilly's actual forecast of projected Hybritech performance but are provided solely for purposes of this case study. Figures may not add because of rounding.

578

EXHIBIT 6 Stock Prices (dollars per share)

	1984			1985								
	Oct	Nov	Dec	Jan	Feb	Mar	Apr	May	Jun	Jul	Aug	Sep 13
Biotechnology Companies:												
Cambridge	1.75	1.38	1.50	2.88	2.63	2.75	3.63	4.38	4.75	4.50	4.25	3.68
Centocor	10.75	9.25	9.75	12.00	14.00	12.25	15.25	16.00	18.50	19.00	18.00	16.00
Cetus	10.25	8.88	8.75	11.68	12.25	10.38	11.00	12.13	10.68	13.25	16.25	13.68
Cooper	3.25	2.88	3.00	3.88	4.88	3.88	3.50	3.50	2.38	1.75	1.75	1.68
Damon	5.25	4.88	4.50	5.88	6.00	5.00	4.75	6.38	6.38	6.50	6.00	5.68
DNA Plant Technology	5.13	4.25	3.75	5.00	6.25	7.25	6.88	7.75	8.50	8.38	8.50	7.75
Genetic Systems	6.63	6.00	5.50	6.88	7.88	7.63	7.00	8.00	7.38	7.68	7.68	6.68
Molecular Genetics	7.25	6.25	7.25	10.00	10.00	8.00	7.50	7.50	6.75	6.50	7.75	6.88
Monoclonal Antibodies	11.25	9.00	8.75	11.50	10.00	9.00	9.00	9.13	9.00	10.50	10.25	11.75
Ventrex	4.63	4.13	3.75	3.88	4.25	4.25	4.13	3.63	3.38	3.68	5.00	4.75
HYBRITECH	14.75	15.25	16.50	19.75	18.00	18.00	20.50	23.75	25.25	25.00	25.25	24.75
Pharmaceutical Companies:												
Abbott Labs	41.13	41.25	41.00	47.25	47.88	53.00	51.00	54.13	57.38	56.75	57.88	55.00
American Home Products	50.00	50.00	50.50	55.88	58.63	62.13	58.38	64.88	63.88	59.75	58.75	59.38
Bristol Myers	49.13	47.88	52.25	54.38	55.50	57.50	56.88	61.00	61.38	60.13	59.50	57.88
Merck	86.75	88.75	94.00	96.00	99.88	104.88	101.75	108.68	112.68	112.88	114.13	112.25
Pfizer	38.00	39.00	42.25	39.50	40.25	42.88	44.50	50.00	49.50	48.25	48.13	45.50
Squibb	49.75	52.63	53.88	53.88	53.63	56.50	55.50	63.13	63.13	69.50	68.75	66.25
Syntex	49.00	46.75	48.63	53.75	56.88	59.00	57.00	62.25	63.88	62.00	60.50	61.50
Upjohn	63.75	66.75	70.13	71.88	75.25	80.50	83.88	107.25	108.25	115.00	107.75	105.00
Warner Lambert	34.00	32.88	34.75	36.50	37.13	39.63	37.00	41.25	43.38	39.75	38.88	38.75
ELI LILLY*	30.63	31.63	33.00	35.68	39.00	38.88	42.75	43.25	42.50	43.25	41.88	41.88
S&P 500	167.49	163.58	167.24	179.63	181.18	180.66	179.83	189.55	191.85	192.11	188.63	182.08

*Adjusted for 2-for-1 stock split 12/31/85.

Source: *ISL Daily Stock Price Index.*

EXHIBIT 7 Financial Data (fiscal year except stock data)

Biotechnology Companies:

	Latest Book Val. /Share ($/share)	Share-holders' Equity (MM $)	Shares Out. (MM)	Market Value of Equity	Income Before Taxes	Taxes	Earn. Per Share	Market/ Book	Cash Balance	Cash/ Share	Debt/ Equity	Price Earnings	Up-Market Beta*
Cambridge	$0.6	$2.7	4.2	$16	($2,031)	$0	($0.49)	5.8	1.5	0.36	7%	NMF	NA
Centocor	3.3	25.5	7.2	130	703	304	0.06	5.5	9.8	1.36	0	267	NA
Cetus	6.1	140	22.9	364	1,061	68	0.04	2.6	85.2	3.72	1	341	1.18
Cooper	2	35.4	17.8	27	1,573	148	0.08	0.8	1.9	0.11	39	20	NA
Damon	1.2	23.3	19.3	116	(3,506)	(1,891)	(0.09)	5	32.3	1.67	9	NMF	1.08
DNA Plant Technology	1.6	16.1	9.9	84	(657)	0	(0.07)	5.2	14.7	1.48	0	NMF	NA
Genetic Systems	2.3	54.5	23.2	177	(3,885)	0	(0.20)	3.2	48.0	2.07	NA	NA	2.4
Molecular Genetics	4.3	26.9	6.2	47	(641)	0	(0.13)	1.7	23.6	3.81	0	NMF	NA
Monoclonal Antibodies	0.6	2.6	2.6	26	(3,622)	0	(1.50)	17.3	0.7	0.27	15	NMF	NA
Ventrex	2	21	10.4	53	(6,069)	158	(0.59)	2.5	5.2	0.5	7	NMF	NA
HYBRITECH	4.6	49.5	10.7	268	1,118	750	0.04	5.4	21.8	2.03	11	413	1.72

Pharmaceutical Companies:

	Latest Book Val. /Share ($/share)	Share-holders' Equity (MM $)	Shares Out. (MM)	Net Income	Earn. Per Share	Working Capital (MM $)	Debt Equity	R&D/ Sales	Price Earnings	Market/ Book	Beta
Abbott Labs	$13.3	$1,602.7	120.2	$403	$3.34	$743.3	29%	7.0%	13	3.0	1.05
American Home Prod.	13.7	2,088.6	152.0	656	4.26	1,439.7	0	4.2	12	3.6	0.85
Bristol Myers	15.6	2,145.9	137.4	472	3.45	1,307.7	5	5.1	13	3.2	0.95
Merck	35.3	2,544.2	72.1	493	6.71	1,076.5	7	11.0	13	2.6	0.80
Pfizer	15.5	2,484.5	160.8	508	3.08	1,354.8	14	6.5	12	2.7	1.05
Squibb	24.9	1,328.4	53.4	197	3.68	683.3	15	8.0	13	2.2	0.90
Syntex	10.8	705.1	64.4	150	2.33	460.8	28	13.5	12	3.0	0.85
Upjohn	37.0	1,134.2	30.7	173	5.67	393.4	34	10.5	11	1.9	1.00
Warner Lambert	18.2	1,433.2	78.8	224	2.81	549.3	36	6.2	12	2.0	0.95
ELI LILLY	19.9	2,221.2	145.7	457	3.37	760.3	5	11.0	9	2.1	0.85

*An internal analyst believed an up-market beta was appropriate, given the current market.

Sources: Hambrecht & Quist, Inc., October 1985; *Value Line Investment Survey*, November 1985; *Media General Financial Weekly Industriscope*, September 1985.

EXHIBIT 8   Average Interest Rates and Yields

| | Treasuries | | | | | | Moody's* | |
| | Bills | | | Notes and Bonds | | | | |
	3-Mo	6-Mo	1-Yr	3-Yr	10-Yr	20-Yr	Aaa	Baa
1982	10.61%	11.07%	11.07%	12.92%	13.00%	12.92%	13.79%	16.11%
1983	8.61	8.73	8.80	10.45	11.10	11.34	12.04	13.55
1984	9.52	9.76	9.92	11.89	12.44	12.48	12.71	14.19
1985 Jan	7.76	8.00	8.33	10.43	13.38	11.58	12.08	13.26
Feb	8.27	8.39	8.56	10.55	11.51	11.70	12.13	13.23
March	8.52	8.90	9.06	11.05	11.86	12.06	12.56	13.69
April	7.95	8.23	8.44	10.49	11.44	11.69	12.23	13.51
May	7.48	7.65	7.85	9.75	10.85	11.19	11.72	13.15
June	6.95	7.09	7.27	9.05	10.16	10.57	10.94	12.40
July	7.08	7.20	7.31	9.18	10.31	10.68	10.97	12.43
August	7.14	7.32	7.48	9.31	10.33	10.73	11.05	12.50
Sept 6	7.14	7.31	7.49	9.36	10.29	10.71	10.94	12.40
Sept 13	7.23	7.42	7.62	9.51	10.48	10.52	11.13	12.41

*Based on yields to maturity on selected long-term corporate bonds.

Sources: *Federal Reserve Bulletin*; *Economic Report of the President*.

Hybritech, Incorporated (B)

On February 14, 1986, Ted Greene, chairman and chief executive officer of Hybritech, Inc., was flying back to San Diego from a meeting in Indianapolis with Eli Lilly and Company. In September 1985, Hybritech, a biotechnology firm specializing in monoclonal antibody (MoAb) research, had agreed to be acquired by Lilly, a large ethical pharmaceutical company. Greene and Tim Wollaeger, Hybritech's chief financial officer, represented Hybritech in the negotiations. Although Hybritech had been in no hurry to be acquired, the strategic business advantages to be gained, the unique deal structure, and the operating autonomy for Hybritech made the offer attractive. Representing Lilly in the lengthy but cordial negotiations were its CFO James Cornelius and the president of the Pharmaceutical Division, Gene Step. The negotiations had been carried on in secret until September, but the acquisition became public knowledge when the two sides reached an agreement that month.

Greene had flown to Indianapolis to discuss the form of payment in the acquisition. The original discussions regarding the merger had ended before a major run-up in the market and both firms' stock prices. Additionally, Lilly and Hybritech had seen continued research success in their separate monoclonal programs. Although Greene and Wollaeger had agreed with Lilly on a price of $32 per share, the form of payment had not been determined.

THE COMPANIES

Hybritech, founded in 1978, was one of the first U.S. biotechnology companies and went public in late 1981. By year-end 1983, it had the largest equity base of any MoAb company. The company was located in San Diego, California, biotechnology's answer to Silicon Valley. Lilly had facilities in nearby La Jolla, and the scientists at the two companies knew each other well. Hybritech was the first firm to develop, produce, and market MoAb products, and it remained the industry leader. Under the leadership of Ted Greene, Hybritech was considered the MoAb flagship—from the quality of its venture capitalists to its research and development team.

By 1985, the company had developed a line of 21 low-cost, simple-to-use diagnostic tests known as Tandem® and Icon® tests. Tandem tests gave a quantitative measurement of a substance associated with a disease or condition. Icon tests indicated qualitatively if a substance was present at all. By September 1985, the most important uses of Tandem and Icon tests were for pregnancy, thyroid disorders, prostate cancer, infertility, allergies, heart attacks, colon cancer, anemia, and dwarfism. CFO Cornelius of Lilly had commented, "Hybritech is really three components; its diagnostics business is in place, while the imaging and therapy research efforts represent uncertain but potentially large growth for the future."

Case written by Casey S. Opitz at the Darden Graduate School of Business Administration, under the direction of Robert F. Bruner and with the assistance of Eli Lilly and Company management. Copyright (c) 1988 by the Darden Graduate Business School Sponsors, Charlottesville, VA.

The employees of Hybritech, many of whom had large personal stakes in the company, believed that continued growth for the company would come from applying monoclonal antibody technology to therapeutics, as well as diagnostics and instrumentation. Most believed the cure for cancer was no more than 5 or 10 years away and that Hybritech was poised on the verge of its discovery. Financial information for Hybritech is provided in Exhibits 1 and 2; ownership information is given in Exhibit 3.

Eli Lilly and Company, a leading therapeutics and pharmaceuticals firm, was founded in 1876 and incorporated in 1901. Until the 1970s, the company had been closely managed by members of the Lilly family; the firm was still conservatively managed and boasted a triple-A bond rating from both agencies. The company's 28,000 employees were involved in research, production, and marketing of human health products, agricultural products, and cosmetics. In 1985, human health products were responsible for two-thirds of Lilly's $3.3 billion in sales, and the remainder was from the sale of agricultural chemicals, animal health products, and cosmetics. The company's pharmaceuticals included pain relievers, an antiarthritis agent, antibiotics, antidiabetic agents, cardiovascular drugs, hormones, sedatives, and vitamins. Its medical instruments included patient vital-signs measurement and monitoring systems, intravenous-fluid delivery and control systems, pacemakers, and a variety of cardiovascular surgical devices. A summary of Lilly's financial statements is given in Exhibit 4.

Lilly was beginning to experience competition from the recent growth in generic drugs. In addition, hospitals were instituting serious cost-cutting programs, which, in turn, were cutting medical suppliers' margins.

Lilly was one of the leading research firms in the pharmaceutical industry, spending 11 percent of revenues on R&D (major pharmaceutical companies' R&D spending ranged from 4.2 percent to 13.5 percent of sales). Lilly was already doing some work in the field of biotechnology. When it licensed the gene-expression method for recombinant human insulin from Genentech, Inc., it developed, ran clinical trials, scaled-up manufacture, and brought the first gene-spliced product to market. Management believed that acquiring a monoclonal antibody firm, which would again take Lilly beyond the traditional realm of the other pharmaceutical companies, would be faster than developing the capability from within.

Lilly could offer and acquire funds to support R&D, medical and clinical experience, a scientific base, and an infrastructure for scale-up to bring products to market. As one analyst said of the proposed acquisition,

> The marketing of therapeutic products is more demanding and has different requirements than, for example, the marketing of computers. Lilly's organization and, more importantly its credibility as a pharmaceutical company, will simplify new product introductions and sell more products.[1]

Lilly could also offer Hybritech manufacturing know-how, which was important, because the mass-production methods necessary to make MoAb production cost effective was outside the experience of most biotechnology firms.

Another analyst stated,

---

[1]*Venture Capital Journal*, October 1985.

Currently among the lower-P/E drug stocks, Lilly is fast becoming the best big-company bet on biotechnology, a factor which argues for higher valuation.... We believe that Eli Lilly is on the verge of a substantial technological surge in the 1987-89 period and that over the next 12 months the market will gain greater confidence in the company's long-term outlook and will adjust the stock's P/E multiple premium upward.[2]

In fact, the predicted market response occurred; Lilly's stock price rose from $42 after the merger announcement in September 1985 to about $57 in early February—a 36 percent increase. (The Standard & Poor's composite index rose 17 percent over the same period.) Another analyst projected an 11 percent increase in Lilly's sales of human health care products in 1986, followed by increases of 8 percent and 9 percent in the following two years. Cosmetics sales were expected to increase 14 percent in 1986, followed by two 11 percent years. The analyst did not expect agriculture product sales to fare as well, however—an increase of between only 2 percent and 5 percent annually. Overall, Lilly earnings per share were expected to increase between 9 percent and 13 percent a year for the next three years.[3]

THE NEGOTIATIONS

Hybritech and Lilly had been in and out of negotiations for about a year. In 1984, Hybritech's stock had traded for between $11 and $22.75 per share. In February 1985, Greene had thought the company was undervalued by the market and was worth $30 per share, but Lilly disagreed, suggesting that $20 was more appropriate. Negotiations broke off, but on friendly terms. Then, as shown in Exhibit 5, from February to September, the market value of most biotechnology and pharmaceutical companies, including Hybritech and Lilly, rose.

When negotiations commenced again in late summer, issues were easily settled, except price and form of payment. Hybritech and Lilly were working with very different forecasted sales and cash-flow assumptions. From the scenarios shown in Exhibits 6 and 7, Hybritech could be a $1 billion company by 1992, but Lilly thought it might be only half that size by 1995. In addition, the companies were using vastly different assumptions as to working-capital needs and capital expenditures.

When the two sides finally agreed to $32 per share in mid-September, it was with provisos. In the current market, Lilly actually did not believe that Hybritech was worth much more than about $29 per share. Conversely, Hybritech management, based on its expectations of future earnings, now believed the company was worth in excess of $32. Therefore, the $32 price was to include a form of payment that would allow each side to meet its expectations.

When news of the Lilly merger reached Hybritech employees, those familiar with Lilly through mutual therapeutic research interests cheered. Other employees, not familiar with Lilly, gave approval as they learned of Lilly's arms-length management philosophy for healthy acquisitions. Under Greene's

---

[2]A. H. Snider, Kidder, Peabody & Co., Inc., Investment Report, September 23, 1985.

[3]R. R. Stover, et al., Smith Barney, Harris Upham & Co., Inc., Investment Report, October 25, 1985.

leadership, Hybritech, flush with cash and full of good scientists, was indeed a healthy acquisition. Greene was quoted in *Business Week*, October 14, 1985, as saying, "Lilly is a money machine that generates a huge amount of cash. We're a black hole into which money is pouring." One analyst noted:

> If this acknowledged biotechnology leader decided its future could be best served joining forces with Lilly, it seems logical that the 300 plus independent biotechnology companies have to be thinking about their own viability. Hybritech may have started a wave of biotechnology acquisitions. In this industry, it may be that it will be the strong that will be acquired.[4]

THE OFFER

Greene had been met with a firm offer in Indianapolis on this trip. As a result of the merger, Hybritech would become a wholly owned subsidiary of Lilly. The offer for each of Hybritech's shares consisted of three parts:

1. at the shareholder's election:

   - $22.00 in cash, or

   - $22.00 of principal amount of Lilly convertible notes bearing interest at the rate of 6.75 percent per annum, and a conversion price of $66.31 per share one year after effective date of the merger. Lilly could not redeem the notes prior to March 31, 1989, at which time they would be callable at 104.725 percent, decreasing to 100 percent by March 31, 1996, when they would mature; or

   - any combination of cash and principal amount of convertible notes equal to $22.00; plus

2. one and four-tenths warrants to purchase Lilly common stock at $75.98 at any time following the merger and through March 31, 1991; the warrants were expected to be listed on the New York Stock Exchange; plus

3. one contingent payment unit (CPU) issued by Lilly; each unit was expected to be listed on the American Stock Exchange.

Each warrant was intended to have an initial trading value of $5.00; therefore, 1.4 warrants would be equivalent to $7.00 per share of Hybritech common stock. Each CPU was eligible to receive up to $22.00 in cash payments during the next ten years if Hybritech's sales and gross profits increased sufficiently. Each CPU was expected to have an initial trading value of approximately $3.00. On this basis, the package of cash and securities being offered by Lilly for each share of Hybritech common stock was believed to have an initial market value of approximately $32.00. However, there was no assurance that the warrants or CPUs would initially trade at these projected values.

---

[4]*Venture Capital Journal*, October 1985.

TERMS OF THE CONTINGENT PAYMENT UNITS

The CPUs provided for annual cash payments based on the operating results of Hybritech as a wholly owned subsidiary of Lilly for each of the 12-month periods ending December 31, 1986, through December 31, 1995. The cash payments with respect to each CPU for each calendar year would be equal to:

- 6 percent of Hybritech's sales, *plus*

- 20 percent of Hybritech's gross profits, *minus*

- a deductible amount, which was to be $11 million for 1986 and which would increase at a compound rate of 35 percent annually for each of the calendar years 1987 through 1995; this total *divided by*

- 12,933,894, which was the total number of shares of Hybritech common stock outstanding, on a fully diluted basis, on January 2, 1986.

The maximum amount that Lilly offered to pay with respect to each CPU was $22.00. The CPUs would be canceled when $22.00 had been paid with respect to each unit, or on March 31, 1996, whichever occurred first.

The CPUs would be issued under an indenture as unsecured obligations of Lilly and would rank equally with all other unsecured indebtedness of Lilly. In addition, Lilly would not be obligated to support Hybritech as an operating subsidiary in order to generate payments on the CPUs. Holders of CPUs would have no equity interest in Lilly or Hybritech and would not derive any economic benefit from Lilly's general business activities.

Lilly had made two acquisitions using some form of contingent payments within the past two years. On May 31, 1984, it purchased Advanced Cardiovascular Systems, Inc. (ACS), for 2.8 million shares[5] with a possibility of issuing up to 1.25 million more to ACS's shareholders. By December 31, 1984, Lilly had issued 41,000 more shares as a result of ACS's performance, and by December 31, 1985, it had issued 160,000 more. Also, Lilly acquired Intec Systems in May 1985 for $47.7 million in cash and $500,000 in convertible debentures, with the possibility of paying up to $85 million more. To date, no such contingency payments had been made.

The offer intrigued Greene; he found the CPUs especially interesting, because they gave Hybritech shareholders the opportunity either to liquidate their holdings for approximately $32 per share or to hold onto their positions and share in the future growth and profitability of the combined firm. Lilly was willing to pay more if Hybritech's results warranted additional payments.

Now Greene had to value the offer, not only for himself, but so he could present it to the venture capitalists. Specifically, he had to determine whether the offer would have a current market value of at least $32 per share.

Greene also wondered whether alternative structures for the deal might satisfy Lilly and yet result in an effectively higher payment to Hybritech's investors. In 1985, 71 percent of all acquisitions of public companies were paid for in cash; 5 percent were paid for entirely with stock; 23 percent involved some combination; and 1 percent were paid for with debt. Also in 1985, 65 acquisitions had involved the use of contingent payments, up from 39 in 1984

---

[5]Adjusted for a 2-for-1 stock dividend 12/31/85.

and 37 in 1983[6]; virtually none of the firms was publicly traded, however. Exhibit 8 provides data (not available to Greene in February 1986) on types of stock and debt used in acquisitions.

When Greene got to his office, he reviewed the financial market data provided in Exhibit 9. His investment banker provided the data on stock prices and standard deviations given in Exhibit 10 to help with his review of their analysis of the warrants and CPUs. The data suggested that the recent volatility of Lilly's stock was about 33 percent. However, another researcher found that Lilly's long-term volatility was 23 percent.

---

[6]*Mergerstat Review*, W. T. Grimm & Company, 1985.

EXHIBIT 1 Consolidated Income Statements (dollars in thousands except per share data)

| | Year Ended December 31 | | | |
	1982	1983	1984	Est. 1985
Operating revenues				
Product sales	$1,841	$6,859	$14,599	$34,150
Contract revenues	1,297	5,735	16,227	24,200
Total operating revenues	3,138	12,594	30,826	58,350
Operating costs and expenses				
Cost of sales	1,741	2,660	6,881	14,950
Research and development	4,987	6,293	13,700	23,100
Marketing	3,348	4,947	8,067	11,970
General and administrative	1,918	2,466	3,891	6,000
Other	9	29	120	180
Total operating expenses	12,003	16,395	32,659	56,200
Operating income (loss)	(8,865)	(3,801)	(1,833)	2,150
Other income (expenses)				
Interest income	1,618	3,371	3,107	1,200
Foreign exchange loss	0	(37)	(121)	(150)
Other loss	(21)	(7)	(35)	(50)
Total other income, net	1,597	3,327	2,951	1,000
Income (loss) before income Taxes and extraordinary item	(7,268)	(474)	1,118	3,150
Provision for income taxes	0	0	750	1,501
Income (loss) before extraordinary item	(7,268)	(474)	368	1,649
Extraordinary item--use of operating-loss carryforward	0	0	708	0
Net income	($7,268)	($474)	$1,076	$1,649
Per share of common stock				
Net income (loss) before extraordinary item	($0.82)	($0.05)	$0.04	$0.15
Net income (loss)	($0.82)	($0.05)	$0.10	$0.15

EXHIBIT 2 Consolidated Balance Sheets (dollars in thousands)

	Year Ended December 3	
	1983	1984
Current assets		
Cash and cash investments	$32,884	$21,792
Accounts receivable	1,815	3,772
Inventories, at cost	3,077	5,891
Other current assets	1,830	3,201
Total current assets	39,606	34,656
Equipment at cost		
Leasehold improvements	2,449	5,931
Equipment and furniture	5,174	17,039
Total equipment	7,623	22,970
Depreciation and amortization	(1,151)	(2,918)
Net equipment	6,472	20,052
Investments	44	3,019
Other assets	1,944	3,354
Total assets	$48,066	$61,081
Current liabilities		
Accounts payable	$959	$2,605
Accrued liabilities	1,008	2,204
Deferred revenue	670	46
Notes payable to bank	0	949
Current portion of long-term debt	36	1,847
Total current liabilities	2,673	7,651
Long-term debt	666	5,231
Total liabilities	3,339	12,882
Common stock, 1984: 10.25MM shares outstanding	59,470	59,858
Series B common, 1984: 0 shares outstanding*	392	0
Series C common, 1984: 0.49MM shares outstanding*	1,178	1,472
Common stock warrants	0	2,453
Accumulated deficit	(14,807)	(13,731)
Foreign currency adjustment	(25)	(119)
Notes receivable: sale of stock	(1,481)	(1,734)
Total shareholders' equity	44,727	48,199
Total liabilities and equity	$48,066	$61,081

*Series B and Series C common stock were sold to employees, directors, and consultants; a maximum of 250,000 and 500,000 shares, respectively, could be sold. No dividends could be paid on Series B, and dividends of one-twentieth the amount paid on common stock could be paid on Series C.

EXHIBIT 3   Hybritech Stock Ownership as of February 1986

	Shares	Percentage
Wilmington Investments, Inc.	2,677,001	26.0%
Kleiner, Perkins and six major investors	2,346,540	22.9
Other institutions (total of 24)	1,473,640	14.3
Total institutions	6,497,181	63.2
Officers and directors	640,585	6.2
Other insiders	318,725	3.1
Total insiders	959,310	9.3
All other investors	2,823,937	27.5
Total shares outstanding	10,280,428	100.0%
Also outstanding:		
Series C stock*	489,162	
Warrants**	1,401,500	
Options†	766,396	
	12,937,486	

*Each share of Series C common stock would convert into one share of common stock upon the merger or acquisition of the company.

**The company issued warrants to the limited partners of Hybritech Clinical Partners, Ltd., to purchase a total of 1,401,500 shares of the company's common stock. These warrants were exercisable between March 31, 1987, and March 31, 1989, at $17.09 per share; on April 1, 1989, the exercise price would increase to $22.09 per share. The warrants expired on March 31, 1992.

†Options were granted to employees, consultants, and advisors, with exercise prices ranging between $2.85 and $26.43 per share.

EXHIBIT 4   Eli Lilly and Company and Subsidiaries Selected Financial Data
(dollars in millions except per share data)

| | Year Ended December 31 | | |
	1982	1983	1984
Net sales	$2,962.7	$3,033.7	$3,109.2
Operating costs and expenses	2,291.8	2,308.8	2,364.9
Other income, net	13.3	29.9	26.4
Net income	$411.8	$457.4	$490.3
Earnings per common share	$2.71	$3.07	$3.36
Dividends paid per common share	1.30	1.375	1.4875
Average common shares outstanding (thousands)*	151,868	149,248	145,710
Cash and marketable securities	$303.8	$491.0	$445.3
Current assets	1,680.5	1,830.1	1,827.5
Current liabilities	873.6	988.3	1,067.2
Property and equipment	1,135.6	1,212.6	1,280.4
Total assets	3,155.1	3,413.8	3,643.9
Long-term obligations	49.4	90.7	116.6
Shareholders' equity	$2,055.5	$2,121.0	$2,221.2
Return on average assets	13.6%	13.9%	13.9%
Return on shareholders' equity	20.9%	21.9%	22.6%
Number of employees	29,300	29,200	28,700
Research and development	$267.4	$293.6	$341.3
Capital expenditures	236.6	199.9	205.3
Depreciation and amortization	83.1	98.3	120.7

*Adjusted for 2-for-1 stock split 12/31/85.

EXHIBIT 5 Stock Prices

	1984			1985								
	Oct	Nov	Dec	Jan	Feb	Mar	Apr	May	Jun	Jul	Aug	Sep 13
Biotechnology Companies:												
Cambridge	1.75	1.38	1.50	2.88	2.63	2.75	3.63	4.38	4.75	4.50	4.25	3.68
Centocor	10.75	9.25	9.75	12.00	14.00	12.25	15.25	16.00	18.50	19.00	18.00	16.00
Cetus	10.25	8.88	8.75	11.68	12.25	10.38	11.00	12.13	10.68	13.25	16.25	13.68
Cooper	3.25	2.88	3.00	3.88	4.88	3.88	3.50	3.50	2.38	1.75	1.75	1.68
Damon	5.25	4.88	4.50	5.88	6.00	5.00	4.75	6.38	6.38	6.50	6.00	5.68
DNA Plant Technology	5.13	4.25	3.75	5.00	6.25	7.25	6.88	7.75	8.50	8.38	8.50	7.75
Genetic Systems	6.63	6.00	5.50	6.88	7.88	7.63	7.00	8.00	7.38	7.68	7.68	6.68
Molecular Genetics	7.25	6.25	7.25	10.00	10.00	8.00	7.50	7.50	6.75	6.50	7.75	6.88
Monoclonal Antibodies	11.25	9.00	8.75	11.50	10.00	9.00	9.00	9.13	9.00	10.50	10.25	11.75
Ventrex	4.63	4.13	3.75	3.88	4.25	4.25	4.13	3.63	3.38	3.68	5.00	4.75
HYBRITECH	14.75	15.25	16.50	19.75	18.00	18.00	20.50	23.75	25.25	25.00	25-2	24-6
Pharmaceutical Companies:												
Abbott Labs	41.13	41.25	41.00	47.25	47.88	53.00	51.00	54.13	57.38	56.75	57.88	55.00
American Home Products	50.00	50.00	50.50	55.88	58.63	62.13	58.38	64.88	63.88	59.75	58.75	59.38
Bristol Myers	49.13	47.88	52.25	54.38	55.50	57.50	56.88	61.00	61.38	60.13	59.50	57.88
Merck	86.75	88.75	94.00	96.00	99.88	104.88	101.75	108.68	112.68	112.88	114.13	112.25
Pfizer	38.00	39.00	42.25	39.50	40.25	42.88	44.50	50.00	49.50	48.25	48.13	45.50
Squibb	49.75	52.63	53.88	53.88	53.63	56.50	55.50	63.13	63.13	69.50	68.75	66.25
Syntex	49.00	46.75	48.63	53.75	56.88	59.00	57.00	62.25	63.88	62.00	60.50	61.50
Upjohn	63.75	66.75	70.13	71.88	75.25	80.50	83.88	107.25	108.25	115.00	107.75	105.00
Warner Lambert	34.00	32.88	34.75	36.50	37.13	39.63	37.00	41.25	43.38	39.75	38.88	38.75
ELI LILLY*	30.63	31.63	33.00	35.68	39.00	38.88	42.75	43.25	42.50	43.25	41.88	41.88
S&P 500	167.49	163.58	167.24	179.63	181.18	180.66	179.83	189.55	191.85	192.11	188.63	182.08

*Adjusted for 2-for-1 stock split 12/31/85.

Source: *ISL Daily Stock Price Index.*

EXHIBIT 6 Hybritech Forecast of Hybritech Income Statements and Cash Flow (dollars in millions except per share data)

Income	Actual 1984	1985	1986	1987	1988	1989	1990	1991	1992	1993	1994
Sales											
Cancer diagnostics	0	5	23	56	107	181	249	274	282	281	268
Other diagnostics	15	23	32	45	75	110	135	165	190	210	225
Imaging	0	0	2	13	52	106	146	166	174	186	184
Therapy	0	0	0	0	8	57	171	307	400	375	305
Total sales	15	28	57	114	242	454	701	912	1,046	1,052	982
Cost of sales	7	10	21	41	84	159	224	294	332	336	322
% of sales	47%	36%	37%	36%	35%	35%	32%	32%	32%	32%	33%
Gross profits	8	18	36	73	158	295	477	618	714	716	660
% of sales	53%	64%	63%	64%	65%	65%	68%	68%	68%	68%	67%
Contract revenue	16	21	23	15	12	4	3	3	3	3	3
Operating expenses											
R&D	14	20	24	18	21	21	32	43	51	52	50
% of sales	96%	71%	42%	16%	9%	5%	5%	5%	5%	5%	5%
SG&A	12	15	24	45	93	176	259	323	369	372	349
% of sales	82%	54%	42%	39%	38%	39%	37%	35%	35%	35%	36%
Total expenses	26	35	48	63	114	197	291	366	420	424	399
Interest inc. (exp.)	3	2	2	0	(3)	(10)	(25)	(38)	(43)	(37)	(20)
Income before taxes	1	6	13	25	53	92	164	217	254	258	244
Taxes	0	2	5	9	19	32	57	76	89	90	85
Tax rate (%)	35%	35%	35%	35%	35%	35%	35%	35%	35%	35%	35%
Net income	1	4	8	16	35	60	107	141	165	168	159
Primary average											
shares outstanding	10.28	10.28	10.28	10.50	10.50	10.50	10.50	10.50	10.50	10.50	10.50
Earnings/share	0.09	0.58	0.82	1.54	3.29	5.70	10.15	13.44	15.72	15.97	15.10

EXHIBIT 6 (continued)

	Actual 1984	1985	1986	1987	1988	1989	1990	1991	1992	1993	1994
Cash Flow											
Gross profits and											
contract revenue	24	39	59	88	170	299	480	621	717	719	663
Less: total expenses	26	35	48	63	114	197	291	366	420	424	399
EBIT	(2)	4	11	25	56	102	189	255	297	295	264
EBIT(1-tax)	(2)	3	7	16	36	66	123	166	193	192	172
Plus: Noncash items	0	1	2	2	6	10	18	19	15	8	(1)
Less: Working capital	(4)	(8)	(12)	(22)	(63)	(101)	(118)	(100)	(61)	1	39
Less: Capital expend.	(15)	(6)	(5)	(23)	(53)	(93)	(111)	(98)	(66)	(10)	(10)
Free cash flow	(21)	(10)	(8)	(27)	(74)	(118)	(88)	(13)	81	191	200

594

EXHIBIT 7 One Lilly Forecast* of Hybritech Income Statements and Cash Flows (dollars in millions except per share data)

INCOME	Actual 1984	1985	1986	1987	1988	1989	1990	1991	1992	1993	1994	1995
Sales												
Cancer diagnostics	0	0	4	8	15	20	31	45	61	72	77	81
Other diagnostics	15	32	40	60	90	120	150	170	175	180	185	190
Imaging	0	0	1	2	7	15	25	50	60	75	91	95
Therapy	0	0	0	0	0	0	0	8	48	80	100	120
Total sales	15	32	45	70	112	155	206	273	344	407	453	486
Cost of sales	7	17	20	25	39	54	72	96	124	142	154	160
% of sales	47%	53%	44%	36%	35%	35%	35%	35%	36%	35%	34%	33%
Gross profits	8	15	25	45	73	101	134	177	220	265	299	326
% of sales	53%	47%	56%	64%	65%	65%	65%	65%	64%	65%	66%	67%
Contract revenue	16	22	22	15	12	4	4	4	4	4	4	4
Operating expenses												
R&D	14	23	25	27	29	33	37	44	52	53	54	55
% of sales	93%	72%	62%	39%	26%	21%	18%	16%	15%	13%	12%	11%
SG&A	12	21	25	32	44	64	87	104	127	138	136	136
% of sales	80%	66%	56%	46%	39%	41%	42%	38%	37%	34%	30%	28%
Total expenses	26	44	50	59	73	97	124	148	179	191	190	191
Other income	3	0	0	1	(1)	(2)	(2)	(3)	(2)	0	0	3
Income before taxes	1	(7)	(3)	2	11	6	12	31	43	77	113	142
Taxes	0	0	0	1	4	2	4	11	15	27	40	49
Tax rate (%)	4%	8%	10%	35%	35%	35%	35%	35%	35%	35%	35%	35%
Net income	1	(7)	(3)	1	7	4	8	20	28	50	74	92
Avg. primary shares outstanding (millions)	10.28	10.28	10.28	10.50	10.50	10.50	10.50	10.50	10.50	10.50	10.50	10.50
Earnings per share	0.09	-0.69	-0.34	0.14	0.69	0.41	0.76	1.92	2.68	4.78	6.98	8.56

EXHIBIT 7 (continued)

	Actual 1984	1985	1986	1987	1988	1989	1990	1991	1992	1993	1994	1995
Gross profits and contract revenue	24	37	47	61	85	105	138	181	224	269	303	330
Less: Total expenses	(26)	(44)	(50)	(59)	(73)	(97)	(124)	(147)	(179)	(191)	(190)	(191)
EBIT	(2)	(7)	(3)	2	12	8	14	34	45	77	113	139
EBIT(1-taxes)	(2)	(7)	(3)	1	8	6	9	22	29	50	73	88
Plus: Noncash items	2	3	3	3	4	6	8	10	14	18	20	23
Less: Working capital add.	(4)	(6)	(6)	(7)	(14)	(17)	(19)	(20)	(28)	(16)	(6)	(6)
Less: Capital expenditures	(15)	(9)	(9)	(9)	(10)	(11)	(15)	(18)	(24)	(27)	(28)	(30)
Free cash flow	(19)	(19)	(15)	(12)	(12)	(16)	(17)	(6)	(9)	25	59	75

*These numbers do not represent Lilly's actual forecast of projected Hybritech performance but are provided solely for purposes of this case study.

Figures may not add due to rounding.

EXHIBIT 8 Means of Payment for Acquisitions, 1973–83

Cash	29.7%
Common stock	18.7
Common stock and cash	5.8
Common stock and other	4.4
Convertible preferred with or without cash	8.7
Preferred with or without cash	1.2
Debt with or without cash	4.4%

Source: Paul Asquith, Robert F. Bruner, David W. Mullins, Jr., "Merger Returns and the Form of Financing," working paper, June 1987.

EXHIBIT 9   Average Interest Rates and Yields

| | | Treasuries | | | | | | | Moody's* |
| | | Bills | | | Notes & Bonds | | | | |
	3-Mo	6-Mo	1-Yr	3-Yr	5-Yr	10-Yr	20-Yr	Aaa	Baa
1982	10.61%	11.07%	11.07%	12.92%	13.01%	13.00%	12.92%	13.79%	16.11%
1983	8.61	8.73	8.80	10.45	10.80	11.10	11.34	12.04	13.55
1984	9.52	9.76	9.92	11.89	12.24	12.44	12.48	12.71	14.19
1985 Jan	7.76	8.00	8.33	10.43	10.93	13.38	11.58	12.08	13.26
Feb	8.27	8.39	8.56	10.55	11.13	11.51	11.70	12.13	13.23
March	8.52	8.90	9.06	11.05	11.52	11.86	12.06	12.56	13.69
April	7.95	8.23	8.44	10.49	11.01	11.44	11.69	12.23	13.51
May	7.48	7.65	7.85	9.75	10.34	10.85	11.19	11.72	13.15
June	6.95	7.09	7.27	9.05	9.60	10.16	10.57	10.94	12.40
July	7.08	7.20	7.31	9.18	9.70	10.31	10.68	10.97	12.43
August	7.14	7.32	7.48	9.31	9.81	10.33	10.73	11.05	12.50
Sept	7.10	7.27	7.50	9.37	9.81	10.37	10.80	11.07	12.48
Oct	7.16	7.33	7.45	9.25	9.69	10.24	10.67	11.02	12.36
Nov	7.24	7.30	7.33	8.88	9.28	9.78	10.24	10.55	11.99
Dec	7.10	7.14	7.16	8.40	8.73	9.26	9.75	10.16	11.58
1986 Jan	7.07	7.17	7.21	8.41	8.68	9.19	9.59	10.05	11.44
Feb 7	7.06	7.11	7.12	8.21	8.52	9.02	9.43	9.90	11.29

AAA Convertible Bonds:

| | | | Conver. | Price/ | Yield To Maturity | | |
	Coupon	Maturity	Price	Share	Dec	Jan	Feb
American Capital Bond Fund	11.35%	1990	$19.20	$21.75	6.98%	7.38%	7.62%
Eastman Kodak	8.250	2007	68.17	48.25	8.25	8.02	7.95
IBM	7.825	2004	153.66	151.50	6.44	6.19	5.88
J.P. Morgan	4.750	1998	40.00	64.25	1.18	--	--

AAA Bonds:

| | | | Yield to Maturity | | | Sinking | Call |
	Coupon	Maturity	Dec	Jan	Feb	Fund	Price
Amoco	14.000%	1991	11.17%	11.14%	11.32%	No	100
Bank of North Dakota	9.250	1993	10.56	9.82	9.06	Yes	--
Bristol-Myers	5.700	1992	9.26	8.78	8.87	Yes	100.57
Bristol-Myers	8.625	1995	9.7	9.29	9.37	No	102.094
Diamond State Telephone	4.625	2005	10.51	9.91	9.92	Yes	101.88
Exxon	6.000	1997	9.8	9.44	9.57	No	101.5
Exxon Finance	10.500	1989	9.33	9.58	9.41	No	100
General Electric	5.300	1992	9.21	9.19	8.9	Yes	100.48
IBM	10.250	1995	9.92	9.17	9.58	No	100
Proctor & Gamble	7.000	2002	10.15	9.84	9.69	Yes	102.88

*Based on yields to maturity on selected long-term corporate bonds.

Sources: *Federal Reserve Bulletin; Standard & Poor's Bond Guide*.

EXHIBIT 10 Calculation of Standard Deviation of Daily Percentage Changes in Stock Price: February 14, 1986

Date	Lilly Stock Price (St)*	Price Relative**	Natural Logarithm of Price Relative	Deviation from Average (Log Rt - Log Rt)	Squared Deviation
12/30/85	55.500				
12/31	55.750	1.005	0.00449	0.004	0.00001
1/02/86	54.875	0.984	-0.01582	-0.017	0.00027
1/03	54.750	0.998	-0.00228	-0.003	0.00001
1/06	55.625	1.016	0.01586	0.015	0.00023
1/07	56.125	1.009	0.00895	0.008	0.00007
1/08	54.500	0.971	-0.02938	-0.030	0.00091
1/09	53.825	0.988	-0.01246	-0.013	0.00017
1/10	53.625	0.996	-0.00372	-0.004	0.00002
1/13	53.125	0.991	-0.00937	-0.010	0.00010
1/14	53.125	1.000	0.00000	-0.001	0.00000
1/15	52.750	0.993	-0.00708	-0.008	0.00006
1/16	52.500	0.995	-0.00475	-0.005	0.00003
1/17	52.500	1.000	0.00000	-0.001	0.00000
1/20	52.250	0.995	-0.00477	-0.006	0.00003
1/21	51.875	0.993	-0.00720	-0.008	0.00006
1/22	50.875	0.981	-0.01947	-0.020	0.00041
1/23	51.125	1.005	0.00490	0.004	0.00002
1/24	52.250	1.022	0.02177	0.021	0.00044
1/27	52.375	1.002	0.00239	0.002	0.00000
1/28	53.125	1.014	0.01422	0.013	0.00018
1/29	53.125	1.000	0.00000	-0.001	0.00000
1/30	53.000	0.998	-0.00236	-0.003	0.00001
1/31	54.500	1.028	0.02791	0.027	0.00074
2/03	57.000	1.046	0.04485	0.044	0.00195
2/04	57.125	1.002	0.00219	0.001	0.00000
2/05	56.500	0.989	-0.01100	-0.012	0.00014
2/06	54.000	0.956	-0.04526	-0.046	0.00212
2/07	54.625	1.012	0.01151	0.011	0.00012
2/10	55.875	1.023	0.02263	0.022	0.00048
2/11	56.750	1.016	<u>0.01554</u>	0.015	<u>0.00022</u>

Average log of price relative = 0.0007424   Variance = 0.00029

Average squared deviation * (30/29) = 0.00030
To convert to annual variance: * 365 or: 0.11074
SIGMA = Annual volatility = square root or: <u>0.33278</u>

Another source placed Lilly's stock volatility between 1980 and 1983 at 23%.

---

*12/30/85 through 1/29/86 adjusted for 2-for-1 stock split.
**(St/(St-1)) = Rt.
Source: *ISL Daily Stock Price Index*; Cox and Rubinstein, *Options Markets*, 1985, p. 352.

Hybritech, Incorporated (B)

SYNOPSIS AND OBJECTIVES

This case is a companion to the "Lilly"/"Hybritech" merger-negotiation cases (47 and 51) and presents the terms of payment that Lilly proposed to Ted Greene, the CEO of Hybritech. The students' task is to evaluate the terms by (1) appraising the package and (2) judging how well the package serves the interests of Lilly and Hybritech shareholders. This case is a useful vehicle for reviewing the valuation of bonds, options, and complicated contingent payments.

STUDY QUESTIONS

1. Why did Lilly propose such a complicated form of payment?

2. What is a "contingent payment unit"?

3. What is Lilly's offer worth?

4. Should Howard Greene support and advocate Lilly's terms of payment? Would other terms be more attractive?

TEACHING PLAN

A wide range of teaching objectives may be served by the following series of discussion questions to be posed by the instructor:

(20 minutes) Here is the structure of the proposed transaction; why is it so complicated?

*   Why isn't it all cash?
*   Why give investors a choice between cash and the convertible note?
*   Why divide the payment 2/3 cash/bonds and 1/3 warrants and CPUs?
*   What incentives do the warrant and CPU create?

(20 minutes) What is the value of the convertible bond?

15 minutes) What is the value of the warrant?

(15 minutes) What is the value of the CPU?

(5 minutes) What value did Lilly management think it was paying? What value did Ted Greene think he was receiving?

If time permits, the instructor can close with some summary comments on valuation and a presentation of the epilogue.

Teaching note written by Robert F. Bruner. Copyright (c) 1988 by the Darden Graduate Business School Sponsors, Charlottesville, VA.

ANALYSIS

The Complexities of the Deal

Presumably the unusual terms of this deal were designed to achieve the goals of both Lilly and Hybritech investors, which suggests that any analysis of the terms is an attempt to guess at the needs being satisfied.

- The choice of cash versus convertible debentures is probably stimulated by the desire of some (not all) of the investors for a tax-free exchange of securities.

- The layering of the deal probably reflects Lilly's estimation of the relative proportions of value currently in place versus value to come: cash and notes represent existing value, while warrants and CPUs exploit value yet to be created.

The structure of the deal may have some strong motivational effects on the Hybritech employees who own 6 percent of the common stock. The warrant and CPU tie their efforts to clear potential payoffs.

Value of the Convertible Bond[1]

The convertible bond may be valued as the sum of the value of the simple bond (yielding 6.25 percent) and a call option.[2] Regarding the bond valuation, the main issue is the choice of a discount rate for the cash flows. The proper rate is the yield to maturity available on other "straight" bonds of similar risk and duration. An average yield to maturity on comparable issues (Bristol-Myers, Exxon, and IBM) is about 9.5 percent. Using this rate results in a market value of $825 for each bond (i.e., having a par value of $1,000).

The call option embedded in the convertible bond may be valued using an option-pricing model.[3] Three of the parameters are certain: stock price is $56.75; exercise price is $66.31; and annual dividend is $1.4875. Two other issues, however, will merit some discussion.

---

[1] The convertible bonds were nontransferable, rendering them illiquid from a trading standpoint. The valuation approach here does not reflect any illiquidity discount.

[2] This approach is used in leading advanced textbooks (such as Copeland and Weston), is consistent with the concept of value additivity, and assumes that the values of the bond and the option are independent. Jonathan Ingersoll has pointed out, however, an interdependence between the bond and the option based on interest rates. To correct for this interdependence requires a model that is beyond the scope of many MBA courses in corporate finance. One could point out to students that the estimate based on the disaggregation approach is only an approximation, but that this approach will generally bring the student closer to the "true" value than will the next best approach (i.e., anecdotal comparison).

[3] Used in this analysis was the Black-Scholes option-pricing model.

Volatility. Case Exhibit 10 computes the volatility as 33 percent, based on the last 30 trading days. The footnote to that exhibit indicates, however, that the long-term historical volatility has been 23 percent.

Time. The conversion option lasts for the life of the bond, which is 10 years, but the bond is callable after 3 years. Students may argue that Lilly will force the conversion after 3 years by calling the bond. Since the *risk-free rate* used in the analysis must be contemporaneous with the life of the option, this assumption could also vary.

These assumptions call for a sensitivity analysis of the value of the conversion option. Exhibit A presents the range of warrant values for the 3- and 10-year terms, by volatilities of .33, .23, and .20. The resulting values vary from $30.58 to $7.78. Using assumptions of a 3-year term, no dilution adjustment, and volatility of .33, the resulting value is $12.55 per option. Since each $1,000 bond is convertible at $66.31 per share, the option embedded in the bond is really worth 15.08 (i.e., 1,000/66.31) times as much or $189.25. Using the value of the conversion option, the value of the convertible bond is $1,014.25 (i.e., $825 + 189.25). Practically speaking, the bond appears to have been about fairly priced.

Warrant Valuation

The warrant may be valued using an option-pricing model, taking care to recognize that three assumptions will differ from the convertible option: term (5 years), exercise price ($75.98), and contemporaneous risk-free rate (.095). Under these assumptions, a warrant for each share is worth $15.77 (if volatility is .33) or $11.47 (if volatility is .23).[4] Since each share of Hybritech will receive warrants for 1.4 Lilly shares, the warrant feature in this deal is worth from $16.05 to $22.08 per Hybritech share. As indicated on page 5 of the case, Lilly expected these warrants to have an initial trading value of $5.00—the volatility implied by this value is 11.71 percent.

Valuing the Contingent Payment Unit

The CPU is a compound option that is not easily valued by any of the straightforward option-pricing models. The analyst can still discount the potential cash flows under various scenarios, however, to determine the sensitivity of payouts to future performance. Exhibit B calculates and discounts the payments under the forecasts by the Lilly and Hybritech sides. The analysis reveals that the payment under Hybritech's forecast is large (discounted cash flow of $9.24), while the payment under Lilly's forecast is virtually nil (DCF of $0.29).

The Value of the Package

As the preceding sections have shown, the value of the entire package of securities offered is contingent on a number of assumptions. A range of possible outcomes is summarized in Exhibit C. Without some firm rationale for accepting one set of assumptions and excluding the others, it is impossible to

---

[4]If all warrants were exercised, 15 million new Lilly shares would be created, diluting share values by 9 percent. Adjusted for dilution, the warrant values are $15.41 and $10.97, respectively.

determine finally what the package is worth, because the range of values is considerable: $29.29 to $53.32. If time permits, the instructor may want to stimulate a discussion of assumptions and scenarios.

On its own, however, the range of total values given in Exhibit C presents an important teaching point. Students should understand that the same package was possibly worth something very different to each side of the transaction. Specifically, all the Hybritech values are higher than the comparable Lilly values. This difference is attributable to the differing values placed on the CPU, which, in turn, is the result of differing expectations about Hybritech's future performance. In short, creative transaction design (i.e., of the CPU) enabled the two sides to bridge their differing views of the business and consummate a deal.

Exhibit C also augments the discussion in The Complexities of the Deal section about the layering of the deal. The cash/notes layer is invariant in value and represents a foundation for the total value of the package. The warrants layer varies according to *Lilly's* risk. The CPU layer varies according to *Hybritech's* performance. The deal structure ties the new shareholders coming in from Hybritech to the fortunes of both Lilly and Hybritech.

EPILOGUE

The acquisition was consummated on the terms of payment described in the case. Hybritech's first year under the Lilly umbrella failed to clear the hurdle embedded in the CPU. Although the hurdle was to rise at an aggressive rate (35 percent per year), a major research breakthrough could still entitle the holders of the CPUs to receive significant payments.

In the two years following the acquisition, the values of the various Lilly securities traded at the following prices:

	Common Stock	Warrant	CPU
March 1986	75.500	18.625	4.500
June	80.875	27.875	3.750
Sept.	65.375	18.500	2.750
Dec.	74.250	19.875	2.375
March 1987	91.500	37.375	3.000
June	93.875	35.875	2.625
Sept.	96.250	42.875	1.375
Dec.	78.000	24.750	0.500

EXHIBIT A   Sensitivity Analysis of the Value of the Conversion Option in the Convertible Notes

	Not Adjusted for Dilution		Adjusted for Dilution*	
Time:	3 Years	10 Years	3 Years	10 Years
Interest rate:	.0821	.0943	.0821	.0943
Volatility				
.33	$12.55	$30.58	$12.26	$29.88
.23	9.03	27.52	8.82	26.89
.20	$ 7.96	$26.73	$ 7.78	$26.12

---

*Potential dilution would dampen the option value. The magnitude of dilution depends on how many investors opt to receive the convertible notes instead of cash. If few investors choose notes, dilution will not be material. This column assumes no investors select cash; it represents the hypothetical maximum effect of dilution. The dilution adjustment is

$$D = \frac{1}{(1 + \frac{M}{N})} = .977$$

where M = number of new shares to be received upon exercise, 3.559 million, and N = number of shares currently outstanding, 151.868 million.

EXHIBIT B   Present-Value Analysis of the Cash Flows to Investors Under the CPU (dollars in millions except per share data)

Hybritech's Forecast of Hybritech Income Statements and Cash Flows

	1984	1985	1986	1987	1988	1989	1990	1991	1992	1993	1994	1995
Sales												
Cancer diagnostics	$ 0	$ 5	$ 23	$ 56	$107	$181	$249	$274	$ 282	$ 281	$268	
Other diagnostics	15	23	32	45	75	110	135	165	190	210	225	
Imaging	0	0	2	13	52	106	146	166	174	186	184	
Therapy	0	0	0	0	8	57	171	307	400	375	305	
Total sales	$ 15	$ 28	$ 57	$114	$242	$454	$701	$912	$1,046	$1,052	$982	982
Cost of sales	$ 7	$ 10	$ 21	$ 41	$ 84	$159	$224	$294	$ 332	$ 336	$322	
% of sales	47%	36%	37%	36%	35%	35%	32%	32%	32%	32%	33%	
Gross profits	$ 8	$ 18	$ 36	$ 73	$158	$295	$477	$618	$ 714	$ 716	$660	660
% of sales	53%	64%	63%	64%	65%	65%	68%	68%	68%	68%	67%	
Cash payments:												
6% of sales			$ 3.42	$ 6.84	$14.52	$27.24	$ 42.06	$ 54.72	$ 62.76	$ 63.12	$ 58.92	$ 58.92
20% gross profits			7.20	14.60	31.60	59.00	95.40	123.60	142.80	143.20	132.00	132.00
Less: Hurdle			11.00	14.85	20.05	27.06	36.54	49.32	66.59	89.89	121.36	163.83
Total cash payment			$-0.38	$ 6.59	$26.07	$59.18	$100.92	$129.00	$138.97	$116.43	69.56	$ 27.09
Shares outstanding		12.933										
Cash payment/share*			$0.00	$0.51	$2.02	$4.58	$7.80	$7.09				
PV at 20% through 1991		$9.24										

Lilly's Forecast of Hybritech Income Statements and Cash Flows

	1984	1985	1986	1987	1988	1989	1990	1991	1992	1993	1994	1995
Sales												
Cancer diagnostics	$ 0	$ 0	$ 4	$ 8	$ 15	$ 20	$ 31	$ 45	$ 61	$ 72	$ 77	$ 81
Other diagnostics	15	32	40	60	90	120	150	170	175	180	185	190
Imaging	0	0	1	2	7	15	25	50	60	75	91	95
Therapy	0	0	0	0	0	0	0	8	48	80	100	120
Total sales	$ 15	$ 32	$ 45	$ 70	$112	$155	$206	$273	$344	$407	$453	$486

EXHIBIT B (continued)

	1984	1985	1986	1987	1988	1989	1990	1991	1992	1993	1994	1995
Cost of sales	$ 7	$ 17	$ 20	$ 25	$ 39	$ 54	$ 72	$ 96	$124	$142	$154	$160
% of sales	47%	53%	45%	35%	35%	35%	35%	35%	36%	35%	34%	33%
Gross profits	$ 8	$ 15	$ 25	$ 45	$ 73	$101	$134	$177	$220	$265	$299	$326
% of sales	53%	47%	56%	64%	65%	65%	65%	65%	64%	65%	66%	67%
Cash payments												
6% of sales			$ 2.70	$ 4.20	$ 6.72	$ 9.30	$12.36	$16.38	$20.64	$24.42	$ 27.18	$ 58.92
20% gross profits			5.00	9.00	14.60	20.20	26.80	35.40	44.00	53.00	59.80	132.00
Less: Hurdle			11.00	14.85	20.05	27.06	36.54	49.32	66.59	89.89	121.36	163.83
Total cash payment			$ 0.00	$ 0.00	$ 1.27	$ 2.44	$ 2.62	$ 2.46	$ 0.00	$ 0.00	0.00	$ 27.09
Shares outstanding		12.93										
Cash payment/share*		$0.29	$0.00	$0.00	$0.10	$0.19	$0.20	$0.19	$0.00	$0.00	$0.00	$2.09
PV at 20% through 1991		$0.29										

*Cash payments to a total of $22 per CPU. Discounting assumes 1986 represents a full year.

606

EXHIBIT C   Summary of Valuation of Package of Securities Offered by Lilly per
            Share of Hybritech

		Lilly's View			Hybritech's View		
Volatility is:		.33*	.23**	.117†	.33*	.23**	.117†
1.	Higher of cash or convertible notes	$22.00	$22.00	$22.00	$22.00	$22.00	$22.00
2.	1.4 Warrants	$22.08	$16.05	$ 7.00	$22.08	$16.05	$ 7.00
3.	Contingent payment unit	$ .29	$ .29	$ .29	$ 9.24	$ 9.24	$ 9.24
	Total value	$44.37	$38.34	$29.29	$54.32	$47.29	$38.24

*The volatility as calculated over the preceding 30-trading days (case Exhibit 10).

**The long-term historical volatility calculated over 1980–84 by Cox and Rubinstein.

†The volatility implied by the terms of the warrant.

Colt Industries

> "God made man and Colonel Samuel Colt made them equal."
>
> Anonymous

On Sunday afternoon July 20, 1986, at 4:00, Fred Graham, an analyst with Goldman Sachs, was enjoying a cookout with his family when the phone interrupted. Graham's boss, Jack Roberts, informed him that one of his companies, Colt Industries, had just declared a startling major recapitalization.

The basics of the plan called for each shareholder to receive $85 in cash and one share of stock in the recapitalized Colt, whose common stock had closed on Friday at $66.75 per share. Shares held in the employee pension fund, 7 percent of the new outstanding shares, would not receive cash, but would receive one new share plus new shares worth $85; the actual number would be determined by dividing the average trading price for the 15 days following the exchange of the publicly held shares.

Colt was going to finance the cash payout by issuing $1.5 billion in new debt. The company said that it expected $900 million to be provided by a group of banks led by Bankers Trust Company, which had agreed to provide $400 million itself, and an additional $525 million was expected to be raised through the sale of debt securities.

Roberts advised Graham to get to the office as soon as possible to assess what impact this announcement would have on Colt's stock price the next day when the market opened. A staff meeting was scheduled for Monday, and he would be expected to answer questions and present some firm recommendations before the market opening.

COLT INDUSTRIES

Colt Industries was best known for its firearms division, founded in 1836 by Colonel Samuel Colt. The division manufactured the M16 military rifle and manufactured and marketed a line of single- and double-action revolvers, pistols, and sporting rifles for the commercial and law-enforcement markets. The division was only a small part of a large diversified company, however. In fact, the original Colt Firearms was acquired in 1954 by the Penn-Texas Corporation, a diversified company whose primary subsidiary was the Pratt & Whitney Company and which, until that year, had operated under the name of Pennsylvania Coal & Coke Corporation. Not until 1964 was the company name officially changed to Colt Industries.

Colt had sales of almost $1.5 billion in 1985. Its diversified operations could be separated into three business segments: aerospace/government, automotive, and industrial. Exhibit 1 lists the divisions and their products. Most of the growth in the company since the 1950s had come from acquisitions (noted on Exhibit 1), although the company had actively divested over the same

---

Case written by Robert M. Conroy, Associate Professor of Business Administration. Copyright (c) 1989 by the Darden Graduate Business School Sponsors, Charlottesville, VA.

period. As recently as 1985, Colt had sold two subsidiaries--Crucible Materials Corporation and Crusteel, Ltd.--to management and employees in a leveraged buyout. During the same period, Colt acquired Lewis Engineering and Walbar, Inc., for cash. Management viewed this process of acquisition and divestiture as a way of constantly updating Colt's product lines.

The last few years had been good for Colt, as shown in Exhibit 2. Sales were level at about $1.5 billion, but in 1985, earnings increased by about 8 percent. Earnings per share increased from $3.95 in 1981 to $6.91 in 1985. Return on equity increased to about 34 percent in 1985. Dividends had increased every year since 1981. Much of the improvement in equity performance came, however, from Colt's aggressive share-repurchase plan. Colt had reduced its share base by about 30 percent over the preceding four years. Colt Industries' stock price nonetheless rose consistently over that period, as shown in Exhibit 3.

During 1985, Standard and Poor's and Moody's both raised their ratings of Colt senior debt from A to A+ and from A3 to A2, respectively. As of the end of that year, cash and marketable securities had increased to $215 million, while at the same time, because of the acquisitions in 1985, long-term debt increased to $342 million (see Exhibit 4). Most of the long-term debt was added in December 1985 when Colt had two new bond issues, of $150 million each. The bond issues were: 10 1/8 percent notes due 1995 and 11 1/4 percent debentures due 2015. Most of the other long-term debt was the capitalized value of long-term leases.

Colt also had a $270-million revolving-credit agreement with various banks. Under this agreement, the company could borrow, repay, and reborrow, at any time until June 30, 1988, amounts aggregating up to the committed amount of $270 million. Upon the loan's maturity, Colt could convert the outstanding balance to a four-year term loan payable in equal semi-annual principal installments commencing December 30, 1988. At the option of the company, interest on the unpaid principal balances was calculated upon either the prime rate, the certificate-of-deposit rate, or the London interbank rate. A commitment fee of 1/4 of 1 percent per annum was payable quarterly on the average daily unused portion.

Although Colt had performed well during the past several years, as the data in Exhibit 5 summarize, the financial community had some concerns about its potential for growth over the next few years. Some of its business segments were experiencing increased competition and technical obsolescence. Exhibit 6 presents financial performance by business segment, and the following comments from the 1985 annual report summarize the company's assessment of prospects in each segment:

> Aerospace/Government segment operating income in 1985 was level with that of a year ago on an eight percent gain in sales. The segment accounted for 34 percent of total company sales in 1985 and 36 percent of operating income.

> Both sales and operating income from the company's Automotive industry segment were down in 1985 from the previous year, reflecting primarily the continuing trend away from carburetion and toward fuel injection as the industry's major fuel management system. The segment accounted for 34 percent of total company sales and 39 percent of operation income.

This general assessment was reflected in the latest Paine Webber report on Colt, dated July 15, 1988:

> We expect a moderate recovery in earnings in 1987 to approximately $6.60 per share, primarily because of the absence on the effect of the 1986 strike at Firearms. We believe that Colt's automotive segment will again trail the prior year reflecting further customer switching from carburetion to fuel injection and probably reduction in U.S. manufacturer new car assemblies. Colt Aerospace/ Defense should be up again. In fact the longer term outlook for this segment is very good and should be an ongoing source of earnings growth for Colt. Industrial segment operations are likely to be about flat at a relatively high level.

THE TAX ENVIRONMENT

A vigorous discussion of tax reform had been going on in Washington. The House of Representatives passed a tax reform bill in December 1985, and the Senate passed its version of the bill in June 1986. On Friday, July 18, 1986, a committee was formed to reconcile the differences in the two bills. An important provision expected to emerge as part of the final tax bill was the lowering of the statutory maximum corporate tax rate of 46 percent to approximately 34 percent.

THE PROBLEM

After reviewing his material, Fred Graham decided there were three major issues he had to address by the opening of the financial markets on Monday. The first was what he thought the Colt stock would sell for when the market opened. An important element in this question was the characteristics of the new equity shares that would remain after the restructuring. The second related to the impact of the announced restructuring on the outstanding debt. His boss had not explicitly asked for such on analysis, but Graham believed it was an important question that was sure to be raised. Finally, what would be the impact of the restructuring on Colt's strategy? Specifically, would the restructuring affect the operational aspects of Colt fundamentally, or was it just a financial restructuring?

EXHIBIT 1 Divisions by Business Segment

Business Segment (acquisition year)	Products
Aerospace/Government	
Chandler Evans Control Systems	Jet engine fuel controls
Colt Firearms (1954)	Military and commemorative arms
Delvan Gas Turbine Products (1983)	Gas turbine products
Fairbanks Morse Engine (1955)	Deisel engines
Lewis Engineering (1985)	Aircraft instrumentation
Menasco Aerospace (1977)	Aircraft landing gear
Walbar (1985)	Jet-engine turbine blades
Automotive	
Colt Automotive Products	Automotive products
Fairbanks Morse	Ignition systems
Holley Special Products (1968)	Carburetors and replacement parts
Farnum Sealing Systems (1979)	Gaskets
Stemco Truck Products	Trucks and bus products and instrumentation
Industrial	
Central Moloney Transformer (1968)	Distribution transformers
Woodville Polymer Engineering	Molded rubber products
Pratt & Whitney Machine Tools	Machine and cutting tools
Garlock (1975)	Mechanical packaging
Elox (1967)	Electrical discharge machining
France Compressor	Compressor components
Quincy Compressor (1966)	Air compressors

EXHIBIT 2   Colt Industries Income Statements 1983-85 (as of December 31; in thousands, except per share data)

	1983	1984	1985
Net sales	$1,343,130	$1,581,750	$1,579,325
Cost of sales	1,003,130	1,170,770	1,579,264
Selling and admin. expense	172,099	192,607	187,614
Interest expense	17,228	14,275	14,331
Interest income	(24,556)	(15,705)	(8,724)
Total costs and expenses	1,167,901	1,361,947	1,352,485
Earnings from continuing operations before taxes	175,229	219,803	226,300
Provision for taxes	77,834	99,834	97,540
Earnings from continuing operations after taxes	97,395	119,969	129,300
Discontinued operations	1,860	12,260	8,733
Net earnings	$ 99,255	$ 132,229	138,033

Per Share Data

	1983	1984	1985
Earnings per share:			
Continuing operations	$ 3.93	$ 5.43	$ 6.47
Discontinued operations	.08	.56	.44
Net earnings per share	$ 4.01	$ 5.99	$ 6.91
Average number of common shares (000s)	24,778	22,093	19,979
Cash dividend per share	$ 2.00	$ 2.27	$ 2.50
Market closing price per share (7/18/86)			$ 66.75
Common shares outstanding (7/18/86)		19,404	

EXHIBIT 3   End-of-Quarter Closing Stock Prices for Colt Industries

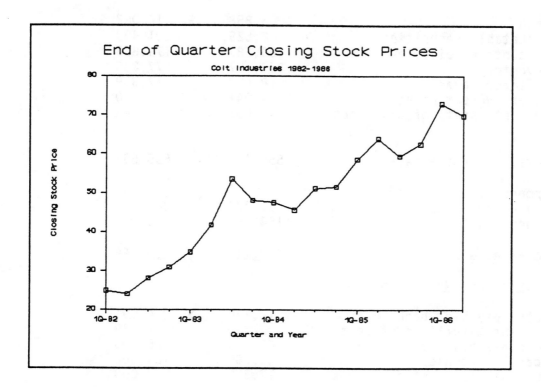

End of Quarter Closing Stock Prices
Colt Industries 1982-1986

EXHIBIT 4   Balance Sheets for December 31, 1984 and 1985 (in thousands)

Assets	1984	1985
Cash	$ 3,858	$ 14,082
Marketable securities	2,529	201,499
Accounts receivable	180,587	179,867
Inventory	266,107	277,230
Deferred taxes	18,493	17,339
Other current assets	4,941	5,520
Current assets of disc. ops.	77,667	--
Total current assets	554,182	695,537
Property, plant, and equipment (net)	251,775	301,932
Other assets	154,156	253,075
Total assets	$960,113	$1,250,544

Liabilities and Net Worth	1984	1985
Notes payable, bank	$ 12,120	$ 4,091
Current maturities of debt	3,889	4,489
Accounts payable	89,639	85,803
Accrued expenses	158,280	184,568
Current liabs. of disc. ops.	17,350	7,008
Total current liabilites	281,278	285,959
Long-term debt	108,589	342,414
Deferred income taxes	(8,919)	5,612
Other liabilities	231,332	198,216
Common stock ($1 par)	20,584	19,374
Retained earnings	335,133	405,664
Foreign currency translation	(11,998)	(10,734)
Total stockholders' equity	343,719	414,304
Total liabilities and net worth	$960,113	$1,250,544

EXHIBIT 5 Selected Colt Industries Financial Data, 1981-85 (in thousands except per share and employee data)

	1981	1982	1983	1984	1985
Sales	$1,451,611	$1,277,736	$1,343,130	$1,581,750	$1,579,325
Earnings from continuing operations	122,709	81,865	97,395	119,969	129,300
Earnings (loss) of discontinued operations:					
Crucible Materials Corp. and Crusteel, Ltd.	17,141	677	1,860	12,260	(1,067)
Discontinued steelmaking facility	(30,000)	(243,000)	--	--	9,800
Net earnings (loss)	$1,561,161	$1,116,378	$1,442,385	$1,713,979	$1,717,358
Earnings (loss) per share					
Continued operations	$4.43	$3.21	$3.93	$5.43	$6.47
Discontinued operations					
Crucible Materials Corp. and Crusteel Ltd.	0.62	0.03	0.08	0.56	(0.05)
Discontinued steelmaking facility	(1.1)	(9.57)	--	--	0.49
Net earnings per share	$3.95	$(6.33)	$4.01	$5.99	$6.91
Common share dividends:					
Total paid	$ 41,470	$ 44,834	$ 48,484	$ 48,766	$ 49,262
Per share	1.54	1.80	2.00	2.28	2.50
Cash and marketable securities	181,494	143,919	163,038	6,387	215,581
Working capital	$ 594,411	$ 513,131	$ 409,974	$ 272,904	$ 409,578
Current ratio	3.16	3.16	2.43	1.97	2.43
Quick ratio	1.31	1.56	1.15	0.66	1.38
Interest-coverage ratio	8	5.9	8.4	11.5	11.2
Total assets	$1,312,773	$1,128,006	$1,113,748	$ 960,113	$1,250,544

Exhibit 5 (continued)

	1981	1982	1983	1984	1985
Long-term debt	$221,398	$175,223	$129,255	$108,589	$342,414
Long-term debt to capitalization	23.1%	28.3%	21.7%	24.0%	45.2%
Shareholders' equity	$735,715	$443,490	$466,831	$343,719	$414,304
Return on average shareholders' equity:					
Continuing operations	17.4%	17.5%	21.4%	29.6%	34.1%
Return on sales:					
Continuing operations	8.5%	6.4%	7.0%	7.6%	8.2%
Book value per common share	$27.06	$18.51	$19.65	$17.58	$21.39
Capital expenditures	$ 40,391	$ 27,482	$ 27,473	$ 40,960	$ 41,278
Depreciation and amortization	24,653	27,347	29,408	33,208	31,626
Order backlog	$647,116	$595,342	$756,491	$800,971	$962,743
Number of employees	21,900	18,400	19,400	19,600	19,700

EXHIBIT 6   Industrial-Segment Information (in millions)

	1981	1982	1983	1984	1985
Sales					
Aerospace/Government	$ 461	$ 424	$ 441	$ 497	$ 539
Automotive	441	405	478	580	542
Industrial	560	458	427	506	501
Intersegment elimination	(10)	(9)	(3)	(1)	(3)
Total	$1,452	$1,278	$1,343	$1,582	$1,579
Operating Income					
Aerospace/Government	$ 81.8	$ 74.4	$ 78.3	$ 91.8	$ 91.8
Automotive	59.0	45.3	81.6	106.4	97.8
Industrial	65.2	31.7	40.3	57.6	61.9
Total segments	$206.0	$151.4	$200.2	$255.8	$251.5
Interest expense	(23.8)	(21.1)	(17.2)	(14.3)	(14.3)
Interest income	28.1	19.2	24.6	15.7	8.7
Corporate unallocated	(21.2)	(16.9)	(32.4)	(37.4)	(19.1)
Gain on sale of leasehold	19.3	--	--	--	--
Earnings from cont. ops. before income taxes	$208.4	$132.6	$175.2	$219.8	$226.8
Operating Margin					
Aerospace/Government	17.7%	17.5%	17.8%	18.5%	17.0%
Automotive	13.4%	11.2%	17.1%	18.3%	18.0%
Industrial	11.6%	6.9%	9.4%	11.4%	12.4%
Total	14.2%	11.8%	14.9%	16.2%	19.0%
Total Assets					
Aerospace/Government	$ 254	$ 246	$ 311	$ 303	$ 535
Automotive	188	186	214	198	189
Industrial	324	279	272	275	244
Corporate unallocated	211	234	189	46	283
Discontinued operations	336	183	128	135	--
Total	$1,313	$1,128	$1,114	$960	$1,251
Depreciation and Amortization					
Aerospace/Government	$ 6.3	$ 7.7	$ 10.1	$ 11.9	$ 13.4
Automotive	7.4	8.4	8.3	11.4	13.4
Industrial	10.8	11.2	10.9	10.2	10.9
Corporate unallocated	0.2	--	0.1	--	--
Total	$ 24.7	$ 27.3	$ 29.4	$ 33.2	$ 31.6
Capital Expenditures					
Aerospace/Government	$ 13.8	$ 12.8	$ 10.6	$ 17.3	$ 18.9
Automotive	12.6	6.6	6.9	8.1	10.0
Industrial	13.9	8.1	9.9	15.5	12.2
Corporate unallocated	0.1	--	0.1	0.1	0.1
Total	$ 40.4	$ 27.5	$ 27.5	$ 41.0	$ 41.3

Colt Industries

SYNOPSIS AND OBJECTIVES

This case asks the student to estimate what the selling price of Colt stock would be on the day following the announcement of a drastic financial restructuring. Colt stock was selling for $66.75 per share, and Colt has just announced a plan that calls for a shareholder to receive $85 and one new share of stock in the recapitalized company for each share of existing stock held. The cash payout is to be financed by issuing $1.5 billion of new debt. This problem involves estimating what the value of the tax shield from the debt is worth. Specific objectives are:

• To provide an exercise in forecasting the balance sheet of a firm that is undergoing a major recapitalization.

• To establish a relationship between value and capitalization.

• To provide an exercise in estimating the value of the tax shelter associated with the use of debt.

STUDY QUESTIONS

1. What do you think is the purpose of the recapitalization?

2. Assuming the recapitalization takes place and that Colt is able to borrow the additional debt at 11 percent, project the income statements and balance sheets for Colt for 1986 and 1987.

3. At what price do you think Colt stock will open on Monday?

4. If you were the banker, would you lend Colt the money for this recapitalization?

TEACHING PLAN

The easiest way to begin the discussion of Colt is to focus on the potential reasons for the recapitalization. A major reason on which students should focus is that Colt is generating cash at a rate far in excess of its ability to reinvest it profitably, which is why Colt has been repurchasing shares over the last few years.

An important factor is that Colt has relatively little debt. If you net out the marketable securities against the long-term debt, the debt-to-equity ratio (using market values) is only 11 percent. Most students should recognize that,

---

Teaching note written by Robert Conroy, Associate Professor of Business Administration. Copyright (c) 1989 by the Darden Graduate Business School Sponsors, Charlottesville, VA.

given the relative stability of Colt's sales, this ratio is very low. It should be clear that Colt is underutilizing debt in its capital structure.

The key question is: why make such a drastic change? The only reason must be to prevent a takeover. The class might discuss if this move is a good idea.

Forecasted income statements and balance sheets for 1986 and 1987 are shown in Exhibits A and B. You can discuss what the negative book value of equity means in this case.

The market value of the firm is (in thousands):

Market value of equity	($66.75 x 19,404)	$1,295,217
Market value of debt	(case Exhibit 4)	342,414
Total market value		$1,637,631

The estimate of the new share price is based on the value of the tax shield. If Colt issues $1.5 billion in debt and keeps it outstanding in perpetuity, the value of the tax shield would be

$$.34 \times \$1.5 \text{ billion} = \$510 \text{ million}.$$

Thus, the new market value of the firm after the recapitalization would be $1,637,631,000 + $510,000,000, or approximately $2.148 billion.

If we deduct the market value of the debt, the equity value of the recapitalized firm after paying the $85 cash dividend is $305.585 million. The price per share depends on the number of shares outstanding, which depends on the number of shares allocated to the employee pension fund. An exact formula for the per share price (P) is

$$\frac{\$305.585 \text{ million}}{[19,404 + 1,358 \times (85/P)]} = P.$$

Solving for P yields

$$P = (\$305.585 \text{ million} - 1,358 \times \$85)/19,404, \text{ or}$$
$$P = \$9.80 \text{ per share}.$$

Thus we have the per share price after the $85 dividend. The estimate of the opening price for Monday should consider this figure, and a reasonable estimate would be $94.80. This price can be tempered by the fact that the recapitalization might not go through.

Other points can be raised that affect this estimate. The first is the impact on the existing debt. Clearly, the addition of this much debt will have a detrimental effect on the existing debt. This situation has the potential to create a wealth gain for the equityholders at the expense of the debtholders. A negative aspect of the recapitalization is that it will make it difficult for Colt to engage in any acquisitions in the near future. Thus, another effect of the recapitalization might be a change in strategy. Here we could have financing having an impact on the operations of the firm.

The discussion of whether the student would make the loan should raise a number of issues about the viability of the deal. There are questions about the ability of Colt to generate enough cash to repay a significant portion of the new loans in the near term without some radical changes.

EPILOGUE

On Monday, July 21, 1986, Colt opened at about $95 per share and closed the day at $93.50. It traded in this range for the next two months. The shares in the recapitalized firm closed at $11.75 on November 8, 1986, immediately after the $85 cash dividend was paid. In early 1988, Colt was the object of a leveraged buyout in which management purchased the outstanding shares for $17 per share.

	1986	1987
Net sales	$1,600,000	$1,600,000
Cost of sales (75%)	1,200,000	1,200,000
Selling and admin. (11.5%)	184,000	184,000
Interest expense*	55,000	179,000
Interest income	0	0
Total costs and expenses	1,439,000	1,563,000
Earnings from continuing operations before taxes	161,000	37,000
Provision for taxes	71,840	12,580
Earnings from continuing operations after taxes	71,679	24,420
Discontinued operations	0	0
Net earnings	$ 71,679	$ 24,420

*Colt was able to borrow the $1.5 billion at an average rate of 11%. The 1986 figure is based on borrowing the $1.5 billion for 3 months plus the $14,000 on the old debt. The 1987 figure is $1.5 billion at 11% plus $14,000 on the old debt.

EXHIBIT B Projected Balance Sheets for December 31, 1986 and 1987 (in thousands)

Assets	1986	1987
Cash	$ 8,000	$ 8,000
Marketable securities	0	0
Accounts receivable	180,000	180,000
Inventory	270,000	270,000
Deferred taxes	20,000	20,000
Other current assets	5,000	5,000
Total current assets	483,000	483,000
Property, plant, and equipment, net	300,000	300,000
Other assets	250,000	250,000
Total assets	$1,033,000	$1,033,000

Liabilities and Net Worth		
Notes payable, bank	$ 0	$ 0
Current maturities of debt	5,000	5,000
Accounts payable	85,000	85,000
Accrued expenses	185,000	185,000
Total current liabilities	275,000	275,000
Long-term debt	1,838,000	1,833,000
Deferred income taxes	8,000	10,000
Other liabilities	200,000	278,580
Common stock ($1 par)	20,763	20,763
Retained earnings	(1,308,763)	(1,284,343)
Total stockholders' equity	(1,288,000)	(1,263,580)
Total liabilities and net worth	$1,033,000	$1,033,000

Case 54

Enigma Engineering, Inc.

In August 1987, George Smiley, managing director at Cypher National Bank, was considering an opportunity that had never arisen before at CNB. He had been approached by a childhood friend, Katherine Bell, president of Olympic Strategic Investments, Inc., in Seattle, Washington, about financing the leveraged buyout (LBO) of Enigma Engineering, Inc., a manufacturer of precision robotic manufacturing systems.

Olympic Strategic Investments, an investment company, was planning to form a limited partnership with Enigma's current management, provide subordinated debt, and take an equity interest in the LBO. Mr. Smiley was now considering whether CNB should become the senior lender by providing $31.5 million in the form of term debt and revolving credit. In addition, Olympic was looking for a second investor to provide an additional $12.002 million of mezzanine (subordinated) debt and take a $1.499 million equity interest (for 20 percent of the shareholder votes). Mr. Smiley thought that, if the deal was attractive, Cypher National Capital Corporation (CNCC), a subsidiary of the bank holding company and provider of mezzanine debt, might be interested. The bank and CNCC had never before provided financing to the same client.

CYPHER NATIONAL BANK

CNB was a large regional commercial bank in the Pacific Northwest of the United States. The corporation's consolidated assets totaled $9.5 billion, and net income in 1986 was $91.8 million. CNB's return on assets in 1986 was 9.6 percent; return on equity was 19.8 percent. The holding company of the bank merged with another regional bank in March 1987, creating an institution with combined assets of about $14 billion. CNB's lending limit to any single client was $80 million ($140 million including the new acquisition). CNB had been interested in entering the venture-capital market for some time and was doing so in a small way through CNCC.

OLYMPIC STRATEGIC INVESTMENTS, INC.

Olympic, one of the largest thrift institutions in the country, was founded as a savings bank, but it had diversified in recent years beyond consumer banking into real estate and mortgage banking, corporate finance, and insurance-related services. Strategic Investments, Inc., was established in 1983 as a wholly owned subsidiary of Olympic and provider of mezzanine financing to LBOs. In its first year of operations, Strategic Investments closed 4 deals; in 1986, its staff of 20 closed 16. Investments totaled $13.7 million in 1983 and $113.1 million by 1986. By year-end 1986, it had invested in the equity and subordinated debt of 41 leveraged buyouts in the areas of manufacturing, publishing, retailing, wholesale distribution, and real estate.

Case prepared by Robert F. Bruner and Casey Opitz with the assistance of a corporation that prefers to remain anonymous. Copyright (c) 1988 by the Darden Graduate Business School Sponsors, Charlottesville, VA.

THE ENIGMA COMPANY

Enigma Engineering, located in Portland, Oregon, designed and manufactured precision robotic manufacturing systems. These systems were guaranteed to perform manufacturing functions within plus-or-minus 50 microns of a target location.[1] Such machines were finding increasing use in several industries, including semiconductors, defense electronics, biotechnology, and in many research-intensive applications.

Enigma held about 25 percent (the market leader) of the pharmaceutical/biotechnology robotics market and 14 percent (third largest producer) of the semiconductor market. The company was either the second or third largest seller of precision robotics in the United States, with a 25 percent market share.

Enigma had competition from 36 other firms. Most were small and lacked a full product line, but some were large, and precision robotic systems were not their primary line of business. The company's three most important competitors were Presley, Orbison, and Vandella (see Exhibit 1). Presley held 25 percent of the market—slightly more than Enigma—but emphasized different product applications. Orbison, a privately held company, competed directly in most product lines, but the privately held company's management team had not kept up with market changes, and the company was losing market share; it was still a strong competitor in the semiconductor industry, however. Vandella was listed on the American Stock Exchange, had sales of $350 million, and was the world leader in precision automotive-related robotics. Vandella and Enigma used many of the same strategies, and they competed directly in sales of very large robotic systems.

Enigma was founded in 1962 by Dr. Karla Gerstmann, an engineer and Russian emigre. In time, he turned control over to the company's management, especially Bill Haydon, its president and general manager. By 1987, Dr. Gerstmann and his wife, Irina, who together owned 48 percent of the company (see Exhibit 2), were ready to "cash out" and retire to a home in Palm Springs.

Enigma produced its entire output from its one Portland plant. The building was leased through Enigma Realty, Inc., which was controlled by Irina Gerstmann, through February 1988. Concurrent with the close of the LBO transaction, a long-term lease was to be consummated.

Enigma had established a European presence in 1976 in Great Britain, followed in 1977 by a French operation and in 1978 by a plant in the Netherlands. A West German sales office that opened in 1982 had recently been closed, and a large portion of the British manufacturing volume had been transferred to the Netherlands—both part of a consolidation effort. In December 1986, the Dutch operations had total assets of $8.55 million, equity of $2,664,000, and net income of $688,500 on sales of $13.05 million. The French operation was about to be sold to its general manager, who would continue to operate the business as an independent Enigma distributor. Proceeds from the sale were expected to be only $225,000.

Research and development accounted for between 5 and 8 percent of annual revenues, and 75 of the company's 100 products were patented. Product evolution in precision robotics was beginning to moderate after a period of high R&D expenditures. Any single product would take an average of 2 years to develop and commercialize and could then have a product life of between 3 and 15 years. Enigma management and Olympic believed the company could survive on the strength of its current product line with no new introductions for 2 or 3 years; the

---

[1]A micron is a unit of measure equal to one-thousandth of a millimeter.

company's goal, however, was for its 15-man engineering staff to develop products and applications at a rate that would ensure that 50 percent of revenues would be generated from products less than 5 years old.

The company's plant in Portland operated on a one-shift basis and had capacity to produce about $160 million in net sales. Management believed that total capital expenditures could remain below $1,125,000 per year for the foreseeable future. The company's 810 domestic and 53 European employees were nonunionized. The work environment was so clean and safe that OSHA had exempted the facility from periodic inspection. A recently installed, highly sophisticated computer-aided design and manufacturing (CAD/CAM) system, the software for which alone cost $775,000, was expected to contribute to Enigma's growth for at least the next 10 years. In addition to manufacturing, the system was used to tie production to sales forecasts, resulting in a finished-goods inventory turnover of 15 times a year on a gross sales basis.

As shown in Exhibit 3, Enigma sold 50 percent of its products through a distributor network serviced by a staff of nine Enigma employees, two regional sales managers, and four customer-service representatives. Exhibit 3 also details Enigma's sales by end-use industry. The company sold the remaining 50 percent of its product through a direct-calling national sales force head-quartered in Portland.

Company Performance

Enigma's historical financial statements are provided in Exhibits 4 and 5. For this industry, net sales were a better indication of trends than gross sales, because companies used sales commissions that averaged 33 percent of the list prices. Enigma's net sales rose from $55.6 million in 1982 to $72.2 million in 1986. Growth in 1986 appeared low, but the company believed that a sales-force incentive promotion resulted in a shift of about $3,375,000 gross sales ($2,250,000 net) to 1985 from 1986. Interim 1987 results suggested that the company would do $79.2 million of business in 1987. The 10 percent compounded growth stemmed primarily from increased volume, although price increases on existing products averaged between 2 and 3 percent a year.

Total gross margins remained steady over the years at between 43 and 45 percent. High margins resulted from a combination of cost reductions, new high-priced product introductions, and the development of new high-technology replacement products for sale at higher prices. The company's operating income was strong because of improvements in selling, general, and administrative expenses (SG&A) from 28.4 percent of sales in 1982 to 23.9 percent in 1986.

On the balance sheet, the "other assets" category included $2,340,000 invested in an equity securities fund that could be liquidated within a week and could therefore be considered a cash equivalent. The company's long-term debt consisted of an industrial revenue bond (IRB on Exhibit 6) contracted in 1982 at 75 percent of the prime lending rate; Enigma made monthly installments of $34,500 and had $5.2 million outstanding on the loan at the end of 1986. Through 1985, it also had $303,750 outstanding under a convertible debenture, originally due in 1990 at 5.5 percent and convertible at the rate of 13.3 shares per $1,000 face value. The conversion took place on December 18, 1986. Maturing long-term debt was estimated to be $390,870 in 1987, increasing steadily to $488,219 in 1991.

The company repurchased shares of its common stock in 1984, 1985, and 1986. Enigma's stock bonus plan invested in the company's preferred shares and would often repurchase retirees' shares.

Company Management

Bill Haydon, Enigma's 43-year-old president and general manager, had been with the company for 18 years and had worked in sales, marketing, and engineering positions. Percy Alleline, the engineering manager, had been with Enigma for 16 years and was 39 years old. The administrative and manufacturing managers were both 40 years old and had been with Enigma for 5 and 6 years; the 39-year-old marketing manager had worked at Enigma a year.

Principal shareholders Karla and Irina Gerstmann were on the payroll but did not participate in day-to-day management. Their expenses ranged between $1,800,000 and $2,250,000; after the LBO, Enigma would pay them a $1,125,000 annual noncompete/consulting fee for four years.

THE FINANCING PROPOSAL

The management of Enigma Engineering and Olympic were planning to form a limited partnership. Olympic and a second investor (perhaps CNCC) would provide a total of $25.65 million in the form of subordinated debt and partners' capital. Enigma's existing management, primarily Mr. Haydon, would also provide $2,250,000 of partners' capital. Equity ownership in the partnership would be 30 percent management, 70 percent divided between Olympic (50 percent) and the second investor (20 percent). The other outside investor was called "investor X."

As shown in Exhibit 6, the total acquisition price was $81,613,000, including transaction expenses and debt assumption. The total amount to be financed with new debt was $51.9 million; CNB was being asked to provide $31.5 million in the form of an $18 million term loan and a $13.5 million revolver. According to Olympic, the company would amortize $2,250,000 of the term loan in October 1988, $3,375,000 in Octobers 1989 and 1990, and $4.5 million the following two years. If CNB issued the loan, Mr. Smiley thought a fair rate would be 50 basis points over prime plus a 1/2 percent annual fee on the average outstandings under the term loan; for the revolver, he was leaning toward prime plus 125 basis points and a 1 percent fee at closing. Between mid-1984 and early 1987, the prime rate had fallen from 13 percent to 7.5 percent. In August 1987, it was 8.25 percent and was expected to reach 9 percent before the year was over; most sources were projecting slightly higher rates over the next two years.

The senior subordinated debentures held by investor X would have a coupon of 12 percent, payable quarterly, and would mature in October 1994. The debentures would be junior to the term debt and revolving credit but senior to the partnership capital and Olympic's subordinated debt (also at 12 percent).

The stock bonus plan for employees, currently worth $5.562 million, would be refinanced into preferred stock of the new company.

EXPECTED ENIGMA PERFORMANCE

The projected income statements, balance sheets, and cash flows provided in Exhibits 7, 8, and 9 were developed by Olympic and were based on an expected growth rate of 7 percent each year. Olympic adjusted the company's historical financial data to reconcile it with the investment company's standard computer model. The projections assumed that Enigma would pay off the term loan as stated previously and $113,000 of the revolver in 1989, $1,125,000 in 1990 and 1991, and $3,375,000 in 1992. The subordinated debt would not be amortized within the first five years.

*   *   *   *   *   *

Mr. Smiley wondered whether the cash flows were strong enough to support the projected amortization schedule. He was also concerned about the possible effects of a recession on the company's performance and wanted to assure himself that Enigma could still meet its obligations.

Mr. Smiley thought that a combination OF CNB and CNCC financing could be attractive to Olympic and Enigma management, because the "one-stop" financing would simplify the transaction to some extent. Before presenting the proposal to CNCC and his own credit-review committee, however, he wanted to be certain the plan was viable and a worthwhile investment for both parties. In addition, he wanted to satisfy himself that Enigma management and current shareholders were paying and receiving a fair price. As part of his analysis, he studied the interest rates, recent debt issues, and market data provided in Exhibits 10, 11, and 12, and the industry data previously given in Exhibit 1.

EXHIBIT 1   Comparative Industry Data: Robotics Industry,* August 1987

	Earnings/ Share	Payout Ratio	Price/ Earnings	Return on Sales	Return on Assets	Return on Equity	Debt/ Equity	Beta
Kenosha Metrics	$ 0.85	56%	22.6	2.1%	3.2%	6.3%	36%	1.05
Cooper Analogics	-0.83	0	NMF	-23.5	-17.0	-26.2	22	1.15
General Robotics	2.30	69	25.4	4.2	4.5	7.1	13	0.95
Millibot	1.52	19	27.1	8.9	10.8	14.8	4	1.20
Vandella Corp.	1.25	23	27.7	12.3	10.3	20.6	19	1.10
Presley Robots	1.70	4	21.8	7.2	10.7	30.7	88	1.05
ENIGMA	$46.94	25%	4.1**	6.4%	12.7%	18.2%	14%	NAv

NMF = Not a meaningful figure.
NAv = Not available.

*Excluded from this exhibit is Orbison Engineering, Inc., a private firm for which financial data were unavailable.

**Enigma's P/E ratio was based on a treasury stock purchase price of $192 in 1986.

Sources: *Media General Industriscope*, September 1987; *Value Line Investment Survey*.

EXHIBIT 2 Ownership Prior to Buyout

Shareholder	Position	Percentage Ownership
Dr. Karla Gerstmann	Chairman	35%
Irina Gerstmann	Corporate secretary	13
Consomol AG*	Inactive	18
Bill Haydon	President and general manager	5
Other management		4
Peter Guillam	Inactive	9
Toby Esterhase	Inactive	7
Others	Inactive	9
		100%

*Karla Gerstmann voted Consomol's stock by proxy.

EXHIBIT 3   Enigma Sales Information

Sales by Source	Percentage of Gross Sales
Independent Distributors (50 firms):	
Manufacturing-equipment suppliers	10%
Industrial distributors	15
CAD/CAM distributors	25
Total independent distributors	50%
Direct Sales:	50%
Grand total	100%

Sales by Industry End User	
Semiconductors	19%
Machinery and equipment [original equipment/ manufacturers (OEM)]	13
Biotechnology	13
Defense electronics	13
Instruments	12
Process controls (OEM)	5
Automotive	2
Other	23
	100%

EXHIBIT 4 Consolidated Income Statements (dollars in thousands except per share amounts)

| | For the Years Ended December 31, | | | | 6 Months, |
	1983	1984	1985	1986	1987
Net sales	$55,643	$65,912	$71,694	$72,221	$38,340
Cost of goods sold	31,581	36,680	40,806	39,789	21,627
Gross profit	24,062	29,232	30,888	32,432	16,713
Operating expenses	15,818	17,753	18,527	19,332	10,220
Operating income	8,244	11,480	12,362	13,100	6,494
Other income	639	954	1,035	995	
Other expenses	3,177	3,569	3,879	3,794	
Income before taxes and income of subsidiaries	5,706	8,865	9,518	10,301	
Income taxes	2,705	4,055	4,451	4,847	
Income after taxes	3,002	4,811	5,067	5,454	
Equity in income of foreign subsidiaries	0 716	0 392	0 761	0 1,440	
Net income	$3,717	$5,202	$5,828	$6,894	
Earnings per share					
Primary	$121.37	$168.44	$189.00	$211.23	
Fully diluted*	$107.46	$149.18	$167.31	$211.23	

*Fully diluted earnings per share computed on the average shares outstanding, adjusted for the conversion on December 18, 1986, of the 5 1/2% convertible debenture.

EXHIBIT 5 Consolidated Balance Sheets (dollars in thousands)

	For the Years Ended December 31			
	1983	1984	1985	1986
Cash and equivalents	$ 7,205	$ 8,195	$11,592	$16,916
Accounts receivable	8,717	10,233	9,864	11,138
Inventory	6,012	7,754	8,055	8,712
Prepaid expenses	275	203	630	607
Other	68	76	54	23
Total current assets	22,277	26,461	30,195	37,396
Investments in subsidiaries	3,177	3,015	4,635	6,453
Property, plant, and equipment (PP&E)	17,330	18,711	18,968	19,328
Depreciation and amortization	5,220	6,687	7,862	9,329
Net PP&E	12,110	12,024	11,106	9,999
Other assets	648	666	2,732	297
Total assets	$38,212	$42,166	$48,668	$54,145
Accounts payable	$ 2,480	$ 3,060	$ 3,240	$ 3,978
Dividends payable	279	279	554	1,737
Accruals	3,686	2,520	2,439	1,647
Current debt maturities	257	252	324	392
Other current liabilities	576	765	1,143	2,332
Total current liabilities	7,277	6,876	7,700	10,086
Long-term debt	6,494	6,332	5,922	5,211
Deferred taxes	581	801	977	976
Common stock—no par value, 32,637 shares in 1986	5,562	5,562	5,562	5,562
Retained earnings	15,871	19,588	25,416	32,310
Currency translation adjustment and unrealized loss on securities	3,426	3,007	3,091	0
Total shareholders' equity (pfd. and common)	23,859	28,157	34,070	37,872
Total liabilities and equity	$38,212	$42,166	$48,668	$54,145

EXHIBIT 6   Sources and Uses of Buyout Financing

Sources of Cash		Uses of Cash	
Senior financing*	$31,500	Cash to seller	$67,500
Debt assumption—IRB**	5,400	Debt assumption—IRB	5,400
Subordinated debt†:		Refinance long-term	
Olympic	8,397	employee obligations††	5,562
Investor X	12,002	Transaction costs	3,151
Refinance long-term			
employee obligations††	5,562		
Partners' capital:			
Olympic (50% voting			
interest)	3,753		
Management (30% voting			
interest)	2,250		
Investor X (20% voting			
interest)	1,499		
Excess cash on hand	11,250		
	$81,613		$81,613

*The acquisition portion of the senior financing package. An additional $4.5 million in revolver availability was being requested for future working-capital needs. The $18 million term-loan portion would be amortized at a rate of $2,250,000 in 1988, $3,375,000 in 1989 and 1990, and $4.5 million the following two years. The $13.5 million revolver would be amortized at a rate of $113,000 in 1989, $1,125,000 in 1990 and 1991, and $3,375,000 in 1992. The interest rate on both portions was yet to be determined.

**At 75% of prime and with installments of $34,500 per month.

†At 12%, maturing in 1994 (balloon maturity).

††The stock bonus plan for employees would be carried into preferred stock of the new company.

EXHIBIT 7   Projected Income Statements (dollars in thousands)

	Actual 1986	Forecast 1987	Year 1	Year 2	Year 3	Year 4	Year 5
Net sales	$72,221	$79,200	$84,744	$90,675	$97,025	$103,815	$111,083
Cost of goods	39,789	44,100	47,457	50,778	54,333	58,136	62,208
Gross profit	32,432	35,100	37,287	39,897	42,692	45,679	48,875
SG&A	17,262	18,900	20,340	21,762	23,288	24,917	26,658
Depreciation	1,652	1,665	1,688	1,688	1,688	1,688	1,688
Incentive sav. plan	675	900	900	900	900	900	900
Operating income	12,843	13,635	14,359	15,547	16,816	18,174	19,629
Interest income	581	540	0	0	0	0	0
Other expense	666	675	383	383	383	383	383
Gerstmanns' income/ 4-yr. noncompete	2,057	2,025	1,125	1,125	1,125	1,125	0
Interest expense:							
Existing debt	396	338	357	345	343	333	289
Senior revolver	0	0	1,418	1,483	1,584	1,570	1,375
Senior term	0	0	1,895	1,709	1,447	1,093	497
Olympic	0	0	1,008	1,008	1,008	1,008	1,008
Second investor	0	0	1,440	1,440	1,440	1,440	1,440
Preferred*	0	0	279	293	306	320	338
Total interest	396	338	6,397	6,278	6,128	5,764	4,947
Other expense	0	0	1,260	1,260	1,260	1,260	1,260
Pretax income	10,305	11,137	5,194	6,501	7,920	9,642	13,039
Taxes**	4,851	4,950	426	533	650	791	1,069
Equity in subs. income	1,440	2,025	1,800	2,025	2,250	2,475	2,699
Net income	6,894	8,212	6,568	7,993	9,520	11,326	14,669
Distribution for federal tax liab.†	0	0	(2,097)	(2,102)	(2,682)	(3,344)	(4,464)
Retained earnings	$6,894	$8,212	$4,471	$5,891	$6,838	$7,983	$10,205
Assumed prime rate			9.5%	10.0%	11.0%	12.0%	12.0%

*"Preferred interest expense" represented noncash payments by the company to employees under the stock bonus plan. Such payments were deductible for tax purposes and were to be delivered in the form of preferred stock of the company.

**The reorganization as a partnership accounted for the decline in tax expense. Despite the fact that it would be a partnership after the buyout, the business entity would continue to pay certain state and local taxes.

†In years 1 through 5, partners would receive funds sufficient to cover their tax liability on the income of the firm.

EXHIBIT 8 Projected Balance Sheets (dollars in thousands)

	1986	Adj.	Pre-Buyout	Buyout Adj.	Post-Buyout	Year 1	Year 2	Year 3	Year 4	Year 5
Cash/securities	$16,916	($3,416)	$13,500	($11,250)	$2,250	$2,561	$3,180	$3,396	$3,195	$2,867
Receivables	11,138	338	11,476	0	11,476	13,050	13,964	14,940	15,989	17,105
Inventories	8,712	167	8,879	1,022	9,901	11,439	12,245	13,100	14,013	14,994
Other	630	108	738	(207)	531	540	540	540	540	540
Current assets	37,396	(2,803)	34,593	(10,435)	24,158	27,590	29,929	31,976	33,737	35,506
Gross fixed assets	19,328	419	19,747	(10,085)	9,662	10,557	11,570	12,582	13,707	14,832
Depreciation	(9,329)	(756)	(10,085)	10,085	0	(1,688)	(3,375)	(5,063)	(6,750)	(8,438)
Net fixed assets	9,999	(337)	9,662	0	9,662	8,870	8,195	7,519	6,957	6,394
Sub. investments	6,453	1,764	8,217	0	8,217	10,017	12,042	14,292	16,767	19,467
Other assets	297	(173)	124	0	124	135	135	135	135	135
Goodwill	0	0	0	32,477	32,477	31,667	30,852	30,042	29,228	28,418
Organization costs	0	0	0	2,250	2,250	1,800	1,350	900	450	0
Total assets	$54,145	($1,549)	$52,596	$24,292	$76,888	$80,078	$82,503	$84,864	$87,274	$89,920
Accounts payable	$3,978	($617)	$3,361	$0	$3,361	$4,239	$4,536	$4,851	$5,193	$5,553
Current portion:										
Existing debt	392	0	392	0	392	414	437	464	486	0
Senior revolver	0	0	0	0	0	113	1,125	1,125	3,375	0
Senior term	0	0	0	2,250	2,250	3,375	3,375	4,500	4,500	0
Accruals	1,647	(315)	1,332	0	1,332	1,505	1,591	1,675	1,770	1,872
Other	4,068	(2,538)	1,530	(675)	855	1,125	1,125	1,125	1,125	1,125

EXHIBIT 8 (Continued)

	1986	Adj.	Pre-Buyout	Buyout Adj.	Post-Buyout	Year 1	Year 2	Year 3	Year 4	Year 5
Current liabs.	10,085	(3,470)	6,615	(1,595)	8,190	10,771	12,189	13,740	16,449	8,520
Deferred tax	977	0	977	0	977	734	491	243	0	0
Long-term debt:										
Existing debt	5,211	(203)	5,008	0	5,009	4,595	4,158	3,695	3,209	3,209
Senior revolver	0	0	0	13,500	13,500	13,388	12,263	11,138	7,763	7,763
Senior term	0	0	0	15,750	15,750	12,375	9,000	4,500	0	0
Olympic	0	0	0	8,397	8,397	8,397	8,397	8,397	8,397	8,397
Second investor	0	0	0	12,002	12,002	12,002	12,002	12,002	12,002	12,002
Preferred stock	0	0	0	5,562	5,562	5,841	6,134	6,440	6,759	7,097
Common--Olympic	0	0	0	3,753	3,753	3,753	3,753	3,753	3,753	3,753
Other	0	0	0	3,749	3,749	3,749	3,749	3,749	3,749	3,749
Existing	5,562	0	5,562	(5,562)	0	0	0	0	0	0
Retained earnings	32,310	2,124	34,434	(34,434)	0	4,473	10,367	17,207	25,193	35,400
Total equity	37,872	2,124	39,996	(32,494)	7,502	11,975	17,869	24,709	32,695	42,902
Total liabs. and equity	$54,145	($1,549)	$52,596	$24,292	$76,888	$80,078	$82,503	$84,864	$87,274	$89,920

EXHIBIT 9 Projected Cash-Flow Statements (dollars in thousands)

| | Forecast | | | | | | |
	1986	1987	Year 1	Year 2	Year 3	Year 4	Year 5
Sources of Cash							
Net income	$6,894	$8,213	$6,570	$7,996	$9,522	$11,329	$14,671
Depreciation	1,652	1,665	1,688	1,688	1,688	1,688	1,688
Amort. of org. fees	0	0	450	450	450	450	450
Amort. of goodwill	0	0	810	815	810	815	810
Total sources	$8,546	$9,878	$9,518	$10,949	$12,470	$14,282	$17,619
Uses of Cash							
Accounts receivable	($1,436)	NAv	($1,574)	($914)	($976)	($1,049)	($1,116)
Inventories	(657)	NAv	(1,538)	(806)	(855)	(913)	(981)
Other current assets	216	NAv	(9)	0	0	0	0
Accounts payable	1,161	NAv	878	297	315	342	360
Accruals	144	NAv	173	86	84	95	102
Other current liabs.	1,017	NAv	270	0	0	0	0
Net working cap.	445	NAv	(1,800)	(1,337)	(1,432)	(1,525)	(1,635)
Subtotal	8,991	NAv	7,716	9,612	11,038	12,757	15,984
Other Sources (Uses)							
Capital expenditures	(576)	NAv	(895)	(1,013)	(1,012)	(1,125)	(1,125)
Disposals/(acquis.)	36	NAv	0	0	0	0	0
Sub. investments	(1,818)	NAv	(1,800)	(2,025)	(2,250)	(2,475)	(2,700)
Other assets	176	NAv	(11)	0	0	0	0
Deferred tax	0	NAv	(243)	(243)	(248)	(243)	0
Distribution: Partners'taxes*	0	NAv	(2,097)	(2,102)	(2,682)	(3,343)	(4,464)
Pre-amortization	$6,809	NAv	$2,670	$4,229	$4,846	$5,571	$7,695
Other equity changes	($3,096)	NAv	0	0	0	0	0

EXHIBIT 9 (Continued)

	Forecast						
Amortization	1986	1987	Year 1	Year 2	Year 3	Year 4	Year 5
Existing debt	($644)	NAv	($392)	($414)	($437)	($464)	($486)
Senior revolver	0	NAv	0	(113)	(1,125)	(1,125)	(3,375)
Senior term loan	0	NAv	(2,250)	(3,375)	(3,375)	(4,500)	(4,500)
Olympic	0	NAv	0	0	0	0	0
Second investor	0	NAv	0	0	0	0	0
Preferred	0	NAv	279	293	306	319	338
Subtotal amortization	($644)	NAv	($2,363)	($3,609)	($4,631)	($5,770)	($8,023)
Change in cash	$ 3,069	NAv	$ 307	$ 621	$ 214	($ 202)	($ 328)
Opening cash balance	13,847	NAv	2,250	2,567	3,180	3,392	3,194
Closing cash balance	$16,916	NAv	$2,557	$3,180	$3,394	$3,194	$2,866

*Under the terms of the proposed buyout, the equity partners were to be reimbursed for their tax expense resulting from their equity interest in Enigma Engineering.

EXHIBIT 10   Interest Rates and Yields

| | Treasuries | | | | Moody's | | Prime Lending Rate |
| | Bills | | Notes and Bonds | | | | |
	3-Mo.	1-Yr.	10-Yr.	30-Yr.	Aaa	Baa	
1982	10.61%	11.07%	13.00%	12.76%	13.79%	16.11%	14.86%
1983	8.61	8.80	11.10	11.18	12.04	13.55	10.79
1984	9.52	9.92	12.44	12.39	12.71	14.19	12.04
1985	7.48	7.81	10.62	10.79	11.37	12.72	9.93
1986	5.98	6.08	7.68	7.80	9.02	10.39	8.33
1987 Jan	5.43	5.46	7.08	7.39	8.36	9.72	7.50
Feb	5.59	5.63	7.25	7.54	8.38	9.65	7.50
March	5.59	5.68	7.25	7.55	8.36	9.61	7.50
April	5.64	6.09	8.02	8.25	8.85	10.04	7.75
May	5.66	6.52	8.61	8.78	9.33	10.51	8.00
June	5.67	6.35	8.40	8.57	9.32	10.52	8.25
July	5.69	6.24	8.45	8.64	9.42	10.61	8.25
Aug	6.04	6.54	8.76	8.97	9.67	10.80	8.25

Sources: *Federal Reserve Bulletin; Economic Report of the President*.

EXHIBIT 11   Subordinated Debt Data

Company	Issue	Maturity	Rating	Amount Outstanding (dollars in millions)	Yield to Maturity
Associates Corp.	Sub notes	1992	A+	150	9.29
Avco Finance	Sr sub notes	1993	A−	42	10.60
Avco Finance	Sr sub notes	1994	A−	9	10.48
Borg Warner Accept.	Sr sub sf deb	1993	A−	6	9.81
General Defense	Sr sub debent	1995	CCC−	58	15.38
General Homes	Sub notes	1995	CCC	50	17.47
General Host	Sub debent	1994	B	14	11.65
Hovnanian Enter.	Sub notes	1994	B	25	13.15
Integ. Resources	Sr sub notes	1995	BBB−	125	12.21
Litton	Sub notes	1995	BBB+	436	10.61
Nortek	Sr sub debent	1994	B	50	12.83
Orion Pictures	Sub debent	1994	B	50	13.51
Rapid American	Sub debent	1994	CCC−	50	14.05
Southmark	Sr sub notes	1994	BB−	300	13.67
Vagabond Hotels	Sub debent	1995	CCC	30	13.80

Source: *Standard & Poor's Bond Guide*, August 1987.

EXHIBIT 12 Historical Average Market Returns (1926-87)

	Arithmetic Means	Geometric Means
Common stock	12.1%	10.0%
Treasury bills	3.5	3.5
Long-term Treasuries	4.7%	4.4%

Source: *Stocks, Bonds, Bills, and Inflation*, 1987 Yearbook (Chicago: Ibbotson Associates) p. 25.

Enigma Engineering, Inc.

SYNOPSIS AND OBJECTIVES

A lending officer at a large regional bank is asked to participate in financing the leveraged buyout (LBO) of a successful manufacturer of precision industrial robots. The bank can participate as a senior lender and as an investor in a package of subordinated debt and equity. The task of the student is to value the firm, estimate the risk of the transaction, and structure the debt and equity investment properly to compensate the bank for the risk incurred.

The case is useful as (1) a comprehensive survey of techniques of valuing debt and equity securities, (2) an illustration of the use of tax shields in creating shareholder value, (3) a vehicle for sensitivity analysis of operating and financing assumptions, and (4) a basis for discussing structuring of leveraged acquisitions.

STUDY QUESTIONS

1. Exhibit 5 summarizes the structure of the proposed transaction. Why is the financing so complicated? In particular, why is subordinated debt part of the deal?

2. From the buyer's perspective (i.e., Olympic, management, and investor X), what is the maximum price for Enigma that is economically justified? The buying group is structured as a partnership; however, the financial plans and forecasts assume that the partners will receive funds sufficient to cover their tax liability on the earnings of the firm. That is, the forecasted cash flows for Enigma are analogous to those for a corporation. Please value Enigma as if it were a corporation.

3. What return should investor X require on the strip of debt and equity (i.e., senior subordinated notes plus 20 percent equity interest in the partnership)? Is the cost of this strip fair?

4. Assuming the loan was structured as suggested in The Financing Proposal section of the case, how profitable would it be? You might assume that Cypher's spread between prime and cost of funds is 175 basis points.

5. How is the value allocated in this deal? Who gains the most? Why?

6. What should George Smiley recommend that Cypher National Bank do?

Teaching note written by Robert F. Bruner. Copyright (c) 1989 by the Darden Graduate Business School Sponsors, Charlottesville, VA. WPO538c

Note: Case Exhibit 1 provides some information on comparable companies to help you develop equity discount rates. Use the capital asset pricing model. Remember that an LBO will dramatically change the capital structure. Therefore, you should relever the beta to estimate a cost of equity for the firm after buyout.

TEACHING PLAN

The following plan offers the standard instructor-led outline. An alternative for managing the discussion would be to assign students to teams to evaluate the transaction from the perspectives of (1) senior lender, (2) a pure equity investor, (3) Olympic, and (4) investor X.

(20 minutes) Why is this transaction so complicated? Why so many layers of financing? This way of opening clarifies the terms of the transaction and introduces the financial-engineering theme of this case.

(10 minutes) How attractive would this transaction be to a senior lender? The focus here should be on estimating the internal rate of return (IRR) of the loan and should touch on some credit-risk considerations.

(30 minutes) What is the value of the equity? Has Olympic fairly priced the equity investment?

(15 minutes) What is the net present value (NPV) of Olympic's investment? Of the investment of investor X?

(5 minutes) How can everyone win? What creates the value in this deal?

The instructor can close with some comments about the effect of debt tax shields in motivating highly leveraged acquisitions.

ANALYSIS

The Structure of the Transaction

The elaborate financial structure of this acquisition invites scrutiny. To the naive observer, the structure looks unnecessarily complicated, but with some discussion, the instructor can help students understand why relatively complicated financial structures arise.

The industrial revenue bond (IRB) is a holdover from the seller. The buyers choose to assume this debt probably because it is cheap.

Long-term employee obligations are refinanced into preferred stock. The choice of preferred as a repository for these obligations is interesting: common would dilute the regular equity investors, and debt would lever the firm more highly. Preferred looks like equity to the lenders, so it has the virtue of enhancing the balance sheet.

The presence of mezzanine debt is probably the result of trying to satisfy two conflicting goals: providing "cushion" to the senior lenders, yet not diluting the returns of the equity investors. One general hypothesis for the presence of mezzanine debt is that the firm does not have sufficient asset and cash-flow coverage to consummate the deal simply with bank debt and equity.

The packaging of the mezzanine debt into "strips" with equity is also interesting. In essence, mezzanine investors cannot participate without also being equity investors. From an agency-theory perspective, the effect is to align the mezzanine investors with the interests of the equity investors. If the firm defaults, it is liable to default first on the subordinated debt. Aligning the subordinated creditors with the equity-holders discourages the former from taking any precipitous action in the event of default.

Finally, the mix of subordinated debt and equity differs for Olympic and investor X. Early in the case discussion, the instructor might leave the motives for this difference to be resolved later. One hypothesis is that the package for investor X has been tailored according to some general idea of what an institutional investor might like to buy. A second, more cynical, hypothesis, supported by analysis discussed later, is that Olympic is the designer of the deal and appropriates a larger risk-adjusted return for itself than for its erstwhile co-investor.

The fundamental point of this review is that to understand the structuring of a complex transaction, one must delve into the incentives and motivations of the prospective participants.

Senior Credit Perspective

Exhibit A presents an estimate of the after-tax return on assets to the senior lender. Net interest income for the term loan and revolver is computed based on average outstandings for each year. Fee income is added in; tax expense is deducted. Repayment of principal is a positive cash flow. The sum of these individual flows is the total cash flow of the loan.[1]

The exhibit reveals a 2.17 percent return on the loan. Compared to the returns banks ordinarily see (e.g., .75 to 1.25 percent) this is extremely attractive.

Common Equity-Holder's Perspective

Exhibit B gives an NPV analysis of the cash flows to equity. The annual cash flows are drawn from case Exhibit 9. The terminal value is estimated using the perpetual-growth model. An IRR to equity-holders is estimated to be about 49 percent, which is within a range of reasonable target returns one hears in conversations with venture capitalists and LBO investors.

Estimating an NPV is complicated slightly by the fact that Enigma's capital structure changes through time. Exhibit B estimates the average debt/equity ratio each year and uses that to estimate the levered beta and cost of equity for that year. The discount factor is the compound product of the varying annual equity costs. By this method, the geometric mean required equity return is 37.5 percent, well below the IRR of the investment. The NPV is $3.448 million.

The size of the NPV value will hinge on small variations in operating and financing assumptions. Students should be encouraged to perform sensitivity analyses to determine breakeven levels for various key assumptions and to gauge the value under different scenarios.

---

[1]Details not reflected here are reserves for potential loan losses perhaps in the amount of 50 basis points annually, and loan-origination expenses of perhaps $10,000. These details do not materially alter the results.

Mezzanine Investors' Perspective

With the equity valuation in hand, the evaluation of Olympic's and investor X's potential returns is relatively straightforward. Exhibit C presents IRRs and geometric mean required returns for both investors.

The IRRs are computed on cash flows consisting of the sum of interest, principal payments, and percentage interest in equity cash flows. The required rates of return are estimated as a weighted average of the cost of equity (computed in Exhibit B) and a target debt return of 12 percent.[2] Again, because the mix of debt and equity securities in each investor's portfolio changes, the weighted average changes. So, once again, the discount factor for each year is computed as the compound product of the varying annual weighted-average required returns.

The results in Exhibit C are:

	Expected Return (IRR)	Geometric Required Return
Olympic	29.5%	25.7%
Investor X	19.8%	18.5%

Olympic might earn a 3.8 percent risk-adjusted rate of return, while investor X will earn a 1.3 percent risk-adjusted return. The disparity is caused by the fact that investor X's bundle of securities is weighted more heavily with debt, which is presumed to earn merely the required rate of return. In this deal, equity-holders appropriate the new value. Why the returns to Olympic and X are allocated this way is interesting. One guess is that Olympic, as designer of the transaction, sought to appropriate a disproportionate risk-adjusted return as compensation for its entrepreneurship. (The case is vague about any advisory fees paid to Olympic. *In toto*, Olympic's entrepreneurship was presumably very well rewarded.)

Sensitivity Analysis Varying the Perpetual Growth Rate

Exhibit D lends some insight into the relative robustness of the returns to the mezzanine investors and equity-holders. In this exhibit, the IRRs are tabulated by the perpetual growth rate assumed in the calculation of the terminal value. A table such as this helps identify the breakeven growth rates (i.e., the rates at which the participants just earn their geometric required returns).

The exhibit reveals that the breakeven perpetual growth rates are relatively modest: less than 0 percent for pure equity investors, 2 percent for Olympic, and 4 percent for investor X. Apparently, optimistic assumptions about perpetual growth are not necessary to forecast results where the participants earn their required returns.

---

[2]Case Exhibits 10 and 11 afford students an opportunity to judge the adequacy of the subordinated debt coupon. A rate of 12 percent appears to be in the reasonable range.

Conclusion

The transaction appears to create value for all participants. Unknown is the extent of any operating efficiencies embedded in the forecast. However, the savings from debt tax shields are manifest. In any event, 18 months after the transaction, Enigma was performing well ahead of plan--despite the stock market crash--thanks to a decline in interest rates, the decline of the dollar, and the unexpected pick-up in foreign orders. Debt was being amortized ahead of plan, and management was beginning to discuss an initial public offering to recapitalize the company.

EXHIBIT A Senior Credit Perspective (dollars in thousands)

		Year				
		0	1	2	3	4	5
Term-loan outstandings	Beginning	$18,000	$15,750	$12,375	$ 9,000	$ 4,500
	Amortiz.	(2,250)	(3,375)	(3,375)	(4,500)	(4,500)
	Ending	15,750	12,375	9,000	4,500	0
Revolving-loan outstandings	Beginning	$13,500	$13,500	$13,387	$12,262	$11,137
	Amortiz.	0	(113)	(1,125)	(1,125)	(3,375)
	Ending	13,500	13,387	12,262	11,137	7,762
Average total outstandings	Term loan	16,875	14,063	10,688	6,750	2,250
	Revolver	13,500	13,444	12,825	11,700	9,450
Net Interest Income (assumes prime cost of funds = 175 basis points)						
Term loan (175 + 50 b.p.)			380	316	240	152	51
Revolver (175 + 125 b.p.)			540	538	513	468	378
Fee income							
Term-loan (.005 x outstandings)			84	70	53	34	11
Revolver (.01 at closing)		$ 135	0	0	0	0	0
Pretax income			1,004	924	807	654	440
Tax (@ .34)			(341)	(314)	(274)	(222)	(150)
After-tax income			663	610	533	431	290
Amortization							
Term-loan			2,250	3,375	3,375	4,500	4,500
Revolving loan			0	113	1,125	1,125	11,137*
Face value of loan		(31,500)					
Cash flow to senior creditor		($31,365)	$2,913	$4,098	$5,033	$6,056	$15,927

After-tax return on assets (IRR) = 2.17%

---

*Amortization assumes entire remaining balance is paid at end of year 5.

EXHIBIT B Common Equity-Holders' Perspective (dollars in thousands)

Assumption: Growth rate in terminal value = 0.07.

		Year				
	0	1	2	3	4	5
Cash flow to equity (case Ex. 9)		$ 307	$ 621	$ 214	$ (202)	$ (328)
Terminal value						51,730*
Total cash flow to equity	(7,502)	307	621	214	(202)	51,402
Equity IRR = 49.03%						
Short-term debt	$ 2,642	$ 3,902	$ 4,937	$ 6,089	$ 8,361	0
Long-term debt	54,658	50,757	45,820	39,732	31,371	31,371
Equity (pfd. and common)	$13,064	$17,816	$24,003	$31,149	$39,454	$49,999
Debt/equity (uses avg. bal.)		8.57	5.92	4.02	2.75	1.80
Levered beta (where B_u = .92)		6.12	4.51	3.36	2.59	2.01
Cost of equity		58.70%	44.85%	34.96%	28.29%	23.36%

R_f = 0.0604 (from case Ex. 10)
$R_m - R_f$ = 0.086 (from case Ex. 12)

	1	2	3	4	5
Discount factor for the year**	0.251	0.630	0.435	0.322	0.204
Present values		$193	$270	$69	($51)
$10,468					

Net present value $ 3,448

*Terminal value is calculated by increasing pre-amortization cash flow for year 5 at 10% to give cash flow to equity. This figure is capitalized at the difference between 23.4% (the cost of equity for year 5) and a long-term growth rate of 7%.

**The geometric mean cost of equity is 37.5%

EXHIBIT C   Mezzanine Investors' Perspective

	Year					
	0	1	2	3	4	5
Book value of common equity	$7,502	$11,975	$17,869	$24,709	$32,695	$42,902
Olympic's Cash Flows						
Interest	$0	$1,008	$1,008	$1,008	$1,008	$1,008
Principal	(8,397)	0	0	0	0	8,397
Equity	(3,751)	154	311	107	(101)	25,701
Total	(12,148)	1,162	1,319	1,115	907	35,106

Olympic's IRR = 29.5%

Olympic's Discount Rate						
Loan balance	$8,397	$8,397	$8,397	$8,397	$8,397	$8,397
Equity investment	3,751	5,988	8,935	12,355	16,348	21,451
Total	12,148	14,385	17,332	20,752	24,745	29,848
Percent equity	31%	42%	52%	60%	66%	72%
Cost of equity	59%	59%	45%	35%	28%	23%
Percent debt	69%	58%	48%	40%	34%	28%
Target debt return	12%	12%	12%	12%	12%	12%
Weighted average	26%	31%	29%	26%	23%	20%
Discount factor	1.000	0.761	0.590	0.470	0.382	0.318

Arithmetic mean cost = 25.8%
Geometric mean cost = 25.7%

Second Investor's Cash Flows						
Interest	$0	$1,440	$1,440	$1,440	$1,440	$1,440
Principal	(12,002)	0	0	0	0	12,002
Equity	(1,500)	61	124	43	(40)	10,280
Total	(13,502)	1,501	1,564	1,483	1,400	23,722

Second investor's IRR = 19.8%

Second Investor's Discount Rate						
Loan balance	$12,002	$12,002	$12,002	$12,002	$12,002	$12,002
Equity investment	1,500	2,395	3,574	4,942	6,539	8,580
Total	13,502	14,397	15,576	16,944	18,541	20,582
Percent equity	11%	17%	23%	29%	35%	42%
Cost of equity	59%	59%	45%	35%	28%	23%
Percent debt	89%	83%	77%	71%	65%	58%
Target debt return	12%	12%	12%	12%	12%	12%
Weighted average	17%	20%	20%	19%	18%	17%
Discount factor	1.000	0.835	0.698	0.588	0.500	0.428

Arithmetic mean cost = 18.5%
Geometric mean cost = 18.5%

EXHIBIT D   Sensitivity Analysis of Returns to Mezzanine Investors and
            Equity-Holders

Growth Rate After Year 5	Resulting Terminal Value	Equity		Mezzanine IRRs to:	
		IRR	NPV	Olympic	Second Investor
11%	$68,467	57.5%	$6,857	34.6%	22.5%
10%	63,344	55.1%	5,813	33.2%	21.7%
9%	58,933	52.9%	4,915	31.8%	21.0%
8%	55,097	50.9%	4,134	30.6%	20.4%
7%	51,730	49.0%	3,448	29.5%	19.8%
6%	48,751	47.3%	2,841	28.5%	19.3%
5%	46,096	45.7%	2,301	27.6%	18.8%
4%	43,715	44.2%	1,816	26.7%	18.4%
3%	41,568	42.8%	1,378	25.9%	18.0%
2%	39,623	41.4%	982	25.2%	17.6%
1%	37,851	40.1%	621	24.5%	17.3%
Required returns:		37.5%		25.7%	18.5%